THE
GREAT FRENCH
REVOLUTION

PETER KROPOTKIN

THE
GREAT FRENCH REVOLUTION

*introduction by
George Woodcock*

Montréal - New York

Copyright © 1989
Black Rose Books

No part of this book may be reproduced or transmitted in any form by means, electronic or mechanical, including photocopying and recording, or by any information storage or retrieval system, without written permission from the publisher, except for brief passages quoted by a reviewer in a newspaper or magazine.

Black Rose Books R 133
Hardcover — ISBN: 978-0-921689-39-3
Paperback — ISBN: 978-0-921689-38-6

> **Canadian Cataloguing in Publication Data**
>
> Kropotkin, Petr Alekseevich, kniaz, 1842-1921
>   The great French Revolution
>
> Translation of: La grande Révolution.
>
>   ISBN: 978-0-921689-39-3 (bound) -
>   ISBN: 978-0-921689-38-6 (pbk.)
>
>   1. France—History—Revolution, 1789-1791. I. Title.
>
> DC148.K8213 1989   944.04′1   C89-090121-X

Cover design: ZEBRA Communications Inc.

Mailing Address: Black Rose Books C.P.
35788, Succ. Leo-Pariseau Montreal, Quebec,
H2X 0A4 Canada

Website Address: www.blackrosebooks.com

Printed and bound in Québec, Canada

CONTENTS

An Introduction by George Woodcock	X
Preface	XXIX
I. The Two Great Currents of the Revolution	1
II. The Idea	5
III. Action	11
IV. The People before the Revolution	16
V. The Spirit of Revolt: the Riots	19
VI. The Convocation of the States-General becomes Necessary	30
VII. The Rising of the Country Districts during the Opening Months of 1789	35
VIII. Riots in Paris and its Environs	46
IX. The States-General	50
X. Preparations for the Coup d'État	57
XI. Paris on the Eve of the Fourteenth	67
XII. The taking of the Bastille	78
XIII. The Consequences of July 14 at Versailles	88
XIV. The Popular Risings	94
XV. The Towns	98
XVI. The Peasant Rising	109
XVII. August 4 and its Consequences	118
XVIII. The Feudal Rights remain	129
XIX. Declaration of the Rights of Man	141
XX. The Fifth and Sixth of October 1789	146
XXI. Fears of the Middle Classes—The New Municipal Organisation	158

CONTENTS

XXII.	FINANCIAL DIFFICULTIES—SALE OF CHURCH PROPERTY...	168
XXIII.	THE FETE OF THE FEDERATION	174
XXIV.	THE "DISTRICTS" AND THE "SECTIONS" OF PARIS	180
XXV.	THE SECTIONS OF PARIS UNDER THE NEW MUNICIPAL LAW	189
XXVI.	DELAYS IN THE ABOLITION OF THE FEUDAL RIGHTS	195
XXVII.	FEUDAL LEGISLATION IN 1790	205
XXVIII.	ARREST OF THE REVOLUTION IN 1790	213
XXIX.	THE FLIGHT OF THE KING—REACTION—END OF THE CONSTITUENT ASSEMBLY	226
XXX.	THE LEGISLATIVE ASSEMBLY—REACTION IN 1791-1792	237
XXXI.	THE COUNTER-REVOLUTION IN THE SOUTH OF FRANCE	247
XXXII.	THE TWENTIETH OF JUNE 1792	255
XXXIII.	THE TENTH OF AUGUST: ITS IMMEDIATE CONSEQUENCES	268
XXXIV.	THE INTERREGNUM—THE BETRAYALS	282
XXXV.	THE SEPTEMBER DAYS	297
XXXVI.	THE CONVENTION—THE COMMUNE—THE JACOBINS	309
XXXVII.	THE GOVERNMENT—CONFLICTS WITH THE CONVENTION—THE WAR	318
XXXVIII.	THE TRIAL OF THE KING	330
XXXIX.	THE "MOUNTAIN" AND THE GIRONDE	340
XL.	ATTEMPTS OF THE GIRONDINS TO STOP THE REVOLUTION	348
XLI.	THE "ANARCHISTS"	353
XLII.	CAUSES OF THE RISING ON MAY 31	361
XLIII.	SOCIAL DEMANDS—STATE OF FEELING IN PARIS—LYONS	370
XLIV.	THE WAR—THE RISING IN LA VENDÈE—TREACHERY OF DUMOURIEZ	379
XLV.	A NEW RISING RENDERED INEVITABLE	391
XLVI.	THE INSURRECTION OF MAY 31 AND JUNE 2	399
XLVII.	THE POPULAR REVOLUTION—ARBITRARY TAXATION	407
XLVIII.	THE LEGISLATIVE ASSEMBLY AND THE COMMUNAL LANDS	413
XLIX.	THE LANDS RESTORED TO THE COMMUNES	421
L.	FINAL ABOLITION OF THE FEUDAL RIGHTS	427
LI.	THE NATIONAL ESTATES	432
LII.	THE STRUGGLE AGAINST FAMINE—THE MAXIMUM—PAPER-MONEY	437

CONTENTS

LIII. Counter-Revolution in Brittany—Assassination of Marat	445
LIV. The Vendee—Lyons—The Risings in Southern France	453
LV. The War—The Invasion Beaten Back	462
LVI. The Constitution—The Revolutionary Movement	470
LVII. The Exhaustion of the Revolutionary Spirit	478
LVIII. The Communist Movement	484
LIX. Schemes for the Socialisation of Land, Industries, Means of Subsistence and Exchange	493
LX. The End of the Communist Movement	500
LXI. The Constitution of the Central Government—Reprisals	508
LXII. Education—The Metric System–The New Calendar–Anti-Religious Movement	518
LXIII. The Suppression of the Sections	528
LXIV. Struggle against the Hebertists	533
LXV. Fall of the Hebertists—Danton Executed	542
LXVI. Robespierre and his Group	550
LXVII. The Terror	555
LXVIII. The 9th Thermidor—Triumph of Reaction	562
Conclusion	573

AN INTRODUCTION

The Great French Revolution is Kropotkin's longest book and, apart from the chapters in *Mutual Aid* dealing with barbarian societies and medieval cities, it is his most important piece of historical writing. But it is something more than the history of a single event, however important, for Kropotkin uses his observations on what happened during the French Revolution to speculate on the reasons for its ultimate failure and to draw from his conclusions lessons about the nature of revolution, and the possible course of a future successful revolution. Such lessons he regarded as of great importance to himself and his fellow anarchists in their search for a means to transform society, to replace a coercive order by a co-operative order. Thus, though it rarely speaks explicitly of anarchism, *The Great French Revolution* has as important a place in libertarian polemics as it does in the historiography of the Revolution, which it views from a standpoint rarely taken by writers in Kropotkin's day, that of the ordinary people who provided the manpower for the revolution and the passion that inspired it during its most dynamic days.

The Great French Revolution was the fruition of half a century of preoccupation with the events that transformed France and Europe at the end of the eighteenth century. Peter Kropotkin's childhood tutor, Monsieur Poulain, was a veteran of Napoleon's Grande Armée who had been stranded in Russia after the French retreated from Moscow in 1812. Though he was an Orleanist

AN INTRODUCTION

— a supporter of the now deposed King Louis Philippe and a great admirer of Napoleon — Poulain retained his respect for the ideals of the French Revolution, and was profoundly shocked that in Russia the serfdom which had come to an end in France after the events of 1789 was still in existence. He told Kropotkin and his brother Alexander about the noblemen — and particularly Mirabeau — who had renounced their titles in the name of democracy; this so impressed Kropotkin that he decided no longer to call himself Prince.

He sustained this decision, despite the disapproval of his superiors, when he was admitted to the élite Corps of Pages. Indeed it was in 1860, while he was in the Corps of Pages, that young Peter began his first readings on the French Revolution in the house of his sister Helen, who was now living in St. Petersburg and, with her husband, had accumulated a library of French books forbidden by the Tsarist censors. Later, during his years of military service in Siberia, Kropotkin's interest in French revolutionary ideas was sustained through his introduction to Proudhon's writings by the exiled *narodnik*, M.K. Mikhailov. Later in the 1860s Kropotkin and his brother Alexander resigned their army commissions in protest against the brutal treatment of Polish prisoners who had attempted a mutiny.

Back in St. Petersburg, Peter became a member of the Chaikovsky circle, which was greatly influenced by the mid-nineteenth-century French socialist thinkers. At this time his interest in the Revolution was revived by reading some of the books in the library of a student, Nizovkin, who temporarily belonged to the Chaikovtsi. But his life as a radical propagandist among the St. Petersburg factory workers was too active for him to study very deeply, and once he was imprisoned in 1874 in the Peter-and-Paul Fortress it was impossible for him to obtain any kind of book that even smelt of revolution.

However, after his sensational escape from prison in 1876, and his decision to remain in Western Europe and participate in the anarchist movement there, Kropotkin's interest in the French Revolution revived. He lived first in England, and it was there in 1877 that he began in the British Museum his serious study of the Revolution. He continued it somewhat more desultorily in the Bibliothèque Nationale in Paris when he arrived there later in the year. His intent at this point was to gain some insight into the way revolutions begin. He was already seeking ways in which the phenomenon of revolution could be fitted into the concept of human society as an evolving entity which he had already developed from his reading of Darwin in the early 1860s.

This was a practical as well as a theoretical intent, for as soon as he reached Paris, Kropotkin had become involved in the activities of the clandestine anarchist groups operating there. Later in the year he moved to Switzerland where, with the help of some Geneva working men, he began to publish a propaganda sheet, *Le Revolté*. In October 1878 he gave an address to a congress of the Jura sections of the International which he later published in *Le Revolté* under the title of "The Anarchist Idea from the Point of View of its Practical Realization." It dealt largely with the revolutionary techniques which should be used in the international uprising which at this period Kropotkin regarded as imminent. His stress on the need for the revolution to be based on the activities of local communes, which would carry out expropriations and transform society by collectivising the means of production, coincided so remarkably with the views of the positive aspects of the revolution to which he would give expression in *The Great French Revolution* that one can hardly doubt the article emerged from his studies of revolutionary history in London and Paris in 1877.

Once again there was a period of intense propagandist activity, first in Switzerland and then, after his expulsion from that country, in France; once again the activity was terminated by imprisonment, this time after a shamefully rigged trial in 1883, in which Kropotkin was charged with membership of an illegal organization, the International, that had actually come to an end in 1877. Despite widespread indignation both in France and abroad at the injustice of the sentence, which provoked a widely signed petition from British scientists, writers and artists, Kropotkin remained in prison until 1886, when he was released and took refuge in

England, which remained his home until he returned to Russia in 1917.

In spite of all he had suffered from the reactionary regime that held power in France at the time of his imprisonment, Kropotkin was remarkably lacking in bitterness towards the French people or France regarded as a nation. Perhaps because, as a Russian aristocrat brought up in the manner initiated by Peter the Great, he had always spoken French fluently, he felt more at home there than in the England that accepted him with friendship and honour. Despite his imprisonment, he still regarded France as a country that had been irremediably changed by the revolution. Even if that revolution had not gained its objectives completely, it resulted in a society renewed where, as Kropotkin said in the last pages of *The Great French Revolution*, "for the first time in centuries the peasant ate his fill, straightened his back and dared to speak back." The revolution had broken feudalism, it had given land to the people, and in so doing it had transformed French society and the French economy. France, Kropotkin would declare in the last pages of *The Great French Revolution*, had become the richest country in Europe as a result of the changes in relations the revolution had precipitated, and with so much — in his view — gained socially he obviously regarded the political squalor of late nineteenth century France as a temporary phase that would pass because the people had learnt the lesson of freedom. Thus, like Bakunin, he always took the side of France in its recurrent disputes with Germany, which he regarded as an irremediably conservative society. In the end such an intense transfer of patriotism would lead him to abandon the anti-militarist tradition sustained by the anarchists, and in 1914 actively, to support the Allied cause, which would end in to his tragic isolation from the comrades of a life of struggle. But in the 1880s all that lay in the unanticipated future.

Not long after Kropotkin's return to England, his interest in the French Revolution was stimulated by its coming centenary, and during 1889 it became his principal preoccupation as he began to write the series of articles and essays on which *The Great French Revolution* would eventually be based.

In 1889 he published two articles on "Le Centenaire de la révolution" in *La Révolte*, the French anarchist journal which appeared after the suppression of *Le Révolté*, and was edited by Jean Grave with some distant collaboration from Kropotkin. In the same year Kropotkin wrote "The Great French Revolution and Its Lessons" for *The Nineteenth Century*, whose editor, James Knowles, was one of his staunchest non-anarchist supporters. Four years later, in 1893, *La Révolte* published a pamphlet (an expansion of the 1889 essays) entitled *Un Siécle d'attente, 1789-1889*. In 1894 *La Révolte* in its turn was suppressed during the French anti-anarchist panic of that period; it was followed in 1895 by *Temps Nouveaux*, also edited by Jean Grave, and in 1903 Kropotkin published two further articles in its columns on "Les Anarchistes et la grande révolution."

In preparing these articles and in carrying on the further research needed for his book, Kropotkin was unable to consult the manuscript and archival sources in France, since he was *persona non grata* there for many years after his release from prison. He did go to Paris in 1887, and on the 20th December gave a lecture on "The Moral Influence of Prisons on Prisoners" to a large audience in the Rue de Rivoli, but there is no record of his having done anything else at this time than deliver the lecture, and it is possible he was subjected to the attentions of the French police, for he made no attempt to visit France again, despite his love of the country, until 1896. Then he went to Dieppe, intending to speak under anarchist auspices in Paris, but was excluded because the Tsarevich (the future Nicholas II) happened to be visiting Nice, and the admission of so distinguished an opponent of the autocracy as Kropotkin would have displeased the authorities in St. Petersburg at a time when France was eager to sustain good relations with Russia as a counterbalance to Germany.

Not until 1905 was Kropotkin in fact able to visit France without interference. On this occasion, after a vacation on the north coast, he went to Paris and stayed with the great impressionist painter, Camille Pissaro, who was also a dedicated anarchist. But there is no evidence that he spent any of his time on research, and his own statement that he depended on the rich collection

AN INTRODUCTION   xv

of printed material in the British Museum can be accepted as generally correct. What little information he received from the French records came through James Guillaume, the printer from the Jura who had introduced him to the Swiss anarchists in 1872 and who had since moved to Paris where he took an active part in the revolutionary syndicalist movement which was emerging among French factory workers at this period and in which the anarchists were playing a leading role.

It was twenty years after his first article in *La Révolte* that Kropotkin finally published *The Great French Revolution*. He wrote it in French and it was this version that was issued in Paris by Stock, who also published the works of Bakunin and other anarchists. The English version, brought out by Heinemann, was translated by Nannie Florence Dryhurst, with whom Kropotkin was on friendly terms for his whole period in England until his departure to Russia in 1917. N.F. Dryhurst, the wife of a British Museum official, was one of the group Kropotkin gathered around him to found the English anarchist journal, *Freedom*, in 1886, and she remained close to the whole Kropotkin family for thirty years. There is no doubt that Kropotkin carefully supervised her translation, which is used in this edition. Shortly afterwards an Italian version was published in Switzerland by the Ticinese Luigi Bertoni, who brought out many anarchist books which at that time could not be published in Italy. Kropotkin was particularly impressed by the "brilliant translation"; the translator, it now seems ironical to observe, was the young Benito Mussolini, then a militant revolutionary socialist.

* * *

The Great French Revolution is essentially a popular history, untrammeled by any great pedantic apparatus, and this may be why academic historians have paid it so little attention. The approach was deliberate on Kropotkin's part; he wrote very consciously for the common reader, seeking to reach the worker as well as to convince the intellectual, and he set great store by clarity of presentation. Considering that he wrote most of his major works in languages that were not his own, either French or English, he succeeded remarkably well (with some scantily acknowledged help from native-speakers who corrected his manuscripts) for his books have a readability and an accessibility rare among political writers in his time. Even Proudhon's prose, vigorous though it may be, is dense in comparison with Kropotkin's.

Essentially, *The Great French Revolution* applies to a particular historic event the generalization that Kropotkin had already developed in the chapters of *Mutual Aid* which deal with human society when it reaches the level beyond primitive tribal groupings. Belonging to the generation of scientists which created the great guiding concepts that changed our view of the universe and of human destiny and which preceded the more recent age of specialization, Kropotkin set great store by generalization, which he saw as the result of an intuitive leap — rather like what the poets call "inspiration" — by which the scholar suddenly understands the natural law that underlies a whole complex of phenomena.

The generalization he drew out of his facts when he was writing *Mutual Aid* was that there is a natural tendency towards sociability which plays its part in the process of evolution, shaping human societies as well as animal species, and that by and large this tendency governs the relations among primitive peoples, whose societies depend on the maintenance of communal institutions to ensure survival in the struggle against adverse natural circumstances. When life becomes more settled, and larger, more prosperous, and technologically advanced communities emerge, a specialization of function appears, with largely negative results, for classes of warriors and priests and rulers emerge who seek to appropriate power and authority to themselves. At the same time, the real force that holds society together is the voluntary co-operation — or mutual aid — that still persists on a vast scale among the ordinary people. Thus two currents appear in every advanced society — that towards a class order based on private property and a hierarchy of power, and that towards free co-operation based on the needs and the natural tendencies of the populace.

AN INTRODUCTION

In *The Great French Revolution* Kropotkin saw a dramatic example of these two currents brought into action and opposition through the breakdown of an autocratic and still largely feudal order.

> For in the Paris insurrection leading to July 14, as all through the Revolution, there were two separate currents of different origin: the political movement of the middle classes and the popular movement of the masses. At certain moments during the great days of the Revolution, the two movements joined hands in a temporary alliance, and then they gained their great victories over the old régime. But the middle classes always distrusted their temporary ally, the people, and gave clear proof of this in July 1789. The alliance was concluded unwillingly by the middle classes; and on the morrow of the 14th, and even during the insurrection itself, they made haste to organize themselves, in order that they might be able to bridle the revolted people.

On the one side were the representatives of the rising middle class, the so-called Third Estate, who were largely inspired by the liberal thinkers of the Enlightenment, but who at the same time were anxious to make use of events to enrich themselves at the expense of the old aristocracy, and who therefore favoured either a limited monarchy or an oligarchical republic based on an electorate defined by property rights. On the other side were the poor, represented by the Parisian *sans culottes* (those who did not wear the knee-breeches and silk stockings of gentlemen), mainly labourers, craftsmen, mechanics and small shopkeepers, and also by the peasants in the countryside. The city workers — hardly yet a proletariat in the sense used by the Marxists — strove for a complete democracy in which every man would have the full rights of a citizen and would share in political power. The local "sections" in which the people of a *quartier* came together to decide their immediate concerns, and the Commune of Paris, were their means of organizing the revolution and giving expression to their demands; as Kropotkin convincingly demonstrates, the famous clubs which figure so notably in the political histories of the revolution were — even the Jacobin Club — overwhelmingly middle class in membership and also in orientation except when the people shouldered them in a radical direction. But it was the peasants, the most oppressed class of the *ancien régime*, whose role in the revolution was perhaps the most vital.

> The insurrection of the peasants for the abolition of the feudal rights and the recovery of the communal lands which had been taken away from the village communes, since the seventeenth century, by the lords, lay and ecclesiastical, is the very essence, the foundation of the Great Revolution. Upon it the struggle of the middle classes for their political rights was developed.

As he traces the popular elements of the revolution, the peasant risings, with the intent of repossessing the land and destroying the feudal records, and the various revolts of the Parisian poor that punctuated the revolutionary years, Kropotkin develops in this special context a number of themes that run through the general body of his work.

One of these is the importance of the local centre of activity, the commune, in keeping alive the spirit of a revolution. He saw the people working at this local level — often little known to history — as the real radicals who tried to relate events to the true needs of the country and the people.

> They made a bold attempt at organizing France as an aggregate of forty thousand communes, regularly corresponding amongst themselves, and representing so many centres of extreme democracy, which should work to establish the real equality — *l'égalité de fait*, as used then to be said — the "equalization of incomes."

The common people who sought to establish communes so that the revolution would have its local bases from which to halt attempts to impede the progress of the revolution were in fact, he suggests, re-establishing the traditional communalism of French peasant life — the kind of communalism dating from the middle ages which he had already praised in *Mutual Aid*. During the revolution

> ...it was the commune which took back from the lords the lands that were formerly communal, resisted the nobles, struggled against the priests, supported the patriots and later on the *sans-culottes*, arrested the returning emigrés, and stopped the runaway king.

In doing so, the communes acted against the centralizing tendencies of the middle class revolutionaries, who actually sought

AN INTRODUCTION xix

to curtail rights the people had retained even under the monarchy so that the attempts of the newly rich to take over the lands appropriated by the nobles should be unimpeded.

> As to the villages, they had preserved, as we have seen, under the old *régime*, in nearly the while of France, up to the Revolution, the general assembly of the inhabitants, like the Mir in Russia... But now these general assemblies of the village communes were forbidden by the Municipal Law of December 22 to 24, 1789.

The idea of the commune as an institution offering an alternative to state centralization recurs throughout the anarchist tradition, appearing in Proudhon as the basic unit of a federal system, and even in Godwin as the parish which he sees as the essential organic unit on which society could be organized. Already, in his earliest pamphlets and in his sketch of an anarchist revolution, *The Conquest of Bread*, Kropotkin had made the commune the basis of the kind of anarchism that has always been especially associated with him, anarchist communism, with its stress on the primacy of the economic and the social rather than the political factors in a revolution, and on the need to organize production and consumption on a free basis that will both stimulate the producer and satisfy the consumer with adequate provision to meet his true needs.

Closely linked with Kropotkin's concern with the organization of production and consumption was the idea of bread both as a pressing need during times of revolution and as a symbol of the well-being of the people. For Kropotkin, as a Russian, bread had a special significance; bread and salt were given as earnests of brotherhood and hospitality in Russian peasant communes (a custom persisting among the Doukhobors in Canada even to this day). But when he used *The Conquest of Bread* as the title for his most militantly anarchist book, it was because he saw the paramount importance of securing the economic base of the revolution, of keeping the people from starving, before anything more ambitious could be achieved. Such a conviction led him to write yet another of his important books, *Fields, Factories and Workshops*, which shows how the wastefulness of agricultural and industrial undertakings, under a system of private ownership, could be replaced by plenty for all under a system controlled by the workers and making full use of scientific knowledge to increase production rather than restricting it to serve special interests.

There is much of this talk of bread and of agricultural productivity in *The Great French Revolution*. Kropotkin notes that even before 1789 "the lack of bread always remained one of the principal causes of the risings." Generalizing from the experience of the French and other revolutions, he remarks that: "One of the great difficulties in every Revolution is the feeding of the large towns," and he argues that the desperation and even savagery of some of the manifestations of popular anger in Paris during the years of the revolution were due to the failure of those who tried to take control of events to satisfy the pressing material needs of the people. And he accused the Third Estate, so intent on using the revolution for the conquest of power on behalf of the middle classes, of failing to recognize:

> yet another problem, infinitely more important to solve — that of giving back the land to the peasant, in order that, possessing a land freed from heavy feudal exactions, he might double and treble the production of its soil, and so put an end to the incessant periods of scarcity that were undermining the strength of the French nation.

Perhaps the one tangible victory of the revolution, in Kropotkin's eyes, came from the fact that incessant pressure from the people forced the middle-class revolutionaries in the Convention, and particularly the Jacobins, finally to return their land to the peasants free of feudal exactions, thus creating a situation when even the Bourbons, returning in 1815, were unable to reverse, and ensuring France's pre-eminence in productivity among the agrarian nations of Europe.

As was his custom, Kropotkin sought in *The Great French Revolution* to generalize from the particulars, and much of the book is concerned — in a manner consonant with the scientific style of the time — with finding the "laws" under which revolutions proceed, laws that seemed to him embodied in the failures and successes of the French Revolution. For example, he saw in the progression of a revolution a kind of recapitulative

AN INTRODUCTION xxi

process similar to that which contemporary evolutionists saw in the development of the human embryo.

> When a revolution has begun, each event in it not merely sums up the events hitherto accomplished; it also contains the chief elements of what is to come.

For him revolutions were really accelerations of the evolutionary process, rather like the mutations by which species will show dramatic changes in a short period of time.

> This is the 'anarchic' revolution, the only way pertaining to free Nature. It is the same even with institutions when they are the organic product of life, and this is why revolutions have such immense importance in the life of societies. They allow men to start with the organic reconstruction work without being hampered by an authority which, perforce, always represents the past ages.

At another point, seeming to reverse Proudhon's famous dictum that "anarchy is order", he declared the necessity of what one might call creative insurrectionism, when he remarked:

> In fact, the triumph of the committees over the Commune of Paris was the triumph of *order*, and during a revolution the triumph of order is the termination of the *revolutionary* period. There might be a few more convulsions, but the Revolution was at an end.

The "committees" to which he referred were the Committee of Public Welfare and the Committee of Public Safety, the sinister tribunals that increasingly directed the Terror towards the establishment of a centralized authoritarian republic, represented at its most extreme by the inflexible doctrinaire Saint Just. Kropotkin believed that the Committees and the interests they represented had disastrously impeded the natural processes of the revolution.

> The fact is, that a revolution that stops half-way is sure to be soon defeated, and at the end of 1793 the situation in France was, that the Revolution, having been arrested in its development, was now wearing itself out in internal struggles.

Nevertheless, there was a central paradox in the operation of revolutions that Kropotkin never fully reconciled; it was that of the dedicated and often lonely revolutionary and the masses who might benefit from his actions. Kropotkin has few illusions about the masses, even when they became involved in a revolution, being able without some kind of guidance to carry events to positive conclusions. He realized from experience how few the militants always were, how cautious, except at critical moments, was the support they received from the general populace.

> Revolutions, we must remember, are always made by minorities, and when a revolution has begun, and a part of the nation accepts its consequences, there is always only a very small minority who understand what still remains to be done to ensure the triumph of what has been obtained, and who have the courage of action.

As he well knew, the impetus of an occasion like the taking of the Bastille, when the people came out in the dawn of the revolution, full of enthusiasm and resolution, was less and less likely to be repeated as the revolution continued. Yet any diminution in the vigilance, not only of militants, but also of the people in general, any lessening of the maximalist urge towards entire social and economic equality, was bound to open the revolution to the politically minded, the men seeking personal power and wealth.

> A revolution should include *the welfare of all*, otherwise it is certain to be crushed by those very persons whom it has enriched at the expense of the nation. Where a shifting of wealth is caused by a revolution, it ought never to be for the benefit of *individuals* but always for the benefit of *communities*.

Here Kropotkin was writing with an eye partially on the experience of dedicated anarchists in the nineteenth century: of Malatesta and Cafiero trying to rouse the peasants of southern Italy to burn the tax records and seize the land; of Bakunin in Lyons of 1870 trying to recreate the revolutionary commune; of Proudhon in the 1860s attempting to convince the working men of their own political capability which took another direction from that of party politics. And although *The Great French Revolution* is not openly a manifesto for anarchism, it is very clear that Kropotkin is trying to find the roots of the movement to which be belonged in the French Revolution, and also to draw from that revolution lessons for anarchists in the present. He may, through ill health, have withdrawn largely from active participation in the movement itself, which in England was in any case small and devoted mainly to rather sedate propaganda, but he still believed in the possibility of revolutionary changes in society, he thought the anarchists were the only people calling themselves revolutionaries who had the right will and awareness to avoid the errors of the French Revolution, and he sought in his own way to prepare them for the revolutionary opportunities which he still believed, and with renewed expectations after the abortive Russian revolution of 1905, would emerge in the not distant future.

In the actions of the people of France in 1789 Kropotkin saw anarchism in action even before its principles were worked out theoretically by William Godwin, the first of the anarchist thinkers, whose strong roots in the English dissenting tradition Kropotkin chose to ignore. For him *Political Justice* was a brilliant production of its own times and most significant as a development of ideas originating in the French Revolution.

In fact, as he had already done in great detail in the original Russian version of *Modern Science and Anarchism* (published in London in 1901), Kropotkin was seeking, even as he wrote his own version of the history of the French Revolution, to give anarchism an ancestry, a tradition. This of course accorded with the approach he necessarily took in *Mutual Aid*, where he presented his libertarian communist ideal of a society, united by voluntary social and economic links, as part of a great natural continuity stretching back far before the dawn of human history or even of the existence of man as a species.

As more recent scientists might say, Kropotkin saw man as part of a great ecosystem whose laws must be rediscovered, and so he differed from the eschatological kind of revolutionary, who seeks to establish a new Earth if not a new Heaven, by contending that we do not need the radically changed world of Utopia, because what we are searching for is what is already there, waiting to be revived and reactivated. The real aim of the French Revolution, as he saw it, was to take people back to a past from which they had strayed, to return to the people what they had lost: the common land, the liberties shredded away by feudalism, and to let them start again creating a sane society.

Kropotkin devotes a chapter to those whom their enemies — notably the Girondins — called "the anarchists", and he shows how these men, like Jacques Roux and Jean Varlet, did anticipate the anarchists of later periods by their continuous selfless agitation, and by their recognition that the revolution had not ended and would not continue unless the Convention were continually forced by the people whom they — the "anarchists" — considered it their duty both to support and to incite.

One senses anxiety and foreboding in *The Great French Revolution* whenever Kropotkin seems to be using the event as an example. He tells how, at the time of the Terror:

> The creative, constructive spirit of a popular revolution, which was feeling its way, was now confronted by the spirit of police management, which was soon to crush it.

In other words, he was showing a revolution that failed. He was aware that other revolutions had failed in the same way, as the English one did when Cromwell suppressed the Levellers, as the 1848 revolutions and the Commune of 1871 also failed and, most pertinent in 1909 when the *Great French Revolution* appeared, the Russian revolution of 1905. He foresaw, as we know from his correspondence, a renewal of the revolutionary ferment in Russia, and the lessons he drew from the French experience were largely directed at his comrades there, members of a small movement that would play little part in the events of 1917.

When Kropotkin returned to Russia in 1917, an old and wornout man, to play what part he could in the revolution, he found — as he wrote to his friend Georg Brandes in 1919 — that the Bolsheviks were following a similar path of centralism and authoritarianism to that pursued by the Jacobins between 1792 and 1794. He felt that, unless the "social revolution" were allowed to find its "right path", the constructive work of the people would be negated, and "a furious and evil reaction" would follow, as it did under Stalin. Lenin, who seems to have had some kind of personal regard for the old anarchist, tried to persuade him to allow *The Great French Revolution* to be republished in Russian; Kropotkin refused because he did not want his work to be brought out by a State publishing house, and at that time there was no alternative.

There remain some aspects of *The Great Revolution* which seem to mar the consistency of the work, and which suggest the confusion of Kropotkin's loyalties. At one point he remarks that "in revolution it is only the accomplished facts that count." Yet a few pages earlier he had complained that: "What the historians have chiefly studied on this period is the War and the Terror. Yet these are not the essentials." But it would seem, even from reading Kropotkin's account, that the War and the Terror are not only "accomplished facts", but that they are *essential* facts to the extent that they offer the principal reasons why the popular movement failed.

Kropotkin's attitude to the revolutionary wars is ambivalent. There are times when he glorifies the romantic aspects of the formation of a citizen army — "the tocsin sounding all over Paris, the drums beating in the streets, the alarum gun, the reports of which rang out every quarter of an hour, the songs of the volunteers setting out for the frontier..." — and others when he saw the war as a convenience both for the supporters of the old regime and for the middle-class leaders seeking to establish their own power. The fact is that he himself was trapped between his transferred loyalty to France, which would take on militaristic aspects when he supported the Allies in World War I, and the anti-militarism of the anarchists. He never at any point really faced the fact that war — even defensive war — has always been the death of revolutions, for the simple fact that war needs for its continuance the very disregard of human life and human freedom that re-establishes authority and reaction. This happened during the French revolutionary wars that ended in Bonapartist imperialism, it happened in Russia during the civil war which ended in a State run by the secret police, it happened in Spain, where the anarchists never really stood a chance against their ruthlessly authoritarian and military more efficient opponents of the left and right alike. "War," as Randolph Bourne said, "is the health of the State." It is the wasting sickness of the Revolution.

Kropotkin's equivocal view of terror in the French Revolution was bred of his indecision during the 1890s about the anarchist assassins of the period. His feelings were repelled by their actions, and yet on principle — since he himself allowed for violent methods — he found himself unable to condemn them, particularly as he admired their suicidal courage. Tolstoy defined Kropotkin's uneasy position astutely when he remarked to their common friend, Vladimir Chertkov:

> His arguments in favour of violence do not seem to me to be the expression of his real opinions, but only of his fidelity to the banner under which he has served so honestly all his life.

It is hard, in fact, to find a consistent line in Kropotkin's attitude to terror during the revolution, since he seems to condemn its use in some hands but not in others. For example, he rightly denounces the indiscriminate execution of people from both right and "anarchist" left, of innocent and guilty, of opponents and former comrades in action, by the Committee of Public Safety and its pitiless henchmen. But towards the September massacres of 1792 he is much more ambivalent, even though many among the thousand odd people slaughtered in the Paris prisons at this time were innocent of intrigue against the revolution; they included no less than 300 common law prisoners who had the ill luck to be incarcerated with the political "suspects". Kropotkin treats these massacres as a popular uprising, coming from the anger of the people, and blames them on the failure of the Convention to move quickly enough in fulfilling the aims of the revolution.

> In these hesitations, in this pusillanimity, this want of honesty among the statesmen in power, lies the true cause of the despair that seized upon the people of Paris on September 2.

But he does not give due importance to the fact — which he offers himself — that the people slaughtered, often very cruelly, on September 2, were not killed by an angry popular "mob", but cold-bloodedly by a group of at most three hundred self-appointed "executioners". From such "popular" killings of people whose guilt was unproven, to the State-supported killings of "suspects" by the Jacobin dictators in 1783 was not a great step.

Perhaps Kropotkin shows in the poorest light, from his own anarchist viewpoint, when he is dealing with the trial of Louis XVI. Since anarchists do not support the right of the State to exist, one would have expected a trial for treason to arouse at least some uneasiness in Kropotkin. What *is* treason, if one condemns political loyalties? Furthermore, having already written books, pamphlets and articles condemning the legal process and the idea of punishment, it seems extraordinary that Kropotkin should write of a trial of any kind, particularly one resulting from the death penalty, with equanimity. Yet he did so, not merely without revulsion, but also with a kind of gloating approval that does not sit well with his repute as a "gentle" anarchist.

> From the legal point of view, there is... nothing wherewith to reproach the Convention...
> On the contrary, by sending Louis to the scaffold, the Revolution succeeded in killing a principle, which the peasants had begun to kill at Varennes. On January 21, 1793, the revolutionary portion of the French people knew well that the pivot of all the power, which for centuries had oppressed and exploited the masses, was broken at last...

Surely, for a consistent anarchist, there can be no "legal point of view," and there seems a lapse in libertarian logic when killing a "principle" is used as an excuse for killing a human being. Kropotkin might have considered the arguments Tom Paine put forward in 1793, at the risk of his own life (he was saved from the guillotine only by Robespierre's fall) when he claimed that the revolution would harm itself by killing the king and that banishment was preferable to execution. Kropotkin must have known of Paine's arguments and his courageous stand, but he mentions neither.

Kropotkin's attitude in these crucial issues of anarchist morality shows that, though he performed an immensely useful task in stressing the social and economic aspects of the events, and the importance of the communal strain in bringing about some fundamental changes in French society even if the revolution was not wholly successful, he still remained in part a prisoner of the political myths that have coloured our view of the dramatic years from 1789 to 1794. Much as he hated the Jacobins for their centralizing authoritarianism, he did not entirely escape their spell.

George Woodcock

PREFACE

The more one studies the French Revolution the clearer it is to see how incomplete is the history of that great epoch, how many gaps in it remain to be filled, how many points demand elucidation.

How could it be otherwise ? The Great Revolution, that set all Europe astir, that overthrew everything, and began the task of universal reconstruction in the course of a few years, was like the working of cosmic forces dissolving and re-creating a world. And if in the writings of the historians who deal with that period, and especially of Michelet, we admire the immense work they have accomplished in disentangling and co-ordinating the innumerable facts of the various parallel movements that made up the Revolution, we realise at the same time the vastness of the work which still remains to be done.

The investigations made during the past thirty years by the school of historical research represented by M. Aulard and the Société de la Révolution française, have certainly furnished most valuable material. They have shed a flood of light upon the acts of the Revolution, on its political aspects, and on the struggles for supremacy that took place between the various parties. But the study of the economic side of the Revolution is still before us, and this study, as M. Aulard rightly says, demands an entire lifetime. Yet without this study the history of the period remains incomplete and in many points wholly incomprehensible. In fact, a long series of totally new problems presents itself to the historian as soon as he turns his attention to the economic side of the revolutionary upheaval.

It was with the intention of throwing some light upon these economic problems that I began in 1886 to make separate studies of the earliest revolutionary stirrings among the peasants; the peasant risings in 1789; the struggles for and against the feudal laws; the real causes of the movement of May 31, and so on. Unfortunately I was not able to make any researches in the National Archives of France, and my studies have, therefore, been confined to the collections of printed matter in the British Museum, which are, however, in themselves exceedingly rich.

Believing that it would not be easy for the reader to appreciate the bearing of separate studies of this kind without a general view of the whole development of the Revolution understood in the light of these studies, I soon found it necessary to write a more or less consecutive account of the chief events of the Revolution. In this account I have not dwelt upon the dramatic side of the episodes of these disturbed years, which have been so often described, but I have made it my chief object to utilise modern research so as to reveal the intimate connection and interdependence of the various events which combined to produce the climax of the eighteenth century's epic.

This method of studying separately the various parts of the work accomplished by the Revolution has necessarily its own drawbacks: it sometimes entails repetition. I have preferred, however, to take the risk of reproach for this fault in the hope of impressing more clearly upon the reader's mind the mighty currents of thought and action that came into conflict during the French Revolution—currents so intimately blended with the very essence of human nature that they must inevitably reappear in the historic events of the future.

All who know the history of the Revolution will understand how difficult it is to avoid errors in facts when one tries to trace the development of its impassioned struggles. I shall, therefore, be extremely grateful to those who will be good enough to point out any mistakes I may have made. And I wish to express here my sincerest gratitude to my friends, James Guillaume and Ernest Nys, who have had the kindness to read my manuscript and to help me in this work with their knowledge and their criticisms.

PETER KROPOTKIN

CHAPTER I

THE TWO GREAT CURRENTS OF THE REVOLUTION

Main causes of Great Revolution—Previous risings—Union of middle classes and people necessary—Importance of part played by people

Two great currents prepared and made the Great French Revolution. One of them, the current of ideas, concerning the political reorganisation of States, came from the middle classes; the other, the current of action, came from the people, both peasants and workers in towns, who wanted to obtain immediate and definite improvements in their economic condition. And when these two currents met and joined in the endeavour to realise an aim which for some time was common to both, when they had helped each other for a certain time, the result was the Revolution.

The eighteenth-century philosophers had long been sapping the foundations of the law-and-order societies of that period, wherein political power, as well as an immense share of the wealth, belonged to the aristocracy and the clergy, whilst the mass of the people were nothing but beasts of burden to the ruling classes. By proclaiming the sovereignty of reason; by preaching trust in human nature—corrupted, they declared, by the institutions that had reduced man to servitude, but, nevertheless, certain to regain all its qualities when it had reconquered liberty—they had opened up new vistas to mankind. By proclaiming equality among men, without distinction of birth; by demanding from every citizen, whether king or peasant, obedience to the law, supposed to express the will of the nation when it has been made by the representatives of the people; finally, by demanding freedom of contract between free men, and the abolition of feudal taxes and services—by putting forward all these claims, linked together with the system and method characteristic of French thought, the philosophers had undoubtedly prepared, at least in men's minds, the downfall of the old *régime*.

This alone, however, would not have sufficed to cause the outbreak of the Revolution. There was still the stage of passing from theory to action, from the conception of an ideal to putting it into practice. And the most important point in the study of the history of that period is to bring into relief the circumstances that made it possible for the French nation at a given moment to enter on the realisation of the ideal—to attempt this passage from theory to action.

On the other hand, long before 1789, France had already entered upon an insurrectionary period. The accession of Louis XVI. to the throne in 1774 was the signal for a whole series of hunger riots. These lasted up to 1783; and then came a period of comparative quiet. But after 1786, and still more after 1788, the peasant insurrections broke out again with renewed vigour. Famine had been the chief source of the earlier disturbances, and the lack of bread always remained one of the principal causes of the risings. But it was chiefly disinclination on the part of the peasants to pay the feudal taxes which now spurred them to revolt. The outbreaks went on increasing in number up to 1789, and in that year they became general in the east, north-east and south-east of France.

In this way the disaggregation of the body social came about. *A jacquerie* is not, however, a revolution, even when it takes such terrible forms as did the rising of the Russian peasants in 1773 under the banner of Pougatchoff. A revolution is infinitely more than a series of insurrections in town and country. It is more than a simple struggle between parties, however sanguinary; more than mere street-fighting, and much more than a mere change of government, such as was made in France in 1830 and 1848. A revolution is a swift overthrow, in a few years, of institutions which have taken

THE TWO GREAT CURRENTS

centuries to root in the soil, and seem so fixed and immovable that even the most ardent reformers hardly dare to attack them in their writings. It is the fall, the crumbling away in a brief period, of all that up to that time composed the essence of social, religious, political and economic life in a nation. It means the subversion of acquired ideas and of accepted notions concerning each of the complex institutions and relations of the human herd.

In short, it is the birth of completely new ideas concerning the manifold links in citizenship—conceptions which soon become realities, and then begin to spread among the neighbouring nations, convulsing the world and giving to the succeeding age its watchword, its problems, its science, its lines of economic, political and moral development.

To arrive at a result of this importance, and for a movement to assume the proportions of a revolution, as happened in England between 1648 and 1688, and in France between 1789 and 1793, it is not enough that a movement of ideas, no matter how profound it may be, should manifest itself among the educated classes; it is not enough that disturbances, however many or great, should take place in the very heart of the people. The revolutionary action coming from the people must coincide with a movement of revolutionary thought coming from the educated classes. There must be a union of the two.

That is why the French Revolution, like the English Revolution of the preceding century, happened at the moment when the middle classes, having drunk deep at the sources of current philosophy, became conscious of their rights, and conceived a new scheme of political organisation. Strong in their knowledge and eager for the task, they felt themselves quite capable of seizing the government by snatching it from a palace aristocracy which, by its incapacity, frivolity and debauchery, was bringing the kingdom to utter ruin. But the middle and educated classes could not have done anything alone, if, consequent on a complete chain of circumstances, the mass of the peasants had not also been stirred, and, by a series of constant insurrections lasting for four years, given to the dissatisfied among the middle classes the possibility of combating both King and Court, of upsetting old institutions and changing the political constitution of the kingdom.

The history of this double movement remains still to be written. The history of the great French Revolution has been told and re-told many times, from the point of view of as many different parties; but up to the present the historians have confined themselves to the political history, the history of the triumph of the middle classes over the Court party and the defenders of the institutions of the old monarchy.

Thus we know very well the principles which dominated the Revolution and were translated into its legislative work. We have been enraptured by the great thoughts it flung to the world, thoughts which civilised countries tried to put into practice during the nineteenth century. The Parliamentary history of the Revolution, its wars, its policy and its diplomacy, has been studied and set forth in all its details. But the *popular* history of the Revolution remains still to be told. The part played by the *people* of the country places and towns in the Revolution has never been studied and narrated in its entirety. Of the two currents which made the Revolution, the current of *thought* is known; but the other, the current of *popular action*, has not even been sketched.

It is for us, the descendants of those called by their contemporaries the "anarchists," to study the popular current, and to try to reconstruct at least its main features.

CHAPTER II

THE IDEA

Modern States—Influence of English and American Revolutions on French Revolution—Condition and aims of middle classes—Centralisation of authority—Attitude towards peasants—Influence of eighteenth-century philosophy

To understand fully the idea which inspired the middle classes in 1789 we must consider it in the light of its results—the modern States.

The structure of the law-and-order States which we see in Europe at present was only outlined at the end of the eighteenth century. The system of the centralised authority, now in full working order, had not then attained either the perfection or uniformity it possesses to-day. That formidable mechanism, by which an order sent from a certain capital puts in motion all the men of a nation, ready for war, and sends them out to carry devastation through countries, and mourning into families; those territories, overspread with a network of officials whose personality is completely effaced by their bureaucratic apprenticeship, and who obey mechanically the orders emanating from a central will; that passive obedience of citizens to the law; that worship of law, of Parliament, of judges and their assistants, which we see about us to-day; that mass of hierarchically organised and disciplined functionaries; that system of schools, maintained or directed by the State, where worship of power and passive obedience are taught; that industrial system, which crushes under its wheels the worker whom the State delivers over to its tender mercies; that commerce, which accumulates incredible riches in the hands of those who monopolise the land, the mines, the ways of communication and the riches of *Nature*, upon which the State is nourished; and finally, that science, which liberates thought and immensely increases the productive powers of men, but which at the same time aims at subjecting them to the authority of the strongest and to the State—all this was non-existent before the Revolution.

However, long before the Revolution had by its mutterings given warning of its approach, the French middle classes—the Third Estate—had already developed a conception of the political edifice which should be erected on the ruins of feudal royalty. It is highly probable that the English Revolution had helped the French middle class towards a comprehension of the part they would be called on to play in the government of society. And it is certain that the revolution in America stimulated the energies of the middle-class revolutionaries. Thanks to Hobbes, Hume, Montesquieu, Rousseau, Voltaire, Mably, d'Argenson and others, ever since the beginning of the eighteenth century the study of Politics and the constitution of organised societies based on elective representation had become popular, and to this Turgot and Adam Smith had just added the study of economic questions and the place of property in the political constitution of a State.

That is why, long before the Revolution broke out, the idea of a State, centralised and well-ordered, governed by the classes holding property in lands or in factories, or by members of the learned professions, was already forecast and described in a great number of books and pamphlets from which the men of action during the Revolution afterwards drew their inspiration and their logical force.

Thus it came to pass that the French middle classes in 1789, at the moment of entering upon the revolutionary period, knew quite well what they wanted. They were certainly not republicans—are they republicans even to-day? But they no longer wanted the King to have arbitrary powers, they refused to be ruled by the princes or by the Court, and they did not recognise the right of the nobility to seize on all the best places in the Government, though they were only capable of plundering the State as they had plundered their vast properties without adding anything to their value. The middle classes were perhaps republican in sentiment, and desired republican simplicity of manners, as in the growing republic of America; but they desired, above all things, government by the propertied classes.

They inclined to free thought without being Atheists, but they by no means disliked the Catholic form of religion. What they detested most was the Church, with its hierarchy and its bishops, who made common cause with the princes, and its priests who had become the obedient tools of the nobility.

The middle classes of 1789 understood that the moment had arrived in France, as it had arrived one hundred and forty years before in England, when the Third Estate was to seize the power falling from the hands of royalty, and they knew what they meant to do with it.

Their ideal was to give France a constitution modelled upon the English constitution, and to reduce the King to the part of a mere enregistering scribe, with sometimes the power of a casting-vote, but chiefly to act as the symbol of national unity. As to the real authority, that was to be vested in a Parliament, in which an educated middle class, which would represent the active and thinking part of the nation, should predominate.

At the same time, their ideal was to abolish all the local powers which at that time constituted so many autonomous units in the State. They meant to concentrate all governmental power in the hands of a central executive authority, strictly controlled by the Parliament, but also strictly obeyed in the State, and combining every department—taxes, law courts, police, army, schools, civic control, general direction of commerce and industry—everything. By the side of this political concentration, they intended to proclaim complete freedom in commercial transactions, and at the same time to give free rein to industrial enterprise for the exploitation of all sorts of natural wealth, as well as of the workers, who henceforth would be delivered up defenceless to any one who might employ them.

All this was to be kept under the strict control of the State, which would favour the enrichment of the individual and the accumulation of large fortunes—two conditions to which great importance was necessarily attached by the middle classes, seeing that the States General itself had been convoked to ward off the financial ruin of the State.

On economic matters, the men of action belonging to the Third Estate held ideas no less precise. The French middle classes had studied Turgot and Adam Smith, the creators of political economy. They knew that the theories of those writers had already been applied in England, and they envied their middle-class neighbours across the Channel their powerful economic organisation, just as they envied them their political power. They dreamed of an appropriation of the land by the middle classes, both upper and lower, and of the revenue they would draw from the soil, which had hitherto lain unproductive in the hands of the nobility and the clergy. In this they were supported by the lower middle class settled in the country, who had become a power in the villages, even before the Revolution increased their number. They foresaw the rapid development of trade and the production of merchandise on a large scale by the help of machinery; they looked forward to a foreign trade with distant lands, and the exportation of manufactured goods across the seas to markets that would be opened in the East, to huge enterprises and colossal fortunes.

But before all this could be realised they knew the ties that bound the peasant to his village must be broken. It was necessary that he should be free to leave his hut, and even that he should be forced to leave it, so that he might be impelled towards the towns in search of work. Then, in changing masters, he would bring gold to trade, instead of paying to the landlords all sorts of rents, tithes and taxes, which certainly pressed very heavily upon him, but which after all were not very profitable for the masters. And finally, the finances of the State had to be put in order; taxation would be simplified, and, at the same time, a bigger revenue obtained.

In short, what they wanted was what economists have called freedom of industry and commerce, but which really meant the relieving of industry from the harassing and repressive supervision of the State, and the giving to it full liberty to exploit the worker, who was still to be deprived of his freedom. There were to be no guilds, no trade societies; neither trade wardens nor master craftsmen; nothing which might in any way check the exploitation of the wage-earner. There was no longer to be any State supervision which might hamper the manufacturer. There were to be no duties on home industries, no prohibitive laws. For all the transactions of the employers, there was to be complete freedom, and for the workers a strict prohibition against combinations of any sort. *Laisser faire* for the one; complete denial of the right to combine for the others.

Such was the two-fold scheme devised by the middle classes. Therefore when the time came for its realisation, the middle classes, strengthened by their knowledge, the clearness of their views and their business habits, without hesitating over their scheme as a whole or at any detail of it, set to work to make it become law. And this they did with a consistent and intelligent energy quite impossible to the masses of the people, because by them no ideal had been planned and elaborated which could have been opposed to the scheme of the gentlemen of the Third Estate.

It would certainly be unjust to say that the middle classes were actuated only by purely selfish motives. If that had been the case they would never have succeeded in their task. In great changes a certain amount of idealism is always necessary to success.

The best representatives of the Third Estate had, indeed, drunk from that sublime fount, the eighteenth-century philosophy, which was the source of all the great ideas that have arisen since. The eminently scientific spirit of this philosophy; its profoundly moral character, moral even when it mocked at conventional morality; its trust in the intelligence, strength and greatness of the free man when he lives among his equals; its hatred of despotic institutions—were all accepted by the revolutionists of that time. Whence would they have drawn otherwise the powers of conviction and the devotion of which they gave such proofs in the struggle? It must also be owned that even among those who worked hardest to realise the programme of enriching the middle classes, there were some who seriously believed that the enrichment of the individual would be the best means of enriching the nation as a whole. Had not the best economists, with Adam Smith at their head, persuasively preached this view ?

But however lofty were the abstract ideas of liberty, equality and free progress that inspired the sincere men among the middle classes of 1789–1793, it is by their practical programme, by the application of their theories, that we must judge them. Into what deeds shall the abstract idea be translated in actual life ? By that alone can we find its true measure.

If, then, it is only fair to admit that the middle classes of 1789 were inspired by ideas of liberty, equality (before the law), and political and religious freedom, we must also admit that these ideas, as soon as they took shape, began to develop exactly on the two lines we have just sketched ; liberty to utilise the riches of Nature for personal aggrandisement, as well as liberty to exploit human labour without any safeguard for the victims of such exploitation, and political power organised so as to assure freedom of exploitation to the middle classes. And we shall see presently what terrible struggles were evolved in 1793 when one of the revolutionary parties wished to go further than this programme.

CHAPTER III

ACTION

The people—Revolution and Socialism—Equal rights of all to land—" Communism "—Situation not clearly understood by people—Hatred of poor towards aristocracy and clergy—Hatred of feudalism—People's readiness to take up arms

But what of the people ? What was their idea ?

The people, too, had felt to a certain extent the influence of the current philosophy. By a thousand indirect channels the great principles of liberty and enfranchisement had filtered down to the villages and the suburbs of the large towns. Respect for royalty and aristocracy was passing away. Ideas of equality were penetrating to the very lowest ranks. Gleams of revolt flashed through many minds. The hope of an approaching change throbbed in the hearts of the humblest. " Something was to be done by some great folk for such poor ones "; she did not know who, nor how; " but God send us better," said an old woman, in 1789, to Arthur Young,* who travelled through France on the eve of the Revolution. That " something " was bound to bring an alleviation of the people's misery.

The question whether the movement which preceded the Revolution, and the Revolution itself, contained any element of Socialism has been recently discussed. The word " Socialism " was certainly not in either, because it dates only from the middle of the nineteenth century. The idea of the State as Capitalist, to which the Social-Democratic fraction of the great Socialist party is now trying to reduce Socialism, was certainly not so much in evidence as it is to-day, because the founders of Social-Democratic " Collectivism," Vidal and Pecqueur, did not

* Arthur Young, *Travels in France*, p. 167 (London, 1892).

write until the period between 1840 and 1849. But it is impossible to read the works of the pre-Revolutionary writers without being struck by the fact that they are imbued with ideas which are the very essence of modern Socialism.

Two fundamental ideas—the equal rights of all citizens to the land, and what we know to-day under the name of communism—found devoted adherents among the more popular writers of that time, Mably, d'Argenson, and others of less importance. Manufacturing production on a large scale was in its infancy, so that land was at that time the main form of capital and the chief instrument for exploiting human labour, while the factory was hardly developed at all. It was natural, therefore, that the thoughts of the philosophers, and later on the thoughts of the revolutionists, should turn towards *communal possession of the land*. Did not Mably, who much more than Rousseau inspired the men of the Revolution, declare about 1768, in his *Doutes sur l'ordre naturel et essentiel des sociétés*, that there should be equal rights to the land for all, and communist possession of it ? The rights of the nation to all landed property, and to all natural wealth—forests, rivers, waterfalls, &c.—was not this the dominant idea of the pre-Revolutionary writers, as well as of the left wing of the revolutionary masses during the period of upheaval ?

Unfortunately, these communistic aspirations were not formulated clearly and concretely in the minds of those who desired the people's happiness. While among the educated middle classes the ideas of emancipation had taken the form of a complete programme for political and economic organisation, these ideas were presented to the people only in the form of vague aspirations. Often they were mere negations. Those who addressed the people did not try to embody the concrete form in which their *desiderata* could be realised. It is even probable that they avoided being precise. Consciously or not, they seemed to say : "What good is there in speaking to the people of the way in which they will be organised later on ? It would only chill their revolutionary ardour. All they want is the strength to attack and to march to the assault of the old institutions. Later on we shall see what can be done for them."

Are there not many Socialists and Anarchists who act still in the same way? In their hurry to push on to the day of revolt they treat as soporific theorising every attempt to throw some light on what ought to be the aim of the Revolution.

It must be said, also, that the ignorance of the writers—city men and bookmen for the most part—counted for much in this. Thus, in the whole of that gathering of learned or experienced business men who composed the National Assembly—lawyers, journalists, tradesmen, and so forth—there were only two or three legal members who had studied the feudal laws, and we know there were among them but very few representatives of the peasants who were familiar by personal experience with the needs of village life.

For these reasons the ideas of the masses were expressed chiefly by simple negations. "Let us burn the registers in which the feudal dues are recorded! Down with the tithes! Down with 'Madame Veto'! Hang the aristocrats!" But to whom was the freed land to go? Who were to be the heirs of the guillotined nobles? Who was to grasp the political power when it should fall from the hands of "Monsieur Veto," the power which became in the hands of the middle classes a much more formidable weapon than it had been under the old *régime?*

This want of clearness in the mind of the people as to what they should hope from the Revolution left its imprint on the whole movement. While the middle classes were marching with firm and decided steps towards the establishment of their political power in a State which they were trying to mould, according to their preconceived ideas, the people were hesitating. In the towns, especially, they did not seem to know how to turn to their own advantage the power they had conquered. And later, when ideas concerning agrarian laws and the equalising of incomes began to take definite form, they ran foul of a mass of property prejudices, with which even those sincerely devoted to the cause of the people were imbued.

A similar conflict was evoked by the conceptions of the political organisation of the State. We see it chiefly in the antagonism which arose between the governmental prejudices of the democrats of that time and the ideas that dawned in the hearts of the people as to political decentralisation, and the prominent place which the people wished their municipalities to take both in the division of the large towns and in the village assemblies. This was the starting-point of the whole series of fierce contests which broke out in the Convention. Thence, too, arose the indefiniteness of the results obtained by the Revolution for the great mass of the people in all directions, except in the recovery of part of the land from the lords, lay and clerical, and the freeing of all land from the feudal taxes it formerly had to pay.

But if the people's ideas were confused on constructive lines, they were, on the other hand, extremely clear on certain points in their negations.

First of all, the hatred felt by the poor for the whole of the idle, lazy, perverted aristocracy who ruled them, while black misery reigned in the villages and in the dark lanes of the great towns. Next, hatred towards the clergy, who by sympathy belonged more to the aristocracy than to the people who fed them. Then, hatred of all the institutions under the old *régime*, which made poverty still harder to bear because they denied the rights of humanity to the poor. Hatred for the feudal system and its exactions, which kept the labourer in a state of servitude to the landowners long after personal serfdom had ceased to exist. Lastly, the despair of the peasant who in those years of scarcity saw land lying uncultivated in the hands of the lord, or serving merely as a pleasure-ground for the nobility while famine pressed hard on the villages.

It was all this hatred, coming to a head after long years as the selfishness of the rich became more and more apparent in the course of the eighteenth century. And it was this *need of land*—this *land hunger*, the cry of the starving in revolt against the lord who refused them access to it—that awoke the spirit of revolt ever since 1788. And it was the same hatred, and the same need, mingled with the hope of success, which stimulated the incessant revolts of the peasants in the years 1789–1793, revolts which enabled the middle classes to overthrow the old *régime* and to organise its own power under the new one, that of representative government.

Without those risings, without that disorganisation of authority in the provinces which resulted in never-ceasing *jacqueries*, without that promptitude of the people of Paris and other towns in taking up arms, and in marching against the strongholds of royalty whenever an appeal to the people was made by the revolutionaries, the middle classes would certainly not have accomplished anything. But it is to this true fount and origin of the Revolution—the people's readiness to take up arms—that the historians of the Revolution have not yet done justice—the justice owed to it by the history of civilisation.

CHAPTER IV

THE PEOPLE BEFORE THE REVOLUTION

Condition of people previous to 1789—Wanton luxury of aristocrats—Poverty of majority of peasants—Rise and importance of well-to-do peasant class

It would be waste of time to describe here at any length the condition of the peasants in the country and of the poorer classes in the towns on the eve of 1789.

All the historians who have written about the great French Revolution have devoted eloquent pages to this subject. The people groaned under the burden of taxes levied by the State, rents and contributions paid to the lord, tithes collected by the clergy, as well as under the forced labour exacted by all three. Entire populations were reduced to beggary and wandered on the roads to the number of five, ten or twenty thousand men, women and children in every province; in 1777, one million one hundred thousand persons were officially declared to be beggars. In the villages famine had become chronic; its intervals were short, and it decimated entire provinces. Peasants were flocking in hundreds and thousands from their own neighbourhood, in the hope, soon undeceived, of finding better conditions elsewhere. At the same time, the number of the poor in the towns increased every year, and it was quite usual for food to run short. As the municipalities could not replenish the markets, bread riots, always followed by massacres, became a persistent feature in the everyday life of the kingdom.

On the other hand might be seen the superfine aristocrat of the eighteenth century squandering immense fortunes—hundreds of thousands and millions of francs a year—in unbridled and absurd luxury. To-day a Taine can go into

THE PEOPLE BEFORE THE REVOLUTION 17

raptures over the life they led because he knows it only from a distance, a hundred years away, and through books; but, in reality, they hid under their dancing-master manners roisterous dissipations and the crudest sensuality; they were without interest, without thought, without even the simplest human feeling. Consequently, boredom was always tapping at the doors of the rich, boredom at the Court of Versailles, boredom in their châteaux; and they tried in vain to evade it by the most futile and the most childish means. We also know what they were worth, these aristocrats, when the Revolution broke out; how they left "their" King, and "their" Queen to defend themselves, and hastened to emigrate, calling for a foreign invasion to protect their estates and privileges against the revolted people. Their worth and their "nobility" of character can be estimated by the colonies of *émigrés*, which they established at Coblentz, Brussels and Mitau.

Those extremes of luxury and misery with which life abounded in the eighteenth century have been admirably depicted by every historian of the Great Revolution. But one feature remains to be added, the importance of which stands out especially when we study the condition of the peasants at this moment in Russia on the eve of the great Russian Revolution.

The misery of the great mass of French peasants was undoubtedly frightful. It had increased by leaps and bounds, ever since the reign of Louis XIV., as the expenditure of the State increased and the luxury of the great lords became more exquisite in the extravagancies revealed for us in certain memoirs of that time. What helped to make the exactions of the nobility unendurable was that a great number of them, when ruined, hiding their poverty under a show of luxury, resorted in desperation to the extortion of even the least of those rents and payments in kind, which only custom had established. They treated the peasants, through the intermediary of their stewards, with the rigour of mere brokers. Impoverishment turned the nobility, in their relations with their ex-serfs, into middle-class money-grubbers, incapable, however, of finding any other source of revenue than the exploitation of ancient privileges, relics of the feudal age.

This is why we find in certain documents, during the fifteen years of Louis XVI.'s reign which preceded the Revolution, indisputable traces of a recrudescence of seigneurial exactions.

But though the historians are right in depicting the condition of the peasants in very dark colours, it would be a mistake to impeach the veracity of those who, like Tocqueville, mention *some amelioration* in the conditions of the country during those very years preceding the Revolution. The fact is, that a double phenomenon became apparent in the villages at that time: the impoverishment of the great mass of the peasants and the bettering of the condition of a few among them. This may be seen to-day in Russia since the abolition of serfdom.

The great mass of the peasants grew poorer. Year after year their livelihood became more and more precarious: the least drought resulted in scarcity and famine. But a new class of peasant, a little better off and with ambitions, was forming at the same time, especially in districts where aristocratic estates were disintegrating rapidly. The village middle classes, the well-to-do peasants, came into being, and as the Revolution drew near these furnished the first speakers against feudal rights, and demanded their abolition. It was this class which, during the four or five years the Revolution lasted, most firmly insisted that these feudal rights should be abolished without compensation, and that the estates of the royalist nobles should be confiscated and sold in small parcels. It was this class, too, which was most bitter, in 1793, against *les ci-devants*, the dispossessed nobles, the ex-landlords.

For the time being, at the approach of the Revolution, it was through the peasant who had become of some importance in his village that hope filled men's hearts and inspired the spirit of revolt.

Traces of this awakening are evident, for since the accession of Louis XVI., in 1774, revolts were continually on the increase. It may be said, therefore, that if despair and misery impelled the people to riot, it was the hope of obtaining some relief that incited them to revolt.

Like every other revolution, that of 1789 was inspired by the hope of attaining certain important results.

CHAPTER V

THE SPIRIT OF REVOLT: THE RIOTS

Reforms at beginning of reign of Louis XVI.—Turgot—Question of National Representation—Character of Louis XVI.—Revolution in America—Riots on accession of Louis—Their consequences—Large towns revolt in turn—" Parliaments " and " Plenary Courts "—Paris parliament refuses to grant money to Court—Action of King—Insurrections in Brittany—Grenoble—Queen's letter to Count de Mercy—Gradual awakening of revolutionary spirit—Louis compelled to convoke Assembly of Notables and States-General

As is usual in every new reign, that of Louis XVI. began with some reforms. Two months after his accession Louis XVI. summoned Turgot to the ministry, and a month later he appointed him Controller-General of Finance. He even supported him at first against the violent opposition that Turgot, as an economist, a parsimonious middle-class man and an enemy of the effete aristocracy, was bound to meet with from the Court party.

Free trade in corn was proclaimed in September 1774,* and statute labour was abolished in 1776, as well as the old corporations and guilds in the towns, which were no longer of any use except to keep up a kind of industrial aristocracy, and by these measures hopes of reform were awakened among the people. The poor rejoiced to see the breaking down of the toll-gates, which had been put up all over France, and prevented the free circulation of corn, salt and other objects of prime necessity. For them it meant the first breach in the odious privileges of the landowners; while the peasants who

* Before that the farmer could not sell his corn for three months after the harvest, the lord of the manor alone being entitled to do that. It was one of the feudal privileges, which enabled the lord to sell it at a high price.

were better off rejoiced to see the joint liability of the taxpayers abolished.* Finally, in the August of 1779, mortmain and personal servitude were suppressed upon the King's private estates, and the following year it was decided to abolish torture, which was used in the most atrocious forms established by the Ordinance of 1670.† "Representative Government," such as was established by the English after their revolution, and was advocated in the writings of the contemporary philosophers, also began to be spoken of. With this end in view, Turgot had even prepared a scheme of provincial assemblies, to be followed later on by representative government for all France in which the propertied classes would have been called upon to constitute a parliament. Louis XVI. shrank from this proposal, and dismissed Turgot; but from that moment all educated France began to talk of a Constitution and national representation.‡ However, it was no longer possible to elude the question of national representation, and when Necker became minister in July 1777, it came up again for discussion. Necker, who understood very well the wishes of his master, and tried to bring his autocratic ideas

---

* This has been abolished in Russia also.

† Statute of August 24, 1780. Breaking on the wheel existed still in 1785. The parliaments, in spite of the Voltaireanism of the period, and the general refinement in the conception of life, enthusiastically defended the use of torture, which was abolished definitely only by the National Assembly. It is interesting to find (E. Seligman, *La justice en France pendant la Révolution*, p. 97) that Brissot, Marat and Robespierre by their writings contributed to the agitation for the reform of the penal code.

‡ The arguments upon which Louis XVI. took his stand are of the highest interest. I sum them up here according to E. Samichon's *Les réformes sous Louis XVI.: assemblées provinciales et parlements*. The King found Turgot's schemes dangerous, and wrote: "Though coming from a man who has good ideas, his constitution would overthrow the existing State." And again, further on: "The system of a rent-paying electorate would tend to make malcontents of the non-propertied classes, and if these were allowed to assemble they would form a hot-bed of disorder. . . . The transition from the abolished system to the system M. Turgot now proposes ought to be considered: we see well enough what is, but only in our thoughts do we see what does not yet exist, *and we must not make dangerous experiments if we do not see where they will end.*" *Vide* also, in Samichon's Appendix A, the very interesting list of the chief laws under Louis XVI. between 1774 and 1789.

THE SPIRIT OF REVOLT

into some accord with the requirements of finance, attempted to manœuvre by proposing the introduction of provincial assemblies only and relegating the possibility of a national representation to the distant future. But he, too, was met by a formal refusal on the part of the King. "Would it not be a happy contingency," wrote the crafty financier, "that your Majesty, having become an intermediary between your estates and your people, your authority should only appear to mark the limits between severity and justice?" To which Louis replied: "*It is of the essence of my authority not to be an intermediary, but to be at the head.*" It is well to remember these words in view of the sentimentalities concerning Louis XVI. which have been propagated by historians belonging to the party of reaction. Far from being the careless, inoffensive, good-natured person, interested only in hunting, that they wished to represent him, Louis XVI. for fifteen years, until 1789, managed to resist the necessity, felt and declared, for new political forms to take the place of royal despotism and the abominations of the old *régime*.

The weapon used by Louis XVI., in preference to all others was deceit. Only fear made him yield, and, using always the same weapons, deceit and hypocrisy, he resisted not only up to 1789, but even up to the last moment, to the very foot of the scaffold. At any rate, in 1778, at a time when it was already evident to all minds of more or less perspicacity, as it was to Turgot and Necker, that the absolute power of the King had had its day, and that the hour had come for replacing it by some kind of national representation, Louis XVI. could never be brought to make any but the feeblest concessions. He convened the provincial assemblies of the provinces of Berri and Haute-Guienne (1778 and 1779). But in face of the opposition shown by the privileged classes, the plan of extending these assemblies to the other provinces was abandoned, and Necker was dismissed in 1781.

The revolution in America had, meanwhile, helped also to awaken minds, and to inspire them with a breath of liberty and republican democracy. On July 4, 1776, the English colonies in North America had proclaimed their independence, and the new United States were recognised by France in 1778, which led to a war with England that lasted until 1783. All historians mention the effect which this war had on men's minds. There is, in fact, no doubt that the revolt of the English colonies and the constitution of the United States exercised a far-reaching influence in France, and helped powerfully in arousing the revolutionary spirit. We know, too, that the Declaration of Rights, drawn up by the young American States influenced the French Revolutionists profoundly, and was taken by them as a model for their declaration. It might be said also that the war in America, during which France had to build an entire fleet to oppose England's, completed the financial ruin of the old *régime* and hastened its downfall. But it is nevertheless certain that this war was also the beginning of those terrible wars which England soon waged against France, and the coalitions which she organised against the Republic. As soon as England recovered from her defeats and felt that France was weakened by internal struggles, she used every means, open and secret, to bring about the wars which we shall see waged relentlessly from 1793 till 1815.

All these causes of the Great Revolution must be clearly indicated, for like every event of primordial importance, it was the result of many causes, converging at a given moment, and creating the men who in their turn contributed to strengthen the effect of those causes. But it must be understood that in spite of the events which prepared the Revolution, and in spite of all the intelligence and ambitions of the middle classes, those ever-prudent people would have gone on a long time waiting for a change if the people had not hastened matters. The popular revolts, growing and increasing in number and assuming proportions quite unforeseen, were the new elements which gave the middle class the power of attack they themselves did not possess.

The people had patiently endured misery and oppression under Louis XV., but as soon as that King died, in 1774, they began to revolt, knowing well that, with a change of masters at the palace, there comes an inevitable slackening of authority. A continuous series of riots broke out between 1775 and 1777.

These were the riots of hunger that had been repressed until then only by force. The harvest of 1774 had been bad, and bread was scarce. Accordingly rioting broke out in April 1775. At Dijon the people took possession of the houses of the monopolists, destroyed their furniture and smashed up their flour-mills. It was on this occasion that the governor of the town—one of the superfine gentlemen of whom Taine has written with so much complacence—said to the people those fatal words which were to be so often repeated during the Revolution: " The grass has sprouted, go to the fields and browse on it." Auxerre, Amiens, Lille, followed Dijon. A few days later the " robbers," for so the majority of historians designate the famished rioters, having assembled at Pontoise, Passy and Saint-Germain with the intention of pillaging the granaries, turned their steps towards Versailles. Louis XVI. wanted to go out on the balcony of the palace to speak to them, to tell them that he would reduce the price of bread ; but Turgot, like a true economist, opposed this. The reduction in the price of bread was not made. The " robbers," in the meantime, entered Paris and plundered the bakeries, distributing whatever food they could seize among the crowd ; but they were dispersed by the troops, and two of the rioters were hanged at the Place de la Grève, and as they were being hanged they cried out that they were dying for the people. Since that time the legend began to circulate in France about " robbers " overrunning the country—a legend which had such an important effect in 1789, as it furnished the middle classes in the towns with a pretext for arming themselves. And from that time also began the placards insulting the King and his ministers which were pasted up at Versailles, containing threats to execute the King the day after his coronation, and even to exterminate the whole of the royal family if bread remained at the same price. Forged governmental edicts, too, began to be circulated through the country. One of them asserted that the State Council had reduced the price of wheat to twelve livres (francs) the measure.

These riots were of course suppressed, but they had far-reaching consequences. Strife was let loose among the various parties. It rained pamphlets. Some of these accused the minister, while others spoke of a plot of the princes against the King, or made fun of the royal authority. In short, with men's minds already in a state of ferment, the popular outbreaks were the sparks which ignited the powder. Concessions to the people, never dreamed of before, were openly discussed; public works were set on foot; taxes on milling were abolished, and this measure led the people of Rouen to declare that *all* manorial dues had been abolished, so that they rose in July to protest against ever paying them again. The malcontents evidently lost no time and profited by the occasion to extend the popular risings.

We have not the necessary documents for giving a full account of the popular insurrections during the reign of Louis XVI.—the historians did not trouble about them; the archives have not been examined, and it is only by accident that we learn that in such-and-such a place there were "disorders." Thus, there were riots of a somewhat serious nature in Paris, after the abolition of the trade-guilds in 1776—and all over France, in the course of the same year—as a result of the false reports respecting the abolition of all obligations in the matter of statute labour and dues claimed by the landowners. But, according to the printed documents, it would appear also that there was a decrease in the rioting in the years 1777 to 1783, the American war having perhaps something to do with this.

However, in 1782 and 1783, the riots recommenced, and from that time went on increasing until the Revolution. Poitiers revolted in 1782; in 1786 it was Vizille's turn; from 1783 to 1789 rioting broke out in the Cevennes, the Vivarais and the Gévaudan. The malcontents, who were nicknamed *mascarats*, wanting to punish the "practitioners" who sowed dissension among the peasants to incite them to go to law, broke into the law courts and into the houses of the notaries and attorneys and burned all the deeds and contracts. Three of the leaders were hanged, others were sent to penal servitude, but the disorders broke out afresh, as soon as the closing of the *parlements* (Courts of Justice) furnished them with a new pretext.* In 1786 it was Lyons that revolted.† The silk-weavers went on strike; they were promised an increase of wages, but troops were called out, whereupon there was a fight and three of the leaders were hanged. From that moment, up to the Revolution, Lyons became a hotbed of revolt, and in 1789 it was the rioters of 1786 who were chosen as electors.

Sometimes these risings had a religious character; sometimes they were to resist military enlistment—every levy of soldiers led to a riot, says Turgot; or it might be the salt tax against which the people rebelled, or the exactions of the tithes. But revolts went on without intermission, and it was in the east, south-east and north-east—future hotbeds of the Revolution—that these revolts broke out in the greatest number. They went on steadily growing in importance, and at last, in 1788, after the dissolution of the Courts of Justice, which were called *parlements* and were replaced by "Plenary Courts," insurrections broke out in every part of France.

It is evident that for the mass of the people there was not much to choose between a *parlement* and a "Plenary Court." If the *parlements* had refused sometimes to register edicts made by the King and his minister, they had on the other hand displayed no solicitude for the people. But the *parlements* had shown opposition to the Court, that was enough; and when emissaries of the middle classes sought popular support for rioting, they were given it willingly, because it was a way of demonstrating against the Court and the rich.

In the June of 1787 the Paris *parlement* had made itself very popular by refusing a grant of money to the Court. The law of the country was that the edicts of the King should be registered by the *parlement*, and the Paris *parlement* unhesitatingly registered certain edicts concerning the corn trade, the convocation of provincial assemblies and statute labour. But it refused to register the edict which was to establish fresh taxes—a new "territorial subvention," and a new stamp duty. Upon this the King convoked what was called a "Bed of

---

* C. de Vic and J. de Vaissete, *Histoire générale du Languedoc*, continued by du Mège, 10 vols., 1840–1846.

† Chassin, *Génie de la Révolution*.

Justice," and compelled his edicts to be registered. The *parlement* protested, and so won the sympathy of the middle classes and the people. There were crowds round the Courts at every sitting; clerks, curious idlers and common men collected there to applaud the members. To stop this, the King banished the *parlement* to Troyes, and then riotous demonstrations began in Paris. The popular hatred was then being directed against the princes chiefly, especially against the Duke d'Artois and the Queen, who was nicknamed " Madame Déficit."

The Exchequer Court of Paris (*Cour des Aides*), supported by the popular outburst, as well as by the provincial *parlements* and the Court of Justice, protested against this act of royal power, and, as the agitation was growing, the King was compelled to recall the exiled *parlement*. This was done on September 9, and evoked fresh demonstrations in Paris, during which the minister Calonne was burnt in effigy.

These disturbances were chiefly confined to the lower middle classes. But in other localities they assumed a more popular character.

In 1788 insurrections broke out in Brittany. When the military Commander of Rennes and the Governor of the province went to the Breton *parlement* to announce the edict by which that body was abolished, the whole town turned out immediately. The crowd insulted and hustled the two functionaries. The people in their hearts hated the Governor, Bertrand de Moleville, and the middle classes profited by this to spread a rumour that the edict was all owing to the Governor. " He is a monster that deserves to be strangled," said one of the leaflets distributed among the crowd. When he came out of the palace, therefore, they pelted him with stones, and after several attempts some one threw a cord with a slip-knot over him. Fighting was about to begin—the young men in the crowd breaking through the ranks of the soldiers—when an officer threw down his sword and fraternised with the people.

By degrees troubles of the same kind broke out in several other towns in Brittany, and the peasants rose in their turn when grain was being shipped at Quimper, Saint-Brieuc,

Morlaix, Pont-l'Abbé, Lamballe and other places. It is interesting to note the active part taken in these disorders by the students at Rennes, who from that time fraternised with the rioters.* In Dauphiné, especially at Grenoble, the insurrection assumed a still more serious character. As soon as the military commander, Clermont-Tonnerre, had promulgated the edict which dissolved the *parlement* the people of Grenoble rose. The tocsin was rung, and the alarm spreading quickly to the neighbouring villages, the peasants hastened in crowds to the town. There was a sanguinary affray and many were killed. The commander's guard was helpless and his palace was sacked. Clermont-Tonnerre, with an axe held over his head, had to revoke the royal edict.

It was the people, and chiefly the women, who acted on this occasion. As to the members of the *parlement*, the people had a good deal of trouble to find them. They hid themselves, and wrote to Paris that the people had risen against their will, and when the people laid hands on them they were kept prisoners—their presence giving an air of legality to the insurrection. The women mounted guard over these arrested members, unwilling to trust them even to the men, lest they should be allowed to escape.

The middle classes of Grenoble were in a state of terror. During the night they organised a militia of citizens that took possession of the town gates as well as of some military posts, which they yielded to the troops soon after. Cannon were trained on the rebels, while the *parlement* took advantage of the darkness to disappear. From June 9 to 14 reaction triumphed, but on the 14th news came that there had been a rising at Besançon and that the Swiss soldiers had refused to fire on the people. Upon this the people's spirit revived, and it was proposed to convoke the Estates of the province. But fresh reinforcements of troops having been sent from Paris the disturbance subsided by degrees. The agitation, however, kept up chiefly by the women, lasted some time longer.†

---

* Du Châtellier, *Histoire de la Révolution dans les départements de l'ancienne Bretagne*, 6 vols., 1836; vol. ii. pp. 60–70, 161, &c.

† Vic and Vaissete, vol. x. p. 637.

Besides these two risings mentioned by the majority of the historians, many others broke out at the same time in Provence, Languedoc, Rousillon, Béarn, Flanders, Franche-Comté and Burgundy. Even where no serious riots occurred advantage was taken of the prevailing excitement to keep up the discontent and to make demonstrations.

At Paris, after the dismissal of the Archbishop of Sens, there were numerous demonstrations. The Pont Neuf was guarded by troops, and several conflicts occurred between them and the people, of whom the leaders were, as Bertrand de Moleville remarks,* " those who later on took part in all the popular movements of the Revolution." Marie-Antoinette's letter to the Count de Mercy should also be read in this connection. It is dated August 24, 1788, and in it she tells him of her fears, and announces the retirement of the Archbishop of Sens and the steps she had taken to recall Necker; the effect produced on the Court by those riotous crowds can therefore be understood. The Queen foresaw that this recall of Necker would lessen the King's authority; she feared " that they may be compelled to nominate a prime minister," but " the moment is pressing. It is very essential that Necker should accept." †

Three weeks later, September 14, 1788, when the retirement of Lamoignon became known, the riotings were renewed. The mob rushed to set fire to the houses of the two ministers, Lamoignon and Brienne, as well as to that of Dubois. The troops were called out, and in the Rue Mélée and the Rue de Grenelle there was a horrible slaughter of poor folk who could not defend themselves. Dubois fled from Paris. " The people themselves would execute justice," said *Les deux amis de la liberté*. Later still, in October 1788, when the *parlement*

* Vic and Vaissete, p. 136.
† J. Feuillet de Conches, *Lettres de Louis XVI., Marie-Antoinette et Madame Elisabeth* (Paris, 1864), vol. i. pp. 214–216; " The *Abbé* has written to you this evening, sir, and has notified my wish to you," wrote the Queen. " I think more than ever that the moment is pressing, and that it is very essential that he (Necker) should accept. The King fully agrees with me, and has just brought me a paper with his own hand containing his ideas, of which I send you a copy." The next day she wrote again; " We must no longer hesitate. If he can get to work to-morrow all the better. It is most urgent. I fear that we may be compelled to nominate a prime minister."

that had been banished to Troyes was recalled, "the clerks and the populace" illuminated the Place Dauphine for several evenings in succession. They demanded money from the passers-by to expend on fireworks, and forced gentlemen to alight from their carriages to salute the statue of Henri Quatre. Figures representing Calonne, Breteuil and the Duchess de Polignac were burned. It was also proposed to burn the Queen in effigy. These riotous assemblies gradually spread to other quarters, and troops were sent to disperse them. Blood was shed and many were killed and wounded in the Place de la Grève. Those who were arrested, however, were tried by the *parlement* judges, who let them off with light penalties.

In this way the revolutionary spirit awoke and developed in the van of the Great Revolution.* The initiative came from the middle classes certainly—chiefly from the lower middle classes—but, generally speaking, the middle classes took care not to compromise themselves, and the number of them who opposed the Court, more or less openly, before the convoking of the States-General was very limited. If there had been only their few attempts at resistance France might have waited many years for the overthrow of royal despotism. Fortunately a thousand circumstances impelled the masses to revolt. And in spite of the fact that after every outbreak there were summary hangings, wholesale arrests and even torture for those arrested, the people did revolt, pressed on one side by their desperate misery, and spurred on the other by those vague hopes of which the old woman spoke to Arthur Young. They rose in numbers against the governors of provinces, tax-collectors, salt-tax agents and even against the troops, and by so doing completely disorganised the governmental machine.

From 1788 the peasant risings became so general that it was impossible to provide for the expenses of the State, and Louis XVI., after having refused for fourteen years to convoke the representatives of the nation, lest his kingly authority should suffer, at last found himself compelled to convoke, first the two Assemblies of Notables, and finally the States-General.

* For fuller information, see Félix Roquain, *L'esprit révolutionnaire avant la Révolution.*

CHAPTER VI

THE CONVOCATION OF THE STATES-GENERAL BECOMES NECESSARY

Irresponsibility of old *régime*—Miserable condition of peasants—Discontent of middle classes—They encourage riots among the people—Change in political system of France—Necker—Financial crisis—Assembly of Notables convoked—Louis convokes States-General—Increased representation granted to Third Estate

To any one who knew the condition of France it was clear that the irresponsible *régime* of the Court could not last. The misery in the country districts went on increasing year by year, and it became more and more difficult to levy the taxes and at the same time compel the peasants to pay rent to the landlords and perform *the innumerable statute labours* exacted by the provincial government. The taxes alone devoured half and often two-thirds of what the peasants could earn in the course of the year. Beggary and rioting were becoming normal conditions of country life. Moreover, it was not only the peasants who protested and revolted. The middle classes, too, were loudly expressing their discontent. They profited certainly by the impoverishment of the peasants to enrol them in their factories, and they took advantage of the administrative demoralisation and the financial disorders of the moment to seize on all kinds of monopolies, and to enrich themselves by loans to the State.

But this did not satisfy the middle classes. For a while they managed to adapt themselves to royal despotism and Court government. A moment came, however, when they began to fear for their monopolies, for the money they had invested in loans to the State, for the landed property they had acquired, for the factories they had established, and afterwards to encourage the people in their riots in order that they might break down the government of the Court and establish their own political power. This evolution can be plainly traced during the first thirteen or fourteen years of Louis XVI.'s reign, from 1774 to 1788.

An important change in the entire political system of France was visibly taking place. But Louis XVI. and his Court resisted that change, and they opposed it so long that when the King at last decided to yield, it was just when those modest reforms that would have been so welcome at the beginning of his reign had already been found insufficient by the nation. Whereas, in 1775, a *régime* of autocracy mingled with national representation would have satisfied the middle classes, twelve or thirteen years later, in 1787 and 1788, the King was confronted by a public opinion which would no longer hearken to compromise, but demanded representative government with all the limitation of royal power which it involved.

We have seen how Louis XVI. rejected Turgot's very modest proposals. The mere thought of limiting the royal power was repugnant to him. Therefore Turgot's reforms—abolition of statute labour, abolition of trade-wardens and a timid attempt to make the two privileged classes—the nobility and clergy—pay some of the taxes, had no substantial results. Everything is interdependent in a State, and everything under the old *régime* fell in ruins together.

Necker, who followed closely on Turgot, was more a financier than a statesman. He had the financier's narrow mind which sees things only in their petty aspects. His proper element was financial transactions—raising loans. To read his *Pouvoir exécutif* is to understand how his mind, accustomed only to reason about *theories* of government, instead of clearing itself in the shock of human passions and *desiderata* that find expression in a society at a given moment, was incapable of comprehending the vast problem, political, economic, religious and social, that was thrust upon France in 1789.*

* *Du pouvoir exécutif dans les grands états*, 2 vols., 1792. The idea of this book is, that if France was passing through a revolutionary

Necker, moreover, never dared to use to Louis XVI. the clear, exact, severe and bold language which the occasion required. He spoke to him very timidly about representative government, and he limited his reforms to what could neither solve the difficulties nor satisfy any one, while they made every one feel the necessity of a fundamental change.

The provincial assemblies, eighteen of which Necker added to those already instituted by Turgot, leading in turn to the establishment of district and parish councils, were evidently brought to discuss the most difficult questions and to lay bare the hideous corruption of the unlimited power of royalty. And these discussions, which could not but spread all over the country down to the villages, no doubt helped powerfully in the fall of the old *régime*. In this way the provincial assemblies, which in 1776 might have acted as lightning conductors and lessened the force of the storm, were helping towards the insurrection of 1788. Likewise the famous *Compte rendu*, the report upon the state of the provinces, that Necker published in 1781, a few months before quitting office, was a heavy blow to royal autocracy. As always happens on such occasions, he helped to shake down the system which was already tottering to its fall, but he was powerless to prevent the fall from becoming a revolution: probably he did not even perceive that it was impending.

The financial crash came after Necker's first dismissal, in the years 1781 to 1787. The finances were in such a miserable condition that the debts of the State, the provinces, the State

---

crisis in 1792, it was the fault of her National Assembly for having neglected to arm the King with a strong executive power. "Everything would have gone its course more or less perfectly if only care had been taken to establish in our midst a tutelary authority," says Necker, in the preface to this work; and he enlarges in these two volumes on the boundless rights with which the royal power should be invested. It is true that in his book, *Sur la législation et le commerce des grains*, published in 1776, he had developed, by way of protesting against a system of free trade in corn, supported by Turgot, some ideas showing sympathy with the poor, in advocating that the State should intervene to fix the price of wheat for their benefit, but that was the limit of his "State-Socialism." The essential thing, in his opinion, was a strong Government, a throne respected and surrounded with that object by high functionaries and a powerful executive.

departments and even of the King's household were accumulating in an alarming fashion. At any moment the bankruptcy of the State might have been declared, a bankruptcy which the middle classes, now interested in the State finances as creditors, did not want at any price. With all this, the mass of the people were already so impoverished that they could no longer pay the taxes—they did not pay, and revolted; while the clergy and the nobility refused to make any sacrifice in the interests of the State. Under such conditions the risings in the villages necessarily brought the country nearer to the Revolution. And it was in the midst of these difficulties that the minister Calonne convoked an Assembly of the Notables at Versailles for February 22, 1787.

To convoke this Assembly of Notables was to do exactly what ought not to have been done at that moment: it was exactly the half-measure which on one side made the National Assembly inevitable, and on the other hand inspired distrust of the Court and hatred of the two privileged orders, the nobility and the clergy. Through that Assembly it was learned that the national debt had mounted up to sixteen hundred and forty-six millions—an appalling sum at that time—and that the annual deficit was increasing by one hundred and forty millions annually. And this in a country ruined as France was! It came to be known—every one talked of it; and after every one had talked about it, the Notables, drawn from the upper classes and practically a ministerial assembly, separated on May 25 without having done or decided anything. During their deliberations Calonne was replaced by Loménie de Brienne, Archbishop of Sens. But the new minister, by his intrigues and his attempted severity, only succeeded in stirring up the *parlements*, in provoking widely spread riots when he wished to disband them, and in exciting public opinion still more against the Court. When he was dismissed on August 25, 1788, there was general rejoicing all over France. But as he had proved clearly the impossibility of despotic government there was nothing for the Court but to submit. On August 8, 1788, Louis XVI. was at last obliged to convoke the States-General, and to fix the opening for May 1, 1789.

Even in this the Court and Necker, who was recalled to the ministry in 1788, managed so as to displease every one. It was the general opinion in France that in the States-General, in which the three classes would be separately represented, the Third Estate ought to have twice as many members as the two others, and that the voting should be by individuals. But Louis XVI. and Necker were opposed to this, and even convoked a second Assembly of Notables on November 6, 1788, which would, they were sure, reject the doubling of numbers in the Third Estate and the individual vote. This was exactly what happened; but in spite of that, public opinion had been so predisposed in favour of the Third Estate by the provincial Assemblies that Necker and the Court were obliged to give in. The Third Estate was granted a double representation—that is to say, out of a thousand deputies the Third would have as many as the clergy and nobility combined. In short, the Court and Necker did everything they possibly could to turn public opinion against them, without gaining any advantage for themselves. The Court's opposition to the convocation of a national representative Assembly was in vain. The States-General met at Versailles on May 5, 1789.

CHAPTER VII

THE RISING OF THE COUNTRY DISTRICTS DURING THE OPENING MONTHS OF 1789

Heroism of middle classes at beginning of Revolution overrated—Abolition of serfdom—Statute labour and other impositions upon peasants—Failure of crops in 1789—Riots follow—Nature of riots—" Vive la Liberté ! "—Riots at Agde —Concessions granted to people—Effect of riots on elections —Agitation in rural districts—Importance of peasant insurrection.

NOTHING could be more erroneous than to imagine or describe France as a nation of heroes on the eve of·1789, and Quinet was perfectly right in destroying this legend, which some historians had tried to propagate. It is evident that if we were to collect into a few pages the occasional instances, very rare after all, of open resistance to the old *régime* on the part of the middle classes—such as d'Espréménil's opposition—we could compose a tolerably impressive picture. But what is particularly apparent in making a survey of the conditions of the time is the absence of serious protests, of assertions of the individual, the servility of the middle classes. " Nobody makes himself known," says Quinet, very justly. There is no opportunity even to know oneself.* And he asks : " What were they doing—Barnave, Thouret, Sieyès, Vergniaud, Guadet, Roland, Danton, Robespierre, and all the others, who were so soon to become the heroes of the Revolution ? "

Dumbness, silence, prevailed in the provinces and in the towns. The central power had to summon men to vote, and invite them to say aloud what they had been saying in whispers, before the Third Estate issued their famous *cahiers*. And

* Quinet, *La Révolution*, ed. 1869, vol. i. p. 15.

even then! If in some of the *cahiers* we find daring words of revolt, what submissiveness and timidity appear in most of them, what moderation in their demands! For, after the right to carry arms, and some legal guarantees against arbitrary arrests, it was chiefly a little more liberty in municipal affairs that was asked for in the *cahiers* of the Third Estate.* It was later on, when the deputies of the Third saw themselves supported by the people of Paris, and when the mutterings of the peasant insurrection began to be heard, that they grew bolder in their attitude towards the Court.

Fortunately, the people began to revolt everywhere, after the disturbances provoked by the *parlements* during the summer and autumn of 1788, and the tide of revolt, gathering force, swept onward to the rising of the villages in July and August of 1789.

It has already been said that the condition of the peasants and workers in the towns was such that a single bad harvest sufficed to bring about an alarming increase in the price of bread in the towns and sheer famine in the villages. The peasants were no longer serfs, serfdom having long been abolished in France, at least on private estates. After Louis XVI. had abolished it within the royal domains in 1779, there remained in 1788 only about 80,000 persons held by mortmain in the Jura, at most about 1,500,000 in the whole of France, perhaps even less than a million; even those subject to mortmain were not serfs in the strict meaning of the term. As to the majority of the French peasants, they had long ceased to be serfs. But they went on paying in money, and in working for their personal liberty with statute labour as well as with

---

* With regard to the demands which afterwards excited the fury of the landowners, it is well to note these: The tax on bread and meat to be fixed according to the average prices, demanded by Lyons, Troyes, Paris and Châlons; that " wages should be regulated periodically according to the daily needs," demanded by Rennes; that work should be guaranteed to all able-bodied poor, demanded by several towns. As to the Royalist-Constitutionalists, who were numerous, it can be seen by the proposals of the " *Cahier général*," analysed by Chassin (*Les élections et les cahiers de Paris en* 1789, vol. iii., 1889, p. 185), that they wished to limit the deliberations of the States-General to questions of finance and of retrenchments in the household expenditures of the King and the princes.

work of other kinds. These dues were extremely heavy and variable, but they were not arbitrary, and they were considered as representing payments for the right of holding land, whether collectively by the community or privately as farm-land. And each parcel of land or farm had its dues, as varied as they were numerous, carefully recorded in the feudal registers, the *terriers*.

Besides, the right of manorial justice had been retained, and over large districts the lord was still judge, or else he nominated the judges ; and in virtue of this ancient prerogative he retained all kinds of personal rights over his ex-serfs.* When an old woman bequeathed to her daughter one or two trees and a few old clothes—for example, " my black quilted petticoat," a bequest such as I have seen—" the noble and generous lord or the noble and generous lady of the castle levied so much on the bequest. The peasant paid also for the right of marriage, of baptism, of burial ; he paid likewise on everything he bought or sold, and the very right of selling his crops or his wine was restricted. He could not sell before the lord had sold his own. Lastly, there were all manner of tolls (*banalités*) —for the use of the mill, of the wine-press, the public bakehouse, the washing-places, on certain roads or particular fords—all maintained since the days of serfdom, as well as contributions of nuts, mushrooms, linen, thread, formerly considered as gifts for festive occasions."

As to statute labour, it took an infinite variety of forms : work in the fields of the lord, work in his parks and his gardens, work to satisfy all sorts of whims. In some villages there was even an obligation to beat the pond during the night in order that the frogs should not prevent his lordship from sleeping.

* In an excellent pamphlet, *Les fléaux de l'agriculture, ouvrage pour servir à l'appui des cahiers des doléances des campagnes*, by D. . . . (April 10, 1789), we find this statement of causes preventing the development of agriculture : The enormous taxes, the tithes, joint and individual, " solites " and " insolites," and these always increasing ; the large quantities of game preserved through abuse of privileges and sport ; and the vexation and abuse of the seigneurial law courts. It is here shown that " it was by means of the attachment of manorial law courts to the fief that the landlords had made themselves despots and held the inhabitants of the country districts in the chains of slavery " (p. 95).

Personally the man was free, but all this network of dues and exactions, which had been woven bit by bit through the craft of the lords and their stewards in the centuries of serfdom—all this network still clung round the peasant.

More than that, the State was there with its taxes, its fines, its twentieths, its statute labours ever increasing, too, and the State, as well as the steward of my lord, was always ready to exercise ingenuity in devising some new pretext for introducing some new form of taxation.

It is true that, since Turgot's reforms, the peasants had ceased paying certain feudal taxes, and some provincial governors had even refused to resort to force to levy certain dues, which they considered to be injurious exactions. But the principal feudal dues attaching to the land were exacted in full, and they became all the heavier as the State and provincial taxes, to which they were added, continually increased. There is, therefore, not a word of exaggeration in the gloomy pictures of life in the villages drawn by every historian of the Revolution. But neither is there any exaggeration in saying that in each village there were some peasants who had created for themselves a certain amount of prosperity, and that these were the men who especially wished to shake off all feudal obligations, and to win individual liberty. The two types depicted by Erckmann and Chatrian in their *Histoire d'un paysan*—the middle-class man of the village, and the peasant crushed beneath the burden of his poverty—are true to life. Both of them existed. The former gave political strength to the Third Estate; while the bands of insurgents that, since the winter of 1788–1789 had begun to force the nobles to relinquish the feudal dues inscribed in the *terriers*, were recruited from among the starving poor in the villages, who had only mud cabins to live in, and a few chestnuts or the gleanings of the fields for food.

The same remark applies also to the towns, to which the feudal rights extended, as well as to the villages. The poorer classes in the towns were just as much crushed beneath feudal taxes as the peasants. The right of seigneurial justice remained to its full extent in many a growing city, and the hovels of the artisans and mechanics paid the same dues, in cases of sales or

THE RISINGS OF 1789

inheritance, as the huts of the peasants. Several towns had even to pay a perpetual tribute as redemption from their former feudal subjection. Besides this, the majority of the towns paid the *don gratuit*—the voluntary gift—to the King, just to maintain a shadow of municipal independence, and the burden of these taxes pressed hardest on the poor. If we add to all this the heavy royal taxes, the provincial contributions, the fines, the salt tax and the rest, as well as the caprices of the functionaries, the heavy expenses incurred in the law courts, and the impossibility of a mere commoner's obtaining justice against a noble, even if he were a rich member of the middle classes, and if we take into consideration the many forms of oppression, insult and humiliation to which the lower classes were subject, we shall be able to form some idea of the condition of the poor on the eve of 1789.

It was, however, these poorer classes who, by revolting in the towns and villages, gave the representatives of the Third Estate in the States-General courage to oppose the King and to declare the Assembly a constituent body.

Drought had caused a failure of the crops in 1788, and the winter was very severe. Before that there had certainly been winters as severe, and crops quite as bad, and even riots among the people. Every year there was scarcity in some part of France, and often it affected a fourth or a third part of the kingdom. But this time hopes had been awakened by preceding events—the provincial assemblies, the Convocation of Notables, the disturbances connected with the *parlements* in the towns, which spread, as we have seen, at least in Brittany, to the villages also. And these insurrections in 1789 soon became alarming both in extent and character.

I learn through Professor Karéeff, who has studied the effect of the Great Revolution upon the French peasants, that in the National Archives there is a huge bundle of documents bearing on the risings of the peasants which preceded the taking of the Bastille.* For my own part, never having been able to study

* It is now known that Taine, who pretended that he had studied the reports of the Governors of the provinces concerning these insurrections, had only glanced through twenty-six referring to 1770, as M. Aulard has shown (*Taine : historien de la Révolution française*, Paris, 1907).

the archives in France, but having consulted many provincial histories of that period,* I had already, in former works, arrived at the conclusion † that a great number of riots had broken out in the villages after January 1789, and even after December 1788. In certain provinces the situation was terrible on account of the scarcity, and everywhere a spirit of revolt, until then but little known, was taking possession of the people. In the spring, the insurrection became more and more frequent in Poitou, Brittany, Touraine, Orléanais, Normandy, Ile de France, Picardy, Champagne, Alsace, Burgundy, Nivernais, Auvergne, Languedoc and Provence.

Nearly all these riots were of the same character. The peasants, armed with knives, scythes, cudgels, flocked in a body to the town, and compelled the labourers and farmers who had brought the corn to the market to sell it at a certain " honest " price, such as three livres the bushel ; or else they went to the corn merchants, took out the wheat and " divided it among themselves at a reduced price," promising to pay for it after the next harvest. In other places they forced the landowner to forego his dues upon flour for a couple of months, or they compelled the municipality to tax bread, and sometimes " to increase by four sous the daily wage." Where famine was severest, as at Thiers, the town workers went to collect wheat in the country districts. Often they broke open the granaries belonging to religious communities and merchant monopolists, or even those belonging to private persons, and provided the bakers with flour. Moreover, from this time, too, dated the formation of bands composed of peasants, wood-cutters, sometimes even of contrabandists, who went from village to village seizing the corn. By degrees they began also to burn the land registers and to force the landlords to abdicate their feudal rights—these were the same bands which gave the middle classes the pretext for arming their militias in 1789.

* *La Jura*, by Sommier; *Le Languedoc*, by Vic and Vaissete ; *Castres*, by Combes ; *La Bretagne*, by du Châtellier; *La Franche-Comté*, by Clerc ; *L'Auvergne*, by Dulaure; *Le Berry*, by Regnal ; *Le Limousin*, by Leymarie ; *L'Alsace*, by Strobel ; &c.

† *La Grande Révolution* (pamphlet), Paris, 1893 ; " The Great French Revolution and its Lesson," anniversary article in *The Nineteenth Century*, June 1889 ; articles on the Revolution in *La Révolte*.

Ever since January there was heard, too, in these riots the cry of " Vive la Liberté ! " and from that time, and still more markedly after the month of March, we find the peasants here and there refusing to pay the tithes and feudal dues, or, indeed, even the taxes. Outside the three provinces, Brittany, Alsace and Dauphiné, which are cited by Taine, traces are to be found of similar movements nearly all over the eastern part of France.

In the south, at Agde, after the riots of April 19, 20 and 21, " the people foolishly persuaded themselves that they were everything," wrote the mayor and the consuls, " and they may do everything according to the pretended will of the King concerning the equality of rank." The people threatened to sack the town if the price of all provisions was not lowered, and the provincial dues on wine, fish and meat suppressed ; furthermore—and here we see already the *communalist* good sense of the masses of the people in France—" they wished to nominate consuls, some of whom would be drawn from their own class," and these demands were acceded to the insurgents. Three days after the people demanded that the duty on milling should be reduced by one-half, and this also was granted.*

This insurrection was the counterpart of a hundred others. To obtain bread was the prime cause of the movement, but soon there were also demands in the direction where economic conditions and political organisation meet, the direction in which popular agitation always goes forward with the greatest confidence and obtains some immediate results.

In Provence, at least in March and April of 1789, more than forty large villages and towns, among them Aix, Marseilles and Toulon, abolished the tax on flour, and here and there the mob pillaged the houses of officials whose duty was to levy the taxes on flour, hides, butcher's meat, &c. The prices of provisions were reduced and a maximum established for all provisions, and when the gentlemen of the upper middle classes protested, the mob replied by stoning them, or else a trench was dug before their eyes which might serve for their grave. Sometimes even a coffin was brought out the better to impress the refractory

* Taine, vol. ii. 22, 23.

who apparently hastened to comply. All this took place in April 1789, without the shedding of a drop of blood. It is "a kind of war declared on proprietors and property," say the reports from the governors and municipalities. "The people still declare that they will pay nothing, neither taxes, nor dues, nor debts."*

Before that, since April, the peasants began to plunder the great country houses and to compel the nobility to renounce their rights. At Peinier, they forced the lord " to sign a document by which he renounced his seigneurial rights of every kind." † At Riez they wanted the bishop to burn the records. At Hyères and elsewhere they burned the old papers concerning the feudal rents and taxes. In short, in Provence, from the month of April, we can already see the beginning of the great rising of the peasants which forced the nobility and clergy to make their first concessions on August 4, 1789.

It is easy to discern the influence that these riots and this excitement exercised upon the elections for the National Assembly. Chassin, in his *Génie de la Révolution*, says that in some localities the nobility exercised a great influence on the elections, and that in these localities the peasant electors dared not make any complaints. Elsewhere, especially at Rennes, the nobles took advantage even of the sitting of the States-General of Brittany at the end of December 1788, and in January 1789, to try to stir up the starving people against the middle classes. But what could these last convulsive efforts of the nobles do against the pouplar tide, which rose steadily ? The people saw more than half the land lying idle in the hands of the nobility and clergy, and they understood better than if statisticians had demonstrated it to them, that so long as the peasants did not take possession of the land to cultivate it famine would be always present among them.

The very need to live made the peasant rise against the monopolisers of the soil. During the winter of 1788–1789, says Chassin, no day passed in the Jura without convoys of wheat being plundered.‡ The military authorities could think of

---

* Letters in the National Archives, 1453, cited by Taine, vol. ii. p. 24. † Letter in the Archives.   ‡ Chassin, p. 162.

nothing but "Suppression of the riots"; but the tribunals refused to sentence or even to judge the famished rioters. Similar riots broke out everywhere, north, south, east and west, says Chassin.*

The elections brought with them a renewal of life and of hope in the villages. The lordly influence was great everywhere, but now in every village there was to be found some middle-class man, a doctor or lawyer, who had read his Voltaire, or Sieyès, or the famous pamphlet—*Qu'est-ce que le tiers état?* Everything was changing wherever there was a weaver or a mason who could read and write, were it only the printed letters. The peasants were eager to put "their grievances" on paper. It is true that these grievances were confined for the greater part to things of secondary importance; but throughout we see cropping up, as in the insurrection of the German peasantry in 1523, the demand that the lords should prove their *right* to the feudal exactions.† When the peasants sent in their *cahiers*, they waited patiently for the result. But the tardiness of the States-General and the National Assembly exasperated them, and as soon as that terrible winter of 1788–1789 came to an end, as soon as the sun shone again, and brought with it hope of a coming harvest, the riots broke out afresh, especially after the spring work in the fields was over.

The intellectual middle classes evidently took advantage of the elections to propagate revolutionary ideas. "A Constitutional Club" was formed, and its numerous branches spread themselves even into the smallest towns. The apathy which had struck Arthur Young in the eastern towns no doubt existed; but in some of the other provinces the middle classes extracted all the profit they desired from the electoral agitation. We can even see how the events which took place in June at Versailles in the National Assembly were prepared severla months before in the provinces. Thus the union of the Three Estates and the vote by head had been agreed to in Dauphiné since the month of August 1788 by the States of the province, under pressure of the local insurrections.

* Chassin, p. 163.
† Doniol, *La Révolution française et la féodalité.*

It must not be thought, however, that the middle-class people who took a prominent part in the elections were in the least degree revolutionary. They were moderates, "peaceful rebels," as Chassin says. As regards revolutionary measures, it was usually the people who spoke of them, since secret societies were found among the peasants, and unknown persons began to go about appealing to the people to pay taxes no longer, but to make the nobles pay them. Or else emissaries went about declaring that the nobles had already agreed to pay the taxes, but that this was only a cunning trick on their part. "The people of Geneva were emancipated in a day.... Tremble, ye nobles!" There were also pamphlets addressed to the peasants and secretly distributed, such as *L'Avis aux habitants des campagnes*, distributed at Chartres. In short, as Chassin says, and no one has more carefully studied this aspect of the Revolution: "Such was the agitation in the rural districts that even if the people of Paris had been vanquished on July 4, it was no longer possible to restore the condition in which the country had been previous to January 1789." To do that, it would have been necessary to conquer each village separately. After the month of March the feudal taxes were no longer paid by any one.*

The importance of this profound agitation in the country districts can be easily understood. Although the educated middle classes did undoubtedly profit by the conflicts with the Court and the *parlements* to arouse political ferment, and although they worked hard to disseminate discontent, it is nevertheless certain that the peasant insurrection, winning over the towns also, made the real basis of the Revolution, and gave the deputies of the Third Estate the determination, presently to be expressed by them at Versailles, to reform the entire system of the government in France, and to initiate a complete revolution in the distribution of wealth.

Without the peasant insurrection, which began in winter and went on, ever growing, until 1793, the overthrow of royal despotism would never have been effected so completely, nor would it have been accompanied by so enormous a change,

* Chassin, p. 167 *et seq.*

political, economic and social. France might, indeed, have had a sham parliament, even as Prussia had in 1848; but this innovation would not have assumed the character of a revolution: it would have remained superficial, as it did in the German States after 1848.

CHAPTER VIII

RIOTS IN PARIS AND ITS ENVIRONS

Activity in Paris—" Réveillon Affair "—First conflict between people of Paris and rich—" English gold "—Paris becomes centre of Revolution

UNDER such conditions it is easy to imagine that Paris could not remain quiet. Famine had set its grip upon the rural districts in the neighbourhood of the great city, as elsewhere. Provisions were as scarce in Paris as in the other large towns, and those who came in search of work could do nothing more than simply increase the multitude of the poor, especially in prospect of the great events which every one felt were on the way.

Towards the end of winter—in March and April—some hunger-riots and pillagings of corn are mentioned in the reports of the Governors of the provinces at Orléans, Cosnes, Rambouillet, Jouy, Pont-Sainte-Maxence, Bray-sur-Seine, Sens, Nangis, Viroflay, Montlhéry, &c. In other places within the region, in the forests around Paris, the peasants, as early as March, were exterminating all the rabbits and hares; even the woods belonging to the Abbey of Saint-Denis were cut down and carried away in the full view and knowledge of every one.

Paris was devouring revolutionary pamphlets, of which ten, twelve, or twenty were published every day, and passed rapidly from the hands of those who could afford to buy them into those of the poorest. People were excitedly discussing the pamphlet by Sieyès, *Qu'est-ce que le tiers?* Rabaud de Saint-Etienne's *Considérations sur les intérêts du tiers état*, which was tinctured with Socialism, *Les droits des états-généraux*, by d'Entraigues, and a hundred other less famous, but often more mordant. All Paris was becoming excited against the Court and the nobles, and soon the middle-class revolutionaries went to the poorest suburbs and into the taverns on the outskirts to recruit the hands and the pikes that they needed to strike at royalty. Meanwhile, on April 28, the insurrection, known later as "The Réveillon Affair" broke out, an affair which seemed like one of the forerunners of the great days of the Revolution.

On April 27, the Electoral Assemblies met in Paris, and it seems that during the preparation of the *cahiers* in the Faubourg Saint-Antoine there was a disagreement between the middle classes and the working-men. The workers stated their grievances and the middle-class men replied with insults. Réveillon, a paper-manufacturer and stainer, formerly a workman himself, now by skilful exploitation come to be the employer of three hundred operatives, made himself especially prominent by the brutality of his remarks. They have been repeated many times since. "The working man can live on black bread and lentils : wheat is not for the likes of him," &c.

Is there any truth in the connection which was made later on by the rich people, after the inquiry into "The Réveillon Affair," between the insurrection itself, and this fact mentioned by the toll-keepers, who declared that an immense multitude of suspicious-looking poor people clothed in rags had entered Paris just at that time ? On this point there can only be conjectures, vain conjectures after all. Given the prevalent state of mind, with revolt simmering in the neighbourhood of Paris, was not Réveillon's attitude towards the workers quite enough in itself to explain what happened the following day ?

On April 27, the people, infuriated by the opposition of the rich manufacturer and his brutal speeches, carried his effigy to the Place de la Grève for sentence and execution. At the Place Royale a rumour spread that the Third Estate had just condemned Réveillon to death. But evening came, and the crowds dispersed, spreading terror among the rich by their cries, which resounded in the streets all through the night. Finally, on the morning of the 28th, the crowds went to Réveillon's factory and compelled the workers to stop work ; they then attacked the warehouse and plundered it. The troops arrived, and the people forthwith defied them by throwing stones, slates and furniture from the windows and the roof. On this the troops opened fire and for several hours the people defended themselves with great fury. The result was that twelve soldiers were killed and eighty wounded; and on the people's side there were two hundred killed and three hundred wounded. The workers took possession of their comrades' dead bodies and carried them through the streets of the suburbs. Several days after a riotous mob of five or six hundred men gathered at Villejuif, and tried to break open the doors of the Bicêtre prison.

Here, then, was the first conflict between the people of Paris and the rich, a conflict which produced a deep impression. It was the first sight of the people driven to desperation, a sight which exercised a powerful influence on the elections by keeping away the reactionaries.

Needless to say that the gentlemen of the middle classes tried to prove that this outbreak was arranged beforehand by the enemies of France. Why should the good people of Paris have risen against a manufacturer? "It was English money that incited them to revolt," said some; "the gold of the aristocrats," said the middle-class revolutionaries. No one was willing to admit that the people revolted simply because they suffered, and had endured enough of the arrogance of the rich, who added insults to their sufferings! * From that time we see the growth of the legend which later on was to be used to reduce the Revolution to its parliamentary work, and to represent all the popular insurrections during the four years of the Revolution as *accidents*—the work of brigands or of agents paid either by Pitt or by the party of reaction. Still later the historians revived the legend: "Since the Court was able to use this riot as a pretext for rejecting the overtures of the States-General, therefore it must have been only the work of reactionaries." How often have we not heard the same methods of reasoning used in our own time!

* Droz (*Histoire du règne de Louis XVI.*), a reactionary historian, has remarked aptly that the money found on some of the slain men may well have been the proceeds of plunder.

In reality the days from April 24 to 28 were merely forerunners of the days of July 11 to July 14. A revolutionary spirit began to manifest itself among the people of Paris from that time onwards. Close by the Palais Royal, the revolutionary focus of the middle classes, were the faubourgs, the centres of the popular risings. Henceforth Paris became the focus of the Revolution, and the States-General, which were about to assemble at Versailles, came to rely upon Paris for the support they needed in pressing their demands and in their struggles against the Court.

CHAPTER IX

THE STATES-GENERAL

Opening of States-General—King's distrust—People not represented—"Third Estate"—Establishment of National Assembly—Oath in Tennis Court—King annuls resolutions of Assembly—Speech of Mirabeau—People threaten force

On May 4, 1789, the twelve hundred deputies of the States-General assembled at Versailles, repaired to the church of Saint Louis to hear Mass in connection with the opening ceremony, and the next day the King opened the session in the presence of a crowd of spectators. And already from this opening meeting the tragic inevitability of the Revolution began to unfold itself.

The King felt nothing but distrust towards the representatives of the nation whom he had convoked. He had at last resigned himself to convoking them, but he complained before the deputies themselves of "the restlessness of spirit," the general ferment throughout the country, as if such restlessness was in itself factitious, and not caused by the actual condition of France; as if that assemblage had been a useless and capricious violation of kingly rights.

France, too long held back from reform, had at last come to feel the necessity of a complete revision of *all* her institutions—and the King only mentioned a few trifling reforms in finance, for which a little economy in expenditure would have sufficed. He demanded "the agreement of the Orders" at a time when the provincial assemblies had already proved to men's minds that the existence of separate Orders was superannuated—a dead weight, a survival of the past. At a time, too, when everything, as in Russia to-day, needed reconstruction, the King expressed his fear above all things of "innovation"! Thus, in the

King's speech, the life-and-death struggle about to begin between royal autocracy and representative power was already foreshadowed.

As to the nation's representatives, they themselves in their divisions were already displaying signs of the deep cleavage which was to manifest itself throughout the Revolution between those who would cling to their privileges and those who would strive to demolish them.

The national representation, in fact, even then showed its chief defect. *The people were not represented at all, the peasants were absent.* It was the middle classes who took it upon themselves to speak for the people in general; and with regard to the peasantry, in the whole of this assembly, made up of lawyers, notaries, attorneys, there were perhaps five or six who knew anything about the real position, much less the legal position of the immense mass of the peasants. All of them, being townsmen, were well able to defend the townsman; but as to the peasant, they did not even know what he required, or what would be injurious to him.

Civil war already exists within these precincts, where the King, surrounded by nobles, speaks as master to the Third Estate, and reminds them of his " benefits." The Keeper of the Seals, Barentain, disclosing the real intention of the King, dwells upon the part to which the States-General should confine themselves. They are to consider the taxes which they will be asked to vote, they are to discuss the reform of civil and criminal law, they are to vote on a law concerning the Press, to check the liberties which it had recently arrogated to itself, and that will be all. There were to be no dangerous reforms: " All just demands have been granted; the King has not been stopped by indiscreet murmurs; he has indulgently deigned to ignore them; *he has pardoned even the expression of those false and extravagant matters under cover of which it was intended to substitute harmful chimeras for the unalterable principles of the monarchy.* Gentlemen, you will reject with indignation these dangerous innovations."

All the struggles of the four succeeding years lay in these words, and Necker, who followed the King and the Keeper of the Seals, in his speech lasting three hours, added nothing to advance either the great question of representative government, which absorbed the middle classes, or that of the land and the feudal exactions, which interested the peasants. The adroit Comptroller of Finance knew how to make a three-hours' speech without compromising himself either with the Court or the people. The King, faithful to the views he had already expressed to Turgot, did not understand the seriousness of the moment, and left to the Queen and princes the task of intriguing to prevent the concessions which were demanded of him.

But neither did Necker comprehend that it was a question of surmounting not merely a financial crisis, but a political and social crisis of the utmost seriousness, and that under these circumstances a policy of manœuvring between the Court and the Third Estate was bound to be fatal. For if it was not already too late to prevent a Revolution, it was at least necessary to make some attempt at an honest, straightforward policy of concessions in the matter of government; the time had come to bring forward, in their most important aspects, the great land problems on which the misery or well-being of a whole nation depended.

And as to the representatives themselves, neither the two privileged orders, nor yet "the Third," grasped the full extent of the problem which was confronting France. The nobility dreamed of regaining their ascendency over the Crown; the clergy thought only of maintaining their privileges; and the Third Estate, although it knew quite well what steps to take for the conquest of power in favour of the middle classes, did not perceive that there was yet another problem, infinitely more important to solve—that of giving back the land to the peasant, in order that, possessing a land freed from heavy feudal exactions, he might double and treble the production of the soil, and so put an end to the incessant periods of scarcity which were undermining the strength of the French nation.

Could there be any way out of these conditions but by conflict and struggle? The revolt of the people: the rising of the peasants, the Jacquerie, the insurrection of the workers in the towns, and of the poor in general—in a word, the Revolution, with all its struggles, its hatreds, its terrible conflicts and its revenges, were they not all inevitable?

For five weeks the "deputies of 'the Third'" tried by parleying to induce the deputies of the other two Orders to sit together, while the Royalist committees on their side worked to maintain the separation. The negotiations led to nothing. But as the days went by the people of Paris assumed a more and more menacing attitude. In Paris, the Palais Royal, turned into an open-air club to which every one was admitted, voiced the general exasperation. It rained pamphlets for which the people scrambled. "Every hour produces something new," says Arthur Young. "Thirteen came out to-day, sixteen yesterday and ninety-two last week. . . . Nineteen-twentieths of these productions are in favour of liberty. . . . The ferment at Paris is beyond conception." * The orators who harangued openly in the streets, standing on a chair in front of a *café*, already spoke of seizing upon the palaces and châteaux of the noble landlords. One heard already, like the rumbling of a coming storm, threatenings of the coming Terror, while at Versailles the people collected at the doors of the Assembly to insult the aristocrats.

The deputies of the "Third" felt that they were being supported. By degrees they grew bolder, and on June 17, upon a motion of Sieyès, they declared themselves at last a "National Assembly." In this way the first step towards the abolition of the privileged classes was taken, and the people of Paris greeted this first step with thunderous acclamations. Thus encouraged, the Assembly voted that the established taxes, being illegal, should be levied only provisionally, and only for as long as the Assembly sat. The people should not be any longer bound to pay them when once the Assembly should be dissolved. A "Committee of Subsistence" was appointed to combat the famine, and capitalists were reassured by the Assembly's consolidation of the National Debt—an act of the greatest prudence at that moment, since the National representation had to maintain itself at any cost, and to disarm a

* Arthur Young, *Travels in France*, pp. 153, 176 (London, 1892).

power, the power of the money-lender, who would be dangerous if he took sides with the Court.

But this meant revolt against the Royal authority. Accordingly the princes, d'Artois, Condé and Conti, together with the Keeper of the Seals, began to plan a *coup d'état*. On a given day the King was to go in great state to the Assembly. There he would annul all the resolutions of the Assembly, he would decree the separation of the Orders, and would himself fix the few reforms, which should be passed by the Three Orders sitting separately. And what did Necker, that perfect representative of the middle classes of the period, oppose to this stroke of authority, to the *coup d'état* prepared by the Court ? Compromise ! He, too, wanted a display of authority, a Royal Session, and in this session the King was to grant the capitative vote without distinction between the Three Orders in the matter of taxes; but for everything concerning the privileges of the nobility and clergy separate sittings of the Orders were to be maintained. Now, it is evident that this measure was still less possible to realise than that of the princes. A *coup d'état* is not risked for a half-measure, which, moreover, could not be maintained for more than a fortnight. How could taxation have been reformed without impinging on the privileges of the two superior Orders ?

It was on June 20, therefore, that the deputies of "the Third," emboldened by the more and more threatening attitude of the people in Paris, and even at Versailles, decided to resist the plans for dismissing the Assembly, and for that purpose to bind themselves together by solemn oath. Seeing their Assembly Hall closed on account of the preparations that were being made for the Royal Session, they went in procession to a kind of private hall, the hall of the Tennis Court in the Rue Saint-François. A crowd lmarched with the procession through the streets of Versailes, headed by Bailly. Some volunteer soldiers offered their services to mount guard for them. The enthusiasm of the crowds which surrounded them on all sides upheld the deputies.

Arrived at the hall of the Tennis Court, excited and touched by a fine emotion, they all but one took a solemn oath not to separate before they had given France a Constitution.

THE STATES-GENERAL

No doubt these were but words; there was even something theatrical in this oath; but that matters little. There are moments when words are required to make hearts vibrate. And the oath taken in the hall of the Tennis Court made the hearts of revolutionary youth vibrate throughout the length and breadth of France. Woe to the Assemblies that are incapable of such an attitude and such words.

Besides, this act of courage on the part of the Assembly bore immediate fruit. Two days later the Third Estate, being obliged to sit in the church of Saint Louis, found the clergy coming to take part in their deliberations.

The great blow of the Royal Session was struck the following day, June 23, but its effect was already weakened by the oath in the Tennis Court and the sitting in the church of Saint Louis. The King appeared before the deputies. He annulled all the resolutions of the Assembly, or rather of the Third Estate; he decreed the maintenance of the Orders, determined the limits of the reforms to be accomplished, threatened the States-General with dissolution if they did not obey, and ordered all the deputies to separate for the time being. Upon this the nobility and clergy obediently left the hall, but the deputies of "the Third" kept their places. Then it was that Mirabeau uttered his beautiful and famous speech, in which he said that the King was only their mandatory, that they held their authority of the people, and having taken the oath they could not separate without having framed a Constitution. Being here by the will of the people they would leave only by the force of the bayonet.

Now, it was exactly this force which the Court no longer possessed. Necker had already told them, in February, and very truly, that obedience was nowhere to be found, and that they could not be sure even of the troops.

As to the people of Paris, we have seen in what kind of humour they were on April 27. Every moment a general rising of the people against the rich was feared in Paris, and a few ardent revolutionaries had not hesitated to go into the gloomy faubourgs in search of reinforcements against the Court. Even at Versailles, on the eve of the Royal Session, the people had almost killed a clerical deputy, the Abbé Maury, as well as d'Espréménil, a deputy of "the Third," who had come over from the nobility. On the day of the Royal Session the Keeper of the Seals and the Archbishop of Paris were so "hooted, abused and scoffed at, so overwhelmed with shame and rage," that the King's secretary, Passeret, who accompanied the minister, "died of the shock the same day." On the 24th, the Bishop of Beauvais was nearly killed by a blow on the head from a stone. On June 25, the crowd hissed the deputies of the nobility and clergy. All the windows were broken in the palace of the Archbishop of Paris. "The troops refused to fire on the people," says Arthur Young bluntly. The King's threat was therefore meaningless. The people's attitude was too menacing for the Court to resort to bayonets, and this is why Louis XVI. uttered this exclamation, "After all . . . let them stay!"

As to the Assembly of the Third Estate itself, was it not deliberating under the watchful eyes and menaces of the people who filled the galleries? As early as June 17, when the Third Estate declared itself a National Assembly, that memorable decision was arrived at amidst the acclamations of the galleries and of the two or three thousand persons who surrounded the Hall of Assembly. The list of the three hundred deputies of "the Third" who were opposed to it went the round of Paris, and there was even some talk of burning their houses. And when the oath was being taken in the Tennis Court, and Martin Dauch opposed it, Bailly, the president of the Assembly, prudently made him escape by a back door to avoid facing the people gathered at the front of the hall, and for several days he had to remain in hiding.

Without this pressure put upon the Assembly by the people, it is quite possible that the brave deputies of "the Third," whose names are remembered in history, might never have succeeded in overcoming the resistance of the timorous who had ranged themselves with Malouet.

As to the people of Paris, they made open preparations for the revolt, which was their reply to the military *coup d'état* prepared by the Court against Paris for July 16.

CHAPTER X

PREPARATIONS FOR THE COUP D'ETAT

The 14th of July—Middle classes distrust people—Royalists prepare *coup d'état*—Middle classes urge people to arm—People seize Bastille—Middle classes restore order—King and feudal rights—Effect of Royal Session—Atmosphere of conspiracy at Court—Foundation of Breton Club—Mirabeau and people—Necker tries to avert famine—Incompetence of National Assembly—Royalist plotting continues—Petition of Assembly

THE accepted account of July 14 runs as follows : The National Assembly was sitting. At the end of June, after two months of parleying and hesitations, the Three Orders were at last united. The power was slipping from the grasp of the Court, which began, therefore, to prepare a *coup d'état*. Troops were summoned and massed round Versailles ; they were to disperse the Assembly and bring Paris to its senses.

On July 11, the accepted version goes on to say, the Court decided to act. Necker was dismissed and exiled, Paris heard of this on the 12th, and the citizens formed a procession, which passed through the streets carrying a statue of the dismissed minister. At the Palais Royal, Camille Desmoulins made his famous speech ending with an appeal to arms. The faubourgs rose and 50,000 pikes were forged in thirty-six hours ; on the 14th the people marched upon the Bastille, which presently lowered its drawbridge and surrendered. The Revolution had gained its first victory.

Such is the usual account, which is repeated at the Republic's festivals. It is, however, only a half-truth. It is true so far as the dry statement of facts is concerned ; but it does not tell what should be told about the part played by the people in the rising; nor yet about the true connection between the two elements of the movement, the people and the middle classes. For in the Paris insurrection leading to July 14, as all through the Revolution, there were two separate currents of different origin: the political movement of the middle classes and the popular movement of the masses. At certain moments during the great days of the Revolution, the two movements joined hands in a temporary alliance, and then they gained their great victories over the old *régime*. But the middle classes always distrusted their temporary ally, the people, and gave clear proof of this in July 1789. The alliance was concluded unwillingly by the middle classes; and on the morrow of the 14th, and even during the insurrection itself, they made haste to organise themselves, in order that they might be able to bridle the revolted people.

Ever since the Réveillon affair, the people of Paris, suffering from scarcity, seeing bread grow dearer day by day, and deceived by empty promises, had been trying to revolt. But not feeling themselves supported, even by those of the middle classes who had become prominent in the struggle with royal authority, they could only chafe the bit. In the meantime, the Court party, led by the Queen and the princes, decided to strike a great blow, which would put an end to the Assembly and to the popular agitation in Paris. They concentrated troops whose attachment to the King and Queen they stimulated by every means, and openly prepared a *coup d'état* against the Assembly and against Paris. Then the Assembly, feeling themselves threatened, gave free rein to those of their members and friends in Paris who wanted "the appeal to the people"; that is to say, the appeal for a popular rising. And the people of the faubourgs, desiring nothing better, responded to the appeal. They did not wait for the dismissal of Necker, but began to rise as early as July 8, and even on June 27. Taking advantage of this the middle classes urged the people to open insurrection, and allowed them to arm themselves. At the same time they took care to be armed, too, so that they could control the popular outbreak and prevent its going "too far." But as the insurrection gathered force, the people, contrary

PREPARATIONS FOR THE COUP D'ETAT

to the will of the middle classes, seized the Bastille, the emblem and support of the royal power; whereupon the middle classes, having meanwhile organised their militia, lost no time in suppressing the men with pikes and re-establishing order.

That is the twofold movement which has to be described.

We have seen that the purpose for holding the Royal Session of June 23 was to declare to the States-General that they were not the power they wished to be; that the absolute power of the King remained unimpaired; that there was nothing for the States-General to change in it;* and that the two privileged orders, the nobility and the clergy, would of themselves enact whatever concessions they should deem useful for a more just distribution of the taxes. The benefits which were to be granted to the people *would come therefore from the King in person*, and those benefits would be the abolition of statute labour, in great part already accomplished, of mortmain and of *franc-fief*, restriction of the game laws, the substitution of a regular enlistment instead of drawing lots for the militia, the suppression of the word *taille* and the organisation of the provincial authorities. All this, however, belonged to the realm of empty promises, or indeed was but the mere naming of reform, for all that these reforms implied, all the substance for making these changes, had still to be provided; and how could it be provided without laying the axe to the privileges of the two superior orders? But the most important point in the royal speech, since the whole revolution was soon to turn upon the matter, was the King's declaration concerning the inviolability of the feudal rights. He declared that the tithes, redemptions, rents of all kinds and seigneurial and feudal rights were property rights absolutely and for ever inviolable.

By such a pronouncement the King was evidently placing the nobility on his side against the Third Estate. But to make a promise of this extent was to circumscribe the Revolution in advance, in such a way as to render it powerless to

* Necker's original project allowed the Assembly a right to push the Revolution as far as the establishment of a charter, in imitation of the English, says Louis Blanc; they took care to exclude from all joint deliberations the form of constitution to be given by the next States-General (*Histoire de la Révolution française*, 4vo, vol. i. p. 120).

accomplish any substantial reform in the finances of the State and in the entire internal organisation of France. It meant maintaining intact the old France, the old *régime*, and we shall see later how, in the course of the Revolution, *royalty and the maintenance of feudal rights*—the old political form and the old economic form—came to be associated in the mind of the nation.

It must be admitted that this manœuvre of the Court succeeded up to a certain point. After the Royal Session the nobility accorded the King, and especially the Queen, an ovation at the palace, and the next day there remained only forty-seven nobles who adhered to the two other Orders. Only a few days later, when the rumour spread that a hundred thousand Parisians were marching on Versailles, the people at the palace were in a state of general consternation at hearing this news, and on an order from the King, confirmed by the weeping Queen—for the nobility no longer relied upon the King—most of the nobles rejoined the representatives of the clergy and the Third Estate. But even then they scarcely concealed their hope of soon seeing those rebels dispersed by force.

Meanwhile, all manœuvrings of the Court, all its conspiracies, and even all conversations of such-and-such a prince or noble, were quickly made known to the revolutionaries. Everything reached Paris by a thousand secret ways of communication carefully established, and the rumours coming from Versailles helped to increase the ferment in the capital. The moment always arrives when those in power can no longer depend even upon their servants, and such a moment had come at Versailles. Thus, while the nobility were rejoicing over the little success gained by the Royal Session, some middle-class revolutionaries were founding at Versailles itself a club, the Breton Club, which soon became a great rallying centre and was later on the famous club of the Jacobins. To this club the servants, even those of the King and Queen, went to report what was said behind closed doors at the Court. Some Breton deputies, among them Le Chapelier, Glezen and Lanjuinais, were the founders of this Breton Club, and Mirabeau, the Duke

PREPARATIONS FOR THE COUP D'ETAT

d'Aiguillon, Sieyès, Barnave, Pétion, the Abbé Grégoire and Robespierre were members of it.

Since the States-General had been sitting at Versailles the greatest excitement prevailed in Paris. The Palais Royal, with its gardens and *cafés*, had become an open-air club, whither ten thousand persons of all classes went every day to exchange news, to discuss the pamphlets of the hour, to renew among the crowd their ardour for future action, to know and to understand one another. Here flocked together the lower middle classes and the intellectuals. All the rumours, all the news collected at Versailles by the Breton Club, were immediately communicated to this open-air club of the Parisians. Thence the rumours and news spread to the faubourgs, and if sometimes on the way fiction was added to fact, it was, as is often the case with popular legends, truer than the truth itself, since it was only forestalling, and revealing under the guise of legend, the secret springs of action, and intuitively judging men and things often more correctly than do the wise. Who better than the obscure masses of the faubourgs knew Marie-Antoinette, the Duchess de Polignac, the perfidious King and the treacherous princes ? Who has understood them better than the people did ?

Ever since the day following the Royal Session, the great city was simmering with revolt. The Hôtel de Ville had sent congratulations to the Assembly. The Palais Royal had forwarded an address couched in militant language. For the famished people, despised and rejected until then, the popular triumph was a gleam of hope, and insurrection represented in their eyes the means of procuring the bread they needed. At the time when the famine was growing more and more severe, and even the supply of bad flour, yellow and burnt, reserved for the poor, continually failed, the people knew that in Paris and the vicinity there was enough food to feed everybody, and the poor said to one another that without an insurrection the monopolists would never leave off starving the people.

But, as the murmurs of the people in their dark quarters grew louder, the Paris middle classes and the representatives of the people at Versailles became more and more alarmed about a possible rising in the provinces. Better the King and Court than the people in revolt.* The very day the three Orders were united, June 27, after the first victory of the Third Estate, Mirabeau, who until then was appealing to the people, separated himself completely from them, and advocated the separation of the representatives from them. He even warned the members to be on their guard against "seditious auxiliaries." In this we can already see the future programme of "the Gironde" evolving in the Assembly. Mirabeau wished the Assembly to contribute "to the maintenance of order, to the public tranquillity, to the authority of the laws and their ministers." He went even further. He wanted the deputies to rally round the King, saying that the King meant well; if it happened that he did any wrong, it was only because he was deceived and badly advised!

The Assembly loudly applauded this speech. "The truth is," says Louis Blanc very aptly, "that far from wishing to overturn the throne, the middle classes were already trying to shelter themselves behind it. Deserted by the nobility, it was in the ranks of his commons, at one time so obstinate, that Louis XVI. would have found his most faithful and most alarmed servitors. He was ceasing to be the King of gentlemen, he was becoming the King of the property-owners."

This primordial defect in the Revolution weighed it down, all the time, as we shall see, up to the moment when reaction got the upper hand.

The distress in the city, however, increased from day to day. It is true that Necker had taken measures to avert the dangers of a famine. On September 7, 1788, he had suspended

* Those who make speeches on the anniversaries of the Revolution prefer to keep silent on this delicate subject, and speak of the touching unanimity which they pretend to have existed between the people and their representatives. But Louis Blanc has already pointed out the fears of the middle classes as the 14th of July drew near, and modern research only confirms this point of view. The additional facts which I give here, concerning the days from the 2nd to the 12th of July, show also that the insurrection of the people of Paris followed up to the 12th its own line of conduct, independent of the middle-class members of the Third Estate.

the exportation of corn, and he was protecting the importation by bounties; seventy million livres were expended in the purchase of foreign wheat. At the same time he gave widespread publicity to the decree of the King's Council of April 23, 1789, which empowered judges and officers of the police to visit private granaries to make an inventory of the grain, and in case of necessity to send the grain to market. But the carrying out of these orders was confided to the old authorities and—no more need be said!

Now in July the Government was giving bounties to those who brought wheat to Paris; but the imported wheat was secretly re-exported, so that it could be brought in again and so obtain the bounty à second time. In the provinces, monopolists were buying up the corn with a view to these speculations; they bought up even the standing crops.

It was then that the true character of the National Assembly was revealed. It had been worthy of admiration, no doubt, when it took the oath in the Tennis Court, but above all things it still maintained towards the people a middle-class attitude. On July 4, when the report of the "Committee of Subsistence" was presented, the Assembly discussed the measures to be taken for guaranteeing food and work to the people. They talked for hours and made proposition after proposition. Pétion proposed a loan, others proposed authorising the provincial assemblies to take the necessary measures, but nothing was decided, nothing undertaken. And, when one of the members raised the question of the speculators and denounced some of them, he had the entire Assembly against him. Two days later, July 6, Bouche announced that the culprits were known, and that a formal accusation would be made the next day. "A general panic took possession of the Assembly," says Gorsas, in the *Courrier de Versailles et de Paris*, which he had just started. But the next day came and not a word more was uttered on this subject. The affair was suppressed in the interim. Why? For fear—as subsequent events go to prove—of compromising revelations.

In any case, so much did the Assembly fear the popular outbreak, that on the occasion of a riot in Paris, on June 30, after the arrest of the eleven French Guards who had refused to load their muskets to fire on the people, the Assembly voted an address to the King, conceived in the most servile terms and protesting its " profound attachment to the royal authority." *

However grudgingly the King might have consented to give the middle classes the smallest share in the Government, they would have rallied to him and helped with all their power of organisation to keep the people down. But—and let this serve as a warning in future revolutions—in the life of the individual, of parties, and even of institutions, there is a logic which is beyond any one's power to change. The royal despotism could not come to terms with the middle classes, who demanded from it their share in the Government. It was logically destined to fight them, and once the battle began it had to succumb and yield its place to representative government—the form which was best suited to the rule of the middle classes. On the other hand, without betraying its natural supporters, the nobility, it could not make terms with democracy, the people's party, and it did its best to defend the nobles and their privileges, to see itself later on betrayed in return by those self-same persons, privileged from their birth.

Meanwhile information concerning the plots of the Court was coming from all quarters, both to the partisans of the Duke of Orléans, who used to meet at Montrouge, as well as to the revolutionaries, who frequented the Breton Club. Troops were concentrating at Versailles, and on the road from Versailles to Paris. In Paris itself they took possession of the most important points in the direction of Versailles. Thirty-five thousand men were said to be distributed within this compass, and twenty thousand more were to be added to them in a few days. The princes and the Queen, it was rumoured, were planning to dissolve the Assembly, to crush Paris in case of a rising, to arrest and kill, not only the principal leaders

* " The National Assembly deplores the troubles which are now agitating Paris. . . . It will send a deputation to the King to beg him of his grace to employ for the re-establishment of order the infallible means of the clemency and kindness that are so native to his heart, with the confidence which his good people will always deserve."

PREPARATIONS FOR THE COUP D'ETAT

and the Duke of Orléans, but also those members of the Assembly, such as Mirabeau, Mounier and Lally-Tollendal, who wished to transform Louis XVI. into a constitutional monarch. Twelve members, said La Fayette later on, were to be immolated. The Baron de Breteuil and Marshal de Broglie had been summoned to put this project into execution—both of them quite ready to do it. "If it is necessary to burn Paris, Paris will be burnt," said the former. As to Marshal de Broglie, he had written to the Prince de Condé that a whiff of grape-shot would soon "disperse these argufiers and restore the absolute power which is going out, in place of the republican spirit which is coming in." *

It must not be believed that those rumours were only idle tales, as some reactionary historians have asserted. The letter of the Duchess de Polignac, addressed on July 12 to Flesselles, the Provost of the Merchants, which was found later on, and in which all the persons implicated were mentioned under assumed names, is sufficient proof of the plot hatched by the Court for July 16. If there could still be any doubt on this matter, the words addressed to Dumouriez at Caen on July 10 by the Duchess de Beuvron, in the presence of sixty exulting nobles, should suffice to prove it:

"Well, Dumouriez," said the Duchess, "do you not know the great news? Your friend Necker is turned out, and the result is that the King reascends the throne and the Assembly is dispersed. Your friends, 'the forty-seven,' are at this very moment in the Bastille, perhaps, with Mirabeau, Turgot, and a hundred or so of those insolent fellows of the Third Estate, and for certain Marshal de Broglie is in Paris with thirty thousand men." †

The Duchess was mistaken. Necker was not dismissed until the 11th, and Broglie took care not to enter Paris.

But what was the Assembly doing then? It was doing what Assemblies have always done, and always will do. It decided on nothing. What could it decide?

The very day that the people of Paris began to rise, that

---

* Louis Blanc, *Histoire de la Révolution française.*
† Dumouriez, *Mémoires,* vol. ii. p. 35.

is, on July 8, the Assembly charged no other than Mirabeau, the people's tribune, with the drawing up of a humble petition to the King, and while praying the King to withdraw the troops the Assembly filled their petition with the grossest adulation. It spoke of a people who dearly loved their King, and thanked Heaven for the gift bestowed upon them in his love. How many times similar words and flatteries will be addressed to the King by the representatives of the people during the progress of the Revolution? The fact is that the Revolution cannot be understood at all if these repeated efforts on the part of the propertied classes to win over Royalty to their side as a buckler against the people are passed by unnoticed. All the dramas which will be enacted later on, in 1793, within the Convention, were already contained in germ in this petition from the National Assembly, signed but a few days before July 14.

CHAPTER XI

PARIS ON THE EVE OF THE FOURTEENTH

Revolution centred in Paris, not in Assembly—Paris ready to rise—Districts organise people—Arrest of soldiers of *Gardes françaises*—Scarcity of bread—Fury of people increases—Dismissal of Necker—Camille Desmoulins appeals to arms—Struggle begins—Tocsin rung—People procure food and arms — Permanent Committee instituted — Formation of National Guard—Middle classes try to disarm people

THE attention of the historians is generally absorbed by the National Assembly. The representatives of the people assembled at Versailles seem to personify the Revolution, and their last words or acts are chronicled with pious devotion. Nevertheless, it was not there that the passionate heart of the Revolution was throbbing during those July days: it was throbbing in Paris.

Without Paris, without her people, the Assembly was naught. If the fear of Paris in revolt had not restrained the Court, the Assembly would have been most certainly dispersed, as has been seen so many times since—on the 18th Brumaire and December 2 in France, and also recently in Hungary and in Russia. No doubt the deputies would have protested; no doubt they would have uttered some fine speeches, and some of them perhaps might have tried to raise the provinces; but without a people ready to rise, without a preliminary revolutionary work accomplished among the masses, without an appeal to the people for revolt made direct from man to man and not by manifestoes, a representative Assembly can do little when it has to face an established government backed by its legions of functionaries and its army.

Fortunately Paris was awake. Whilst the National Assembly

slumbered in fancied security, and on July 10 tranquilly resumed the discussion on the scheme for a Constitution, the people of Paris, to whom the boldest and most clear-sighted of the middle classes had at last appealed, prepared for insurrection. Details of the military trap which the Court was preparing for the 16th were repeated in the faubourgs. Everything was known, even the King's threat to retire to Soissons and deliver up Paris to the army; and Paris, *la grande fournaise*, organised itself in its various sections to answer force by force. The "seditious auxilliaries" with which Mirabeau had threatened the Court had been appealed to indeed, and in the gloomy wineshops of the suburbs the Paris proletarians discussed the means of "saving the country." They armed themselves as best they could.

Hundreds of patriotic agitators, "unknown persons," of course, did everything to keep up the ferment and to draw the people into the streets. Squibs and fireworks were, according to Arthur Young, one of the means used; they were sold at half-price, and whenever a crowd collected to see the fireworks let off at a street corner, some one would begin to harangue the people—tell them news of the Court plots. "Lately a company of Swiss would have crushed all this; a regiment would do it now if led with firmness; but let it last a fortnight, and an army will be wanting,"* said Arthur Young on the eve of July 14.

In fact, by the end of June the people of Paris were in full ferment and preparing for insurrection. At the beginning of the month there had already been riots on account of the dearness of corn, writes Hardy, the English bookseller; and if Paris remained calm until the 25th, it was only because, until the Royal Session, the people were always hoping that the Assembly would do something. But since the 25th, Paris understood already that no other hope remained but insurrection.

One party of Parisians marched that day towards Versailles, ready to fight the troops. In Paris itself, bands were formed "prepared to proceed to the direst extremities," as we read

* Young, *Travels in France*, p. 184 (London, 1892).

in the secret Notes addressed to the Minister of Foreign Affairs, which were published by Chassin.* "The people have been in commotion all night, they have made bonfires and let off a prodigious number of rockets in front of the Palais Royal and the General Comptroller's Office. They were shouting, ' Long live the Duke of Orléans ! ' "

The same day, the 25th, soldiers of the French Guards deserted their barracks, fraternising and drinking with the people, who carried them off to various quarters, shouting through the streets as they passed : " *A bas la calotte !* "

Meanwhile the "districts" of Paris, that is, the primary bodies of electors, especially those of the workmen's quarters, assembled regularly and took measures for organising resistance in Paris. The "districts" were kept in touch with each other, and their representatives made repeated efforts to constitute an independent municipal body. Even on the 25th Bonneville appealed to arms at an Assembly of the electors, and proposed that they should form themselves into a Commune, quoting historical precedent to give weight to his proposal. The next day, after having met first in the Museum, Rue Dauphine, the representatives of the "districts" at last transferred themselves to the Hôtel de Ville, and on July 1 they were already in their second session, a verbatim report of which is given by Chassin.† Thus they constituted the "Permanent Committee," which we shall see acting on the day of July 14.

On June 30, a simple incident, the arrest of eleven soldiers of the *Gardes françaises*, who had been sent to the Abbaye prison for refusing to load their muskets, sufficed to cause a serious riot in Paris. When Loustalot, editor of the *Révolutions de Paris*, mounted a chair in front of the Café Foy in the Palais Royal, and harangued the crowd on this matter, four thousand men went immediately to the Abbaye and set the arrested soldiers at liberty. The jailers, seeing the crowd arrive, realised that resistance was useless, and handed over the prisoners ; and the dragoons, riding full gallop to cut down the people,

---

* Chassin, *Les élections et les cahiers de Paris* (Paris, 1889), vol. iii. p. 453.   † Chassin, vol. iii. pp. 439-444, 458, 460.

halted, thrust back their sabres into their sheaths, and fraternised with the crowd. A shudder ran through the Assembly when they learned next day of this fraternisation of the troops and the rioters. "Are we to be the tribunes of a people in revolt?" these gentlemen asked one another.

But revolt was already growing in the outskirts of Paris. At Nangis the people had refused to pay the taxes, so long as they were not fixed by the Assembly, and as there was a scarcity of bread (only two bushels of wheat were sold to each buyer) and the people were in an uproar, the market was surrounded by dragoons. But notwithstanding the presence of the troops there were several riots at Nangis and in other little towns on the outskirts. "The people quarrel with the bakers," says Young, "and then run away with the bread and wheat for nothing." *

The *Mercure de France* (July 27) even mentions some attempts made in several places, especially at Saint-Quentin, to cut the green crops, so great was the scarcity.

In Paris, on June 30, the patriots were already enrolling themselves at the Café du Caveau for insurrection, and when they heard the next day that Broglie had taken command of the army, the people, say the secret reports, openly declared and posted up everywhere that "should the troops fire a single shot they would put everything to fire and sword." "Many other things much stronger than that were said," adds the official. "Wise men dare not show themselves."

On July 2 the fury of the populace broke out against the Count d'Artois and the Polignacs. There was talk of killing them and sacking their palaces. There was talk also of seizing upon all the cannon distributed through Paris. The crowds in the streets were larger and the fury of the people inconceivable, say the same reports. "This very day," said Hardy, the bookseller, in his journal, "a raging multitude was on the point of setting out from the Palais Royal to rescue the deputies of the Third Estate, who it was said were exposed to the danger of being assassinated by the nobles." The people now began to talk of seizing on the arms at the Hôtel des Invalides.

* Arthur Young, p. 189.

PARIS ON THE EVE OF THE FOURTEENTH

The fury inspired by hunger kept pace with the fury against the Court. Consequently, on July 4 and 6, fearing an attack on the bakers, parties of *Gardes françaises* had to be sent out to patrol the streets and superintend the distribution of bread.

On July 8, a prelude to the insurrection broke out in Paris itself, at the camp of twenty thousand unemployed workmen engaged by the Government in road-making at Montmartre. Two days after, on the 10th, blood was already flowing, and on the same day they began to set fire to the toll-gates. The one in the Chaussée d'Antin was burnt, and the people took advantage of this by letting in provisions and wine free of duty.

Would Camille Desmoulins ever have made his appeal to arms on the 12th if he had not been sure that the people would listen to him, if he had not known that Paris was already in revolt, that only twelve days before Loustalot had stirred up the crowd over a matter of less importance, and that Paris and the faubourgs were even then merely waiting for the signal for some one to begin and it would flame into insurrection ?

The impetuosity of the princes, who were certain of success, precipitated the *coup d'état* planned for the 16th, and the King was compelled to act before reinforcements for the troops had arrived at Versailles.*

Necker was dismissed on the 11th, the Count d'Artois shaking his fist in the minister's face as he passed into the council chamber of the ministers, and the King, with his usual duplicity, pretending to know nothing about it, although he had already signed the dismissal. Necker submitted to his master's orders without a word. He even fell in with his plans, and arranged for his departure for Brussels in such a way that it passed unnoticed at Versailles.

Paris only learned about it towards noon the next day, Sunday, the 12th. Every one had been expecting this dismissal, which was to be the beginning of the *coup d'état*. The people were already repeating the saying of the Duke de Broglie,

* *Vide* the Letters of Salmour, the Envoy from Saxony, to Stutterheim, on July 19 and August 20 (Archives of Dresden), cited by Flammermont ; *La journée du 14 Juillet* 1789, by Pitra (Publications de la Société de l'Histoire de la Révolution française, 1892).

who, with his thirty thousand soldiers massed between Paris and Versailles, was "answerable for Paris," and as sinister rumours were circulating all the morning concerning the massacres prepared by the Court, "all revolutionary Paris" rushed in a body to the Palais Royal. Just then the courier had arrived bringing news of Necker's exile. The Court had decided to open hostilities. . . . Whereupon Camille Desmoulins, coming out of one of the *cafés* in the Palais Royal, the Café Foy, with a sword in one hand and a pistol in the other, mounted upon a chair and made his appeal to arms. Breaking a branch from a tree, he took, as is known, a green leaf as a badge, a rallying-sign. And his cry, "There is not a moment to lose, haste to arms!" spread through the faubourgs.

In the afternoon an immense procession, carrying the busts of the Duke of Orléans and Necker, veiled in crape (it was said that the Duke of Orléans also had been banished), passed through the Palais Royal, along the Rue Richelieu, and turned towards the Place Louis XV. (now Place de la Concorde), which was occupied by troops—Swiss, French Infantry, Hussars and Dragoons—under the command of the Marquis de Besenval. The troops soon found themselves surrounded by the people. They tried to keep them back with sabre-thrusts; they even fired upon them, but before an innumerable crowd that pushed and jostled, pressing in and breaking through their ranks on every side, the soldiers were forced to retire. From other sources we learn that the French Guards fired a few shots at the "Royal German" regiment, which adhered to the King, and that the Swiss refused to fire on the people. Besenval, who seems not to have had much confidence in the Court, withdrew, therefore, before an overwhelming torrent of the people and went to camp on the Champ-de-Mars.*

Thus the struggle began. But what would be the final

---

* "The French Guards, having sided with the populace, fired upon a detachment of the Royal German regiment, posted on the boulevard, under my windows. Two men and two horses were killed," wrote Simolin, Plenipotentiary of Catherine II. in Paris, to the Chancellor Osterman, on July 13. And he added: "Yesterday and the day before they burned the *barrière blanche* and that of the Faubourg Poissonnière" (Conches, *Lettres de Louis XVI.*, &c., p. 223).

PARIS ON THE EVE OF THE FOURTEENTH 73

outcome of it if the troops, still faithful to the King, received orders to march on Paris ? In this eventuality, the middle classes decided to accept, with reluctance, the supreme measure, the appeal to the people. The tocsin was rung throughout Paris, and the faubourgs began to forge pikes.*

By degrees armed men began to appear in the streets. All night long men of the people compelled the passers-by to give them money to buy powder. The toll-gates were in flames. All the gates on the right bank, from the Faubourg Saint-Antoine to that of Saint-Honoré, as well as those at Saint-Marcel et Saint-Jacques, were burnt, and provisions and wine entered Paris freely. All night the tocsin rang and the middle classes trembled for their possessions, because men armed with pikes and cudgels spread themselves through every quarter and plundered the houses of some monopolists, known to be enemies of the people, and knocking at the doors of the rich they demanded money and arms.

The next day, the 13th, the people went first of all to the places where there was food. They attacked the monastery of Saint-Lazare, with cries of "Bread, bread !" Fifty-two carts were laden with flour, which, instead of being emptied then and there, were dragged to the Halles, so that the food might be used by every one. It was to the Halles that the people also sent the provisions let into Paris without paying duty.†

At the same time the people seized the prison of La Force, where debtors were imprisoned, and the liberated prisoners went about the city thanking the people ; but an outbreak of prisoners in the Châtelet was quelled, apparently by some of the middle classes who had armed in hot haste and were already

---

* Of these 50,000 were made, as well as "all kinds of small arms, at the expense of the town," says Dusaulx ("L'œuvre de sept jours," p. 203).

† "From all parts there came to the Hôtel de Ville an infinite number of carriages, chariots and carts, stopped at the gates of the town, and loaded with all sorts of supplies, plates and dishes, furniture, food-stuffs, &c. The people, who only clamoured for arms and ammunition, . . . came to us in crowds and became more insistent every minute." It was July 13 (Dusaulx, "L'œuvre de sept jours," in *Mémoires sur la Bastille*, published by H. Monin, Paris, 1889, p. 397).

patrolling the streets. By six o'clock the middle-class militia were already formed and marching towards the Hôtel de Ville, and at ten o'clock that evening, says Chassin, they were on duty.

Taine and his followers, faithful echoes of the fears of the middle class, try to make us believe that, on the 13th, Paris was in the hands of thieves. But this allegation is contradicted by all contemporary evidence. There were, no doubt, wayfarers stopped by men with pikes, who demanded money to procure arms; and there were also, on the nights between the 12th and 14th, armed men who knocked at the doors of the well-to-do to ask for food and drink, or for arms and money.

It is also averred that there were attempts at pillage, since two credible witnesses mention persons executed at night, between the 13th and 15th, for attempts of that kind.* But here, as elsewhere, Taine exaggerates.

Whether the modern middle-class Republicans like it or not, it is certain that the revolutionaries of 1789 did appeal to the " compromising auxiliaries " of whom Mirabeau spoke. They went to the hovels on the outskirts to find them. And they

* The citations given by M. Jules Flammermont, in a note in his work on the Fourteenth (*La journée du* 14 *Juillet* 1789), are conclusive on this subject—more conclusive than his text, which seems to us up to a certain point to contradict itself on pages clxxxi. and clxxxii. " In the afternoon," says the Count de Salmour, " the guard of the middle classes, already formed, began to disarm all the vagabonds. It is they and the armed middle-class men who, by their vigilance, saved Paris again this night. . . . The night passed quietly and with much order: thieves and vagabonds were arrested, and for the more serious offences they were hanged on the spot " (Letter of the Count de Salmour, dated July 10, 1789, in the Archives of Dresden). The following passage from a letter of Dr. Rigby, which M. Flammermont gives as a note, p. clxxxiii., says the same thing: " As night came on very few of the persons who had armed themselves the preceding evening were to be seen. Some, however, had refused to give up their arms, and proved in the course of the night how just were the suspicions of the inhabitants concerning them, for they began to plunder; but it was too late to do it then with impunity. They were soon discovered and apprehended, and we were told the following morning that several of these unhappy wretches, who had been taken in the act, had been executed " (Dr. Rigby's Letters, pp. 56–57). On reading these pages we admit there is some truth in the testimony of Morellet, according to which, " on the night between the 13th and 14th some excesses were committed against persons and property."

were quite right to do so, because even if there were a few cases of pillaging, most of these "auxilliaries," understanding the seriousness of the situation, put their arms at the service of the general cause, much more than they used them to gratify their personal hatreds or to alleviate their own misery.

It is at any rate certain that cases of pillage were extremely rare. On the contrary, the spirit of the armed crowds became very serious when they learned about the engagement that had been entered into by the troops and the middle classes. The men with the pikes evidently looked upon themselves as the defenders of the town, upon whom a heavy responsibility rested. Marmontel, a declared enemy of the Revolution, nevertheless notices this interesting feature. " The thieves themselves, seized with the general terror [?], committed no depredations. The armourers' shops were the only ones broken open, and only arms were stolen," he says in his *Mémoires*. And when the people brought the carriage of the Prince de Lambesc to the Place de la Grève to burn it, they sent back the trunk and all the effects found in the carriage to the Hôtel de Ville. At the Lazarite Monastery the people refused money and took only the flour, arms and wine, which were all conveyed to the Place de la Grève. " Nothing was touched that day, either at the Treasury or at the Bank," remarks the English Ambassador in his account.

What is quite true is the fear felt by the middle classes at the sight of these men and women, ragged, pinched with hunger and armed with clubs and pikes " of all shapes." The terror inspired by these spectres of famine thronging the streets was such that the middle classes could not get over it. Later on, in 1791 and 1792, even those among them who wanted to put an end to Royalty preferred reaction rather than make a fresh appeal to the popular revolution. The memory of the famished people swarming in the streets of whom they had caught a glimpse on July 12, 13 and 14 haunted them.

" Arms ! " was the cry of the people after they had found a little bread. They sought everywhere for them, without finding any, while night and day in the faubourgs pikes of every kind were being forged from any iron that came to hand.

The middle classes, meanwhile, without losing a moment, were constituting their executive power in the municipality at the Hôtel de Ville, and their militia.

We know that the elections for the National Assembly took place in two degrees; but the elections over, the electors of the Third Estate, to whom were added some of the electors of the clergy and of the nobility, had continued to meet at the Hôtel de Ville, since June 27, with the authorisation of the Town Council and the "Ministers for Paris." Now these electors took the lead in organising the middle-class militia. We have already seen them holding their second sitting on July 1.

On July 12 they instituted a Permanent Committee, presided over by Flesselles, the Provost of the Merchants, and they decided that each of the sixty districts should choose two hundred well-known citizens, capable of bearing arms, which should form a body of militia numbering 12,000 men, to watch over the public safety. This militia was to be increased in four days to a total of 48,000 men; meanwhile the same Committee was trying to disarm the people.

In this way, Louis Blanc says very truly, the middle classes obtained for themselves a Pretorian Guard of 12,000 men and at the risk of supporting the Court they wanted to disarm the mass of the people.

Instead of the green badge of the earlier days, this militia had now to wear the red and blue cockade, and the Permanent Committee took measures to prevent the people, who were arming themselves, from invading the ranks of this militia. It was decreed that any one with arms and wearing the red and blue cockade, without having been registered in one of the districts, should be brought for judgment before the Committee. The general commandant of this National Guard had been nominated by the Permanent Committee on the night of July 13 and 14; he was a noble, the Duke d'Aumont. He would not accept the post, and another nobleman, the Marquis de la Salle, who had been nominated second in command, took his place.

In short, while the people were forging pikes and arming

themselves, while they were taking measures to prevent the ammunition from being sent out of Paris, while they were seizing the bread-stuffs and sending them to the Halles or to the Place de la Grève, while on the 14th they were constructing barricades to prevent the troops entering Paris, and had seized the arms at the Hôtel des Invalides and were marching in a body towards the Bastille to compel it to capitulate, the middle classes were mainly preoccupied in taking measures for keeping the newly acquired power entirely in their own hands. They constituted the middle-class Commune of Paris, which tried to restrain the popular movement, and at the head of this Commune they placed Flesselles, the Provost of the Merchants, who was corresponding with the Duchess de Polignac about checking the insurrection in Paris. We know, indeed, that on the 13th, when the people went to ask Flesselles for arms, he sent them boxes containing old linen instead of muskets, and the next day he used all his influence to prevent the people from taking the Bastille.

Thus began on the side of the adroit middle-class leaders the system of betraying the Revolution, which, as we shall see, developed so much during the next few years.

CHAPTER XII

THE TAKING OF THE BASTILLE

"*A la Bastille !*"—Importance of Bastille—Popular hatred of prisons—Guns taken from Hôtel des Invalides—Deputations sent to de Launey—Attack on Bastille begins—Defenders fire on people—Another deputation sent—Firing continues—Cannon arrives for people—Garrison capitulates—Deaths of de Launey and Flesselles—First victory of people

FROM the dawn of July 14, the attention of the Paris insurrection was directed upon the Bastille, that gloomy fortress with its solid towers of formidable height which reared itself among the houses of a populous quarter at the entrance of the Faubourg Saint-Antoine. Historians are still inquiring how the thoughts of the people came to be turned in this direction, and some of them suggest that it was the Permanent Committee at the Hôtel de Ville, who wanted to furnish an objective for the insurrection in directing it against this emblem of royalty. There is nothing, however, to confirm this supposition, whilst several important facts contradict it. It is more probable that the popular instinct, which, ever since the 12th or 13th, understood that in the plans of the Court to crush the people of Paris the Bastille would play an important part, decided in consequence to get possession of it.

We know, indeed, that in the west the Court had Besenval camped with his thirty thousand men in the Champ-de-Mars, and that in the east it relied for support upon the towers of the Bastille, with their cannon trained on the revolutionary Faubourg Saint-Antoine and its principal thoroughfare, as well as on that other great artery, the Rue Saint-Antoine, which leads to the Hôtel de Ville, the Palais Royal and the Tuileries. The importance of the Bastille was, therefore, only too evident, and from the morning of the 14th, according to the *Deux amis de la liberté*, the words "*A la Bastille!*" flew from mouth to mouth from one end of the town to the other.*

It is true that the garrison of the Bastille numbered only one hundred and fourteen men, of whom eighty-four were pensioners and thirty Swiss, and that the Governor had done nothing towards victualling the place; but this proves only that the possibility of a serious attack on the fortress had been regarded as absurd. The people, however, knew that the Royalist plotters counted on the fortress, and they learned from inhabitants of the quarter that ammunition had been transferred from the arsenal to the Bastille on the night between the 12th and 13th. They perceived, also, that the Governor, the Marquis de Launey, had already placed his cannon in position on the morning of the 14th, so that the people could be fired on if they massed themselves in the direction of the Hôtel de Ville.

It must also be said that the people had always detested prisons, such as the Bicêtre, the donjon of Vincennes and the Bastille. During the riots of 1783, when the nobility protested against arbitrary imprisonments, the minister Bréteuil decided to abolish incarceration at Vincennes. This famous donjon was then transformed into a granary, and to conciliate public opinion Bréteuil permitted visitors to inspect the terrible *oubliettes*. There was much talk, says Droz, about the horrors that were to be seen there, and of course it was also said that in the Bastille there were even worse things to be seen.†

In any case, it is certain that on the evening of the 13th some musket shots were being exchanged between the detachments of armed Parisians, who passed close to the fortress and its

---

* In several of the *cahiers* the electors had already demanded "that the Bastille be pulled down and destroyed"—Cahiers des Halles; also those of Les Mathurins, Cordeliers, Sépulcre, &c., cited by Chassin (*Les élections et les cahiers de Paris*, vol. ii. p. 449 *et seq.*). The electors had cause for their demand, as, after the Réveillon affair, the order had been given to fortify the Bastille. Therefore, already on the night of June 30 there was some talk of seizing this fortress (*Récit de l'élargissement . . . des gardes françaises*, cited by Chassin, p. 452 note).

† Droz, *Histoire de Louis XVI.*, vol. i. p. 417.

defenders, and that on the 14th, from the earliest hours of the morning, the crowds, more or less armed, who had been moving about the streets all through the preceding night, began to assemble in the thoroughfares which led to the Bastille. Already during the night the rumour ran that the King's troops were advancing from the side of the Barrière du Trône, in the Faubourg Saint-Antoine, and the crowds moved off eastwards and barricaded the streets north-east of the Hôtel de Ville.

A successful attack on the Hôtel des Invalides gave the people an opportunity of arming themselves and provided them with some cannon. Since the previous day middle-class men, delegated by their districts, had been calling at the Hôtel des Invalides to ask for arms, saying that their houses were in danger of being plundered by the thieves, and Baron de Besenval, who commanded the royal troops in Paris, happening to be at the Invalides, promised to obtain authorisation for this from Marshal de Broglie. The authorisation had not yet arrived when, on the 14th, by seven o'clock in the morning—the pensioners, commanded by Sombreuil, being at their guns with match in hand ready to fire—a mob of seven or eight thousand men suddenly poured out of the three neighbouring streets at a quick pace. Helping one another, " in less than no time " they crossed the fosse, eight feet in depth and twelve feet wide, which surrounded the esplanade of the Hôtel des Invalides, swarmed over the esplanade and took possession of twelve pieces of cannon, 24-, 18- and 10-pounders, and one mortar. The garrison, already infected with a " seditious spirit," made no defence, and the mob, spreading everywhere, soon found their way into the cellars and the church, where they discovered 32,000 muskets concealed, as well as a certain quantity of powder.* These muskets and cannon were used the same day in the taking of the Bastille. As to the powder, on the previous day the people had already stopped thirty-six barrels which were being sent to Rouen; these had been carried off to the Hôtel de Ville, and all night long powder had been distributed to the people, who were arming themselves.

* I here follow the letter of the Count de Salmour, as well as Mathieu Dumas, both quoted by M. Flammermont.

THE TAKING OF THE BASTILLE

The removal of the guns by the mob from the Hôtel des Invalides was done very slowly. At two o'clock in the afternoon it was not yet completed. There would therefore have been quite enough time to bring up troops and disperse the people, especially as infantry, cavalry, and even artillery were stationed close by at the Military School and in the Champ-de-Mars. But the officers of these troops did not trust their soldiers; and besides, they must themselves have hesitated when they were confronted with this innumerable multitude, composed of persons of every age and every condition, of which more than 200,000 had flooded the streets for the last two days. The people of the faubourgs, armed with a few muskets, pikes, hammers, axes, or even with simple cudgels, were moving about in the streets, thronging in crowds to the Place Louis XV. (now the Place de la Concorde) surrounding the Hôtel de Ville and the Bastille, and filling the thoroughfares between. The middle classes of Paris were themselves seized with terror on seeing these masses of armed men in the street.

Hearing that the approaches to the Bastille were invaded by the people, the Permanent Committee at the Hôtel de Ville, of which mention has been made, sent on the morning of the 14th some persons to parley with de Launey, the Governor of the fortress, to beg him to withdraw the cannon levelled on the streets, and not to commit any act hostile to the people; in return, the Committee, usurping powers they did not possess, promised that the people " would not set on foot any vexatious proceedings against the place." The delegates were received very affably by the Governor, and even stayed to breakfast with him until nearly midday. De Launey was probably trying to gain time while waiting for definite orders from Versailles, which did not come, as they had been intercepted in the morning by the people. Like all the other military chiefs, de Launey must have realised that it would be difficult for him to stand against the whole people of Paris assembled in the streets, and so he temporised. For the time being he ordered the cannon to be drawn back four feet and closed the embrasures with wooden planks, so that the people should not see through them.

About midday the district of Saint-Louis-la-Culture on its own account sent two delegates to speak in its name to the Governor; one of them, the advocate Thuriot de la Rosière, obtained from the Marquis de Launey the promise that he would not give the order to fire if he was not attacked. Two more deputations were sent to the Governor by the Permanent Committee at one and three o'clock; but they were not received. Both of them demanded of the Governor the surrender of the fortress to a body of the middle-class militia, which would guard it jointly with the soldiers and the Swiss.

Luckily, all these compromises were baffled by the people, who understood that the Bastille must be captured, cost what it might. Being in possession of the muskets and the cannon from the Hôtel des Invalides, their enthusiasm was steadily increasing.

The mob thronged the streets adjacent to the Bastille, as well as the different courtyards which surrounded the fortress itself. Presently a fusillade began between the people and the soldiers posted on the ramparts. Whilst the Permanent Committee were striving to allay the ardour of the assailants and making arrangements for proclaiming at the Place de la Grève that de Launey had promised not to fire if they refrained from attacking him, the crowds, shouting " We want the Bastille! Down with the bridges! " rushed towards the fortress. It is said that on seeing from the top of the walls the whole Faubourg Saint-Antoine and the street leading to it quite black with people marching against the Bastille, the Governor, who had ascended thither with Thuriot, almost swooned. It appears even that he was on the point of surrendering the fortress immediately to the Committee of Militia, but that the Swiss opposed it.*

The first drawbridges of that exterior part of the Bastille which was called the Forecourt (*l'Avancée*) were soon battered down, thanks to one of those audacious deeds of some few persons who are always forthcoming at such moments. Eight or ten men, with the help of a tall, strong fellow, Pannetier, a grocer, took advantage of a house that was built against the

* Letter of De Hue to his brothers, German text, quoted by Flammermont, p. cxcviii. note.

exterior wall of the Forecourt to climb this wall, astride of which they moved along as far as a guard-house standing close to the little drawbridge of the Forecourt, and thence they leaped into the first court of the Bastille proper, the Government Court in which was the Governor's house. This court was unoccupied, the soldiers having retreated with de Launey into the fortress itself, after the departure of Thuriot.

The eight or ten men, having dropped into this courtyard, with a few blows of an axe lowered first the little drawbridge of the Forecourt and opened its gate, and afterwards the larger one. More than three hundred men then rushed into the Government Court, and ran to the other two drawbridges, the greater and the lesser, which, when lowered, served to cross the wide fosse of the actual fortress. These two bridges, of course, had been raised.

Here took place the incident which wrought the fury of the people of Paris to its full pitch, and afterwards cost de Launey his life. When the crowd thronged into the Government Court, the defenders of the Bastille began to fire upon them, and there was even an attempt to raise the great drawbridge of the Forecourt, so as to prevent the crowd from leaving the Government Court and obviously with the intention of either imprisoning or massacring them.* Thus, at the very moment when Thuriot and Corny were announcing to the people in the Place de la Grève that the Governor had promised not to fire, the Government Court was being swept by the musketry of the soldiers posted upon the ramparts, and the guns of the Bastille began to hurl cannon-balls into the adjoining streets. After all the parleying which had taken place that morning, this opening fire upon the people was evidently interpreted as an act of treason on the part of De Launay, whom the people accused of having lowered the two first drawbridges

* This attempt was made, it is now said, not by order of de Launey, but spontaneously by some soldiers, who had gone out to buy provisions and were returning. A highly improbable thing, it seems to me, for three or four soldiers to attempt, isolated as they were, in the midst of that crowd. Besides, what would have been the good of imprisoning the crowd if it was not intended to use the prisoners as hostages against the people?

of the Forecourt, for the purpose of drawing the mob under the fire from the ramparts.*

It was then about one o'clock. The news that the cannon of the Bastille were firing on the people spread through Paris and produced a two-fold effect. The Permanent Committee of the Paris militia hastened to send another deputation to the Commandant, to ask him if he would receive there a detachment of militia who would guard the Bastille jointly with the troops. But this deputation never reached the Commandant, for a close fusillade was going on all the time between the soldiers and their assailants, who, crouched along some of the walls, were firing at the soldiers serving the guns. Besides, the people knew that the deputations from the Committee would only throw cold water on the attack. " It is no longer a deputation they want ; it is the siege of the Bastille ; it is the destruction of this horrible prison ; it is the death of the Governor for which they are loudly clamouring "—reported the deputies when they returned.

This did not prevent the Committee at the Hôtel de Ville from sending a third deputation. M. Ethis de Corny, Procureur of the King and of the town, and several citizens were charged once more to allay the people's ardour, to check the assault, and to parley with de Launey, for the purpose of persuading him to receive a guard from the Committee into the fortress. The intention of preventing the people taking possession of the Bastille was evident.†

---

* Various explanations have been given of this sudden opening of hostilities. As the people who had thronged into the Court de l'Orme and the Government Court began to plunder the Commandant's house and those of the soldiers' quarters, it was said that this had decided the defenders of the Bastille to open fire. For the military, however, the taking of the Forecourt by assault, which gave the people access to the drawbridges of the fortress and even to the gates, was quite sufficient reason. But it is also possible that the order to defend the Bastille to the last was at that moment transmitted to de Launey. We know that one order was intercepted, which does not prove that no other was delivered. It is, in fact, supposed that de Launey had received this order.

† " They were charged to induce all persons found near the Bastille *to withdraw to their respective districts in order that they might there be at once admitted into the Paris militia ;* to remind de Launey of the promises he had made to M. Thuriot de la Rozière and to M. Bellon . . ."

THE TAKING OF THE BASTILLE 85

As to the people, as soon as the news of the firing spread through the town, they acted without any one's orders, guided by their revolutionary instinct. They dragged the cannon which they had taken from the Hôtel des Invalides to the Hôtel de Ville, and about three o'clock, when Corny's deputation was returning to report their failure, they met about three hundred French Guards, and a number of armed men belonging to the middle class under the command of an old soldier named Hulin, marching to the Bastille, followed by five pieces of artillery. The firing by this time had been going on for more than three hours. The people, not in the least dismayed by the great number killed and wounded,* were maintaining the siege by resorting to various expedients. One of these was the bringing up of two cartloads of straw, to which they set fire, using the smoke as a screen to facilitate their attack on the two entrances, the greater and lesser drawbridges. The buildings of the Government Court were already in flames.

The cannon arrived just at the moment they were wanted. They were drawn into the Government Court and planted in front of the drawbridges and gates at a distance of only 90 feet.

It is easy to imagine the effect that these cannon in the hands of the people must have produced on the besieged. It was evident that the drawbridges must soon go down, and that the gates would be burst open. The mob became still more threatening and was continually increasing in numbers.

The moment soon came when the defenders realised that to resist any longer was to doom themselves to certain destruction. de Launey decided to capitulate. The soldiers, seeing that

(Flammermont, *loc. cit.*, p. clviii.). Having entered the Forecourt, which was full of people armed with muskets, axes, &c., the deputation spoke to the soldiers on the walls. These latter demanded that the people should first withdraw from the Government Court, whereupon the deputation tried to induce the people to do so (*cf.* Boucheron, cited by Flammermont, p. ccxiv. note). Fortunately the people were wise enough not to comply with their wishes. They continued the assault. They understood so well that it was no longer any time for parleying, that they treated the gentlemen of the deputation rather badly, and even talked of killing them as traitors (*loc. cit.*, p. ccxvi. note, and *Procès-verbal des électeurs*).

* Eighty-three killed on the spot, fifteen dead of their wounds, thirteen disabled and sixty injured.

they would never get the better of the whole of Paris which was coming to besiege them, had some time before advised capitulation, and so about four o'clock, or between four and five, the Governor ordered the white flag to be hoisted and the drums to beat the *chamade* (the order to cease fire), and descend from the battlements.

The garrison capitulated and demanded the right of marching out with their arms. It may be that Hulin and Elie, standing close to the great drawbridge, would have agreed to these terms in the name of the people; but the people would have none of them. A furious cry of " Down with the bridges! " was raised. At five o'clock, therefore, the Commandant passed out through one of the loopholes near the lesser drawbridge a note in which it was said, " We have twenty-thousand-weight of gunpowder; we shall blow up the whole quarter, with the garrison, if you do not accept the terms of capitulation." However, even if de Launey thought of so doing, the garrison would never have permitted him to put this threat into effect. At any rate, the fact is that de Launey himself gave up the key that opened the entrance of the lesser drawbridge.

Immediately, the mass of the besiegers took possession of the fortress. They disarmed the Swiss and the Invalides, and seized de Launey, who was dragged towards the Hôtel de Ville. On the way the mob, furious at his treachery, heaped every kind of insult on him; twenty times he was nearly killed, despite the heroic efforts of Cholat and another.* These two men protected him with their own bodies, but, when only a hundred steps from the Hôtel de Ville, he was dragged out of their hands and decapitated. De Hue, the Commandant of the Swiss, saved his life by declaring that he was devoted to the Town and the Nation, and by drinking to them, but three officers of the Bastille staff and three soldiers were slain. As to Flesselles, the Provost of the Merchants, who was in correspondence with Besenval and the Duchess de Polignac, and who had, as appears by a passage in one of his letters, many other secrets to hide that were very compromising for the Queen, the people

* Was not this other Maillard? We know that it was he who arrested de Launey.

were about to execute him when an unknown man shot him dead. Did this unknown man think that dead men tell no tales?

As soon as the bridges of the Bastille had been lowered the crowd rushed into the courtyards and began to search the fortress and free the prisoners entombed in the *oubliettes*. There was great emotion, and tears were shed at the sight of the phantoms who issued from their cells, bewildered by the light of the sun and by the sound of the many voices that welcomed them. These poor martyrs of royal despotism were carried in triumph by the people through the streets of Paris. The whole town was soon delirious with joy on hearing that the Bastille was in the hands of the people, and their determination to keep their conquest was redoubled. The *coup d'état* of the Court had failed.

In this way the Revolution began. The people had won their first victory. A material victory of this kind was essential. It was necessary that the Revolution should endure a struggle and come out from it triumphant. Some proof of the strength of the people had to be given, so as to impress their enemies, to arouse courage throughout France, and to push forward everywhere towards revolt, towards the conquest of liberty.

CHAPTER XIII

THE CONSEQUENCES OF JULY 14 AT VERSAILLES

Fête at Versailles—State of Court—Conduct of people—Middle classes—King visits Paris—His plans of armed resistance come to nothing—Insurrection in Paris spreads—Emigration of nobles—Foulon and others put to death

WHEN a revolution has once begun, each event in it not merely sums up the events hitherto accomplished; it also contains the chief elements of what is to come; so that the contemporaries of the French Revolution, if they could only have freed themselves from the momentary impressions, and separated the essential from the accidental, might have been able, on the morrow of July 14, to foresee whither events as a whole were thenceforth trending.

But even on the evening of the 13th, the Court attached no importance to the movement in Paris.

That evening there was a *fête* at Versailles. There was dancing in the Orangery, and glasses were filled to drink to the coming victory over the rebellious capital; and the Queen, her friend the Duchess de Polignac and the rest of the Court beauties, with the princes and princesses, were lavishing favours on the foreign soldiers in their barracks to stimulate them for the coming fight.* In their madness and terrible frivolity, no one in that world of shams and conventional lies, which constitute every Court, perceived that it was too late to attack Paris, that the opportunity for doing so was lost. And

---

* Mirabeau, in his speech before the Assembly, which resumed its sitting on the 15th at eight o'clock in the morning, spoke as if this *fête* had taken place the day before. He was alluding, however, to the *fête* of the 13th.

Louis XVI. was no better informed on the matter than the Queen and the princes. When the Assembly, alarmed by the people's rising, hurried to him on the evening of the 14th, to beg him in servile language to recall the ministers and send away the troops, he replied to them in the language of a master certain of victory. He believed in the plan that had been suggested to him of putting some reliable officers at the head of the middle-class militia and crushing the people with their help, after which he would content himself with sending some equivocal orders about the retirement of the troops. Such was that world of shams, of dreams more than of reality, in which both King and Court lived, and in which, in spite of brief intervals of awakening, they continued to live up to the moment of ascending the steps of the scaffold.

How clearly they were revealing their characters even then! The King hypnotised by his absolute power, and always ready on account of it to take exactly the step which was to lead him to the catastrophe. Then he would oppose to events inertia—nothing but inertia, and finally yield, for form's sake, just at the moment when he was expected to resist obstinately. The Queen, too, corrupt, depraved to the very heart as absolute sovereign, hastening the catastrophe by her petulant resistance, and then suddenly yielding the next moment, only to resume, an instant after, the childish tricks of a courtesan. And the princes? Instigators of all the most fatal resolutions taken by the King, and cowards at the very first failures of them, they left the country, flying immediately after the taking of the Bastille to resume their plottings in Germany or Italy. How clearly all these traits of character were revealed in those few days between July 8 and 15.

On the opposite side we see the people, filled with ardour, enthusiasm and generosity, ready to let themselves be massacred that Liberty might triumph, but at the same time asking to be led; ready to allow themselves to be governed by the new masters, who had just installed themselves in the Hôtel de Ville. Understanding so well the Court schemes, and seeing with the utmost clearness through the plot which had been growing into shape ever since the end of June, they allowed themselves to be entangled in the new plot—the plot of the propertied classes, who were soon to thrust back into their slums the hungry people, "the men with the pikes" to whom they had appealed for a few hours, when it was necessary to set the force of popular insurrection against that of the army.

And finally, when we consider the conduct of the middle classes during these early days, we see already foreshadowed the great dramas of the Revolution which were to come. On the 14th, in proportion as Royalty gradually lost its menacing character, it was the people who, in a corresponding degree, inspired terror in the representatives of the Third Estate assembled at Versailles. In spite of the vehement words uttered by Mirabeau concerning the *fête* at the Orangery, the King had only to present himself before the Assembly, recognise the authority of the delegates, and promise them inviolability, for the whole of the representatives to burst into applause and transports of joy. They even ran out to form a guard of honour round him in the streets, and made the streets of Versailles resound with cries of "*Vive le Roi !*" And this at the very moment when the people were being massacred in Paris in the name of this same King, and while at Versailles the crowd was insulting the Queen and the Duchess de Polignac, and the people were asking themselves if the King was not at one of his old tricks.

In Paris the people were not deceived by the promise to withdraw the troops. They did not believe a word of it. They preferred to organise themselves in a huge insurgent commune, and this commune, like a commune of the Middle Ages, took all the necessary measures of defence against the King. The streets were torn up in trenches and barricades, and the people's patrols marched through the town, ready to sound the tocsin at the first alarm.

Nor did the King's visit to Paris greatly reassure the people. Seeing himself defeated and abandoned, he decided to go to Paris, and to the Hôtel de Ville, to be reconciled with his capital, and the middle classes tried to turn this visit into a striking act of reconciliation between themselves and the King. The middle-class revolutionaries, of whom very many belonged to

THE CONSEQUENCES AT VERSAILLES

the Freemasons, made an "arch of steel" with their swords for the King on his arrival at the Hôtel de Ville; and Bailly, elected Mayor of Paris, fastened in the King's hat the tricolour cockade. There was talk even of erecting a statue to Louis XVI. on the site of the demolished Bastille, but the mass of the people preserved an attitude of reserve and mistrust, which were not dispelled even after the visit to the Hôtel de Ville. King of the middle classes as much as they liked, but not a King of the people.

The Court, for its part, knew very well that after the insurrection of July 14 there would never be peace between royalty and the people. They induced the Duchess de Polignac to leave for Switzerland, despite the tears of Marie-Antoinette, and the following day the princes began to emigrate. Those who had been the life and soul of the defeated *coup d'état* made haste to leave France. The Count d'Artois escaped in the night, and so much was he in fear for his life that, after stealing secretly through the town, he took a regiment and two cannon for escort the rest of the way. The King promised to rejoin his dear emigrants at the first opportunity, and began to make plans of escaping abroad, in order to re-enter France at the head of an army.

In fact, on July 16, all was ready for his departure. He was to go to Metz, place himself at the head of the troops, and march on Paris. The horses were already put to the carriage which were to convey Louis XVI. to the army, then concentrated between Versailles and the frontier. But de Broglie refused to escort the King to Metz, and the princes were in too great a hurry to be off, so that the King, as he said himself afterwards, seeing himself abandoned by the princes and the nobles, relinquished his project of an armed resistance, which the history of Charles I. had suggested to him, and went to Paris to make his submission instead.

Some Royalist historians have tried to cast a doubt on the preparation by the Court of a *coup d'état* against the Assembly and Paris. But there are plenty of documents to prove the reality of the plot. Mignet, whose moderation is well known, and who had the advantage of writing soon after the events, had not the slightest doubt on this point, and later researches have confirmed his position. On July 13, the King was to have revived the declaration of June 23, and the Assembly was to have been dissolved. Forty thousand copies of this declaration were already printed for sending throughout France. The commander of the army massed between Versailles and Paris had been given unlimited powers for the massacre of the people of Paris and for extreme measures against the Assembly in case of resistance.

A hundred million of State notes had been manufactured to provide for the needs of the Court. Everything was ready, and when they heard that Paris had risen, the Court considered this rising as an outbreak which aided their plans. A little later on, when it was known that the insurrection was spreading, the King was still on the point of setting out and leaving to his ministers the task of dispersing the Assembly with the help of foreign troops. It was the ministers who dared not put this plan into execution when they saw the tide rising. This is why so great a panic seized the Court after July 14, when they heard of the taking of the Bastille and the execution of de Launey, and why the Duchess de Polignac, the princes, and so many other nobles, who had been the leading spirits of the plot, afraid of being denounced, had to emigrate in a hurry.

But the people were on the alert. They vaguely understood what the emigrants were going to seek on the other side of the frontier, and the peasants arrested the fugitives, among whom were Foulon and Berthier.

We have already made mention of the misery which reigned in Paris and the environs, and of the monopolists, into whose crimes the Assembly refused to inquire too closely. The chief of these speculators in the people's misery was said to be Foulon, who had made an immense fortune as financier and in his position as contractor for the army and navy. His detestation of the people and the revolution was also well known. Broglie wanted him to be minister when he was preparing the *coup d'état* for July 16, and if the crafty financier refused this post, he had not been sparing of his counsel. His advice was to get

THE CONSEQUENCES AT VERSAILLES

rid, at one blow, of all those who had acquired influence in the revolutionary camp.

After the taking of the Bastille, when he learned how de Launey's head had been carried through the streets, he knew that it was best for him to follow the princes and emigrate; but as this was not an easy thing to do, owing to the watchfulness of the District Commune, he took advantage of the death of one of his servants to pretend that he was dead and buried, while he quitted Paris and took refuge in a friend's house at Fontainebleau.

There he was discovered and arrested by the peasants, who avenged their long endurance of misery upon him. With a bundle of grass tied on his shoulders, in allusion to the grass he had promised to make the people of Paris eat, the wretched monopolist was dragged to Paris by an infuriated crowd. At the Hôtel de Ville Lafayette tried to save him, but the angry people hanged him on a lamp-iron.

His son-in-law, Berthier, equally guilty in the *coup d'état*, and contractor for the Duke de Broglie's army, was arrested at Compiègne and also dragged to Paris, where they were going to hang him likewise, but, struggling to save himself, he was overpowered and trampled to death.

Other guilty individuals who were on the way to foreign lands were arrested in the north and north-east and brought back to Paris.

The terror excited in the breasts of the Court's familiar friends by these executions on the people's side can easily be imagined. Their pride and their resistance to the Revolution were shattered; they wished only to be forgotten.

CHAPTER XIV

THE POPULAR RISINGS

Necessity of popular risings outside Paris—Effect of taking of Bastille over-estimated—Difference between French and English peasant risings—Importance of peasant insurrection

PARIS, by frustrating the plans of the Court, had struck a mortal blow at royal authority. Besides this, the appearance in the streets of people in rags, as an active force in the Revolution, was giving a new character, a new tendency of equality to the whole movement. The rich and powerful understood perfectly the meaning of what had been going on in Paris during those days, and the emigration, first of the princes, then of the favourites and the monopolists, accentuated the victory. The Court was already seeking the aid of the foreigner against revolutionary France.

If, however, the insurrection had been confined to the capital, the Revolution could never have developed to the extent of resulting in the demolition of ancient privileges. The insurrection at the centre had been necessary to strike at the central Government, to shake it down, to demoralise its defenders. But to destroy the power of the Government in the provinces, to strike at the old *régime* through its governmental prerogatives and its economic privileges, a widespread rising of the people was necessary in cities, towns and villages. This is exactly what came about in the course of July throughout the length and breadth of France.

The historians, who all, whether consciously or not, have followed very closely the *Deux amis de la liberté*, have generally represented this movement of the towns and rural districts as a result of the taking of the Bastille. The news of this success is supposed to have roused the country parts. The châteaux were burned, and this rising of the peasants diffused so much terror that the nobles and clergy abdicated their feudal rights on August 4.

This version is, however, only half true. As far as the towns are concerned, it is correct that a great number of urban risings took place under the influence of the taking of the Bastille. Some of them, as at Troyes on July 18, at Strasbourg on the 19th, at Cherbourg on the 21st, at Rouen on the 24th, and at Maubeuge on the 27th, followed close upon the Paris insurrection, whilst the others went on during the next three or four months, until the National Assembly had voted the municipal law of December 14, 1789, which legalised the constitution of a democratic middle-class municipal government to a considerable extent independent of the Central Government.

With regard to the peasants, it is clear that with the then existing slowness of communications, the space of twenty days which passed between July 14 and August 4 are absolutely insufficient to account for the effect of the taking of the Bastille on the rural districts and the subsequent effect of the peasants' insurrection on the decisions of the National Assembly. In fact, to picture events in such a fashion is to belittle the profound importance of the movement in the country.

The insurrection of the peasants for the abolition of the feudal rights and the recovery of the communal lands which had been taken away from the village communes, since the seventeenth century, by the lords, lay and ecclesiastical, is the very essence, the foundation of the great Revolution. Upon it the struggle of the middle classes for their political rights was developed. Without it the Revolution would never have been so thorough as it was in France. The great rising of the rural districts which began after the January of 1789, even in 1788, and *lasted five years*, was what enabled the Revolution to accomplish the immense work of demolition which we owe to it. It was this that impelled the Revolution to set up the first landmarks of a system of equality, to develop in France the republican spirit, which since then nothing has been able to suppress, to proclaim the great principles of agrarian communism, that we shall see emerging in 1793. This rising, in fact, is what gives the true character to the French Revolution, and distinguishes it radically from the Revolution of 1648–1657 in England.

There, too, in the course of those nine years, the middle classes broke down the absolute power of royalty and the political privileges of the Court party. But beyond that, the distinctive features of the English revolution was the struggle for the right of each individual to profess whatever religion he pleased, to interpret the Bible according to his personal conception of it, to choose his own pastors—in a word, the right of the individual to the intellectual and religious development best suited to him. Further, it claimed the right of each parish, and, as a consequence, of the townships, to autonomy. But the peasant risings in England did not aim so generally, as in France, at the abolishing of feudal dues and tithes, or the recovery of the communal lands. And if Cromwell's hosts demolished a certain number of castles which represented true strongholds of feudalism, these hosts unfortunately did not attack either the feudal pretensions of the lords over the land, or even the right of feudal justice, which the lords exercised over their tenants. What the English revolution did was to conquer some precious rights for the individual, but it did not destroy the feudal power of the lord, it merely modified it whilst preserving his rights over the land, rights which persist to this day.

The English revolution undoubtedly established the political power of the middle classes, but this power was only obtained by sharing it with the landed aristocracy. And if the revolution gave the English middle classes a prosperous era for their trade and commerce, this prosperity was obtained on the condition that the middle classes should not profit by it to attack the landed privileges of the nobility. On the contrary, the middle classes helped to increase these privileges, at least in value. They helped the nobility to take legal possession of the communal lands by means of the Enclosure

Acts, which reduced the agricultural population to misery, placed them at the mercy of the landowners, and forced a great number of them to migrate to the towns, where, as proletarians, they were delivered over to the mercy of the middle-class manufacturers. The English middle classes also helped the nobility to make of their immense landed estates sources, not only of revenue often fabulous, but also of political and local juridical power, by re-establishing under new forms the right of manorial justice. They helped also to increase their revenues tenfold by allowing them through the land laws, which hamper the sale of estates, to monopolise the land, the need of which was making itself felt more and more among a population whose trade and commerce were steadily increasing.

We now know that the French middle classes, especially the upper middle classes engaged in manufactures and commerce, wished to imitate the English middle classes in their revolution. They, too, would have willingly entered into a compact with both royalty and nobility in order to attain to power. But they did not succeed in this, because the basis of the French Revolution was fortunately much broader than that of the revolution in England. In France the movement was not merely an insurrection to win religious liberty, or even commercial and industrial liberty for the individual, or yet to constitute municipal authority in the hands of a few middle-class men. It was above all a *peasant* insurrection, a movement of the people to regain possession of the land and to free it from the feudal obligations which burdened it, and while there was all through it a powerful individualist element—the desire to possess land individually—there was also the communist element, the right of the whole nation to the land—a right which we shall see proclaimed loudly by the poorer classes in 1793.

This is why it would be a strange reduction of the importance of the agrarian insurrection in the summer of 1789 to represent it as an episode of brief duration brought about by enthusiasm over the taking of the Bastille.

CHAPTER XV

THE TOWNS

Condition of municipal institutions—Feudal rights still exist—Need of municipal reform—Townspeople revolt—New municipality voted—Importance of communalist movement—Paris Commune—Other cities follow—Troubles at Strasbourg—New corporation constituted—Middle classes freed from feudalism—Riots in Troyes, Amiens and other cities—Significance of popular action during Revolution

In the eighteenth century the municipal institutions had fallen to utter decay, owing to the numerous measures taken by royal authority against them for two hundred years.

Since the abolition of the plenary assembly of the townspeople, which formerly had the control of urban justice and administration, the affairs of the large cities were going from bad to worse. The posts of "town councillors" introduced in the eighteenth century had to be bought from the commune, and, often enough, the patent so purchased was for life.* The councils met seldom, in some towns about once in six months, and even then the attendance was not regular. The registrar managed the whole business, and as a rule did not fail to make those interested in it pay him handsomely. The attorneys and advocates, and still more the governor of the province, continually interfered to obstruct all municipal autonomy.

Under these conditions the affairs of the city fell more and more into the hands of five or six families, who shared a good deal of the revenues among themselves. The patrimonial revenues which some towns had retained, the proceeds of the *octrois*, the city's trade and the taxes all went to enrich them.

---

* Babeau, *La ville sous l'ancien régime*, p. 153 *et seq.*

THE TOWNS

Besides this, mayors and officials began to trade in corn and meat, and soon became monopolists. As a rule, the working population hated them. The servility of the officials, councillors and aldermen towards " Monsieur l'Intendant " (the Governor) was such that his whim became law. And the contributions from the town towards the governor's lodging, towards increasing his salary, to make him presents, for the honour of holding his children at the baptismal font, and so forth, went on growing larger—not to mention the presents which had to be sent every year to various personages in Paris.

In the towns, as in the country, the feudal rights still existed. They were attached to property. The bishop was still a feudal lord, and the lords, both lay and ecclesiastical—such, for instance, as the fifty canons of Brioude—maintained not only honorary rights, or even the right of intervening in the nomination of aldermen, but also, in some towns, the right of administering justice. At Angers there were sixteen manorial tribunals. Dijon had preserved, besides the municipal tribunals, six ecclesiastical courts—" the bishopric, the chapter, the monks of Saint-Bénigne, La Sainte-Chapelle, La Chartreuse and the commandery of La Madeleine." All of these were waxing fat in the midst of the half-starved people. Troyes had nine of these tribunals, beside " two royal mayoral courts." So that the police did not always belong to the towns, but to those who administered "justice." In short, it was the feudal system in full swing.*

But what chiefly excited the anger of the citizens was that all kinds of feudal taxes, the poll tax, the twentieths, often the *taille* and the "voluntary gifts" (imposed in 1758 and abolished only in 1789), as well as the *lods et ventes* (which were the dues levied by the lord on all sales and purchases made by his vassals), weighed heavily upon the homes of the citizens, and especially on those of the working classes. Not so heavily, perhaps, as in the country, but still very eavily when added to all the other urban taxes.

* *Vide* Babeau, *La Ville*, pp. 323, 331, &c. Rodolphe Reuss, *L'Alsace pendant la Révolution*, vol. i., gives the *cahier* of the Strasbourg Third Estate, very interesting in this connection.

What made these dues more detestable was that when the town was making the assessment hundreds of privileged persons claimed exemption. The clergy, the nobles and officers in the army were exempt by law, as well as the " officers of the King's household," " honorary equerries," and others who paid for those offices without service, to flatter their own vanity and to escape from the taxes. An indication of their titles inscribed over the door was enough to excuse their paying anything to the town. One can readily imagine the hatred that these privileged persons inspired in the people.

The entire municipal system had, therefore, to be reformed. But who can tell how many years it would have lasted yet, if the task of reforming it had been left to the Constituent Assembly. Happily enough, the people undertook to do it themselves, the more so that during the summer of 1789 a fresh cause of discontent was added to all those which have just been enumerated. This cause was the famine—the exorbitant price of bread, for lack of which bread the poorer classes were suffering in most of the towns. Even in those places where the municipality did its best to lower the price of it by purchasing corn, or by proclaiming a fixed price, bread was always scarce, and the hungry people formed in long queues outside the bakers' doors.

But in many of the towns the mayor and the aldermen followed the example of the Court and the princes, and speculated themselves in the dearth. This is why, after the news of the taking of the Bastille, as well as of the executions of Foulon and Berthier, had spread into the provinces, the townspeople began to revolt more or less everywhere. First, they exacted a fixed price on bread and meat; they destroyed the houses of the principal monopolists, often of the municipal officials; they took possession of the Town Hall and nominated by election on the popular vote a new municipality, without heeding the limitations fixed by law or the legal rights of the old municipal body, or yet the offices purchased by the " councillors." A movement of the highest revolutionary importance was thus set on foot, for the town affirmed, not only its autonomy, but also its determination to take an active part in

THE TOWNS

the general government of the nation. It was, as Aulard has aptly remarked, a communalist movement of the very greatest importance,* in which the province imitated Paris, where, as we have seen, the Commune had been established on July 13. It is evident that this movement was far from being general. It displayed itself clearly only in a certain number of cities and small towns, chiefly in the east of France. But everywhere the old municipality of the ancient *régime* had to submit to the will of the people, or, at least, to the will of the electorate in the local assemblies.

Thus was accomplished, at the outset, in July and August, the great Communalist Revolution, which the Constituent Assembly legalised later on by the municipal laws of December 14, 1789, and June 21, 1790. Obviously this movement gave the Revolution a powerful access of life and vigour. The whole strength of the Revolution concentrated, as we shall see, in 1792 and 1793, in the municipalities of the towns and villages, of which the revolutionary Commune of Paris was the prototype.

The signal for this reconstruction came from Paris. Without waiting for the municipal law, which some day would be voted by the Assembly, Paris gave herself a Commune. Her Municipal Council, her Mayor (Bailly), and the Commander of her National Guard (Lafayette) were elected. Better still, her sixty districts were organised—" sixty republics," as Montjoie happily terms them : for if these districts did delegate authority to the assembled representatives of the Commune and to the Mayor, they at the same time retained some of it. " Authority is everything," said Bailly, " and there is none at the centre." " Each district is an independent power," declare with regret the friends of the rule and compass, without understanding that this is how revolutions are made.

While the National Assembly had to struggle against its own dissolution, and had its hands full of so many things, when could it have been able to enter on the discussion of a law concerning the reorganisation of the Courts of Justice ? It hardly got as far as that at the end of ten months of its existence.

* Aulard, *Histoire politique de la Révolution française*, 2nd edition, 1903.

But "the district of the Petits-Augustins decided on its own account," says Bailly, in his *Mémoires*, "that justices of the peace should be established." And the district proceeded then and there to elect them. Other districts and other cities, Strasbourg especially, did the same, and when the night of August 4 arrived and the nobility had to abdicate their rights of seigneurial justice, they had lost it already in several towns, where new judges had been appointed by the people. The Constituent Assembly had thus nothing else to do but incorporate the accomplished fact in the Constitution of 1791.

Taine and all the admirers of the administrative order of the somnolent ministers are shocked no doubt at the thought of these districts forestalling the Assembly by their votes and pointing out to it the will of the people by their decisions; but it is in this way human institutions develop when they are not the product of bureaucracy. In this way all the great cities were built up; we can see them still being thus built. Here a group of houses and a few shops beside them; this will be an important point in the future city; there a track, as yet scarcely discernible, and that one day will be one of its great streets. This is the "anarchic" evolution, the only way pertaining to free Nature. It is the same even with institutions when they are the organic product of life, and this is why revolutions have such immense importance in the life of societies. They allow men to start with the organic reconstructive work without being hampered by an authority which, perforce, always represents the past ages.

Let us therefore glance at some of these communal revolutions.

In 1789 news spread with what would seem to us almost inconceivable slowness. Thus at Château-Thierry on July 12, and at Besançon on the 27th, Arthur Young did not find a single *café* or a single newspaper. The news that was being talked about was a fortnight old. At Dijon, nine days after the great rising in Strasbourg and the taking of the Town Hall by the insurgents, no one knew anything about it. Still the news that was coming from Paris, even when it came in the form of legend, could not but stimulate the people to rise.

THE TOWNS

All the deputies, it was said, had been put in the Bastille; and as to the "atrocities" committed by Marie-Antoinette, every one was discussing them with perfect assurance.

At Strasbourg the troubles began on July 19, as soon as the news of the taking of the Bastille and the execution of de Launey spread through the town. The people had already a grudge against the municipal council for their slowness in communicating to the people's "representatives"—that is, to the electors—the results of their deliberations over the *cahier de doléances*, the "writ of grievances," drawn up by the poorer classes. The people, therefore, attacked the house of Lemp, the Mayor (or *Ammeister*), and destroyed it.

Through the organ of its "Assembly of Burgesses" the people demanded measures—I quote from the text—" for assuring the political equality of the citizens, and their influence in the elections of the administrators of the public property and of the freely elected judges freely eligible." *

They insisted upon no notice being taken of the existing law, and upon electing by universal suffrage a new town council, as well as all the judges. The Magistracy, or Municipal Government, on its side had no great wish to do this, "and opposed the observance of several centuries to the proposed change." Whereupon the people gathered to besiege the Town Hall, and a storm of stones began to fall in the apartment where negotiations were taking place between the Magistracy and the revolutionary representatives, and to this argument the Magistracy at once yielded.

Meanwhile, seeing poor and starving persons assembling in the streets, the well-to-do middle classes armed themselves against the people, and going to the house of Count Rochambeau, the governor of the province, they asked his permission for the respectable citizens to carry arms, and to form themselves into a police, jointly with the troops, a request which the officer in command, "imbued with aristocratic ideas," unhesitatingly refused, as de Launey had done at the Bastille.

* *Lettre des représentants de la bourgeoisie aux députés de Strasbourg à Versailles*, July 28, 1789 (R. Reuss, *L'Alsace pendant la Révolution française*, Paris, 1881, "Documents," xxvi).

The next day, a rumour having spread in the town that the Magistracy had revoked their concessions, the people went again to attack the Town Hall, demanding the abolition of the town-dues and subsidies (*octrois* and *bureaux des aides*). Since this had been done in Paris, it could very well be done in Strasbourg. About six o'clock masses of " workmen, armed with axes and hammers," advanced from three streets towards the Town Hall. They smashed open the doors with their hatchets, broke into the vaults, and in their fury destroyed all the old papers accumulated in the offices. " They have wreaked a blind rage upon the papers: they have been all thrown out of the windows and destroyed," wrote the new Magistracy. The double doors of all the archives were forced open in order to burn the old documents, and in their hatred of the Magistracy the people even broke the furniture of the Town Hall and threw it out into the streets. The Record Office, " the depôt of estates in litigation," met with the same fate. At the tax-collector's office the doors were broken open and the receipts carried off. The troops stationed in front of the Town Hall could do nothing; the people did as they liked.

The Magistracy, seized with terror, hurriedly lowered the prices of meat and bread: they fixed the six-pound loaf at twelve sous.* Then they opened amicable negotiations with the twenty *tribus* (or guilds) of the city for the elaboration of a new municipal constitution. They had to hurry, as rioting still went on in Strasbourg and in the neighbouring districts, where the people were turning out the " established " provosts of the communes, and were nominating others at will, while formulating claims to the forests and claiming other rights directly opposed to legally established property. " It is a moment when every one believed himself in a fair way to obtain the restoration of pretended rights," said the Magistracy in the letter dated August 5.

On top of this the news of the night of August 4 in the Assembly arrived at Strasbourg on the 11th, and the disturbance

---

* Wheat was then 19 livres the sack. The prices rose at the end of August to 28 and 30 livres, so that the bakers were forbidden to bake cakes or fancy bread.

THE TOWNS

became still more threatening, all the more as the army made common cause with the rebels. Whereupon the old Corporation resolved to resign.* The next day, August 12, the three hundred aldermen in their turn resigned their " offices," or rather their privileges. New aldermen were elected, and they appointed the judges.

Thus, on August 14, a new Corporation was constituted, a provisional Senate, which was to direct the affairs of the city until the Assembly at Versailles should establish a new municipal constitution. Without waiting for this constitution Strasbourg had in this way given herself a Commune and judges to her liking.

The old *régime* was thus breaking up at Strasbourg, and on August 17 M. Dietrich congratulated the new aldermen in these terms:

" Gentlemen, the revolution which has just taken place in our town will mark the epoch of the return of the confidence that should unite the citizens of the same commune. This august assembly has just been freely elected by their fellow citizens to be their representatives. . . . The first use that you have made of your powers has been to appoint your judges. . . . What strength may grow from this union!" Dietrich, moreover, proposed to decree that August 14, the day of the revolution in Strasbourg, should be an annual civic *fête*.

An important fact stands out in this revolution. The middle classes of Strasbourg were freed from the feudal system. They had given themselves a democratic municipal government. But they had no intention of giving up the feudal (patrimonial) rights which belonged to them over certain surrounding lands. When the two deputies from Strasbourg in the National Assembly were pressed by their fellows to abdicate their rights, during the night of August 4, they refused to do so. And when later on one of these two deputies, Schwendt, urged the matter before the Strasbourg middle classes, begging them not to oppose the current of the Revolution, his constituents persisted nevertheless in claiming their feudal rights. Thus

* Reuss, *L'Alsace*, p. 147.

we see forming in this city, since 1789, a party which will rally round the King, " the best of kings," " the most conciliatory of monarchs," with the purpose of preserving their rights over " the rich seignories," which belonged to the city under feudal law. The letter* in which the other Strasbourg deputy, Türckheim, sent in his resignation after escaping from Versailles on October 5, is a document of the highest interest in this connection; one sees there already how and why the Gironde will rally under its middle-class flag the " defenders of property " as well as the Royalists.

What happened at Strasbourg gives us a clear enough idea of what was going on in the other large towns. For instance, at Troyes, a town about which we have also sufficiently complete documents, we see the movement made up of the same elements. The people, with the help of the neighbouring peasants, rebelled since July 18, after they had heard about the burning of the toll-gates at Paris. On July 20, some peasants, armed with pitchforks, scythes and flails, entered the town, probably to seize the wheat they needed for food and seed, which they expected to find there in the warehouses of the monopolists. But the middle classes formed themselves into a National Guard and repulsed the peasants, whom they already called " the brigands." During the ten or fifteen days following, taking advantage of the panic which was spreading, five hundred " brigands " were talked of as coming from Paris to ravage everything; the middle classes organised their National Guard, and all the small towns armed themselves likewise. But the people were ill-pleased at this. On August 8, probably on hearing news of the night of August 4, the people demanded arms for all volunteers, and a maximum price for bread. The municipality hesitated. Whereupon the people deposed the members on August 19, and, as had been done at Strasbourg, a new municipality was elected.

The people overran the Town Hall, seized the arms and distributed them among themselves. They broke into the Government salt-stores; but here, too, they did not plunder, " they only caused the salt to be served out at six sous."

* Published by Reuss.

Finally, on September 9, the disturbance, which had never ceased since August 19, reached its culminating-point. The people seized upon the Mayor (Huez), whom they accused of having tried to defend the trading monopolists, and killed him. They sacked his house, and also a notary's, and the house of the old Commandant Saint-Georges, who a fortnight before had given the order to fire on the people, as well as that of the lieutenant of the mounted police, who had caused a man to be hanged during the preceding riot; and they threatened, as they had done in Paris after July 14, to sack many others. After this, for about a fortnight, terror reigned among the upper middle classes. But they managed during that time to reorganise their own National Guard, and on September 26 they ended by getting the upper hand of the unarmed people.

As a rule the anger of the people was directed much more against the representatives of the middle classes who monopolised the food-stuffs than against the nobility who monopolised the land. Thus at Amiens, as at Troyes, the insurgent people almost killed three merchants; whereupon the middle classes hastened to arm their militia. We may even say that this formation of militias in the towns, which was carried out everywhere in August and September, would probably have never taken place if the popular rising had been confined to the country parts, and had been directed solely against the nobility.

At Cherbourg on July 21, at Rouen on the 24th, and in many other towns of less importance, almost the same thing happened. The hungry people rose with cries of "Bread! Death to the monopolists! Down with the toll-gates!" which meant free entrance of all supplies coming in from the country. They compelled the municipality to reduce the price of bread, or else they took possession of the monopolists' storehouses and carried off the grain; they sacked the houses of those who were known to have trafficked in the price of bread-stuffs. The middle classes took advantage of this movement to turn out the old municipal government imbued with feudalism, and to set up a new municipality elected on a democratic basis. At the same time, taking advantage of the panic produced by the rising of the " lower classes" in the towns, and of the "brigands" in the country, they armed themselves and organised their Municipal Guard. After that they "restored order," executed the popular leaders, and very often went into the country to restore order there, where they fought with the peasants and hanged the "leaders" of the revolted peasantry.

After the night of August 4, these urban insurrections spread still more. Indications of them are seen everywhere. The taxes, the town-dues, the levies and excise were no longer paid. "The collectors of the *taille* are at their last shift," said Necker, in his report of August 7. "The price of salt has been compulsorily reduced one-half in two of the revolted localities," the collection of taxes "is no longer made," and so forth. "An infinity of places" was in revolt against the treasury clerks. The people would no longer pay the indirect tax; as to the direct taxes, they are not refused, but conditions were laid down for their payment. In Alsace, for instance, "the people generally refused to pay anything until the exempts and privileged persons had been added to the lists of tax-payers."

In this way the people, *long before the Assembly*, were making the Revolution on the spot; they gave themselves, by revolutionary means, a new municipal administration, they made a distinction between the taxes that they accepted and those which they refused to pay, and they prescribed the mode of equal division of the taxes that they agreed to pay to the State or to the Commune.

It is chiefly by studying this method of *action* among the people, and not by devoting oneself to the study of the Assembly's legislative work, that one grasps the genius of the Great Revolution—the Genius, in the main, of all revolutions, past and to come.

CHAPTER XVI

THE PEASANT RISING

Peasants begin to rise—Causes of risings—Châteaux destroyed—Rising in Alsace—Franche-Comté—Castres—Auvergne—Characteristics of rising—Middle classes and their fears—Picardy revolts — Terror throughout France — National Assembly meets

EVER since the winter of 1788, and especially since March 1789, the people, as we have said, no longer paid rent to the lords. That in this they were encouraged by the revolutionaries of the middle classes is undoubtedly true; there were many persons among the middle classes of 1789 who understood that without a popular rising they would never have the upper hand over the absolute power of the King. It is clear, also, that the discussions in the Assembly of the Notables, wherein the abolition of the feudal rights was already spoken about, encouraged the rising, and that the drawing up in the parishes of the *cahiers*, which were to serve as guides for the assemblies of electors, tended in the same direction. Revolutions are never the result of despair, as is often believed by young revolutionists, who think that good can come out of an excess of evil. On the contrary, the people in 1789 had caught a glimpse of the light of approaching freedom, and for that reason they rose with good heart. But to hope was not enough, to act was also necessary; the first rebels who prepare a revolution must be ready to give their lives, and this the people did.

Whilst rioting was being punished by pillory, torture and hanging, the peasants were already in revolt. From November, 1788, the Governors of the provinces were writing to the ministers that if they wished to put down all the riotings it was no longer possible to do so. Taken separately, none was of great importance; together, they were undermining the very foundations of State.

In January 1789, writs of plaints and grievances (the *cahiers de doléances*) were drawn up, the electors were elected, and from that time the peasants began to refuse to furnish statute labour to the lords and the State. Secret associations were formed among them, and here and there a lord was executed by the "Jacques Bonhommes." In some places the tax-collectors were received with cudgels; in others, the lands belonging to the nobles were seized and tilled.

From month to month these risings multiplied. By March the whole of the east of France was in revolt. The movement, to be sure, was neither continuous nor general. An agrarian rising is never that. It is even very probable, as is always the case in the peasant insurrections, that there was a slackening n the outbreaks at the time of field work in April, and afterwards at the beginning of the harvest time. But as soon as the first harvests were gathered in, during the second half of July 1789, and in August, the risings broke out with fresh force, especially in the east, north-east and south-east of France.

Documents bearing with exactitude on this rising are wanting. Those that have been published are very incomplete, and the greater part bear traces of a partisan spirit. If we take the *Moniteur*, which, we know, only began to appear on November 24, 1789, and of which the ninety-three numbers, from May 8 to November 23, 1789, were compiled later on in the Year IV.,* we find in them a tendency to show that the whole movement was the work of the enemies of the Revolution—of heartless persons who took advantage of rustic ignorance. Others go so far as to say that it was the nobles, the lords, or, indeed, even that it was the English, who had incited the peasants to rise. As for the documents published by the Committee for Investigations in January 1790, they tend rather to represent the whole affair as the result of an unfortunate chance—the work of "brigands," who had devastated the

---

* Moreover, the numbers from November 24, 1789, to February 3, 1790, were also retouched in the Year IV.

country parts, and against whom the middle classes had taken up arms, and whom they had exterminated.

We know to-day how false this representation is, and it is certain that if a historian took the trouble to study carefully the documents in the archives, a work of the highest value would result from it, a work the more necessary as the risings of the peasants continued until the Convention abolished feudal rights, in August 1793, and until the village communes were granted the right of resuming the communal land which had been taken from them during the two preceding centuries. For the time being, this work among the archives not being done, we must confine ourselves to what can be gleaned from some local histories from certain memoirs, and from a few authors, always explaining the rising of 1789 by the light which the better-known movements of the following year sheds on this first outbreak.

That the dearth of food counted for much in these risings is certain. But their chief motive was the desire to get possession of the land and the desire to get rid of the feudal dues and the tithes.

There is, besides, one characteristic trait in these risings. They appear only sporadically in the centre of France and in the south and west, except in Brittany. But they are very general in the east, north-east and south-east. The Dauphiné, the Franche-Comté and the Mâconnais are especially affected by them. In the Franche-Comté nearly all the châteaux were burned, says Doniol; * three out of every five were plundered in Dauphiné. Next in proportion comes Alsace, the Nivernais, the Beaujolais, Burgundy and the Auvergne. As I have remarked elsewhere, if we trace on a map the localities where these risings took place, this map will in a general way present a striking resemblance to the map " of the three hundred and sixty-three," published in 1877, after the elections which gave to France the Third Republic. It was chiefly the eastern part of France which espoused the cause of the Revolution, and this same part is still the most advanced in our own day.

Doniol has remarked very truly that the source of the risings

* *La Révolution française*, p. 48.

was already set forth in the *cahiers*, which were written for the elections of 1789. Since the peasants had been asked to state their grievances, they were sure that something would be done for them. Their firm belief that the King to whom they addressed their complaints, or the Assembly, or some other power, would come to their aid and redress their wrongs, or at least let them take it upon themselves to redress these wrongs—this was what urged them to revolt as soon as the elections had taken place, and before even the Assembly had met. When the States-General began to sit, the rumours which came from Paris, vague though they were, necessarily made the peasants believe that the moment had come for obtaining the abolition of feudal rights and for taking back the land.

The slightest encouragement given to them, whether on the part of the revolutionaries or from the side of the Orléanists, by no matter what kind of agitators, coupled with the disquieting news which was coming from Paris and from the towns in revolt, sufficed to make the villages rise. There is no longer the slightest doubt that use was made more than once of the King's name, and of the Assembly's, in the provinces. Many documents, indeed, allude to the circulation among the villages of false decrees of the King and of the Assembly. In all their risings, in France, in Russia and in Germany, the peasants have always tried to decide the hesitating ones—I shall even say to persuade themselves by maintaining that there was some force ready to back them up. This gave them cohesion, and afterwards, in case of defeat and of proceedings being taken against them, there was always a safe excuse. They had thought, and the majority thought so sincerely, that they were obeying the wishes, if not the orders, of the King or of the Assembly. Therefore, as soon as the first harvests were reaped in the summer of 1789, as soon as people in the villages began to eat again after the long months of scarcity, and the rumours arriving from Versailles began to inspire hope, the peasants rose. They turned upon the châteaux in order to destroy the charter-rooms, the lists and the title-deeds; and houses were burned down if the masters did not relinquish with a good grace the feudal rights recorded in the charters, the rolls and the rest.

THE PEASANT RISING

In the neighbourhood of Vesoul and Belfort the war on the country houses began on July 16, the date when the château of Sancy, and then those of Luce, Bithaine and Molans, were plundered. Soon all Loraine had risen. "The peasants, believing that the Revolution was going to bring in equality of wealth and rank, were especially excited against the lords," says the *Courrier français*.* At Saarlouis, Forbach, Sarreguemines, Phalsbourg and Thionville the excise officers were driven away and their offices pillaged and burnt. Salt was selling at three sous the pound. The neighbouring villages followed the example of the towns.

In Alsace the peasant rising was almost general. It is stated that in eight days, towards the end of July, three abbeys were destroyed, eleven châteaux sacked, others plundered, and that the peasants had carried off and destroyed all the land records. The registers of feudal taxes, statute-labours and dues of all sorts were also taken away and burnt. In certain localities flying columns were formed, several hundred and sometimes several thousand strong, of peasants gathered from the villages round about; they marched against the strongest châteaux, besieged them, seized all the old papers and made bonfires of them. The abbeys were sacked and plundered for the same reason, as well as houses of rich merchants in the towns. Everything was destroyed at the Abbey of Mürbach, which probably offered resistance.†

In the Franche-Comté the first riots took place at Lons-le-Saulnier as early as July 19, when the news of the preparations for the *coup d'état* and Necker's dismissal reached that place, but the taking of the Bastille was still unknown, says Sommier.‡ Rioting soon began, and at the same time the middle classes armed its militia (all wearing the tricolour cockade) to resist

* P. 242 *et seq.*
† According to Strobel (*Vaterländische Geschichte des Elsass*), the rising took place generally in this way: a village rose, and straightway a band was formed composed of the inhabitants of various villages, which went in a body to attack the châteaux. Sometimes these bands concealed themselves in the woods.
‡ *Histoire de la Révolution dans le Jura* (Paris, 1846), p. 22. The bent of men's minds in the Jura is revealed in a song given in the *Cahier d'Aval*.

"the incursions of the brigands who infest the kingdom."* The rising soon spread to the villages. The peasants divided among themselves the meadows and woods of the lords. Besides this, they compelled the lords to renounce their right over land which had belonged formerly to the communes. Or else, without any formalities, they retook possession of the forests which had once been communal. All the title-deeds held by the Abbey of the Bernardins in the neighbouring communes were carried off.† At Castres the risings began after August 4. A tax of *coupe* was levied in kind (so much per *setier*) in this town on all wheats imported into the province. It was a feudal tax, granted by the King to private individuals. As soon, therefore, as they heard in Castres the news of the night of August 4, the people rose, demanding the abolition of this tax; and immediately the middle classes, who had formed the National Guard, six hundred strong, began to restore "order." But in the rural districts the insurrection spread from village to village, and the châteaux of Gaix and Montlédier, the Carthusian Convent of Faix, the Abbey of Vielmur and other places were plundered and the records destroyed.‡

In the Auvergne the peasants took many precautions to put the law on their side, and when they went to the châteaux to burn the records, they did not hesitate to say to the lords that they were acting by order of the King.§ But in the eastern provinces they did not refrain from declaring openly that the

---

* Sommier, pp. 24–25.

† Edouard Clerc, *Essai sur l'histoire de la Franche-Comté*, 2nd edition (Besançon, 1870).

‡ Anacharsis Combes, *Histoire de la ville de Castres et de ses environs pendant la Révolution française* (Castres, 1875).

§ M. Xavier Roux, who published in 1891, under the title *Mémoire sur la marche des brigandages dans le Dauphiné en 1789*, the complete depositions of an inquiry made in 1879 on this subject, attributes the whole movement to a few leaders: "To call upon the people to rise against the King would have had no results," says this writer; "they attained their end in a roundabout way. A singularly bold plan was adopted and carried out over the whole province. It is summed up in these words: to stir up the people against the lords in the name of the King; the lords once crushed, the throne was to be attacked, which, then being defenceless, could be destroyed" (p. iv. of the introduction). Well, we take from M. Roux himself this admission, that all the inquiries made have never led" to the disclosure of a single leader's name " (p. v.). The whole people were included in this conspiracy.

time had come when the Third Estate would no longer permit the nobles and priesthood to rule over them. The power of these two classes had lasted too long, and the moment had come for them to abdicate. For a large number of the poorer nobles, residing in the country and perhaps loved by those round them, the revolted peasantry showed much personal regard. They did them no harm; but the registers and title-deeds of feudal landlordism they never spared. They burned them, after compelling the lord to swear that he would relinquish his rights.

Like the middle classes of the towns, who knew well what they wanted and what they expected from the Revolution, the peasants also knew very well what they wanted; the lands stolen from the communes should be given back to them, and all the dues begotten by feudalism should be wiped out. The idea that the rich people as a whole should be wiped out, too, may have filtered through from that time; but at the moment the *jacquerie* confined its attention to *things*, and if there were cases where the persons of some lords were ill-treated, they were isolated cases, and may generally be explained by the fact that they were speculators, men who had made money out of the scarcity. If the land-registers were given up and the oath of renunciation taken, all went off quietly: the peasants burned the registers, planted a May-tree in the village, hung on its boughs the feudal emblems, and then danced round the tree.*

Otherwise, if there had been resistance, or if the lord or his steward had called in the police, if there had been any shooting —then the château was completely pillaged, and often it was set on fire. Thus, it is reckoned that thirty châteaux were plundered or burnt in the Dauphiné, nearly forty in the Franche-Comté, sixty-two in the Mâconnais and the Beaujolais, nine only in the Auvergne, and twelve monasteries and five châteaux in the Viennois. We may note, by the way, that the peasants made no distinctions for political opinions. They attacked, therefore, the houses of " patriots " as well as those of " aristocrats."

* Sometimes in the south they hung up also this inscription: " By order of the King and of the National Assembly, a final quittance of rents" (Mary Lafon, *Histoire politique du Midi de la France*, 1842-1845, vol. iv. p. 377).

What were the middle classes doing while these riots were going on?

There must have been in the Assembly a certain number of men who understood that the rising of the peasants at that moment represented a revolutionary force; but the mass of the middle classes in the provinces saw only a danger against which it was necessary to arm themselves. What was called at the time *la grande peur* (" the great fear ") seized, in fact, on a good many of the towns in the region of the risings. At Troyes, for example, some countrymen armed with scythes and flails had entered the town, and would probably have pillaged the houses of the speculators, when the middle classes, " all who were honest among the middle classes," * armed themselves against " the brigands " and drove them away. The same thing happened in many other towns. The middle classes were seized with panic. They were expecting " the brigands." Some one had seen " six thousand " on the march to plunder everything, and the middle classes took possession of the arms which they found at the Town Hall or at the armourers', and organised their National Guard, for fear lest the poor folk of the town, making common cause with " the brigands," might attack the rich.

At Péronne, the capital of Picardy, the inhabitants had revolted in the second half of July. They burnt the toll-gates, threw the Custom House officers into the water, carried off the receipts from the Government offices and set free all the prisoners. All this was done before July 28. " After receiving the news from Paris on the night of the 28th," wrote the Mayor of Péronne, " Hainault, Flanders and all Picardy have taken up arms; the tocsin is ringing in all the towns and villages." Three hundred thousand middle-class men were formed into permanent patrols—and all this to be ready for two thousand " brigands," that, they said, were overrunning the villages and burning the crops. In reality, as some one aptly remarked to Arthur Young, all these " brigands " were nothing more than peasants,† who were, indeed, rising, and, armed with pitchforks, cudgels and scythes, were compelling the lords to abdicate their

---

* *Moniteur*, i. 378.   † *Travels in France*, p. 225.

THE PEASANT RISING

feudal rights, and were stopping passers-by to ask them if they were "for the nation." The Mayor of Péronne has also aptly said: "We are willing to be in the Terror. Thanks to the sinister rumours, we can keep on foot an army of three millions of middle-class men and peasants all over France."

Adrien Duport, a well-known member of the Assembly and of the Breton Club, even boasted of having armed in this way the middle classes in a great many towns. He had two or three agents, "resolute but not well-known men," who avoided the towns, but on arriving at a village would announce that "the brigands were coming." "There are five hundred, a thousand, three thousand of them," said these emissaries, "they are burning all the crops round about, so that the people may starve." Thereupon the tocsin would be rung and the villages would arm themselves. And by the time that the sinister rumour reached the towns, the numbers would have grown to six thousand brigands. They had been seen about a league off in such a forest; then the townspeople, especially the middle classes, would arm themselves and send patrols into the forest—to find nothing there. But the important point was that the peasants were thus being armed. Let the King take care! When he tries to escape, in 1791, he will find the armed peasants in his way.

We can imagine the terror which these risings inspired all through France; we can imagine the impression that they made at Versailles, and it was under the domination of this terror that the National Assembly met on the evening of August 4 to discuss what measures should be taken to suppress the *jacquerie*.

CHAPTER XVII

AUGUST 4 AND ITS CONSEQUENCES

Night of August 4—Aristocracy pretends to relinquish feudal rights—Assembly begs King to take action—D'Aiguillon and de Noailles take up cause of peasants—Their great speeches—Le Guen de Kérangall—Scene in Assembly—Extent of actual concessions—Effect of news in provinces—Middle classes take up arms against peasants.

THE night of August 4 is one of the great dates of the Revolution. Like July 14 and October 15, 1789, June 21, 1791, August 10, 1792, and May 31, 1793, it marked one of the great stages in the revolutionary movement, and it determined the character of the period which follows it.

The historic legend is lovingly used to embellish this night, and the majority of historians, copying the story as it has been given by a few contemporaries, represent it as a night full of enthusiasm and saintly abnegation.

With the taking of the Bastille, the historians tell us, the Revolution had gained its first victory. The news spread to the provinces, and provoked everywhere somewhat similar insurrections. It penetrated to the villages, and, at the instigation of all kinds of vagabonds, the peasants attacked their lords and burnt the châteaux. Whereupon the clergy and nobility, filled with a patriotic impulse, seeing that they had as yet done nothing for the peasant, began to relinquish their feudal rights during this memorable night. The nobles, the clergy, the poorest parish priest and the richest of the feudal lords, all renounced upon the altar of their country their secular prerogatives. A wave of enthusiasm passed through the Assembly; all were eager to make their sacrifice. "The sitting was a holy feast, the tribune an altar, the Assembly

AUGUST 4 AND ITS CONSEQUENCES

Hall a temple," says one of the historians, who are usually calm enough. "It was a Saint Bartholomew of property," say the others. And when the first beams of day broke over France on the morrow the old feudal system no longer existed. "France was a country born anew, having made an *auto-da-fé* of all the abuses of its privileged classes."

That is the legend. It is true that a profound enthusiasm thrilled the Assembly when two nobles, the Viscount de Noailles and the Duke d'Aiguillon, put the demand for the abolition of feudal rights, as well as of the various privileges of the nobility, and when two bishops—those of Nancy and of Chartres—spoke demanding the abolition of the tithes. It is true that the enthusiasm went on ever increasing, and that during this all-night sitting nobles and clergy followed one another to the tribune and disputed who should first give up their seignorial courts of justice. Pleas were to be heard, made by the privileged persons, for justice—free, unbought, and equal for all. Lords, lay and ecclesiastic, were seen relinquishing their game laws. The Assembly was carried away by its enthusiasm, and in this enthusiasm nobody remarked the clause for *redeeming* the feudal rights and tithes, which the two nobles and the two bishops had introduced into their speeches—a clause terrible even in its vagueness, since it might mean all or nothing, and did, in fact, postpone, as we shall see, the abolition of feudal rights for four years—until August 1793. But which of us in reading the beautiful story of that night, written by its contemporaries, has not been carried away by enthusiasm in his turn ? And who has not passed over those traitorous words, "*rachat au denier* 30" (redemption at a thirty-years' purchase), without understanding their terrible import ? This is also what happened in France in 1789.

The evening sitting of August 4 had at first begun with panic, not with enthusiasm. We have just seen that a number of châteaux had been burnt or plundered during the previous fortnight. Beginning in the east, the peasant insurrection spread towards the south, the north and the centre ; it threatened to become general. In a few places the peasants had acted savagely towards their masters, and the news which came in from the provinces exaggerated what had happened. The nobles ascertained with alarm that there was not any force on the spot capable of checking the riots.

The sitting opened, therefore, with the reading of a scheme for issuing a proclamation against the risings. The Assembly was invited to pronounce an energetic condemnation of the rioters and to command most emphatically respect for property, whether feudal or not, while waiting for the Assembly to legislate on the matter.

"It appears that property, of no matter what nature, is the prey of the most culpable brigandage," said the Committee of Inquiry. "On all sides châteaux are burnt, convents destroyed and farms given over to pillage. The taxes and seignorial dues all are done away with. The laws are powerless, the magistrates are without authority. . . ." And the report demanded that the Assembly should censure severely the disturbances and declare "that the old laws (the feudal laws) were in existence until the authority of the nation had abrogated or modified them, that all the customary dues and payments should be paid as in the past, until it should have been ordained otherwise by the Assembly."

"They are not brigands who do that!" exclaimed the Duke d'Aiguillon; "in several provinces the whole of the people have entered into a league to destroy the châteaux to ravage the lands, and above all to get possession of the record-rooms where the title-deeds of the feudal properties are deposited." It is certainly not enthusiasm that speaks here: it is more like fear.*

The Assembly proceeded in consequence to beg the King to take stringent measures against the rebellious peasants. This had already been spoken of the day before, August 3. But for some days past a certain number of the nobility—a few more advanced in their ideas than the rest of their class, and who saw more clearly all that was happening: the Viscount de

* "To ravage the lands" would probably mean that in certain places the peasants reaped the harvests belonging to the lords while they were yet green. Besides, it was the end of July, the corn was nearly ripe, and the people, who had nothing to eat, cut the corn belonging to the lords.

AUGUST 4 AND ITS CONSEQUENCES

Noailles, the Duke d'Aiguillon, the Duke de La Rochefoucauld, Alexandre de Lamotte and some others—were secretly consulting together as to the attitude to be taken towards the *jacquerie*. They had understood that the only means of saving the feudal rights was to sacrifice the honorary rights and prerogatives of little value, and to demand *the redemption* by the peasants of the feudal dues *attached to the land and having a real value*. They commissioned the Duke d'Aiguillon with the development of these ideas, and this is how it was done by the Viscount de Noailles and the Duke d'Aiguillon.

Ever since the Revolution began the country folk had demanded the abolition of the feudal rights.* At the present time, said the two spokesmen of the liberal nobility, the rural districts, dissatisfied that nothing has been done for them during these three months, are in a state of revolt; they are no longer under control, and the choice now lies " between the destruction of society and certain concessions." These concessions were formulated by the Viscount de Noailles thus : Equality of all persons under taxation, which should be paid in proportion to the income; all public expenses to be contributed to by all; " all the feudal rights to be redeemed by the (village) communes by means of a yearly rent " ; and lastly, " the abolition without redemption of the seignorial statute-labours, of mortmain and other kinds of personal servitude." † It must also be said that

---

* " The marks of transport and effusion of generous sentiment which made the picture presented by the Assembly more lively and spirited from hour to hour, scarcely left time for coming to some agreement over the prudential measures thought advisable for carrying into effect those beneficent projects, which had been voted in so many memorials of both provincial and parochial assemblies—wherever the citizens had been able to meet for the last eighteen months—amid touching expressions of opinion and ardent protestations."

† " All the feudal rights were to be redeemable by the communes, either by money or exchange," said the Viscount de Noailles. " Every one will be subject to all the public charges, all the State charges (*subsides*), without any distinction," said d'Aiguillon. " I demand the redemption for the ecclesiastical funds," said Lafare, Bishop of Nancy, " and I demand that the redemption be not turned to the profit of the ecclesiastical lord, but that it may be invested usefully for the poor." The Bishop of Chartres demanded the abolition of the game laws, and renounced those rights for his own part. Whereupon both nobles and clergy rise at the same time to follow his example. De Richer demanded not only the abolition of the manorial courts of

for some time past the personal services had been no longer paid by the peasants. We have very clear evidence on that head from the governors of the provinces. After the revolt of July it was plain that they would never be paid again, whether the lord renounced them or not.

These concessions, proposed by the Viscount de Noailles, were, however, cut down, both by the nobles and by the middle-class deputies, of whom a great number possessed landed property comprising feudal rights. The Duke d'Aiguillon, who followed de Noailles in the tribune, and whom the above-mentioned nobles had chosen as their spokesman, spoke of the peasants with sympathy; he excused their insurrection, but his conclusion was that " the barbarous remnants of the feudal laws which still exist in France are—there is no need for dissimulation—a *species of property, and all property is sacred.*" "*Equity*," said he, " *forbids us to exact the renunciation of any property without granting a just indemnity to the owner.*" He also softened down the Viscount de Noailles' phrase about the taxes, by saying that all citizens should contribute " in proportion to their means." And as to the feudal rights, he demanded that all these rights—the personal rights as well as the others—might be redeemed by the vassals " if they so desired," the compensation being " *au denier* 30"—that is, thirty times the annual payment. This was to make redemption a sham, because for land rents it was heavy enough at twenty-five years, and in business transactions rent is generally reckoned at twenty, or even seventeen.

These two speeches were received by the gentlemen of the Third Estate with enthusiasm, and they have come down to posterity as sublime acts of abnegation on the part of the nobility, while in reality the National Assembly, which followed the programme laid down by the Duke d'Aiguillon, created thereby the very conditions of the terrible struggles which later on steeped the Revolution in blood. The few peasants who were in this Assembly did not speak, and nobody called

justice, but also that justice should be dispensed gratuitously. Several priests asked that they might be allowed to sacrifice their perquisites (*casuel*), but that a tax in money should take the place of the tithe.

AUGUST 4 AND ITS CONSEQUENCES

attention to the small value of the "renunciations" of the nobles. As to the mass of the deputies of the Third Estate, who were city men for the most part, and therefore probably had only a very vague idea about the feudal rights as a whole, as well as about the significance of the peasant rising, in their eyes, to renounce the feudal rights, even on terms of redemption, was to make a sublime sacrifice to the Revolution.

Le Guen de Kérangall, a Breton deputy, "dressed as a peasant," then uttered some beautiful and moving words. These words, when he spoke of the "infamous parchments" which registered the obligations of personal servitude, survivals of serfdom, made, and still make, hearts throb. But he, too, did not speak against a redemption of all the feudal rights, including those same "infamous" services, imposed "in times of darkness and ignorance," the injustice of which he so eloquently denounced.

It is certain that the spectacle presented by the Assembly during that night must have been fine—representatives of the nobility and clergy coming forward to relinquish the privileges they had exercised without question for centuries. The action and the word were magnificent when the nobles rose to renounce their privileges in the matter of taxes, and the priests to renounce their tithes, the poorest curates among them giving up the *casuel*, the greatest lords giving up their courts of manorial justice, and all of them relinquishing the hunting rights, asking for the suppression of the pigeon-houses, which had been such a plague to the peasants. It was fine to see, also, whole provinces renouncing privileges which had created for them an exceptional position in the kingdom. The category of *pays d'états* endowed with special rights was thus suppressed, and the privileges of the towns, several of which held feudal rights over the neighbouring country, were abolished. The representatives of the Dauphiné (where, as we have seen, the rising had been strong and widespread) having led the way for the abolition of provincial distinctions, the others followed them.

All the eye-witnesses of this memorable sitting have given glowing descriptions of it. When the nobility accepted in principle the redemption of the feudal rights, the clergy were called upon to declare themselves. They accepted fully the redemption of the ecclesiastical feudalities on the condition that the price of redemption should not create personal fortunes amongst the clergy, but that the whole should be employed in works of general utility. A bishop then spoke about the injuries done in the peasants' fields by the packs of hounds kept by the lords, and demanded the abolition of the hunting privileges, and immediately the nobility gave their assent by a loud and impassioned shout. The enthusiasm reached a very high pitch during the sitting, and when the Assembly separated at two o'clock in the morning, every one felt that the foundations of a new society had been laid.

It would not be fair to try to diminish the importance of that night. Enthusiasm of this kind is needed to push on events. It will be needed again when a Social Revolution comes. In a revolution enthusiasm must be provoked, and words which make hearts vibrate must be pronounced. The fact that the nobility, the clergy and the privileged persons of every kind had recognised during that night's sitting the progress of the Revolution, that they decided to submit to it instead of taking up arms against it—this fact by itself was already a conquest of the human mind. It was all the greater as the renunciation was made with enthusiasm. It is true that it was done in the light of the burning châteaux, but how many times had that same light merely provoked in the privileged classes an obstinate resistance, and led to hatred and massacre! That night in August those distant flames inspired other words—words of sympathy for the rebels; and other acts—acts of conciliation.

Ever since July 14, the spirit of the Revolution, born of the ferment which was working through the whole of France, was hovering over everything that lived and felt, and this spirit, created by millions of wills, gave the inspiration that we lack in ordinary times.

But having pointed out the effects of the enthusiasm which only a revolution could inspire, the historian must also consider calmly how far all this enthusiasm did actually go, and what was the limit it dared not pass; he must point out what it gave the people and what it refused to grant them.

Well, that limit can be indicated in very few words. The Assembly only sanctioned in principle and extended to France altogether what the people had accomplished themselves in certain localities. It went no further.

We have seen what the people had already done in Strasbourg and in so many other towns. They had compelled all the citizens, noble and middle-class, to share the taxation, and had proclaimed the necessity of an income tax—and the National Assembly accepted that. The people had abolished all honorary offices, and the nobility agreed to renounce those offices on August 4; by so doing, they again accepted a revolutionary act. The people had also abolished the manorial courts of justice and appointed judges by election; the Assembly accepted this in its turn. Finally, the people had abolished the privileges of the towns and the provincial toll-gates—it was actually done in the eastern provinces—and now the Assembly made a general principle of a fact already accomplished in a part of the kingdom.

For the rural districts the clergy admitted in principle that the tithes should be redeemable; but in how many places were the people paying them! And when the Assembly tried afterwards to exact payment up to 1791, it had to resort to threats of execution to compel the peasants to obey. Let us rejoice, certainly, that the clergy yielded to the abolition of the tithes—under the condition that they should be redeemed—but let us also say that the clergy would have done infinitely better had they not insisted on redemption. What struggles, what hatreds, what bloodshed had been spared if they had given up the tithes and had left the payment of their salaries to the nation or their parishioners. As to the feudal rights, how much strife would have been avoided if the Assembly, instead of accepting the motion of the Duke d'Aiguillon, had simply adopted on August 4, 1789, that of the Viscount de Noailles, which after all was a very modest proposal: the abolition without indemnity of the personal dues, and redemption for the rents attaching to land. But, to arrive at this latter measure, in 1792, how much blood had to flow during three years, not to mention the savage struggles which had to be gone through to attain in 1793 the total abolition of feudal rights without redemption?

But let us for the moment do as the men of 1789 did. Every one was filled with joy after that sitting. Every one congratulated themselves upon that Saint Bartholomew of feudal abuses, which proves how important it is during a revolution to recognise, or at least to proclaim, a new principle. Couriers were despatched from Paris, carrying the great news to every corner of France: "All the feudal rights are abolished!" For it was so that the decisions of the Assembly were understood by the people, and it was so stated in the first article of the resolution of August 5. All the feudal rights are abolished! No more tithes! No more quit-rents! No more dues on the sales of inheritance, no more payments in kind, nor statute-labours, nor subsidies! The game laws are gone! Done with the pigeon-houses: all game is henceforth free to everybody! There were to be no more nobles, no privileged persons of any sort: every one was equal before the judge elected by all!

At least this was how the night of August 4 was understood in the provinces. And before the resolutions of August 5 and 11 had been published, before the line of demarcation between what should be redeemed and what should disappear since that day had been marked out—long before those acts and renunciations had been formulated into paragraphs of law, messengers had already brought the good news to the peasant. Henceforth, whether he was shot down or not, he would no longer pay anything.

The peasant insurrection took, therefore, a new force. It spread through the provinces, such as Brittany, which until then had remained quiet. And if the landowners demanded payment of any kind of dues, the peasants went to their châteaux and burnt all the records and land-registers. They did not care to submit to the decrees of August and distinguish between redeemable rights and abolished rights, says Du Châtellier.* Everywhere, all over France, the pigeon-houses and game were destroyed. In the villages the peasants ate their fill therefore,

* *Histoire de la Révolution dans les départements de l'ancienne Bretagne*, 8 vols., vol. i. p. 422.

and they also took possession of those lands which, though formerly belonging to the village communities, had been seized by the lords.

It was then that in the east of France one could see what has happened later on more or less all over France—namely, the middle classes interposing against the peasants in favour of the landlords. Liberal historians have passed this by in silence, but it is a fact of the highest importance for the comprehension of the history of the next few years.

We have seen that the peasant rising attained its greatest vigour in the Dauphiné and in eastern France generally. The rich people and the lords fled, Necker complaining that he had to furnish six thousand passports to the richest inhabitants in a fortnight. Switzerland was inundated with them. But the middle-class people who remained armed themselves and organised their militia, and the National Assembly soon voted a draconian measure against the peasants (August 10).* Under the pretext that the insurrection was the work of brigands, it authorised the municipalities to call out the troops, to disarm all men without profession and without domicile, to disperse the bands and to deal with them summarily. The middle classes of the Dauphiné profited largely by these laws. When bands of peasants in revolt passed through Burgundy, burning the châteaux, the middle-class men in the towns and villages leagued themselves against them. One of these bands, says the *Deux amis de la liberté*, was defeated at Cormatin on July 27, when twenty were killed and sixty taken prisoners. At Cluny there were a hundred killed and one hundred and sixty prisoners. The municipality of Mâcon made war in due form upon the peasants, who refused to pay the tithe, and they hanged twenty of them. Twelve peasants were hanged at Douai; at Lyons the middle classes, while fighting the peasants, killed eighty of them and took sixty prisoners. In the Dauphiné the Provost-Marshal went all over the country hanging the rebellious peasants.† In the Rouergue, the town of Milhaud appealed

* Buchez and Roux, *Histoire parlementaire*, vol. ii. p. 254.
† After the defeat of two large bands of peasants, one of which threatened to attack the châteaux of Cormatin, the other the town of Cluny, and after punishments of a frightful severity had been inflicted,

to the neighbouring towns, inviting them to arm themselves against the brigands and those who refused to pay the taxes.*

In short, we see by these several acts, of which it would be easy to increase the list, that wherever the rising of the peasants was the most violent, there the middle classes undertook to crush it; and they would have undoubtedly helped considerably to do it if the news which came from Paris after the night of August 4 had not given a new impetus to the insurrection.

The peasant rising apparently slackened only in September or October, perhaps on account of the ploughing; but in January 1790 we learn, from the account of the Feudalism Committee, that the peasant insurrection had begun again with renewed vigour, probably because of the claims for payment. The peasants were unwilling to submit to the distinction made by the Assembly between the dues attached to the land and the personal services, and they rose in order that they should pay nothing at all.

We shall return to this very important subject in one of the succeeding chapters.

the war went on, but in a scattered way, say Buchez and Roux. "However the Permanent Committee of Mâcon illegally constituted itself into a tribunal, by order of which twenty of these unhappy peasants were executed for the crime of hunger and for having rebelled against the tithe and feudal laws" (p. 244). Everywhere the rising was clearly provoked by acts of minor importance, by disputes with the lord or the chapter about a meadow or a fountain, and in one château, to which the rights of plenary jurisdiction belonged, several vassals were hanged for marauding offences, &c. The pamphlets of the time, which Buchez and Roux consulted, say that the *parlement* (the Court) of Douai ordered twelve leaders of bands to be executed; the Committee of Electors (middle-class men) at Lyons sent out a flying column of volunteer National Guards. One contemporary pamphlet states that this little army in a single engagement killed eighty of the so-called brigands, and took sixty prisoners. The Provost-Marshal of the Dauphiné, at the head of a body of middle-class militia, marched through the country and executed as he went (Buchez and Roux, vol. ii. p. 245).

* *Courrier parisien*, sitting of August 19, 1789, p. 1729.

CHAPTER XVIII

THE FEUDAL RIGHTS REMAIN

Assembly and feudal privileges—Survivals of serfdom—Obligations to feudal lord—Lords try to back out of their promises—Church tithes abolished in theory but not in practice—Disappointment of peasants—Game laws—Feudal rights—Personal servitude alone abolished—Other dues remain—Redemption of land rendered impossible—Effect of vagueness of Assembly—Article of August 4, 1789, not to be taken literally—Peasants refuse to pay—King the rallying-point of feudalism—Tactics of Assembly—Its resolutions finally published by the King

WHEN the Assembly met again on August 5 to draw up, under the form of resolutions, the list of renunciations which had been made during the historic night of the 4th, one could see up to what point the Assembly was on the side of property, and how it was going to defend every one of the pecuniary advantages attached to those same feudal privileges, which it had made a show of abandoning a few hours before.

There were still in France, under the name of *mainmortes*, *banalités*,* &c., a few survivals of the ancient serfdom. There were still peasants subject to mortmain in the Franche-Comté, the Nivernais and the Bourbonnais. They were serfs in the true sense of the word; they could not sell their goods, nor transmit them by inheritance, except to those of their children who lived with them. They remained therefore attached to the soil.† How many they were we do not exactly know, but

---

* The common oven, mill, press, &c., belonging to the lord, for the use of which the peasants had to pay, besides suffering much loss of food, grain and wine.

† The fact of being attached to the land is what constitutes the essence of serfdom. Wherever serfdom has existed for several centuries, the lords have also obtained from the State rights over the person of the serf, which made serfdom (in Russia, for example, at the

it is thought that the number given by Boncerf as three hundred thousand *mainmortables* is the most probable.*

Besides these *mainmortables* there were a very large number of peasants and also of free townsmen, who were, nevertheless, still held under personal obligations either to their former lords or else to the lords of the lands they had bought or held on lease.

It is estimated that as a rule the privileged classes—the nobility and clergy—held half the lands of every village, but that besides these lands, which were their property, they still retained various feudal rights over the lands owned by the peasants. Small proprietors were even then very numerous in France, but there were very few of them, adds M. Sagnac, who "held by right of freehold, who did not owe at least a quit-rent, or some other due, in recognition of the seigniory." Nearly all lands paid something, either in money or in a portion of the crops, to some or other lord.

These obligations varied very much, but they may be divided into five classes: (1) The personal obligations, often humiliating—relics of serfdom; † (2) payments of all sorts in money, in kind or in work, which were due for a real or supposed concession of land; these were the mortmain and the real statute-labours,‡ the quit-rent, the field-rent, the land-tax, the fines on sales and on inheritance; (3) various payments resulting from the lords' monopolies; that is to say, the lords levied certain customs-revenues, certain town-dues, or certain rents from those who used their markets or their measures,

beginning of the eighteenth century) a state closely akin to slavery, and in the current language of the day allowed serfdom to be confounded with slavery.

* Sagnac, *La législation civile de la Révolution française*, pp. 59, 60.

† Arthur Young, writing of these vexatious and ruinous dues, says: "What are these tortures of the peasantry in Bretagne, which they call *chevanchés, quintaines, soule, saut de poisson, baiser de mariées, chansons; transporte d'œuf sur un charette; silence des grenouilles, corvée à miséricorde; milode; leide; couponage; cartilage; barrage; forage; maréchaussé; bauvin; ban d'août; trousses; gelinage; civerage; taillabilité; vingtain; sterlage; bordelage; minage; ban de vendanges; droit d'accapt . . . ?* The very terms . . . are unknown in England, and consequently untranslatable" (*Travels in France*, p. 319; London, 1892).

‡ "Real" opposed to "personal" means here an obligation attached to *things*, that is to say, to the possession of the land.

mills, wine-presses, common ovens and the rest; (4) the fees of justice levied by the lord wherever the court belonged to him, the taxes, fines and so on; and (5) the lord possessed the exclusive right of hunting over his land and those of the neighbouring peasantry, as well as the right of keeping pigeon-houses and rabbit-warrens, which conferred a much-coveted honour with the privilege.

All these rights were vexatious to the last degree, and they cost the peasant dear, even when they mattered little or nothing to the lord. And it is a fact, upon which Boncerf lays stress in his remarkable work, *Les inconvénients des droits féodaux* * that ever since 1776 the impoverished lords, and especially their stewards, began to squeeze the farmers, the tenants and the peasants generally, in order to get out of them as much as possible. In 1786 there was even a pretty wide revision of the land-registers for the purpose of augmenting the feudal dues.

The Assembly, therefore, after pronouncing the abolition of all the survivals of the feudal system, halted when it became a question of wording these renunciations and putting them into the written law.

Thus it seemed as if the lords having sacrificed their *main-mortes*, there was nothing more to be said about it; they had only to put their renunciation into the form of a decree. But even on this question they raised discussions. They tried to establish a distinction between the personal mortmainable serfdom, a condition which should be abolished without indemnity, and the real mortmainable serfdom attached to the land and transmitted with the leasing or purchase of it: serfs of the latter class might redeem themselves. And if the Assembly decided in the end to abolish without indemnity all the rights and dues, feudal as well as manorial, " which pertained to mortmain, real or personal, and to personal services," they managed so as to cast a doubt even on this—especially in every case where it was difficult to separate the rights of *mortmain* from *feudal* rights in general.

There was the same shuffling over the question of the

* P. 52.

Church tithes. It is known that the tithes very often amounted to a fifth or even a quarter of all harvests, and that the clergy claimed a share of the very grasses and nuts which the peasants gathered. These tithes weighed very heavily upon the peasants, especially upon the poorer ones. But then, on August 4, the clergy had declared their renunciation of all tithes in kind, on condition that these tithes should be redeemed by those who paid them. But as they did not indicate the conditions of redemption, nor the rules of procedure under which the redemption should be made, the renunciation in reality was reduced to a simple declaration of principle. The clergy accepted the redemption; they permitted the peasants to redeem the tithes if they wished to do so, and to debate the price with the holders of the tithes. But, on August 6, when it was proposed to draw up the resolutions concerning the tithes, a difficulty presented itself.

There were tithes which the clergy had sold in the course of the centuries to private individuals, and these tithes were called lay or *enfeoffed*. For such as these redemption was considered absolutely necessary, in order to maintain the right of property for the last purchaser. Worse than that: the tithes paid by the peasants to the clergy themselves were represented to the Assembly by certain speakers, as *a tax* which the nation paid in support of its clergy; and by degrees, during the discussion, the opinion prevailed that there might be a question of redeeming the tithes if the nation undertook to give a regular salary to the clergy. This discussion lasted five days, until the 11th, and then several priests, backed by the archbishops, declared that they relinquished the tithes to the country, and left themselves to the justice and generosity of the nation.

It was decided, therefore, that the tithes paid to the clergy should be abolished; but while means were being found for providing from some other source the expenses for religion, the *tithes should be paid as formerly*. As to the enfeoffed tithes, they were to be paid until they were redeemed.

It can be imagined what a terrible disappointment this was for the rural populations, and what a cause of disturbance.

In theory the tithes were suppressed, but in reality they were to be collected as usual. "Until when ?" asked the peasants; and the answer was, "Until we find some other means of paying the clergy!" And as the finances of the kingdom were going from bad to worse, the peasant was justified in asking if the tithes would ever be abolished. The stoppage of work and the revolutionary agitation manifestly prevented the collection of the taxes, whilst the cost of the new law and the new administration tended necessarily to increase the difficulty. Democratic reforms are expensive and it is only with time that a nation in revolution is able to pay the cost of its reforms. Meanwhile the peasant had to pay the tithes, and up to 1791 they were exacted from him in a very harsh way, and as he did not want to pay, law upon law and penalty upon penalty were decreed by the Assembly against the defaulters.

The same remark applies to the game laws. On the night of August 4 the nobles had renounced their hunting rights. But when it came to the formulation of what had been said, it was perceived that this would give the right of hunting to every one. Whereupon the Assembly retracted, and only extended the right of hunting to all proprietors, or rather to the owners of real estate upon their own lands. But here again they left rather vague the formula at which they finally stopped. The Assembly abolished the *exclusive* right of hunting and that of the unenclosed warrens, but they said that every proprietor had the right to destroy and to cause to be destroyed, only upon his inherited land, all kinds of game. Did this authorisation apply to the farmers ? It is doubtful. The peasants, however, did not wait for, nor require, the permission of tricky lawyers. Immediately after August 4 they began everywhere to destroy the game belonging to the lords. After having seen for many years their crops devoured by the game, they themselves destroyed the depredators without waiting for any authorisation.

Finally as to what concerned the essential thing, the great question which so deeply interested more than twenty millions of Frenchmen—the feudal rights—the Assembly, when it was formulating in resolutions the renunciations of the night of August 4, confined itself simply to the enunciation of a principle.

"The National Assembly destroys entirely the feudal system," said the first article of the resolutions of August 5. But the following articles of August 5 to 11 explain that only the personal servitude degrading to honour should disappear entirely. *All the other dues, whatsoever their origin or nature, remained.* They might be redeemed one day, but there was nothing in the resolutions of August to indicate either when or under what conditions that could be done. No limit was imposed. Not the slightest suggestion was made as to the legal procedure by means of which the redemption would be made. Nothing—nothing but the principle, the *desideratum*. And, meanwhile, the peasant had to pay everything, as before.

There was something worse in these resolutions of August 1789. They opened the door to a measure by which redemption would be made impossible, and this was passed by the Assembly seven months later. In February 1790 they made redemption absolutely impossible for the peasant to accept, by imposing the joint redemption of all land rents, personal and real. M. Sagnac has remarked, on page 90 of his excellent work that Demeunier had already proposed on August 6 or 7 a measure of this kind. And the Assembly, as we shall see, made a law in February 1790, after which it became impossible to redeem the dues upon the *land* without redeeming at the same time, in the same lot, the *personal* services, abolished though they were since August 5, 1789.

Carried away by the enthusiasm with which Paris and France received the news of that all-night sitting of August 4, the historians have not given sufficient prominence to the extent of the restrictions which the Assembly put against the first clause of its decree by means of clauses voted in the sittings from August 5 to 11. Even Louis Blanc, who furnishes, however, in his chapter *La propriété devant la Révolution*,* the ideas necessary for the appreciation of the tenor of the resolutions passed in August, seems to hesitate at destroying the beautiful legend, and he glosses over the restrictions, or

* Book II. chap. i.

THE FEUDAL RIGHTS REMAIN

else tries even to excuse them in saying that "the logical sequence of facts in history is not so rapid, indeed far from it, as that of the ideas in the head of a thinker." But the fact remains that this vagueness, these doubts, these hesitations, which the Assembly flung to the peasants when they asked for measures, clear and precise, to abolish the old abuses, became the cause of the terrible struggles which were evolved during the four following years. It was not until after the expulsion of the Girondins that the question of the feudal rights came up again boldly and in its entirety, in the sense of Article 1 of the resolution of August 4.*

It is no use now, and at a distance of a hundred years, to declaim against the National Assembly. Indeed, the Assembly did all that could have been hoped for from an assembly of property owners and well-to-do middle-class men; perhaps it did even more. It gave forth a principle, and by so doing it invited, so to say, a further step. But it is very important to take into account these restrictions, for if the article which declared the total destruction of the feudal system is taken literally, we cannot fail to understand completely the four years of the Revolution which follow, and still more the struggles which broke out in the very midst of the Convention in 1793.

The resistance to these resolutions was immense. If they could not satisfy the peasants and if they became the signal for a powerful recrudescence of the peasant risings, to the nobles,

* Buchez and Roux (*Histoire parlementaire de la Révolution française*, vol. ii. p. 243) see in the abdications of August 4 only concessions rendered necessary by the debates on the "Declaration of the Rights of Man." The majority being in favour of this declaration, their vote would have infallibly carried with it the abolition of privileges. It is also interesting to note how Madame Elisabeth announced the night of August 4 to her friend, Madame de Mombelles: "The nobility," she writes, "with an enthusiasm worthy of the French heart, have renounced everything, the feudal rights and their hunting rights. Fishing will also be comprised, I believe. The clergy have likewise renounced the tithes and perquisites and the possibility of holding several benefices. This decree has been sent into all the provinces. *I hope this will put an end to the burning of the châteaux.* They have burned seventy." (Conches, *loc. cit.* p. 238.)

the higher clergy and the King these resolutions signified the spoliation of Church and nobility. From that day began the hidden agitation, which was fomented unceasingly and with an ever-growing ardour against the Revolution. The Assembly believed it could safeguard the rights of landed property, and in ordinary times a law of that kind might have attained this end. But in the villages people understood that the night of August 4 had dealt a tremendous blow at all feudal rights, and that the resolutions of August 5 to 11 had stripped the landlords of them, even though redemption of these rights was imposed upon the peasants. The general spirit of these resolutions, which included the abolition of the tithes, the rights of hunting and other privileges, clearly indicated to the people that the interests of the people are superior to the rights which property-owners may have acquired in the course of history. They contained the condemnation, in the name of justice, of all the hereditary privileges of feudalism. And henceforth nothing could rehabilitate those rights in the mind of the peasant.

The peasants understood that those rights were condemned and they rightly declined to buy them out. They just simply ceased to pay. But the Assembly, having neither the courage to abolish the feudal rights altogether, nor the inclination to work out a method of redemption that would be acceptable to the peasants, created in that way the equivocal conditions which were to bring forth civil war throughout France. On the one hand, the peasants understood that they need not buy anything, nor pay anything; that the Revolution had only to go on in order to abolish the feudal rights without redemption. On the other hand, the rich people understood that the resolutions of August had as yet abolished nothing except the mortmain and the sacrificed hunting rights; so that, by rallying themselves to the counter-revolution, and to the King as its representative, they would perhaps succeed in maintaining their feudal rights and in keeping the land that they and their ancestors had, under various pretexts, robbed from the village communes.

The King, probably by the advice of his counsellors, had

thoroughly understood the part assigned to him in the counter-revolution as a rallying-point for the defence of feudal privileges, and he hastened to write to the Archbishop of Arles to tell him that he would never give, except under compulsion, his sanction to the resolutions of August. "The sacrifice of the two first orders of the State is fine," he said; "but I can only admire it; I will never consent to the spoliation of my clergy and my nobility. I will not give my sanction to decrees which would despoil them."

And he continued to refuse his assent until he was led a prisoner to Paris by the people. And even when he gave it, he did everything, in conjunction with the property-owning clergy, nobles and middle classes, to couch his sanction in such a form as to render the resolutions of the Assembly dead letters.

My friend, James Guillaume, who has been so kind as to read my manuscript, has made a note on the question of the sanction of the resolutions (*arrêtés*) of August 4, which I here reproduce in entirety:

The Assembly at the time exercised both *constituent* and *legislative* power: and it had several times declared that its enactments, as a constituent power, were independent of the royal authority; only the *laws* had need of the King's sanction (they were called *decree* before the sanction, *law* after it).

The acts of August 4 were of a *constituent* nature: the Assembly had worded them as resolutions (*arrêtés*), but it did not think for a moment that it was necessary to obtain a permission from the King to state that the privileged persons had renounced their privileges. The character of these resolutions—or of this *resolution*, for sometimes they speak of it in the plural and sometimes in the singular—is indicated in the 19th and last Article, which says: "The National Assembly will occupy itself, immediately *after the constitution*, with drawing up the *laws* necessary for the development of the *principles* which it has *determined* by the present *resolution*, which will be forthwith sent by Messieurs the Deputies into all the provinces," &c. It was on August 11 that the publication of the resolutions was definitely adopted; at the same time the Assembly accorded to the King the title of "Restorer of French Liberty," and ordered that a *Te Deum* should be sung in the chapel of the palace.

On the 12th the president (Le Chapelier) went to ask the King when he would receive the Assembly for the *Te Deum;* the King replied that it would be on the 13th at noon. On the 13th the whole of the Assembly went to the palace; the president made a speech; he did not in the least ask for sanction; he explained to the King what the Assembly had done, and announced to him the title that had been accorded to him: Louis XVI. replied that he accepted the title with gratitude; he congratulated the Assembly and expressed his confidence in it. Then the *Te Deum* was sung in the chapel.

It mattered little that the King had written secretly to the archbishop to express a different sentiment: just then only public actions mattered.

Therefore *there was not the least public opposition* from the King, during the early days, against the resolutions of August 4.

But on Saturday, September 12, concerned at the disturbances which were agitating all France, the party of the "patriots" judged that, to put an end to them, it was necessary to make a solemn proclamation of the resolutions of August 4, and to this end the majority decided *that the resolutions should be presented for the King's sanction*, in spite of the opposition made to this decision by the counter-revolutionists, who would have preferred not to mention them further.

However, on Monday the 14th the patriots perceived that there might be some misunderstanding over this word "*sanction.*" Just at that point the Assembly discussed the "suspensive veto" of the King, and Barnave remarked that the veto could not be applied to the resolutions of August 4. Mirabeau spoke to the same effect. "The resolutions of August 4," he said, "were enacted by the constituent power, since when they cannot be subjected to sanction. The resolutions of August 4 are not laws, but principles and constitutional bases. Consequently, when you sent for sanction the acts of August 4, it was *for promulgation only* that you should have forwarded them." Le Chapelier, indeed, proposed to replace the word "sanction" in all concerning these resolutions by the word "promulgation," and added: "I maintain that it is useless to receive royal sanction for what his Majesty has already given authentic approbation to, as much by the letter, which he sent me when I had the honour to be the spokesman of the Assembly. (when president), as by the solemn acts of grace and the *Te Deum* sung in the King's Chapel."

It was proposed, therefore, to decree that the Assembly should suspend its order of the day (the question of the veto) until the promulgation of the resolutions of August 4 had been made by the King.

THE FEUDAL RIGHTS REMAIN

(Great noise and disorder.) The sitting was ended without arriving at any decision.

On the 15th there was a fresh discussion, without results. On the 16th and 17th other things were discussed, the succession to the Throne occupying attention.

At last, on the 18th, the King's reply arrived. He approved the general spirit of the articles of August 4, but there were some of them to which he could only give a conditional assent; and he concluded in these terms: "Therefore, I approve the greater number of these articles, and I will sanction them *when they shall be worded as laws*." This dilatory reply produced great discontent; it was repeated that the King had been asked only to *promulgate*, which he could not refuse to do. It was decided that the president should go to the King to beg him to order the promulgation at once. Confronted by the threatening language of the speakers in the Assembly, Louis XVI. knew that he must yield; but while yielding he cavilled over the words: he sent back to the president (Clermont Tonnerre) on the evening of September 20 a reply saying: "You have asked me to invest with my sanction the resolutions of August 4 . . . I have communicated to you the criticisms to which they seem to me to be susceptible . . . You ask me now to promulgate these same decrees; *promulgation* belongs to *laws*. . . . But I have already said that I approved of the general spirit of these resolutions. . . . I am going to order their *publication* throughout the kingdom. . . . I do not doubt but that I shall be able to invest with my sanction all the laws which you will decree upon the various matters contained in these resolutions."

If the resolutions of August 4 contained only principles, or theories, if we seek in them vainly for practicable *measures*, &c., it is so, because such must be the character of these *resolutions*, so clearly marked by the Assembly in Article 19. On August 4 the Assembly had proclaimed, in principle, the destruction of the feudal system; and it was added that the Assembly *would make* the *laws*, for the application of the *principle*, and that they would make these laws *when the Constitution should be completed*. We may reproach the Assembly for this method if we wish; but we must acknowledge that it deceived no one, and in no way broke its word by not making the laws *immediately*, since it had promised to make them *after the Constitution*. But, once the Constitution was completed, the Assembly had to dissolve and bequeath its work to the Legislative Assembly.

This note by James Guillaume throws a new light upon the

tactics of the Constituent Assembly. When the war against the châteaux had raised the question of feudal rights the Assembly had two courses before it. Either it could elaborate some scheme of laws upon feudal rights, schemes which would have taken months, or rather years, to discuss, and, seeing the diversity of opinions held by the representatives on this subject, would have ended only in dividing the Assembly. Or else the Assembly might have confined itself to proposing *only some principles*, which should serve as bases for the enactment of future laws.

It was this second alternative which was ordained by the Assembly. It hastened to compile in several sittings the *resolutions* which the King was finally obliged to publish. And in the provinces these declarations of the Assembly had the effect of so shaking the feudal system that, four years after, the Convention was able to vote for the complete aboliton of the feudal rights without redemption. Whether this was foreseen or not we do not know, but this alternative was, after all, preferable to the first.

CHAPTER XIX

DECLARATION OF THE RIGHTS OF MAN

Meaning and significance of Declaration—Modelled on Declaration of Independence—Its defects—Its influence—"Preamble to the Constitution"—Defiance of feudalism

A FEW days after the taking of the Bastille the Constitution Committee of the National Assembly met to discuss the "Declaration of the Rights of Man and of the Citizen." The idea of issuing such a declaration, suggested by the famous Declaration of Independence of the United States, was perfectly right. Since a revolution was in course of accomplishment, and a complete change in the relations between the various ranks of society would result from it, it was well to state its general principles before this change was expressed in the form of a Constitution. By this means the mass of the people would be shown how the revolutionary minorities conceived the revolution, and for what new principles they were calling on the people to struggle.

It would not be fine phrases merely; it would be a brief summary of the future that it was proposed to conquer; and under the solemn form of a declaration of rights, made by an entire people, this summary would be invested with the significance of a national oath. Proclaimed in a few words, the principles that they were going to put into practice would kindle the people's courage. It is always ideas that govern the world, and great ideas presented in a virile form have always taken hold of the minds of men. In fact the young North American republicans, at the time when they were intending to conquer their independence, had issued just such declarations, and ever since, the Declaration of Independence of the United States had become the charter, one might almost say the Decalogue, of the young North American nation.*

Consequently, as soon as the Assembly nominated (on July 9) a committee for the preparatory work of the Constitution, it was found necessary to draw up a Declaration of the Rights of Man, and the work was begun after July 14. The committee took for their model the Declaration of Independence of the United States, which had already become famous, since 1776, as a statement of democratic belief.† Unfortunately the defects in it were also copied ; that is to say, like the American Constitutionalists assembled in the Congress of Philadelphia, the National Assembly kept out of its declaration all allusions to the economic relations between citizens ; it confined itself to affirming the equality of all before the law, the right of the nation to give itself whatever government it wished, and the constitutional liberties of the individual. As to property, the French Declaration took care to affirm its "inviolable and sacred" character and it added that "nobody could be deprived

* "When in the course of human events," said the Declaration of Independence of the United States, "it becomes necessary for one people to dissolve the political bands which have connected them with another, and to assume among the Powers of the Earth the separate and equal station to which the Laws of Nature and of Nature's God entitle them, a decent respect to the opinions of mankind requires that they should declare the causes which impel them to the separation.

"We hold these Truths to be self-evident, that all men are created equal, that they are endowed by their Creator with certain unalienable Rights, that among these are Life, Liberty and the Pursuit of Happiness—that to secure these rights, Governments are instituted among men, deriving their just powers from the consent of the governed, *that whenever any form of government becomes destructive of these ends it is the right of the people to alter or to abolish it*, and to institute new government, laying its foundation on such principles, and organising its powers in such form, as to them shall seem most likely to effect their safety and happiness" (Declaration made in Philadelphia, July 4, 1776). This declaration certainly does not correspond to the communist aspirations proclaimed by numerous groups of citizens. But it expresses and indicates exactly their ideas concerning the political form which they wished to obtain, and it inspired the America s with a proud spirit of independence.

† James Guillaume has recalled this fact in his work, *La déclaration des droits de l'homme et du citoyen*, Paris, 1900, p. 9. The Reporter of the Constitutional Committee had indeed mentioned this fact. To be assured of this one has only to compare the texts of the French drafts with those of the American declaration given in J. Guillaume's book.

of his property if it were not that public necessity, *legally established*, clearly exacted it, and under the condition of a *just* and *previous* indemnity." This was to repudiate the right of the peasants to the land and to the abolition of the exactions of feudal origin.

The middle classes put forth in this way their liberal programme of equality before the law in judicial matters and of government controlled by the nation and existing only by its will. And, as in all minimum programmes, this signified implicitly that the nation must not go further; it must not touch upon the rights of property established by feudalism and despotic royalty.

It is probable that during the discussions raised by the drawing-up of the Declaration of the Rights of Man, some ideas of a social and equalising character were brought forward. But they must have been set aside. In any case we find no trace of them in the Declaration of 1789.* Sieyès' proposal that " if men are not equal in *means*, that is in riches, intellect, and strength, &c., it does not follow that they may not be equal in *rights* " †—even this idea, so modest in its claim, is not to be found in the Declaration of the Assembly. Instead of the foregoing words of Sieyès, the first article of the Declaration was conceived in these terms : " Men are born and live free and equal under the laws. Social distinctions may be established only on grounds of common utility " ; which allows that social distinctions might be established by law in the interest of the community, and, by means of that fiction, opens the door to all inequalities.

Altogether, when reading to-day the " Declaration of the Rights of Man and of the Citizen," we are tempted to ask if this declaration had really the influence over the minds of the period which historians attribute to it. It is evident that Article 1, which affirms the equality of rights for all men; Article

---

* In America the people of certain States demanded the proclamation of the common right of the whole nation to the whole of the land; but this idea, detestable from the middle-class point of view, was excluded from the Declaration of Indepndence.

† Article 16 of Sieyès' proposal (*La déclaration des droits de l'homme et du citoyen*, by James Guillaume, p. 30).

6, which says that the law should be "the same for all," and that "all the citizens have a right to co-operate, either personally or through their representatives, in its formation"; Article 10, by virtue of which "no one should be molested for his opinions, provided that their manifestation does not disturb the public order established by law"; and finally, Article 12, which declares that the public force was "instituted for the advantage of all—not for the special use of those to whom it is entrusted"—these affirmations, made in the midst of a society wherein feudal subjection still existed, and while the Royal family still considered itself the owner of France, worked a complete revolution in the minds of men.

But it is also certain that the Declaration of 1789 would have never had the influence it exercised later on in the course of the nineteenth century if the Revolution had stopped short at the limits of this profession of middle-class liberalism. Luckily the Revolution went much further. And when, two years later, in September 1791, the National Assembly drew up the Constitution, it added to the Declaration of the Rights of Man a "Preamble to the Constitution," which contained already these words: "The National Assembly . . . abolishes irrevocably the institutions that are hurtful to liberty and the equality of rights." And further, "There no longer exists either nobility, or peerage, or hereditary distinctions, or distinctions of orders, or *feudal system*, or *patrimonial courts of justice*, nor are there any titles, denominations and prerogatives which were derived from them, nor any order of chivalry, nor any such corporations which required proofs of nobility for entering them, or decorations which supposed distinctions of birth, *nor any other superiority except that of the public functionaries in the exercise of their functions.* There are no longer any guilds, nor corporations of professions, arts and crafts [the middle-class ideal of the State Omnipotent appears in these two paragraphs]. *The law does not recognise any longer either religious vows or any other pledge which would be contrary to natural laws and to the Constitution.*"

When we think that this defiance was flung to a Europe still plunged in the gloom of all-powerful royalty and feudal subjection, we understand why the French Declaration of the Rights of Man, often confounded with the Preamble of the Constitution which followed it, inspired the people during the wars of the Republic and became later on the watchword of progress for every nation in Europe during the nineteenth century. But it must not be forgotten that it was not the Assembly, nor even the middle classes of 1789 who expressed their desires in this Preamble. It was the popular revolution which was forcing them bit by bit to recognise the rights of the people and to break with feudalism—at the cost of what sacrifices we shall see presently.

CHAPTER XX

THE FIFTH AND SIXTH OF OCTOBER 1789

King refuses to sanction Declaration—Middle classes and people in opposition to royalty—Influence of people on upper classes—Power of King's *veto* during Revolution—Assembly refuse King the *veto*, but grant him the *suspensive veto*—Weakness of Assembly—Scarcity of food in Paris—Accusations against royal family and people at Court—Danger of national bankruptcy—Plans for King's escape—Influence of history of Charles I. on Louis XVI.—His terror of Revolution—Plotting continues—Preparations for march on Versailles—Precautions of King—Outbreak of insurrection—March on Versailles—Queen chief object of people's animosity—Entry of women into Versailles—King sanctions Declaration of Rights of Man—Lafayette sets out for Versailles—Terror at Court—End of Monarchy of Versailles

EVIDENTLY to the King and the Court the "Declaration of the Rights of Man and of the Citizen" must have seemed a criminal attempt upon all the laws, human and divine. The King, therefore, bluntly refused to give it his sanction. It is true that, like the "resolutions" passed between August 4 and 11, the Declaration of Rights represented only an affirmation of principles; it had, therefore, as they said then, a "constituent character" (*un caractère constituant*), and as such it did not need the royal sanction. The King had but to promulgate it.

Now this is what he refused to do under various pretexts. On October 5 he wrote again to the Assembly to say that he wished to see how the maxims of the Declaration would be applied before giving it his sanction.*

* "I do not quite understand the Declaration of the Rights of Man: it contains very good maxims, suitable for guiding your labours. But it contains some principles that require explanations, and are even

He had opposed, as we have seen, by a similar refusal, the resolutions of August 4 to 11, concerning the abolition of the feudal rights, and it can be imagined what a weapon the Assembly made of these two refusals. What! the Assembly was abolishing the feudal system, personal subjection and the pernicious prerogatives of the lords, it was proclaiming the equality of all before the law—and see how the King, but especially the princes, the Queen, the Court, the Polignacs, the Lamballes and all the rest of them, are opposing it! If it were only a matter of speeches in favour of equality, the circulation of which had been prevented! But no, the whole Assembly, including the nobles and the bishops, were all agreed to make a law favourable to the people and to do away with all privileges (for the people who do not pay much heed to legal terms, the "resolutions" were as good as "laws"), and now the Court party are going to prevent these laws coming into force! The King would have accepted them; he came to fraternise with the people of Paris after July 14; but it is the Court, the princes, the Queen, who are opposed to the attempt of the Assembly to secure the happiness of the people.

In the great duel between royalty and the middle classes, the latter thus had got the people on their side. At this moment public opinion was really inflamed against the princes, the Queen, and the upper classes on account of the Assembly, whose labours they began to follow with interest.

At the same time the people themselves were influencing those labours in a democratic sense. Thus the Assembly might perhaps have accepted the scheme of two Chambers "in the English fashion." But the people would not have it. They understood instinctively what learned jurists have since so well explained—that in revolution a second Chamber was impossible: it could only act when the revolution was exhausted and a period of reaction had begun.

Similarly, it was also the people of Paris who were more vehemently opposed to the royal *veto* than those who sat in

liable to different interpretations, which cannot be fully appreciated until the time when their true meaning will be fixed by the laws to which the Declaration will serve as the basis. Signed: Louis."

the Assembly. Here, too, the masses understood the situation quite clearly; for if, in the normal course of affairs, the power of the King to check a decision of the parliament loses much of its importance, it is quite another thing in a revolutionary period. Not that the royal power becomes less dangerous in the long run; but in ordinary times a parliament being the organ of privileged persons will seldom pass anything that the King would have to veto in the interest of the privileged classes; while during a revolutionary period the decisions of a parliament, influenced as they are by the popular spirit of the moment, may often tend towards the destruction of ancient privileges, and, consequently, they will encounter opposition from the King. He will use his *veto*, if he has the right and the strength to use it. This is, in fact, what happened with the Assembly's " resolutions " of August, and even with the Declaration of Rights.

In spite of this, there was in the Assembly a numerous party who desired the absolute *veto*—that is to say, they wished to give the King the possibility of legally preventing any measure he might choose to prevent; and it took lengthy debates to arrive at a compromise. The Assembly refused the absolute *veto*, but they accepted, against the will of the people, the *suspensive veto*, which permitted the King to suspend a decree for a certain time, without altogether annulling it.

At a distance of a hundred years the historian is naturally inclined to idealise the Assembly and to represent it as a body that was ready to fight for the Revolution. In reality it was not. The fact is that even in its most advanced representatives the National Assembly remained far below the requirements of the moment. It must have been conscious of its own impotence. Far from being homogeneous, it contained, on the contrary, more than three hundred deputies—four hundred according to other estimates; that is to say, more than one-third, ready to come to terms with royalty. Therefore, without speaking of those members who were pledged to the Court, and there were several of them, how many feared the revolution much more than the royal power! But the revolution had begun, and there was the direct pressure of the people and the fear of their rage ; there was also that intellectual atmosphere which dominates the timorous and forces the prudent to follow the more advanced ones. Moreover the people maintained their menacing attitude, and the memory of de Launey, Foulon and Bertier was still fresh in their minds. In the faubourgs of Paris there was even talk of massacring those members of the Assembly whom the people suspected of having connections with the Court.

Meanwhile the scarcity of food in Paris was always terrible. It was September, the harvest had been gathered in, but still there was a lack of bread. Long files of men and women stood every night at the bakers' doors, and after long hours of waiting the poor often went away without any bread. In spite of th purchase of grain that the Government had made abroad, and the premium paid to those who imported wheat to Paris, bread was scarce in the capital, as well as in all the large towns, and in the small towns near Paris. The measures taken for revictualling were insufficient, and what was done was paralysed by fraud. All the vices of the *ancien régime*, of the centralised State which was growing up since the sixteenth century, became apparent in this question of bread. In the upper circles the refinement of luxury had attained its limits ; but the mass of the people, flayed without mercy, had come to the point of not being able to produce its own food on the rich soil and in the productive climate of France !

Besides, the most terrible accusations were being circulated against the princes of the royal family and personages in the highest positions at Court. They had re-established, it was said, the " famine compact," and were speculating on the rise of prices of the bread-stuffs. And these rumours, as it appeared later on, were not quite unfounded.

To complete all, the danger of national bankruptcy was imminent. Interest on State debts had to be paid immediately, but the expenses were increasing, and the Treasury was empty. No one dared now to resort to the abominable means which were habitual under the old *régime* for levying the taxes, when everything in the peasant's home was seized by the tax collector; whilst the peasants, on their side, in the expectation of a more just assessment of the taxes, preferred not to pay, and the rich, who hated the Revolution, with secret joy refrained from paying anything whatever. Necker, again in the Ministry since July 17, 1789, had tried various ingenious expedients for avoiding bankruptcy—but without success. In fact, one cannot well see how bankruptcy could be prevented without either resorting to a forced loan from the rich, or seizing the wealth of the clergy. The middle classes understood it, and became resigned to such drastic measures, since they had lent their money to the State and did not wish to lose it. But the King, the Court and the higher ecclesiastics, would they ever agree to this seizure of their properties by the State?

A strange feeling must have taken possession of men's minds during the months of August and September 1789. At last the desire of so many years was realised. Here was a National Assembly which held in its hands the legislative power. An Assembly which had already proved itself not quite hostile to a democratic, reforming spirit; and now it was reduced to impotence, and to the ridicule attendant on impotency. It could make decrees to avoid bankruptcy, but the King, the Court, the princes would refuse to sanction them. Like so many ghosts of the past, they had the power to strangle the representation of the French people, to paralyse its will, to prolong to infinity the provisional unsettled state of affairs.

More than that: these ghosts were preparing a great *coup*. In the King's household they were making plans for his escape from Versailles. The King would shortly be carried off to Rambouillet, or to Orléans, where he would put himself at the head of the armies, and thence he would threaten Versailles and Paris. Or else he might fly towards the eastern frontier and there await the arrival of the German and Austrian armies which the *émigrés* had promised him. All sorts of influences were thus intermingling at the palace: that of the Duke of Orléans, who dreamed of seizing the throne after the departure of Louis; that of "Monsieur," the brother of Louis XVI., who would have been delighted if his brother, as well as Marie-Antoinette, whom he hated personally, had disappeared.

Since the month of September the Court meditated the escape of the King; but if they discussed many plans, they dared not carry out any one of them. It is very likely that Louis XVI. and his wife dreamed of repeating the history of Charles I., and of waging a regular war against the parliament only with better success. The history of the English King obsessed them: it fascinated them; but they read it, as prisoners awaiting trial read police stories. They drew from it no instruction as to the necessity of yielding in time: they only said to themselves: "Here they ought to have resisted; there it was necessary to plot; there again daring was required!" And so they made plans, which neither they nor their courtiers had the courage to put into execution.

The Revolution held them spell-bound; they saw the monster that was going to devour them, and they dared neither submit nor resist. Paris, which was already preparing to march upon Versailles, filled them with terror and paralysed their efforts. "What if the army falters at the supreme moment, when the battle has begun? What if the commanders betray the King, as so many of them have done already? What would be left to do then if not to share the fate of Charles I.?"

And yet they plotted. Neither the King nor his courtiers, nor the privileged classes as a whole could understand that the time for compromise was far away; that now the only way was frankly to submit to the new force and to place the royal power under its protection—for the Assembly asked nothing better than to grant its protection to the King. Instead of that, they plotted, and by so doing they impelled those members of the Assembly who were, after all, very moderate, into counter-plots: they drove them towards revolutionary action. This is why Mirabeau and others, who would have willingly worked at the establishing of a moderately constitutional monarchy, had to throw in their lot with the advanced sections. And this is why moderates, like Duport, constituted "the confederation of the clubs," which allowed them to keep the people in a state of ferment, for they felt they would soon have need of the masses.

The march upon Versailles on October 5, 1789, was not as spontaneous as it was supposed to be. Even in a Revolution every popular movement requires to be prepared by men of the people, and this one had its forerunners. Already on August 30 the Marquis of Saint-Huruge, one of the popular orators of the Palais Royal, had wanted to march on Versailles with fifteen hundred men to demand the dismissal of the "ignorant, corrupt and suspected" deputies, who were defending the suspensive *veto* of the King. Meanwhile they threatened to set fire to the châteaux of those deputies, and warned them that two thousand letters had been sent into the provinces to that effect. The gathering was dispersed, but the idea of a march upon Versailles was thrown out, and it continued to be discussed.

On August 31 the Palais Royal sent to the Hôtel de Ville five deputations, one of which was headed by Loustalot, the most sympathetic of republican writers, asking the municipality of Paris to exercise pressure upon the Assembly to prevent its acceptance of the royal *veto*. Some of those who took part in these deputations went to threaten the deputies, others to implore them. At Versailles the crowd, in tears, begged Mirabeau to abandon the defence of the absolute *veto*, justly remarking that if the King had this right he would no longer have need of the Assembly.*

From this time, the idea began to grow that it would be well to have the Assembly and the King at hand in Paris. In fact, since the first days of September, there was open speaking already at the Palais Royal about bringing the King and "M. le Dauphin" to Paris, and for this purpose all good citizens were exhorted to march on Versailles. The *Mercure de France* made mention of it on September 5 (page 84), and Mirabeau spoke of women who would march on Versailles a fortnight before the event.

The banquet given to the Guards on October 3, and the

* Buchez and Roux, p. 368 *et seq.* Bailly, *Mémoires*, ii. 326, 341.

OCTOBER 5 AND 6, 1789

plots of the Court, hastened events. Every one had a foreboding of the blow which the party of reaction was preparing to strike. Reaction was raising its head; the Municipal Council of Paris, essentially middle class, became bold in reactionary ways. The royalists were organising their forces without troubling much to conceal the fact. The road from Paris to Metz having been lined with troops, the carrying off of the King and his going to Metz were discussed openly. The Marquis de Bouillé, who commanded the troops in the East, as well as de Breteuil and de Mercy were in the plot, of which de Breteuil had taken the direction. For this end the Court collected as much money as possible, and October 5 was spoken of as the possible date of the flight. The King would set out that day for Metz, where he would place himself in the midst of the army commanded by the Marquis de Bouillé. There he would summon to him the nobility and the troops which still held faithful, and would declare the Assembly rebellious.

With this movement in view they had doubled at the palace the number of the body-guards (young members of the aristocracy charged with the guarding of the palace), and the regiment of Flanders had been summoned to Versailles, as well as the dragoons. The regiment came, and on October 1 a great banquet was given by the body-guard to the regiment of Flanders, and the officers of the dragoons and of the Swiss in garrison at Versailles were invited to this banquet.

During the dinner Marie-Antoinette and the Court ladies, as well as the King, did all they could to bring the royalist enthusiasm of the officers to a white heat. The ladies themselves distributed white cockades, and the National cockade was trodden underfoot. Two days later, on October 3, another banquet of the same kind took place.

These banquets precipitated events. The news of them soon reached Paris—exaggerated perhaps on the way—and the people of the capital understood that if they did not march immediately upon Versailles, Versailles would march upon Paris.

The Court was evidently preparing a great blow. Once the King, having left Versailles, was safe somewhere in the midst of his troops, nothing would be easier than to dissolve the Assembly, or else compel it to return to the Three Orders —that is to say, to the position before the Royal Session of June 23. In the Assembly itself there was a strong party of some four hundred members, the leaders of whom had already held confabulations with Malouet for the transference of the Assembly to Tours, far from the revolutionary people of Paris. If this plot of the Court succeeded, then all the hitherto obtained results would be upset. The fruits of July 14 would be lost; lost, too, the results of the rising of the peasants and of the panic of August 4.

What was to be done to prevent such a disaster? *The people had to be roused—nothing less than that would do!* And therein lies the glory of the prominent revolutionists of that moment; they understood the necessity of a popular rising and accepted it, though usually the middle classes recoil before such a measure. To rouse the people—the gloomy, miserable masses of the people of Paris—this is what the revolutionists undertook to do on October 4; Danton, Marat and Loustalot, whose names we have already mentioned, being the most ardent in the task. A handful of conspirators cannot fight an army; reaction cannot be vanquished by a band of men, howsoever determined they may be. To an army must be opposed an army, and, failing an army—the people, the whole people, the hundreds of thousands of men, women and children of a city. They alone can be victorious, they alone have conquered armies by demoralising them, by paralysing their brute force.

On October 5 the insurrection broke out in Paris to the cry of "Bread! Bread!" The sound of the drum beaten by a young girl served to rally the women. Soon a troop of women was formed; it marched to the Hôtel de Ville, forced the doors of the Communal Hall, demanding bread and arms, and, as a march upon Versailles had already been talked of for several days, the cry "To Versailles!" attracted crowds of women. Maillard, known in Paris since July 14 for the part he had taken in the siege of the Bastille, was declared leader of the column, and the women set out.

A thousand diverse ideas no doubt crossed their minds, but that of bread must have dominated all others. It was at Versailles that the conspiracies against the happiness of the people were hatched; it was there that the famine compact had been made, there that the abolition of the feudal rights was being prevented—so the women marched on Versailles. It is more than probable that among the mass of the people the King, like all Kings, was regarded as a good enough creature, who wished the welfare of his people. The royal prestige was then still deeply rooted in the minds of men. But even in 1789 they hated the Queen. The words uttered about her were terrible. "Where is that rip? Look at her, the dirty whore; we must catch hold of that bitch and cut her throat," said the women, and one is struck by the ardour, the pleasure, I might say, with which these remarks were written down in the inquiry at the Châtelet. Here again the people judged soundly. If the King had said, on learning about the fiasco of the Royal Session on June 23, " After all, let these wretches stay!"—Marie-Antoinette was wounded to the heart by it. She received with supreme disdain the "plebeian" King when he came on his return from his visit to Paris on July 17, wearing the tricolour cockade, and since then she had become the centre of all the intrigues. The correspondence which later she carried on with Count Fersen about bringing the foreign armies to Paris originated from that moment. Even this night of October 5, when the women invaded the palace —this very night, says the extremely reactionary Madame Campan, the Queen received Fersen in her bedchamber.

The people knew all this, partly through the palace servants; and the crowd, the collective mind of the people of Paris, understood what individuals were slow to comprehend—that Marie-Antoinette would go far in her hatred of the Revolution, and that, in order to prevent all the plottings of the Court, it was necessary that the King and his family, and the Assembly as well, should be kept in Paris under the eye of the people.

At first, on entering Versailles, the women, crushed by

fatigue and hunger, soaked through with the downpour of rain, contented themselves with demanding bread. When they invaded the Assembly they sank exhausted on the benches of the deputies; but nevertheless, by their presence alone these women had already gained a first victory. The Assembly profited by this march upon Versailles to obtain from the King his sanction for the Declaration of the Rights of Man.

After the women had started from Paris, men had also begun to march, and then, about seven o'clock in the evening, to prevent any mishap at the palace, Lafayette set out for Versailles at the head of the National Guards.

Terror seized upon the Court. "It is all Paris, then, that is marching against the palace?" The Court held a council, but without arriving at any decision. Carriages had already been ordered out to send off the King and his family, but they were discovered by a picket of National Guards, who sent them back to the stables.

The arrival of the middle-class National Guards, the efforts of Lafayette, and above all, perhaps, a heavy rain, caused the crowd which choked the streets of Versailles, the Assembly and the purlieus of the palace, to diminish by degrees. But about five or six in the morning some men and women found at last a little gate open which enabled them to enter the palace. In a few moments they had found out the bedchamber of the Queen, who had barely time to escape to the King's apartment; otherwise she might have been hacked to pieces. The body-guard were in similar danger when Lafayette rode up, just in time to save them.

The invasion of the palace by the crowd was one of those defeats of royalty from which it never recovered. Lafayette obtained from the crowds some cheering for the King when he appeared upon a balcony. He even extracted from the crowd some cheers for the Queen by making her appear on the balcony with her son, and by kissing respectfully the hand of her whom the people called "the Medicis" . . . but all that was only a bit of theatricality. The people had realised their strength, and they used it to compel the King to set out for Paris. The middle classes then tried to make all sorts of royalist demonstrations on the occasion of the entrance of the King into his capital, but the people understood that *henceforth the King would be their prisoner*, and Louis XVI. on entering the Tuileries, abandoned since the reign of Louis XIV., had no illusions about it. " Let every one put himself where he pleases ! " was his reply when he was asked to give orders, and he asked for the history of Charles I. to be brought to him from his library.

The great monarchy of Versailles had come to an end. For the future there would be " Citizen Kings " or emperors who attained the throne by fraud ; but the reign of the " Kings by the Grace of God " was gone.

Once more, as on July 14, *the people*, by solidarity and by their action, had paralysed the plots of the Court and dealt a heavy blow at the old *régime*. The Revolution was making a leap forward.

CHAPTER XXI

FEARS OF THE MIDDLE CLASSES—THE NEW MUNICIPAL ORGANISATION

Unexpected reaction sets in—Exultation of revolutionists—Their misconception of the situation—Reaction *versus* Revolution—Aims of middle classes—Assembly, afraid of people, strengthens its position—Council of Three Hundred establishes its authority—Importance of Bailly and Lafayette—Martial law voted—Marat, Robespierre and Buzot alone protest—Intrigues of Duke of Orléans and Count de Pro ence—Mirabeau—Aims of educated middle class—Duport, Charles de Lameth and Barnavo—Bailly and Lafayette—Alarm of middle classes at insurrection—Proposal of Sieyès accepted—Ancient feudal divisions abolished—France divided into departments—Electoral Assemblies—Difference between *passive* and *active* citizens—General assemblies of village communes forbidden—Importance to Revolution of municipal centres—Parliaments abolished—Formidable opposition to new organisation

ONCE more one might have thought that the Revolution would now freely develop of itself. Royal reaction was vanquished; "Monsieur and Madame Veto" had given in, and were held as prisoners in Paris; and the National Assembly would surely use now the axe in the forest of abuses, hew down feudalism, and apply the great principles it had proclaimed in the Declaration of the Rights of Man, the mere reading of which had made all hearts throb.

There was, however, nothing of the sort. Against all expectations, it was reaction that began after October 5. It organised its powers, and went on, growing in strength until the month of June 1792.

After having accomplished its task, the people of Paris retreated to their hovels; the middle classes disbanded them and made them leave the streets. And had it not been for the peasant insurrection, which followed its course until the feudal rights were actually abolished in July 1793, had it not been for the numerous insurrections in the provincial towns which prevented the government of the middle classes from firmly establishing itself, the final reaction, which triumphed in 1794, might have been already triumphant in 1791 or even in 1790.

"The King is at the Louvre, the National Assembly at the Tuileries, the channels of circulation are cleared, the marketplace is full of sacks of corn, the National exchequer is being replenished, the mills are turning, the traitors are flying, the shavelings are down, the aristocracy is expiring," thus Camille Desmoulins wrote in the first number of his journal (November 28). But in reality reaction was everywhere raising its head. While the revolutionaries exulted, believing that the Revolution was almost accomplished, the reactionaries knew that the great struggle, the real one, between the past and the future, was only to begin in every provincial town, great and small, in every little village; that now was the time for them to act in order to get the upper hand in the revolution.

The reactionaries understood something more. They saw that the middle classes, who until then had sought the support of the people, in order to obtain constitutional laws and to dominate the higher nobility, were going, now that they had seen and felt the strength of the people, to do all they could to dominate the people, to disarm them and to drive them back into subjection.

This fear of the people made itself felt in the Assembly, immediately after October 5. More than two hundred deputies refused to go to Paris, and demanded passports for returning to their homes. They met with a refusal, and were treated as traitors, but a certain number of them sent in their resignations all the same: they were not thinking of going so far! There was now a new series of emigrations, as there had been after July 14. But this time it was not the Court which gave the signal, it was the Assembly.

However, there was in the Assembly strong nucleus of middle-class representatives who knew how to profit by the first moments of success—to establish the power of their own class upon a solid foundation. Consequently, even before moving to Paris, the Assembly voted, on October 19, the responsibility of the ministers, as well as of administrative officials before the National representation, and the assessment of all taxes by the Assembly. These two first conditions of a Constitutional Government were thus established. The title of the " King of France " was also changed into " King of the French."

Whilst the Assembly was thus profiting by the movement of October 5 to establish itself as the sovereign power, the middle-class municipality of Paris, *i.e.*, the Council of the Three Hundred, which had set itself up after July 14, also took advantage of events to establish its authority. Sixty directors, chosen from among the Three Hundred, and divided between eight departments—food, police, public works, hospitals, education, land and revenues, taxes and the National Guard—were going to take over all these important branches of administration, and thus to become a respectable power, especially as the municipality had under its orders a National Guard of 60,000 men, drawn solely from well-to-do citizens.

Bailly, the Mayor of Paris, and Lafayette, the chief commander of the National Guard, were becoming important personages. As to the municipal police functions, the middle classes assumed the right of supervision in everything: meetings, newspapers, the selling of literature in the streets, the advertisement posters, and so on ; so as to be able to suppress all that might be hostile to their interests.

And finally, the Council of the Three Hundred, taking advantage of the murder of a baker on October 21, went to the Assembly to beg for martial law, which was voted at once. Henceforth it was sufficient for a municipal official to unfurl the red flag for martial law to be proclaimed ; after that every crowd had to disperse, and the troops, when required by the municipal official, could fire upon the people if they did not disperse after three summonses had been made. If the people dispersed peaceably without resistance, before the last summons, only the ringleaders of the disturbance were arrested and sent to prison for three years—if the crowd was unarmed; otherwise the sentence was death. But in case of any violence committed by the people, it was death for all concerned in the riot. It was death, too, for any soldier or officer of the National Guard who should stir up any rioting.

A murder committed in the street was thus sufficient excuse for this law to be passed, and, as Louis Blanc has aptly remarked, in the whole press of Paris there was but one voice, that of Marat, to protest against this atrocious law, and to say that in a time of revolution, when a nation had still to break its chains and to fight to the bitter end against its enemies, martial law had no right to exist. In the Assembly, Robespierre and Buzot were the only ones to protest, and these not on a point of principle. It was not advisable, they said, to proclaim martial law before having established a court which could try the criminals for felony against the nation.

Profiting by the slackening of the people's ardour, which necessarily followed after the movement of October 5 and 6, the middle classes began, also in the Assembly, as in the municipality, to organise their new power—not, it is true, without some collisions between the personal ambitions which clashed and conspired against each other.

The Court on its side saw no reason for abdicating; it conspired and struggled also, and made profit out of the necessitous and ambitious, such as Mirabeau, by enrolling them in its service.

The Duke of Orléans, having been compromised in the movement of October 5, which he had secretly supported, was sent in disgrace, by the Court, as ambassador to England. But then it was "Monsieur," the Count of Provence, the King's brother, who began intriguing to send away the King— "the log" (*soliveau*), as he wrote to a friend. Once the King had gone, Orléans could pose as a candidate for the throne of France. Mirabeau, always in want, and who, ever since June 23, had acquired a formidable power over the Assembly, was intriguing on his side to get into the Ministry. When his plots were thwarted by the Assembly, which voted that none of its members should accept a place in the Ministry, he threw himself into the arms of the Count of Provence, in the hope of getting into power by his intervention. Finally, he sold himself to the King and accepted from him a pension of fifty thousand francs a month for four months, and the promise of an embassy; in return for which M. de Mirabeau pledged himself "to aid the King with his knowledge, his power and his eloquence, in whatever Monsieur will judge useful to the State and in the interest of the King." All this, however, only became known later on, in 1792, after the taking of the Tuileries, and, meanwhile, Mirabeau kept, until his death on April 2, 1791, his reputation as a champion of the people.

Historians will never unravel the tissue of intrigues which was then being woven round the Louvre and in the palaces of the princes, as well as round the Courts of London, Vienna and Madrid, and in the various German principalities. Quite a world fermented round the royalty which was perishing. And even in the midst of the Assembly, how many ambitions were struggling to grasp the power! But after all, these are but incidents of small value. They help to explain certain facts, but they could change nothing in the progress of events, marked out by the very logic of the situation and the forces in the conflict.

The Assembly represented the educated middle classes on their way to conquer and organise the power which was falling from the hands of the Court, the higher clergy, and the great nobles. And it contained in its midst a number of men marching straight towards this end with intelligence and a certain audacity, which increased every time that the people gained a fresh victory over the old *régime*. There was in the Assembly a "triumvirate" composed of Duport, Charles de Lameth, and Barnave, and at Paris there were the Mayor Bailly and the commander of the National Guard, Lafayette, upon whom all eyes were turned. But the real power of the mement was represented by the compact forces of the Assembly which were elaborating the laws to constitute the government of the middle classes.

This was the work which the Assembly resumed with ardour,

as soon as it was installed in Paris and could go on with its work with a certain amount of tranquillity.

This work was begun, as we have seen, the very day after the taking of the Bastille. The middle classes were seized with alarm when they saw the people arming themselves with pikes in a few days, burning the toll-gates, seizing the breadstuffs wherever they found them, and all the while showing as much hostility to the rich middle classes as towards the "red heels" (*talons rouges*). They made haste to arm themselves and to organise *their* National Guard—to array the "beaver hats" against the "woollen caps" and the pikes, so that the popular insurrections could be kept in hand. And after the insurrection on October 5, they passed without delay the law about rioting, of which we have just spoken.

At the same time they made haste to legislate in such a way that the political power which was slipping out of the hand of the Court should not fall into the hands of the people. Thus, eight days after July 14, Sieyès, the famous advocate of the Third Estate, had already proposed to the Assembly to divide the French into two classes, of which one only, the *active* citizens, should take part in the government, whilst the other, comprising the great mass of the people under the name of the *passive* citizens, should be deprived of all political rights. Five weeks later the Assembly accepted this division as the basis for the Constitution. The Declaration of Rights, of which the first principle was Equality of Rights for all citizens, was thus flagrantly violated as soon as proclaimed.

Now, on resuming the work of political organisation for France, the Assembly abolished the ancient feudal division into provinces, of which each one preserved certain privileges for the nobility and the *parlements*. It divided France into departments, and suspended the ancient *parlements*, *i.e.*, the ancient tribunals, which also possessed certain judicial privileges—and it went on to the organisation of an entirely new and uniform administration, always maintaining the principle of excluding the poorer classes from the Government.

The National Assembly, which had been elected under the old *régime* under a system of elections in two degrees, was nevertheless the outcome of an almost universal suffrage. That is to say, that the *primary assemblies*, which had been convoked in every electoral division, were composed of nearly all the citizens of the locality. These primary assemblies had nominated the *electors*, who made up in each division one *electoral* assembly, and this, in its turn, chose its representative in the National Assembly. It is well to note that after the elections the electoral assemblies continued to meet, receiving letters from their deputies and keeping watch over their votes.

Having now attained power, the middle classes did two things. They extended the prerogatives of the electoral assemblies, by confiding to them the election of the local councils (the *directoires* of each department), the judges and certain other functionaries. They gave them thus a great power. But, at the same time, they excluded from the primary assemblies the mass of the people, whom by this means they deprived of all political rights. They admitted into them only the *active* citizens, that is, those who paid in direct contributions at least three days' work.* The rest became *passive* citizens, who could no longer take part in the primary assemblies, and accordingly had no right to nominate the electors, or the municipality, or any of the local authorities. Besides, they could no longer form part of the National Guard.†

Furthermore, to be eligible as an elector, it was necessary to pay, in direct taxes, the value of *ten* days' work, which made these assemblies entirely middle class. Later on, in 1791, when reaction was emboldened by the massacre on the Champ-de-Mars, the Assembly made an additional restriction: electors must possess landed property. And to be nominated a representative of the people in the National Assembly, it was necessary to pay in direct taxation the value of a *marc* of silver (eight ounces), that is to say, fifty livres.‡

* Each municipality fixed the value, in money, of the day, and it was agreed to take for a basis the day of a journeyman.
† The municipal law of December 14, 1789, not only excluded the *passive* citizens from all the elections of municipal officers (paragraphs 5, 6, 8, &c.), but it also forbade the electoral assemblies to meet " by trades, professions or guilds." They could only meet by quarters, or districts.
‡ The *livre* had the value of about one franc.

And finally, the *permanence* of the electoral assemblies was interdicted. Once the elections were over, these assemblies were not to meet again. Once the middle-class governors were appointed, they must not be controlled too strictly. Soon the right even of petitioning and of passing resolutions was taken away—" Vote and hold your tongue ! "

As to the villages, they had preserved, as we have seen, under the old *régime*, in nearly the whole of France, up to the Revolution, the general assembly of the inhabitants, like the *mir* in Russia. To this general assembly belonged the administration of the affairs of the commune, such as the re-division and the use of the communal lands—cultivated fields, meadows and forests, and also the waste lands. But now these general assemblies of the village communes were forbidden by the municipal law of December 22 to 24, 1789. Henceforth only the well-to-do peasants, the *active* citizens, had the right to meet, *once a year*, to nominate the mayor and the municipality, composed of three or four middle-class men of the village.

A similar municipal organisation was given to the towns, where the *active* citizens met to nominate the general council of the town and the municipality, that is to say, the legislative power in municipal matters and the executive power to whom was entrusted the administration of the commune's police and the command of the National Guard.

Thus the movement described as taking place in the towns in July 1789, and which consisted in obtaining by revolutionary means an elective municipal administration at a time when the laws of the old *régime*, still in full force, authorised nothing of the kind—this movement was sanctioned by the municipal and administrative law of December 22 to 24, 1789. And, as we shall see, an immense power was conferred on the Revolution by the creation, at its very outset, of these thirty thousand municipal centres, independent in a thousand matters of the central government, and capable of revolutionary action, when the revolutionaries succeeded in seizing upon them.

It is true that the middle classes surrounded themselves with every precaution in order to keep the municipal power in the hands of the well-to-do members of the community, and the municipalities themselves were placed under the supervision of the councils of the department, which, being chosen by electors in the second degree, thus represented the wealthier section of the middle classes and were the support and the right hand of the counter-revolutionists during the Revolution. On the other hand, the municipality itself, which was elected by the *active* citizens only, also represented the middle classes more than the masses of the people, and in towns like Lyons and so many others it became a centre of reaction. But with all that, the municipalities were not dependent upon the royal power, and it must be recognised that the municipal law of December 1789 contributed to the success of the Revolution more than any other law. During the insurrection against the feudal lords, in August 1789, many municipalities were hostile to the revolted peasants, and we saw how the municipalities of the Dauphiné took the field against the peasants and hanged the rebels without mercy. But in proportion as the Revolution developed, the people came to get hold of the municipalities, and in 1793 and 1794 the municipalities in several parts of France became the real centres of action for the popular revolutionaries.

Another very important step was made by the National Assembly when it abolished the old courts of justice—the *parlements*—and introduced judges elected by the people. In the rural districts, each canton, composed of five or six parishes, appointed, through its *active* citizens, its own magistrates; and in the large towns this right was given to the electoral assemblies. The old *parlements* naturally strove to maintain their prerogatives. In the south, for instance at Toulouse, eighty members of the *parlements*, supported by eighty-nine gentlemen, even started a movement to restore to the monarch his legitimate authority and "liberty," and to religion "its useful influence." At Paris, Rouen and Metz, and in Brittany the *parlements* would not submit to the levelling power of the Assembly, and they headed conspiracies in favour of the old *régime*.

But they found no support among the people, and they

were compelled to yield to the decree of November 3, 1789, by which they were sent on vacation until a new order was given. The attempts to resist led only to a new decree, on January 11, 1790, by which it was declared that the resistance to the law by the magistrates of Rennes " disqualified them from fulfilling any functions of the active citizen, until, having sent in their request to the legislative body, they had been admitted to take the oath of fidelity to the Constitution, as decreed by the National Assembly and accepted by the King."

The National Assembly, it can be seen, meant to make its decisions concerning the new administrative organisation for France respected. But this new organisation encountered a formidable opposition on the part of the higher clergy, the nobility and the upper middle classes, and it took years of a revolution, much more far-reaching than the middle classes had intended, to break down the old organisation for the admission of the new.

CHAPTER XXII

FINANCIAL DIFFICULTIES—SALE OF CHURCH PROPERTY

Necessity of avoiding bankruptcy—Assembly determine to seize Church property—Value of Church revenue—Its unequal distribution—Proposals of Bishop of Autun—Alarm of wealthy clergy—Delight of middle classes—Expropriation voted—Suppression of monastic orders—Paper currency—Administration of Church property transferred to municipalities—Clergy henceforward deadly enemies of Revolution—Organisation of French Church—Effects of new organisation—Constituent Assembly works essentially for middle class—Need of " wind from the street "

THE greatest difficulty for the Revolution was that it had to make its way in the midst of frightful economic circumstances. State bankruptcy was still hanging threateningly over the heads of those who had undertaken to govern France, and if this bankruptcy came indeed, it would bring with it the revolt of the whole of the upper middle classes against the Revolution. If the deficit had been one of the causes which forced royalty to make the first constitutional concessions, and gave the middle classes courage to demand seriously their share in the Government, this same deficit weighed, like a nightmare, all through the Revolution upon those who were successively pushed into power.

It is true that, as the State loans were not international in those times, France had not the fear of foreign nations coming down upon her in the guise of creditors, to seize upon her provinces, as would be done to-day if a European State in revolution was declared bankrupt. But there were the home money-lenders to be considered, and if France had suspended payment, it would have been the ruin of so many middle-class

FINANCIAL DIFFICULTIES

fortunes that the Revolution would have had against it all the middle class, both upper and lower—in fact every one except the workers and the poorest of the peasantry. So it was that the Constituent Assembly, the Legislative Assembly, the Convention, and, later on, the Directory, had to make unheard-of efforts during a succession of years to avoid bankruptcy.

The solution arrived at by the Assembly at the close of 1789 was that of seizing the property of the Church, putting it up for sale, and in return paying the clergy by fixed salaries. The Church revenues were valued in 1789 at a hundred and twenty million *livres* for the tithes, eighty millions in other revenues brought in by various properties (houses and landed property, of which the value was estimated at a little more than two thousand millions), and thirty millions or thereabout from the subsidy that was added every year by the State; a total, let us say, of about two hundred and thirty millions a year. These revenues were evidently shared in a most unjust way among the different members of the clergy. The bishops lived in the most refined luxury, and rivalled in their expenditure the richest lords and princes, whilst the priests in the towns and villages "reduced to a suitable portion," lived in poverty. It was proposed, therefore, by Talleyrand, Bishop of Autun, after October 10, to take possession of all Church property in the name of the State, to sell it, to endow the clergy adequately, by giving 1200 livres a year to each priest, plus his lodging, and with the rest to cover part of the public debt, which had mounted to fifty millions in life-interests, and to sixty millions in rents for ever. This measure enabled the deficit to be filled in, the remainder of the salt tax (*gabelle*) to be abolished, and a stop put to the selling of the *charges* or posts of officials and functionaries, which used to be sold to contractors by the State.

This scheme, of course, did not fail to evoke great alarm on the part of those who were landed proprietors. "You are leading us on to an agrarian law!" they told the Assembly. "Every time you go back to the origin of property, the nation will go back with you!"—which meant recognising that the foundation of all landed property lay in injustice, usury, fraud or theft.

But the middle classes who did not own land were delighted with this scheme. Bankruptcy was avoided by it, and the *bourgeois* would be enabled to buy property. But as the word " expropriation " frightened the pious souls of the landowners, means were found to avoid it. It was said that the Church property was " put at the disposal of the nation," and it was decided to put it up for public sale to the value of four hundred millions. November 2, 1789, was the memorable date when this immense expropriation was voted in the Assembly by five hundred and sixty-eight voices against three hundred and forty-six. Three hundred and forty-six were against it. And these opposers became, henceforth, the bitter enemies of the Revolution, always agitating to do the greatest possible and imaginable harm to the constitutional *régime* and later on to the Republic.

But the middle classes, taught by the Encyclopedists on the one hand, and haunted on the other hand by the ineluctability of the bankruptcy, did not allow themselves to be daunted. When the enormous majority of the clergy and especially of the monastic orders began to intrigue against the expropriation of the Church property, the Assembly voted, on February 12, 1790, for the suppression of perpetual vows and of the monastic orders of both sexes. Only it did not dare to touch for the time being the religious bodies entrusted with public education and the care of the sick. These were not abolished until August 18, 1792, after the taking of the Tuileries.

We can understand the hatred these decrees excited in the breasts of the clergy, as well as of those—and in the provinces they were very numerous—upon whom the clergy had a hold. So much, however, did the clergy and the religious orders hope to retain the *administration* of their enormous properties, which would be considered in such case merely as guarantees for the State loans, that they did not at first display all their hostility. But this state of affairs could not last. The Treasury was empty, the taxes were not coming in. A loan

FINANCIAL DIFFICULTIES

of thirty millions, voted on August 9, 1789, was not successful; another, of eighty millions, voted on the 27th of the same month, had brought in even much less. Finally, an extraordinary tax of a fourth of the revenue had been voted on September 26 after one of Mirabeau's famous speeches. But this tax was immediately swallowed up in the gulf of interests on old loans, and then followed the idea of a forced paper currency, of which the value would be guaranteed by the national property confiscated from the clergy, and which should be redeemed according as the sale of the lands brought in money.

One can imagine the colossal speculations to which these measures for the sale of the national property upon a large scale gave rise. One can easily guess the element which they introduced into the Revolution. Nevertheless, even now the economists and the historians ask whether there was any other method for meeting the pressing demands of the State. The crimes, the extravagance, the thefts and the wars of the old *régime* weighed heavily upon the Revolution; and starting with this enormous burden of debt, bequeathed to it by the old *régime*, it had to bear the consequences. Under menace of a civil war, still more terrible than that which was already breaking out, under the threat of the middle classes turning their backs upon it—the classes which, although pursuing their own ends, were nevertheless allowing the people to free themselves from their lords, but would have turned against all attempts at enfranchisement if the capital they had invested in the loans was endangered, set between these two dangers, the Revolution adopted the scheme for a paper currency (*les assignats*), guaranteed by the national property.

On December 21, 1789, on the proposition of the districts of Paris,* the administration of the Church property was transferred to the municipalities, which were commissioned to put up for sale four hundred millions' worth of this property. The great blow was struck. And henceforth the clergy, with the exception of some village priests who were real friends of the people, vowed a deadly hatred to the Revolution—a

* *Vide* chap. xxiv.

clerical hatred, which the abolition of monastic vows helped further to envenom. Henceforward all over France we see the clergy becoming the centres of conspiracies made to restore the old *régime* and feudalism. They were the heart and soul of the reaction, which we shall see bursting forth in 1790 and in 1791, threatening to put an end to the Revolution before it had realised anything substantial.

But the middle classes resisted it, and did not allow themselves to be disarmed. In June and July 1790 the Assembly opened the discussion upon a great question—the internal organisation of the Church of France. The clergy being now paid by the State, the legislators conceived the idea of freeing them from Rome, and putting them altogether under the Constitution. The bishoprics were identified with the new departments: their number was thus reduced, and the two boundaries, that of the diocese and that of the department, became identical. This might have been allowed to pass; but the election of the bishops was by the new law entrusted to the Assemblies of electors—to those same Assemblies which were electing the deputies, the judges and the officers of the State.

This was to despoil the bishop of his sacerdotal character and to make a State functionary of him. It is true that in the Early Churches the bishops and priests were nominated by the people; but the electoral Assemblies which met for the elections of political representatives and officials were not the ancient assemblies of the people—of the believers. Consequently the believers saw in it an attempt made upon the ancient dogmas of the Church, and the priests took every possible advantage of this discontent. The clergy divided into two great parties: the constitutional clergy who submitted, at least for form's sake, to the new laws and took the oath to the Constitution, and the unsworn clergy who refused the oath and openly placed themselves at the head of a counter-revolutionary movement. So it came about that in every province, in each town, village and hamlet, the question put to the inhabitants was—whether they were for the Revolution or against it? The most terrible struggles sprang, therefore,

SALE OF CHURCH PROPERTY

into existence in every locality, to decide which of the two parties should get the upper hand. The Revolution was transported from Paris into every village : from being parliamentary it became popular.

The work done by the Constituent Assembly was undoubtedly middle-class work. But to introduce into the customs of the nation the principle of political equality, to abolish the relics of the rights of one man over the person of another, to awaken the sentiment of equality and the spirit of revolt against inequalities, was nevertheless an immense work. Only it must be remembered, as Louis Blanc has remarked, that to maintain and to kindle that fiery spirit in the Assembly, " the wind that was blowing from the street was necessary." " Even rioting," he adds, " in those unparalleled days, produced from its tumult many wise inspirations ! *Every rising was so full of thoughts !* " In other words, it was the street, the man in the street, that each time forced the Assembly to go forward with its work of reconstruction. Even a revolutionary Assembly, or one at least that forced itself upon monarchy in a revolutionary way, as the Constituent Assembly did, would have done nothing if the masses of the people had not impelled it to march forward, and if they had not crushed, by their insurrections, the anti-revolutionary resistance.

CHAPTER XXIII

THE FETE OF THE FEDERATION

End of first period of Revolution—Duel between King and Assembly—King bribes Mirabeau—He finds tools among middle class—Enemies of Revolution among all classes—Period of plots and counter-plots—The Fête of the Federation—Meaning of the fête—Joy of the people

WITH the removal of the King and the Assembly from Versailles to Paris the first period—the heroic period, so to speak, of the Great Revolution—ended. The meeting of the States-General, the Royal Session of June 23, the Oath of the Tennis Court, the taking of the Bastille, the revolt of the cities and villages in July and August, the night of August 4, and finally the march of the women on Versailles and their triumphal return with the King as prisoner; these were the chief stages of the period.

Now, when both the "legislative" and the "executive" power—the Assembly and the King—settled at Paris, a period of hidden, continuous struggle began between moribund royalty and the new Constitutional power which was being slowly consolidated by the legislative labours of the Assembly and by the constructive work done on the spot, in every town and village.

France had now, in the National Assembly, a constitutional power which the King had been forced to recognise. But, if he recognised it officially, he saw in it only a usurpation, an insult to his royal authority, of which he did not wish to admit any diminution. So he was always on the alert to find a thousand petty means of belittling the Assembly, and for disputing with it the smallest fragment of authority. Even to the last moment he never abandoned the hope of

THE FETE OF THE FEDERATION

one day reducing to obedience this new power, which he reproached himself for having allowed to grow by the side of his own.

In this struggle every means seemed good to the King. He knew, by experience, that the men of his own surroundings easily sold themselves—some for a trifle, others demanding a high price—and he exerted himself to obtain money, plenty of money, borrowing it in London, so as to be able to buy the leaders of the parties in the Assembly and elsewhere. He succeeded only too well with one of those who stood in the forefront, with Mirabeau, who in return for heavy sums of money became the counsellor of the Court and the defender of the King, and spent his last days in an absurd luxury. But it was not only in the Assembly that royalty found its tools; the great number were outside it. They were found among those whom the Revolution had deprived of their privileges, of the handsome pensions which had been allotted to them in former days, and of their colossal incomes; among the clergy who saw their influence perishing; among the nobles who were losing, with their feudal rights, their privileged position; among the middle classes who were alarmed for the capital they had invested in manufactures, commerce and State loans—among those self-same middle classes who were now enriching themselves during and by means of the Revolution.

They were numerous, indeed, the enemies of the Revolution. They included all those who formerly had lived on the higher ecclesiastics, the nobles and the privileged members of the upper middle class. More than one-half of that active and thinking portion of the nation which contains the makers of its historic life stood in the ranks of these enemies. And if among the people of Paris, Strasbourg, Rouen and many other towns, both large and small, the Revolution found ardent champions—how many towns there were, like Lyons, where the centuries-old influence of the clergy and the economic servitude of the workers were such that the poor themselves supported the priests against the Revolution. How many towns, like the great seaports, Nantes, Bordeaux, Saint-Malo, where the great merchants and all the folk depending on them were already bound up with reaction.

Even among the peasants, whose interests should have lain with the Revolution—how many lower middle-class men there were in the villages who dreaded it, not to mention those peasants whom the mistakes of the revolutionists themselves were to alienate from the great cause. There were too many theorists amongst the leaders of the Revolution, too many worshippers of uniformity and regularity, incapable, therefore, of understanding the multiple forms of landed property recognised by the customary law; too many Voltaireans, on the other hand, who showed no toleration towards the prejudices of the masses steeped in poverty; and above all, too many politicians to comprehend the importance which the peasants attached to the land question. And the result was that in the Vendée, in Brittany and in the south-east, the peasants themselves turned against the Revolution.

The counter-revolutionists knew how to attract partisans from each and all of these elements. A Fourteenth of July or a Fifth of October could certainly displace the centre of gravity of the ruling power; but it was in the thirty-six thousand communes of France that the Revolution had to be accomplished, and that required some time. And the counter-revolutionists took advantage of that time to win over to their cause all the discontented among the well-to-do classes, whose name was legion. For, if the radical middle classes put into the Revolution a prodigious amount of extraordinary intelligence, developed by the Revolution itself—intelligence, subtleness and experience in business were not wanting either among the provincial nobility or the wealthy merchants and clergy, who all joined hands for lending to royalty a formidable power of resistance.

This relentless struggle of plots and counter-plots, of partial risings in the provinces and parliamentary contests in the Constituent Assembly, and later on in the Legislative—this concealed struggle lasted nearly three years, from the month of October 1789 to the month of June 1792, when the Revo-

THE FETE OF THE FEDERATION 177

lution at last took a fresh start. It was a period poor in events of historic import—the only ones deserving mention in that interval being the recrudescence of the peasants' rising in January and February 1790, the *Fête* of the Federation, on July 14, 1790, the massacre at Nancy on August 31, 1790, the flight of the King on June 20, 1791, and the massacre of the people of Paris on the Champ-de-Mars on July 17, 1791.

Of the peasants' insurrections we shall speak in a later chapter, but it is necessary to say something here about the *Fête* of the Federation. It sums up the first part of the Revolution. Its overflowing enthusiasm and the harmony displayed in it show what the Revolution might have been if the privileged classes and royalty, comprehending how irresistible was the change, had yielded with a good grace to what they were powerless to prevent.

Taine disparages the festivals of the Revolution, and it is true that those of 1793 and 1794 were often too theatrical. They were got up *for* the people, not *by* the people. But that of July 14, 1790, was one of the most beautiful popular festivals ever recorded in history.

Previous to 1789 France was not unified. It was an historic entity, but its various parts knew little of each other and cared for each other even less. But after the events of 1789, and after the axe had been laid at the roots of the survivals of feudalism, after several glorious moments had been lived together by the representatives of all parts of France, there was born a sentiment of union and solidarity between the provinces that had been linked together by history. All Europe was moved to enthusiasm over the words and deeds of the Revolution—how could the provinces resist this unification in the forward march towards a better future ? This is what the *Fête* of the Federation symbolised.

It had also another striking feature. As a certain amount of work was necessary for this festival, the levelling of the soil, the making of terraces, the building of a triumphal arch, and as it became evident, eight days before the *fête*, that the fifteen thousand workmen engaged in this work could never finish it in time—what did Paris do ? Some unknown person suggested that every one should go to work in the Champ-de-Mars; and all Paris, rich and poor, artists and labourers, monks and soldiers, went to work there with a light heart. France, represented by the thousands of delegates arrived from the provinces, found her national unity in digging the earth—a symbol of what equality and fraternity among men should one day lead to.

The oath that the scores of thousands of persons present took " to the Constitution, as decreed by the National Assembly and accepted by the King," the oath taken by the King and spontaneously confirmed by the Queen for her son, are of little importance. Every one took his oath with some " mental reservations "; every one attached to it certain conditions. The King took his oath in these words : " I, King of the French, swear to use all the power reserved to me by the constitutional Act of the State to maintain the Constitution decreed by the National Assembly and accepted by me." Which meant that he would indeed maintain the Constitution, but that it would be violated, and that he would not be able to prevent it. In reality, at the very moment the King was taking the oath he was thinking only of how he was to get out of Paris—under the pretence of going to review the army. He was calculating the means of buying the influential members of the Assembly, and discounting the help that should come from the foreigners to check the Revolution which he himself had let loose through his opposition to the necessary changes and the trickery in his dealings with the National Assembly.

The oaths were worth little, but the important thing to note in this *fête*—beyond the proclamation of a new nation having a common ideal—is the remarkable good humour of the Revolution. One year after the taking of the Bastille, Marat had every reason for writing : " Why this unbridled joy ? Why these evidences of foolish liveliness ? The Revolution, as yet, has been merely a sorrowful dream for the people ! " But although nothing had yet been done to satisfy the wants of the working people, and everything had been done, as we shall see presently, to prevent the real abolition of the feudal abuses, although the people had everywhere paid

THE FETE OF THE FEDERATION 179

with their lives and by terrible sufferings every progress made in the political Revolution—in spite of all that, the people burst into transports of joy at the spectacle of the new democratic *régime* confirmed at this *fête*. Just as fifty-eight years later, in February 1848, the people of Paris were to place " three years of suffering at the service of the Republic," so now the people showed themselves ready to endure anything, provided that the new Constitution promised to bring them some alleviation, provided that it held in it for them a little goodwill.

If then, three years later, the same people, so ready at first to be content with little, so ready to wait, became savage and began the extermination of the enemies of the Revolution, it was because they hoped to save, at least, some part of the Revolution by resorting to extreme means. It was because they saw the Revolution foundering before any substantial economic change had been accomplished for the benefit of the mass of the people. In July 1790 there was nothing to forecast this dark and savage character. " The Revolution, as yet, has been only a sorrowful dream for the people." " It has not fulfilled its promises. No matter. *It is moving. And that is enough.*" And everywhere the people's hearts were filled with life.

But reaction, all armed, was watchful, and in a month or two it was to show itself in full force. After the next anniversary of July 14, on July 17, 1791, it was already strong enough to shoot down the people of Paris on this same Champ-de-Mars.

CHAPTER XXIV

THE "DISTRICTS" AND THE "SECTIONS" OF PARIS

Creation of Communes—Their power—Village Communes—Municipal Communes—Commune of Paris—Soul of Revolution—Erroneous conceptions of Communes—Electoral divisions of Paris—Districts useful for organisation of Revolution—Varied constitution of districts—Germ of Commune—Lacroix on districts—Independence of districts—Link between Paris and provincial towns—Sections become instruments of federation

WE have seen how the Revolution began with popular risings ever since the first months of 1789. To make a revolution it is not, however, enough that there should be such risings —more or less successful. It is necessary that after the risings there should be left something new in the institutions, which would permit new forms of life to be elaborated and established.

The French people seem to have understood this need wonderfully well, and the something new, which was introduced into the life of France, since the first risings, was the popular Commune. Governmental centralisation came later, but the Revolution began by creating the Commune—autonomous to a very great degree—and through this institution it gained, as we shall see, immense power.

In the villages it was, in fact, the peasants' Commune which insisted upon the abolition of feudal dues, and legalised the refusal to pay them; it was the Commune which took back from the lords the lands that were formerly communal, resisted the nobles, struggled against the priests, protected the patriots and later on the *sans-culottes*, arrested the returning *émigrés*, and stopped the runaway king.

In the towns it was the municipal Commune which reconstructed the entire aspect of life, arrogated to itself the right of appointing the judges, changed on its own initiative the apportioning of the taxes, and further on, according as the Revolution developed, became the weapon of sans-culottism in its struggle against royalty and against the royalist conspirators and the German invaders. Later still, in the Year II. of the Republic, it was the Communes that undertook to work out the equalisation of wealth.

And it was the Commune of Paris, as we know, that dethroned the King, and after August 10 became the real centre and the real power of the Revolution, which maintained its vigour so long only as that Commune existed.

The soul of the Revolution was therefore in the Communes, and without these centres, scattered all over the land, the Revolution never would have had the power to overthrow the old *régime*, to repel the German invasion, and to regenerate France.

It would, however, be erroneous to represent the Communes of that time as modern municipal bodies, to which the citizens, after a few days of excitement during the elections, innocently confide the administration of all their business, without taking themselves any further part in it. The foolish confidence in representative government, which characterises our own epoch, did not exist during the Great Revolution. The Commune which sprang from the popular movement was not separated from the people. By the intervention of its "districts," "sections" or "tribes," constituted as so many mediums of popular administration, it remained of the people, and this is what made the revolutionary power of these organisations.

Since the organisation and the life of the "districts" and the "sections" is best known for Paris,* it is of the City of Paris that we shall speak, the more so as in studying the life of the Paris "sections" we learn to know pretty well the life of the thousands of provincial Communes.

From the very beginning of the Revolution, and especially

* The "districts" were described as "sections" after the municipal law of June 1790 was passed.

since events had roused Paris to take the initiative of rebellion in the first days of July 1789, the people, with their marvellous gift for revolutionary organisation, were already organising in view of the struggle which they would have to maintain, and of which they at once felt the import.

The City of Paris had been divided for electoral purposes into sixty districts, which were to nominate the electors of the second degree. Once these were nominated, the districts ought to have disappeared; but they remained and organised themselves, on their own initiative, as permanent organs of the municipal administration, by appropriating various functions and attributes which formerly belonged to the police, or to the law courts, or even to different government departments under the old *régime*.

Thus they rendered themselves necessary, and at a time when all Paris was effervescing at the approach of July 14 they began to arm the people and to act as independent authorities; so much so that the Permanent Committee, which was formed at the Hôtel de Ville by the influential middle classes,* had to convoke the districts to come to an understanding with them. The districts proved their usefulness and displayed a great activity in arming the people, in organising the National Guard, and especially in enabling the capital to repulse an attack upon it.

After the taking of the Bastille, we see the districts already acting as accepted organs of the municipal administration. Each district was appointing its Civil Committee, of from sixteen to twenty-four members, for the carrying out of its affairs. However, as Sigismond Lacroix has said in the first volume of his *Actes de la Commune de Paris pendant la Révolution*,† each district constituted itself " how it liked." There was even a great variety in their organisation. One district, " anticipating the resolutions of the National Assembly concerning judicial organisation, appointed its justices of peace and arbitration." But to create a common understanding between them, " they formed a central corresponding bureau where special delegates met and exchanged communications."

* See chap. xii. † Vol. i., Paris, 1894, p. vii.

"DISTRICTS" AND "SECTIONS" OF PARIS

The first attempt at constituting a Commune was thus made *from below upward*, by the federation of the district organisms; it sprang up in a revolutionary way, from popular initiative. The Commune of August 10 was thus appearing in germ from this time, and especially since December 1789, when the delegates of the districts tried to form a Central Committee at the Bishop's palace.*

It was by means of the " districts " that henceforth Danton, Marat and so many others were able to inspire the masses of the people in Paris with the breath of revolt, and the masses, accustoming themselves to act without receiving orders from the national representatives, were practising what was described later on as Direct Self-Government.†

Immediately after the taking of the Bastille, the districts had ordered their delegates to prepare, in consultation with the Mayor of Paris, Bailly, a plan of municipal organisation, which should be afterwards submitted to the districts themselves. But while waiting for this scheme, the districts went on widening the sphere of their functions as it became necessary.

When the National Assembly began to discuss municipal law, they did so with painful slowness. "At the end of two months," says Lacroix, "the first article of the new Municipality scheme had still to be written." ‡ These delays naturally seemed suspicious to the districts, and from this time began to develop a certain hostility, which became more and more apparent, on behalf of part of the population of Paris and the official Council of its Commune. It is also important to note that while trying to give a legal form to the Municipal Government, the districts strove to maintain their own independence. They sought for unity of action, not in subjection to a Central Committee, but in a federative union.

Lacroix says: "The state of mind of the districts . . .

---

* Most of the " sections " held their general assemblies in churches, and their committees and schools were often lodged in buildings which formerly belonged to the clergy or to monastic orders. The Bishopric became a central place for the meetings of delegates from the sections.

† Sigismond Lacroix, *Actes de la Commune*, vol. iii. p. 625. Ernest Mellié, *Les Sections de Paris pendant la Révolution*, Paris, 1898, p. 9.

‡ Lacroix, *Actes*, vol. ii. p. xiv.

displays itself both by a very strong sentiment of communal unity and by a no less strong tendency towards direct self-government. Paris did not want to be a federation of sixty republics cut off haphazard each in its territory; the Commune is a unity composed of its united districts. . . . Nowhere is there found a single example of a district setting itself up to live apart from the others . . . But side by side with this undisputed principle, another principle is disclosed . . . which is, that the Commune must legislate and administer for itself, directly, as much as possible. Government by representation must be reduced to a minimum; everything that the Commune can do directly must be done by it, without any intermediary, without any delegation, or else it may be done by delegates reduced to the *rôle* of special commissioners, acting under the uninterrupted control of those who have commissioned them . . . the final right of legislating and administrating for the Commune belongs to the districts—to the citizens, who come together in the general assemblies of the districts."

We thus see that the principles of anarchism, expressed some years later in England by W. Godwin, already dated from 1789, and that they had their origin, not in theoretic speculations, but in the *deeds* of the Great French Revolution.

There is still another striking fact pointed out by Lacroix, which shows up to what point the districts knew how to distinguish themselves from the Municipality and how to prevent it from encroaching upon their rights. When Brissot came forward on November 30, 1789, with a scheme of municipal constitution for Paris, concocted between the National Assembly and a committee elected by the Assembly of Representatives (the Permanent Committee of the Paris Commune, founded on July 12, 1789), the districts at once opposed it. Nothing was to be done without the direct sanction of the districts themselves,* and Brissot's scheme had to be abandoned. Later on, in April 1790, when the National Assembly began to discuss the municipal law, it had to choose between two proposals: that of an assembly—free and illegal, after all—of delegates from the districts, who met at the Bishop's palace,

* Lacroix, *Actes*, vol. iii. p. iv.

"DISTRICTS" AND "SECTIONS" OF PARIS

a proposal which was adopted by the majority of the districts and signed by Bailly, and that of the legal Council of the Commune, which was supported by some of the districts only. The National Assembly decided in favour of the first. Needless to say that the districts did not limit themselves to municipal affairs. They always took part in the great political questions of the day. The royal *veto*, the imperative mandate, poor-relief, the Jewish question, that of the " marc of silver " *—all of these were discussed by the districts. As for the " marc of silver," they themselves took the initiative in the matter, by convoking each other for discussion and appointing committees. " They vote their own resolutions," says Lacroix, " and ignoring the official representatives of the Commune, they are going themselves on February 8 (1790) to present to the National Assembly the first *Address of the Paris Commune in its sections*. It is a personal deonstration of the districts, made independently of any official representation, to support Robespierre's motion in the National Assembly against the " marc of silver." †

What is still more interesting is that from this time the provincial towns began to put themselves in communication with the Commune of Paris concerning all things. From this there developed a tendency to establish a *direct link* between the towns and villages of France, outside the National Parliament, and this direct and spontaneous action, which later became even more manifest, gave irresistible force to the Revolution.

It was especially in an affair of capital importance—the liquidation of the Church property—that the districts made their influence felt, and proved their capacity for organisation. The National Assembly had ordained on paper the seizing of the Church property and the putting it up for sale, for the benefit of the nation; but it had not indicated any practical means for carrying this law into effect. At this juncture it was the Paris districts that proposed to serve as intermediaries for the purchase of the property, and invited all the munici-

---

* *Vide* chap. xxi.
† Lacroix, *Actes*, vol. iii. pp. xii. and xiii.

palities of France to do the same. They thus found a practical method of applying the law.

The editor of the *Actes de la Commune* has fully described how the districts managed to induce the Assembly to entrust them with this important business: " Who speaks and acts in the name of that great personality, the Commune of Paris ? " demands Lacroix. And he replies: " The Bureau de Ville (Town Council) in the first place, from whom this idea emanated; and afterwards the districts, who have approved it, and who, having approved it, have got hold of the matter *in lieu* of the Town Council, for carrying it out, *have negotiated* and *treated directly with the State*, that is to say, with the National Assembly, and at last *effected the proposed purchase directly*, all contrarily to a formal decree, but with the consent of the Sovereign Assembly."

What is even more interesting is that the districts, having once taken over this business, also took no heed of the old Assembly of Representatives of the Commune, which was already too old for serious action, and also they twice dismissed the Town Council that wanted to interfere. " The districts," Lacroix says, " prefer to constitute, with a view to this special object, a special deliberate assembly, composed of sixty delegates, and a small executive council of twelve members chosen by these sixty representatives." *

By acting in this way—and the libertarians would no doubt do the same to-day—the districts of Paris laid the foundations of a new, free, social organisation.†

---

* Lacroix, *Actes*, iv. p. xix.

† S. Lacroix, in his Introduction to the fourth volume of the *Actes de la Commune*, gives a full account of this affair. But I cannot resist reproducing here the following lines of the " Address to the National Assembly by the deputies of the sixty sections of Paris, relative to the acquisition to be made, in the name of the Commune, of national domains." When the members of the Town Council wanted to act in this affair of the purchases, instead of the sections, the sections protested and they expressed the following very just idea concerning the representatives of a people : " How would it be possible for the acquisition consummated *by the Commune itself, through the medium of its commissioners, specially appointed ' ad hoc,' to be less legal than if it were made by the general representatives.* . . . *Are you no longer recognising the principle that the functions of the deputy cease in the presence*

We thus see that while reaction was gaining more and more ground in 1790, on the other side the districts of Paris were acquiring more and more influence upon the progress of the Revolution. While the Assembly was sapping by degrees the royal power, the districts and afterwards the "sections" of Paris were widening by degrees the sphere of their functions in the midst of the people. They thus prepared the ground for the revolutionary Commune of August 10, and they soldered at the same time the link between Paris and the provinces.

"Municipal history," says Lacroix, "is made outside official assemblies. It is by means of the districts that the most important acts in the communal life, both political and administrative, are accomplished: the acquisition and selling of the national estates (*biens nationaux*) goes on, as the districts had wished, through the intermediary of their special commissioners; the national federation is prepared by a meeting of delegates to whom the districts have given a special mandate. . . . The federation of July 14 is also the exclusive and direct work of the districts," their intermediary in this case being an assembly of delegates from the sections for concluding a federative compact.*

It has often been said that the National Assembly represented the national unity of France. When, however, the question of the *Fête* of the Federation came up, the politicians, as Michelet has observed, were terrified as they saw men surging from all parts of France towards Paris for the festival, and the Commune of Paris had to burst in the door of the National Assembly to obtain its consent to the *fête*. "Whether it liked or not, the Assembly had to consent," Michelet adds.

Besides, it is important to note that the movement was born first (as Buchez and Roux had already remarked) from the need of assuring the food-supply to Paris, and to take measures against the fears of a foreign invasion; that is to say, this movement was partly the outcome of an act of local

of the deputer?" Proud and true words, unfortunately buried nowadays under governmental fictions.
* Lacroix, vol. i. pp. ii. iv. and 729, note.

administration, and yet it took, in the sections of Paris,* *the character of a national confederation*, wherein all the cantons of the departments of France and all the regiments of the army were represented. The sections, which were created for the individualisation of the various quarters of Paris, became thus the instrument for the federate union of the whole nation.

* S. Lacroix, *Les Actes de la Commune*, 1st edition, vol. vi., 1897, pp. 273 *et seq.*

CHAPTER XXV

THE SECTIONS OF PARIS UNDER THE NEW MUNICIPAL LAW

Commune of Paris—Permanence of sectional assemblies—Distrust of executive power—Local power necessary to carry out Revolution—National Assembly tries to lessen power of districts—Municipal law of May-June 1790—Impotence of attacks of Assembly—Municipal law ignored—Sections the centre of revolutionary initiative—Civic committees—Increasing power of sections—Charity-bureaux and charity-workshops administered by sections—Cultivation of waste land

OUR contemporaries have allowed themselves to be so won over to ideas of subjection to the centralised State that the very idea of communal independence—to call it " autonomy " would not be enough—which was current in 1789, seems strange nowadays. M. L. Foubert,* when speaking of the scheme of municipal organisation decreed by the National Assembly on May 21, 1790, was quite right in saying that "the application of this scheme would seem to-day a revolutionary act, even anarchic—so much the ideas have changed " ; and he adds that at the time this municipal law was considered insufficient by the Parisians who were accustomed, since July 14, 1789, to a very great independence of their " districts."

The exact delimitation of powers in the State, to which so much importance is attached to-day, seemed at that time to the Parisians, and even to the legislators in the National Assembly, a question not worth discussing and an encroachment on liberty. Like Proudhon, who said "The Commune will

* *L'idée autonomiste dans les districts de Paris en 1789 et en 1790*, in the review *La Révolution française*," Year XIV., No. 8, February 14, 1895, p. 141 *et seq.*

be all or nothing," the districts of Paris did not understand that the Commune was not *all*. "A Commune," they said, "is a society of joint-owners and fellow inhabitants enclosed by a circumscribed and limited boundary, and it has collectively the same rights as a citizen." And, starting from this definition, they maintained that the Commune of Paris, like every other citizen, "having liberty, property, security and the right to resist oppression, has consequently every power to dispose of its property, as well as that of guaranteeing the administration of this property, the security of the individuals, the police, the military force—*all*." The Commune, in fact, must be sovereign within its own territory: the only condition, I may add, of real liberty for a Commune.

The third part of the preamble to the municipal law of May 1790 established, moreover, a principle which is scarcely understood to-day, but was much appreciated at that time. It deals with the direct exercise of powers, without intermediaries. "The Commune of Paris"—so says this preamble—"in consequence of its freedom, *being possessed of all its rights and powers, exercises them always itself—directly as much as possible, and as little as possible by delegation*."

In other words, the Commune of Paris was not to be a governed State, but a people governing itself directly—when possible—without intermediaries, without masters.

It was the General Assembly of the section, and not the elected Communal Council, which was to be the supreme authority for all that concerned the inhabitants of Paris. And if the sections decided to submit to the decision of a majority amongst themselves in general questions, they did not for all that abdicate either their right to federate by means of freely contracted alliances, or that of passing from one section to another for the purpose of influencing their neighbours' decisions, and thus trying by every means to arrive at unanimity.

The "permanence" of the general assemblies of the sections —that is, the possibility of calling the general assembly whenever it was wanted by the members of the section and of discussing everything in the general assembly—this, they said, will educate every citizen politically, and allow him, when it is necessary, "to elect, with full knowledge, those whose zeal he will have remarked, and whose intelligence he will have appreciated." *

The section in permanence—the forum always open—is the only way, they maintained, to assure an honest and intelligent administration.

Finally, as Foubert also says, distrust inspired the sections: *distrust of all executive power.* "He who has the executive power, being the depository of force, must necessarily abuse it." "This is the opinion of Montesquieu and Rousseau," adds Foubert—it is also mine!

The strength which this point of view gave to the Revolution can be easily understood, the more so as it was combined with another one, also pointed out by Foubert. "The revolutionary movement," he writes, "is just as much against centralisation as against despotism." The French people thus seem to have comprehended from the outset of the Revolution that the immense work of transformation laid upon them could not be accomplished either constitutionally or by a central power; it had to be done by the local powers, and to carry it out they must be free.

Perhaps they also thought that enfranchisement, the conquest of liberty, must begin in each village and each town. The limitation of the royal power would thus be rendered only the more easy.

The National Assembly evidently tried all it could to lessen the power of the districts, and to put them under the tutelage of a communal government, which the national representatives might be able to control. Thus the municipal law of May 27 to June 27, 1790, suppressed the districts. It was intended to put an end to those hotbeds of Revolution, and for that purpose the new law introduced a new subdivision of Paris into forty-eight sections—*active* citizens only being allowed to take part in the electoral and administrative assemblies of the new "sections."

The law had, moreover, taken good care to limit the duties

* Section des Mathurins, quoted by Foubert, p. 155.

of the sections by declaring that in their assemblies they should occupy themselves "with no other business than that of the elections and the administration of the civic oath." * But this was not obeyed. The furrow had been ploughed more than a year before, and the "sections" went on to act as the "districts" had acted. After all, the municipal law was itself obliged to grant to the sections the administrative attributes that the districts had already arrogated to themselves. We find, therefore, under the new law the same sixteen commissioners whom we saw in the districts—elected and charged not only with police and even judicial functions, but also trusted by the administration of the department "with the reassessment of the taxes in their respective sections." † Furthermore, if the Constituent Assembly abolished the "permanence"—that is to say, the permanent right of the sections to meet without a special convocation—it was compelled nevertheless to recognise their right of holding general assemblies, at the demand of fifty active citizens.‡

That was sufficient, and the citizens did not fail to take advantage of it. For instance, scarcely a month after the installation of the new municipality, Danton and Bailly went to the National Assembly, on behalf of forty-three out of the forty-eight sections, to demand the instant dismissal of the ministers and their arraignment before a national tribunal.

The sections parted with none of their sovereign power. Although they had been deprived of it by law, they retained it, and proudly displayed it. Their petition had, in fact,

---

* Division I., Article 2.   † Division IV., Article 12.
‡ Danton understood thoroughly the necessity of guarding for the sections all the rights which they had attributed to themselves during the first year of the Revolution, and this is why the *General Ruling for the Commune of Paris*, which was elaborated by the deputies of the sections at the Bishopric, partly under the influence of Danton, and adopted on April 7, 1790, by forty districts, abolished the General Council of the Commune. It left all decisions to the *citizens assembled in their sections*, and the sections retained the right of *permanence*. On the contrary, Condorcet, in his "municipality scheme," remaining true to the idea of representative government, personified the Commune in its elected General Council, to which he gave all the rights (Lacroix, *Actes*, 2nd series, vol. i. p. xii.).

nothing municipal about it, but they took action, and that was all. Besides, the sections, on account of the various functions they had assumed, became of such importance that the National Assembly listened to them and replied graciously.

It was the same with the clause of the municipal law of 1790, which entirely subjected the municipalities "to the administration of the department and the district for all that concerned the functions they should have to exercise by delegation from the general administration." * Neither the sections nor the Commune of Paris nor the provincial Communes would accept this clause. They simply ignored it and maintained their independence.

Generally speaking, the sections gradually took upon themselves the part of being centres of revolutionary initiative, which had belonged to the "districts"; and if their activity relaxed during the reactionary period which France lived through in 1790 and 1791, it was still, as we shall see by the sequel, the sections which roused Paris in 1792 and prepared the revolutionary Commune of August 10.

By virtue of the law of May 21, 1790, each section had to appoint sixteen commissioners to constitute their civic committees, and these committees entrusted at first with police functions only, never *ceased*, during the whole time of the Revolution, extending their functions in every direction. Thus, in September 1790, the Assembly was forced to grant to the sections the right which the Strasbourg sections had assumed in August 1789, namely, 'the right to appoint the justices of the peace and their assistants, as well as the *prud'hommes* (conciliation judges). And this right was retained by the sections until it was abolished by the revolutionary Jacobin government, which was instituted on December 4, 1793.

On the other hand, these same civic committees of the sections succeeded, towards the end of 1790, after a severe struggle, in obtaining the power of administering the affairs of the charity-bureaux, as well as the very important right of inspecting and organising the distribution of relief, which enabled them to replace the charity workshops of the old

* Article 55.

régime by relief-works, under the direction of the sections themselves. In this way they obtained a great deal. They undertook by degrees to supply clothes and boots to the army. They organised milling and other industries so well that in 1793 any citizen, domiciled in a section, had only to present him- or her-self at the sectional workshop to be given work.*
A vast powerful organisation sprang up later on from these first attempts, so that in the Year II. (1793-1794) the sections tried to take over completely the manufacture as well as the supply of clothing for the army.

The "Right to Work," which the people of the large towns demanded in 1848, was therefore only a reminiscence of what had existed during the Great Revolution in Paris. But then in 1792-93, it was organised from below, not from above, as Louis Blanc, Vidal and other authoritarians who sat in the Luxembourg from March till June 1848 *intended* it to be.†

There was something even better than this. Not only did the sections throughout the Revolution supervise the supply and the sale of bread, the price of objects of prime necessity, and the application of the maximum when fixed by law, but they also set on foot the cultivation of the waste lands of Paris, so as to increase agricultural produce by market gardening.

This may seem paltry to those who think only of bullets and barricades in time of revolution; but it was precisely by entering into the petty details of the toilers' daily life that the sections of Paris developed their political power and their revolutionary initiative.

But we must not anticipate. Let us resume the current of events. We shall return again to the sections of Paris when we speak of the Commune of August 10.

* Meillé, p 289.
† We must say "intended," because in 1848 nothing was *done* besides talk and discussion.

CHAPTER XXVI

DELAYS IN THE ABOLITION OF THE FEUDAL RIGHTS

The people desire to abolish feudal system—Aims of middle classes—Gradual estrangement of middle classes and people—" Anarchists "—" Girondins "—Importance of feudal question in Revolution—August 4, 1789—Reactionary party gains ground—*Honorary rights* and *profitable rights*—Decrees of February 27, 1790—Feudalism still oppresses peasants—Difficulties of peasants

ACCORDING as the Revolution progressed, the two currents of which we have spoken in the beginning of this book, the popular current and the middle-class current, became more clearly defined—especially in economic affairs.

The people strove to put an end to the feudal system, and they ardently desired equality as well as liberty. Seeing delays, therefore, even in their struggle against the King and the priests, they lost patience and tried to bring the Revolution to its logical development. They foresaw that the revolutionary enthusiasm would be exhausted at no far distant day, and they strove to make the return of the landlords, the royal despotism, and the reign of the rich and the priests impossible for all time. And for that reason they wished—at least in very many parts of France—to regain possession of the lands that had been filched from the village communities and demanded agrarian laws which would allow every one to work on the land if he wanted, and laws which would place the rich and the poor on equal terms as regarded their rights as citizens.

They revolted when they were compelled to pay the tithes, and they made themselves masters of the municipalities, so that they could strike at the priests and the landlords. In short, they maintained revolutionary conditions in the greater part of France, whilst in Paris they kept close watch over the law-makers from the vantage-points of the galleries in the Assembly, and in their clubs and meetings of the "sections." Finally, when it became necessary to strike a heavy blow at royalty, the people organised the insurrection and fought arms in hand, on July 14, 1789, and on August 10, 1792.

The middle classes, on their side, worked with all their might to complete "the conquest of power"—the phrase, as is seen, dates from that time. According as the power of the King and the Court crumbled and fell into contempt, the middle classes developed their own. They took up a firm position in the provinces, and at the same time hastened to establish their present and future wealth.

If in certain regions the greater portion of the property confiscated from the *émigrés* and the priests passed in small lots into the hands of the poor (at least this is what may be gathered from the researches of Loutchitzky,*)—in other regions an immense portion of these properties served to enrich the middle classes, whilst all sorts of financial speculations were laying the foundations of many a large fortune among the Third Estate.

But what the educated middle classes had especially borne in mind—the Revolution of 1648 in England serving them as a model—was that now was the time for them to seize the government of France, and that the class which would govern would have the wealth—the more so as the sphere of action of the State was about to increase enormously through the formation of a large standing army, and the reorganisation of public instruction, justice, the levying of taxes, and all the rest. This had been clearly seen to follow the revolution in England.

It can be understood, therefore, that an abyss was ever widening between the middle classes and the people in France; the middle classes, who had wanted the revolution and urged the people into it, so long as they had not felt that "the

---

* *Izvestia* (*Bulletin*) of the University of Kieff, Year XXXVII., Nos. 3 and 8 (Russian).

DELAYS IN ABOLITION OF FEUDAL RIGHTS

conquest of power" was already accomplished to their advantage; and the people, who had seen in the Revolution the means of freeing themselves from the double yoke of poverty and political disability.

Those who were described at that time by the "men of order" and the "statesmen" as "the anarchists," helped by a certain number of the middle class—some members of the Club of the Cordeliers and a few from the Club of the Jacobins—found themselves on one side. As for the "statesmen," the "defenders of property," as they were then called, they found their full expression in the political party of those who became known later on as "the Girondins": that is to say, in the politicians who, in 1792, gathered round Brissot and the minister Roland.

We have told in chap. xv. to what the pretended abolition of the feudal rights during the night of August 4 was reduced by the decrees voted by the Assembly from August 5 to 11, and we now see what further developments were given to this legislation in the years 1790 and 1791.

But as this question of feudal rights dominates the whole of the Revolution, and as it remained unsolved until 1793, after the Girondin chiefs had been expelled from the Convention, I shall, at the risk of a little repetition, sum up once more the legislation of the month of August 1789, before touching upon what was done in the two following years. This is the more necessary as a most regrettable confusion continues to prevail about this subject, although the abolition of the feudal rights was the principal work of the Great Revolution. Over this question the main contests were fought, both in rural France and in the Assembly, and out of all the work of the Revolution, it was the abolition of these rights which best survived, in spite of the political vicissitudes through which France passed during the nineteenth century.

The abolition of the feudal rights certainly did not enter the thoughts of those who called for social renovation before 1789. All they intended to do was to amend the abuses of these rights. It was even asked by certain reformers whether it would be possible "to diminish the seigniorial prerogative," as Necker said. It was the Revolution that put the question of abolition pure and simple of these rights.

"All property, without any exception, shall be always respected"—they made the King say at the opening of the States-General. And it was added that "his Majesty expressly understands by the word property the feudal and seigniorial tithes, levies, rents, rights and dues and, generally speaking, all rights and prerogatives profitable or honorary, attached to the estates and to the fiefs belonging to any person."

None of the future revolutionists protested then against this interpretation of the rights of the lords and the landed proprietors altogether.

"But," says Dalloz—the well-known author of the *Répertoire de jurisprudence*, whom certainly no one will tax with revolutionary exaggeration—"the agricultural populations did not thus interpret the liberties promised to them; everywhere the villages rose up; the châteaux were burned, and the archives and the places where the records of feudal dues were kept were destroyed; and in a great many localities the landlords gave their signatures to documents renouncing their rights." *

Then, in the dismal blaze of the burning châteaux and the peasant insurrection which threatened to assume still greater proportions, took place the sitting of August 4, 1789.

As we have seen. the National Assembly voted during that memorable night a decree, or rather a declaration of principles, of which the first article was "The National Assembly destroys completely the feudal system."

The impression produced by those words was immense. They shook all France and Europe. The sitting of that night was described as a "Saint Bartholomew of property." But the very next day, as we saw already, the Assembly changed its mind. By a series of decrees, or rather of resolutions passed on August 5, 6, 8, 10 and 11, they re-established and placed under the protection of the Constitution all that was essential in the feudal rights. Renouncing, with certain exceptions, the personal services that were due to them, the

* Dalloz, article *Féodalisme*.

DELAYS IN ABOLITION OF FEUDAL RIGHTS 199

lords guarded with all the more care those of their rights, often quite as monstrous, which could in the slightest way be made to represent rents due for the possession or the use of the land—the *real* rights, as the law-makers said (rights over things—*res* in Latin signifying things). These were not only the rents for landed property, but also a great number of payments and dues, in money and in kind, varying with the province, established at the time of the abolition of serfdom and attached thenceforth to the possession of the land. All these exactions had been entered in the *terriers* or landed-estate records, and since then these rights had often been sold or conceded to third parties.

The *champarts*, the *terriers*, the *agriers comptants* and so on * and the tithes too—everything, in short, that had a pecuniary value—*were maintained in full*. The peasants obtained *only the right to redeem these dues*, if some day they would come to an agreement with the landlord about the price of the redemption. But the Assembly took good care neither to fix a term for the redemption nor to determine its rate.

In réality, except that the idea of feudal property was shaken by Article 1 of the resolutions of August 5 to 11, everything which concerned dues reputed to be attached to the use of the *land* remained just as it was, and the municipalities were ordered to bring the peasants to reason if they did not pay. We have seen how ferociously certain of them carried out these instructions.†

* Shares of the produce of the land, taxes on it, court rolls, &c.
† These facts, which are in complete contradiction to the unmeasured praise lavished on the National Assembly by many historians, I first published in an article on the anniversary of the Great Revolution in the *Nineteenth Century*, June 1889, and afterwards in a series of articles in *La Révolte* for 1892 and 1893, and republished in pamphlet form under the title *La Grande Révolution*, Paris, 1893. The elaborate work of M. Ph. Sagnac (*La législation civile de la Révolution française, 1789–1804: Essai d'histoire sociale*, Paris, 1898) has since confirmed this point of view. After all, it was not a question of a more correct *interpretation of facts*, it was a question of *the facts themselves*. And to be convinced of this, one has only to consult any collection of the laws of the French State—such as is contained, for instance, in the well-known *Répertoire de jurisprudence*, by Dalloz. There we have, either in full or in a faithful summary, all the laws concerning landed property,

We have seen, furthermore, in the note written by my friend James Guillaume * that the Assembly, by specifying in one of its acts of August 1789 that these were only " resolutions," gave themselves, by this, the advantage of not having to require the King's sanction. But at the same time, the acts were thus deprived of the character of law, so long as their provisions had not been put into the shape of constitutional decrees. No obligatory character was attached to them: legally, nothing had been done.

However, even these "resolutions" seemed too advanced to the landlords and to the King. The latter tried to gain time, so as not to have them promulgated, and on September 18 he was still addressing remonstrances to the National Assembly asking them to reconsider their resolutions. He only decided on their promulgation on October 6, after the women had brought him back to Paris and placed him under the supervision of the people. But then it was the Assembly that turned a deaf ear. They made up their minds to promulgate the resolutions only on November 3, 1789, when they sent them out for promulgation to the provincial *parlement*s (courts of justice); so that in reality the resolutions of August 5 to 11 were never actually promulgated.

In such conditions the peasants' revolt had necessarily to go on, and that is what happened. The report of the Feudal Committee, made by Abbé Grégoire in February 1790, stated, in fact, that the peasant insurrection was still going on and that it had gained in strength since the month of January. It was spreading from the East to the West.

But in Paris the party of reaction had already gained much ground since October 6. Therefore, when the National Assembly undertook the discussion of the feudal rights after Grégoire's report, they legislated in a reactionary spirit. In reality the decrees which they passed from February 28 to March 5 and on June 18, 1790, had as consequence the re-

both private and communal, which are not to be found in the histories of the Revolution. From this source I have drawn, and it was by studying the texts of these laws that I have come to understand the real meaning of the Great French Revolution and its inner struggles.

* *See* above, chap. xviii.

DELAYS IN ABOLITION OF FEUDAL RIGHTS

establishing of the feudal system in all that was of importance.

That, as can be seen by the documents of the period, was the opinion of those who wished for the abolition of feudalism. They described the decrees of 1790 as *re-establishing feudalism.*

To begin with, the distinction between the *honorary* rights, abolished without redemption, and the *profitable* rights which the peasants had to redeem, was maintained completely, and confirmed; and, what was worse, several personal feudal rights, having been classed as *profitable* rights, were now " completely assimilated with the *simple rents and charges on the land.*" *
Some rights, therefore, that were mere usurpations, mere vestiges of personal servitude and should have been condemned on account of their origin, were now put upon the same footing as obligations resulting from the location of the land.

For non-payment of these dues, the lord, even though he had lost the right of "feudal seizure"† could exercise constraint of all kinds, according to the common law. The following article confirms this: " The feudal dues and taxes (*droits féodaux et censuels*), together with all sales, rents and rights that are redeemable by their nature, shall be subject, until their redemption, to the rules that the various laws and customs of the kingdom have established."

The Constituent Assembly went still further. In their sitting of February 27, following the opinion of Merlin, they confirmed, in a great number of cases, *the right of serfdom in mortmain.* They decreed that " the landed rights of which the tenure in mortmain had been converted into tenure by annual rent, not being representative of the mortmain, should be preserved."

So much did the middle classes hold to this heritage of serfdom that Article 4 of chap. iii. of the new law declared, that "if the mortmain, *real* or *mixed*, has been converted

---

* " All honorary distinctions, superiority and power resulting from the feudal system are abolished. *As for those profitable rights which will continue to exist until they are redeemed,* they are completely assimilated to the simple rents and charges on the land " (Law of February 24, Article 1 of chap. i.).   † Article 6.

since the enfranchisement into dues on the land, or into rights of mutation, these dues shall continue to be owed."

Altogether, the reading of the discussion in the Assembly on the feudal rights suggests the question—whether it was really in March 1790, after the taking of the Bastille, and on August 4 that these discussions took place, or were they still at the beginning of the reign of Louis XVI. in the year 1775.

Thus, on March 1, 1790, certain rights "of fire, . . . *chiennage* (kennels), *monéage* (coining), of watch and ward," as well as certain rights over the sales and purchases by the vassals were abolished. One would have thought, however, that these rights had been abolished, without redemption, during the night of August 4. But it was nothing of the kind. Legally, in 1790, the peasants, in many parts of France, still dared not buy a cow, nor even sell their wheat, without paying dues to the lord. They could not even sell their corn before the lord had sold his and had profited by the high prices that prevailed before much of the corn had been threshed.

However, one might think that at last these rights were abolished on March 1, as well as all the dues levied by the lords on the common oven, the mill, or the wine-press. But we must not jump to conclusions. They were abolished, true enough, but with the exception of those cases where they had formerly been the subject of a written agreement between the lord and the peasant commune, or were considered as payable in exchange for some concession or other.

Pay, peasant! always pay! and do not try to gain time, for there would be an immediate distraint, and then you could only save yourself by winning your case before a law-court.

This seems hard to believe, but so it was. Here is the text of Article 2, chap. iii., of the new feudal laws. It is rather long, but it deserves to be reproduced, because it lets us see what slavery the feudal law of February 24 to March 15, 1790, left still crushing down the peasant.

"Article 2.—And are presumed redeemable, except there is proof to the contrary (which means 'shall be paid by the peasant until he has redeemed them'):

"(1) All the seigniorial annual dues, in money, grain,

poultry, food-stuffs of all kinds, and fruits of the earth, paid under the denomination of quit-rents, over-rents, feudal rents, manorial or emphyteutic, *champerty, tasque, terrage, agrier* (rights on the produce of lands and fields, or on the tenant's labour), *soète*, actual forced labour, or any other denomination whatsoever, which are payable or due only by the proprietor or holder of a piece of land, so long as he is proprietor or holder, and has the right of continuing in possession.

"(2) All the occasional fees (*casuels*) which, under the name of *quint* (fifth), *requint* (twenty-fifth), *treizains* (thirteenth), *lods* (dues on sales of inheritance), *lods et ventes, mi-lods*, redemptions, *venterolles, reliefs, relevoisons*, pleas, and any other denominations whatsoever, are due on account of supervening mutations in the property or the possession of a piece of land.

"(3) The rights of *acapts* (rights on succession), acapts in arrears (*arrière-acapts*) and other similar rights due on the mutation of the former lords."

On the other hand, the Assembly, on March 9, suppressed various rights of toll on the high roads, canals, &c., which were levied by the lords. But immediately afterwards they took care to add the following clause:

"It is not to be understood, however, that the National Assembly includes, as regards the present, in the suppression declared by the preceding article, the authorised toll-gates . . . &c., and the duties mentioned in the article aforesaid *which may have been acquired as compensation*." This meant that many of the lords had sold or mortgaged certain of their rights; or else, in cases of inheritance, the eldest son having succeeded to the estate or the châteaux, the others, more especially the daughters, received *as compensation* certain rights of toll over the highways, the canals, or the bridges. In these cases, therefore, *all the rights remained, although recognised as being unjust*, because, otherwise, it would have meant a loss to some members of noble or middle-class families.

Cases like these recurred all through the new feudal law. After each suppression of feudal right some subterfuge was inserted to evade it. So that the result would have been lawsuits without end.

There was only one single point where the breath of the Revolution really made itself felt, and this was on the question of the tithes. It was decided that all tithes, ecclesiastical and enfeoffed (which means sold to the laity), should cease from January 1791. But here again the Assembly decreed that for the year 1790 they were to be paid to whom they were due, " and in full."

This is not all. They did not forget to impose penalties on those who might disobey this decree, and on opening the discussion of chap. iii. of the feudal law, the Assembly enacted: "No municipality or administration of district or department shall be able, on pain of nullity *and of being prosecuted as a guilty party and having to pay the damages, as such*, to prohibit the collection of any of the seigniorial dues, *of which payment shall be asked* under the pretext that they have been implicitly or explicitly suppressed without compensation."

There was nothing to fear from the officials of either the districts or the departments; they were, especially the latter, body and soul with the lords and the middle-class landowners. But there were municipalities, especially in the East of France, of which the revolutionists had taken possession, and these would tell the peasants that such and such feudal dues had been suppressed, and that, if the lords claimed them, they need not be paid.

Now, under penalty of being themselves prosecuted or distrained upon, the municipal councillors of a village will not dare to say anything, and the peasant will have to pay, and they must distrain upon him. He will only be at liberty, if the payment was not due, to claim reimbursement later on from the lord, who, by that time, may have emigrated to Coblentz.

This was introducing—as M. Sagnac has well said—a terrible clause. The *proof* that the peasant no longer owed certain feudal dues, that they were personal, and not attached to the land—this proof, so difficult to make, rested with the peasant. If he did not make it, if he could not make it—as was nearly always the case—he had to pay!

CHAPTER XXVII

FEUDAL LEGISLATION IN 1790

New laws support feudal system—Sagnac's opinion of them—Attempts to collect feudal dues resisted—Insurrection spreads—Spurious decrees excite further risings—Peasants demand "Maximum" and restoration of communal lands—Revolution fixes price of bread—Middle-class suppressions—Draconian laws against peasants (June 1790)—Tithes to be paid one year longer—Summary of laws to protect property—Articles of peasants' demands

THUS it was that the National Assembly, profiting by the temporary lull in the peasant insurrections during the winter, passed, in 1790, laws which in reality gave a new legal basis to the feudal system.

Lest it should be believed that this is our own interpretation of the legislation of the Assembly, it should be enough to refer the reader to the laws themselves, or to what Dalloz says about them. But here is what is said about them by a modern writer, M. Ph. Sagnac, whom it is impossible to accuse of sans-culottism, since he considers the abolition without redemption of the feudal rights, accomplished later on by the Convention, as an "iniquitous and useless spoliation." Let us see, then, how M. Sagnac estimates the laws of March 1790.

"The ancient law," he writes, "weighs, with all its force, in the work of the Constituent Assembly, upon the new law that is being worked out. It is for the peasant—if he does not wish to pay a tribute of forced labour, or to carry part of his harvest to the landlord's barn, or to leave his field in order to go and work in his lord's—it is for the peasant to bring proof that his lord's demand is illegal. But if the lord has possessed some right for forty years—no matter what was its origin under the old system—this right becomes legal under the law of March 15. Possession is enough. It matters little what precisely is this possession, the legality of which the tenant denies: he will have to pay all the same. And if the peasants, by their revolt in August 1789, have compelled the lord to renounce certain of his rights, or if they have burned his title-deeds, it will suffice for him now to produce proof of possession during thirty years for these rights to be re-established." *

It is true that the new laws allowed the cultivator to purchase the lease of the land. But " all these arrangements, undoubtedly favourable to one who owed the payment of *real* dues (*droits réels*), were turned now against him," says M. Sagnac; " because the important thing for him was, first of all, to pay only the legal dues, while now, if he could not show proof to the contrary, he had to acquit and redeem even the usurped rights." †

In other words, nothing could be redeemed unless all the dues were redeemed: the dues for the possession of the land, retained by the law, and the personal dues which the law had abolished.

Furthermore, we read what follows in the same author, otherwise so moderate in his estimations:

" The framework of the Constituent Assembly does not hold together. This Assembly of landlords and lawyers, by no means eager, despite their promises, to destroy completely the seigniorial and domanial system, after having taken care to preserve the more considerable rights [all those which had any real value], pushed their generosity so far as to permit redemption; but immediately it decrees, in fact, the impossibility of that redemption. . . . The tiller of the soil had begged for reforms and insisted upon having them, or rather upon the registration in law of a revolution already made in his mind and inscribed—so at least he thought—in deeds; but the men of law gave him only words. He felt that once more the lords had got the upper hand." ‡

" Never did legislation unchain a greater indignation,"

---

* Ph. Sagnac, *La législation civile de la Révolution française* (Paris, 1898), pp. 105-106.
† Sagnac, p. 120.   ‡ Sagnac, p. 120.

continues M. Sagnac. "On both sides people apparently decided to have no respect for it." *

The lords, feeling themselves supported by the National Asssembly, began, therefore, angrily to exact all the feudal dues which the peasants had believed to be dead and buried. They claimed the payment of all arrears; writs and summonses rained in thousands on the villages.

The peasants, on their side, seeing that nothing was to be got from the Assembly, continued in certain districts to carry on the war against the lords. Many châteaux were sacked or burned, while elsewhere the title-deeds were destroyed and the offices of the fiscal officials, the bailiffs and the recorders were pillaged or burnt. The insurrection spread also westward, and in Brittany thirty-seven châteaux were burnt in the course of February 1790.

But when the decrees of February to March 1790 became known in the country districts, the war against the lords became still more bitter, and it spread to regions which had not dared to rise the preceding summer. Thus, at the sitting of the Assembly on June 5, mention was made of risings in Bourbon-Lancy and the Charolais, where false decrees of the Assembly had been spread, and an agrarian law was demanded. At the session of June 2, reports were read about the insurrections in the Bourbonnais, the Nivernais and the province of Berry. Several municipalities had proclaimed martial law; there had been some killed and wounded. The "brigands" had spread over the Campine, and at that very time they were investing the town of Decize. Great "excesses" were also reported from the Limousin, where the peasants were asking to have the maximum price of grain fixed. "*The project for recovering the lands granted to the lords for the last hundred and twenty years is one of the articles of their demand,*" says the report. The peasants evidently wanted to recover the communal lands of which the village communes had been robbed by the lords.

Spurious decrees of the National Assembly were seen everywhere. In March and April 1790, several were circulated

* Sagnac, p. 121.

in the provinces, ordering the people not to pay more than one *sou* for a pound of bread. The Revolution was thus getting ahead of the Convention, which did not pass the law of the "Maximum" until 1793.

In August, the popular risings were still going on. For instance, in the town of Saint-Étienne-en-Forez, the people killed one of the monopolists, and appointed a new municipality which was compelled to lower the price of bread; but thereupon the middle classes armed themselves, and arrested twenty-two rebels. This is a picture of what was happening more or less everywhere—not to mention the greater struggles at Lyons and in the South of France.

But what did the Assembly do ? Did they do justice to the peasants' demands ? Did they hasten to abolish without redemption those feudal rights, so hateful to those who cultivated the land, that they no longer paid them except under constraint ?

Certainly not ! The Assembly only voted new Draconian laws against the peasants. On June 2, 1790, "the Assembly, informed and greatly concerned about the excesses which have been committed by troops of brigands and robbers" [for which read "peasants"] in the departments of the Cher, the Nièvre and the Allier, and are spreading almost into the Corrèze, enact measures against these "promoters of disorder," and render the communes jointly responsible for the violences committed.

"All those," says Article 1 of this law, "who stir up the people of the towns and the country to accomplish acts of violence and outrages against the properties, possessions and enclosures, or the life and safety of the citizens, the collection of the taxes, the free sale and circulation of food-stuffs, are declared enemies of the Constitution, of the work of the National Assembly, of Nature, and of the King. Martial law will be proclaimed against them." *

A fortnight later, on June 18, the Assembly adopted a decree even still harsher. It deserves quotation.

Its first article declares that all tithes, whether ecclesiastical

* *Moniteur*, June 6.

or lay, hold good "for payment during the present year only to those to whom the right belongs and in the usual manner...."
Whereupon the peasants, no doubt, asked if a new decree was not going to be passed by-and-by for yet another year or two —and so they did not pay.

According to Article 2, "those who owe payments in field- and land-produce (*champart, terriers*), in cash, and in *other dues payable in kind*, which have not been suppressed without indemnity, will be held to pay them during the present year and the years following in the usual way ... in conformity with the decrees passed on March 3 and on May 4 last."

Article 3 declares that no one can, under pretext of litigation, refuse to pay either the tithes or the dues on field-produce, &c.

Above all, it was forbidden "to give any trouble during the collecting" of the tithes and dues. In the case of disorderly assemblies being formed, the municipality, by virtue of the decree of February 20–23, must proceed to take severe measures.

This decree of February 20–23, 1790, was very characteristic. It ordained that the municipality should intervene and proclaim martial law whenever a disorderly assembly takes place. If they neglect to do this, the municipal officials were to be held responsible for all injury suffered by the owners of the property. And not only the officials, but "all the citizens being able to take part in the re-establishment of public order, the whole community shall be responsible for two-thirds of the damage done." Each citizen shall be empowered to demand the application of martial law, and then only shall he be relieved of his responsibility.

This decree would have been still worse if its supporters had not made a tactical error. Copying an English law, they wanted to introduce a clause which empowered the calling out of the soldiers or militia, and in such case "royal dictature" had to be proclaimed in the locality. The middle classes took umbrage at this clause, and after long discussions the task of proclaiming martial law, in support of one another, was left to the municipalities, without any declaration in the King's name. Furthermore, the village communes were to be held responsible for any damages which might accrue to the lord, if they had not shot or hanged in good time the peasants who refused to pay the feudal dues.

The law of June 18, 1790, confirmed all this. All that had any real value in the feudal rights, all that could be represented by any kind of legal chicanery as attached to the possession of the land, was to be paid as before. And every one who refused was compelled by the musket or the gallows to accept these obligations. To *speak* against the payment of the feudal dues was held to be a crime, which called forth the death penalty, if martial law was proclaimed.*

Such was the bequest of the Constituent Assembly, of which we have been told so many fine things; for everything remained in that state until 1792. The feudal laws were only touched to make clear certain rules for the redemption of the feudal dues, or to complain that the peasants were not willing to redeem anything,† or else to reiterate the threats against the peasants who were not paying.‡

The decrees of February 1790 were all that the Constituent Assembly did for the abolition of the odious feudal system, and it was not until June 1793, after the insurrection of May 31, that the people of Paris compelled the Convention, in its " purified " form, to pronounce the actual abolition of the feudal rights.

Let us, therefore, bear these dates well in mind.

On August 4, 1789.—Abolition in principle of the feudal system; abolition of personal mortmain, the game laws, and patrimonial justice.

From August 5 to 11.—Partial reconstruction of this system by acts which imposed redemption for all the feudal dues of any value whatsoever.

End of 1789 and 1790.—Expeditions of the urban munici-

---

* During this discussion Robespierre uttered a very just saying which the revolutionists of all countries should remember: " As for me, I bear witness," he cried, " that no revolution has ever cost so little blood and cruelty." The bloodshed, indeed, came later, through the counter-revolution.

† Law of May 3 to 9, 1790.

‡ Law of June 15 to 19, 1790.

palities against the insurgent peasantry, and hangings of the same.

February 1790.—Report of the Feudal Committee, stating that the peasant revolt was spreading.

March and June 1790.—Draconian laws against the peasants who were not paying their feudal dues, or were preaching their abolition. The insurrections still spreading.

June 1791.—These laws were confirmed once more. Reaction all along the line. The peasant insurrections continuing.

Only in July 1792, as we shall see, on the very eve of the invasion of the Tuileries by the people, and in August 1792, after the downfall of royalty, did the Assembly take the first decisive steps against the feudal rights.

Lastly, it was only in August 1793, after the expulsion of the Girondins, that the definite abolition, without redemption, of the feudal rights was enacted.

This is the true picture of the Revolution.

One other question, of immense importance for the peasants, was clearly that of the communal lands.

Everywhere, in the east, north-east and south-east of France, wherever the peasants felt themselves strong enough to do it, they tried to regain possession of the communal lands, of which the greater part had been taken away from them by fraud, or under the pretext of debt, with the help of the State, chiefly since the reign of Louis XIV.* Lords, clergy, monks and the middle-class men of both towns and villages—all had had their share of them.

There remained, however, a good deal of these lands still in communal possession, and the middle classes looked on them with greedy eyes. So the Legislative Assembly hastened to make a law, on August 1, 1791, which authorised the sale of communal lands to private persons. This was to give a free hand for pilfering these lands.

The Assemblies of the village communes were at that time, in virtue of the municipal law passed by the National Assembly in December 1789, composed exclusively of the middle-class

* Decree of 1669.

men of the village—of *active citizens*—that is, of the wealthier peasants, to the exclusion of the poor householders. And these village assemblies were evidently eager to put up the communal lands for sale, of which a large part could be acquired at a low price by the better-off peasants and farmers.

As to the mass of the poor peasants, they opposed with all their might the destruction of the collective possession of the land, as they are to-day opposing it in Russia.

On the other hand, the peasants, both the rich and the poor, did all they could to regain possession of the communal lands for the villages ; the wealthier ones in the hope of securing some part for themselves, and the poor in the hope of keeping these lands for the commune. All this, let it be well understood, offering an infinite variety of detail in different parts of France.

It was, however, this re-taking by the communes of the communal lands of which they had been robbed in the course of two centuries, that the Constituent and the Legislative Assemblies, and even the National Convention, opposed up to June 1793. The King had to be imprisoned and executed, and the Girondin leaders had to be driven out of the Convention before it could be accomplished.

CHAPTER XXVIII

ARREST OF THE REVOLUTION IN 1790

Insurrections necessary—Extent of reaction—Work of Constituent and Legislative Assemblies—New Constitution—Local government opposed to centralisation—Difficulties in applying new laws—*Directoires* on side of reaction—"Disorder wanted"—Active and passive citizens—The gains of insurrection—Equality and agrarian law—Disappearance of manorial courts—Workers' demands answered by bullets—Middle classes' love of order and prosperity—"Intellectuals" turn against people—Success of counter-revolution—Plutocracy—Opposition to republican form of government—Danton and Marat persecuted and exiled—Discontent and dishonesty in army—Massacres at Nancy—Bouillé's "splendid behaviour"

WE have seen what the economic conditions in the villages were during the year 1790. They were such that if the peasant insurrections had not gone on, in spite of all, the peasants, freed in their persons, would have remained economically under the yoke of the feudal system—as happened in Russia, where feudalism was abolished, in 1861, by law, and not by a revolution.

Besides, all the *political* work of the Revolution not only remained unfinished in 1790, but it actually suffered a complete set-back. As soon as the first panic, produced by the unexpected breaking-out of the people, had passed, the Court, the nobles, the rich men and the clergy promptly joined together for the reorganisation of the forces of reaction. And soon they felt themselves so well supported and so powerful that they began to see whether it would not be possible to crush the Revolution, and to re-establish the Court and the nobility in their rights.

All the historians undoubtedly mention this reaction; but still they do not show all its depth and all its extent. The reality was that for two years, from the summer of 1790 to the summer of 1792, the whole work of the Revolution was suspended. People were asking if it was the Revolution which was going to get the upper hand or the counter-revolution. The beam of the balance wavered between the two. And it was in utter despair that the revolutionist "leaders of opinion" decided at last, in June 1792, once more to appeal to popular insurrection.

Of course it must be recognised that while the Constituent Assembly, and after it the Legislative, opposed the revolutionary abolition of the feudal rights and popular revolution altogether, they nevertheless accomplished an immense work for the destruction of the powers of the King and the Court, and for the creation of the political power of the middle classes. And when the legislators in both these Assemblies undertook to express, in the form of laws, the new Constitution of the Third Estate, it must be confessed that they went to work with a certain energy and sagacity.

They knew how to undermine the power of the nobility and how to express the rights of the citizen in a middle-class Constitution. They worked out a local self-government which was capable of checking the governmental centralisation, and they modified the laws of inheritance so as to democratise property and to divide it up among a greater number of persons.

They destroyed for ever the political distinctions between the various "orders"—clergy, nobility, Third Estate, which for that time was a very great thing; we have only to remember how slowly this is being done in Germany and Russia. They abolished all the titles of the nobility and the countless privileges which then existed, and they laid the foundations of a more equal basis for taxation. They avoided also the formation of an Upper Chamber, which would have been a stronghold for the aristocracy. And by the departmental law of December 1789, they did something which helped on the Revolution enormously: they abolished every representative of the central authority in the provinces.

Lastly, they took away from the Church her rich possessions,

ARREST OF THE REVOLUTION IN 1790

and they made the members of the clergy simple functionaries of the State. The army was reorganised; so were the courts of justice. The election of judges was left to the people. And in all these reforms the middle-class legislators avoided too much centralisation. In short, judged from the legislative point of view, they appear to have been clever, energetic men, and we find in their work certain elements of republican democratism, and a tendency towards local autonomy, which the advanced parties of the present day do not sufficiently appreciate.

However, in spite of all these laws, nothing was yet done. *The reality was not on the same level as the theory*, for the simple reason that *there lies always an abyss between a law which has just been promulgated and its practical carrying out in life*—a reason which is usually overlooked by those who do not thoroughly understand from their own experience the working of the machinery of State.

It is easy to say: "The property of the religious bodies shall pass into the hands of the State." But how is that to be put into effect? Who will go, for example, to the Abbey of Saint Bernard at Clairvaux, and tell the abbot and the monks that they have to go? Who is to drive them out if they do not go? Who is to prevent them from coming back to-morrow, helped by all the pious folk in the neighbouring villages, and from chanting the mass in the abbey? Who is to organise an effective sale of their vast estates? And finally, who will turn the fine abbey buildings into a hospital for old men, as was actually done later on by the revolutionary government? We know, indeed, that if the "sections" of Paris had not taken the sale of the Church lands into their hands, the law concerning these sales would never have begun to take effect.

In 1790, 1791, 1792, the old *régime* was still there, intact, and ready to be reconstituted in its entirety—with but slight modifications—just as the Second Empire of Napoleon III. was ready to come back to life at any moment in the days of Thiers and MacMahon. The clergy, the nobility, the old officialism, and above all the old spirit, were all ready to lift up their heads again, and to clap into gaol those who had dared to put on the tri-colour sash. They were watching for the opportunity; they were preparing for it. Moreover the new Directories (*directoires*) of the departments, established by the Revolution, but drawn from the wealthy class, were the framework, always ready for the re-establishment of the old *régime*. They were the citadels of the counter-revolution.

Both the Constituent and the Legislative Assembly had certainly drawn up a number of laws, of which people admire the lucidity and style to this day; but nevertheless, the greater majority of these laws remained a dead letter. It must not be forgotten that for more than two-thirds of the fundamental laws made between 1789 and 1793 no attempt was even made to put them into execution.

The fact is, that it is not enough to make a new law. It is necessary also, nearly always, to create the mechanism for its application; and as soon as the new law strikes at any vested interest, some sort of revolutionary organisation is usually required in order to apply this law to life, with all its consequences. We have only to think of the small results produced by the laws of the Convention concerning education, which all remained a dead letter.

To-day even, in spite of the present bureaucratic concentration and the armies of officials who converge towards their centre at Paris, we see that every new law, however trifling it may be, takes years before it passes into life. And again, how often it becomes completely mutilated in its application! But at the time of the Great Revolution this bureaucratic mechanism did not exist; it took more than fifty years for its actual development.

How then could the laws of the Assembly enter into everyday life without a *revolution by deed being accomplished* in every town, in every village, in each of the thirty-six thousand communes all over France.

Yet such was the blindness of the middle-class revolutionists that, on the one hand, they took every precaution to prevent the people—the poor people, who alone were throwing themselves with all their heart into the Revolution—from having

ARREST OF THE REVOLUTION IN 1790

too much share in the direction of communal affairs, and on the other hand, they opposed with all their might the breaking-out and the successful carrying-through of the Revolution in every town and village.

Before any vital work could result from the decrees of the Assembly, *disorder* was wanted. It was necessary that in every little hamlet, men of action, the patriots who hated the old *régime*, should seize upon the municipality; that a revolution should be made in that hamlet; that the whole order of life should be turned upside down; that all authority should be ignored; that the revolution should be a *social* one, if they wished to bring about the *political* revolution.

It was necessary for the peasant to take the land and begin to plough it without waiting for the orders of some authority, which orders evidently would never have been given. It was necessary for an entirely new life to begin in the village. But without disorder, without a great deal of *social* disorder, this could not be done.

Now it was precisely this disorder the legislators wanted to prevent.

Not only had they eliminated the people from the administration, by means of the municipal law of December 1789, which placed the administrative power in the hands of the *active citizens only*, and under the name of *passive citizens* excluded from it all the poor peasants and nearly all the workers in towns. And not only did they hand over all the provincial authority to the middle classes: they also armed these middle classes with the most terrifying powers to prevent the poor folk from continuing their insurrections.

And yet it was only these insurrections of the poor people which later on permitted them to deal mortal blows at the old *régime* in 1792 and 1793.*

---

* It is interesting to read in M. Aulard's *Histoire politique de la Révolution française* (2nd edition, Paris, 1903) the pages 55 to 60, in which he shows how the Assembly laboured to prevent the power falling into the hands of the people. The remarks of this writer, concerning the law of October 14, 1790, prohibiting the assembling of the citizens of the communes to discuss their affairs more than once a year for the elections, are very true.

Altogether the Revolution appeared at this period under the following aspect: The peasants realised that nothing was yet done. The abolition of the *personal* services had only awakened their hopes, and they claimed now the abolition of their economic servitude, for good, and without redemption. Besides, they wanted to regain possession of their communal lands.

What they had already gained, here and there, in 1789, by means of their insurrections, they wanted to keep, and to have their gains sanctioned by the National Assembly. And what they had not yet succeeded to obtain, they wanted to have without falling under the thunders of the martial law.

But these two wants of the people the middle classes opposed with all their might. They had taken advantage of the revolts against feudalism to begin their first attack on the power of the King, the nobles and the clergy. But as soon as a first outline of a middle-class Constitution had been worked out and accepted by the King—with every scope for the violation of it—the middle classes halted, terrified at the rapid conquests made by the spirit of revolution in the hearts of the people.

They knew, moreover, that the landed property of the nobility was going to pass into their hands; and they wanted to have that property intact, with all the additional revenues that stood for the ancient feudal services transformed into payments in money. Some day, later on, they would see if it would not be advantageous to abolish the rest of these dues, and then it would be done legally, "methodically," and "in order." Because if disorder be tolerated, who knows where the people would stop? Were they not already talking of "equality," of "agrarian law," of "equalisation of fortunes," of "farms not exceeding a hundred and twenty acres"?

As to the towns and the artisans, and the entire working population of the cities, the same thing was going on as in the villages. The guilds and corporations of which royalty had contrived to make so many instruments of oppression had been abolished. The survivals of the feudal system which still existed, in the towns as in the country, had been sup-

ARREST OF THE REVOLUTION IN 1790

pressed since the popular insurrections of the summer of 1789. The manorial courts had disappeared and the judges were elected by the people and taken from the propertied middle class.

But after all this did not really mean much. Work was slack and bread was selling at famine prices. The great mass of the workers would indeed have waited patiently if only there was a chance of the reign of Liberty, Equality and Fraternity being established. But as that was not being done, they lost patience. The workers began to demand that the Commune of Paris, like the municipalities of Rouen, Nancy and Lyons, and elsewhere, should take charge of the victualling so as to sell the wheat and the rye at cost price. They demanded that maximum prices for the sale of the bread-stuffs should be established, and that sumptuary laws should be made, so that the rich might be taxed by a forced and progressive tax. But then the middle classes, who had armed themselves since 1789, while the passive citizens had been disarmed, came forth, unfurled the red flag, and bidding the people disperse, they shot those who did not obey at once. This was done in Paris, as it was very nearly everywhere else throughout France.

The progress of the Revolution was thus stopped. Royalty began to revive. The emigrant nobles at Coblentz, Turin and Mitau rubbed their hands. They plucked up courage and indulged in wild speculation. From the summer of 1790 until June 1792, the counter-revolution had every reason to believe that it would soon be victorious.

It was quite natural, after all, that such an important revolution as that which had been accomplished between 1789 and 1793 should have its periods of check and even of recoil. The forces at the disposal of the old *régime* were immense, and having experienced a first defeat, they could not but try to reconstitute themselves, in order to set up a barrier in opposition to the new spirit. There was therefore nothing unforeseen in the wave of reaction which appeared in 1790. But if this reaction was so strong that it could last until June 1792, and if, in spite of all the crimes of the Court, it became so powerful that in 1791 the whole Revolution was set back, this was because the middle classes had joined hands with the nobility and the clergy who had rallied round the banner of royalty. The new force constituted by the Revolution itself—the middle classes—brought their business ability, their love of "order" and of property, and their hatred of popular tumult to lend support to the forces of the old *régime*. Moreover, the majority of the "intellectuals," in whom the people had put their trust, as soon as they perceived the first glimmer of a rising, turned their backs on the masses, and hurried into the ranks of the defenders of "order" to join them in keeping down the people and in opposing the popular tendencies towards equality.

Reinforced in this fashion, the counter-revolutionists succeeded so well, that if the peasants had not continued their risings in the provinces, and if the people in the towns, on seeing the foreigners invading France, had not risen again during the summer of 1792, the progress of the Revolution would have been stopped, without anything lasting having been effected.

Altogether, the situation was very gloomy in 1790. "A plutocracy is already established shamelessly," wrote Loustallot on November 28, 1789, in the *Révolution de Paris*. Who knows if it is not already a treasonable crime to say, "The nation is the sovereign." * But since then reaction had gained a good deal of ground, and it was still visibly progressing.

In his great work upon the political history of the Great Revolution, M. Aulard has described at some length the opposition that the idea of a republican form of government encountered among the middle classes and the "intellectuals" of the period—even when the abolition of monarchy was rendered unavoidable by the treacheries of the Court and the monarchists. In fact, while in 1789 the revolutionists had acted as if they wished to get rid of royalty altogether, a

---

* Aulard, *Histoire politique de la Révolution française*, p. 72. A detailed analysis of what had been done by the Assembly against the spirit of democracy will be found in Aulard.

ARREST OF THE REVOLUTION IN 1790

decidedly monarchical movement began now, among these very revolutionists, in proportion as the constitutional power of the Assembly was asserted.* Even more may be said. After October 5 and 6, 1789, especially after the flight of the King in June 1791, every time that the people displayed themselves as a revolutionary force, the middle classes and the "leaders of opinion" of the Revolution became more and more monarchical.

That is a very important fact; but neither must it be forgotten that the essential thing for both middle class and intellectuals was the "preservation of property," as they used to say in those days. We see, in reality, this question of the *maintenance of property* running like a black thread all through the Revolution up to the fall of the Girondins.† It is also certain that if the idea of a Republic so greatly frightened the middle classes, and even the ardent Jacobins (while the Cordeliers accepted it willingly), it was because the popular masses linked it with that of *equality*, and this meant for them *equality of fortune and the agrarian law*—that is, the ideal of the Levellers, the Communists, the Expropriators, the "Anarchists" of the period.

It was therefore chiefly to prevent the people from attacking the sacrosanct principle of property that the middle classes were anxious to put a check on the Revolution. After October 1789, the Assembly had passed the famous martial law which permitted the shooting of the peasants in revolt, and later on, in July 1791, the massacre of the people of Paris. They put obstacles also in the way of the men of the people coming

---

* Among others, a very interesting instance of this may be found in the letters of Madame Jullien (de la Drôme): "I am cured, therefore, of my Roman fever, which did not, however, go as far as republicanism for fear of civil war. I am shut up with animals of all sorts in the sacred Ark of the Constitution. . . . One is somewhat of a Huron squaw (North American Indian) when playing the Spartan or Roman woman in Paris." Elsewhere she asks her son: "Tell me if the Jacobins have become Feuillants" (the Club of the Feuillants was the monarchist club). *Journal d'une bourgeoise pendant la Révolution*, published by Edouard Lockroy, Paris, 1881, 2nd edition, pp. 31, 32, 35.

† Marat alone had dared to put in his newspaper the following epigraph: "*Ut redeat miseris abeat fortuna superbis.*" (May fortune desert the rich and come back to the poor.)

to Paris for the *Fête* of the Federation, on July 14, 1790. And they took a series of measures against the local revolutionary societies which gave strength to the popular revolution, even at the risk of killing, in so doing, what had been the germ of their own power.

Since the first outbreaks of the Revolution some thousands of political associations had sprung into being throughout France. It was not only the primary or electoral assemblies continuing to meet; it was not only the numerous Jacobin societies, branches of the parent society at Paris—it was the sections chiefly, the Popular Societies and the Fraternal Societies, which came into existence spontaneously and often without the least formality; it was the thousands of committees and local powers—almost independent—substituting themselves for the royal authority, which all helped to spread among the people the idea of social equality by means of a revolution.

Therefore the middle classes eagerly applied themselves to the task of crushing, paralysing, or at least demoralising these thousands of local centres, and they succeeded so well that the monarchists, the clergy, and the nobles began once more to get the upper hand in the towns and boroughs of more than half of France.

Presently they resorted to judicial prosecutions, and in January 1790, Necker obtained an order of arrest against Marat, who had openly espoused the cause of the people, the poorest classes. Fearing a popular outbreak, they despatched both infantry and cavalry to arrest the people's tribune; his printing press was smashed, and Marat, at the high-tide of the Revolution, was forced to take refuge in England. When he returned, four months after, he had to remain hidden all the time, and in December 1791 he had to cross the Channel once more.

In short, the middle classes and the "intellectuals," both defenders of property, did so much to crush the popular movement that they stopped the Revolution itself. According as middle-class authority constituted itself, the authority of the King was seen to recover its youthful vigour.

ARREST OF THE REVOLUTION IN 1790

"The true Revolution, an enemy to licence, grows stronger every day," wrote the monarchist, Mallet du Pan, in June 1790. And so it was. Three months later, the counter-revolution felt itself already so powerful that it strewed the streets of Nancy with corpses.

At first, the revolutionary spirit had touched the army but little, composed, as it then was, of mercenaries, partly foreign—either Germans or Swiss. But it penetrated by degrees. The *Fête* of the Federation, to which delegates from the soldiers had been invited to take part as citizens, helped in this, and in the course of the month of August, a spirit of discontent began to show itself a little everywhere, but especially in the eastern garrisons, in a series of movements among the soldiers. They wanted to compel their officers to give an account of the sums which had passed through their hands, and to make restitution of what had been withheld from the soldiers. These sums were enormous. In the regiment of Beauce they amounted to more than 240,000 livres, and from 100,000 even to two millions in other garrisons. The ferment went on growing; but, as might be expected of men brutalised by long service, part of them remained faithful to the officers, and the counter-revolutionists took advantage of this to provoke conflicts and sanguinary quarrels between the soldiers themselves. Thus, at Lille, four regiments fought among themselves—royalists against patriots—and left fifty dead and wounded on the spot.

It is highly probable that, the royalist plots having redoubled in activity since the end of 1789, especially among the officers of the Army of the East, commanded by Bouillé, it fell in with the plans of the conspirators to take advantage of the first outbreak of the soldiers by drowning it in blood, thus helping the royalist regiments to remain faithful to their commanders.

The occasion was soon found at Nancy.

The National Assembly, on hearing of the agitation among the soldiers, passed, on August 6, 1790, a law, which diminished the effectives in the army and forbade the "deliberate associations" of the soldiers in the service, but at the same time ordered also the money accounts to be rendered without delay by the officers to their respective regiments.

As soon as this decree became known at Nancy on the 9th, the soldiers, chiefly the Swiss of the Châteauvieux regiment, made up mainly of men from the cantons of Vaud and Geneva, demanded the accounts from their officers. They carried off the pay-chest of their regiment and placed it in the safe keeping of their own sentinels; they threatened their officers with violence, and sent eight delegates to Paris to plead their cause before the National Assembly. The massing of Austrian troops on the frontier helped to increase the disturbance.

The Assembly, meanwhile, acting on false reports sent up from Nancy, and incited by the Commandant of the National Guard, Lafayette, in whom the middle class had full confidence, voted on the 16th a decree condemning the soldiers for their breach of discipline, and ordering the garrisons of the National Guard of the Meurthe department to "repress the authors of the rebellion." Their delegates were arrested, and Lafayette, on his part, ssued a circular summoning the National Guards from the towns nearest Nancy to take arms against the revolted garrison in that town.

At Nancy itself, however, everything seemed as if it were going to pass off peaceably, the majority of the men who had rebelled having even signed "a deed of repentance." But apparently that was not what the royalists wanted.*

Bouillé set out from Metz on the 28th, at the head of three thousand faithful soldiers, with the firm intention of dealing the rebels the crushing blow desired by the Court.

The double-dealing of the Directory of the department helped Bouillé, and while everything could yet be arranged peaceably, Bouillé offered the garrison quite impossible conditions, and immediately attacked it. His soldiers com-

---

* Vide *Grands détails par pièces authentiques de l'affaire de Nancy* (Paris, 1790); *Détail très exact des ravages commis . . . à Nancy* (Paris, 1790); *Relation exacte de ce qui s'est passé à Nancy le 31 août 1790*; *Le sens commun du bonhomme Richard sur l'affaire de Nancy* (Philadelphie (?)), *l'an second de la liberté française*, and other pamphlet in the rich collection at the British Museum, vol. vii. pp. 326, 327, 328 962.

ARREST OF THE REVOLUTION IN 1790

mitted the most frightful carnage, they killed the citizens as well as the rebellious soldiers, and plundered the houses.

Three thousand corpses strewed the streets of Nancy as the outcome of the fight, and after that came the "legal" reprisals. Thirty-two rebels were executed by being broken on the wheel, and forty-one were sent to penal servitude.

The King at once expressed his approval by letter of "the splendid behaviour of M. Bouillé"; the National Assembly thanked the assassins; and the municipality of Paris held a funeral service in honour of the *conquerors* who had fallen in the battle. No one dared to protest, Robespierre no more than the others. Thus ended the year 1790. Armed reaction was uppermost.

CHAPTER XXIX

THE FLIGHT OF THE KING—REACTION—END OF THE CONSTITUENT ASSEMBLY

June 21, 1791—Royalist plot—Flight to Varennes—Drouet pursues King—Decision of people—Effect of this decision—France without a King—Middle classes recant—Causes of their reaction—King declared re-established—Massacre of republicans—Danton escapes to England—Robert, Marat and Féron go into hiding—Electoral rights of people further restricted—King takes oath to Constitution—Constituent Assembly dissolved—Legislative Assembly obtains power—Views of Marat and Desmoulins—Reaction continues—Treason in the air

The Great Revolution is full of events, tragic in the highest degree. The taking of the Bastille, the march of the women on Versailles, the attack on the Tuileries, the execution of the King, have resounded all over the world—we were taught the dates of them in our childhood. However, there are also other dates, which are often forgotten, but have an equally great significance, as they sum up the meaning of the Revolution at a given moment, and its further progress.

Thus, as regards the downfall of monarchy, the most significant moment of the Revolution—the moment that most clearly sums up its first part and gives, moreover, to all its further progress a certain popular character—is June 21, 1791: that memorable night when some obscure men of the people arrested the fugitive King and his family at Varennes, just as they were about to cross the frontier and to throw themselves into the arms of the foreigner. On that night royalty was wrecked in France. And from that night the people entered upon the scene, thrusting the politicians into the background.

The episode is well known. A plot had been formed in Paris to enable the King to escape, and to get him across the

THE FLIGHT OF THE KING

frontier, where he was to put himself at the head of the *émigrés* and the German armies. The Court had been concocting this plot since September 1789, and it appears that Lafayette was aware of it.*

That the royalists should have seen in this escape the means of placing the King in safety, and of crushing the Revolution at the same time, was but natural. But many of the revolutionists among the middle classes also favoured the plan: once the Bourbons were out of France, they thought, Philippe, Duke of Orléans, would be put on the throne and he could be made to grant a middle-class Constitution, without having any need of assistance from the always dangerous popular risings.

The people frustrated this plot.

An unknown man, Drouet, ex-postmaster, recognised the King as he passed through a village. But the royal carriage was already off at full speed. Losing no time, Drouet and one of his friends, Guillaume, set off at once, in the dark, in hot pursuit after the carriage. The forests along the road were, they knew, scoured by hussars who had come to meet the royal fugitives at Pont-de-Somme-Vesle, but not seeing the carriage and fearing the hostility of the people had retreated into the woods. Drouet and Guillaume managed, however, to avoid these patrols by following paths known to themselves, but did not overtake the royal carriage until Varennes, where an unexpected delay had detained it—the relay of horses and the hussars not having been met at the exact place which had been appointed. There, Drouet, getting a little ahead, had just time to run to the house of a friendly innkeeper. "You are a good patriot, are you?" "I should think so!" "Very well then, let us arrest the King."

Then, without making any noise, they blocked, first of all, the road for the heavy royal carriage, by placing across the bridge over the Aire a cart laden with furniture, which they found there by chance. After that, followed by four or five

* In the letter of the Count d'Estaing to the Queen, of which the rough draft, found afterwards, was published in the *Histoire de la Révolution*, by the *Deux amis de la liberté*, 1792, vol. iii. pp. 101-104. Also Louis Blanc, 1832, vol. iii. pp. 175-176.

citizens armed with muskets, they stopped the fugitives, just as their carriage, coming down from the upper town towards the bridge, was passing under the archway of the church of Saint Gencoult.*

Drouet and his friends made the travellers alight despite their protestations and, while waiting for the municipality to verify their passports, made them go into the back-parlour of Sauce, the grocer.   There, the King, being openly recognised by a judge residing at Varennes, was compelled to abandon his character of servant to "Madame Korff" (the passport obtained for the Queen from the Russian ambassador bore that name) and with his usual duplicity began to plead the dangers to which his family was exposed in Paris from the Duke of Orléans, to excuse his flight.

But the people of Varennes were in no wise deceived. They understood at once the King's stratagems. The tocsin was rung, and the alarm rapidly spread in the night from Varennes, all round to the country villages, whence there came flocking on every side peasants armed with hay-forks and sticks. They guarded the King until day broke, two peasants, hay-fork in hand, acting as sentinels.

Thousands upon thousands of peasants from the neighbouring villages flocked now on the road leading from Varennes to Paris, and these crowds entirely paralysed the hussars and

* It seems most probable, according to authentic documents collected and analysed by M. G. Lenôtre (*Le Drame de Varennes, Juin* 1791, Paris, 1905, pp. 151 *et seq.*), and a pamphlet, *Rapport sommaire et exact de l'arrestation du roi à Varennes, près Clermont*, by Bayon (Collection of the British Museum, F. 893, 13), that Drouet had at first only suspicions concerning the travellers, that he had hesitated and only dashed through the woods in pursuit after his suspicions had been confirmed by Jean de Lagny. This boy of thirteen, who was the son of the postmaster at Chantrix, J. B. Lagny, arrived at Sainte-Menehould, having ridden full speed, bringing the order for the arrest of the royal carriage, signed by Bayon, one of the volunteers who were sent from Paris in pursuit of the King. Bayon having covered thirty-five leagues in six hours, by changing horses ten times, was probably quite exhausted, and halting for a moment at Chantrix, he hurried off a courier before him. It is also highly probable that Louis XVI. had been already recognised at Chantrix by Gabriel Vallet, who had just married one of J. B. Lagny's daughters, and who had been in Paris during the *Fête* of the Federation. This Vallet drove the royal carriage as far as Châlons, where he certainly did not keep the secret.

THE FLIGHT OF THE KING

dragoons of Bouillé, in whom the King had put his trust for escape. At Sainte-Menehould the tocsin was rung immediately after the departure of the royal carriage; and it was the same at Clermont-en-Argonne. At Sainte-Menehould the people even disarmed the dragoons, who had come to form an escort for the King, and then fraternised with them. At Varennes the sixty German hussars, under the command of sub-lieutenant Rohrig, who had come to escort the King until he would be met by Bouillé, and who had posted themselves in the lower town on the other side of the Aire, scarcely showed themselves. Their officer disappeared without any one ever knowing what had become of him, and the men, after drinking all day with the inhabitants, who did not abuse them, but won them over to their cause in a brotherly way, took no further interest in the King. They were soon shouting "*Vive la Nation!*" as they drank, while the whole town, roused by the tocsin, was crowding into the neighbourhood of Sauce's shop.

The approaches to Varennes were barricaded to prevent Bouillé's uhlans' from entering the town. And as soon as day dawned, the cry of the crowd was "To Paris! To Paris!"

These cries became even more menacing, when, about ten o'clock in the morning, the two commissioners—despatched on the morning of the 21st, one by Lafayette and the other by the Assembly, to stop the King and his family—arrived at Varennes. "Let them set out. They must set out. We shall drag them into the carriage by force!" shouted the peasants, growing furious when they saw Louis XVI. trying to gain time in expectation of the arrival of Bouillé and his uhlans. The King and his family had to obey, and after having destroyed the compromising papers which they carried with them in the carriage, they saw that there was nothing left to do but begin their return to Paris.

The people took them back to Paris as prisoners. All was over with royalty. It was covered with opprobrium.

On July 14, 1789, royalty had lost its fortress, but it had retained its moral force, its prestige. Three months later, on October 6, the King became the hostage of the Revolution, but the monarchical principle was still firm. Louis XVI., around whom the propertied classes had rallied, was still powerful. The Jacobins themselves dared not attack him.

But on that night, when the King, disguised as a servant, passed the night in the back-parlour of a village grocer, elbowed by "patriots" and lighted by a candle stuck in a lantern—that night when the tocsin was rung to prevent the King from betraying the nation, and the peasant crowds brought him back as prisoner to the people of Paris—that night royalty was wrecked for ever. The King, who had been in olden times the symbol of national unity, lost now his right to be so regarded by becoming the symbol of an international union of tyrants against the peoples. All the thrones of Europe felt the shock.

Moreover, on that same night, the people entered the political arena, to force the hand of the political leaders. The ex-postmaster Drouet, who, on his own initiative, stopped the King and thus frustrated the deep-laid plots of politicians; this villager, who, obeying his own impulse at dead of night, urged his horse and made him gallop over hills and dales in pursuit of the secular traitor—the King—is a symbol of the people who from that day, at every critical juncture of the Revolution, took the lead and dominated the politician.

The invasion of the Tuileries by the people on June 20, 1792, the march of the faubourgs of Paris against the Tuileries on August 10, 1792, the dethronement of Louis XVI. with all its consequences—all these great events were to follow each other now, as a historic necessity.

The King's intention, when he tried to escape, was to put himself at the head of the army commanded by Bouillé, and supported by a German army, to march on Paris. Once the capital should be reconquered, we know exactly what the royalists intended to do. They were going to arrest all the "patriots": the proscription lists were already drawn up. Some of them would have been executed, and the others deported or imprisoned. All the decrees voted by the Assembly for the establishment of the Constitution or against the clergy were going to be abolished; the ancient *régime*, with its orders and its classes, was to be re-established; the mailed fist would have been re-introduced, and, by means of summary executions, the tithes, the feudal laws, the game laws, and all the feudal rights of the old *régime* would have been reinstituted.

Such was the plan of the royalists; they did not trouble to conceal it. "Just wait, you gentlemen patriots," said they, to whoever would listen to them, "soon you will pay for your crimes."

The people, as we have said, frustrated this plan. The King, arrested at Varennes, was brought back to Paris and placed under the guardianship of the patriots of the faubourgs.

One might think that now was the time for the Revolution to pursue its logical development with giant strides. The King's treachery having been proved, were they not going to proclaim his dethronement, overthrow the old feudal institutions and inaugurate the democratic republic?

But nothing of the sort happened. On the contrary, it was reaction that triumphed definitely a few weeks after the King's flight to Varennes, and the middle classes handed over to royalty a new patent of immunity.

The people had grasped at once the situation. It was evident that the King could not be left on the throne. Reinstated in his palace, would he not resume all the more actively the web of his conspiracies and plots with Austria and Prussia? Since he had been prevented from leaving France, he would doubtless the more zealously hasten the foreign invasion. This was obvious, the more so as he had learned nothing by his Varennes adventure. He continued to refuse his signature to the decrees directed against the clergy, and the prerogatives of the nobles. Evidently the only possible solution was to declare his dethronement without further delay.

This is how the people of Paris and a large part of the provinces understood the situation. At Paris they began, the day after June 21, to demolish the busts of Louis XVI. and to efface the royal inscriptions. The crowd rushed into the Tuileries, openly inveighing against royalty and demanding the dethronement. When the Duke of Orléans took his drive through the streets of Paris, with a smile on his lips, believing as he did that he would pick up a crown there, people turned their backs on him: they did not want any King. The Cordeliers openly demanded the republic and signed an address in which they declared themselves to be all against the King —all "tyrannicides." The municipal body of Paris issued a similar declaration. The sections of Paris proclaimed their permanence; the woollen caps and the men with pikes reappeared in the streets; every one felt that it was the eve of another July 14. The people of Paris were, in fact, ready to rise for the definite overthrow of royalty.

The National Assembly, under the pressure of the popular movement, went ahead: they acted as if there was no longer a King. Had he not, in effect, abdicated by his flight? They seized the executive power, gave orders to the ministers and took over the diplomatic correspondence. For about a fortnight France existed without any King.

But then the middle classes suddenly changed their mind; they recanted, and set themselves in open opposition to the republican movement. The attitude of the Assembly changed in the same way. While all the popular and fraternal societies declared themselves in favour of dethronement, the Jacobin Club, composed of the middle-class statists, repudiated the idea of a republic, and declared for the maintenance of a constitutional monarchy. "The word republic frightened the haughty Jacobins," said Réal from the platform of their club. The most advanced among them, including Robespierre, were afraid of compromising themselves: they did not dare to declare for dethronement, they said it was calumny when they were called republicans.

The Assembly which were so decidedly anti-royalist on June 22, now suddenly reversed their decisions, and on July 15 they published in great haste a decree which declared the King to be blameless and pronounced against his dethronement; and therefore against the republic. Thenceforth, to demand a republic became a crime.

What had happened during those twenty days that the leaders should have tacked so suddenly and formed the resolution of keeping Louis XVI. on the throne? Had he shown any signs of repentance ? Had he given any pledges of submission to the Constitution ? No, nothing of the kind! The explanation lies in the fact that the middle-class leaders had again seen the spectre which had haunted them since July 14 and October 6, 1789 : *the rising of the people !* The men with the pikes were out in the streets and the provinces seemed ready to rise, as in the month of August 1789. Thousands of peasants were hastening from their villages, at the sound of the tocsin, on the road to Paris, and bringing the King back to the capital ; the mere sight of this had given them a shock. And now they saw the people of Paris ready to rise, arming themselves and demanding that the Revolution should go on : asking for the republic, for the abolition of the feudal laws, for equality pure and simple. The agrarian law, the bread tax, the tax upon the rich, were they not going to become realities ?

No, rather the traitor King, the invasion of the foreigner, than the success of the popular Revolution !

This is why the Assembly hastened to make an end of all republican agitation, in hurrying through, on July 15, the decree which exculpated the King, re-established him on the throne, and declared all those who wished to push forward the Revolution to be criminals.

Whereupon the Jacobins, those pretended leaders of the Revolution, after one day of hesitation, abandoned the republicans, who were proposing to get up a huge popular demonstration against royalty, on July 17, in the Champ-de-Mars. And then, the middle-class counter-revolutionists, sure of their position, assembled their National Guard commanded by Lafayette, and brought them up against the masses as they assembled, unarmed, in the Champ-de-Mars, round the " altar of the fatherland," to sign a republican petition. The red flag was unfurled, martial law proclaimed, and the people, the republicans, were massacred.

From that time began a period of open reaction, which went on increasing until the spring of 1792.

The republicans, authors of the Champ-de-Mars petition which demanded the dethronement of the King, were fiercely persecuted. Danton had to cross over to England (August 1791), Robert, a declared republican and editor of the *Révolutions de Paris*, Fréron, and above all Marat, had to go into hiding.

Profiting by this period of terror, the middle classes took care to limit further the electoral rights of the people. Henceforth, to be an elector, besides paying in direct contributions ten days' labour, a man had to possess, either as owner, or in usufruct, property valued at 150 to 200 days' work, or to hold as a farmer property valued at 400 days' labour. The peasants, as we see, were deprived absolutely of all political rights.

After July 17, 1791, it became dangerous to call oneself or to be called a republican, and soon some of the revolutionists, who had "nothing to lose and everything to gain from disorder and anarchy," themselves began to treat as "depraved men" those who asked for a republic instead of a king.

By degrees the middle classes became still bolder, and it was in the middle of a pronounced royalist movement, to the accompaniment of enthusiastic cheers for the King and Queen from the Paris middle classes, that the King came on September 14, 1791, before the Assembly to accept and solemnly swear fealty to the Constitution which he betrayed the same day.

Fifteen days later, the Constituent Assembly dissolved, and this was made another occasion for the constitutionalists to renew their manifestations of loyalty in honour of Louis XVI. The Government then passed into the hands of the Legislative Assembly, elected on a restricted suffrage, and clearly even more middle class than the Constituent Assembly had been.

And still the reaction grew. Towards the end of 1791 the best revolutionists completely despaired of the Revolution. Marat believed all was lost. "The Revolution," he wrote in his *Ami du peuple*, "has failed. . . ." He demanded that an appeal should be made to the people, but the politicians did not listen to him. "It was a handful of poor folk," he said in his journal, on July 21, "who knocked down the walls of the Bastille. Only set them to work, and they will prove themselves as they did that first day; they ask nothing better than to fight against their tyrants ; *but then they were free to act, now they are chained.*" Chained by the leaders, be it understood. " The patriots dare not show themselves," says Marat again on October 15, 1791, " and the enemies of liberty fill the galleries of the Senate-house, and are seen everywhere."

Similar words of despair were uttered by Camille Desmoulins at the Jacobin Club, on October 24, 1791. The " reactionaries have turned," he said, " the popular movement of July and August 1789, to their advantage. The Court favourites talk to-day about the sovereignty of the people and the rights of man, of equality among the citizens, to deceive the people, and they parade in the uniform of the National Guard to seize or even buy the posts of leaders. Around them gather the tools of the throne. The aristocratic devils have displayed an infernal cleverness."

Prudhomme said openly that the nation was betrayed by its representatives ; the army by its chiefs.

But Prudhomme and Desmoulins could at least show themselves, while a popular revolutionist, such as Marat, had to hide himself for several months, not knowing sometimes where to find a shelter for the night. It has been well said of him that he pleaded the cause of the people with his head upon the block. Danton, on the point of being arrested, had gone to London.

The Queen herself, in her correspondence with Fersen, by whose intermediary she arranged for invasion and prepared for the entry of the German armies into the capital, bore witness to " a marked change in Paris." " The people," she said, " no longer read the papers." " They are only interested in the dearness of bread and the decrees," she wrote on October 31, 1791.

The dearness of bread—and the decrees ! Bread, so that they might live and carry on the Revolution, for bread was scarce already in October ! And the decrees against the priests and the *émigrés*, which the King refused to sanction !

Treason was everywhere, and we know now that at that

very time—at the close of 1791, Dumouriez, the Girondist General who commanded the armies in the East of France, was already plotting with the King. He was drawing up for Louis a secret memorandum on the means for checking the Revolution. This memorandum was found after the taking of the Tuileries in the iron safe of Louis XVI.

CHAPTER XXX

THE LEGISLATIVE ASSEMBLY—
REACTION IN 1791-1792

King and Assembly—Fear of foreign invasion—Feuillants and Girondins—Count d'Artois and Count de Provence—Emigration of nobles—Assembly summon Count de Provence and *émigrés* to return—Declaration of war against Austria—Fall of royalist Ministry—Girondins in power—Was war necessary?—Equalisation of wealth—Socialistic ideas of people—Mayor of Étampes killed by peasants—Robespierre and agrarian law—Middle classes rally round royalty—Royalist *coup d'état* imminent—Lafayette's letter to Assembly

THE new National Assembly, elected by *active* citizens only, which took the name of National Legislative Assembly, met on October 1, 1791, and from the first moment, the King, encouraged by the manifestations of the temper of the middle classes who thronged round him, assumed an arrogant attitude towards it. Now began, just as in the early days of the States-General, a series of malicious petty annoyances on the side of the Court, with feeble attempts at resistance on the part of the representatives. In spite of this, as soon as the King entered the Assembly, he was received with the most servile marks of respect and the liveliest marks of enthusiasm. On such occasions Louis XVI. spoke of an enduring harmony and an inalienable confidence between the legislative body and the King. "May the love of country unite us, and public interest render us inseparable," he would say—and at that very time he would be arranging the foreign invasion which was to overawe the constitutionalists and re-establish representation by Three Orders and the privileges of the nobility and clergy.

Generally speaking, since October 1791—in reality, since the flight of the King and his arrest at Varennes in June, the fear of a foreign invasion obsessed all minds and had become the chief object of consideration. There were, it is true, in the Legislative Assembly two parties: the royalist Right, represented by the *Feuillants*, and the Left, represented by the *Girondins*, serving as a half-way house between those of the middle classes who were partly constitutional and those who were partly republican. But neither one nor the other of them took any interest in the great problems bequeathed to them by the Constituent Assembly. Neither the establishing of a republic nor the abolition of the feudal privileges excited the Legislative Assembly. The Jacobins themselves and even the Cordeliers seemed to have agreed not to mention the republic, and it was about questions of secondary importance, such as who should be mayor of Paris, that the passions of the revolutionists and anti-revolutionists came into collision.

The two great questions of the moment concerned the priests and the emigrated nobles. They dominated everything else on account of the attempts at anti-revolutionary risings organised by the priests and the *émigrés*, and because they were intimately connected with the foreign war, which, every one felt, was close at hand.

The youngest brother of the King, the Count d'Artois, had emigrated, as we know, immediately after July 14, 1789. The other brother, the Count de Provence, had escaped at the same time as Louis XVI., in June 1791, and had succeeded in getting to Brussels. Both of them had protested against the King's acceptance of the Constitution. They declared that the King could not alienate the rights of the ancient monarchy, and that, consequently, his act was null. Their protestation was published by the royalist agents all over France and produced a great effect.

The nobles left their regiments or their châteaux and emigrated *en masse*, and the royalists threatened those who did not do the same that they would be relegated to the middle class when the nobility returned victorious. The *émigrés*

THE LEGISLATIVE ASSEMBLY

assembled at Coblentz, Worms and Brussels were openly preparing a counter-revolution which was to be supported by the foreign invasion; and it became more and more evident that the King was playing a double game, for it was impossible not to see that everything done by the emigrant nobles had his assent.

On October 30, 1791, the Legislative Assembly decided to proceed against the King's younger brother, Louis-Stanislas-Xavier, who had received from Louis XVI., at the time of his flight, a decree conferring upon him the title of regent, in case the King should be arrested. The Assembly, therefore, summoned the Count de Provence to return to France within two months; if not, he was to lose his right of regency. A few days later, on November 9, the Assembly ordered also all *émigrés* to return before the end of the year; if not, they should be treated as conspirators, condemned, sentenced in default, and their revenues should be seized for the profit of the nation—" without prejudice, however, to the rights of their wives, their children and their lawful creditors."

The King sanctioned the decree concerning his brother, but opposed his " veto " to the second, concerning the *émigrés*. He vetoed also a decree which ordered the priests to take the oath to the Constitution, under pain of arrest as suspects, in case of religious disturbances in the communes to which they ministered.

The most important act of the Legislative Assembly was the declaration of war against Austria, which was openly preparing for an invasion, in order to re-establish Louis XVI. in those rights he had held before 1789. The King and Marie-Antoinette urged it upon the Emperor of Austria, and their entreaties became still more urgent after their flight had been stopped. But it is extremely probable that the warlike preparations of Austria would have been prolonged, perhaps until the following spring, if the Girondins had not pressed for war.

Lack of cohesion in the royalist Ministry, one of its members,

Bertrand de Moleville, being strongly opposed to the constitutional *régime*, whilst Narbonne wanted to make it one of the props to the throne, had led to its fall; whereupon, in March 1792, Louis XVI. called into power a Girondist Ministry, with Dumouriez for foreign affairs, Roland, that is to say, Madame Roland, for the Interior, Grave, soon to be replaced by Servan, at the War Office, Clavière for Finance, Duranthon for Justice, and Lacoste for the Marine.

It need not be said, as Robespierre quickly made it appear, that far from hastening the Revolution, the coming of the Girondins into power was on the contrary a weight in the scales for reaction. Henceforth all was for moderation, since the King had accepted what the Court called the " *Ministère sans-culotte*." It was only in the affair of the war that this Ministry showed any ardour, against the advice of Marat and Robespierre, and on April 20, 1792, the Girondins triumphed. War was declared against Austria, or as they said then, " against the King of Bohemia and Hungary."

Was the war necessary? Jaurès* has put the question, and in the answering of it has placed before the reader's eyes many documents of that time. And the conclusion that must be drawn from these documents, and is deduced from them by Jaurès himself, is the same as that which was defended by Marat and Robespierre. The war was *not* necessary. The foreign sovereigns no doubt feared the development of republican ideas in France; but from that to their rushing to the help of Louis XVI. was far enough; they were very far from eager about entering upon a war of that kind. It was the Girondins who wanted the war, because they saw in it the means of combating the royal power.

Marat told the plain truth concerning the matter. "You want the war," he said, "because you do not want to appeal to the people for the giving of a decisive blow to royalty." The Girondins and a mass of the Jacobins preferred indeed a foreign invasion, which, by arousing patriotism and laying bare the treachery of the King, would lead to the downfall of

* *Histoire socialiste, La Législative*, p. 815 *et seq.*

royalty without any popular rising. "We want some great treachery," said Brissot, who hated the people, their disorderly risings, and their attacks upon property.

Thus the Court on one side, and the Girondists on the other, found themselves in agreement in encouraging the invasion of France. Under such conditions war was inevitable. It blazed out, and it raged for twenty-three years with all its fatal consequences, fatal to the Revolution and to European progress. "You do not want to appeal to the people; you do not want the popular revolution—very well, you shall have war, and perhaps the general break-up!" How many times has this truth been verified since.

The spectre of the people, armed and insurgent, demanding from the middle classes their share of the national wealth, never ceased to haunt those members of the Third Estate who had attained power, or who had, through the clubs and newspapers, acquired an influence upon the course of events. It must be said also that, by degrees, the revolutionary education of the people was being accomplished by the Revolution itself, and that the masses were by degrees emboldened to demand measures imbued with a communist spirit, which to some extent would have contributed to efface the economic inequalities.

"Equalisation of wealth" was very much spoken of among the people. The peasants who possessed only miserable little plots, and the town-workers, thrown out of work, began to affirm their right to the land. In the villages, the peasants demanded that no one should possess a farm of more than a hundred and twenty acres, and in the towns it was said that any one who wished to cultivate the land should have a right to a certain quantity.*

A tax upon food-stuffs, to prevent speculation in objects of prime necessity, laws against monopolists, municipal purchasing

* After the decrees of March 15, the objections raised against these decrees had been numerous. They have been pointed out by Doniol (*La Révolution*, &c., pp. 104 *et seq.*), and by Professor N. Karéiev (*Les paysans et la question paysanne en France dans le dernier quart du XVIIIe Siècle* (Paris: Giard, 1899), pp. 489 *et seq.*, and Appendix No. 33.

of food-stuffs which should be delivered to the inhabitants at cost price, a progressive tax on the rich, a forced loan and heavy taxes on all inheritances, these ideas were discussed by the people and found their way into the press. The very instantaneousness with which they manifested themselves each time the people gained a victory, either in Paris or in the provinces, proved that these ideas were widely circulating among the disinherited, even though the revolutionary writers did not dare to express them too openly. "You do not then perceive," said Robert in his *Révolutions de Paris*, in May 1791, "that the French Revolution, for which you are fighting, as you say, *as a citizen*, is a veritable agrarian law put in execution by the people. They are re-entering on their rights. One step more, and they will re-enter upon their possessions . . ."*

It is easy to guess the horror with which these ideas inspired the middle classes, who were eager to enjoy now, and at their ease, their acquired wealth, as well as their new, privileged position in the State. We can imagine the fury which was kindled among them in March 1792, when the news came to Paris that the Mayor of Etampes, Simonneau, had just been killed by the peasants. He, as well as so many other middle-class mayors, had shot down the peasants who had revolted without any legal formalities and no one had said a word. But when the hungry peasants, who asked only that the price of bread should be fixed, killed this mayor with their pikes, a chorus of indignation was raised among the Parisian middle classes.

"The day has come when the landowners of *all classes* must feel at length that they are falling under the scythe of anarchy," groaned Mallet du Pan in his *Mercure de France;* and he demanded a "coalition of the landowners" against the people, against the "brigands," the preachers of agrarian law. Every one began to perorate against the people, Robespierre as well as the others. The priest Dolivier was alone in raising his voice in favour of the masses and to declare that "the nation is really the owner of its land." "There is no law," he said, "which could justly prevent the peasant from eating when

* Quoted by Aulard, p. 91.

he is hungry, so long as the servants and even the beasts of the rich have all they need."

As for Robespierre, he declared that "the agrarian law was only an absurd bogey displayed to stupid men by wicked ones." And he rejected beforehand every attempt that was made in the direction of the "equalisation of wealth." Always careful never to go beyond the opinion of those who represented the dominant power at a given moment, he took care not to side with those who marched with the people but knew that it was the ideas of equalisation and communism which alone could give the Revolution the force that was necessary for the final demolition of the feudal system.

This fear of popular risings and of their economic consequences impelled the middle classes also to rally closer and closer round royalty and to accept whatever kind of Constitution came from the hands of the Constituent Assembly, with all its defects and its compliance with the King's wishes. Instead of progressing in the way of republican ideas, the middle classes and the "intellectuals" developed in a contrary direction. If in 1789, in all the actions of the Third Estate, a decidedly republican and democratic spirit was to be seen, now, according as the people manifested communistic and equalising tendencies, these same men became the defenders of royalty; while the sincere republicans, such as Thomas Paine and Condorcet, represented an infinitesimal minority among the educated members of the middle classes. As the people became republican, the "intellectuals" retrograded towards constitutional royalty.

On June 13, 1792, scarcely eight days before the invasion of the Tuileries by the people, Robespierre was still inveighing against the republic. "It is in vain," he cried on that date, "for any one to wish to seduce ardent and uninstructed minds by the lure of a freer government under the name of a republic : the overthrow of the Constitution at this moment can only kindle civil war, which will lead to anarchy and to despotism."

Did he fear the establishing of a sort of aristocratic republic, as in the Netherlands ? Such is, at least, the supposition of Louis Blanc, and it is possible, after all ; but to us it seems more probable that having remained up till then a fierce defender of property, Robespierre feared at that moment, as nearly all the Jacobins did, the fury of the people, their attempts at levelling down fortunes, "expropriation," as we say to-day. He feared to see the Revolution wrecked in its attempts at Communism. The fact is, that even up to the eve of August 10, at a time when the whole Revolution, unfinished as it was, checked in its onrush, and assailed by a thousand conspiracies, was almost on the point of being defeated, and nothing could save it except the overthrow of royalty by a popular rising, Robespierre, like all the Jacobins, preferred to maintain the King and his Court rather than risk a fresh appeal to the revolutionary fire of the people. Just as the Italian and Spanish republicans of our own times prefer to retain monarchy rather than risk a popular revolution which they foresee would surely be inspired with communistic tendencies.

History thus repeats itself, and how many times it may again repeat itself, when Russia, Germany and Austria begin their great revolution!

The most striking thing in the condition of mind of the politicians of the period is shown by the fact that exactly at this moment, July 1792, the Revolution found itself menaced by a formidable royalist *coup d'état*, long preparing, which was to be supported by widespread insurrections in the south and west, and also by a German, English, Sardinian and Spanish invasion.

Thus in June 1792, after the King had dismissed Roland, Clavière and Servan, the three Girondist ministers, Lafayette, chief of the Feuillants and royalist at heart, at once wrote his famous letter to the Legislative Assembly, dated June 18, in which he offered to make a *coup d'état* against the revolutionists. He openly demanded that France should be purged of the "Jacobins," and he added that in the army "the principles of liberty and equality are cherished, the laws respected, and property sacred"—not as in Paris, for

THE LEGISLATIVE ASSEMBLY 245

example, where attacks were openly made upon it in the Commune and at the Club of the Cordeliers.

Lafayette demanded—and this already gives the measure of the progress of reaction—that the royal power should remain "intact and independent." He desired "a revered King"—and this after the flight to Varennes; this, at the very moment when the King was keeping up an active correspondence with Austria and Prussia, expecting from them his "liberation," and treating the Assembly with more or less contempt, according to the tenor of the news he received concerning the progress of the German invasion.

And to think that the Assembly was upon the point of sending out this letter of Lafayette's to the eighty-three departments, and that only a stratagem of the Girondins prevented it—Gaudet pretending that the letter was a forgery, that it could not have come from Lafayette! All this within two months of August 10.

Paris was inundated at this time by royalist conspirators. The *émigrés* came and went freely between Coblentz and the Tuileries, whence they returned after receiving the caresses of the Court and plenty of money. "A thousand houses of ill-fame were open to the conspirators," wrote Chaumette, then Public Prosecutor of the Commune of Paris, in his Notes.*
The departmental administration of Paris which had Talleyrand and La Rochefoucauld in its midst, belonged entirely to the Court. The municipality, a great many of the Justices of the Peace, "the majority of the National Guard, and all its General Staff, were for the Court, serving it as an escort and as watch-dogs in the frequent excursions that royalty were making in the streets and in the theatres." June 21 was then apparently forgotten.

"The semi-military household of the King, composed very largely of old body-guards, returned *émigrés*, and some of

* *Mémoires sur la Révolution du 10 août*, 1792, with preface by F. A. Aulard (Paris, 1893). Chaumette accused even the Directory of the department of having gathered together sixty thousand counter-revolutionists and lodged them. If there seems to be any exaggeration in the number of sixty thousand, the fact that a great number of counter-revolutionists were assembled in Paris is certain.

those heroes of February 28, 1791, known under the name of "knights of the dagger" (*chevaliers du poignard*), irritated the people by their insolence, insulted the National Representatives and loudly declared their liberticide intentions," continues Chaumette.

The monks, the nuns and an immense majority of the priests stood on the counter-revolutionary side.*

As to the Assembly, this is how Chaumette characterised it: "A National Assembly, without force, without respect, divided against itself, lowering itself in the eyes of Europe by petty and vexatious debates, humiliated by an insolent Court, and replying to insult only by redoubling its servility; without power, without any stability of purpose." In fact, this Assembly, which used to discuss for hours in succession how many members should compose such and such a deputation to the King, and whether one or two wings of the folding-doors should be open for them—which really spent its time, as Chaumette wrote, "in listening to declamatory speeches, all ending in . . . *addressing some new message to the King*"—such an Assembly could inspire nothing but contempt in the Court itself.

Meanwhile, all through the west and the south-east of France, up to the very gates of the revolutionary towns, such as Marseilles, secret royalist committees were at work, collecting arms in the châteaux, enrolling officers and men, and preparing for the levy of a powerful army, which was to march upon Paris, under the command of chiefs who would be sent from Coblentz.

These movements in the south are so characteristic that it is necessary to give at least a general view of them.

* Here is a piece of news of which all Paris was talking at the time, as related by Madame Jullien: "The Superior of the Grey Sisters of Rueil lost her portfolio, which was found and opened by the municipality of the place. It is estimated that they have sent 48,000 livres to the *émigrés* since January 1." (*Journal d'une bourgeoise*, p. 203.)

CHAPTER XXXI

THE COUNTER-REVOLUTION IN THE SOUTH OF FRANCE

Condition of provinces—Coblentz centre of royalist plots—Counter-revolutionary federation—Loyalist activity—Royalists receive money from Pitt, and help from other Powers—Risings and counter-risings in provinces

WHEN studying the Great Revolution, one is so much attracted by the magnitude of the struggles which unfolded themselves in Paris, that one is tempted to neglect the condition of the provinces, and to overlook the power which the counter-revolution possessed there all the time. This power, however, was enormous. The counter-revolution had for it the support of the past centuries, and the interests of the present; and it is necessary to study it in order to understand how small is the power of a representative assembly during a revolution —even if its members could all be inspired with the very best intentions only. When it comes to a struggle, in every town and in every little village, against the forces of the old *régime*, which, after a moment of stupor, reorganise themselves to stop the revolution—it is only the impulse of the revolutionists on the spot which can overcome that powerful resistance.

It would take years and years of study in the local archives to trace out all the doings of the royalists during the Great Revolution. A few episodes will, however, allow us to gain some idea of them.

The insurrection in the Vendée is more or less known. But we are only too much inclined to believe that there, in the midst of a half-savage population, inspired by religious fanaticism, is to be found the only real hotbed of the counter-revolution. Southern France represented a similar hotbed, all the more dangerous as there the country districts and cities had furnished some of the best contingents to the Revolution.

The direction of these various movements emanated from Coblentz, the little German town situated in the Electorate of Trèves, which had become the chief centre of the royalist emigration. Since the summer of 1791, when the Count d'Artois, followed by the ex-minister Calonne, and, later, by his brother, the Count de Provence, had settled in this town, it had become the head centre of the royalist plots. Thence came the emissaries who were organising throughout the whole of France anti-revolutionary risings. Everywhere soldiers were being recruited for Coblentz, even in Paris, where the Editor of the *Gazette de Paris* publicly offered sixty livres for each recruit. For some time these men were almost openly sent to Metz and afterwards to Coblentz.

"Society followed them," says Ernest Daudet, in his monograph, *Les Conspirations royalistes dans le Midi;* "the nobility imitated the princes, and many of the middle class and common people imitated the nobility. They emigrated for fashion, for poverty or for fear. A young woman who was met in a *diligence* by a secret agent of the Government, and questioned by him, replied: "I am a dressmaker; my customers are all gone off to Germany; so I have turned *émigrette* in order to go and find them."

A complete Court, with its ministers, its chamberlains and its official receptions, and also its intrigues and its infamies, was evolved round the King's brothers, and the European sovereigns recognised this Court, and treated and plotted with it. Meanwhile, they were expecting to see Louis XVI. arrive and set himself at the head of the troops formed by the *émigrés*. He was expected in June 1791, when he fled to Varennes, and later, in November 1791, and in January 1792. Finally it was decided to prepare for a great stroke in July 1792, when the royalist armies of western and southern France, supported by English, German, Sardinian and Spanish invasions, were to march on Paris, rousing Lyons and other large towns on the way, whilst the royalists of Paris would strike their great blow, disperse the Assembly and punish the hot-headed Jacobins.

"To replace the King on the throne," which really meant making him again an absolute monarch, and reintroducing the old *régime* as it had existed at the time of the Convocation of the States-General—that was their intention. And when the King of Prussia, more intelligent than those phantoms of Versailles, asked them: "Would it not be justice, as well as prudence, to make the nation the sacrifice of certain abuses of the old government?" "Sire," they replied, "not a single change, not a single favour!" *

It is needless to add that all the cabals, all the tale-bearings, all the jealousies, which characterised Versailles were reproduced at Coblentz. The two brothers had each his Court, his acknowledged mistress, his receptions, his circle, while the nobles indulged in Court gossip which grew more and more malicious according as they grew poorer and poorer.

Around this centre gravitated, quite openly now, those fanatical priests who preferred civil war to the constitutional submission proposed by the new decrees, as well as those noble adventurers who chose to risk a conspiracy rather than resign themselves to the loss of their privileged position. They went to Coblentz, obtained the prince's sanction for their plots, and returned to the mountainous regions of the Cévennes or to the shores of the Vendée, to kindle the religious fanaticism of the peasants and to organise royalist risings.

The historians who sympathise with the Revolution pass, as a rule, too rapidly over these counter-revolutionary resistances, so that many readers may consider them as unimportant events, or as the work of but a few fanatics who could have been easily subdued by the Revolution. But in reality, the royalist plots extended over whole regions, and as they found support among the big men of the middle classes, in the great commercial cities—and, in certain regions, in the religious hatred between Protestants and Catholics as in the south— the revolutionists had to carry on a terrible struggle for life

* Document in the *Archives des affaires étrangères*, quoted by E. Daudet.

in every town and in every little commune to save the Revolution from defeat.

Thus, while the people of Paris were preparing for July 14, 1790, the great *Fête* of the Federation, in which all France took part, and which was to give to the Revolution a firm communal basis—the royalists were preparing the federation of the counter-revolutionists in the south-east. On August 18 of the same year, nearly 20,000 representatives of 185 communes of the Vivarais assembled on the plain of Jalès, all wearing the white cross on their hats. Led by the nobles, they formed that day the nucleus of the royalist federation of the south, which was solemnly constituted in the month of February following.

This federation prepared, first, a series of insurrections for the summer of 1791, and afterwards the great insurrection which was to break out in July 1792, simultaneously with the foreign invasion, and which was expected to give the finishing blow to the Revolution. The Jalès confederation existed in this way for two years, keeping up regular correspondence with both the Tuileries and Coblentz. Its oath was " to reinstate the King in all his glory, the clergy in their possessions, and the nobility in their honours." And when their first attempts failed, they organised, with the help of Claude Allier, the prior of Chambonnaz, a widely spread conspiracy, which was to bring out more than fifty thousand men. Led by a large number of priests, marching under the folds of the white flag, and supported by Sardinia, Spain and Austria, this army would have gone to Paris " to free " the King, to dissolve the Assembly, and to chastise the patriots.

In the Lozère, Charrier, notary and ex-deputy to the National Assembly, whose wife belonged to the nobility, was invested with the supreme command by the Count d'Artois. He openly organised a counter-revolutionary militia, and even got together some artillery.

Chambéry, at that time a town in the kingdom of Sardinia, was another centre of the *émigrés*. Bussy had even formed there a royalist legion which exercised in open day. In this way the counter-revolution was being organised in the south,

THE COUNTER-REVOLUTION

while in the west the priests and nobles were preparing for the rising of the Vendée, with the help of England.

It may perhaps be said that, even all taken together, the conspirators and the confederations of south-eastern France were not very numerous. But the revolutionists, too, those at least who were determined to act, were not numerous either. Everywhere and in all times, the men of action have been an insignificant minority. But thanks to inertia, to prejudice, to acquired interests, to money and to religion, the counter-revolution held entire provinces; and it was this terrible power of reaction which explains the fury of the Revolution in 1793 and 1794, when it had to make a supreme effort to escape from the clutches that were strangling it.

Whether the adherents of Claude Allier, ready to take arms, really amounted to sixty thousand men, as he stated when he visited Coblentz in January 1792, may be doubted. But this much is certain, that in every town in the south, the struggle between the revolutionists and the counter-revolutionists continued without intermission, making the balance sway sometimes to one side and sometimes to the other.

At Perpignan, the military royalists were ready to open the frontier to the Spanish army. At Arles, in the local struggle between the *monnetiers* and the *chiffonistes*, that is, between the patriots and the counter-revolutionists, the latter were victorious. "Warned," says one writer, "that the Marseillais were organising an expedition against them, that they had even pillaged the arsenal of Marseilles the better to be able to make the campaign, they prepared for resistance. They fortified themselves, built up the gates of their town, deepened the fosses along the enclosure, made safe their communications with the sea, and reorganised the National Guard in such a way as to reduce the patriots to impotence."

These few lines borrowed from Ernest Daudet* are characteristic. They give a picture of what was taking place

---

* *Histoire des Conspirations royalistes du Midi sous la Révolution* (Paris, 1881). Daudet is a moderate, or rather a reactionary, but his history is documentary, and he has consulted the local archives.

more or less all through France. Four years of revolution, that is, the absence of a strong government for four years, and incessant fighting on the part of the revolutionists were necessary to paralyse to some extent the reaction.

At Montpellier, the patriots had founded a league of defence against the royalists, in order to protect the priests who had taken the oath to the Constitution, as well as those parishioners who attended mass when the constitutional priests officiated. There was frequent fighting in the streets. At Lunel in the Hérault, at Yssingeaux in the Haute-Loire, at Mende in the Lozère, it was the same. People remained in arms. It might be truly said that in every town in that region similar struggles took place between the royalists, or the "Feuillants" of the place, and the "patriots," and later on between the Girondins and the "anarchists." We may even add that in the vast majority of the towns of the centre and of the west, the reactionaries got the upper hand, and that the Revolution was seriously supported only in thirty out of the eighty-three departments. More than that; the revolutionists themselves, for the most part, began to defy the royalists only by degrees and in proportion as their own revolutionary education was effected by events.

In all these towns the anti-revolutionists joined hands. The rich people had a thousand means, which the generality of the patriots did not possess, of moving about, of corresponding by means of special messengers, of hiding in their châteaux, and of accumulating arms in them. The patriots corresponded undoubtedly with the Popular Societies and the Paris Fraternities, with the Society of the Indigent, as well as with the mother society of the Jacobins; but they were very poor! Arms and means of moving about both failed them.

Besides, those who were against the Revolution were supported from without. England has always followed the policy she pursues to this day: that of weakening her rivals and creating partisans among them. "Pitt's money" was no phantom. Very far from that. With the help of this money the royalists passed quite freely from their centre and depôt

THE COUNTER-REVOLUTION 253

of arms, Jersey, to St. Malo and Nantes, and in all the great seaports of France, especially those of St. Malo, Nantes, Bordeaux, the English money gained adherents and supported the "commercialists" (*les commerçantistes*) who took sides against the Revolution. Catherine II. of Russia did as Pitt did. In reality, all the European monarchs took part in this. If in Brittany, in the Vendée, at Bordeaux, and at Toulon the royalists counted upon England, in Alsace and Lorraine they counted on Germany, and in the south upon the armed help promised by Sardinia, as well as on the Spanish army which was to land at Aigues-Mortes. Even the Knights of Malta were going to help with two frigates in this expedition.

In the beginning of 1792, the department of the Lozère and that of the Ardèche, both rendezvous of the refractory priests, were covered with a network of royalist conspiracies, of which the centre was Mende, a little town hidden away in the mountains of the Vivarais, where the population was very backward, and where the rich and the nobles held the municipality in their hands. Their emissaries went through the villages of the province, enjoining on the peasants to arm themselves with guns, scythes and pitch-forks, and to be ready to turn out at the first call. In this way they were preparing for the insurrection which, they hoped, would raise the Gévaudan and the Velay, and compel the Vivarais to follow suit.

It is true that none of the royalist insurrections which took place in 1791 and 1792, at Perpignan, Arles, Mende, Yssingeaux and in the Vivarais, were successful. It was not enough to shout "Down with the patriots!" to rally a sufficient number of insurgents, and the patriots promptly dispersed the royalist bands. But during those two years the struggle was incessant. There were moments when the whole country was a prey to civil war, and the tocsin rang without intermission in the villages.

There was even a moment when it was necessary that armed bands of the Marseillais should come to hunt out the counter-revolutionists in that region, to take possession of Arles and Aigues-Mortes, and to inaugurate the reign of terror which, later on, attained such vast proportions in the South of Lyons, and in the Ardèche. As to the rising organised by the Count de Saillans, which broke out in July 1792, at the same time as that of the Vendée, and at the moment when the German armies were marching on Paris, it would certainly have had a fatal influence on the progress of the Revolution if the people had not promptly suppressed it. Fortunately, the people took this upon themselves, while Paris, on her side, made preparations to seize, at last, the centre of all royalist conspiracies —the Tuileries.

CHAPTER XXXII

THE TWENTIETH OF JUNE 1792

State of Revolution at beginning of 1792 — Constitution lacks power—Legislative Assembly—Preparations of counter-revolutionists—People recognise dangers of Revolution—Jacobin fears—Great republican demonstration—Effect of demonstration — Republican leaders imprisoned — Assembly and Revolution—"The Lamourette kiss"—People decide to do away with royalty—Critical point of Revolution—Girondins warn King—Their fears of popular revolution—Despair of Marat and patriots—Royalist hopes—Petty disputes of revolutionists

WE see, by what has just been said, in what a deplorable condition the Revolution was in the early months of 1792. If the middle-class revolutionists could feel satisfied with having conquered a share in the government and laid the foundations of the fortunes they were going soon to acquire with the help of the State, the people saw that nothing had yet been done for them. Feudalism still stood erect, and in the towns the great mass of the proletarians had gained nothing to speak of. The merchants and monopolists were making huge fortunes as Government contractors and stock-jobbers, and by means of speculating in the bonds upon the sale of the Church property and buying up the communal lands, but the price of bread and of all things of prime necessity went up steadily, and hunger became permanent in the poorer quarters of the great cities.

The aristocracy meanwhile became bolder and bolder. The nobility, the rich, lifted up their heads and boasted that they would soon bring the *sans-culottes* to reason. Every day they expected the news of a German invasion, advancing triumphantly on Paris to restore the old *régime* in all its splendour. In the provinces, as we have seen, reaction was openly organising its partisans for a general rising.

As to the Constitution, which the middle classes and even the intellectual revolutionaries spoke of preserving at every cost, it existed only for passing measures of minor importance, while all serious reforms remained suspended. The King's authority had been limited, but in a very modest way. With the powers left him by the Constitution—the civil list, the military command, the choice of ministers and the rest—but above all the interior organisation of the local government, which placed everything in the hands of the rich, the people could do nothing.

No one certainly would suspect the Legislative Assembly of radicalism, and it is evident that its decrees concerning the feudal dues and the priests were sufficiently imbued with middle-class moderation; and yet even these decrees the King refused to sign. Every one felt that the nation was living simply from day to day, under a system which offered no stability and could be overthrown at any moment in favour of the old *régime*.

Meanwhile the plot which was concocting in the Tuileries spread further into France itself, and drew in the Courts of Berlin, Vienna, Stockholm, Turin, Madrid and Petersburg. The hour was near when the counter-revolutionists were to strike the great blow they had prepared for the summer of 1792. The King and Queen urged the German armies to march upon Paris; they even named the day when they should enter the capital, and when the royalists, armed and organised, would receive them with open arms.

The people, and those of the revolutionists who, like Marat and the Cordeliers, held by the people—those who brought the Commune of August 10 into existence—understood perfectly well the dangers by which the Revolution was surrounded. The people had always had a true inkling of the situation, even though they could not express it exactly, nor support their premonitions by learned arguments; and the mass of the French people guessed, infinitely better than the politicians, the plots which were being hatched in the

JUNE 20, 1792

Tuileries and in the châteaux of the nobility. But they were disarmed, while the middle classes had organised their National Guard battalions; and what was worse, those of the "intellectuals" whom the Revolution had pushed to the front, those who were held as the spokesmen of the Revolution—among them honest men like Robespierre—had not the necessary confidence in the Revolution, and still less in the people. Just like the parliamentary Radicals of our own times, who dread to see the people come out into the streets, lest they should become masters of the situation, they did not dare to avow their dread of revolutionary equality. They explained their attitude as one of care to preserve, at least, the few liberties acquired by the Constitution. To the indeterminate chances of a new insurrection, they preferred, they said, a constitutional monarchy.

Events of such an importance as the declaration of war (on April 21, 1792) and the German invasion were necessary to change the situation. Then only, seeing themselves betrayed on all sides, even by the leaders in whom they had put their trust, the people began to act for themselves, and to exercise pressure on the "leaders of opinion." Paris began to prepare for a great insurrection which was to allow the people to dethrone the King. The sections, the Popular Societies, and the Fraternal Societies—that is, the "unknown ones," the crowd, seconded by the Club of the Cordeliers, set themselves this task. The keenest and most enlightened patriots, says Chaumette,* assembled at the Club of the Cordeliers and there they used to pass the night, preparing the popular insurrection. There was, among others, one committee which got up a red flag, bearing the inscription: "Martial Law of the People against the Rebellion of the Court." Under this flag were to rally all free men—the true republicans, those who had to avenge a friend, a son or some relative assassinated in the Champ-de-Mars on July 17, 1791.

Most historians, paying a tribute to their authoritarian training, represent the Jacobin Club as the initiator and the head of all the revolutionary movements in Paris and the

* *Mémoires*, p. 13.

provinces, and for two generations every one believed this. But now we know that such was not the case. The initiative of June 20 and August 10 did not come from the Jacobins. On the contrary, for a whole year they were opposed, even the most revolutionary of them, to appealing again to the people. Only when they saw themselves outflanked by the popular movement, they decided, and again only a section of them, to follow it.

But with what timidity! They wished to see the people out in the street, combating the royalists; but they dared not wish for the consequences. What if the people were not satisfied with overthrowing the royal power? If popular wrath should turn against the rich, the powerful, the cunning ones, who saw in the Revolution nothing but a means of enriching themselves? If the people should sweep away the Legislative Assembly, after the Tuileries? If the Commune of Paris, the extremists, the "anarchists"—those whom Robespierre himself freely loaded with his invectives—those republicans who preached "the equality of conditions"— what if they should get the upper hand?

This is why, in all the conferences which took place before June 20, we see so much hesitation on the part of the prominent revolutionists. This is why the Jacobins were so reluctant to approve the necessity of another popular rising. It was only in July, when the people, setting aside the constitutional laws, proclaimed the "permanence" of the sections, ordered the general armament, and forced the Assembly to declare "the country in danger"—it was only then that the Robespierres, the Dantons and, at the very last moment, the Girondins decided to follow the people's lead and declare themselves more or less at one with the insurrection.

It was quite natural that under these circumstances the movement of June 20 could not have either the spirit or the unity that was necessary to make of it a successful insurrection against the Tuileries. The people came out into the streets, but, uncertain as to the attitude of the middle classes, the masses did not dare to compromise themselves too much. They acted as if they wanted to find out first how far they could go in their attack of the palace—leaving the rest to the chances of all great popular demonstrations. If anything comes of this one—all the better; if not, they will at least have seen the Tuileries at close quarters and estimated its strength.

This is, in fact, what happened. The demonstration was perfectly peaceful. Under the pretence of petitioning the Assembly to celebrate the anniversary of the Oath in the Tennis Court, and to plant a tree of Liberty at the door of the National Assembly, an immense multitude of people came out on this day. It soon filled all the streets leading from the Bastille to the Assembly, while the Court filled with its adherents the Place du Carrousel, the great courtyard of the Tuileries and the outskirts of the palace. All the gates of the Tuileries were closed, cannon were trained on the people; cartridges were distributed to the soldiers, and a conflict between the two bodies seemed inevitable.

However, the sight of the ever-increasing multitudes paralysed the defenders of the Court. The outer gates were soon either opened or forced, and the Place du Carrousel as also the courtyards were inundated with people. Many were armed with pikes and sabres, or with sticks at the end of which a knife, a hatchet, or a saw was fixed, but the section had carefully selected the men who were to take part in the demonstration.

The crowd were beginning to break in one of the doors of the palace with the blows of an axe, when Louis XVI. himself ordered it to be opened. Immediately thousands of men burst into the inner courtyards and the palace itself. The Queen, with her son, had been hurried away by her friends into a hall, part of which was barricaded with a large table. The King being discovered in another room, it was filled in a few minutes by the crowd. They demanded that he should sanction the decrees which he had vetoed; that the "patriot ministers"—that is, the Girondist Ministry—whom he had dismissed on June 13, should be recalled; that the rebel priests should be driven out of France; and his choice be made between Coblentz and Paris. The King took off his hat, and allowed a woollen cap to be put on his head; the crowd also made him drink a glass of wine to the health of the nation. But for two hours he withstood the crowd, repeating that he should abide by the Constitution.

As an attack on royalty, the movement had failed. Nothing came of it.

But the rage of the well-to-do classes against the people was only the greater on that account. Since the masses had not dared to attack the palace, and had, by that, shown their weakness, they fell upon them with all the hatred that can be inspired only by fear.

When a letter from Louis XVI., complaining of the invasion of his palace, was read at the sitting of the Assembly, the members broke out into applause, as servile as the plaudits of the courtiers before 1789. Jacobins and Girondins were unanimous in thus disowning any share in the demonstration.

Encouraged undoubtedly by this manifestation of support, the Court had a tribunal set up in the palace of the Tuileries itself, for the punishing of those guilty of the movement. They were thus resuscitating, says Chaumette in his *Mémoires*, the odious methods of procedure which had been resorted to after October 5 and 6, 1789, and after July 17, 1791. This tribunal was composed of justices of the peace in the pay of royalty. The Court sent them their food, and the Wardrobe-Keeper of the Crown had orders to provide for all their wants.*
The most vigorous of the writers were prosecuted and sent to prison. Several presidents and secretaries of the sections shared the same fate. Again it became dangerous to call oneself a republican.

The Directories of the departments and a large number of municipalities joined in the servile protestations of the Assembly and sent letters of indignation against the "faction." In reality, thirty-three out of the eighty-three Directories of departments—that is, the whole west of France—were openly royalist and counter-revolutionary.

Revolutions, we must remember, are always made by minorities, and even when a revolution has begun, and a part

* *Journal de Perlet* of June 27, quoted by Aulard in a note added to the *Mémoires* of Chaumette.

of the nation accepts its consequences, there is always only a very small minority who understands what still remains to be done to assure the triumph of what has been obtained, and who have the courage of action. This is why an Assembly, always representing the average of the country, or rather something below the average, has always been, and will always be, a check upon revolution; it can never be an instrument of revolution.

The Legislative Assembly gives us a striking case in point. On July 7—that is, four days before the country had to be declared in danger in consequence of the German invasion, and one month only before the downfall of royalty—the following occurrence took place in the Assembly. They had been discussing for several days what measures should be taken for the general safety, when, at the instigation of the Court, Lamourette, Bishop of Lyons, proposed, on a motion of order, a general reconciliation of the parties, and to bring it about, he suggested a very simple means : " One party in the Assembly attributes to the other the seditious design of wishing to destroy the monarchy. The others attribute to their colleagues the design of wishing the destruction of constitutional equality and the aristocratic government known under the name of the Two Chambers. Well, gentlemen, let us annihilate by a common execration, and by an irrevocable oath, let us annihilate both the Republic and the Two Chambers." Hats were thrown into the air, members embraced each other, the Right fraternised with the Left, and a deputation was sent at once to the King, who came to join in the general gaiety. This scene is known in history as " the Lamourette kiss." Fortunately public opinion was not captured by such scenes. The same evening Billaud-Varennes protested at the Jacobin Club against this hypocritical attempt at reconciliation, and it was decided to send his speech out to the affiliated societies. The Court on its side had no intention of disarming. Pétion, Mayor of Paris, had been suspended from his office that very day by the royalist Directory of the Seine department, for his negligence on June 20. But then, the people of Paris took up the cause of their mayor passionately, so that six days later, on July 13, the Assembly thought fit to rescind the suspension.

The people had made up their minds. They understood that the moment had come when they must get rid of royalty, and that, if June 20 were not quickly followed by a popular rising, all would be over with the Revolution. But the politicians in the Assembly judged otherwise. "Who could tell what would be the result of a rising?" they asked themselves, and the result was that with but a few exceptions the legislators of the Assembly were already arranging for a way out, in case the counter-revolution should be victorious.

The fears of those who intend to become "statesmen," and their desire of securing for themselves pardon in case of defeat —there lies the danger for every revolution.

For all those who seek instruction from history, the seven weeks which elapsed between the demonstration of June 20 and the taking of the Tuileries on August 10, 1792, are of the highest importance.

Although the demonstration on June 20 had had no immediate result, it produced nevertheless a great awakening all over France. "The revolt ran from town to town," as Louis Blanc says. The foreigner was at the gates of Paris, and on July 11 the country was proclaimed in danger. On the 14th, the Federation was celebrated, and on this occasion the people made a formidable demonstration against royalty. From every side the revolutionary municipalities sent addresses to the Assembly calling on it to take action. Since the King had betrayed his country they demanded his dethronement or, at least, his suspension. The word Republic, however, was not yet mentioned; there was rather an inclination towards a regency. Marseilles was an exception, as it had demanded the abolition of royalty since June 27, and had sent five hundred volunteers who arrived in Paris singing the "Marseillaise Hymn." Brest and other towns also sent some volunteers, and the sections of Paris, sitting in permanence, armed themselves and organised their popular battalions.

It was felt on all sides that the Revolution was approaching a decisive moment.

What, then, did the Assembly do ? And what those middle-class republicans—the Girondins ?

When the strongly worded address from Marseilles was read in the Assembly, demanding that measures in consonance with the seriousness of events should be taken, nearly the whole of the Assembly protested. And when Duhem, on July 27, demanded that the dethronement should be discussed, his proposition was received with howls.

Marie-Antoinette certainly was not mistaken when she wrote, on July 7, to her intimate correspondents abroad, that the patriots were frightened and wanted to negotiate—which is what really came to pass a few days later.

Those who were with the people, in the sections, no doubt felt that they were on the eve of some great event. The sections of Paris had declared themselves permanent, as well as several of the municipalities. Taking no notice of the law concerning the *passive* citizens, they admitted them to their deliberations, and armed them with pikes. It was evident that a great insurrection was on the way.

But the Girondins, the party of "the statesmen," were just then sending to the King, through his *valet de chambre*, Thierry, a letter telling him that a formidable insurrection was preparing, that the dethronement and something yet more terrible might result from it, and that only one way remained to prevent this catastrophe, and that was to recall the Ministry of Roland, Servan and Clavière within eight days at latest.

Certainly it was not "the twelve millions promised to Brissot" which impelled the Girondins to take this step. Neither was it, as Louis Blanc wrote, their ambition to re-grasp the power. The cause was much deeper than that, and Brissot's pamphlet *A ses commettants* discloses clearly what the Girondins thought at this moment. It was their fear of a popular revolution—a revolution which would touch upon property—their fear and their contempt for the people —the mob of ragged wretches, who guided them: their fear of a system in which property and more than that, authoritarian training and the "managing capacity," would lose the privileges they had conferred until then—the fear of seeing themselves reduced to the level of " the Great Unwashed."

This fear paralysed the Girondins as to-day it paralyses all the parties who occupy in Parliaments the same position, more or less Governmental, which the Girondins occupied at that time.

We can comprehend, therefore, the despair which seized upon the true patriots and expressed by Marat in these words:

" For three years," he wrote, " we have striven to regain our liberty, and we are now as far off from it as ever. The Revolution has turned against the people. For the Court and its supporters it is an eternal motive for intrigue and corruption; for the legislators, an occasion for prevarication and trickery. . . . Already it is for the rich and the avaricious nothing but an opportunity for illicit gains, monopolies, frauds and spoliations, while the people are ruined, and the numberless poor are placed between the fear of perishing from hunger and the necessity of selling themselves. . . . Let us not be afraid to repeat: we are further from liberty than ever; for, not only are we slaves, but we are so legally."

" On the stage of the State, the scenery only has been changed," he writes further on. " The same actors, the same intrigues, the same motives have remained." " It was fatal," continues Marat, " for the lower classes of the nation to be left alone to struggle against the highest class. At the moment of an insurrection the people will break down all before them by their weight; but whatever advantage they may gain at first, they will end by succumbing to the machinations of the superior classes, who are full of cunning, craft and artifice. Educated men, those who are well off, and the crafty ones of the superior classes, had at first taken sides against the despot; but that was only to turn against the people, after they had wormed themselves into the people's confidence and had made use of the people's forces to set themselves up in the place of the privileged orders whom they have proscribed."

" Thus," continues Marat—and his words are of gold, since one might say they were written to-day, in the twentieth century—" thus it is that the revolution has been made and maintained only by the lowest classes of society—by the workers, the artisans, the little tradesmen, the agriculturists, by the plebs, by those luckless ones whom the shameless rich call *canaille*, and whom Roman insolence called *proletarians*. But who would ever have imagined that it would be made only in favour of the small landowners, the men of law, the supporters of fraud."

The day after the taking of the Bastille, it would have been easy for the representatives of the people " to have suspended from their offices the despot and his agents," wrote Marat further on. " But for doing that, they ought to have had perspicacity and virtue." As to the *people, instead of arming themselves universally, they permitted one part only of the citizens to arm* (meaning the National Guard composed of *active* citizens). And instead of attacking the enemies of the Revolution without further delay, the people gave up the advantages of their victory by remaining merely in a state of defence.

"To-day," says Marat, "after three years of everlasting speeches from patriotic societies and a deluge of writings . . . the people are further from feeling what they ought to do in order to be able to resist their oppressors, than they were on the very first day of the Revolution. At that time they followed their natural instincts, their simple good sense which made them find the true way for subduing their implacable foes. . . . Now, behold them—chained in the name of the law, tyrannised over in the name of justice; they are constitutional slaves!"

This might have been written yesterday, yet it is taken from No. 657 of the *Ami du peuple*.

A profound discouragement took hold of Marat, and he could see only one exit: "some fit of civic fury" on the part of the people, as on July 13 and 14 and on October 5 and 6, 1789. Despair was devouring him, until the federates came from the departments to Paris. This filled him with new hope.

The chances of the counter-revolution were so great at the end of July 1792, that Louis XVI. curtly refused the proposition of the Girondins. Were not the Prussians already marching upon Paris? And Lafayette and Luckner too, were they not ready to turn their armies against the Jacobins, against Paris? Lafayette, who enjoyed great power in the North, and was the idol of the middle-class National Guards in Paris!

In fact, the King had many reasons to expect a victory. The Jacobins dared not act. And when Marat, on July 18, after the treachery of Lafayette and Luckner became known —they had wanted to carry off the King on July 16, and to set him in the midst of their armies—when Marat proposed to take the King as a hostage for the nation against the foreign invasion, every one turned his back on him, and treated him as a madman: he had none but the *sans-culottes* in the hovels to approve him. Because he had dared to say at that moment what to-day we know to be *the truth*, because he had dared to denounce the plottings of the King with the foreigner, Marat was abandoned by every one, even by those few patriotic Jacobins upon whom he, who is represented as so suspicious, had, however, depended. They refused even to give him an asylum when he was hunted down for arrest and knocked for shelter at their doors.

As to the Girondins, after the King had refused their proposal, they again parleyed with him, through the intermediary of the painter, Boze. They sent him another message on July 25.

Fifteen days only separated Paris from August 10. Revolutionary France was chafing the bit. It knew that the supreme moment had come. Either the finishing blow must be struck at royalty, or else the Revolution would remain unaccomplished. How could they allow royalty to surround itself with troops, and to organise the great plot which was to deliver Paris to the Germans? Who knows how many years longer royalty, slightly rejuvenated, but still very nearly absolute, would have continued to rule France?

And yet, at this supreme moment, the whole care of the politicians was to dispute among themselves as to whose hands the power should fall into if it should drop from the hands of the King!

The Girondins wanted it to go to their Committee of Twelve, which should then become the Executive Power. Robespierre, for his part, demanded fresh elections—a renovated Assembly—a Convention, which should give France a new Republican Constitution.

As to acting, as to preparing the dethronement, nobody thought of that except the people : the Jacobins thought of it as little as all other politicians. It was once more " the unknown men," the favourites of the people—Santerre, Fournier, the American, the Pole, Lazowski, Carra, Simon,* Westermann, at that time a simple law-clerk—who came together at the Soleil d'Or to plan the siege of the palace and the general rising, with the red flag at its head. It was the sections—the majority of the Paris sections, and a few here and there in the north of France—in the department of Maine-et-Loire, and in Marseilles ; and finally, the volunteers from Marseilles and Brest, whom the people of Paris had enlisted in the cause of the insurrection.

The people : always the people !

" There (in the National Assembly) they were like lawyers crazily disputing, without cessation, over trifling matters, under the whip of their masters. . . ."

" Here (in the Assembly of the Sections) the very foundations of the Republic were being laid," as Chaumette expressed it in his notes on August 10.

* J. F. Simon was a German tutor, an old collaborator of Basedow in the Philantropium at Dessau.

CHAPTER XXXIII

THE TENTH OF AUGUST: ITS IMMEDIATE CONSEQUENCES

Peasants ignore feudal system—Change in state of France—Royalist plans—Administration—Army—Lafayette—Feudal laws—King and Germans—Revolutionists fear popular risings—Robespierre—Revolutionary leaders at length join hands—People prepare to strike—New " Commune " springs up—August 10—Royalists anticipate victory—Indecision of Assembly—Abolition of royalty—Triumph of popular revolution—Decrees passed under compulsion by Assembly—Feudal laws—Lands of émigrés—Proposal of Mailhe—Legislative Assembly dissolves—Commune of Paris

WE have seen what was the condition of France during the summer of 1792. For three years the country had been in open revolution and a return to the old state of affairs had been made absolutely impossible. For, if the feudal system still existed according to law, in actuality it was no longer acknowledged by the peasants. They paid the feudal dues no more; they got hold of the lands of the clergy and the emigrant nobles; and in certain places they, themselves, retook from the landlord the lands which formerly belonged to the village communities. In their village municipalities, they considered themselves the masters of their own affairs.

The State institutions were equally upset. The whole of the administrative structure, which seemed so formidable under the old *régime*, was crumbling away under the breath of the popular revolution. Who had any respect now for the ex-governor of the province, or for the Marshals' Courts and the judges of the old *parlement?* The new municipality, closely watched over by the local *sans-culottes*, the Popular

AUGUST 10: ITS CONSEQUENCES

Society of the place, the Primary Assembly, the men with the pikes—these represented the new powers of France.

The whole aspect of the country, the whole spirit of the people, its language, its manners, its ideas, had been changed by the Revolution. *A new nation was born*, and in its political and social conceptions it completely differed from what had been scarce twelve months before.

But still the old *régime* was left standing. Royalty continued to exist and represented an enormous force, round which the counter-revolutionists were ready to rally. The nation was living under provisional conditions. To give back to royalty its former power was clearly a dream in which no one but some Court fanatics believed any longer. But the powers of royalty for evil were still immense. If it could not restore the feudal system, what evil might it not do, all the same, to the liberated peasants, if, after having got the upper hand, its supporters should dispute in every village the land and the liberties the peasants had won. This was, in fact, what the King and a good many of the Constitutional Monarchists, the "Feuillants," proposed to do as soon as the Court party should have crushed those whom they called the "Jacobins."

As to the Administration in two-thirds of the departments, and even in Paris, the departmental administration and that of the districts were against the people, against the Revolution, they were ready to adapt themselves to any simulacrum of a constitution that would have permitted the middle classes to share the power of governing with the King and the Court.

The army, commanded by men like Lafayette and Luckner, could be used at any moment against the nation. In fact, we have seen how, after June 20, Lafayette left his camp and came to Paris to offer the King the support of "his" army against the people, to break up the patriotic societies and to make a *coup d'état* in favour of the Court.

And to crown all, the feudal laws still remained in force. If the peasants had ceased to pay the feudal dues this was a breach of the law; and the moment the King recovered his authority the peasants would have been compelled to pay everything, so long as they had not freed themselves from the clutches of the feudal past by redeeming their servitude—they would have had to restore all the land they had taken from the landlord and even what they had bought from the State.

It was clear that this provisional state of things could not last long. A nation cannot go on living with a sword suspended over its head. And, moreover, the people, guided by their unfailing instincts, knew perfectly well that the King was conniving with the Germans, and inviting them to march on Paris. At that time, it is true, no written proof of his treachery was yet known. The correspondence of the King and Marie-Antoinette had not been discovered, and it was not known how these two traitors were urging the Austrians and the Prussians to hasten their march on Paris; that they were keeping them informed as to all the movements of the French troops; transmitting to them all the military secrets, thus delivering up France to the invaders. All this was only learned later, and even then, rather vaguely, after the taking of the Tuileries, when certain papers of the King's were seized in a secret cupboard made for him by locksmith Gamain. But treason is not easily hidden, and by a thousand indications, upon which the men and women of the people were quick to seize, they were convinced that the Court had made an agreement with the Germans and that France was going to be delivered up to them.

The idea gradually spread then, through Paris and the provinces, that it was necessary to strike a great blow against the Tuileries: that the old *régime* would remain a perpetual menace to France so long as Louis XVI. remained on the throne.

And in order to strike that blow, an appeal had to be made for a rising of the people of Paris—to the men with the pikes—as had been done in 1789 before July 14. And this was what the middle classes refused to do—what they dreaded most. We find, indeed, in the writings of the period a kind of terror of "the men with the pikes." Were they going to reappear, these men so terrible to the rich?

The worst was that this fear was felt not only by the propertied classes, but also by the advanced politicians. Robespierre up to June 1792 also opposed the appeal for a popular rising. "The overthrow of the Constitution at this moment," he said, "can only kindle civil war, which will lead to anarchy and despotism." He did not believe in the possibility of a republic. "What," he exclaimed, "is it in the midst of so many fatal dissensions that they want to leave us suddenly without a Constitution!" The republic, in his opinion, would be "the arbitrary will of the few." He meant of the Girondins. "This is the aim of all the intrigues which have agitated us this long while." And to baffle these intrigues he preferred to retain the King and the intrigues of the Court! This was how he spoke as late as June, two months before August 10.

To convince the revolutionary "leaders of opinion" of the necessity of striking a blow at the Tuileries and of making an appeal, therefore, for a popular rising, nothing less was required than that they should have visible testimony of the reaction which began after June 20—the coming of Lafayette to Paris to offer "his" army for a royalist *coup d'état*, the Germans making ready to march on Paris "to deliver the King" and "to punish the Jacobins," and finally, the active military preparations made by the Court for attacking Paris. Only then did they make up their minds, and understand the necessity of the rising. But once this was decided upon, the people undertook to do the rest.

It is certain that Danton, Robespierre, Marat, Robert and a few others came to a preliminary understanding. Robespierre detested everything about Marat; his military fervour, which he called exaggeration, his hatred of the rich, his absolute distrust of politicians—everything even to the poor and dirty clothing of the man, who since the Revolution had broken out had eaten nothing but the food of the people, bread and water, and had entirely devoted himself to the people's cause. And yet the elegant and punctilious Robespierre, as well as Danton, approached Marat and his followers, approached the men of the Paris sections of the Commune, to come to an understanding with them as to the means of rousing the people again, as on July 14. They at last understood that if the provisional state of things lasted much longer the Revolution would die out without having accomplished anything durable.

Either an appeal should be made to the people, and then full liberty would have to be left to the poor to strike their enemies as it seemed best to them, and to levy what they could upon the property of the rich, or else the royal power would win in the struggle and this would mean the triumph of the counter-revolution, the destruction of the little that had been obtained in the direction of equality—the White Terror of 1794 would have begun in 1792.

An understanding was, therefore, arrived at between a small number of the more advanced Jacobins, and those of the people who wanted to strike a decisive blow at the Tuileries. But the moment they had come to this understanding, from the moment when " the leaders of opinion "—the Robespierres, the Dantons, and their followers—promised to oppose no longer a popular insurrection, and declared their readiness to support it, the rest was left to the people, who understood, much better than the leaders of the parties, the necessity for common action when the Revolution was on the point of striking such a decisive blow.

The people, the Great Unknown, now began to prepare for the rising and they created, spontaneously, for the needs of the moment, the kind of sectional organisation which was judged the fittest to give the necessary cohesion to the movement. As to the details, they were left to the organising spirit of the people of the faubourgs, and when the sun rose over Paris no one could have predicted how that great day would end. The two battalions of federals from Marseilles and Brest, well organised and armed, numbered only about a thousand men, no one except those who had been working the preceding days and nights in the red-hot furnace of the faubourgs could say whether the faubourgs would rise in a body or not.

"And the ordinary leaders, where were they and what were they doing?" asks Louis Blanc. "There is nothing to

AUGUST 10: ITS CONSEQUENCES

indicate," he replies, "what action Robespierre took on this supreme night, or whether he did anything at all." Nor does Danton seem to have taken any active part in the preparations for the rising or in the fight itself on August 10.

It is quite clear that, from the moment that the movement was decided, the people had no need of the politicians. What was necessary was to arm the people, to distribute weapons among those who knew how to use them, to organise the nucleus of each battalion, to form a column in each street of the faubourgs. For this work, the politicians would only have been in the way, and the men of the people told them to go to bed while the movement was being definitely organised on the night of August 9 and 10. That is what Danton did, and he slept peacefully, as we know from Lucile Desmoulin's journal.

New men, "unknown ones," came to the front in those days, when a new General Council, the Revolutionary Commune of August 10, was appointed by the sections. Taking the law into their own hands, each section nominated three commissioners, "to save the country," and the people's choice fell, so the historians tell us, upon obscure men. The "extremist," Hébert, was one of them, that was a matter of course; but we find neither Marat nor Danton among them at first.*

Thus it was that a new "Commune"—the insurrectionary Commune—sprang up in the midst of the people and took upon itself the direction of the rising. And we shall see this Commune exercising a powerful influence over the progress of subsequent events; dominating the Convention and urging "the Mountain" to revolutionary action so as to secure, at least, the conquests already won by the Revolution.

It would be useless to narrate here the whole day's doings on August 10. The dramatic side of the Revolution is what

---

* "How great that Assembly was!" says Chaumette in his *Mémoires*, p. 44. "What sublime outbursts I witnessed during the discussion on the King's dethronement! What was the National Assembly, with its paltry passions, its petty measures, its decrees stifled at birth, then crushed by the veto, what was that Assembly, I say, in comparison with the Assembly of the Commissioners from the Paris sections?"

has been told best by the historians, and excellent descriptions of its events will be found in Michelet and Louis Blanc. We shall, therefore, confine ourselves to recalling the chief features of that day.

Ever since Marseilles had declared for the dethronement of the King, petitions and addresses for the dethronement had come in great numbers to the Assembly. In Paris forty-two sections had pronounced in favour of it. Pétion had even gone on August 4 to bring forward this resolution of the sections at the bar of the Assembly.

As to the politicians they did not realise in the least the gravity of the situation; and though we find in letters written from Paris by Madame Jullien on August 7 and 8, such passages as these: "A terrible storm is coming up on the horizon. . . . At this moment the horizon is heavy with vapours which must produce a terrible explosion"—the Assembly in its sitting of the 8th calmly voted the absolution of Lafayette for his letter as if no such thing as a movement of hatred against royalty existed.

All the while the people of Paris were preparing for a decisive battle. The insurrectionary committee had, however, the good sense not to fix any date for the rising beforehand. They merely sounded the varying moods of the population of Paris, did their best to brace up their minds, and kept watch for the moment when the appeal to arms could be made. Thus, they tried, apparently, to provoke a rising on June 26, after a popular banquet among the ruins of the Bastille, in which the whole faubourg had taken part—people bringing to it their tables and provisions.* And they tried another rising on July 30, but again the attempt did not succeed.

Altogether the preparations for the rising, badly seconded by "the leaders of opinion," would, perhaps, have dragged out to some length, if the plots of the Court had not helped to precipitate matters. With the aid of the courtiers, who had sworn to die for the King, along with some battalions of the National Guard that had remained faithful to the Court

* Mortimer Ternaux, *La Terreur*, vol. ii. p. 130.

AUGUST 10: ITS CONSEQUENCES

and the Swiss, the royalists felt sure of victory. They had fixed August 10 for their *coup d'état*. "That was the day fixed for the counter-revolution," we read in one of the letters of the period; "the following day was to see all the Jacobins of the kingdom drowned in their own blood."

The insurrection, therefore, could not be postponed any longer. On the night of the 9th and 10th, just about midnight, the tocsin rang in Paris. At first, however, its call seemed not to be well attended, and it was asked at the Commune whether the rising should not be countermanded. At seven o'clock in the morning certain quarters were still tranquil. In reality, however, it appears that the people of Paris, with their admirable instinct for revolution, did not want to enter into conflict with the royal troops in the dark, because such a fight might easily have ended in their being routed.

In the meantime the Insurrectionary Commune had taken possession of the Hôtel de Ville during the night, and the legal council of the Commune had abdicated in the presence of this new revolutionary power, which immediately gave an impetus to the insurrection.

About seven o'clock in the morning only some men with pikes, led by the Federates from Marseilles, debouched upon the Place du Carrousel; but an hour later large masses of the people began to move, and the King was informed that "all Paris" was marching on the Tuileries.

It was indeed all Paris, that is, all the Paris of the poor, supported by the National Guards from the workers' and artisans' quarters.

About half-past eight, as these masses were already approaching the palace, the King, haunted by the recent memory of what had happened on June 20, and fearing to be killed this time by the people, quitted the Tuileries, and went to take refuge with the Assembly, leaving his faithful servitors to defend the palace and to massacre its assailants. But as soon as the King had gone, entire battalions of National Guards from the rich middle-class quarters dispersed, so as not to have to face the people in revolt.

Compact masses of the people then thronged into the

approaches to the Tuileries, and their vanguard, encouraged by the Swiss Guards, who flung their cartridges out of the palace windows, penetrated into one of the courtyards of the Tuileries. But here, others of the Swiss, commanded by the officers of the Court and posted on the great staircase of the chief entrance, fired upon the crowd, and in a few minutes four hundred of the assailants lay dead in heaps at the foot of the stairs.

This shooting decided the issue of the day. The cries of "Treachery! Death to the King! Death to the Austrian woman!" rapidly spread all over the town, and the people of Paris ran towards the Tuileries from all sides—the Faubourgs Saint-Antoine and Saint-Marceau rushed there in a body—and soon the Swiss, under the furious assault of the people, were either disarmed or massacred.

Need we recall the fact that even at the supreme moment the Assembly remained undecided, not knowing what to do? They acted only when the armed people burst into the hall where they were sitting threatening to kill the King and his family, as well as the deputies who did not dare to pronounce the dethronement. Even after the Tuileries had been taken and when royalty no longer existed in fact, the Girondins, who formerly had loved to orate about the Republic, still hesitated to face any decisive action. All that Vergniaud dared demand was "a provisional suspension of the head of the executive power"—who, henceforth, should be installed int he Palace of the Luxembourg.

It was only two or three days later that the Revolutionary Commune transferred Louis XVI. and his family from the Luxembourg, whence they might easily have escaped, to the tower of the Temple, and undertook to hold them there as the people's prisoners.

Royalty was thus abolished *de facto*. Henceforth the Revolution was able to develop for awhile without fear of being suddenly checked in its progress by a royalist *coup d'état* or by a massacre of the revolutionists by the "White Terror."

For the politicians the chief interests of the revolution of

AUGUST 10: ITS CONSEQUENCES

August 10 lay in the blow it had struck at royalty. For the people it lay especially in the abolition of that force, which was opposing the carrying out of the decrees against the feudal rights, against the emigrant nobles and against the priests, and which at the same time had appealed to a German invasion to re-establish the feudal monarchy. It lay in the triumph of a popular revolution, in a triumph of the masses, who could now push on the Revolution towards Equality—that dream and aim of the poor. Consequently, on the very day after August 10, the Legislative Assembly, reactionary as it was, had to pass, under pressure from without, some decrees which were to send the Revolution a step forward.

Every priest who had not yet taken the oath (so ran these decrees), and who, within the next fortnight, did not swear to obey the Constitution, and yet was found after that time upon French territory, should be transported to Cayenne.

All the lands of the emigrant nobles, in France and in the colonies, were to be sequestrated, and put up for sale in small lots.

All distinctions between *passive* citizens (the poor) and *active* citizens (the propertied classes) were abolished. Every one became an elector on attaining his twenty-first year, and was eligible for election at twenty-five.

As to the feudal laws, we have seen how the Constituent Assembly, on March 15, 1790, had made a decree, according to which the feudal dues were supposed to represent the price of a certain concession of land, made once upon a time by the landowner to the tenant—which was, of course, false—and, as such, all the feudal dues had to be paid so long as they were not redeemed by the tenant. This decree, by thus confounding the *personal* dues, the outcome of rent, wiped out, *de facto*, the decree of August 4, 1789, which had declared the former to be abolished. By the decree of March 15, 1790, these decrees came up again under the fiction which represented them as payment for the possession of the land. This is what Couthon had made quite evident in his report, read before the Assembly on February 29, 1792.

But on June 14, 1792, that is to say, when June 20 was

close at hand, and it was necessary to conciliate the people, the Left, taking advantage of the accidental absence of certain members of the Right, abolished *without indemnity* some of the personal feudal dues, the most noteworthy being the *casuel*, that is, the right of the lord to levy dues in cases of legacies left by his tenants, on marriages, on sales and on the wine-press, the mill and other communal necessaries.

After three years of revolution a parliamentary trick was thus necessary to obtain from the Assembly the abolition of these odious dues. In reality even this decree did not finally abolish them : in certain cases they still had to be redeemed ; but let us pass over that.

As to the annual feudal levies, such as the quit-rents, the field-tax and so on, which were paid in addition to the rent and represented relics of the ancient servitude, they remained in full force.

But now came August 10. The people had taken possession of the Tuileries, and the King was dethroned and imprisoned. And as soon as this news spread to the villages, petitions from the peasants flooded the Assembly, demanding the total abolition of the feudal rights.

These were the days before September 2, when the attitude of the people of Paris was not altogether reassuring for the Legislative Assembly, which was accused of plotting with royalty, and the Assembly, seeing itself compelled to take some steps forward, issued the decrees of August 16 to 25, 1792.

In virtue of these decrees all prosecution for non-payment of feudal dues was suspended. The feudal and seigniorial rights of all kinds, which were not the price of an original concession of land, were suppressed without indemnity.

And by the decree of August 20, it was permitted to redeem separately, either the *casuel* rights, or the annual rights, the legitimacy of which could be proved by presenting the original title of the concession of land. All this, however, only in case of a *new* purchase by a new owner.

The abolition of the prosecutions represented, undoubtedly, a great step in advance. But the feudal rights still remained.

They had still to be redeemed. The new law only added to the confusion—the result being that, henceforth, the peasants could pay nothing and redeem nothing. And this was what the peasants did while waiting for some new victory for the people and some new concession on the part of the ruling classes.

At the same time all tithes and prestations, or obligatory unpaid labour for the clergy, which had been retained from the days of serfdom or mortmain, were suppressed without indemnity. This was a substantial gain. If the Assembly protected the lands and the middle-class monopolists, they, at least, delivered up the priests, since the King was no longer there to defend them.

But at the same time the Assembly took a measure which, if it had been applied, would have stirred up the whole of the French peasantry against the Republic. It abolished the joint responsibility for payments which existed in the peasant communes,* and accepting the motion of François de Neufchâteau, the Assembly ordered the communal lands to be divided among the citizens. It appears, however, that this decree, expressed in a few lines and in very vague terms, was never taken seriously. Its application, besides, would have involved such difficulties that it remained a dead letter; and when the question came up again, the Legislative Assembly, having finished its term of office, dissolved without coming to any decision.

Concerning the lands of the emigrant nobles it was decided to put them up for sale in small lots of two, three, or not more than four acres. And this sale was to be made, " on lease, at a money rent," always redeemable. That is to say, he who had not the money could purchase all the same, on condition of paying a perpetual rent, which he might, some day, be able to redeem. This was, of course, to the advantage of the poor peasant, but all sorts of difficulties were evidently put in the way of small purchasers. Well-to-do middle-class people preferred to buy the estates of the emigrant nobles

* It was the same thing evidently as that which exists in Russia under the name of *krougovaia porouka*, " responsibility all round."

in bulk and to speculate in the sale of them broken up into lots later on.

Finally—and this, too, was typical—one of the members, Mailhe, took advantage of the condition of men's minds at this moment to propose a measure which was really revolutionary and was accepted later on, in 1793, after the fall of the Girondins. He demanded that the effects of the royal ordinance of 1669 might be broken, and that the lords should be compelled to restore to the village communes the land which they had taken away from them in virtue of that ordinance. His proposal, however, was not accepted; a new revolution was required for that.

These then were the results of August 10: Royalty was overthrown, and now it was possible for the Revolution to turn over a new page in the direction of equality, provided the Assembly and the governing classes in general did not oppose it.

The King and his family were in prison. A new Assembly, a National Convention, was convoked. The elections were to be made by universal suffrage, but still in two degrees.

Some measures were taken against the priests who refused to recognise the Constitution, and against the emigrant nobles. Orders were given to put up for sale the lands of the *émigrés* which had been sequestrated in accordance with the decree of March 30, 1792.

The war against the invaders was to be pushed on vigorously by the *sans-culotte* volunteers.

But the great question—"what was to be done with the traitor King"—and that other great question, which was so vital for fifteen million peasants—the question of the feudal rights—remained in suspense. It was still necessary to redeem those rights in order to do away with them. And the new law concerning the partition of the communal lands threw the villages into alarm.

It was over this that the Legislative Assembly dissolved, after doing all they could to prevent the Revolution from developing normally, and from putting an end to those two heritages of the past: the absolute authority of the King and the feudal laws.

But by the side of the Legislative Assembly there had grown up, since August 10, a new power, the Commune of Paris, which took into its hands the revolutionary initiative and, as we shall see presently, managed to retain it for nearly two years.

CHAPTER XXXIV

THE INTERREGNUM—THE BETRAYALS

People demand justice—*Suspension* of King—Danger of German invasion—Heroism of people—Royalists and Germans—Despair of people—Popularity of Lafayette—Position of middle-class landowners—Royalist plots for King's escape—Activity of Commune—Revolutionary army organised—Character of Revolution changes—Struggle between Assembly and Commune—Surrender of Longwy—Exultation of Royalists—Royalist conspirators acquitted—Royalist houses searched—Nearly two thousand arrests—Assembly orders Great Council of Commune to dissolve—Commune refuses to obey—Royalist plan disclosed—Siege of Verdun—Indignation of revolutionists

THE people of Paris wept for their dead; and loudly demanded justice and punishment on those who had provoked the massacre round the Tuileries.

Eleven hundred men, says Michelet, three thousand according to public rumour, had been slain by the defenders of the Palace. It was chiefly the men with the pikes, the extremely poor folk of the faubourgs who had suffered. They had rushed in crowds on the Tuileries, and had fallen under the bullets of the Swiss and the nobles protected by the strong walls of the Palace.

Tumbrils laden with corpses wended their way to the faubourgs, says Michelet, and there they laid out the dead, so that they might be identified. The crowd gathered round them, and the men's cries for vengeance mingled with the sobs of the women.

On the evening of August 10 and the following day the popular fury was turned chiefly on the Swiss. Had not some of the Swiss thrown their cartridges out of the windows, thereby inviting the crowd to enter the Palace? Were not

THE INTERREGNUM—THE BETRAYALS

the people trying to fraternise with the Swiss, who were posted on the great staircase at the entrance, when at close quarters they opened a steady and murderous fire on the crowd?

But the people soon came to know, however, that it was necessary to strike higher, if they wanted to reach the instigators of the massacre; at the King, the Queen, and "the Austrian Committee" in the Tuileries.

Now, it was just the King, the Queen, and their faithful adherents whom the Assembly protected with their authority. It is true that the King, the Queen, their children and the familiar friends of Marie-Antoinette were shut up in the tower of the Temple. The Commune had obtained their transference to this Tower from the Assembly, by declining all responsibility if they remained in the Luxembourg. But in reality there was nothing done. Nothing was done until September 4.

On August 10 the Assembly had refused even to proclaim the dethronement of Louis XVI. Under the inspiration of the Girondins they had only declared the *suspension* of the King, and they were careful to nominate a governor for the Dauphin. And now the Germans, who had entered France on the 19th, were marching upon Paris to abolish the Constitution, to restore the King and his absolute power, to annul all the decrees of the two Assemblies, and to put the "Jacobins" to death, which meant all the revolutionists.

It is easy to understand the state of mind which must have prevailed in Paris under these conditions; beneath a calm exterior, an uneasy gloom held the faubourgs, which after their victory over the Tuileries, so dearly bought, felt themselves betrayed by the Assembly, and by the revolutionary "leaders of opinion," who hesitated, they also, to declare against the King and the royal power.

Every day new proofs were brought into the tribune of the Assembly, to the meetings of the Commune and to the press, of the plot, which had been hatched at the Tuileries before August 10 and was still going on in Paris and in the provinces. But nothing was done to punish the guilty, or to prevent them from resuming the weaving of their plots.

Every day the news from the frontier became more and more disquieting. The fortresses were not prepared for defence; nothing had been done to prevent the advance of the enemy. It was evident that the weak French contingents, commanded by untrustworthy officers, could never stop the German armies, twice as strong in numbers, accustomed to warfare, and under generals who were trusted by their soldiers. The royalists calculated the day, the hour, when the invading armies would knock at the gates of Paris.

The mass of the people comprehended the danger. All who were young, strong, enthusiastic in republican Paris, hastened to enrol themselves for frontier service. The enthusiasm became heroic. Money, jewellery, and all sorts of gifts of the patriots flowed into the enrolment offices.

But what was the good of all this devotion, when every day brought news of some fresh treachery, and when all these treacheries were to be traced to the King and Queen, who, shut up in the Temple, still continued to direct the plots? In spite of the close watch kept by the Commune, did not Marie-Antoinette know exactly all that went on outside? She was informed of every movement of the German armies; and when workmen went to put bars on the windows of the Temple, she said: "What is the use? In a week we shall not be here." In fact, it was between September 5 and 6 that the royalists expected the entrance of eighty thousand Prussians into Paris.

What is the use of arming and hastening to the frontier, when the Legislative Assembly and the party that is in power are the declared enemies of the Republic? They are doing everything to maintain royalty. A fortnight before August 10, on July 24, had not Brissot actually spoken against the Cordeliers who wanted the Republic? Had he not demanded that they should be punished by the arm of the law?* And now, after August 10, did not the Jacobin Club, which was the meeting-place for the well-to-do middle classes, keep silent,

* "If there exist," he said, "men who are working now to establish the Republic upon the ruins of the Constitution, the arm of the law should punish them, as well as the active partisans of the two Chambers and the counter-revolutionists at Coblentz."

THE INTERREGNUM—THE BETRAYALS

until August 27, on the question which was agitating the people: "Shall royalty, which depends for support upon German bayonets, be maintained—yes or no?"

The powerlessness of the governing classes, the cowardice of the "leaders of thought" in this hour of danger, could not but bring the people to despair. And the depth of this despair can only be gauged if one reads the newspapers of those days, the memoirs, and the private letters, and tries to live through the various emotions that Paris lived through after the declaration of war. This is why I shall briefly recapitulate the chief events.

At the moment when war was declared, Lafayette was still being lauded to the skies, especially in middle-class circles. They rejoiced to see him at the head of an army. It is true that since the massacre in the Champ-de-Mars (July 1791) some doubts about him had been expressed, and that Chabot spoke of them in the Assembly at the beginning of June 1792. But the Assembly treated Chabot as an agitator, as a traitor, and silenced him.

Then, on June 18, the Assembly received from Lafayette his famous letter, in which he denounced the Jacobins and demanded the suppression of all the clubs. This letter arriving a few days after the King had dismissed the Girondist Ministry —the Jacobin Ministry, as it was then called—the coincidence caused people to reflect. Nevertheless, the Assembly condoned it by casting a doubt on the authenticity of the letter, whereupon people naturally wondered if the Assembly were not in league with Lafayette.

In spite of all this, the agitation went on increasing, and on June 20 the people rose. Admirably organised by the "sections," it invaded the Tuileries. No excesses, as we have seen, took place; but the middle classes were seized with terror, and the Assembly flung themselves into the arms of reaction by passing a riot act against public gatherings in the streets. Thereupon Lafayette arrived, on the 23rd; he went to the Assembly, where he acknowledged and stood by his letter of June 18. He disapproved of the doings of June 20 in violent terms, and denounced the "Jacobins" with still more acrimony. Luckner, who commanded the other army, joined with Lafayette in disapproving of June 20 and in testifying his fidelity to the King. After this, Lafayette drove through Paris " with six or eight hundred officers of the Parisian garrison surrounding his carriage." * We know now why he had come to Paris. It was to persuade the King to allow himself to be carried off, and be placed under the protection of the army. It is only now that we know this with certainty, but Lafayette's conduct was at the time already becoming suspicious. A communication was even then laid before the Assembly, asking that he should be prosecuted; but the majority voted for his exculpation. What must the people have thought of this matter ? †

* Madame Jullien to her son (*Journal d'une bourgeoise*, p. 170). If the letters of Madame Jullien may be incorrect in some small details, they are still most valuable for this period, because they tell exactly what revolutionary Paris was saying and thinking on such and such days.

† Lally-Tollendal, in a letter which he addressed to the King of Prussia in 1793, claiming the liberation of Lafayette, enumerated the services that the cunning general had rendered to the Court. After the King had been brought back to Paris from Varennes in June 1791, the principal leaders in the Constituent Assembly met to decide whether the King should not be tried and the Republic established. Lafayette said to them : " If you kill the King, I warn you that the next day I and the National Guard will proclaim the Prince Royal." "He belongs to us, we must forget everything," said Madame Elisabeth (the sister of Louis XVI,) in June 1792, to Madame de Tonnerre, when speaking of Lafayette ; and in the beginning of July 1792, Lafayette wrote to the King, who replied to him. In this letter, dated July 8, he proposed to organise the King's escape. He was to come on the 15th, with fifteen squadrons and eight pieces of horse artillery, to receive the King at Compiègne. Lally-Tollendal, a royalist in virtue of a sort of religion that was hereditary in his family, as he said himself, confirmed what follows, on his conscience : " His [Lafayette's] proclamations to the army, his famous letter to the Legislative body, his unexpected appearance at the bar after the terrible day of June 20 ; *nothing of this was unknown to me, nothing was done without my participation.* . . . The day after his arrival in Paris, I spent part of the night with him ; *we were discussing whether war should be declared against the Jacobins in Paris itself—war, in the full meaning of the word.*" Their plan was to unite " all the landowners who were dissatisfied, and all the oppressed who were numerous," and to proclaim : *No Jacobins, and no Coblentz :* to lead the people to the Jacobin Club, " to arrest their leaders, seize their papers, and pull down their house." M. de Lafayette strongly desired this ; he had said to the King, " *We must destroy the Jacobins physically and morally.*" His timid friends were opposed to

THE INTERREGNUM—THE BETRAYALS

"*Mon Dieu*, my friend, how badly everything is going," wrote Madame Jullien to her husband on June 30, 1793. "For mark how the conduct of the Assembly irritates the people; so much so that when it will please Louis XVI. to take up the whip of Louis XIV. to turn out this flabby parliament, there will be hurrahs on all sides, with very different meanings, it is true; but what does it matter to tyrants, provided they fall in with their plans! The aristocratic middle class are wild with joy, and the people in the depths of despair; consequently the storm brews.*

Let us compare these words with those of Chaumette quoted above, and we shall be able to understand that to the revolutionary element of the population of Paris, the Assembly must have seemed like a cannon-ball attached to the feet of the Revolution.†

August 10, however, came, and the people of Paris in their sections took over the movement. Proceeding revolutionary-wise, they had elected their own Council of the Commune to give unity to the rising. They drove out the King from the Tuileries, made themselves masters of the Palace after a

this. He swore to me that he would, at least, on returning to his army, immediately set to work to find means for the King's deliverance." This letter of Lally-Tollendal's is given in full by Buchez and Roux, vol. xvii. p. 227 *et seq.*

And yet in spite of all, "the commissioners sent to Lafayette after August 10 by the leaders of the Assembly had instructions to offer him the first place in the new order of things." The treachery in the Assembly among the Girondins was thus much deeper than one would have thought.

* *Journal d'une bourgeoise*, p. 164.

† "At this moment the horizon is charged with vapours which must produce an explosion," wrote Madame Jullien on August 8. "The Assembly appears to me too weak to back up the will of the people, and the people appear to me too strong to allow itself to be overmastered by them. Out of this conflict, this struggle, something must come: either liberty or slavery for twenty-five millions of men" (p. 211). And further on: "The dethronement of the King demanded by the majority, and rejected by the minority who dominate the Assembly, will bring about the frightful conflict which is preparing. The Senate will not have the audacity to pronounce it, and the people will not have the baseness to endure the contempt which is shown to public opinion." And when the Assembly acquitted Lafayette, Madame Jullien made this prophecy: "But all that is leading us towards a catastrophe which will cause the friends of humanity to shudder; *for, it will rain blood. I do not exaggerate*" (p. 213).

sharp fight, and their Commune imprisoned the King in the tower of the Temple. But the Legislative Assembly still existed, and soon it became the rallying-point for the royalist elements.

The middle-class landowners saw at once the new popular and equalising turn taken by the insurrection—they clung on all the more to royalty. A thousand plans were set on foot for the transference of the Crown, either to the Dauphin— which would have been done if the regency of Marie-Antoinette had not been generally regarded with so much disgust —or to some other candidate, either French or foreign. There was, as after the flight to Varennes, a recrudescence of sentiment in favour of royalty; and when the people loudly demanded that they should pronounce plainly against royalty, the Assembly, like all assemblies of parliamentarian politicians, being uncertain which side should get the upper hand, took good care not to compromise itself. It inclined rather towards royalty and tried to condone the past crimes of Louis XVI. It was opposed to their being brought to light by any serious prosecutions of his accomplices.

The Commune had to threaten to ring the tocsin, and the sections had to talk of a massacre of all the royalists * before the Assembly decided to give in. At last it ordered, on August 17, the formation of a criminal tribunal, composed of eight judges and eight jurors, who were to be elected by the representatives of the section. But still, they tried to limit the powers of the tribunal. It was not to try and fathom the conspiracy which had been planned in the Tuileries *before* August 10; it was to confine itself to inquiring who was responsible for what took place on the 10th.

Proofs of the conspiracy, however, were forthcoming; every day they became more definite. Among the papers found after the taking of the Tuileries in the desk belonging to Montmorin, Keeper of the Civil List, were many compromising documents. There was, among others, a letter from

* " You appear to be in the dark as to what is happening in Paris," said the spokesman of one of the deputations of the Commune to the Assembly.

THE INTERREGNUM—THE BETRAYALS

the princes, proving they were acting in agreement with Louis XVI. when they sent out the Austrian and Prussian armies against France and organised a corps of cavalry from among the *émigrés*, who were marching with those armies on Paris. There was also found a long list of pamphlets and libels directed against the National Assembly and the Jacobins; libels paid for out of the Civil List, including those which were meant to provoke a riot on the arrival of the Marseillais federates, and inciting the National Guard to slaughter them.*

And finally, there was proof that the "constitutional" minority of the Assembly had promised to follow the King in the case of his leaving Paris, without, however, exceeding the distance prescribed by the Constitution. There were very many other things besides, but they were concealed, lest the popular fury might be directed on the prisoners in the Temple. Probably also on the Assembly, we may add.

At length the betrayals, so long foreseen, broke out in the army. On August 22 the treason of Lafayette became known. He had tried to force his army to follow him and to march on Paris. In reality, his plan had been arranged two months before when he had come to see how the land lay in Paris after June 20. Now he threw off the mask. He ordered the arrest of three commissioners who were sent to him by the Assembly to announce the revolution of August 10, and the old fox Luckner approved of his action. Fortunately, Lafayette's army did not follow its general, and on the 19th, accompanied by his staff, he had to cross the frontier, hoping to make his way to Holland. But he fell into the hands of the Austrians and was clapped into prison by them and treated very rigorously, which shows how the Austrians intended to treat every revolutionist who should have had the misfortune to fall into their power. They executed on the spot those

* In one letter from Switzerland, the punishing the Jacobins was discussed. "We shall execute justice on them; they shall be a terrible example.... War upon the paper money; that is where bankruptcy will begin. The clergy and the *parlements* will be reinstated.... So much the worse for those who have bought the property of the clergy...." In another letter we read: "There is not a moment to lose. We must make the middle classes feel that the King alone can save them."

municipal officers who were "patriots," and whom they succeeded in capturing; and some of them had their ears cut off and nailed to their foreheads by the Uhlans.

The next day after Lafayette's treason, the news came to Paris that Longwy, which had been invested on the 20th, had yielded at once, and among th epapers of the commandant, Lavergne, a letter was found containing offers of betrayal on behalf of Louis XVI. and the Duke of Brunswick.

"Unless a miracle happen, no further dependence can be placed on the army," was now the general opinion.

As to Paris, it was full of *Noirs*.* A crowd of *émigrés* had returned, and the military man was often recognised disguised in a priest's soutane. All kinds of plots, the indications of which the people, who anxiously watched the royal prison, were quick to seize upon, were woven round the Temple. The royalists intended to free the King and Queen, either by an escape or by a sudden attack on the prison, and they were getting up a general rising for the day, either September 5 or 6, when the Prussians would be on the outskirts of Paris. They made no attempt to conceal it. The seven hundred Swiss remaining in Paris were to serve as the military framework for the rising. They were to march upon the Temple, set the King at liberty, and place him at the head of the movement. All the prisons were to be opened, and the prisoners were to be sent out to plunder the city, and so add to the confusion, during which Paris was to be set on fire.†

So, at least, ran public rumour, spread by the royalists themselves. And when Kersaint read the report upon August 10, that report confirmed the rumour. In the words of a contemporary, "it made one tremble . . . so well and so thickly were the nets spread" round the revolutionists. And yet the whole truth was not told.

In the midst of all these difficulties, there was only the activity of the Commune and its sections that responded to the gravity of the situation. They alone, seconded by the Cordeliers'

* So they then called those who later were termed the *Blancs*.

† The prisoners shut up in La Force prison had already tried to set it on fire, says Michelet, according to the inquiry that was made concerning the September days.

Club, acted with a view to rousing the people, and obtaining from them a supreme effort to save the Revolution and the country, the cause of both being at that moment identical.

The General Council of the Commune, revolutionarily elected by the sections on August 9, acting in harmony with the sections themselves, worked with enthusiastic ardour to arm and equip, first 30,000, then 60,000 volunteers, who were to set out for the frontiers. Supported by Danton, they found for their vigorous appeals the words which electrified France. For, casting its municipal attributes behind it, the Commune of Paris spoke then to all France, and, through its volunteers, to the army also. The sections organised the immense work of equipping the volunteers, and the Commune ordered the leaden coffins to be dug up and melted down to make bullets, and the holy vessels from the churches to be made into bronze for cannon. The sections became the burning furnace whereat they furbished up the weapons by which the Revolution was about to vanquish its enemies and make another step forward—a step towards Equality.

For, in fact, a new revolution—a revolution aiming at Equality—taken by the people into their own hands, was already evolving. And it was the glory of the people of Paris to understand that in preparing to repel the invasion they were not acting merely under an impulse of national pride; neither was it a simple question of preventing the restoration of royal despotism. It was a question of consolidating the Revolution, of bringing it to some practical conclusion for the benefit of the mass of the people, by inaugurating a revolution as social as it was political in character; and that meant opening, by a supreme effort on the part of the masses, a new page in the history of civilisation.

But the middle classes, they also had perfectly divined this new character which was appearing in the Revolution and of which the Commune of Paris was making itself the organ. Accordingly the Assembly, which represented chiefly the middle classes, worked with ardour to counteract the influence of the Commune.

Already on August 11, while the smoke of its burning still

hung over the Tuileries, and the corpses still lay in the courtyards of the Palace, the Assembly had commanded the election of a new Directory of the department which they wished to oppose to the Commune. The Commune refused this, and the Assembly had to capitulate ; but the struggle went on— an inexorable struggle, in which the Girondins of the Assembly tried at times to detach the sections from the Commune, and at times to obtain the dissolution of the General Council elected revolutionarily on August 9. Contemptible intrigues in the face of an enemy that drew nearer to Paris each day, plundering shamelessly as it went.

On the 24th, the news that Longwy had surrendered without a fight reached Paris, and the insolence of the royalists grew accordingly. They chanted "Victory." The other towns would do as Longwy did, and they were already announcing that their German allies would arrive within a week; they even prepared lodging for them. Crowds of royalists gathered round the Temple and the royal family joined them in wishing success to the Germans. But the most terrible thing was, that those who were charged with the government of France had not the courage to take any measure to prevent Paris from being forced to capitulate like Longwy. The Commission of Twelve, which represented the pivot of action in the Assembly, fell into consternation. And the Girondin Ministry—Roland, Clavière, Servan and the others—were of the opinion that it was necessary to fly and withdraw to Blois, or else to Southern France, and leave the revolutionary people of Paris to the fury of the Austrians, of the Duke of Brunswick, and the *émigrés*. "The deputies were already flying one by one," * and the Commune openly came to complain of it to the Assembly. This was adding baseness to treachery, and of all the ministers, Danton alone was opposed to it absolutely.

It was only the revolutionary sections and the Commune who understood that victory must be won at all costs, and that to win it, the enemy must be struck on the frontiers, and the counter-revolutionists in Paris—both at the same time.

---

* Aulard, *Etudes et leçons sur la Révolution française*, 2nd series, 1898, p. 49.

THE INTERREGNUM—THE BETRAYALS 293

This was just what the governing classes did not want to admit. After the criminal court, appointed to try those who were guilty of the measures on August 10, had been installed with much solemnity, it soon became apparent that this tribunal did not care to punish the guilty any more than the High Court of Orleans, which had become—to use Brissot's expression—"the safeguard of the conspirators." It sacrificed at first two or three scapegoats for Louis XVI., but immediately after it acquitted one of the most important of the conspirators, the ex-minister Montmorin, as well as Dessonville, who was implicated in d'Angremont's conspiracy, and it hesitated about punishing Bachmann, the general in command of the Swiss. After that, there was nothing further to be expected from it.

An attempt has been made by some writers to represent the population of Paris as composed of cannibals, greedy for blood, who became furious when they saw a victim escaping from them. This is absolutely false. What the people understood by these acquittals was, that the governing class did not wish to bring to light the conspiracies that had been hatched in the Tuileries, because they knew how many of themselves would be implicated, and because these conspiracies were still going on. Marat, who was well informed, was right in saying that the Assembly was afraid of the people, and that it would not have been displeased if Lafayette had come with his army to restore royalty.

The discoveries made three months later, when Gamain informed about the existence of the iron cupboard containing the secret papers of Louis XVI., have in fact proved this. Royalty's strength lay in the Assembly.

Thereupon the people, seeing that it was absolutely impossible to establish the responsibilities of each one of the monarchist conspirators, and realising the danger which these conspirators presented in view of the German invasion, decided to strike indiscriminately at all those who had occupied posts of trust at the Court, and who were considered dangerous by the sections, as well as those at whose houses arms might be found concealed. To do this, the sections compelled the

Commune and the Commune compelled Danton, who had filled the post of Minister of Justice since August 10, to order a general search to be made throughout Paris, in order to seize the arms concealed in the houses of the royalists and priests, and to arrest those who were most suspected of connivance with the invading enemy. The Assembly had to submit and issue the search-warrants.

The search for arms took place on the night of the 29th and 30th, and the Commune displayed in it a vigour which struck terror into the conspirators. On the afternoon of August 29, Paris seemed dead, a prey to gloomy terror. It having been forbidden for any one to go out after six o'clock in the evening, all the streets, by nightfall, were in the possession of the patrols, sixty strong, each man armed with a sabre or an improvised pike. Towards one o'clock, in the night, the searchings began throughout Paris. The patrols entered every apartment, looking for arms and taking away those which they found in the houses of royalists.

Nearly three thousand men were arrested, nearly two thousand muskets were seized. Sometimes the search lasted for hours, but no one could complain about the disappearance of any article of value, whilst at the Eudistes'—priests who had refused to take the Oath of the Constitution—all the silver vessels which had disappeared from the Sainte-Chapelle were found hidden in the fountains.

The next day the greater number of the persons arrested were released by order of the Commune or on the demand of the sections. As to those who were kept in prison, it is highly probable that a sorting of these would have been made and that summary courts would have been formed to try them—if events had not been precipitated at the seat of war and in Paris itself.

While all Paris was arming itself at the vigorous appeal of the Commune; while on every public place "altars to the country" were erected, before which the youth of Paris was enrolled, and upon which citizens, rich and poor, laid their offerings to the country; while the Commune and the sections were displaying an energy truly astounding in the equipment

THE INTERREGNUM—THE BETRAYALS 295

and arming of 60,000 volunteers for the frontier, and although everything and all things were lacking for this purpose, nevertheless they had succeeded in despatching two thousand every day—the Assembly chose this very moment to attack the Commune. Upon the report of the Girondin, Guadet, it issued on August 30 a decree ordering the instant dissolution of the General Council of the Commune and new elections.

If the Commune had obeyed, it would have meant disorganising at a blow, to the advantage of both the royalists and the Austrians, the organisation and the despatch of the volunteers—the only chance there was for repelling the invasion and for vanquishing royalty. It is evident that the only reply which could be given to this by the Revolution was to refuse to obey, and to declare the instigators of this measure to be traitors. This is what the Commune did a few days later by ordering a search to be made at the houses of Roland and Brissot. As to Marat, he frankly demanded the extermination of those traitorous legislators.

The same day the Criminal Court acquitted Montmorin—and this, having learned a few days before, by the trial of d'Angremont, that the royalist conspirators, well paid, enrolled, divided into brigades and subject to a central committee, were only awaiting the signal to appear in the streets and attack the patriots in Paris and in every town of the provinces.

Two days later, on September 1, there came a new revelation. The official paper of the Girondist Ministry, the *Moniteur*, published a " Plan of the forces joined against France "—received, so they said, from a trustworthy source in Germany ; and in this plan it was stated that, while the Duke of Brunswick was fighting the patriot armies, the King of Prussia was to march straight upon Paris ; that after he had made himself master of the city, the inhabitants would be divided into two sections—the revolutionists and the royalists, and all the revolutionists would be put to death ; that in case a town could not be taken, it would be set on fire—" Deserts are preferable to people in revolt," the leagued kings had already said in their manifesto. And, as if to confirm this plan, Guadet discoursed to the Assembly about the great conspiracy discovered in the town of Grenoble and its environs. In the house of a certain Monnier, an agent of the *émigrés*, a list of more than a hundred local leaders of the conspiracy had been seized, and these leaders reckoned on the support of twenty-five to thirty thousand men. The country districts of the Deux-Sèvres and those of the Morbihan had begun an insurrection as soon as they had heard of the surrender of Longwy: that was actually included in the plan of the royalists and of Rome.

The same day, in the afternoon, news came that Verdun was besieged, and every one understood that this town was going to surrender, like Longwy; that then nothing more would remain to check a rapid march of the Prussians on Paris; and that the Assembly would indeed either quit Paris, leaving it to the enemy, or would treat for the restoration of the King to the throne and give him full powers to satisfy his vengeance by the extermination of the patriots.

Finally, on this very day, September 1, the minister Roland issued an address to the administrative bodies, which was stuck up on the walls of Paris, and in which he spoke of a vast conspiracy of the royalists to prevent the free circulation of foodstuffs. Nevers and Lyons were already suffering from it.*

Thereupon the Commune closed the barriers, and ordered the tocsin to be rung and the alarm-gun to be fired. In a strongly worded proclamation, it requested all the volunteers who were prepared to start to sleep that night upon the Champ-de-Mars, so as to be ready to march early the next day.

And at the same time a furious cry of "Let us rush the prisons!" rang throughout Paris. There lay the conspirators who were only waiting for the coming of the Germans to put Paris to fire and sword. Some of the sections, Poissonnière, Postes, Luxembourg, voted that these conspirators should be put to death. "We must finish with them to-day!"—and push on the Revolution in a new path.

* Granier de Cassagnac, *Histoire des Girondins et des massacres de Septembre* (Paris, 1860).

CHAPTER XXXV

THE SEPTEMBER DAYS

People roused to fury—Massacres at Abbaye prison—Commune tries to put an end to massacres—Massacres continue—Attitude of Girondins—Explanation of massacres—Address of Assembly to people—End of massacres

THE tocsin sounding all over Paris, the drums beating in the streets, the alarum-gun, the reports of which rang out every quarter of an hour, the songs of the volunteers setting out for the frontier, all contributed that Sunday, September 2, to rouse the anger of the people to fury.

Soon after midday, crowds began to gather around the prisons. Some priests who were being transferred from the Town Hall to the Abbaye prison, to the number of twenty-five,* in closed carriages, were assailed in the streets by the Federates from Marseilles or Avignon. Four priests were killed before they reached the prison. Two were massacred on arriving there, at the gate. The others were admitted; but just as they were being put through some simple form of interrogation, a multitude, armed with pikes, swords and sabres, forced the door of the prison and killed all the priests with the exception of Abbé Picard, head of the Deaf and Dumb Institution, and his assistant.

This was how the massacres began at the Abbaye—a prison which had a specially bad reputation in the quarter where it stood. The crowd, which had formed around this prison,

* Sixteen, says Méhée fils (Felhémési, *La vérité toute entière sur les vrais acteurs de la journée du 2 septembre, et sur plusieurs journées et nuits secrètes des anciens comités de gouvernement*, Paris, 1794). I maintain the exact orthography of the printed title. "Felhémési" is the anagram of Mébée fils.

composed chiefly of small tradespeople living in that part of the town, demanded that all the royalists arrested since August 10 should be put to death. It was known in the quarter that gold was plentiful among them, that they feasted and received their wives and friends quite freely. The prisoners had made illuminations after the defeat of the French army at Mons, and sang songs of victory after the taking of Longwy. They insulted the passers-by from behind the bars and promised the immediate arrival of the Prussians and the slaughter of the revolutionists. The whole of Paris was talking of the plots concocted in the prisons, of arms introduced, and it was widely known that the prisons had become actual manufactories of false paper-money and false drafts on the "Maison de Secours," by which they were trying to ruin the public credit.

All this was said and repeated among the crowds that gathered round the Abbaye, La Force, and the Conciergerie. Soon these crowds forced the doors and began killing the officers of the Swiss regiments, the King's guards, the priests who were to have been deported because of their refusal to take the Oath to the Constitution, and the royalist conspirators, arrested after August 10.

The spontaneity of this attack seems to have struck every one by its unexpectedness. Far from having been arranged by the Commune and Danton, as the royalist historians are pleased to declare,* the massacres were so little foreseen that the Commune had to take measures in the greatest haste to protect the Temple, and to save those who were imprisoned for debt or for arrears of payments, as well as the ladies attending on Marie-Antoinette. These ladies could only be saved under cover of the night by the commissioners of the Com-

* They quote, to prove this, that persons were liberated, between August 30 and September 2, thanks to the intervention of Danton and other revolutionary personages, and say: "You see very well how they saved their friends!" They forget, however, to say that out of the three thousand persons arrested on the 30th, more than two thousand were released. It was sufficient that any patriot of the prisoners' section should claim his release. For the part played by Danton in the September days, see the careful study of A. Aulard, in his *Etudes et leçons sur la Révolution française*, 1893–1897, 3rd series.

THE SEPTEMBER DAYS

mune, who carried out their tasks with much difficulty and at the risk of perishing themselves by the hands of the crowds that surrounded the prisons, or were stationed in the neighbouring streets.*

As soon as the massacres began at the Abbaye, and it is known that they began at about half-past two A.M.,† the Commune immediately took measures to prevent them. It immediately notified them to the Assembly, which appointed Commissioners to speak to the people; ‡ and at the sitting of the General Council of the Commune, which opened in the afternoon, Manuel, the attorney, was already, by six o'clock, giving an account of his fruitless efforts to stop the massacres. "He stated that the efforts of the National Assembly's twelve commissioners, his own, and those of his colleagues from the

---

* Madame de Tourzel, the Dauphin's governess, and her young daughter Pauline, three of the Queen's waiting-women, Madame de Lamballe and her waiting-woman, had been transferred from the Temple to La Force, and from this prison they were all saved, except Madame de Lamballe, by the Commissioners of the Commune. At half-past two in the night of September 2 and 3, these Commissioners, Truchot, Tallien and Guiraud, came to render an account of their efforts to the Assembly. At the prison of La Force and that of Sainte-Pélagie, they had taken out all the persons detained for debt. After reporting to the Commune, about midnight, Truchot returned to La Force, to take out all the women. "I was able to take out twenty-four," he said. "We have placed especially under our protection Mademoiselle de Tourzel and Madame Sainte-Brice. . . . For our own safety we withdrew, for they were threatening us too. We have conducted those ladies to the section of the 'Rights of Man,' to stay there until they are tried" (Buchez and Roux, xvii. p. 353). These words of Truchot are absolutely trustworthy, because as we know, by the narrative of Pauline de Tourzel, with what difficulty the commissioner of the Commune (she did not know who he was, and spoke of him as a stranger) succeeded in getting her through the streets near the prison, full of people watching to see that none of the prisoners were removed. Madame de Lamballe, too, was about to be saved by Pétion, the mayor, but some forces unknown opposed it. Emissaries of the Duke of Orléans are mentioned, who desired her death, and names even are given. However, one thing only is certain; there were so many influential persons who, since the Diamond Necklace affair, were interested in the silence of this confidante of the Queen's, that the impossibility of saving her need not surprise us.

† *Mon agonie de trente-huit heures*, by Jourgniac de Saint-Méard.

‡ Bazire, Dussaulx, François de Neufchâteau, the famous Girondin Isnard, and Laquinio were among the number. Bazire invited Chabot, who was beloved in the faubourgs, to join them (Louis Blanc, quarto edition, ii. p. 19).

municipality, had been ineffectual to save the criminals from death." At the evening sitting the Commune received the report of its commissioners sent to La Force; and decided that they should be sent there again to calm the minds of the people.*

During the night of the 2nd and 3rd, the Commune had even ordered Santerre, commandant of the National Guard, to send detachments to stop the massacres. But the National Guard *did not wish to interfere;* otherwise, it is clear that the battalions of the moderate sections would have gone. An opinion was evidently forming in Paris that for the National Guard to march upon the crowds would have been to kindle civil war, at the very moment when the enemy was but a few days distant, and when union was most necessary. "They divide you; they disseminate hatred; they want to kindle civil war," said the Assembly in its proclamation of September 3, in which it called on the people to stand united. Under the circumstances there was no other weapon but persuasion. But to the exhortations of the Commune's envoys, who were trying to stop the massacres, a man of the people aptly replied at the Abbaye by asking Manuel, "If those rascals of Prussians and Austrians entered Paris, would *they* try to distinguish between the innocent and guilty." † And another, or

---

* *See* the minutes of the Commune, quoted by Buchez and Roux, xvii. p. 368. Tallien, in his report to the Assembly, which was given in later during the night, confirms the words of Manuel: "The procurator of the Commune," said he, "went first to the Abbaye and used every means suggested to him by his zeal and humanity. He could not make any impression, and saw several victims killed at his feet. He himself was in danger of his life, and they were obliged to force him away for fear that he should fall a victim to his zeal." At midnight, when the people went over to La Force, "our commissioners," says Tallien, "followed them there, but could not gain anything. Some deputations came after them, and when we left to come here, another deputation was then going thither."

† "Tell me, Mr. Citizen, if those rascals of Prussians and Austrians came to Paris, would they too seek out the guilty? Would they not strike right and left, as the Swiss did on August 10? As for me, I am no orator, I put no one to sleep, and I tell you I am a father of a family; I have a wife and five children whom I want to leave here in the keeping of the section, so that I can go and fight the enemy, but I don't intend that these scoundrels who are in prison, for whom the other scoundrels are coming to open the doors, shall be able to go and slaughter my wife and children." I quote from Felhémési (Méhée fils), *La vérité toute entière*, &c.

THE SEPTEMBER DAYS

perhaps the same, added : " This is Montmorin's blood and his companions ! We are at our post, go back to yours ; *if all those whom we set up to do justice had done their duty, we should not be here.*" * This is what the people of Paris and all the revolutionists understood thoroughly that day.

In any case the Watch Committee of the Commune,† as soon as they learned the result of Manuel's mission on the afternoon of September 2, published the following appeal : " In the Name of the People. Comrades,—It is enjoined upon you to try all the prisoners in the Abbaye, without distinction, with the exception of the Abbé Lenfant, whom you shall put in a secure place. At the Hôtel de Ville, September 2. (Signed : Panis, Sergent, Administrators.) "

A provisional tribunal, composed of twelve jurors chosen by the people, was at once set up, and Usher Maillard, so well known in Paris since July 14 and October 5, 1789, was appointed president of it. A similar tribunal was improvised at La Force by two or three members of the Commune, and these two tribunals set themselves to save as many of the prisoners as was possible. Thus Maillard succeeded in saving Cazotte, who was gravely compromised,‡ and Sombreuil, known to be a declared enemy of the Revolution. Taking advantage of the presence of their daughters, Mademoiselle

* Prudhomme, in his journal, gives in these words the reply made by a man of the people, on the first visit to the Abbaye by a deputation from the Legislative Assembly and from the municipality.

† The Watch Committee of the Commune, which had taken the place of the preceding administration, and was composed at first of fifteen members of the municipal police, had been reorganised by a decree of the General Council of the Commune on August 30 : it was then formed of four members, Panis, Sergent, Duplain and Sourdeuil, who, with the authorisation of the Council, and " seeing the critical state of circumstances and the divers and important works to which it was necessary to devote themselves," added on September 2 seven other members : Marat, Deforgues, Lenfant, Leclerc, Durfort, Cailly and Guermeur (Buchez and Roux, vol. xvii. pp. 405, 433 ; vol. xviii. pp. 186, 187). Michelet, who saw the original document, speaks only of six ; he does not mention Durfort ; Robespierre was sitting on the General Council, Marat took part in it " as journalist "—the Commune having decreed that a gallery should be erected in the Council Chamber for a journalist (Michelet, vol. vii. ch. iv.). Danton tried to reconcile the Commune with the executive of the Assembly ; that is to say, with the Ministry of which he was a member.

‡ Michelet, vol. vii. ch. v.

Cazotte and Mademoiselle Sombreuil, who had obtained leave to share their fathers' imprisonment, and also the advanced age of Sombreuil, he succeeded in having them acquitted. Later on, in a document which Granier de Cassagnac * has reproduced in facsimile, Maillard could say with pride that in this way he saved the lives of forty-three persons. Needless to say that "the glass of blood," said to have been drunk by Mademoiselle Sombreuil to save her father, is one of the infamous inventions of the royalist writers.†

At La Force prison there were also many acquittals, and, according to Tallien, there was only one woman who perished, Madame de Lamballe. Every acquittal was hailed with cries of "*Vive la Nation!*" and the acquitted person was escorted to his residence by men of the crowd with every mark of sympathy; but his escort refused absolutely to accept money from either the man set at liberty or his family. Thus they acquitted the royalists against whom there were no established facts, as, for example, the brother of the minister Bertrand de Molleville; and even a bitter enemy of the Revolution, Weber, the Austrian, who was foster-brother to the queen; and they conducted them back in triumph, with transports of joy, to the houses of their relations or friends.

At the Carmelite Convent, priests began to be imprisoned from August 11—among them being the famous Archbishop of Arles, who was accused of having been the cause of the massacre of the patriots in that town. All of them would have been deported but for what happened on September 2. A certain number of men armed with sabres broke into the convent that day and, after a summary trial, killed the archbishop, as well as a great many of the priests who refused to take the civic oath. Several, however, saved themselves by climbing over a wall; others were saved, as is shown in the narrative of the Abbé Berthelet de Barbot, by members of the Luxembourg section, and by some pikemen who were on duty in the prison.

* *Histoire des Girondins et des massacres de Septembre*, 2 vols., 1860.
† *Vide* Louis Blanc, Book viii. ch. ii.; L. Combes, *Episodes et curiosités révolutionnaires*, 1872.

THE SEPTEMBER DAYS

The massacres continued also on the 3rd, and in the evening the Watch Committee of the Commune sent out to the departments, in envelopes of the Ministry of Justice, a circular, drawn up by Marat, in which the Assembly was attacked, the events recounted, and the departments recommended to imitate Paris.

The tumult among the people, however, subsided, Saint-Méard says, and on the 3rd, about eight o'clock, he heard several voices calling out: "Mercy, mercy for those who remain!" Moreover, only a few political prisoners were left in the prisons. But then there happened what must needs happen. With those who had attacked the prison on principle, there began to mingle other elements—the dubious elements. And finally there appeared what Michelet has aptly called "the fury of purification"—the desire to purge Paris, not only of royalist conspirators, but also of coiners, the forgers of bills of exchange, swindlers, and even the prostitutes, who were, they said, all royalists. On the 3rd the thieves in the Grand Châtelet and the convicts at the Bernardins had already been massacred, and on the 4th a band of men went out to kill at the Salpêtrière, and at Bicêtre, even at the "House of Correction" at Bicêtre, which the people ought to have respected as a place of suffering for the poor, like themselves, especially the children. At last the Commune succeeded in putting an end to these massacres, on the 4th, according to Maton de la Varenne.*

More than a thousand persons in all perished, of whom two hundred and two were priests, twenty-six of the Royal Guards, about thirty of the Swiss belonging to the Staff, and more than three hundred prisoners under the common law, some of whom, imprisoned in the Conciergerie, were fabricating during their detention false paper-money. Maton de la Varenne, who has given † an alphabetical list of persons killed during those September days, makes a total of 1086, plus

* M . . . de la Varenne, *Histoire particulière des événements qui ont eu lieu en France pendant les mois de juin, de juillet, d'août et de septembre, et qui ont opéré la chute du trône royal* (Paris, 1806). There were a few more isolated massacres on the 5th.

† *Histoire particulière*, pp. 419–460.

three unknown persons who perished accidentally. Upon which the royalist historians embroidered their romances, and wrote about 8000 and even 12,852 killed.*

All the historians of the Great Revolution, beginning with Buchez and Roux, have given the opinions of various well-known revolutionists concerning these massacres, and one striking trait stands out in the numerous quotations which they have published. This is, that the Girondins, who later on made use of the September days to attack violently and persistently the "Mountain," in no wise departed during those days from this very attitude of *laisser faire* with which later on they reproached Danton, Robespierre and the Commune. The Commune alone, in its General Council and in its Watch Committee, took measures, more or less efficacious, to stop the massacres, or, at least, to circumscribe and legalise them, when they saw that it was impossible to prevent them. The others acted feebly, or thought that they ought not to interfere, and the majority *approved* after the thing was done. This proves up to what point, in spite of the cry of outraged humanity necessarily raised by these massacres, it was generally understood that they were the inevitable consequence of August 10, and of the political equivocations of the governing classes themselves during the twenty days which followed the taking of the Tuileries.

Roland, in his letter of September 3, so often quoted, spoke of the massacres in terms which recognised their necessity.†

* Peltier, arch-royalist writer and liar, giving every detail, put the figure at 1005, but he added that there had been some killed at the Bicêtre and *in the streets*, which permitted him to bring the total up to 8000 ! (*Dernier tableau de Paris, ou récit historique de la Révolution du 10 août*, 2 vols., London, 1792-1793). On this Buchez and Roux have justly remarked that "Peltier is the only one to say that people were killed in other places besides the prisons," in contradiction to all his contemporaries.

† "I know that revolutions are not to be judged by ordinary rules ; but I know, also, that the power which makes them must soon take it place under the ægis of the law, if total annihilation is not desired. The anger of the people and the beginning of the insurrection are comparable to the action of a torrent that overthrows *the obstacles that no other power could have annihilated*, and the ravage and devastation which the flood will carry far onward if it does not soon return to its channel. . . . Yesterday was a day of events over which perhaps we

The essential thing for him was to develop the theory which was to become the favourite theory of the Girondins—namely, that if disorder was necessary before August 10, all must now return again to order. In general, the Girondins, as Buchez and Roux * have well said, "were chiefly preoccupied with themselves. . . . They saw with regret the power passing out of their hands into those of their adversaries . . . but they found no motive for condemning the movement that had been made . . . they did not deny that it alone could save the national independence, and guard themselves from the vengeance of the army directed by the *émigrés.*"

The chief newspapers, such as the *Moniteur* and Prudhomme's *Révolutions de Paris*, approved, whilst the others, such as the *Annales patriotiques* and the *Chronique de Paris*, and even Brissot in the *Patriote français*, limited themselves to a few cold and indifferent words concerning those days. As to the royalist press, it is evident that they seized upon these facts to put in circulation for a whole century the most fantastic tales. We shall not take upon ourselves to contradict them. But there is an error of appreciation deserving of reference, which is to be found among the republican historians.

It is true that the number of those who did the killing in the prisons did not exceed more than three hundred men, wherefore all the republicans have been accused by some writers of cowardice for not having put a stop to it. Nothing

ought to draw a veil; I know that the people, terrible in their vengeance, had in it some kind of justice; they did not take as their victims every one who came in the way of their fury, they directed it upon those whom they believed to have been too long spared by the sword of justice, and who, the peril of circumstances persuaded them, must be immolated without delay. But the safety of Paris demands that all the powers shall return at once to their respective limits."

* P. 397. There is no doubt that the Girondist ministers knew very well what was going on in the prisons. We know that Servan, the Minister of War, on the afternoon of the 2nd, went to the Commune, where he had made an appointment for eight o'clock with Santerre, Pétion, Hébert, Billaud-Varenne and others, to discuss military measures. It is obvious that the massacres must have been mentioned at the Commune, and that Roland was informed about them, but that Servan, as well as the others, thought that they should attend to the most pressing business—the war on the frontiers—and on no account provoke civil war in Paris.

is, however, more erroneous than this reckoning. The number of three or four hundred is correct. But it is enough to read the narratives of Weber, Mademoiselle de Tourzel, Maton de la Varenne and others, to see that if the murders were the work of a limited number of men, there were around each person and in the neighbouring streets crowds of people who approved of the massacres, and who would have taken arms against any one who might have tried to prevent them. Besides, the bulletins of the sections, the attitude of the National Guard, and the attitude even of the best-known revolutionists, proved that every one understood that military intervention would have been the signal for a civil war, and, no matter to which side the victory went, this would have led to massacres still more widespread and still more terrible than those in the prisons.

On the other hand, Michelet has said, and his words have been repeated since, that it was *fear*, groundless fear, always ferocious, which had inspired these massacres. A few hundreds of royalists more or less in Paris did not mean danger for the Revolution. But to reason so is to underrate, it seems to me, the strength of the reaction. These few hundred royalists had on their side the majority, the immense majority of the well-to-do middle classes, all the aristocracy, the Legislative Assembly, the Directory of the department, the greater number of the justices of peace, and the enormous majority of the officials. It was this compact mass of elements opposed to the Revolution which was merely awaiting the approach of the Germans to receive them with open arms, and to inaugurate with their aid the counter-revolutionary Terror, the Black Massacre. We have only to remember the White Terror under the Bourbons, when they returned in 1814 under the powerful protection of armed foreigners.

Besides, there is one fact which is not sufficiently appreciated by the historians, but which sums up the whole situation, and gives the true reason for the movement of September 2.

It was on the morning of September 4, while the massacres were still going on, that the Assembly decided at last, on the motion of Chabot, to utter the word so long awaited from the legislators by the people. In an address to the French people, it declared that respect for the decisions of the future Convention prevented its members "from forestalling by their resolution what they must expect from the French nation"; but that they took now, as individuals, the oath which they could not take as representatives of the people: "*to combat with all their might both kings and royalty!—No king; capitulation, never; a foreign king, never!*" shouted the members. And as soon as this address was voted, despite the restriction just mentioned, certain commissioners of the Assembly went immediately with it to the Sections, where these Commissioners were promptly welcomed, and the sections took upon themselves to put an end at once to the massacres.

But this address was not voted in the Assembly before Marat had advised the people to massacre the royalist knaves of the Legislative Assembly; nor before Robespierre had denounced Carra and the Girondins in general as ready to accept a foreign king, and the Commune had ordered the searching of Roland's and Brissot's dwellings. It was on September 4—only on the 4th—that the Girondin Guadet invited the representatives to swear their readiness to combat with all their might both kings and royalties. If a frank declaration of this kind had been voted immediately after August 10, and if Louis XVI. had been brought to trial there and then, the massacres would certainly not have taken place. The people would have realised the powerlessness of the royalist conspiracy from the moment the Assembly and the Government declared their readiness to combat the supporters of the throne.

Furthermore, Robespierre's suspicions were not pure fancy. Condorcet, the old republican, the only representative in the Legislative Assembly who since 1791 had openly pronounced for the Republic while repudiating on his own account—but only on his own account—all idea of desiring the Duke of Brunswick on the throne of France, admitted, however, in the *Chronique de Paris* that the Duke had been mentioned to him sometimes.* The fact is that during those days of interregnum

---

* Carra, the editor of the *Annales patriotiques*, one of the chief organs of the Girondist party, mentioned Brunswick in these terms, in the

several candidates for the throne of France—the Duke of York, the Duke of Orléans, the Duke of Chartres (who was the candidate of Dumouriez) and the Duke of Brunswick— were undoubtedly discussed, not only by those politicians who, like the Feuillants, did not want to have a republic, but also by those who, like the Girondins, did not believe in the chances of victory for France.

In these hesitations, in this pusillanimity, this want of honesty among the statesmen in power, lies the true cause of the despair which seized upon the people of Paris on September 2.

number dated July 19, 1792: "He is the greatest warrior and the cleverest statesman in Europe, this Duke of Brunswick; he is very learned, very enlightened, very amiable; he wants but one thing, perhaps—a crown—to be, I do not say the greatest king on earth, but to be the true restorer of the liberty of Europe. If he comes to Paris, I wager that his first step will be to come to the Jacobins and put on the *bonnet rouge*."

CHAPTER XXXVI

THE CONVENTION—THE COMMUNE—THE JACOBINS

Convention formed—Its composition—Girondins—" Mountain "—" Plain " or " Marsh "—Activity of sections since their formation—Revolutionary Commune—Jacobin Club and " Mountain "—Jacobins support " Mountain," but oppose Girondins

ON September 21, 1792, the Convention, that Assembly which has been so often represented as the true type, the ideal of a revolutionary Assembly, was at last opened. The elections had been made by all the citizens, both active and passive, but still in two degrees, which means that all the citizens had first elected the electoral assemblies, and these had nominated the deputies to the Convention. Such a mode of election was clearly in favour of the wealthy; but as the elections took place in September, in the midst of the general agitation resulting from the triumph of the people on August 10, and many who were opposed to the Revolution, being terrorised by the events on September 2, preferred not to show themselves at all during the elections, things were not so bad as might have been feared. In Paris, Marat's list, containing all the revolutionaries known at the Cordeliers' and Jacobin Clubs, was accepted in its entirety. The five hundred and twenty-five electors of Paris, who met together on September 2, in the Club of the Jacobins, elected Collot d'Herbois and Robespierre as president and vice-president, excluded from the lists all those who had signed the two royalist petitions known as the Petitions of the Eight Thousand and the Twenty Thousand, and voted for Marat's list.

The "moderantist" element dominated, however, all the same in the new Assembly, and Marat wrote, after the first sitting, that, seeing the character of the majority of the delegates, he despaired of the salvation of France. He foresaw that their opposition to the revolutionary spirit was going to plunge the country into endless struggles : "They will end by bringing everything to destruction," he said, "if the small number of the defenders of the people, who will have to contend with them, do not get the upper hand and crush them." We shall see presently how right were his forebodings.

But the events were impelling France towards the Republic, and the inclinations of the people were such that the moderantists of the Convention did not dare to resist the current which was sweeping away royalty. At its very first sitting the Convention declared unanimously that royalty was abolished in France. Marseilles, as we have seen, and several other provincial towns were already before August 10 demanding a Republic ; and Paris had done so with all solemnity since the first day of the elections. The Jacobin Club had also decided at last, in its sitting of August 27, to declare itself republican, after the publication of the papers found in the Tuileries. The Convention followed the lead of Paris. It abolished royalty at its first sitting on September 21, 1792. The next day, by a second decree, it ordained that from this day all public acts should be dated from the first year of the Republic.

Three very distinct parties met in the Convention : the Mountain, the Gironde and the Plain, or rather the Marsh. The Girondins, although less than two hundred, dominated. They had already, in the Legislative Assembly, furnished the King with the Roland Ministry, and they liked to pose as "statesmen." Composed of well-educated, refined and keen politicians, the Girondist party represented the interests of the commercial, mercantile, and propertied middle classes, who were coming to the front very rapidly under the new *régime*. With the support of the Moderates of the Marsh, the Girondins were at first the strongest, and it was from among them the first republican Ministry was chosen. Danton alone, of the Ministry that had come into power on August 10, had represented the popular revolution: but he sent in his resignation on September 21, when the Convention met, and the power rested in the hands of the Girondins.

The "Mountain," composed of Jacobins, such as Robespierre, Saint-Just and Couthon, of Cordeliers, such as Danton and Marat, and supported by popular revolutionists like Chaumette and Hébert, was not yet constituted into a political party: that was done later through the course of events. For the time being, there rallied round them those who wanted to press on ahead and make the Revolution end in some tangible results—that is to say, to destroy royalty and royalism, to crush the power of the aristocracy and the clergy, to abolish feudalism to establish the Republic.

Lastly, the "Plain" or "Marsh" consisted of those who were undecided—men without settled convictions, always remaining "property-owners" and conservatives by instinct—those who form the majority in all representative assemblies. They numbered about five hundred in the Convention. At first they supported the Girondins, but then deserted them in the moment of danger. Fear made them support for a certain time the Red Terror, with Saint-Just and Robespierre, but afterwards they became partisans of the White Terror, when the *coup d'état* of Thermidor had sent Robespierre and his friends to the scaffold.

One might have thought that now the Revolution was going to develop without further hindrances and follow the natural path dictated by the logic of events. The trial and condemnation of the King, a Republican Constitution in place of that of 1791, war to the death against the invaders; and at the same time the abolition of all that constituted the power of the old *régime*—the feudal laws, the authority of the clergy, the royalist organisation of provincial administrations—all these ought to have been considered as the necessary outcome of the situation.

But the middle classes which had come into power and were represented in the Convention by the "Statesmen" of the Gironde, did not hold this opinion.

The people had dethroned Louis XVI. But as to getting

rid of the traitor who had brought the Germans almost to the gates of Paris, as to executing Louis XVI., the Gironde was very strongly in opposition. Rather civil war than this decisive step! Not from fear of the vengeance of the foreigner—since it was the Girondins themselves who had undertaken to wage war against all Europe; but from fear of the Revolution, of the French people, and especially of the Paris revolutionists who saw in the execution of the King the beginning of the real revolution.

However, the people of Paris, in their sections and their Commune, had been able to form, side by side with the National Assembly, a veritable power, which gave body to the revolutionary tendencies of the Parisian population, and in the end even dominated the Convention. Let us, therefore, pause a moment before touching upon the struggles which rent the National Representation, to cast a retrospective glance on the methods by which this authority, the Commune of Paris, had been constituted.

We have seen in chaps. xxiv. and xxv. how the sections of Paris had assumed importance, as organs of the municipal life, by taking upon themselves, in addition to the police functions and the election of the judges which belonged to them by law, various economic functions of the highest importance—such as the distribution of food-stuffs, public aid, the sale of national lands, and so on, and we saw now these very functions enabled them to exercise a serious influence in the discussion of the great political questions of a general character.

Having become important organs of the public life, the sections necessarily tried to establish a federal link between themselves, and several times already, in 1790 and 1791, they appointed special commissioners with the object of coming to an understanding with each other for common action, outside the regular Municipal Council. However, nothing permanent resulted from these attempts.

In April 1792, when war was declared, the labours of the sections were suddenly augmented by a great many new functions. They had to take upon themselves the enrolment and the choice of the volunteers, the collecting of patriotic

THE CONVENTION

donations, the equipment and provisioning of the battalions sent to the frontiers, the administrative and political correspondence with these battalions, the looking after the needs of the volunteers' families, &c., not to mention the perpetual strife which they had to maintain from day to day against the royalist conspirators who tried to hamper their work. With these new functions, the necessity for a *direct* union between the sections made itself felt more than ever.

Nowadays, looking over the correspondence of the sections and their vast accounts, one cannot but admire the spirit of spontaneous organisation shown by the people of Paris, and the devotion of the men who willingly carried out the whole of this task—usually after finishing their daily labour. Here is where we may appreciate the devotion, more than religious, which was created in the French people by the Revolution. For we must not forget that if each section appointed its military committee and its civil committee, it was to the General Assemblies, held in the evening, that all important questions were generally referred.

We can understand, too, how these men, who were looking on the horrors of war not theoretically, but in reality, and were in daily touch with the sufferings imposed upon the people by the invasion, must have hated the instigators of the invasion —the King, the Queen, the Court, the ex-nobles and the rich, all the rich, who made common cause with the Court. The people of Paris thus joined with the peasants of the frontier departments in their hatred of the supporters of the throne who had called the foreigners into France. When, therefore, the idea of a pacific demonstration for June 20 was suggested, it was the sections that took upon themselves the organisation of this demonstration—it was they who afterwards arranged the attack on the Tuileries on August 10, taking the opportunity, meanwhile, to form at last the much desired direct union for revolutionary action among the sections.

When it became evident that the demonstration on June 20 had resulted in nothing—that the Court had not learned anything, and did not wish to learn anything—the sections themselves took the initiative in demanding from the Assembly the dethronement of Louis XVI. On July 23 the section of Mauconseil passed a resolution to this effect, of which they gave notice to the Assembly; and then they set to work to prepare for a rising on August 5. Other sections hastened to pass a similar resolution, and when the Assembly, in its sitting of August 5, denounced the resolution of the citizens of Mauconseil as illegal, it had already received the approbation of fourteen sections. The same day some members of the Gravilliers section went to the Assembly to declare that they were still leaving to the legislators "the honour of saving the country," but they added: "If you refuse, however, to do it, we shall have to take it upon ourselves." The Quinze-Vingts section, on its part, announced "the morning of August 10 as the extreme limit of the people's patience," and that of Mauconseil declared that "it would wait peaceably and keeping watch until eleven o'clock on the evening of the following Thursday (August 9) in expectation of the decision of the National Assembly; but that, if justice and right was not done to the people by the legislative body, one hour after, at midnight, the fire-drum would be beaten, and every one would rise." *

Finally, on August 7, the same section requested all the others to appoint in each of them "six commissioners, *less orators than good citizens,* who by their meeting together would form a central point at the Hôtel de Ville," which was done on the 9th.† When twenty-eight or thirty out of the forty-six sections had joined the movement, their commissioners met at the Hôtel de Ville, in a hall adjoining the one where the Municipal Council met regularly—it was small in numbers that night—and they took action in a revolutionary manner, as a new Commune. They provisionally suspended the Municipal Council, shut up in a hall the mayor, Pétion, dismissed the staff of the National Guards' battalions, and took

* Mortimer Ternaux, *La Terreur*, vol. ii. pp. 178, 216, 393; Buchez and Roux, vol. xvi. p. 247; Ernest Mellié, *Les Sections de Paris*, p. 144 *et seq.*

† A "corresponding committee" had already been established for communicating with the different sections, and a meeting of the commissioners of several sections had taken place on July 23.

over all the authority of the Commune, as well as of the general direction of the insurrection.*

Thus the new authority, the Revolutionary Commune, was constituted, and installed in the Hôtel de Ville.

The Tuileries Palace was taken, the King dethroned, and immediately the new Commune made it felt that August 10 was not the culmination of the Revolution inaugurated on July 14, 1789, but the beginning of a new popular revolution, marching in the sense of Equality. Henceforth it dated its documents from " the Year IV. of Liberty and the Year I. of Equality." A whole mass of new duties began to devolve upon the new Commune.

During the last twenty days of August, while the Legislative Assembly was hesitating between the various currents, royalist, constitutionalist, and republican, which drew its members hither and thither, and was proving itself absolutely incapable of rising to the height of events, the sections of Paris and the Commune became the true heart of the French nation for the awakening of Republican France, for flinging her against the coalition of kings, and for organising in co-operation with the other Communes the great movement of the volunteers in 1792. And when the hesitations of the Assembly, the hankering of the majority of the members after royalty, and their hatred of the insurrectional Commune had brought the people of Paris to a pitch of mad fury in those September days, it was still the sections and the Commune that tried to appease them. As soon as the Legislative Assembly decided at last to declare, on September 4, against royalty and

* Ernest Mellié has found the minute-book of the Poissonnière section. It met on August 9, at eight o'clock in the evening, in permanent committee in the church of Saint-Lazare; there it dismissed all the officers of the Saint-Lazare battalion, not appointed by the National Guards themselves, and appointed " on the spot other officers under whose orders the section intended to march." It entered into agreement with the other sections as to the order of marching, and at four o'clock in the morning, having appointed its permanent committee " to keep watch over the preparations for arming and to give the orders for security that they should judge to be necessary," the section joined " the brethren of the Saint-Antoine faubourg," and began to march upon the Tuileries. By means of this minute we get a lively impression of the way in which the people of Paris acted on that memorable night.

the various pretenders to the throne of France, and as soon as it signified its decision to the sections, these joined together at once, to put an end to the massacres which threatened to extend from the prisons to the streets, and to guarantee the safety of all the inhabitants.

Likewise, when the Convention met, and though it had decreed the abolition of royalty in France on the morning of September 21, "it did not dare to pronounce the decisive word 'Republic,'" and "seemed to be waiting for some encouragement from without"; * this encouragement came from the people of Paris. They acclaimed the decree in the street with cries of "*Vive la République!*" and the citizens of the Quatre-Nations section went to the Convention, to compel it to take a step further, saying that they would be only too happy to pay with their blood for the "Republic" which was not yet proclaimed, and which was only on the next day officially recognised by the Convention.

The Commune of Paris thus became a power which took upon itself to be the inspirer, if not the rival, of the Convention, and the ally of the party called the "Mountain."

The "Mountain" had, besides, another power on its side which had been formed in the current of the Revolution—the Jacobin Club, in Paris, with the numerous societies in the provinces which were affiliated to it. It is true that this club had none of the power and revolutionary initiative with which modern political writers endow it. The very persons composing the mother-society in Paris were chiefly well-to-do middle-class men. How could they guide the Revolution?

At every epoch, Michelet says, they had flattered themselves with being the wiseacres and political lights of the Revolution, who held the balance of it all. They did not lead the Revolution; they followed it. The tone of the club changed with every fresh crisis. But the club made itself immediately the expression of the tendency which had come to the front at a certain moment among the educated, moderately democratic middle classes; it supported this tendency by cultivating

* Aulard, *Histoire politique de la Révolution*, 2nd edition, p. 272 *et seq.*

THE JACOBINS

opinion in Paris in the directions desired, and it furnished the most important officials under each new *régime*. Robespierre, who, to use Michelet's happy phrase, was "the golden mean of the Mountain," wanted the Jacobins "to serve as an intermediary between the Assembly and the Street, to frighten and reassure the Convention alternately." But he understood that the initiative should come from the Street, from the People.

We have already said that the influence of the Jacobins on the events of August 10 was *nil*, and it so remained until September 1792, the club being nearly deserted at that time. But by degrees, in the course of the autumn, the mother-society of Paris was reinforced by many Cordeliers, and then the club revived and became the rallying-point for the whole of the moderate party among the republican democrats. Marat became very popular there, but not so "the extremists"—which in modern parlance would mean "the Communists." These the club opposed and, later on, fought against them.

When, in the spring of 1793, the struggle entered on by the Girondins against the Commune of Paris reached its critical point, the Jacobins supported the Commune and the Mountain, in the Convention, and helped them to gain the victory over the Girondins, and to consolidate it. By their correspondence with the affiliated clubs in the provinces, the Jacobins supported the advanced revolutionists there, and helped them to checkmate the influence not only of the Girondins, but also of the royalists concealed behind them. This left the Jacobins free to turn later on against the popular revolutionists of the Commune, and so make way for middle-class reaction to accomplish the *coup d'état* of the 9th Thermidor.

CHAPTER XXXVII

THE GOVERNMENT—CONFLICTS WITH THE CONVENTION—THE WAR

New Ministerial Council—Danton, at first its leader, later forced to resign—Roland succeeds him—Council inactive—Real power in hands of Danton, Commune, Sections and Jacobins—Council attacks Danton, Marat, and Robespierre—Conflict between Convention and Commune—Provinces become hostile to Commune and people of Paris—Girondins attack Paris sections—Revolution and war—Girondins desire war—Peasants of frontier enthusiastic—Western France not eager—Country unprepared—Plan of Dumouriez and Lafayette—Germans advance—Battle of Valmy—Danton negotiates with Duke of Brunswick—Further republican successes—Battle of Jemmapes—England—Consequences of war—The Vendée

THE first care of the Convention was not to decide what should be done with the dethroned King, but to determine which party should profit by the people's victory over the Tuileries—who should rule the Revolution. Whereupon there broke out those conflicts which for eight months hindered the regular development of the Revolution and, until June 1793, held in suspense the great questions, such as that of the land, the feudal dues, and so on, and led to the exhaustion of the people's energy, to indifference, to that lassitude which made the hearts of those who witnessed it to bleed, as Michelet has so well expressed it.

On August 10, after pronouncing the "suspension" of the King, the Legislative Assembly had handed over all the functions of central executive power to a council composed of six ministers—chosen from without the Assembly, the majority being Girondins—Roland, Servan, Clavière, Monge, and Le Brun—with the addition of Danton, whom the Revolution had placed in the position of Minister of Justice. This council had no president; each minister presiding for a week in turn.

The Convention confirmed this arrangement; but Danton, who had become the soul of the national defence and diplomacy, and who exercised a preponderating influence on the council, was forced to resign by the attacks of the Girondins. He quitted the Ministry on October 9, 1792, and his place was filled by the insignificant Garat. After this, Roland, the Minister of the Interior, became the most influential man of the Ministerial Council, and kept his post until January 1793, when he resigned after the execution of the King. In this position he exercised all his influence, and permitted the Girondins grouped round him and his wife to employ all their energy to prevent the Revolution from developing along the broad lines which had been marked out for it since 1789: the establishment of a democracy, the definite abolition of the feudal system, and some steps towards an equalisation of conditions. Danton, however, was still the inspirer of diplomacy, and when the Committee of Public Safety was instituted, in April 1793, he became the real Minister of Foreign Affairs on this committee.*

Although in power and dominating the Convention, the Gironde did not know actually what to do. As Michelet truly says, "it perorated," but it did nothing. Not having courage for revolutionary measures, neither had it enough for open reaction. Consequently, the real authority, both for initiative and for action, rested in Danton's hands in the war and diplomacy, and in the hands of the Commune of Paris, the sections, the popular societies, and partly with the Jacobin Club with regard to revolutionary measures in the interior. Powerless to act itself, the Gironde directed furious attacks upon those who did act, chiefly against "the triumvirate" of Danton, Marat, and Robespierre, whom they violently accused of dictatorial tendencies. There were times when it was asked whether these attacks should come to a head—whether Danton was to be ostracised and Marat sent to the guillotine.

* Aulard gives in his *Histoire politique*, 2nd edition, pp. 315-317, an excellent *résumé* of these various changes.

However, as the Revolution had not yet exhausted its vitality, all these attacks failed. They only made the people more ardently in favour of Marat, especially in the faubourgs of Saint-Antoine and Saint-Marceau; they augmented the influence of Robespierre in the eyes of the Jacobins and of the democratic middle class, and they raised Danton still higher in the eyes of all those who loved to see Republican France defying the Kings. To them Danton was the man of action capable of heading off the invasion, of frustrating the royalist plots at home, and of establishing the Republic securely, even at the risk of his life and his political reputation.

Ever since the first sittings of the Convention, its Right, formed by the Girondins, had renewed the shameful conflict with the Commune of Paris, which they had been leading in the Legislative Assembly since August 11. They owed their power to the insurrection, organised by the Commune, and yet they attacked it with a hatred which they had never displayed for the Court conspirators.

It would be wearisome to narrate here in full all these attacks of the Gironde upon the Commune. It will be enough to mention some of them.

The first was over the auditing of the accounts; it was aimed at the Commune and its Watch Committee, as well at Danton. It is evident that during those disturbed months of August and September 1792, under the extraordinary circumstances created by the movement of August 10 and the foreign invasion, money had to be expended by Danton, the only active man in the Ministry, without too much exactitude of accounts, whether for the diplomatic negotiations which led to the retreat of the Prussians, or for getting hold of the threads of the plot of the Marquis de la Rouèrie in Brittany, and that of the princes in England and elsewhere. It is also very plain that it was not easy for ·the Watch Committee of the Commune, which equipped and sent off every day, in haste, several thousand volunteers for the frontier, to keep very exact accounts. But it was just upon this weak point that the Girondins directed their first attack and their insinuations, demanding that a complete account from September 30 should be rendered. The Executive of the Commune, that is, its Watch Committee, sent in an extremely clear statement of its accounts,* and justified its political action.

But in the provinces, doubts as to their honesty remained hanging over Danton and the Commune; and the Girondins in their letters to their friends and agents made as much as possible out of these doubts.

At the same time the Girondins tried to give the Convention an anti-revolutionary guard. They wanted the Directory of each department—the Directories were, as we know, reactionary —to send to Paris four foot-soldiers and two mounted men, making in all 4470 men, to guard the Convention against the possible attacks of the people of Paris and the Commune ! And a powerful agitation was necessary among the sections, which appointed special commissioners to resist the passing of this vote, and to prevent the formation in Paris of a reactionary guard.

But it was chiefly the September massacres that the Girondins never ceased exploiting in order to attack Danton, who in those days acted hand in hand with the Commune and the sections. After "drawing the veil," and almost justifying those days by the mouth of Roland † as they had justified previously the massacres of La Glacière at Lyons by the mouth of Barbaroux,‡ they now manœuvred so well in the Convention that on January 20, 1793, they obtained from it an order of prosecution against the authors of the September massacres, in the hope that the reputation of Danton, Robespierre, and Marat would be blackened by this inquiry.

By degrees, taking advantage of the constitutionalist and

* Out of 713,885 livres received it had expended only 85,529 livres, of which there was a clear account rendered (Louis Blanc, ii. 62). Giraut, on the accusation of the Terror, proved later on that in four months the committee had arrested only 320 persons. If only the Girondins had been as modest after Thermidor !

† *Vide* ch. xxxv.

‡ After long struggles between the revolutionary population of Lyons and the adherents of the priests, and after the murder in a church of the patriot Lescuyer, for having wanted to put up the church's property for sale, in accordance with law, there was an insurrection of the revolutionary working population, which ended in the murder of sixty royalists, whose corpses were thrown into the depths of the Tour de la Glacière. Barbaroux, a Girondist deputy, justified these massacres.

royalist current, which asserted itself among the middle classes after August 10, the Girondins succeeded in creating in the provinces a feeling of hostility towards Paris and its Commune, as well as towards the party of the "Mountain."

Several departments even sent detachments of federates to defend the Convention against "the agitators who wanted to become tribunes and dictators"—Danton, Marat, and Robespierre—and against the people of Paris. At the appeal of Barbaroux, Marseilles—this time "commercialist" Marseilles —sent up to Paris, in October 1792, a battalion of federates, composed of rich young men from the merchant city, who marched through the streets of Paris, demanding the heads of Robespierre and Marat. They were the precursors of the Thermidor reaction; but, fortunately, the people of Paris defeated the plot by winning over these federates to the cause of the Revolution.

Meanwhile the Girondins did not fail to make a direct attack on the federal organisation of the Paris sections. They wanted at any cost to destroy the insurrectional Commune of August 10, and they succeeded in getting new elections for the General Council of the Paris municipality. Pétion, the Girondist mayor, resigned at the same time. Here again, however, the sections frustrated these manœuvres. Not only had the party of the Mountain the majority in the elections, but a revolutionary as advanced and as popular as Chaumette was appointed procurator of the Commune, and the editor of the *Père Duchesne*, Hébert, became his deputy (December 2, 1792). Pétion, who was no longer in sympathy with the revolutionary sentiments of the people of Paris, was not re-elected, and Chambon, a moderate, took his place; but he remained there only two months, and on February 14, 1793, he was replaced by Pache, formerly Minister of War.

This was how the revolutionary Commune of 1793 was constituted—the Commune of Pache, Chaumette, and Hébert, which was the rival of the Convention and played so powerful a part in the movement of May 31–June 2, 1793, which ended in the expulsion of the Girondin leaders from the Convention, and pushed forward with ardour the popular revolution of the

Year II. of the Republic which stood up for Equality and, finally, for Communism.

The great question of the moment was the war. On the successes of the armies depended the future development of the Revolution.

We have seen that the advanced revolutionaries, like Marat and Robespierre, had not wanted the war. But the Court called in the German invaders to save royal despotism: the priests and nobles furiously wanted the war, hoping to regain through it their ancient privileges; and the neighbouring governments saw in a war upon France the means of combating the spirit of revolution which was beginning to show itself in their own dominions, as well as a good opportunity for wresting from France some provinces and colonies. The Girondins, on the other hand, desired the war, because they saw in it the only way to succeed in limiting the authority of the King without appealing to a popular rising. " It is because you do not wish to appeal to the people that you wish for war," said Marat, and he was right.

As to the people, the peasants of the frontier departments, when they saw the German armies headed by the emigrant nobles massing themselves on the Rhine and in the Low Countries, they understood that it was a question for them of taking up arms to defend their rights over the lands they had retaken from the nobles and clergy. Therefore, when the war with Austria was declared on April 20, 1792, an astounding enthusiasm was displayed by the inhabitants of the departments close to the Eastern frontier. The levies for the volunteers, for one year, were made with enthusiasm, to the singing of *Ça ira!* and the patriotic gifts flowed in from all sides. But this was not the case in the regions of western and south-western France: there the people did not want the war at all.

Nothing, moreover, was ready for the war. The forces of France, not numbering more than 130,000 men, spread out from the North Sea to Switzerland, badly equipped and commanded by royalist officers and staffs, were not in a condition to resist an invasion.

Dumouriez and Lafayette at first conceived the bold plan of rapidly invading Belgium, which had already in 1790 tried to detach herself from Austria, but had been vanquished. The Belgian Liberals had appealed to the French, but the attempt failed, and thenceforth the French generals kept on the defensive, the more so because Prussia had joined with Austria and the German princes to invade France, and moreover, this coalition was strongly and openly supported by the Court of Turin, and secretly by the Courts of St. Petersburg and London.

On July 26, 1792, the Duke of Brunswick, who commanded one of the invading armies, composed of 70,000 Prussians and 68,000 Austrians, Hessians and *émigrés*, began to march upon Coblentz, publishing as he went a manifesto which roused the indignation of all France. He threatened to set fire to the towns that dared to defend themselves, and to exterminate their inhabitants as rebels. If Paris dared to break into the palace of Louis XVI., the city would be subjected to an exemplary dragooning that would never be forgotten.

Three German armies were to enter France and march upon Paris, and on April 19, the Prussian army crossed the frontier and took Longwy and Verdun without a struggle.

We have seen the enthusiasm that the Commune succeeded in rousing in Paris when this news arrived, and how it replied by causing the leaden coffins of the rich to be melted down for balls, and the bells, as well as the other church furniture in bronze, to be turned into cannon, whilst the churches were used as vast worksheds, where thousands of people worked making the volunteers' outfits, singing, as they sewed, the *Ca ıra* and the *Marseillaise*, the stirring hymn of Rouget de l'Isle.

The *émigrés* had made the allied kings believe that they would find France ready to receive them with open arms. But the openly hostile attitude of the peasants and the September days in Paris made the invaders pause. The inhabitants of the towns and the peasants of the Eastern departments understood very well that the enemy had come to take away the fruits of all their conquests, and it had been chiefly in the regions to the East that the risings of the town and country parts, in 1789 and 1790, had best succeeded in destroying feudalism.

But enthusiasm was not sufficient to conquer. The Prussian army was advancing, and now with the Austrian army, it had already entered the forest of the Argonne, which extended over a length of eleven leagues, separating the valley of the Meuse from the barren Champagne. Dumouriez' army tried vainly by forced marches to stop the invasion. It succeeded only in occupying just in time an advantageous position at Valmy, at the exit from the great forest, and here the Prussians, on September 20, met with their first check, while trying to gain possession of the hills occupied by the soldiers of Dumouriez. Under the circumstances, the battle of Valmy was an important victory—the first victory of the peoples over the kings—and as such it was hailed by Goethe who accompanied the army of the Duke of Brunswick.

The Prussian army was compelled to make a halt under torrential rains in the forest of the Argonne, and as everything was lacking in the arid plains stretching in front, it became a prey to dysentery, which made frightful ravages among the men. The roads were liquid mud, the peasants on the watch—everything foreboded a disastrous campaign.

It was then that Danton negotiated with the Duke of Brunswick for the retreat of the Prussians. What the conditions were is not known to this day. Did Danton promise him, as it has been later maintained, to save the life of Louis XVI. ? It is possible. But if this promise was made, it must have been conditional, and we do not know what engagements were undertaken in return by the invaders, beyond the immediate retreat of the Prussians. Was the simultaneous retreat of the Austrians promised ? Was a formal renunciation of the throne by Louis XVI. spoken of ? We are only able to make conjectures.

All we really know is that, on October 1, the Duke of Brunswick began his retreat by Grand-Pré and Verdun. Towards the end of the month he recrossed the Rhine at Coblentz, accompanied by the curses of the *émigrés*.

Dumouriez thereupon, after giving Westermann orders to "escort the Prussians back politely," without hurrying them too much, went to Paris, on October 11, evidently to see how the parties were divided and to determine his own line of conduct.

He so arranged it that, although he did not take the oath to the Republic, he was nevertheless very well received by the Jacobins, and from that time he undoubtedly began to press keenly the candidature of the Duke de Chartres for the throne of France.

The insurrection, which had been arranged in Brittany by the Marquis de la Rouêrie to break out at the time when the Germans would be marching on Paris, also came to nothing. Information about it was given to Danton, who was able to grasp the threads of it, in Brittany as well as in London. But London remained the centre of the conspiracies of the princes, and the island of Jersey was made the centre for royalist stores of arms. The intention was to land a small army somewhere on the coast of Brittany, to seize Saint-Malo with the aid of the local royalists, and to hand over this port of great military and commercial importance to the English.

At the same time, the French army of the South, commanded by Montesquiou, entered Savoy the very day the Convention opened. It took Chambéry four days later and introduced into Savoy the peasant revolution against feudal landlords.

At the end of the same month of September, one of the armies of the Republic, commanded by Lauzun and Custine, passed the Rhine and took Spires by assault on the 30th. Worms yielded four days later, and on October 23, Mayence and Frankfort-on-the-Maine were occupied by the armies of the *sansculottes*.

In the North, there was another series of successes. Towards the end of October, the army under Dumouriez entered Belgium, and on November 6, it gained a great victory over the Austrians at Jemmapes, in the environs of Mons—a victory which Dumouriez had arranged in such a way as to bring glory to the son of the Duke de Chartres—and to sacrifice two battalions of Parisian volunteers.

This victory opened up Belgium to the French. Mons was occupied on the 8th, and on the 14th Dumouriez made his entry into Brussels. The people received the soldiers of the Republic with open arms. They were expecting them to initiate a series of revolutionary measures, chiefly concerning property. Snch was also the idea of the "Mountain"—at least of Cambon—the man who had organised the immense business of selling the lands of the clergy as a guarantee for the *assignats*, who was at that moment organising the sale of the estates of the emigrant royalists, and who asked nothing better than to introduce the same system into Belgium. But whether it was that the "Mountain" lacked courage, attacked as it was by the Girondins for its want of respect for property, or that the aims of the Revolution had not found the necessary support in Belgium, where only the proletarians were on the side of the Revolution, while all the well-to-do middle classes and the formidable power of the priests were opposed to it. At any rate, it remains a fact that the Revolution—which might have combined the Belgians with the French, was not accomplished.

With all these successes and victories there was enough to intoxicate the lovers of the war, and the Girondins triumphed. On December 15, the Convention issued a decree in which it defied all the monarchies and declared that peace should not be concluded with any of the Powers until their armies had been expelled from the territory of the Republic. In reality, however, the situation within looked rather gloomy, and the very victories of the Republic only set the seal upon the union between all the monarchies.

The invasion of Belgium decided England as to her *rôle*. The dawn of republican and communist ideas among the English, which was manifested by the foundation of republican societies, and found its literary expression in 1793 through the remarkable work on free communism, by Godwin, "On Political Justice," had inspired the French republicans, especially Danton, with the hope of finding support in an English revolutionary movement.*

But industrial and mercantile interests carried the day in the British Isles. And when republican France invaded Belgium

* The tenor of the negotiations of Brissot in England during January 1793, before the King's execution, is still unknown. Concerning those of Danton, *see* Georges Avenel's article, *Danton et les positivistes religieux*, in his *Lundis révolutionnaires*, 1875, pp. 248 *et seq.* and the work of Albert Sorel, *L'Europe et la Révolution française* (Paris).

and fortified herself in the valley of the Scheldt and Rhine, threatening to take possession of Holland, England's policy was decided.

To take away France's colonies, to destroy her power on the sea, to check her industrial development and her colonial expansion—this was the policy to which the greatest number adhered in England. The party of Fox was crushed and Pitt's was in the ascendant. Thenceforth England, strong in her fleet and still stronger in her money with which she subsidised the continental powers—Russia, Prussia, and Austria among them—became and remained, for a quarter of a century, the head of a European coalition. It was a war of complete exhaustion between the two nations. And this war forcibly brought France to a military dictatorship.

Besides, if Paris, threatened by the invasion, was transported by a sublime enthusiasm and its best elements hastened to join the volunteers from the departments of Eastern France, it was also the war which gave the first impulse to the rising in the Vendée. It furnished the priests with a pretext for exploiting the reluctance of the population to leave their shady groves and go fighting, they knew not where, upon the frontier: it helped to arouse the fanaticism of the Vendéans and to make them revolt, at the very time when the Germans were entering France. We shall see later how much evil was wrought for the Revolution by this rising.

But if it had been only the Vendée! All through France the war created such a terrible condition of things for the great mass of the poor folk that one cannot but ask, how did the Republic succeed in passing safely through such a formidable crisis?

The harvest of 1792 was a good one for wheat; but on account of the rains it was only fairly good for the oats and barley. The exportation of cereals was forbidden, and yet for all that there was a famine. In the towns, for a long time nothing so terrible had been seen. Long files of men and women besieged the bakers and the butchers, spending the whole night in the snow and rain, without the certainty of getting one scrap of bread in the morning even at an exorbitant price. And this, at a time when quite a number of industries had been stopped almost completely, which meant no work.

The fact is that one cannot with impunity take away from a nation of twenty-five millions nearly a million men in the flower of their manhood, and perhaps half a million of beasts of burden, without its being felt in agricultural labour. Neither can the food-stuffs of a nation be subjected to the inevitable wastage of war without making still blacker the misery of the poor—at the same time that a horde of exploiters enrich themselves at the expense of the public treasury.*

Questions concerning all these vital facts were being launched like thunderbolts into the very midst of each popular society in the provinces and into each section of the great towns, to find their way thence to the Convention. And above everything rose the greatest question of all upon which all the others depended: " What was to be done with the King ? "

* The robberies committed by a certain number of officers in the commissariat of the armies of the Republic were scandalous. Some examples will be found in Jaurès' *Histoire socialiste, La Convention.* The speculations in which they indulged can also be imagined from the fact that the commissariat officers purchased immense quantities of wheat precisely in those departments where the harvest had been bad, and the prices were very high. Speculations in the rise of wheat formerly made by Septeuil for the profit of Louis XVI., " the good King," who never neglected this means of filling his privy purse, were now being made by the middle classes.

CHAPTER XXXVIII

THE TRIAL OF THE KING

Fate of King undecided—Reason of delay—Trial determined on—Gamain betrays the King—Obstacles in way of trial—Justification of trial—Marie-Antoinette and Fersen—Girondins try to prevent trial by attacking " Mountain "—King appears before Convention—Death sentence pronounced—Execution of King

THE two months which elapsed between the opening of the Convention and the trial of the King remain up till now an enigma for history.

The first question which confronted the Convention after it had met was naturally that of deciding what was to be done with the King and his family, imprisoned in the Temple. To keep them there for an indefinite time, until the invasion should be repelled and a republican constitution voted and accepted by the people, was impossible. How could the Republic be established, so long as it held the King and his legitimate heir in prison, without daring to do anything with them?

Besides, having become simple individuals, who, taken from the palace, were dwelling *en famille* in prison, Louis XVI., Marie-Antoinette and their children became interesting martyrs, to whom the royalists were devoted, and whom the middle classes and even the *sans-culottes* pitied as they mounted guard over them at the Temple.

Such a situation could not continue. And yet, nearly two months passed, during which the Convention was very much interested in all manner of things without ever broaching the first consequence of August 10—the fate of the King. This delay, in our opinion, must have been intentional, and we can

THE TRIAL OF THE KING

only explain it by supposing that during this time they were carrying on secret conferences with the European Courts—conferences which have not yet been divulged, and which were certainly connected with the invasion and the issue of which depended on the turn that would be taken by the war.

We know already that Danton and Dumouriez had had parleyings with the chief commander of the Prussian army, which in the end decided him to separate from the Austrian and effect his retreat. And we know, too, that one of the conditions imposed by the Duke of Brunswick—although very probably it was not accepted—was that Louis XVI. should not be harmed. But there must have been more than that. Similar negotiations were very likely being carried on with England. And how can the silence of the Convention and the patience of the sections be explained, without supposing that there was an understanding between the "Mountain" and the Gironde?

To-day, however, it is clear to us that parleyings of this kind could come to nothing, and for two reasons. The fate of Louis XVI. and his family was not of sufficient interest to the King of Prussia, nor to the King of England, nor to the brother of Marie-Antoinette, the Emperor of Austria, for them to sacrifice national political interests to the personal interests of the prisoners in the Temple. That was plainly seen through the negotiations, which took place later, concerning the setting at liberty of Marie-Antoinette and Madame Elisabeth. And on the other hand, the allied Kings did not find in France among the educated class, the unity of republican sentiment which should have made their hope of re-establishing royalty vanish. On the contrary, they found the "intellectuals" of the middle classes very much inclined to accept either the Duke of Orléans (Grand Master of the Brotherhood of Freemasons, to which all the revolutionaries of renown belonged) or his son, the Duke de Chartres—the future Louis-Philippe—or even the Dauphin.

But the people became impatient. The popular societies throughout France demanded that the trial of the King should be deferred no longer, and on October 19, the Commune attended at the bar of the Convention to signify that this was the wish of Paris also. At last, on November 3, the first step was taken. A communication was read demanding that Louis XVI. should be put upon his trial, and the principal heads of accusation were formulated the next day. The discussion on this subject was opened on the 13th. The affair, however, would have still dragged out to a great length if, on November 20, the locksmith Gamain, who had formerly taught Louis lock-making, had not revealed to Roland the existence in the Tuileries of a secret cupboard, which Gamain had helped the King to put in one of the walls, for keeping his papers.

This bit of history is well known. One day, in August 1792, Louis XVI. sent for Gamain from Versailles in order that he might help him to fix in a wall, under a panel, an iron door which he had constructed himself, to serve to shut in a kind of secret cupboard. When the work was finished, Gamain set out again in the night for Versailles, after drinking a glass of wine and eating a biscuit given to him by the Queen. He fell on the road, seized with violent colic, and had been ill ever since. Believing himself to have been poisoned, or worked upon, may be, by the fear of being prosecuted some day by the republicans, he gave information concerning the cupboard to Roland, who, without letting any one know, immediately took possession of the papers in it, carried them off to his house and examined them together with his wife, and having affixed his seal to each of them he brought them to the Convention.

The profound sensation produced by this discovery can be understood, especially when it became known through these papers that the King had bought the services of Mirabeau, that his agents had proposed to him to buy eleven influential members of the Legislative Assembly (it was already known that Barnave and Lameth had been won over to his cause), and that Louis XVI. still had in his pay those disbanded members of his guards who had placed themselves at the service of his brothers at Coblentz, and who were then marching with the Austrians upon France.

It is only now, when we have in our hands so many documents

THE TRIAL OF THE KING

that confirm the treacheries of Louis XVI., and can see the forces which were, nevertheless, opposed to his condemnation, that we comprehend how very difficult it was for the Revolution to bring a King to judgment and to execute him.

All the prejudice, the open and latent servility in society, the fear for the property of the rich, and the distrust of the people, were joined together to hinder the trial. The Gironde, faithfully reflecting all these fears, did all that was possible to prevent the trial from taking place, and afterwards to prevent its ending in a condemnation, or, failing this, to see that the condemnation should not be to death, and finally, that the sentence should not be carried out.* Paris had to threaten the Convention with an insurrection to force it to pronounce its judgment when the trial opened, and not to defer the execution. And yet up to the present day what maudlin speeches are uttered, what tears are shed by the historians when they mention this trial !

And what about ? If any general, no matter which, had been convicted of having done what Louis XVI. had done—that is, of calling in the foreign invaders and of supporting them—who, among the modern historians, all of them defenders of " State reasons," would have hesitated a single moment to demand the death of that general ? Why then so much lamentation when high treason was committed by the commander of all the armies of France ?

According to all traditions and all fictions to which our historians and jurists resort for establishing the rights of "the head of the State," the Convention *was* the sovereign at that moment. To it, and to it alone belonged the right of judging the sovereign whom the people had dethroned, as to it alone belonged the right of legislation which had fallen from his hands. Tried by the members of the Convention, Louis XVI. was—to use their own language—tried by his peers. And they, having ascertained the moral certitude of his treason—had no choice. They *had* to pronounce the

* During the trial, some Girondist deputies, those of Calvados in particular, wrote to their constituents that the " Mountain " wanted the King to be put to death only to set the Duke of Orléans upon the throne.

sentence of death. Clemency even was outside the question, at a time when blood was flowing on the frontiers. The allied Kings knew this themselves; they comprehended it perfectly.

As to the theory developed by Robespierre and Saint-Just, according to which the Republic had the right to kill Louis XVI. as its enemy, Marat was quite right to protest against it. That might have been done during or immediately after the conflict of August 10, but not three months after the fight. Now, there was nothing left to do but to try Louis with all the publicity possible, so that the peoples and posterity might themselves judge as to his knavery and his deceit.

In the matter of the act of high treason on the part of Louis XVI. and his wife, we, who have in our hands the correspondence of Marie-Antoinette with Fersen and the letters of Fersen to various personages, must admit that the Convention judged rightly, even though it had not the overwhelming proofs that we possess to-day. But so many facts had accumulated in the course of the last three years, so many avowals had been let drop by royalists and by the Queen, so many acts of the King since his flight to Varennes, which, although amnestied by the Constitution of 1791, served none the less to explain his ulterior acts—that every one was *morally* certain of his treason. Neither had the people of Paris any doubts on the subject.

In fact, this treason began by the letter which Louis XVI. wrote to the Emperor of Austria the very day on which he took the oath to the Constitution in September 1791, amid the enthusiastic acclamations of the Parisian middle classes. Then came the correspondence of Marie-Antoinette with Fersen, written with the King's knowledge. Nothing is more odious than this correspondence. Ensconced in the Tuileries, the two traitors, the Queen and the King, asked for the invasion, planned it, pointed out the road for it, sent information concerning the forces and the military plans. The triumphal entry of the German allies into Paris and the wholesale massacre of all the revolutionists were planned out by the fair and skilful hand of Marie-Antoinette. The people had estimated truly the woman they called the "Médicis," she whom the historians wish to represent to us now as a poor madcap.*

From the legal point of view, there is consequently nothing wherewith to reproach the Convention. As to the often-debated question whether the execution of the King did not do more harm than would have been caused by his presence in the midst of the German or English armies, there is only one remark to make. So long as the royal power was considered by the propertied class as the best means of holding in check those who wish to dispossess the rich and diminish the power of the priests—so long the King, dead or alive, in prison or free, beheaded and canonised, going about as a knight-errant among his fellow Kings, would have always been the hero of a pathetic legend invented by the clergy and all interested persons.

On the contrary, by sending Louis to the scaffold, the Revolution succeeded in killing a principle, which the peasants had begun to kill at Varennes. On January 21, 1793, the revolutionary portion of the French people knew well that the pivot of all the power, which for centuries had oppressed and exploited the masses, was broken at last. The demolition of that powerful organisation which was crushing the people was begun ; its centre was broken, and the popular revolution took a fresh start.

* Fersen, the friend of Marie-Antoinette, has entered in his private diary what these conspirators were preparing for the French patriots. The Minister of Prussia, Baron de Beck—Fersen wrote—disapproved loudly of their not exterminating the Jacobins in the towns through which they passed, and of their having shown too much clemency. As to the Count de Mercy, he said to Fersen that great severity was needful, and *that Paris ought to be set on fire at the four corners.*
On September 11, Fersen wrote to the Baron de Breteuil that, as the territory conquered by the German armies yields only to force, " mercy in such case appears to me extremely pernicious. *This is the moment to destroy the Jacobins.*" To exterminate the leaders in every place through which the allies should pass, seems to him to be the best means : " We must not hope to win them over by kindness ; they must be exterminated, and this is the moment." And Breteuil replies to him that he has spoken of it to the Duke of Brunswick. But the duke is too mild. The King of Prussia appears to be better : " Varennes, for example, will be chastised one of these days." Vide *Le Comte de Fersen et la Cour de France. Extrait de papiers . . . publié par son petit-neveu, le Baron R. M. de Klinckowström* (Paris, 1877), vol. ii. pp. 360 *et seq.*

Since then the right divine of Kings has never been able to re-establish itself in France, even with the support of Europe in coalition, even with the aid of the frightful " White Terror " of the Restoration. And royalties issuing from the barricades or from a *coup d'état*, like Napoleon III., have not succeeded either, as we have seen in 1848 and 1870. The very principle of royalty was slain in France.

Everything was done, however, by the Girondins to prevent the condemnation of Louis XVI. They invoked every judicial argument, they had recourse to every parliamentary wile. There were even moments when the King's trial was nearly changed into a trial of the " Mountain." But nothing availed. The logic of the situation carried the day over the quibbles of parliamentary tactics.

At first, the Girondins put forward the pretext of the King's inviolability, established by the Constitution, to which it was triumphantly replied that this inviolability no longer existed —since the King had betrayed the Constitution and his country.

A special tribunal, formed of representatives of the eighty-three departments, was next demanded ; and when it became evident that this proposal would be set aside, the Girondins wanted to have the sentence submitted to the ratification of the thirty-six thousand communes and all the primary assemblies by a roll-call of each citizen. This was to call in question again the results of August 10 and the Republic.

When the impossibility of thus laying the trial upon the shoulders of the primary Assemblies was demonstrated, the Girondins, who had themselves most eagerly clamoured for the war and advocated war to the bitter end and against all Europe, began now to plead the effect which would be produced on Europe by the King's execution. As if England, Prussia, Austria and Sardinia had waited for the death of Louis XVI. to make their coalition. As if the democratic Republic was not sufficiently odious to them, as if the allurement of the great commercial ports of France, and her colonies and provinces in the East, were not enough to bring the Kings in coalition against France, so that they might profit by the moment when

THE TRIAL OF THE KING

the birth of a new society had weakened his powers of military resistance outside his own territory.

Repulsed again on this point by the "Mountain," the Girondins then made a diversion by attacking the "Mountain" itself, demanding that several members of this party should be brought to trial as "the aiders and abettors of the September massacres," by whom were meant Danton, Marat and Robespierre, the "dictators," the "triumvirate."

In the midst of all these discussions the Convention decided on December 3 that it would itself try Louis XVI.; but scarcely was this declared than everything was again called in question by one of the Girondins, Ducos, and the attention of the Convention was turned in another direction. By demanding the penalty of death for "any person who shall propose to restore Kings or royalty in France, no matter under what denomination," the Girondins flung at the "Mountain" an insinuation that the "Mountain" was trying to bring the Duke of Orléans to the throne. They sought to substitute a trial of the "Mountain" for the trial of the King.

At last, on December 11, Louis XVI. appeared before the Convention. He was subjected to an interrogation, and his replies must have killed any lingering sympathy which may have existed in his favour. Michelet asks how was it possible for a man to lie as Louis lied ? And he can only explain his deceit by the fact that every kingly tradition and all the influence of the Jesuits to which Louis XVI. had been subjected, had inspired him with the idea that State reasons permitted a King to do anything.

The impression produced by this interrogation was so disadvantageous to Louis that the Girondins, comprehending that it would be impossible to save the King, made a fresh diversion demanding the expulsion of the Duke of Orléans. The Convention allowed a vote to be taken on it, and decreed the expulsion, but the next day the decision was revoked after it had been disapproved by the Jacobin Club.

The trial, however, followed its due course, Louis XVI. appeared a second time before the Convention on December 26, with his advocates and his counsellors, Malesherbes, Tronchet and Desèze; his defence was heard, and it was evident that he would be condemned. There was no longer any possibility of interpreting his acts as an error of judgment, or as an act of foolishness. It was treason, deliberate and crafty, as Saint-Just the next day showed it to be.

If, however, the Convention and the people of Paris could thus form a clear opinion concerning Louis XVI.—both as man and king—it is to be understood that such was not the case with the provincial towns and villages. And we can imagine the unloosing of passions which would have resulted, had the pronouncing of the penalty been referred to the Primary Assemblies. The majority of the revolutionists having gone to the frontiers, it would, as Robespierre said, have left the decision "to the rich, the natural friend of monarchy, to the selfish, to the feeble and the cowardly, to all the haughty and aristocratic upper middle class, all of them men born to thrive and to oppress under a King."

We shall never disentangle all the intrigues which were set on foot at that time in Paris between the "statesmen." It is enough to say that on January 1, 1793, Dumouriez hastened to Paris and stayed there until the 20th, occupied in clandestine conference with the various parties, while Danton remained until January 14 with the army of Dumouriez.*

At last, on the 14th, after an extremely stormy discussion, the Convention decided to vote, by name, upon three questions, namely, to know whether Louis XVI. was guilty of "conspiring against the liberty of the nation, and of criminal attempts against the general safety of the State"; whether the sentence should be submitted to the sanction of the people; and what should be the penalty.

The roll-call began the next day, the 15th. Out of 749

* Jaurès has pointed out here an important error in Michelet. It was Daunou who, on January 14, pronounced the speech in favour of the King that Michelet has attributed by mistake to Danton. Returning to Paris on January 15, Danton, on the contrary, made a powerful speech demanding the condemnation of Louis XVI. It would be important to verify the accusation against Brissot, Gensonné, Guadet, and Pétion, formulated by Billaud-Varennes in his speech on January 15, 1793 (Pamphlet of 32 pages, published by order of the Convention. British Museum Collection, vol. F, 1097).

THE TRIAL OF THE KING

members of the Convention, 716 declared Louis XVI. guilty. Twelve members were absent through illness or official business, and five abstained from voting. No one said "not guilty." The appeal to the people was rejected by 423 votes out of the 709 who voted. Paris, during all this time, was in a state of profound agitation, especially in the faubourgs.

The voting by name on the third question—the penalty—lasted twenty-five consecutive hours. Here again, apparently through the influence of the Spanish ambassador, and perhaps with the help of his piastres, one deputy, Mailhe, tried to stir up confusion by voting for a reprieve, and his example was followed by twenty-six members. Sentence of death, without any proviso, was pronounced by 387 out of 721 voters, there being five who abstained from voting and twelve absent. The sentence was therefore pronounced only by a majority of fifty-three voices—by twenty-six only, if we exclude the votes containing conditions of reprieve. And this was at a moment when all the evidence went to prove that the King had plotted treason; and that to let him live was to arm one-half of France against the other, to deliver up a large part of France to the foreigners, and, finally, to stop the Revolution at the time when, after three years of hesitation, during which nothing durable had been effected, an opportunity at last presented itself of broaching the great questions which were of such intense interest to the country.

But the fears of the middle classes went so far that on the day of the King's execution they expected a general massacre.

On January 21, Louis XVI. died upon the scaffold. One of the chief obstacles to all social regeneration within the Republic existed no longer. There is evidence that up to the last moment Louis hoped to be liberated by a rising, and an attempt to carry him off, when on the way to execution, had in fact been arranged. The vigilance of the Commune caused this to fail.

CHAPTER XXXIX

THE "MOUNTAIN" AND THE GIRONDE

Policy of "Mountain"—Royalist tendencies of Girondins—They reject agrarian law, and swear to respect property—Continuous conflict between Gironde and "Mountain"—Socialistic aims of Montagnards—Brissot and Robespierre—Order *versus* Revolution

SINCE August 10 the Commune of Paris had dated its documents from "the Fourth Year of Liberty and the First of Equality." The Convention dated its acts from "the Fourth Year of Liberty and the First Year of the French Republic." And in this little detail already appeared two ideas confronting one another.

Was there to be a new revolution grafted upon the preceding one ? Or would France confine herself to establishing and legalising the political liberties won since 1789 ? Would she be content with consolidating the middle-class government, slightly democratised, without calling upon the mass of the people to take advantage of the immense readjustment of wealth accomplished by the Revolution ?

Two totally different ideas, and these two ideas were represented in the Convention, one by the "Mountain," and the other by the Gironde.

On the one side were those who understood that for the destruction of the ancient feudal system, it was not enough to register a beginning of its abolition in the laws ; and that, to bring the reign of absolutism to an end, it was not enough to dethrone a King, set up the emblem of the Republic on the public buildings, and print its name upon the headings of official papers ; that this was only a beginning, nothing but the creation of certain conditions which would perhaps permit

THE "MOUNTAIN" AND THE GIRONDE

the remodelling of the institutions. And those who thus understood the Revolution were supported by all who wished the great mass of the people to come forth at last from the hideous poverty, so degrading and brutalising, into which the old *régime* had plunged them—all who sought, who strove to discover in the lessons of the Revolution the true means of elevating these masses, both physically and morally. With them were great numbers of the poor, whom the Revolution had taught to think.

And opposed to them were the Girondins—a party formidable in its numbers: for the Girondins were not only the two hundred members grouped around Vergniaud, Brissot and Roland. They were an immense portion of the French nation; almost all the well-to-do middle class; all the constitutionalists whom the force of circumstances had made republicans, but who feared the Republic because they feared the domination of the masses. And behind them, ready to support them, while waiting for the moment to crush them too, for re-establishing royalty, were all those who trembled for their wealth, as well as for their educational privileges—all those whom the Revolution had deprived of their old privileges, and who were sighing for the return of the old *régime*.

In fact, we see quite clearly that not only the "Plain," but also three-fourths of the Girondins were royalists as much as the Feuillants. For, if some of their leaders dreamed of a kind of antique republic, without a king, but with a people obedient to the laws made by the rich and the learned, the greater number would have very willingly accepted a king. They gave ample proof of this by their good fellowship with the royalists after the *coup d'état* of Thermidor. And, all things considered, this attitude of mind of the Girondins is quite comprehensible, because the essential thing for them was *the establishment of government by the middle classes*, who were then rapidly growing in trade and commerce, on the ruins of feudalism, and, as Brissot used to say," the preservation of property " was for them the main point.

Hence their hatred of the people and their love of " order."

To prevent a rising of the people, to constitute a strong government, and to protect property, this was what was essential for the Girondins at this moment; and it is because most historians failed to comprehend this fundamental character of Girondism, that they have sought for so many other secondary circumstances to explain the conflict that broke out between the "Mountain" and the Gironde.

When we see the Girondins "repudiating the agrarian law," "refusing to recognise equality as a principle of republican legislation," and "swearing to respect property," we may perhaps think all that a little too abstract in a hundred years' time. Those formulas had, however, in the time of the Revolution, a very exact meaning.

To reject the agrarian law meant at that time to reject the attempts to place the land in the hands of those who cultivated it. It meant rejecting the idea, so popular among the revolutionists sprung from the people, that no landed property—no farm—should be of more than 120 *arpents* (about 180 acres); that every citizen had a right to the land; and that it was necessary to seize the property of the *émigrés* and the clergy, as well as the large estates of the rich, and to divide them between the poor labourers who possessed nothing.

"To take the oath to respect property" was to deny to the rural communities the right of resuming possession of the lands which had been taken from them for two centuries, by virtue of the royal ordinance of 1669; it was to oppose, in favour of the lords and of the recent middle-class buyers of land, the abolition of the feudal rights without redemption.

Finally, it was to combat any attempt at levying upon the rich commercial class and the stock-jobbers a progressive tax; it was to keep the heavy charges of the war and the Revolution upon the poor only.

The abstract formula had thus, as we see, a very tangible meaning.

In fact, over each of these questions the "Mountain" had to carry on a bitter struggle against the Girondins; so much so, that it was forced to appeal to the people, to approve of insurrection, and to expel the Girondins from the Convention, in order to be able to make even a few steps in the direction just mentioned.

For the time being, this "respect for property" was asserted by the Girondins in the smallest things, even in the inscribing of the words *Liberty, Equality, Property*, on the base of the statues which they carried at a festival; in the embracing of Danton, when he said at the first sitting of the Convention: "Let us declare that all properties, territorial, individual and industrial, shall be for ever respected." At these words the Girondin Kersaint fell upon his neck, saying: "I repent of having called you a sedition-monger this morning," which was as much as to say, "Since you promise to respect middle-class property, let us pass over your responsibility for the September massacres!"

While the Girondins were thus endeavouring to organise the middle-class republic, and to lay the foundations for the enrichment of the middle classes on the model set by England after her revolution of 1646, the members of the "Mountain" —or rather, the advanced group among them, which for a short time took the lead over the moderate section, represented by Robespierre—sketched the broad outlines of what would have been the basis for a socialist society—meaning no offence to those of our contemporaries who wrongfully claim to be the first to have done so. The Montagnards wanted, first, to abolish the last vestiges of feudalism, and then to equalise property, to destroy the great landed estates, and give the land to all, even to the poorest labourers. They intended at the same time to organise the national distribution of the products of prime necessity, estimated at their just value, and, by means of a properly handled taxation, to fight "commercialism"—that is, the whole tribe of rich stock-jobbers, bankers, merchants and captains of industry, who were rapidly multiplying and accumulating large fortunes.

At the same time, they had proclaimed, since 1793, "the universal right of well-being—well-being for all," which the socialists later on turned into "the right to work." This right had been already mentioned in 1789 (on August 27), and again in the Constitution of 1791. But even the most advanced of the Girondins were too fettered by their middle-class education to comprehend this right of universal well-being, which implied the right of all to the land and a complete reorganisation, freed from speculation in the distribution of the products necessary for existence.

The Girondins were generally described by their contemporaries as "a party of refined, subtle, intriguing and, above all, ambitious people," fickle, talkative, combative, but in the manner of barristers. "They want the Republic," said Couthon, "but they want also the aristocracy." "They displayed much tenderness," said Robespierre, "but a tenderness which sighed almost exclusively for the enemies of liberty."

They felt a kind of aversion towards the masses; they were afraid of them.*

At the time when the Convention assembled, the gulf that separated the Girondins from the Montagnards was not yet understood. Many saw only a personal rivalry between Brissot and Robespierre. Madame Jullien, for instance, a true friend of the "Mountain" and a true democrat in sentiment, in her letters, called upon the two rivals to cease their fratricidal struggle. But it had already become a struggle between two opposite principles: the party of order and the party of the Revolution.

The people, in a period of strife, and, later on, the historians, always like to personify every conflict in two rivals. It is briefer, more convenient for conversation, and it is also more "romantic," more "dramatic." This is why the struggle between these two parties was so often represented as the clashing of two ambitions, Brissot's and Robespierre's. As is always the case, the two heroes in whom the people personified the

* It is necessary to read the *Mémoires* of Buzot to understand the hatred and contempt of the Girondins for the people. We constantly meet phrases of this kind: "Paris is made up of September murderers"; "here one wallows in the filth of this corrupt city"; "one must have the vice of the people of Paris to please them," &c. Vide Buzot, *Mémoires sur la Révolution française, précédés d'un précis de sa vie*, by M. Gaudet (Paris, 1828), pp. 32, 45, 141, &c. See also Pétion's letter to Buzot of February 6, 1792, published in the *Révolutions de Paris*, vol. xi. p. 263, from which Aulard has given extracts.

THE "MOUNTAIN" AND THE GIRONDE

conflict were well chosen. They were typical. But, in reality, Robespierre did not accept the principle of equality to the extent it was accepted by the Montagnards after the fall of the Girondins. He belonged to the group of moderates. In March and May 1793, he understood that, if he wanted the Revolution to triumph, he must not separate himself from those who demanded expropriatory measures, and he acted accordingly—leaving himself free to guillotine later the Left wing, the Hébertists, and to crush the "extremists." Brissot, on the other hand, was not always a supporter of order; he admitted "disorder" up to the moment when his party had come to power. But, all things considered, the two men represented the two parties very well.

A struggle to the bitter end was, therefore, inevitable between the middle-class party of order and that of the popular revolution.

The Girondist party, having come into power, wanted that everything should now be restored to order; that the Revolution with its revolutionary proceedings should cease, as soon as they took the helm. No more disturbance in the street; everything was henceforth to be under the orders of the ministers, appointed by a docile parliament.

As to the party of the "Mountain," they wanted the Revolution to accomplish such changes as would really modify the whole of the conditions prevailing in France: especially for the peasants, who represented more than two-thirds of the population, and the poverty-stricken folk in the towns; changes which would make it impossible ever to go back to the royal and feudal past.

Some day, a year or two later, the Revolution would calm itself; the people, being exhausted, would have gone back into their cabins and hovels; the *émigrés* would return; the priests and the nobles would again get the upper hand. Therefore it was all the more urgent that they should find everything changed in France; the land in other hands, already watered with the sweat of its new owners; and these owners regarding themselves not as intruders, but as having the right to plough this land and to reap it. They must find the whole of France transformed in its manners, its habits, its language—a land where every man would consider himself the equal of his fellow men from the moment he handled the plough, the spade, or the tool. But for this it was of absolute necessity that the Revolution should continue even though it had to sacrifice a number of those whom the people had appointed to be their representatives, by sending them to the Convention.

Of course such a struggle would be a struggle to the death. For it must not be forgotten that these men of order and government, the Girondins, nevertheless considered the revolutionary tribunal and the guillotine as the most efficacious wheels of government. But it could not be avoided.

Already on October 24, 1792, when Brissot published his first pamphlet, in which he demanded a *coup d'état* against the disorganisers, the " anarchists " and the " Tarpeian Rock " for Robespierre;* already from October 29, when Louvet made in the Convention his speech of accusation in which he demanded the head of Robespierre, the Girondins were holding the knife of the guillotine suspended over the heads of the " levellers, the abettors of disorder, the anarchists," who had had the audacity to take sides with the people of Paris and their revolutionary Commune.†

Ever since that day the Girondins had not ceased in their efforts to despatch the " Mountain " party to the guillotine. Thus, on March 21, 1793, when the defeat of Dumouriez at Neerwinden became known at Paris, and Marat rose to accuse

---

* " Three Revolutions," he wrote, " were necessary to save France : the first to overthrow despotism ; the second to destroy royalty ; the third to beat down anarchy ! And to this last Revolution I have consecrated my pen and all my efforts *since August* 11 " (J. P. Brissot, député à la Convention Nationale, *A tous les républicains de France, sur la Société des Jacobins de Paris*. Pamphlet dated October 24, 1792). Both Brissot's pamphlets were reprinted in London.

† Louvet made no concealment of the true meaning of his " Robespierride." When he saw that the shot directed by him and his friends had missed fire, and that the Convention had not put Robespierre on his trial, on going home he said to his wife, Lodoiska : " We must be prepared for the scaffold or exile." He tells this in his *Mémoires*, p. 74. He felt that the weapon he had aimed at the " Mountain " was turning against himself.

him of treason, the Girondins nearly killed him in the Convention; he was saved merely by his cool audacity; and three weeks later, on April 12, returning to the charge, they ended by getting the Convention to send Marat before the revolutionary tribunal. Six weeks later, on May 24, it was the turn of Hébert, the vice-procureur of the Commune; of Varlet, the working-man preacher of socialism, and other "anarchists" whom they caused to be arrested in the hope of sending them to the scaffold. In short, it was a regular campaign for turning the members of the "Mountain" out of the Convention, for throwing them down the "Tarpeian Rock."

At the same time the Girondins were organising counter-revolutionary committees everywhere; and they kept up an uninterrupted stream of petitions, directed against the Montagnards coming to the Convention from persons who styled themselves "friends of law and liberty"—we know to-day what that means—while those of them who were in the Convention wrote letters, full of calumnies, to their friends in the provinces, exciting them against the "Mountain," and especially against the revolutionary population of Paris. And while the commissioners of the Convention made superhuman efforts to repel the invasion, and tried to stimulate the ardour of the people by applying measures of equality, the Girondins opposed them at every point, in all directions, by means of the despatches they sent to their electors. They endeavoured even to prevent the collection of necessary information concerning the estates of the *émigrés* which had to be confiscated and put up for sale.

In his *Patriote française*, Brissot conducted a bitter campaign against the revolutionists, and altogether the Girondins demanded—nay, they insisted on—the dissolution of the revolutionary Commune of Paris; and they went even so far as to demand the dissolution of the Convention and the election of a new Assembly in which none of the present members of the Convention could be re-elected. And finally, a "Commission of the Twelve," which lay in wait for the moment when a *coup d'état* should enable them to send the chief members of the "Mountain" to the scaffold

CHAPTER XL

ATTEMPTS OF THE GIRONDINS TO STOP THE REVOLUTION

Girondins represent middle classes—They support Liberty, but oppose Equality—Views of Brissot—Girondins and " anarchists "

So long as it was a question of overthrowing the old *régime* of absolute monarchy, the Girondins were in the front rank. High-spirited, fearless poets imbued with admiration for the republics of antiquity, and desirous of power at the same time—how could they adapt themselves to the old *régime ?*

Therefore, while the peasants were burning the châteaux of the landlords and their tax-registers, while the people were demolishing the relics of feudal servitude, the Girondins were busy chiefly with establishing the new political forms of government. They saw themselves already in power, masters of the destiny of France, sending forth armies to carry Liberty into the four quarters of the earth.

As to bread for the people, did they ever think about that ? Certain it is that they never realised the force of resistance possessed by the old *régime*, and that they never thought that to conquer this force they would have to appeal to the people. The people must pay the taxes, vote at elections, furnish soldiers to the State ; but as to making or unmaking political forms of government, that must be the work of the thinkers, of the governing class, of the statesmen.

Therefore, when the King had summoned the Germans to his aid, and they were on their way to Paris, the Girondins, who had wished for the war to rid them of the Court, refused to appeal to the people in revolt to repel the invasion and

ATTEMPTS TO STOP THE REVOLUTION 349

drive out the traitors from the Tuileries. Even after August 10, the idea of repelling the foreigner by the Revolution seemed so hateful to them, that Roland convoked the leading men, including Danton and his friends, to speak to them about his plan. This was to flee, to transport the Assembly and the prisoner King to Blois first, and thence to the South, thus delivering up the North of France to the invaders, and constituting a little republic somewhere in the Gironde.

The people, the revolutionary enthusiasm of the people which saved France, did not exist for them. They were merely bureaucrats.

Altogether the Girondins were the faithful representatives of the middle classes. According as the people grew bolder, and claimed that the rich should be taxed, and equal chances of wealth be given to all; as soon as they demanded *equality* as the necessary condition of *liberty*—the middle classes began to say it was time to draw the line between themselves and the people and to reduce the popular masses to "order."

The Girondins followed this current. When they came into power, these middle-class revolutionaries, who until then had given themselves heart and soul to the Revolution, separated themselves from the people. The efforts of the people, in striving to set up its own political organisation within the sections of the large cities, and the popular societies throughout France, their desire to march forward on the road of Equality were in their eyes a danger for the whole of the propertied classes, and constituted a crime.

And henceforth the Girondins resolved to stop the Revolution: to establish a strong government and to reduce the people to submission—by means of the guillotine if need be. In order to comprehend the great drama of the Revolution which ended in the insurrection of Paris on May 31, and the "purification" of the Convention, one must read what the Girondins said themselves; and in this respect the two pamphlets of Brissot are especially instructive.*

"I thought, on entering the Convention," says Brissot

* *Brissot à ses commettants* (May 23, 1793), and *A tous les républicains de France* (October 24, 1792).

"that since royalty was annihilated, and since nearly all power was concentrated in the hands of the people or of their representatives, the patriots must change their way of proceeding since their position had changed."

"I thought that the insurrectionary movement must cease, because, when there was no longer a tyranny to be struck down, there ought to be no longer any force in insurrection."*

"I thought," Brissot says further on, "that order alone could produce tranquillity; that order consisted of a religious respect for the laws, the magistrates and the safety of the individual. . . . I thought, consequently, that order, also, was a *truly revolutionary measure*. . . . I thought therefore that the real enemies of the people and of the Republic were the *anarchists, the preachers of agrarian law*, the exciters of sedition."†

"Twenty anarchists," Brissot goes on to say, "have usurped an influence in the Convention which should belong to reason alone." Follow the debates and you shall see on one side men constantly occupied with the care of causing the laws, the constituted authorities and property to be respected; and on the other hand are men constantly occupied in keeping the people agitated, in discrediting by calumny the constituted authorities, in protecting the impunity of crime, and in loosening all the bonds of society."‡

It is true that those whom Brissot called "anarchists" comprised very diverse elements. But they all had this one trait in common: they did not believe the Revolution had ended, and they acted accordingly.

They knew that the Convention would do nothing without being forced by the people. And for that reason they organised the popular rising. In Paris they proclaimed the sovereign power of the Commune, and they tried to establish national unity, not by means of a central government, but by direct relations established between the municipality and the sections of Paris, and the thirty-six thousand communes of France.

Now this is precisely what the Girondins would not allow.

---

* *J. P. Brissot à ses commettants*, p. 7.
† *Supra*, pp. 8, 9. ‡ *Supra*, p. 13.

"I have declared," says Brissot, "since the beginning of the Convention that there was in France a party of disorganisers, which was tending towards the dissolution of the Republic, even while it was in its cradle. . . . I can prove to-day: first, that this party of anarchists has dominated and still dominates nearly all the deliberations of the Convention and the workings of the Executive Council; secondly, that this party has been and still is the sole cause of all the evils, internal as well as the external, which afflict France; and thirdly, that the Republic can only be saved by taking rigorous measures to wrest the representatives of the nation from the despotism of this faction."

For any one who knows the character of the epoch, this language is quite plain. Brissot was simply demanding the guillotine for those whom he called anarchists and who, by wanting to go on with the Revolution and to finish the abolition of the feudal system, were preventing the middle classes, and the Girondins in particular, from manipulating the Convention to their own advantage.

"It is necessary, therefore, to define this anarchy," says the representative Girondin, and here is his definition:

"Laws that are not carried into effect, authorities without force and despised, crime unpunished, *property attacked*, the safety of the individual violated, the morality of the people corrupted, no constitution, no government, no justice, these are the features of anarchy!"

But, is not this precisely the way by which all revolutions are made? As if Brissot himself did not know it, and had not practised it before attaining power! For three years, from May 1789 to August 10, 1792, it had been necessary to despise the authority of the King—and to have an "authority without force," in order to be able to overthrow it on August 10.

Only what Brissot wanted was, that once that point had been reached, and the authority of the King was overthrown, the Revolution might cease the same day.

Since royalty was overthrown and the Convention had become the supreme power, "all insurrectionary movement," he tells us, "ought to have stopped."

What was most distasteful to the Girondins was the tendency of the Revolution towards Equality—the most dominant tendency in the Revolution at this moment, as M. Faguet has clearly demonstrated.* Thus, Brissot could not forgive the Jacobin Club for having taken the name—not "Friends of the Republic," but "Friends of Liberty and Equality"—especially of Equality! And he could not pardon the "anarchists" for having inspired the petitions "of those workers in the camp at Paris who styled themselves *the nation*, and who wished to fix their salary by that of the deputies!"†

"The disorganisers," he says elsewhere, "are those who want to level everything—property, comforts, the price of commodities, *the various services rendered to the State*, &c., who want the workmen in the camp to receive the salary of the legislator; who want to level even talents, knowledge, the virtues, because they have none of these things."‡

* *L'œuvre sociale de la Révolution française*, edited, with introduction, by Emile Faguet. Paris, undated, ? 1900.
† Brissot, *supra*, p. 29.
‡ Brissot, Pamphlet dated October 24, 1792.

CHAPTER XLI

THE "ANARCHISTS"

Anarchists not a party—Their aims and policy—Brissot quoted—He attacks anarchists—Gironde and anarchists—Girondist programme

But who were those anarchists of whom Brissot spoke so much, and whose extermination he demanded with so much rancour?

First of all, the anarchists did not form *a party*. In the Convention there were the parties of the "Mountain," the Gironde, the "Plain," or rather the "Marsh" (sometimes called *le Ventre*), but there were no "anarchists." Danton, Marat, and even Robespierre, or some other Jacobin of the same stamp, could work at times with the anarchists; but they always remained outside the Convention. They were, one might almost say, above it: they dominated it.

The "anarchists" were the revolutionists scattered all over France. They had given themselves to the Revolution body and soul; they understood the necessity for it; they loved it, and they worked for it.

Many of them gathered round the Paris Commune, because it was still revolutionary; a certain number of them were members of the Cordeliers' Club; some of them belonged to the Jacobin Club. But their true domain was *the Section*, and, still more so, the Street. In the Convention, they were to be seen in the galleries, where they guided the debates by their approbation or disapproval. Their effective means of action was the opinion of *the people*, not "the public opinion" of the middle classes. Their real weapon was the insurrection, and with this weapon they influenced the deputies and the executive power.

When it became necessary to make a fresh attempt to inflame the people and to march *with them* against the Tuileries, it was they who prepared the attack and fought in the ranks. And when the revolutionary enthusiasm of the people had cooled—they returned to the obscurity from whence they had sprung, leaving us only the rancorous pamphlets of their adversaries by which we are enabled to discover the immense revolutionary work they have accomplished.

As to their ideas, they were clear and decided. The Republic—of course! They believed in it. Equality before the law was another of their canons. But that was not all: far from it.

To use political liberty as the means for gaining economic liberty, as had been recommended to them by the middle classes! They knew that this could not be done. Therefore, they wanted *the thing itself*. The Land for All—which was what they called "the agrarian law"—and Economic Equality, or to use the language of that period, " the levelling of wealth."

But let us hear what Brissot has to say about them: "They are the men," he says, "who have divided society into two classes, those who have and those who have not—*the unbreeched ones (sans-culottes)*, and *the property-owners*—and who have stirred up the one against the other.

"They are the men," Brissot goes on to say, "who, under the name of sections, have never ceased from wearying the Convention with petitions, demanding a maximum for corn."

They are the men who have incited "the petition of those ten thousand men, who declared themselves in a state of insurrection if the price of wheat was not fixed," and who are stirring up revolts all over France.

These, then, were the crimes of those who were described by Brissot as the "anarchists": to have divided the nation into two classes; the Haves and the Have-Nots; to have stirred up the one against the other; to have demanded bread—and above all, bread for those who worked.

They were unquestionably great criminals. But who of the

learned socialists of the nineteenth century has been able to invent anything better than this demand of our ancestors in 1793: "Bread for all"? Many more words there are to-day, but less action!

As for their methods of putting their ideas into execution, here they are: "The multiplicity of crimes," Brissot tells us, "is produced by impunity; impunity by the paralysis of the law courts; and the anarchists stand up for this impunity, and help to paralyse the courts, either by terrorism or by denouncing and accusing the aristocracy."

"Of repeated outrages on property and individual safety the anarchists of Paris give examples every day; and their private emissaries, as well as those whom they distinguish by the title of commissioners of the Convention, are preaching this violation of the rights of man everywhere."

Brissot then mentions "the anarchists' eternal denunciations of property-owners and merchants, whom they designate by the name of 'monopolists'"; he speaks of "property-owners who are unceasingly branded as robbers," of the hatred the anarchists feel towards every State official. "From the moment," he says, "when a man takes office, he becomes odious to the anarchists, he becomes guilty." And with cause, say we.

But Brissot is superb when he is enumerating the benefits of "order." It is a passage that must be read if one wishes to comprehend what the Girondist middle class would have given the French people, if the "anarchists" had not given a further impulse to the Revolution. "Consider," he says, "the departments where the fury of these men has been restrained; take for example, the department of the Gironde. Order has constantly reigned there; the people there submit to the law, although they are paying ten *sols* a pound for bread. . . . The reason is that from this department the citizens have expelled the preachers of the agrarian law, that they have nailed up the doors of that club * where they teach . . ." &c.

And this was written two months after August 10, when the blindest person could not fail to understand that if the people

* The Jacobin Club.

all over France had "submitted to the law, although they were paying ten *sols* a pound for bread" there would have been no Revolution at all, and royalty, which Brissot feigned to be fighting, as well as feudalism, might perhaps have reigned for still another century, as in Russia.*

We must read Brissot to understand what the middle classes were then preparing for France, and what the "Brissotins" of the twentieth century are still preparing wherever a revolution is going to break out.

"The troubles in the Eure; the Orne and elsewhere," says Brissot, "have been caused by preachings against the rich, against the monopolists, by seditious sermons on the necessity of fixing by force a maximum price for grains and all foodstuffs."

And of Orléans, he says: "This town enjoyed since the beginning of the Revolution a tranquillity that has not even been touched by the disturbances arising elsewhere through the scarcity of grain, although grain was one of the staple commodities of the town. . . . However, this harmony between the poor and the rich was not according to the principles of anarchy; and so one of these men to whom order brings despair, for whom disturbance is the only aim, rushed in to break this happy harmony by exciting the *sans-culottes* against the property-owners."

"Again it is this anarchy," exclaims Brissot, "which has created a revolutionary influence in the army": "Who now can doubt the terrible evil which has been caused in our armies by this anarchist doctrine that would establish under cover of equality in law equality both universal *and in fact*—the scourge of society, just as the other is its support? Anarchic doctrine

* Louis Blanc has defined Brissot extremely well in saying that he was one of those men who are "republicans in advance of the time to-day, and revolutionaries behind the time to-morrow"; people who have not the strength to follow the century, after having had the audacity to outstrip it. After having written in his youth that "property was theft," his respect for property became so great that on the morrow of August 4, he blamed the Assembly for the precipitation with which it had published its decrees against feudalism; and that at a moment when citizens were embracing each other in the street in congratulation of these decrees.

which would bring down to one level learning and ignorance, virtue and vice, offices, salaries, services."

This is what the Brissotins will never pardon in the anarchists : equality in law may be forgiven, but it must never become equality in fact. Had not Brissot, moreover, been sufficiently angered already by the navvies engaged in the camp at Paris, who one day asked that their wages might be made equal to the salary of the deputies ? The idea of such a thing ! Brissot and a navvy put upon the same level—not in law, but "in fact " ! Miserable wretches !

But how did it happen that the anarchists exercised such a great power even to the dominating of the terrible Convention and the dictating of its decisions ?

Brissot tells us how in his pamphlets. " It is," he says, " the galleries of the Convention, the *people* of Paris, and the *Commune* who dominate the position and force the hand of the Convention every time some revolutionary measure is taken."

At the outset, Brissot tells us, the Convention was very wise. " You would see," said he, " the majority of the Convention, sincere, sane, the friends of principles, with their eyes always fixed upon the law." They welcomed " almost unanimously " every proposal which tended to humble and crush " the abettors of disorder."

One can guess the revolutionary results which were to be expected from these representatives who always kept their eyes fixed on the law—the royal and feudal law ; fortunately, the " anarchists " had something to say in the matter. But these " anarchists " knew that their place was not in the Convention, among the representatives—their place was *in the street ;* they understood that if they ever set foot inside the Convention, it must not be to debate with the " members of the Right," or the " Frogs of the Marsh " ; it must be to exact something, either from the top of the galleries where the public sat, or through an invasion of the Convention, with the people at their back.

" In this fashion, little by little the brigands " (Brissot is speaking of the " anarchists ") " have audaciously lifted up their heads. From being the accused, they have transformed themselves into the accusers ; instead of being silent spectators at our debates, they have become the arbiters."—" We are in the midst of a revolution," was their reply.

In fact, those whom Brissot called " anarchists " saw further and were giving proofs of a political wisdom far exceeding that shown by those who were pretending to govern France. If the Revolution had ended in the triumph of the Brissotins, without having abolished the feudal system, and without having given back the land to the Communes—where should we be to-day ?

But perhaps Brissot has formulated somewhere a programme in which he explains how the Girondins proposed to put an end to the feudal system and the struggles it provoked ? At the supreme moment, when the people of Paris were demanding the expulsion of the Girondins from the Convention, he may perhaps have said how the Girondins proposed to satisfy, were it only in part, the most pressing of the popular needs ?

He never says anything, absolutely not a word of the sort. The party of the Gironde cut short the whole of this question by repeating that to touch property, whether it be feudal or middle class, is to do the work of the " leveller," of the " aider and abettor of disorder," of the " anarchist." People of that sort should be simply exterminated.

" Before August 10, the disorganisers were real revolutionists," writes Brissot, " because a republican had to be a disorganiser. But the disorganisers of to-day are the real counter-revolutionists ; they are enemies of the people, because the ' people ' are master now. What is left for them to desire ? Interior tranquillity, since this tranquillity alone assures to the owner his property, to the worker his work, to the poor their daily bread, and to all the enjoyment of liberty." *

Brissot did not even understand that at that time of scarcity, when the price of bread had gone up to six or seven *sous* the pound, the people might well demand an edict to fix the price of bread. Only " anarchists " could make such a demand ! †

For him and for the whole of the Gironde, the *Revolution* was terminated since the movement of August 10 had placed

---
* Pamphlet dated October 24, 1792.
† *Ibid.* p. 19.

their party in power. There was nothing more to be done but to accept the situation and obey whatever political laws the Convention should make. They did not even understand the man of the people, who said that, since the feudal laws remained, since the land had not been given back to the Communes, since in all things concerning the land question there was merely a provisional arrangement, since the poor had still to bear the whole burden of the war—*the Revolution was not ended,* and only revolutionary action could bring it to an end, seeing the immense resistance offered by the old *régime* to every attempt at decisive measures.

The party of the Gironde could not even comprehend this. They admitted only one class of discontented—that of the citizens who feared " either for their riches, their comforts, or their lives." * Any other kind of discontented had no right to exist. And when we know in what a state of uncertainty the Legislative Assembly had left all questions pertaining to the land, we can but ask how such an attitude of mind *could be possible ?* In what sort of unreal world of political intrigue did these men live ? We should not be able to understand them at all, were it not that we know too many like them among our own contemporaries.

Brissot's conclusion, accepted by all the Girondins, was as follows : " We must make a *coup d'état,* a third revolution, which must 'beat down anarchy.' Dissolve the Commune of Paris, and destroy its sections ! Dissolve the clubs which preach disorder and equality ! Close the Jacobin Club, and seal up its papers ! The 'Tarpeian Rock,' that is, the guillotine, for 'the triumvirate' of Robespierre, Danton, and Marat, as well as for all the 'levellers'—all the 'anarchists.' Then, a new Convention will be elected, but not one of the present members shall sit again " (which meant, of course, a certainty of triumph for the counter-revolution). A strong Government, and Order—restored ! Such was the Girondins' programme ever since the fall of the King had carried them into power and made " the disorganisers useless."

What was left, then, for the revolutionists to do if not to take

* Pamphlet dated October 24, 1792, p. 127.

up the fight, and fight for life or death? Either the Revolution must have stopped short—unfinished as it was—and then the counter-revolution of Thermidor would have begun fifteen months sooner, in the spring of 1793, before the abolition of the feudal rights had been accomplished; or else the Girondins had to be expelled from the Convention, notwithstanding all the services they had rendered to the Revolution, so long as royalty had to be fought. It was impossible to ignore these services. "No doubt," exclaimed Robespierre, in the famous sitting of April 10—" they have struck at the Court, at the *émigrés*, at the priests, and that with a heavy hand; but at what time? When they had still to gain power. Once they had gained it, their ardour soon abated. *How quickly they changed the objects of their hatred!*"

The Revolution could not be left unfinished. It had to go on —over their bodies, if necessary. And, therefore, Paris and the revolutionary departments, ever since February 1793, were in the throes of an agitation which culminated in the movement of May 31.

CHAPTER XLII

CAUSES OF THE RISING ON MAY 31

Struggle between "Mountain" and "Gironde"—Momentous questions—Inactivity of Convention —Montagnards—Robespierre—Counter-revolution gains ground—Directories of departments and districts—New Commune—Growth of Popular Societies, Fraternal Societies and Revolutionary Committees—*Federalism*—Centralisation—Gironde and "Mountain"

DURING the early part of 1793, the struggle between the "Mountain" and the "Gironde" grew daily more envenòmed according as these three great questions presented themselves to France.

First: Were all the feudal dues to be abolished without redemption, or were these survivals of feudalism to continue to starve the farmer and paralyse agriculture? This was the burning question which meant so much to an agricultural population of nearly twenty millions, including those who had bought the greater part of the national lands taken from the clergy and the emigrant nobles.

Secondly: Were the villages to retain possession of the communal lands which they had retaken from the lords? Would the right of resuming possession be recognised for those Communes that had not already done so? Would the right of every citizen to the land be admitted?

And thirdly: Was the *maximum* going to be introduced, which meant the fixing of the price of bread and other commodities of prime necessity?

These three great questions were exciting the whole of France and had divided it into two hostile camps. On one side were those who possessed property; on the other, those who possessed nothing—the rich and the poor; those who were enriching themselves in spite of misery, scarcity and war, and those who were supporting the whole burden of the war and yet had to stand for hours, and sometimes for entire nights at the baker's door, without being able in the end to carry home a morsel of food.

And yet months—five to eight months—passed without the Convention having done anything to change the situation or to solve the great social problems evolved by the development of the Revolution itself. Time was spent in endless discussions in the Convention and hatred was increasing between the two parties, of which one stood for the rich, and the other defended the poor, while no agreement, no compromise was possible between those who defended property and those who wished to attack it.

It is true that the " Montagnards " themselves had no very clear ideas about economic questions, and were divided into two groups—the one known as the " Enragés " being the much more advanced of the two. The other group, to which Robespierre belonged, was inclined to take views almost as much in defence of property as were those of the Girondins concerning the three great questions just mentioned. But little as we may sympathise with Robespierre, it must be admitted that he developed with the Revolution and he always felt deeply for the sufferings of the people. In the National Assembly, ever since 1791, he had spoken in favour of restoring the communal lands to the Communes. The more he saw of the property-owning and commercial selfishness of the middle classes the more openly he sided with the people and the revolutionary Commune of Paris—with those who were then called the " anarchists."

" The food necessary for the people," he declared in the Convention, " is as sacred as life itself. All that is necessary to preserve life is property common to the whole of society. It is only what is in excess of this that may become private property, and may be given up to the industrial activities of the traders."

What a pity that this frankly communistic idea did not prevail among the nineteenth-century socialists instead of the

CAUSES OF THE RISING ON MAY 31   363

"collectivism" of Pecqueur and Vidal, which was preached in 1848 and is now being dished up again under the name of "scientific socialism." What might not the trend of the Communist movement in 1871 have been, had it recognised as its principle that "all things necessary for life are as sacred as life itself and represent the common property of the whole nation"—if it had taken as its watchword: "The Commune organising consumption and guaranteeing well-being for all."

Everywhere and always a revolution is made by minorities. Even among those deeply interested in the Revolution it is only a minority that devotes itself entirely to it. This was also the case in France in 1793.

As soon as royalty was overthrown a gigantic movement was set on foot throughout the provinces against the revolutionists who had dared to fling down the head of a King as a defiance to all the reactionaries of Europe. In the manor-house, the drawing-room, the confessional, the cry was: "What scoundrels to have dared to do that! Now they will stop at nothing: they are going to rob us of our wealth, or else guillotine us!" And so the plots of the counter-revolutionists redoubled in vigour.

The Church, every Court of Europe, the English middle classes, all took part in the work of intrigue, propaganda and corruption for organising the counter-revolution.

The maritime towns, especially such as Nantes, Bordeaux and Marseilles, where there were many rich merchants, Lyons, the manufacturer of luxury, Rouen, the centre of trade and industry, became powerful centres of reaction. Whole regions were influenced by priests and *emigres* who had returned under false names, and also by English and Orléanist gold, as well as by emissaries from Italy, Spain, and Russia.

The party of the "Gironde" served as the rallying-point for this mass of reaction, for the royalists knew perfectly well that the Girondins, in spite of their apparent republicansim, were really their allies, and that they were compelled to be so *by the logic of their party*, which is always much more powerful than the party label. And the people, on its side, understood the situation perfectly. It knew that so long as the Girondins remained in the Convention no real revolutionary measure would be possible, and that the war carried on so feebly by these sybarites of the Revolution would be prolonged indefinitely to the utter exhaustion of France. Accordingly, therefore, as the necessity for "purifying the Convention" by the elimination of the Girondins became more and more evident, the people on its side tried to organise itself for the local struggles which were imminent in every large city and every small town and village.

We have already remarked that the Directories of the departments were mostly counter-revolutionary. The Directories of the districts were equally so. But the municipalities, established by the law of 1789, were much more democratic. It is true that when they were first constituted in the summer of 1789, they mercilessly repressed the peasant revolts. But, as the Revolution developed, the municipalities, elected by the people often in the midst of insurrectionary disturbances and under the supervision of the Popular Societies, gradually became more revolutionary.

In Paris, previous to August 10, the council of the Commune had been composed of middle-class democrats. But during the night of August 10, a new revolutionary Commune was elected by the forty-eight sections, and although the Convention, at the instance of the Girondins, had dissolved this Commune, the new Commune elected on December 2, 1792, with its procurator, Chaumette, its deputy-procurator, Hébert, and its mayor, Pache (who was appointed somewhat later), was a frankly revolutionary body.

An elected body of officials invested with powers so extensive and so diverse as those entrusted to the council of the Paris Commune would have certainly inclined by degrees towards a moderate policy. But the people of Paris had, in the sections, centres for revolutionary action. These sections, however, according as they arrogated to themselves various political powers, such as the right of distributing cards of citizenship to show that the recipient was not a royalist conspirator, the appointing of volunteers to fight in La Vendée, and so on—these very sections, whose Committee of Public Welfare and

CAUSES OF THE RISING ON MAY 31   365

the Committee of General Safety were working to make them political organs, in their turn soon inclined to officialism and conservatism. In 1795, they became, in fact, the rallying-points for the middle-class reaction.

This is why a network of Popular Societies and Fraternal Societies, as well as Revolutionary Committees, was constituted side by side with the Commune and the sections to become, after the expulsion of the Girondins in the Year II. of the Republic, a real power for action. All these groups federated with each other, either for momentary purposes or for continuous action, and they endeavoured to put themselves in touch with the thirty-six thousand communes of France. For this purpose they organised a special correspondence-bureau.

A new, freely constituted organisation thus came into existence. And when we study these groupings—these "free understandings," we should say now—we see before us the realisation of what the modern anarchist groups in France are advocating without even knowing that their grandfathers had already put it into practice during so tragic a moment of the Revolution as was the early part of 1793.*

The majority of historians in sympathy with the Revolution, when they come to the tragic struggle which was fought out between the " Mountain " and the " Gironde " in 1793, dwell too much, it seems to me, on the secondary aspects of this struggle. They attach too much importance to the so-called *federalism* of the Girondins.

It is true that after May 31, when the Girondist and royalist insurrections broke out in several departments, the word " federalism " embodied in contemporary documents the chief article of accusation used by the " Mountain " party against the Girondins. But this word had become a mere catch-word, a party badge, and was in reality only a battle-cry good enough

* Mortimer-Ternaux, a rabid reactionary, has pointed out this double organisation in his *Histoire de la Terreur*, vol. vii. Jaurès (*La Convention*, vol. ii. p. 1254) has also a very well written page on this subject ; and Aulard refers to it at some length in his *Histoire politique de la Révolution*, part ii. ch. v.

to use against one's adversaries, and as such it served its purpose well. In reality, as Louis Blanc has remarked, the "federalism of the Girondins consisted chiefly in their hatred of Paris and their desire to oppose the reactionary provinces to the revotionary capital. They were afraid of Paris, and this was all their federalism meant." *

They detested and feared the ascendency gained in the Revolution by the Commune of Paris, the Paris revolutionary committees and the people of Paris. When they talked of transferring the seat of the Legislative Assembly, and later of the Convention itself, to some provincial town, it was not for love of provincial autonomy. It was merely to place the legislative body and the executive authority in the midst of a less revolutionary population than that of Paris—among people less active in the public cause. This was how royalty acted in the Middle Ages when it preferred a growing town, a "royal town," to the older cities accustomed to the *forum*. Thiers wanted to do the same in 1871.†

Instead of federalising, everything done by the Girondins showed them to be as centralising and authoritarian as the Montagnards, perhaps more so; for the latter relied at least upon the Popular Societies when they went on commission into the provinces and not upon organs of bureaucracy—the councils of the departments and the districts. When the Girondins appealed to the provinces against Paris, it was to incite the counter-revolutionary forces of the middle classes in the manufacturing towns and the fanaticism of the peasants in Normandy and Brittany against the revolutionists of Paris. When the reactionaries were victorious and the Girondins returned to power after the 9th Thermidor, they proved, as befits a party of order, that they were centralisers much more than the Montagnards.

M. Aulard, who wrote at some length about the federalism of the Girondins, aptly remarks that before the establishment

* Louis Blanc, 4to, vol. ii. p. 42.
† When the Girondins talked of assembling the commissioners of the departments at Bourges "they would not have stopped at this transference," says Thibaudeau in his *Mémoires:* "It was their intention to form a second Convention."

of the Republic none of the Girondins expressed federalist tendencies. Barbaroux, for example, was an unmistakable centraliser, and declared before the Bouches-du-Rhône Assembly that a Federative Government is not suitable for a great people, because of the slowness of its working and the multiplicity and complexity of its machinery.* We do not, in fact, find any serious attempt at federative organisation in the scheme for a Constitution that the Girondins brought forward in 1793. They show themselves by it to have been thorough centralists.

On the other hand, it seems to me that Louis Blanc lays too much stress on the "fiery impetuosity" of the Girondins, Brissot's ambition clashing with Robespierre's, and the wounding of Robespierre's self-esteem by the reckless Girondins—for which Robespierre never pardoned them. Jaurès expresses similar ideas, at least in the first part of his volume on the Convention,† which, however, does not prevent him, later on, from indicating other causes—when he begins to explain the struggle between the people of Paris and the *bourgeoisie*—causes much more serious than wounded self-esteem, and "the egoism of power."

Of course the "fiery impetuosity" of the Girondins, so well described by Louis Blanc, and the conflict of ambition were present, and they certainly helped to envenom the strife, but in the struggle between the "Gironde" and the "Mountain," there was, as we have already said, one general cause of strife infinitely more serious than all the personal conflicts put together. This cause Louis Blanc had already clearly indicated by quoting from Garat the language used by the "Gironde" to the "Mountain" and the reply of the "Mountain" to the "Gironde":

"It is not for you," said the Gironde, "to govern France,

---

* Aulard, *Histoire politique*, p. 264. "I do not know that any one should have claimed the honour of it," Thibaudeau wrote, when speaking of the federalism of the Girondins, in his *Mémoires sur la Convention et la Directoire*, vol. i. p. 38 (Paris, 1824). As to Marat, he was very explicit on this point in his paper, under the date of May 24, 1793. "They have for a long time been accusing the leaders of this infernal faction with federalism; I confess that I have never held this opinion of them, although I also have sometimes reiterated the charge."

† *La Convention*, pp. 388, 394, 396, and 1458.

you, who are covered with the blood of September. The legislators of a rich and industrial empire *must regard property as one of the most sacred bases of social order*, and the mission of legislating for France cannot be fulfilled by you who preach anarchy, protect plunder and terrify the owners of property. . . . You summon against us all the hired assassins of Paris; we summon against you all the honest folk of Paris."

It is the language of the propertied party—*le parti des honnêtes gens*—those who massacred the people of Paris in June 1848 and in 1871, supported the *coup d'état* of Napoleon III., and who are now ready to do it all over again.

To it the " Mountain " replied : " We accuse you of wanting to use your talents for your own advancement only, and not in the interests of Equality. So long as the King permitted you to govern through the ministers you gave him, so long did he seem honest enough for you. . . . Your secret desire has never been to raise France to the glorious destiny of a Republic, but to keep her under a King whose Mayors of the Palace you would yourselves have been."

We shall see how just this accusation was when we find Barbaroux in the South and Louvet in Brittany both of them hand in glove with the royalists, and when so many of the Girondins entered into an agreement with *les blancs*, after they came back to power through the reaction of Thermidor. But let as continue the quotation.

" You want liberty without equality," said the " Mountain," " and we desire equality because we cannot conceive liberty without it. You who call yourselves statesmen, you want to organise the Republic for the rich ; but we, not pretending to be statesmen, are striving for laws which will lift the poor out of their misery and turn all men, under a state of universal well-being, into happy citizens and ardent defenders of a universally adored republic."

Here we see two absolutely different conceptions of society ; and it was so that the struggle was understood by its contemporaries.*

---

* Numerous quotations could be given to prove this. The two following may serve as examples : " The Girondins wanted the Revolu-

The Revolution had hitherto confined itself to overthrowing the King, without even trying to secure its work by a complete change of the ideas of the nation in a republican direction; it had to stop after its first victory, and leave France to struggle, as best she could, against German, English, Spanish, Italian, and Savoyard invaders, supported from within by the partisans of royalty. Or else, the Revolution, after getting rid of the King, had to make at once, without delay, an effort towards "Equality," as they then called it—towards "Communism," as we should say now. It must complete the work of abolishing the feudal rights, the work of restoring the land to the communes, the work of nationalising the soil, while it would recognise the right of all to the land. It must consolidate the work already so far carried out by the revolted peasantry during those four years, and it would try, with the people's help, " to raise the poor out of their wretchedness." It must try to create, if possible, not absolute equality of riches, but a condition of well-being for all,—" universal welfare." And it would do this by forcibly taking the power of Government from the rich, and transferring it to the Communes and the Popular Societies.

These alternatives suffice to explain the sanguinary struggle which rent asunder the Convention, and with it the whole of France after the downfall of royalty. Everything else is of secondary importance.

tion to stop short of the middle classes," says Baudot. They wanted "quietly to establish a middle-class aristocracy, which should take the place of the nobility and clergy," said Bourdon de l'Oise at the Jacobin Club, on May 31. (*La Société des Jacobins*, Aulard edition, vol. v. p. 220.)

CHAPTER XLIII

SOCIAL DEMANDS—STATE OF FEELING IN PARIS— LYONS

Effect of execution of King—Changed aspect of Revolution—Rise of counter-revolution—Paris Commune tries to keep down price of bread—Varlet—Jacques Roux—Movement against owners of large fortunes—Petition to Convention—Marat tries to stop agitation—Effect of riot—Necessity of crushing "Gironde" becomes evident

NOTWITHSTANDING the violence that the Parliamentary struggle between the "Mountain" and the "Gironde" displayed at times, it would have dragged on had it been strictly confined to the Convention. But since the execution of Louis XVI. events were moving faster, and the gulf between the revolutionists and the counter-revolutionists was becoming so wide that there was no longer any possibility of a vague, indetermined party, half-way between the two others. Opposed as they were to the natural course of development which the Revolution was following, the Girondins soon found themselves, together with the Feuillants and Royalists, in the ranks of the counter-revolutionists, and as such they had to succumb. The Revolution was still in its ascendant phase.

The execution of the King had produced a profound impression in France. If the middle classes were stricken with terror at the daring of the Montagnards, and trembled for their property and their lives, the intelligent portion of the population saw on the contrary the dawn of a new era—the nearing of that "well-being for all" which the revolutionists had promised to the poor.

The greater was their deception! The King had perished,

SOCIAL DEMANDS

royalty had disappeared; but the insolence of the rich was growing. Their insolence sunned itself in the wealthy quarters, it even announced itself impudently in the public galleries of the Convention, while in the poor districts misery grew blacker and blacker, as the sad winter of 1793 crept on, bringing a lack of bread, unemployment, a rise in prices, and the depreciation of paper-money. And, in the meantime, bad news came in from everywhere: from the frontier, where the troops had melted like snow; from Brittany, where a general rising with the help of the English was being prepared; from La Vendée, where a hundred thousand revolted peasants were murdering the patriots with the benediction of the clergy; from Lyons, which had become the stronghold of the counter-revolutionists; from the Treasury, that now existed only by fresh issues of paper-money (*les assignats*); and, finally, from the Convention, which had come to a standstill, and was exhausting its forces in stormy internal struggles.

All this was helping to paralyse the revolutionary spirit. In Paris, the poor workers, the *sans-culottes*, no longer came to the sections in sufficient numbers, and the middle-class counter-revolutionists took advantage of it. In February 1793, the *culottes dorées* invaded the sections. They came in great numbers to the evening meetings, passed reactionary votes—by using their sticks in case of need—displaced the *sans-culotte* functionaries, and had themselves nominated in their stead. The revolutionists were even forced to reorganise their forces, so as to be able to come to the rescue from the neighbouring sections, when one section was invaded by the counter-revolutionists.

In Paris and in the provinces some sections were even compelled to ask the municipal council to guarantee to the poor men of the people who assisted at the sittings, and accepted duties on the committees, a payment of two livres per day. Whereupon the Girondins did not fail, of course, to ask the Convention to dissolve all these organisations of Sections, Popular Societies and Federations of Departments. They did not understand what power of resistance was yet in the old *régime*, and they did not see that such a step, taken at this moment, would have secured the immediate triumph of the counter-revolution and the "Tarpeian Rock" for themselves.

However, the mass of the people was not yet discouraged. The fact is, that new ideas were ripening in many minds, new currents were coming to the surface, and seeking the form which would best express them.

The Paris Commune, having obtained large grants from the Convention for the purchase of flour, succeeded more or less in keeping the price of bread to three-halfpence a pound. But to obtain bread at this price, the people had to spend the night at the bakers' doors, waiting in a queue on the pavement. And then the people understood that the Commune in buying wheat at the price the monopolists extorted only enriched the speculators at the expense of the State. It meant moving for ever in a circle, for the profit of the stock-jobbers. Stock-jobbing had already grown alarmingly. The newly formed *bourgeoisie* rapidly became rich by this means. Not only did the caterers for the armies—the "rice-bread-and-salt" (*les riz-pain-sel*)—make ill-gotten fortunes, but, as everything—wheat, flour, copper, oil, soap, candles, zinc, &c.—induced speculation, to say nothing of the enormous speculations on the sale of national estates, fortunes grew from nothing with an extraordinary rapidity in the sight and hearing of all.

The question: "What is to be done?" was then asked with all the tragic meaning which it acquires in times of crisis.

Those to whom the supreme remedy for all social evils is always "the punishment of the guilty," could only propose the death penalty for the stock-jobbers, the reorganisation of the police system of "public safety," and a revolutionary tribunal—which was in reality merely a return to Maillard's tribunal, without its openness, but certainly not a solution of the problem.

In the faubourgs, however, a deeper current of opinion was also forming, one which sought *constructive solutions*, and this current found expression in the predictions of a workman of the faubourgs, Varlet, and of a former priest, Jacques Roux, supported by all the "nameless ones," who in history go by the name of *Les Enragés* (the extremists). These men understood that the theories on freedom of commerce, defended in the Convention by men like Condorcet and Sieyès, were not true: that those commodities which are scarce in the market are easily to be seized upon by speculators, especially during a period such as the Revolution was now traversing. And they set themselves to spread ideas on the necessity of *communalising and nationalising commerce, and organising the exchange of goods at cost price*—those ideas which later on inspired Fourier, Godwin, Robert Owen, Proudhon, and their subsequent socialist followers.

The *Enragés* had understood—and we will see later how a beginning of practical application was given to their ideas—that it was not enough to guarantee to each man the right to work, or even a right to the land; they saw that so long as commercial exploitation existed, nothing could be done; they maintained that to prevent this, *commerce would have to be communalised.*

At the same time, a pronounced movement was growing among the masses against the owners of great fortunes—a movement similar to that of to-day in the United States against the rapidly amassed fortune of the "trusts." The best minds of the time were struck by the impossibility of establishing a democratic Republic, so long as there was no protection against the monstrous inequality of incomes, which was already asserting itself, and threatened to grow even worse.*

This movement against the monopolists and the stockjobbers was bound to produce also a movement against *speculation in paper-money*, and on February 3, 1792, delegates from the Commune, from the forty-eight sections and from the "United Defenders of the eighty-four departments" came before the Convention, demanding that a limit should be put to the depreciation of paper-money, due to stock-jobbery. They demanded the repeal of the decree of the Constituent

* Michelet's genius has led him to see very clearly the importance of this communist movement of the masses, and he had already drawn attention to its essential points. Jaurès (*Histoire socialiste*, vol. iv. pp. 1003 *et seq.*) has now given more ample and very interesting information on this movement in Paris and Lyons, where L'Ange was a precursor of Fourier.

Assembly which had recognised that money is merchandise, and the death penalty for stock-jobbers.*

This was, as we may see, a revolt of the poor against the wealthy classes, who having got all possible advantages out of the Revolution, were now opposed to its benefiting the poor. And this is why, when the petitioners learned that the Jacobins, Saint-Just included, were opposed to their petition, for fear of alarming the middle classes, they spoke of them as of "those who do not understand the poor, because they themselves dine well every night."†

Marat, too, tried to calm the agitation. He disapproved of the petition and defended the Montagnards and the Paris deputies whom the petitioners attacked; but he knew misery well, and when he heard the pleadings of the working women who came to the Convention on February 24, begging the protection of the legislators against the speculators, he at once took up the cause of the poor. In a very violent article, in the issue of his paper of the 25th, "despairing of seeing the legislators take any effectual measures," he preached "the complete destruction of this accursed brood"—"capitalists, stock-jobbers, monopolists, whom these wretched representatives of the nation encouraged, by not attacking them."

The fury of an enraged mob is felt in this article, in which

* Could stock-jobbing influence the fluctuations in the value of paper-money? Several historians have put to themselves this question, only to reply in the negative. The depreciation, they said, was due to the too great quantity of tokens of exchange which were put into circulation. This is true; but those who have followed closely the fluctuations in the price, let us say, of wheat on the international markets, of cotton on the Liverpool Exchange, or of Russian notes on the Berlin Exchange, some thirty years ago, will not hesitate to recognise that our grandfathers were right in holding stock-jobbers largely responsible for the depreciation of the paper-money. Even to-day, when financial operations cover an infinitely wider area than they did in 1793, stock-jobbing has always the effect of *exaggerating out of all proportion the effects of supply and demand at a given moment.* If, with the present facilities of transport and exchanges, stock-jobbing cannot create a *permanent* rise in the price of a commodity, or in the value of given shares, it always exaggerates nevertheless the natural rise, and swells quite out of proportion the temporary fluctuations in price which are due either to the varying productivity of labour (for instance, in the harvests), or to fluctuations in supply and demand.

† Jaurès, iv. p. 1023.

Marat demands, first, that the principal monopolists be handed over to a State tribunal, and then advocates revolutionary acts, saying that "the looting of a few shops, at the doors of which the monopolists should be hanged, would soon put an end to these malpractices, which reduce twenty-five million people to despair, and cause thousands to perish of want."

On the same day, in the morning, the people did indeed pillage some shops, taking sugar, soap, &c., and there was talk in the faubourgs of recommencing the September massacres among the monopolists and jobbers of the Stock Exchange, and the rich altogether.

One can imagine what was made of this movement, which after all was nothing but a small riot, by the Girondins who wished to convince the provinces that Paris was a raging furnace of terror, in which no one was safe any longer. Happy at having found in Marat's article the sentence about pillage which we have just quoted, they made enough out of it to accuse the "Mountain" and the people of Paris *en masse* of intending to murder the rich. The Commune did not dare to approve the riot, and even Marat had to contradict himself by saying that it was fomented by royalists. As to Robespierre, he did not lose the opportunity of attributing the whole movement to the influence of foreign money.

The riot produced nevertheless the desired effect. The Convention raised, from four to seven millions, the advance it was making to the Commune to enable it to keep bread at three-halfpence the pound, and Chaumette, the *procureur* of the Commune, developed before the Convention the idea which was later introduced into the "law of maximum"—that the question was not solely to obtain bread at a reasonable price. It was also necessary, said he, "that commodities of secondary necessity" should be accessible to the people. There no longer exists "any just ratio between the pay of a day's manual labour and these commodities of secondary necessity." "The poor have done as much as the rich, even more, for the Revolution. The whole life of the rich has changed, he alone (the poor man) has remained in the same position, and all he has gained through the Revolution is the right of complaining of his poverty."*

This movement in Paris at the end of February contributed to a great extent to the fall of the Girondins. While Robespierre was still hoping by legal means to paralyse the party of the "Gironde" in the Convention, the *Enragés* understood that so long as this party ruled in the Assembly, no progress of any sort would be made in matters of economics. They had the courage to say aloud that the aristocracy of money, of the great merchants and financiers, was rising from the ruins of the old aristocracy, and that this new aristocracy was so strong in the Convention that if the coalition of the Kings had not counted on its support, they would never have dared to attack France. It is even very probable that from that time on Robespierre and his faithful Jacobins told themselves that they ought to make sure of the *Enragés* to crush the Girondins, leaving till later, according to the turn events might take, the question whether to follow the *Enragés* or to fight them.

It is certain that ideas such as those advocated by Chaumette were bound to simmer in the people's minds in all large towns. The poor man had indeed done all for the Revolution, and while the *bourgeoisie* got rich, the poor man alone got nothing. Even in those cities where no popular movements similar to those of Paris and Lyons had taken place, the poor must have made similar reflections among themselves. And everywhere

---

* A much keener economist than many professional economists, this most sympathetic man pointed to the root of the question, showing how monopolists exaggerated the results of conditions created by the war and the repeated issues of paper-money. "War at sea," said he, "the disasters in our colonies, the losses on the market value of the paper currency, and above all, the fact that the quantities of notes issued no longer correspond with the needs of the commercial transactions—these are a few of the causes of this considerable rise which we lament. But how great is their influence, how terrible and disastrous is their result, when among us there exist evilly disposed men, monopolists, when the national distress is used as a base for the selfish speculations of a crowd of capitalists who do not know what to do with the immense sums of money they have gained in the recent transactions."

they must have noticed that the Girondins were a centre, round which could rally those who wished to prevent at all costs the Revolution from benefiting the poor.

At Lyons, the struggle took just the same course. It is clear that in this great manufacturing town, where the workmen lived by an industry of luxury, which unavoidably had suffered from the Revolution, the destitution was terrible. There was no work, and bread was at a famine price, threepence a pound.

There were in Lyons, as everywhere, two parties: the popular party, represented by Laussel, and still more by Chalier, and the party of the merchant middle class, which rallied round the Girondins, as an intermediate step before going over to the Feuillants. The mayor, Nivière-Chol, a Girondist merchant, was the man of the middle-class party.

Many priests who had refused to take the oath of obedience to the Constitution were in hiding in this town, where the population had always had a leaning towards mysticism, and agents of the *émigrés* also were there in great numbers. Altogether Lyons was a centre for conspirators coming from Jalès,* Avignon, Chambéry and Turin.

Against all these, the people had but the Commune, in which the two most popular men were Chalier—an ex-priest and mystic communist, and Laussel, another ex-priest. The poor worshipped Chalier, who never ceased to preach against the rich.

It is difficult to disentangle the events which took place in Lyons during the first days of March. We only know that the unemployment and want were terrible, and that there was great unrest among the workmen. They demanded the maximum for grain, and also for those commodities which Chaumette called "commodities of secondary necessity" (wine, wood, oil, soap, coffee, sugar, &c.). They also called for the prohibition of the traffic in tokens of exchange, whether notes, gold or silver, and wished for the establishment of a tariff of wages. The poor discussed the expediency of massacring or guillotining the monopolists, and the Commune of

* Ch. xxxi.

Lyons, going no doubt by the decree of the Legislative Assembly of August 29, 1792, ordered searches to be made all over Lyons, similar to those which took place on August 29, 1792, in Paris, in order to lay hands on the numerous royalist conspirators sojourning in the city. But the royalists and the Girondins, rallying round the mayor, Nivière-Chol, succeeded in seizing the municipality, and proposed to deal severely with the people. The Convention, however, interfered to prevent the slaughter of the " patriots," and for this purpose sent three commissioners to Lyons. Supported by these commissioners, the revolutionists again took possession of the sections which had been invaded by reactionaries. The Girondin mayor was forced to resign, and on March 9, a friend of Chalier was elected in the place of Nivière-Chol.

But the struggle did not end with that, and we shall see later on how, the Girondins again gaining the upper hand at the end of May, the people, the " patriots," were massacred. For the present let us only note that in Lyons, as in Paris, the Girondins served as a rallying-point, not only for those who were opposed to the people's Revolution, but also for all those absolute Royalists and constitutional Feuillants who did not want a Republic.*

The necessity of crushing the political power of the " Gironde " became, however, still more evident when the betrayal of Dumouriez revealed whither their policy was leading.

* On April 15, the *bourgeoisie* of Lyons sent to the Convention a delegation of those sections where they held the upper hand, to report that their city groaned beneath the tyranny of a Jacobin municipal council, which was laying hands on the property of rich merchants. They also asked the *bourgeoisie* of Paris to get hold of the sections. At the end of February the Mayor of Paris, Pétion, published his " Letter to the Parisians," in which he called the *bourgeoisie* to arms against the people, saying : " Your property is threatened, and you close your eyes to the danger. . . . You are subjected to all manner of requisitions and yet you suffer patiently." This was a direct appeal to the middle classes against the people.

CHAPTER XLIV

THE WAR—THE RISING IN LA VENDEE—TREACHERY OF DUMOURIEZ

Need of volunteers—Forces ordered—Money required—Lack of trustworthy generals—Dumouriez—His connection with Girondins and Montagnards—France and England—War declared—Treachery of Dumouriez—Counter-revolutionary movement in Brittany—Rising in La Vendée—Danton recalled from Belgium—Volunteers enlist—Terrible situation —" Mountain " tries to allay panic—Revolutionary tribune—Peasants urge clergy to rise—Savage hunt for republicans—Dumouriez in Belgium—Danton tries to check Dumouriez—Dumouriez outlawed—Committee of Public Welfare created—Danton becomes leading spirit—Fall of Girondins inevitable

IN the early part of 1793, the war began under very unfavourable circumstances, and the advantages obtained during the previous autumn were not maintained. Great reinforcements were necessary in order to enable the army to take the offensive and the free enlistments were far from giving the necessary numbers.*

It was estimated in February 1793, that it would take at least 300,000 men to fill up the gaps in the army and to bring up its effective force to half a million, but volunteers were no longer to be counted on. Certain departments (the Var and the Gironde) willingly sent their battalions—nearly whole armies—but other departments did nothing of the sort.

Then, on February 24, the Convention was compelled to

---

* The people knew, of course, how the volunteers of 1792 had been received in the army by the staff of officers and the generals—all royalists. " None of them wanted to have them," says Avenel, who has consulted the archives of the War Office. The volunteers were treated as " disorganisers " and cowards ; they were shot on the slightest provocation, and the troops were incited against them (*Lundis révolutionnaires*, p. 8).

order a forced levy of 300,000 men, to be raised among all the departments, and in each department by the districts and communes between them. These latter had first to call upon volunteers; but if this appeal was not answered by the required number of men, the communes had to recruit the remainder, in whichever way they considered best—that is to say, either by lot or by personal nomination, with the right, however, of finding a substitute in both cases. To induce men to enlist, the Convention not only promised them pensions, but it also undertook to enable the pensioners to buy portions of the national estates, by paying for them in instalments with their pensions, a tenth part of the total cost of the land or estate purchased to be paid every year. Government lands to the value of 400 million francs were assigned for this purpose.*

Meanwhile money was badly wanted, and Cambon, an absolutely honest man, who held an almost absolute power over the finances, was forced to make a new issue of 800 millions in paper-money. But the best estates of the clergy (which were the guarantee for these notes) had already been sold, and the estates of the *émigrés* did not sell so easily. People hesitated to buy them, fearing that the purchased estates might be confiscated when the *émigrés* would return to France. Therefore the Treasury, under Cambon, found it increasingly difficult to meet the ever-growing needs of the armies.†

However, the greatest difficulty of the war was not this. It lay in the fact that nearly all the generals belonged to the counter-revolution, and the system of the election of officers by the soldiers themselves, which the Convention had just introduced, could furnish superior officers only after the lapse of a certain time. For the present, the generals did not inspire confidence, and in fact the treachery of Lafayette was soon followed by that of Dumouriez.

Michelet was perfectly justified in saying that when Du-

* Everything remained, however, so far as it can be ascertained, as promises (Avenel, *Biens nationaux*, in *Lundis révolutionnaires*).

† A few revolutionary sections of Paris offered thereupon to mortgage all their properties to serve as a guarantee for the notes. This offer was refused, but there was a profound idea in it. When a nation makes war, property owners must bear the weight of it, as much and even more than those whose only incomes are their wages.

mouriez left Paris to rejoin his army a few days after the execution of Louis XVI., he was already meditating his treachery. He had seen the triumph of the " Mountain," and he probably understood that the execution of the King was the beginning of a new phase in the Revolution. For the revolutionists he felt nothing but hatred, and he no doubt foresaw that his dream of re-establishing the Constitution of 1791 in France, with a Duke of Orléans on the throne, could only be realised w th the help of Austria. From that day he must have decided on his treachery.

At this moment Dumouriez was closely connected with the Girondins, and even on intimate terms with Gensonné, with whom he remained in communication till April. However, he did not break with the " Montagnards " either, who already mistrusted him—Marat treated him frankly as a traitor, but did not feel strong enough to attack him. The victories of Valmy and Jemmapes had been so much glorified, and the real facts concerning the retreat of the Prussians were so little known, that the soldiers, especially the rank and file, adored their general. To attack him in these circumstances would have been to risk rousing the army, which Dumouriez could have led against Paris and the Revolution. Consequently there remained nothing for the " Mountain " to do but to wait and watch.

In the meantime France was entering into a war with England. As soon as the news of the execution of Louis XVI. had reached London, the English Government returned his passport and papers to the French Ambassador, ordering him to quit the United Kingdom. But it goes without saying that the execution of the King was only a pretext to break off relations with France. It is in fact now known, through the Count de Mercy, that the English Government felt no affection for the French royalists, and that it was not in the least anxious to strengthen them by its support. England simply considered this the right time to get rid of a maritime rival that had helped the Americans to obtain their independence, to take from France her colonies, and perhaps even some great mil tary port—at any rate, to weaken her sea power.

The English Government simply made the most of the impression produced by the execution of the King to press the war.

Unfortunately, the French politicians did not see how inevitable from the English point of view was this war. Not only the Girondins—especially Brissot, who plumed himself on knowing England—but Danton also, still hoped that the Whigs, of whom a party were enthusiastic supporters of the ideas of liberty, would overthrow Pitt and prevent the war. In reality, the greater part of the British nation was soon united on the question of war when its mercantile advantages were understood. It must also be said that the English diplomatists managed to make very clever use of the ambitions of the French statesmen. They made Dumouriez believe that he was the man for them—the only one with whom they could treat; and they promised to support him, to re-establish a constitutional monarchy. Danton they persuaded that the Whigs might, very possibly, return to power, and they would then make peace with Republican France.*

On the whole they managed to put the onus on France when the Convention declared war with Great Britain on February 1.

This declaration changed the whole of the military situation. To take possession of Holland, to prevent the English from landing there, became an absolute necessity. But this was precisely what Dumouriez, either because he did not consider himself strong enough, or because he had no mind to, had not done during the autumn, although he had been urged by Danton to do it. He had taken up, in December, his winter quarters in Belgium, and this of course did not dispose the Belgians in favour of the French invaders. Liége was his chief military depôt.

Up to the present we do not yet know all about Dumouriez' treachery. Very probably, as Michelet said, he had already made up his mind to betray, when he returned to his army on January 26, 1793. His march at the end of February,

---

* Albert Sorel, *L'Europe et la Révolution française* (Paris, 1891), Book I., ch. ii., pp. 373 *et seq.* Avenel, *loc. cit.*

against Holland, when he took Breda and Gertruydenberge, seems to have been already a manœuvre agreed upon with the Austrians. At any rate, this march served the Austrians admirably. They took advantage of it to enter Belgium, on March 1, and took Liége, where the inhabitants had in vain begged Dumouriez for arms. The patriots of Liége were forced to fly, the French army was completely routed and disbanded; the generals refused to help each other, and Dumouriez was far off in Holland. It was impossible to do the Austrians a better turn.

This news produced a tremendous effect in Paris, especially as it was followed by other news, equally grave. On March 3 it became known that a counter-revolutionary movement was about to begin immediately in Brittany. At the same time, at Lyons, the reactionary battalions of the *fils de famille* (wealthy young men) made a move against the revolutionary Commune—just at the time when the *émigrés*, who had gathered in numbers at Turin, were crossing the frontier and entering France in battle array, backed up by the King of Sardinia. To crown all, the department of La Vendée rose on March 10. It was quite evident that these various movements were, as in 1792, parts of one great counter-revolutionary scheme. And every one in Paris suspected that Dumouriez was won over by the counter-revolutionists, and was working for their advantage.

Danton, who was at that time in Belgium, was recalled in all haste. He arrived in Paris on March 8 and pronounced one of his powerful calls to unity and patriotism—an appeal which made hearts thrill all over France. The Commune hoisted once more the black flag. Again the fatherland was declared in danger.

Volunteers enlisted hurriedly, and on the evening of the 9th a civic feast, at which masses of people assisted, was organised in the streets, on the eve of their departure. But it was no longer the youthful enthusiasm of 1792. A sinister energy goaded them on. A lowering anger gnawed at the hearts of the poor of the faubourgs at the sight of the political struggles tearing France asunder. "A rising in Paris is what is needed,"

Danton is reported to have said, and indeed one was needed to rouse the people and the sections from the torpor into which they were sinking.

To ward off the difficulties, truly terrible, which beset the Revolution, to provide for the immense expenditure imposed on France by the counter-revolutionary leagues without and within, the Revolution had to find resources by levying taxes upon the fortunes which were then being amassed by the middle classes, owing to the Revolution itself. But this was exactly what the governing class refused to admit, partly on principle, the accumulation of large *private* fortunes being considered the way to enrich *the nation*, and partly from the fear with which a more or less general rising in the big towns, of poor against rich, inspired them.

The horror of the September days—especially the 4th and 5th at the Châtelet and the Salpêtrière—was yet fresh in their memories. What would happen then if a whole class rose against another—the poor against the rich, against all the wealthy? It meant civil war in every town. And this, with La Vendée and Brittany rising in the West, supported by England, by the *émigrés* in Jersey, by the Pope, and all the clergy—with the Austrians in the North, and the army of Dumouriez ready to follow its general and march against the people of Paris!

Therefore the leaders of opinion of the "Mountain" and the Commune did their utmost first of all to allay the panic, pretending that they considered Dumouriez a trustworthy republican. Robespierre, Danton and Marat, constituting a sort of triumvirate of opinion, backed up by the Commune, made speeches to this effect, and they all worked at the same time to rouse courage in the people's hearts, so as to be in a position to repel the invasion, which wore a far more serious aspect than it had in 1792. All worked to this end, save the Girondins, who saw but one thing—"the anarchists," who were to be crushed and exterminated!

On March 10, a renewal of the September days was feared in Paris. But the public anger was turned upon the journalist friends of Dumouriez, and a band betook themselves to the chief Girondin printing offices of Gorzas and Fiévé, and smashed their presses.

What the people, inspired by Varlet, Jacques Roux, the American, Fournier, and other *Enragés* really desired was a purification of the Convention. But the more common demand for a revolutionary tribunal had been substituted for this in all the sections. Pache and Chaumette came to the Convention on the 9th, to demand such a tribunal. Whereupon Cambacérès, the future "arch-counsellor" of the Napoleonic Empire, proposed that the Convention should renounce the current ideas on the division of legislative and judicial power and seize the latter as well, so as to be able to establish a special tribunal for the trial of traitors.

Robert Lindet, a lawyer of the old monarchist school, proposed later on to institute a tribunal consisting of judges nominated by the Convention, and bound to judge those whom the Convention would send before them. He insisted upon having no jury in this new tribunal, and it was only after long debates that it was decided to reinforce the five judges, nominated by the Convention, by twelve jurymen and six assistants, taken from Paris and the adjoining departments, and nominated every month by the Convention.

And so, instead of measures calculated to reduce stock-jobbing and place the necessaries of life within reach of the people, instead of a purification of the Convention, which would have eliminated the members always opposed to revolutionary measures, instead of taking military steps rendered imperative by the already almost confirmed treachery of Dumouriez, the insurrection of March 10 obtained nothing beyond a revolutionary tribunal. The creative, constructive spirit of a popular revolution, which was feeling its way, was now confronted by the spirit of police management, which was soon to crush it.

After appointing this tribunal the Convention was going to adjourn, when Danton rushed to the tribune, and stopped the members as they were leaving the hall, to remind them that the enemy was on the frontiers of France, and that nothing had yet been done.

The same day the peasants in La Vendée, urged on by the clergy, rose in insurrection and began to massacre the Republicans. The rising had long been prepared, chiefly by the priests, at the instigation of Rome, and there had already been an attempt at starting it, in August 1792, when the Prussians had entered France. Since then, Angers had become the political centre of the malcontent priests, the Sisters of the Sagesse Order and others serving as emissaries to distribute the appeals to revolt, and to awaken fanaticism by spreading stories about supposed miracles.* The levy of men for the war, promulgated on March 10, became the signal for a general rising. The head council of the insurrection, dominated by the priests, and having at its head the priest Bernier, was established at the demand of Cathelinau, a mason and sacristan of his parish, who had become one of the most audacious chiefs of the bands.

On the 10th the tocsin rang in several hundred parishes, and about 100,000 men left their work to begin the hunting down of the republicans and those priests who had sworn allegiance to the Constitution. It was an actual hunt, with a ringer who sounded the "view halloo," says Michelet, a hunt of extermination, during which the captives were subjected to the most terrible tortures : they were killed slowly, or else were left to be tortured by the women's scissors and the weak hands of the children who prolonged their martyrdom. All this, under the leadership of the priests, with tales of miracles to incite the peasants to kill the wives also of the republicans. The nobles, with their royalist amazons, only came after. And when these "honest folk" decided at last to appoint a tribunal to try the republican prisoners, this tribunal, in six weeks, sent 542 patriots to be executed.†

* Michelet, Book X. ch. v.
† "Each day," wrote a royalist priest, François Chevalier (quoted by Chassin), "each day was marked by bloody expeditions which cannot but horrify every decent soul, and seem justifiable only in the light of philosophy." (They were commanded by priests in the name of religion.) "Matters had come to a pass, when it was said openly that it was unavoidable and essential for peace, not to leave a single republican alive in France. Such was the popular fury that it was sufficient to have attended at a mass said by one of the constitutional clergy,

THE RISING IN LA VENDEE

To resist this savage rising, the Republic had nothing but 2000 men scattered all over the lower part of La Vendée, from Nantes to La Rochelle. It was not till the end of May that the first organised forces of the Republic arrived. Up to then the Convention had only been able to oppose decrees : death penalty and confiscation of property for the nobles and priests who had not left La Vendée at the end of a week! But who was there with the necessary force to carry out these decrees ?

Matters were no better in Eastern France, where the army of Custine was retreating; while in Belgium, Dumouriez was in open rebellion against the Convention since March 12. He sent them from Louvain a letter, which he at once made public, and in which he reproached France with the crime of having annexed Belgium, of wishing to ruin that country by introducing paper-money and the sale of national properties. Six days later he attacked the superior forces of the Austrians at Neerwinden, allowed himself to be beaten by them, and on March 22, supported by the Duke de Chartres and some Orléanist generals, he entered into direct negotiations with the Austrian, Colonel Mack. These two traitors promised to evacuate Belgium without resistance, and to march against Paris to re-establish there the constitutional monarchy. In case of need, they would call on the Austrians to support them, and in the meantime the Austrians occupied Condé, one of the French fortresses near the frontier, as a guarantee.

Danton, staking his head on it, rushed to Dumouriez' camp, to prevent this treason and to attempt to bring back Dumouriez to the Republic. Having failed in persuading two Girondins, Gensonné, a friend of Dumouriez, and Gaudet, to go with him, he left alone, on the 16th, for Belgium, running the risk of being accused himself of treason. He found Dumouriez in full retreat after the Battle of Neerwinden, and understood that the traitor had already made up his mind. He had indeed

to be imprisoned and then murdered, or shot, under the pretext that the prisons were too full, as they were on September 2." At Machecoul, 524 republican citizens had been shot, and there was talk of massacring the women. Charette was urging on his fanatical peasants to do this.

already given his word to Colonel Mack to evacuate Holland without fighting.

Paris was seized with fury when, Danton having returned on the 29th, Dumouriez' treason was established as a certainty. The republican army, which alone might have repulsed the invasion, was perhaps already marching against Paris to re-establish royalty! Under such conditions, the Committee of Insurrection, which had then been meeting for some days at the Bishop's palace, under the leadership of the *Enragés*, won over the Commune. The sections began to arm and seized the artillery; they probably would have marched against the Convention, had not other counsels prevailed to prevent a panic. On April 3, confirmatory news of Dumouriez' treachery was received. He had arrested the commissioners sent to him by the Convention. Happily, his army did not follow him. The decree of the Convention, outlawing Dumouriez and ordering the arrest of the Duke de Chartres, had reached the regiments, and neither Dumouriez nor the Duke de Chartres succeeded in winning over the soldiers. Dumouriez was forced to cross the frontier, as Lafayette had done, and to seek refuge among the Austrians.

On the following day he and the Imperial generals issued a proclamation, in which the Duke of Coburg made known to the French that he was coming to restore to France her constitutional King.

At the height of this crisis, when the uncertainty about the attitude of Dumouriez' army jeopardised the security of the Republic itself, the three most influential men of the "Mountain"—Danton, Robespierre and Marat—in agreement with the Commune led by Pache, Hébert and Chaumette, acted with complete unanimity, to prevent the panic and the sad consequences it might have entailed.

At the same time the Convention, in order to avoid the lack of unity which had hitherto hampered the general management of the war, resolved to take the executive power into their hands, as well as the legislative and judicial powers. They created a Committee of Public Welfare (*Comité de Salut public*), with very extensive powers, almost dictatorial—a measure

THE TREACHERY OF DUMOURIEZ

which was evidently of an immense importance for the subsequent development of the Revolution.

We have seen that after August 10 the Legislative Assembly had founded, under the name of "Provisory Executive Council," a body of ministers invested with all the functions of the executive power. Besides, in January 1793, the Convention had created a "Committee of General Defence," and, war being at that moment the most important matter, this committee obtained control over the Provisory Executive Council, and thus became the chief machinery of the administration. Now, to give the Government more unity, the Convention created a "Committee of Public Welfare" (*Comité de Salut public*), elected by it and renewable every twelve months. This committee was to supplant both the Defence Committee and the Executive Council.

In reality it was the Convention itself supplanting the Ministry, but little by little, as was to be expected, the Committee of Public Welfare overruled the Convention and acquired in all the branches of administration a power which it shared only with the Committee of Public Safety (*Comité de Sûreté générale*), entrusted with the control of the State police.

In the middle of the crisis which was developing in April 1793, Danton, who had until then taken a most active part in the war, became the leading spirit of the Committee of Public Welfare, and he retained this influence until July 10, 1793, when he retired.

Finally, the Convention, which had sent, since September 1792, several of its members to the provinces and to the armies, with the title of Commissioned Deputies (*Représentants en mission*), armed with very extensive powers, decided to send eighty more deputies to rouse enthusiasm in the provinces and to supervise the war. And, as the Girondins generally refused to accept this function, they willingly agreed to appoint members of the "Mountain" on these difficult missions, perhaps with the idea of having a freer hand in the Convention after their departure.

It was certainly not these measures of reorganisation of the

Government which prevented the treachery of Dumouriez having the disastrous effect it might have had, if the army had followed its general. There was a higher force in action. For the French nation the Revolution possessed a charm, and gave it a vigour, which it was not possible for a general to destroy at his will and pleasure. On the contrary, this betrayal had the effect of giving a new character to the war— that of a popular, democratic war. But every one understood that Dumouriez alone would never have dared what he did. He obviously had strong support in Paris. It was there that the root of the treachery lay. "The Convention betrays," said the address of the Jacobin Club, signed by Marat, who presided that night.

Henceforth the fall of the Girondins and the removal of their leaders from the Convention became inevitable. The treachery of Dumouriez gave the final impetus to the insurrection which broke out on May 31.

CHAPTER XLV

A NEW RISING RENDERED INEVITABLE

Rising of May 31—Significance of rising—Summary of situation—Convention and Dumouriez—Girondins vote arrest of Marat—People take his part—Character of Marat—He is acquitted—Famine in large towns—Extraordinary tax levied—Indignation of Girondins—Commission of Twelve appointed—Hébert and Varlet arrested — Isnard's threat — Sections demand expulsion of Girondins from Convention

MAY 31 is one of the great dates of the Revolution, and quite as full of significance as July 14 and October 5, 1789, June 21, 1791, and August 10, 1792—but, perhaps, the most tragic of them all. On this day the people of Paris rose for the third time, making its last effort to impress upon the Revolution a really popular character ; and, to bring this about, it had to stand up—not against the King and the Court, but against the child of the Revolution itself—the National Convention—in order to eliminate from it the leaders of the Girondin party.

June 21, 1791, the day of the King's arrest at Varennes, had brought one epoch to a close ; the fall of the Girondins on May 31, 1793, was the close of another epoch. At the same time it became a symbol for all revolutions to come. Henceforth, for a long time to come, no revolution will be possible unless it culminates in its May 31. Either there will be in the revolution a day when the proletarians will separate themselves from the middle-class revolutionists, and will advance then to a point where the others will not be able to follow them without ceasing to be middle class ; or this separation will not take place, and then there will be no revolution.

Even to this day we feel the tragedy of the situation which presented itself to the Republicans of that time. On the eve of May 31, it was no longer a question of a perjured, treacherous king to be set aside : it was against their comrades in the fight that the revolutionists had to proceed, because it had become evident that unless this was done, the reaction would have got the upper hand already in June 1793, while the chief work of the Revolution—the destruction of the feudal system and of "the right divine of royalty"—had not yet been accomplished. The dilemma was this: either to proscribe the Girondin republicans, who had up till then fought so bravely against despotism, but were now saying to the people: "Thus far, but no farther!"; or else to rouse the people for the purpose of eliminating them, and passing over their dead bodies to try and accomplish the great work which the Revolution had begun.

This tragic situation is very clearly revealed in Brissot's pamphlet "To his Constituents," dated May 26, which we have already mentioned. We cannot, in fact, read these pages without feeling that it is a question of life or death that is debated. Brissot was evidently hazarding his head in publishing this pamphlet, in which he implacably demanded that those whom he called the "anarchists" should be sent to the scaffold. After its appearance there remained but two issues: either the "anarchists" should let themselves be guillotined by the Girondins, which would open the door to the royalists; or else the Girondins should be expelled from the Convention, and in that case it was they who must perish.

It is evident that the members of the "Mountain" did not decide with a light heart to appeal to an insurrection in order to compel the Convention to thrust out from its midst the chief leaders of the Right. For more than six months they had been trying to come to some agreement. Danton especially laboured to negotiate a compromise. Robespierre, for his part, worked to render the Girondins powerless "parliamentarily," without resorting to force. Marat himself stifled his anger in order to avoid civil war. In this way they managed to delay the separation for several months. But at what a price ! The Revolution was entirely stopped ; nothing was being done to secure what had been already gained. It was living from hand to mouth.

In the provinces, the old *régime* had maintained much of its strength. The privileged classes were lying in wait for the moment to recapture their wealth and position, to restore royalty and the feudal rights that the law had not yet abolished. The first serious check of the armies would have brought about the victorious return of the old *régime*. In the South, the South-West and the West of France, the mass of the people were with the priests, with the Pope, and through them with royalty. It is true that a great deal of the land taken from the clergy and the dispossessed nobles had already passed into the hands of the upper and lower middle classes, as well as to some extent to the peasants. The feudal dues were neither redeemed nor paid. But all that was merely provisional. And what if to-morrow the people, exhausted by poverty and famine, weary of the war, should retreat to their hovels and leave a free hand to the old *régime?* Would it not be triumphant everywhere in a few months?

After Dumouriez' treachery the situation in the Convention became quite untenable. Feeling how deeply they were implicated by this treason of their favourite general, the Girondins redoubled the bitterness of their attacks against the "Mountain." Accused of conniving with the traitor, they could only reply by flinging down a demand for the prosecution of Marat for the address the Jacobins had published on April 3, on hearing the news of Dumouriez' treachery, which Marat had signed as the president of the club for that week.

Taking advantage of the absence of a great many members of the Convention—mostly members of the "Mountain"—who were acting as commissioners to the armies and in the departments at that time, the Girondins demanded of the Convention, on April 12, an order of prosecution against Marat, and then a warrant for his arrest, in order to send him for trial before the criminal tribunal, for having advocated murder and pillage. The decree for his arrest was voted on April 13, by 220 voices against 92, out of 367 voters—seven being for an adjournment, and forty-eight abstaining from voting.

The blow however failed. The people of the faubourgs loved Marat too much to allow him to be condemned. The poor felt that Marat was one of the people and never would betray them. And the more one studies the Revolution the more one knows what Marat did and what he said, the more one discovers how unmerited was his reputation as a sinister exterminator which the historians, admirers of the middle-class Girondins, have created for him. Nearly always, since the very first weeks of the Convocation of the States-General, and especially in critical moments, Marat saw more clearly and more justly than the others, clearer and better even than the two other great leaders of revolutionary opinion—Danton and Robespierre.

From the day that Marat threw himself into the Revolution, he gave himself entirely to it, and lived in absolute poverty, driven continually into hiding while the others entered into power. Up to his death, in spite of the fever which racked him, Marat never changed his way of living. His door was always open to the men of the people. He thought that a dictatorship would help the Revolution through its difficulties, but he never thought of dictatorial powers for himself.

Bloodthirsty as his language was with regard to the creatures of the Court—especially at the outset of the Revolution, when he said that if they did not strike off thousands of heads there would be nothing done and the Court would crush the Revolution—he always respected those who were devoted to the Revolution, even when they in their turn began to be an obstacle to the development of the movement. He saw from the outset that the Convention, having a strong Girondin party in its midst, would never be capable of accomplishing its mission, but he tried at first to avoid the elimination of the Girondin leaders by violence, and he only became its advocate and organiser when he saw that it was necessary to choose between the " Gironde " and the Revolution. If he had lived, it is probable that the Terror would not have assumed the ferocity imprinted on it by the members of the Committee

A NEW RISING RENDERED INEVITABLE

of Public Safety. They would not have been allowed to use it to strike, on the one side, the advanced party—the Hébertists—and, on the other, the conciliators, such as Danton.*

The more the people loved Marat, the more the middle-class members of the Convention detested him. This is why the Girondins, who wished to break down the "Mountain," decided to begin with him: he would be defended less than any other Montagnard.

But as soon as Paris learned that a writ was out for Marat's arrest, the excitement was immense. The insurrection would have broken out on April 14 if the "Mountain," including Robespierre and Marat himself, had not preached calmness. Marat, who did not let himself be arrested at once, appeared before the tribunal on April 24, and was acquitted off-hand by the jury. He was then carried in triumph to the Convention, and from thence into the streets on the shoulders of the *sans-culottes*, under a cascade of flowers.

The attempt of the Girondins had thus failed, and they understood at once that they never would recover from that blow. It was "a day of mourning" for them, as one of their newspapers said, and Brissot began to write his last pamphlet, "To his Constituents," in which he did his best to arouse the passions of the well-to-do middle classes against the "anarchists."

Under these conditions, the Convention, whose sittings were becoming furious battles between the two parties, lost the people's respect: and the Commune of Paris took naturally the lead in the initiation of revolutionary measures.

As the winter of 1793 advanced, famine in the large towns grew worse and worse. The municipalities found the greatest difficulty in the world in procuring bread, were it only a pound,

* Marat was right in saying that the works he had published at the beginning of the Revolution, *Offrande à la Patrie, Plan de Constitution, Législation criminelle*, and the first hundred numbers of the *Ami du peuple*, were full of tenderness, prudence, moderation, love of mankind, liberty, justice (Chèvremont, *Marat*, vol. ii. p. 215). Jaurès, who has read *Marat* carefully, has done much towards showing him in a true light, especially in the fourth volume of his *Histoire de la Révolution*.

or a quarter of a pound—four ounces—a day, for each inhabitant. To do that even, the municipalities, and especially that of Paris, had to run into the most frightful debt.

The Commune of Paris then ordered a progressive income tax of twelve million livres to be levied on the rich, for the expenses of the war. An income of fifteen hundred livres for the head of each family, and a thousand livres for every other member, were considered as "necessary" and therefore freed from this taxation. But everything above this amount was treated as "superfluity," and had to pay a progressive tax: thirty livres for a superfluity of two thousand livres; fifty livres on a superfluity of from two to three thousand livres; and so on, up to twenty thousand livres on a superfluity of fifty thousand livres.

For sustaining the war in which France was engaged, in the midst of a Revolution and a famine, such an extraordinary tax, to be levied this special year only, was very modest, after all. It was only the large incomes which were touched by it, whereas a family of six persons who had an income of ten thousand livres would have paid less than one hundred livres. But the rich protested loudly, while Chaumette, the promoter of this tax, whom the Girondins wanted to attack after Marat, said justly: "Nothing will make me change my principles. Even with the knife at my neck I shall still declare, *up to this day, the poor have done everything; it is time for the rich to take their turn.* I shall declare that the selfish people, the young idlers, must be made useful, whether they like it or not, and some respite be procured for the useful and respectable worker."

The Gironde redoubled its hatred for the Commune that had suggested the idea of such a taxation. But one can imagine the general explosion of hatred that broke forth among the middle classes, when Cambon, supported by the public in the galleries, proposed in the Convention, and put to the vote a forced loan of a thousand millions to be levied throughout France on the rich people, and assessed on nearly the same principles as the tax of the Commune—a loan to be reimbursed later on by the money raised on the *émigrés'* lands, according as they were sold. In the difficult circumstances through

A NEW RISING RENDERED INEVITABLE

which the Republic was passing, it had no other possible way out except a tax of this kind. But in the Convention the defenders of property were ready to slay the Montagnards when the latter supported the project of a forced loan; they almost came to blows.

If proofs were still necessary to show the impossibility of anything being done to save the Revolution, so long as the Girondins remained in the Convention, and the two parties continued to neutralise each other, these debates upon the loan would have given a striking demonstration of it.

But what exasperated the people of Paris most of all was that to stop the Revolution, of which Paris had up to that time been the chief forcing-bed, the Girondins did all they could to incite the departments against the capital, not even hesitating before the necessity this involved of marching hand in hand with the royalists. They preferred royalty rather than that any step should be made towards the Social Republic. Better to inundate Paris with blood and to rase the accursed town to the ground, than to allow the people of Paris and their Commune to initiate a movement which would threaten the middle-class property-owners. Thiers and the Bordeaux Assembly of 1871 had, we see, their ancestors in 1793.

On May 19, the Girondins, at the suggestion of Barère, decreed the formation of a Commission of Twelve to examine into the decisions passed by the Commune, and this commission, appointed on the 21st, became the driving-wheel of the Government. Two days later, on the 23rd, it caused Hébert to be arrested, the deputy-procurator of the Commune, beloved by the people for the frank republicanism of his *Père Duchesne*, and Varlet, the favourite of the Paris poor, for whom the Convention was but a "law-shop," and who preached the social revolution in the streets. But the arrests were not meant to stop there. The Commission of Twelve proposed also to prosecute the sections; it demanded that the register of the sections should be given up, and it procured the arrest of the president and secretary of the City section for having refused to give up their registers.

The Girondin, Isnard, who presided over the Convention

during these days, an authoritarian in whom Thiers was foreshadowed—on his part added to the ferment by his threats. He threatened the Parisians, if they made any attack on the National representation, that Paris would be destroyed. "People would be searching soon on the banks of the Seine, to see if Paris had ever existed." These stupid threats, which recalled only too well those of the Court in 1791, brought the popular indignation to its full height. On the 26th there was fighting in nearly every section. The insurrection became inevitable, and Robespierre, who until then had discouraged the rising, went to the Jacobins on the 26th to say that if need be he was ready to rise alone against the conspirators and traitors who sat in the Convention.

Thirty-five sections of Paris out of thirty-eight had already asked the Convention to expel from its midst twenty-two Girondin representatives, whose names were given. The sections were now rising to compel the Convention to obey the will of the people of Paris.

CHAPTER XLVI

THE INSURRECTION OF MAY 31 AND JUNE 2

Preparations for rising—Activity of sections—Commission of Twelve—Want of union among revolutionists—*Les Enragés*—New class of middle-class property-owners—May 31—Failure of insurrection—Preparations for fresh revolt—June 2—News of rising at Lyons—Fury against Gironde—Letter to Convention—Speech of Marat to Jacobin Club—Girondins join counter-revolutionists—Convention outlaws Girondins

ONCE more the people, in their sections, got ready for insurrection as on August 10. Danton, Robespierre and Marat held frequent consultations with each other during those days; but still they hesitated, and again action came from the "unknown ones," who constituted an insurrectionary club at the Bishop's Palace, and appointed a Commission of "Six" for that purpose.

The sections took an active part in the preparations. The section of the Quatre Nations had already, in March, declared itself in a state of insurrection, and had authorised its Watch Committee to issue mandates of arrest against citizens suspected of anti-revolutionary opinions, whilst other sections, those of Mauconseil and Poissonnière, openly demanded the arrest of the "Brissotin" deputies. The following month, that is to say, on April 8 and 9, after the treachery of Dumouriez, the sections of Bonconseil and the Halle-aux-Blés insisted on the general's accomplices being prosecuted, and on the 15th, thirty-five sections published a list of the twenty-two members of the Gironde, whose expulsion from the Convention they demanded.

From the beginning of April, the sections had also been trying to constitute their own federation, for action, outside the Council of the Commune, and on April 2 the Gravilliers section, always in the vanguard, took the lead in the creation of a "General Committee." This committee acted only in an intermittent way, but it was reconstituted on the approach of danger, on May 5, and on the 29th it undertook the direction of the movement. As to the influence of the Jacobin Club, it was never very great, and its members themselves admitted that the centre of action lay in the sections.*

On May 26, numerous gatherings of the people besieged the Convention, into which they speedily forced their way, and those who entered the hall demanded, with the support of the galleries, that the Commission of Twelve should be suppressed. But the Convention resisted this demand, and it was not until after midnight that, wearied out, it at last yielded, and the Commission was broken up.

This concession was, however, only for the moment. The very next day, on the 27th, profiting by the majority they had in the Convention owing to the absence of a great many of the "Montagnards," who were on commissions in the provinces, the "Gironde," supported by the "Plain," re-established the Commission of Twelve. The insurrection had thus had no effect.

What had rendered the insurrection powerless was that there was no agreement among the revolutionists themselves. One party of the sections, inspired by those known as the "Extremists" (*les Enragés*), wanted a measure that would strike terror into the counter-revolutionists. They wanted, after rousing the people, to kill the principal Girondins: they even spoke of slaying the aristocrats in Paris.

But this scheme met with strong opposition. The National Representation was a trust confided to the people of Paris; how could they betray the trust of all France? Danton, Robespierre and Marat opposed it strenuously. The council of the Commune with Pache, the mayor, also refused to agree to this scheme; and the Popular Societies would not support it either.

There was another thing to be taken into account. It was

* *Vide* Aulard, *Jacobins*, vol. v. p. 209.

THE INSURRECTION OF MAY 31 AND JUNE 2

necessary to consider the middle classes who were at that time already very numerous in Paris, and whose battalions of National Guards would have put down the insurrection if it became a question of defending their property. Guarantees had thus to be given that property should not be touched. This is why Hassenfratz, one of the Jacobins, who declared that there was nothing in theory against the pillage of the scoundrels—for so he called the rich—nevertheless tried to prevent the insurrection from being accompanied by pillage. "There are a hundred and sixty thousand men having their homes in Paris, who are armed and ready to repress pillage. It is clear that it is an *absolute impossibility* to make an attack on property," said Hassenfratz to the Jacobins; and he therefore called on all the members of the club to "pledge themselves to perish, rather than allow attacks to be made on property."

A similar oath was taken on the night of the 31st, in the Commune, and even at the Bishop's Palace, by the "extremists," the sections doing likewise.

The fact is, that a new class of middle-class property-owners had already sprung up at this time—a class which has increased so enormously during the nineteenth century—and the revolutionists were compelled to take them into consideration, so as not to be opposed by them.

On the eve of an insurrection one can never tell whether the people will rise or not. This time there was also the fear that the *Enragés* would try to kill the Girondins in the Convention, and so compromise Paris in the eyes of the departments. Three days, therefore, were spent in conferences, until it was agreed that the insurrection should be directed by a union of the different revolutionary elements—the Council of the Commune, the Council of the Departments, and the General Revolutionary Council at the Bishop's Palace; that no personal violence should be committed, and that property should be respected. They were to confine themselves to a *moral insurrection*, to putting pressure on the Convention, so as to force it to hand over the guilty deputies to the revolutionary tribunal.

Marat, on leaving the Convention on the evening of the 30th, explained this decision at the Bishop's Palace, and afterwards at the Commune. And apparently it was he who, braving the law which punished with death any one who rang the tocsin, rang the first peal at midnight from the belfry of the Hôtel de Ville. The insurrection thus began.

The delegates who sat at the Bishop's Palace, and who were representing the centre of the movement, first deposed, as had been done on August 10, the mayor and the council of the Commune; but instead of dismissing the mayor and appointing another council, they reinstated both, after first making them take an oath to join the insurrection. They did the same with the council of the department, and that night the revolutionists from the Bishop's Palace, the Department, and the Commune met together, constituting a " General Revolutionary Council " which undertook the direction of the movement.

This council appointed Hanriot, the commander of one of the battalions, that of the *sans-culottes* section, to be General Commander of the National Guard. The tocsin was rung and drums were beating the " alarm " throughout Paris. But still indecision was the most noticeable thing in this rising. Even after the alarm-gun on the Pont-Neuf had begun to fire, about one o'clock in the afternoon, the armed sectionaries, pouring into the streets, did not seem to have any fixed plan. Two battalions, faithful to the Girondins, had been the first to hasten to the Convention, and they took up a position in front of the Tuileries. Hanriot, with forty-eight cannon from the sections, surrounded the Tuileries and the Assembly Hall.

Hours passed by without anything being done. All Paris was on foot, but the majority of the people only wanted to put some pressure on the Convention, so that the Girondin Vergniaud, seeing that they went no further, put a resolution to the effect that the sections had merited well of the country. He no doubt hoped by this to mitigate their hostility towards the " Gironde." It looked almost as if the day were lost, when new crowds of people came up in the evening and invaded the Hall of the Convention. Then, the Montagnards feeling

THE INSURRECTION OF MAY 31 AND JUNE 2

themselves reinforced, Robespierre demanded not only the suppression of the Commission of Twelve and the trial of its members, but also the trial of the principal members of the ".Gironde," whom they called "the Twenty-Two" and who did not include the Twelve.

This proposition was not discussed. All that the Convention decided to do was to break up the Commission of Twelve once more, and to have all its papers settled and sent to the Committee of Public Welfare, for a report to be made on them within three days. For the rest, the Convention approved of a resolution of the Commune which directed that the workmen who remained under arms, until public tranquillity was restored, should be paid forty sous a day. Upon this the Commune levied a tax on the rich, so as to be able to pay the workmen for the first three days of the insurrection. It was decided, also, that the galleries of the Convention should be thrown open to the people, without tickets being required for admission.

All this meant, however, very little. The "Gironde" was still there, and continued to have a majority in the Convention. The insurrection had failed. But then the people of Paris, comprehending that nothing had been done, set to work to prepare for a fresh rising for the next day but one, June 2.

The revolutionary committee formed within the General Council of the Commune gave the order for the arrest of Roland and his wife. He had gone away, and she was arrested alone. It furthermore demanded very plainly that the Convention should have twenty-seven of its Girondist members arrested. That evening the tocsin was rung, and the measured reports of the alarm-gun began again to resound.

On June 2 all Paris had risen, this time to finish matters. More than a hundred thousand armed men assembled round the Convention. They had with them one hundred and sixty-three pieces of artillery, and they asked that the Girondist leaders should hand in their resignations, or, failing this, that twenty-two of them, the number being afterwards raised to twenty-seven, should be expelled from the Convention.

The horrible news that arrived that day from Lyons reinforced the popular insurrection. It became known that on May 29 the famished people of Lyons had risen, but that the counter-revolutionists—that is, the Royalists supported by the Girondins—had gained the upper hand and had restored order by murdering eight hundred patriots!

This was unfortunately only too true, and the share taken by the Girondins in the counter-revolution was only too evident. The news roused the people to fury; it was the doom of the "Gironde." The people who were besieging the Convention declared that they would let no one pass out so long as the expulsion of the principal Girondins, in some fashion or other, was not pronounced.

It is known that the Convention, or at least the Right, the "Plain" and part of the "Mountain," declaring that their deliberations were no longer free, tried to get out, hoping to overawe the people, and so make their way through the crowd. Whereupon Hanriot, drawing his sword, gave the famous order: "Gunners, to your guns!"

After a three days' resistance, the Convention was thus obliged to do as it was bidden. It voted the exclusion of thirty-one of the Girondist members; whereupon a deputation of the people brought to it the following letter:

"The whole of the people of the departments of Paris have deputed us to tell you, citizen legislators, that the decree which you have just made is the salvation of the Republic; we come to offer hostages from among us, in numbers equalling those of whom the Assembly has ordered the arrest, so as to answer their departments for their safety."

On the other hand, Marat gave an address to the Jacobins on June 3, in which he summed up as follows the meaning of the movement that had just been carried out, and proclaimed the right of well-being for all.

"We have given a great impetus to the Revolution," he said, speaking of the expulsion of the thirty-one Girondin deputies, "it is for the Convention now to confirm the bases of the public happiness. Nothing is easier; you only must make up your minds definitively. We wish that all the citizens spoken of as *sans-culottes* may enjoy happiness and comfort. We wish that this useful class should be helped by the rich in proportion to their capacities. We do not wish to attack property. But what is the most sacred property? It is that of existence. We wish this property to be respected. . . .

"We wish that all men who have not a hundred thousand livres' worth of property should have an interest in the maintenance of our work. As to those who have more than a hundred thousand, let them cry out as much as they like. . . . We shall tell these men: 'Acknowledge that we are the great number, and if you do not help us to turn the wheel, we shall drive you out of the Republic, we shall take possession of your property, and divide it among the *sans-culottes*.'"

And to this he added another idea which was soon to be put into execution:

"Jacobins," he went on to say, "I have a truth to tell you. You do not know your most deadly enemies; *they are the constitutional priests.* It is they who declaim most in the provinces against anarchists, disorganisers, Dantonism, Robespierrism, Jacobinism. . . . Do not cherish any longer the popular errors; cut at the roots of superstition! Declare openly that the priests are your enemies."*

At that moment Paris did not in the least desire the death of the Girondist deputies. All that the people wanted was that the revolutionary members of the Convention should have a liberty of action for carrying the Revolution further on. The arrested deputies were not sent to the Abbaye prison; they were guarded in their own homes. Their pay even, of eighteen francs a day, allotted to each member of the Convention, was continued, and every one of them could move about Paris, accompanied by a gendarme, whom he had to feed.

If these deputies, acting in accordance with the principles of antique citizenship, which they so much liked to vaunt, had withdrawn into private life, it is certain that they would have been let alone. But instead of that, they hurried off to their departments to stir them up against the Convention,

* Aulard, *Jacobins*, vol. v. p. 227.

and when they saw that in order to excite the counter-revolution and to rouse the departments against Paris, they would have to march hand in hand with the royalists, they allied themselves with the royalist traitors, rather than give up their plans. They marched with these traitors against the Revolution.

Then, and only then—in July 1793—the Convention outlawed them as rebels.

CHAPTER XLVII

THE POPULAR REVOLUTION—ARBITRARY TAXATION

Immediate result of expulsion of Girondins—Importance of period, May 1793 to July 1794—Famine continues—War against coalition—Difficulties of *sans-culottes*—Forced loan necessary—*Superfluous* and *necessary* incomes—Impossibility of levying loan

IF any one doubts the necessity under which the Revolution lay, of expelling the chief men of the " Gironde " from the Convention, he should cast a glance at the legislative work which the Convention set itself to accomplish, as soon as the opposition of the Right was broken.

The taxation of the rich to help towards the enormous expenses of the war; the establishment of a maximum price for all commodities; the restoration to the communes of the lands which the nobility had taken from them since 1669; the definite abolition, without redemption, of the feudal rights; the laws concerning inheritance, intended to spread and equalise wealth; the democratic Constitution of 1793—all these measures came in rapid succession after the Right had been weakened by the expulsion of the Girondist leaders.

This period, which lasted from May 31, 1793, to July 27, 1794 (9th Thermidor of the Year II. of the Republic), represents the most important period of the whole Revolution. The great changes in the relations between citizens, the programme which the Assembly had sketched during the night of August 4, 1789, were, after four years of resistance, at last carried out by the purified Convention, under the pressure of the popular revolution. And it was the people—the *sans-*

culottes—who not only forced the Convention to legislate in this way, after they had given it the power of doing so by the insurrection of May 31; but it was also they who put these measures into execution locally, by means of the popular societies to whom the commissioned members of the Convention applied, when they had to create local executive power.

Famine still reigned during this period, and the war, maintained by the Republic against the coalition of the King of Prussia, the Emperor of Austria, the King of Sardinia and the King of Spain, urged on and financed by England, assumed terrible proportions. The requirements of this war were enormous, and one can have no idea of them without noting the minute details that are to be found in the documents of the time, so as to conceive the actual penury and ruin to which France was brought by the invasion. Under these truly tragic circumstances, when all things were lacking—bread, shoes, beasts of burden, iron, lead, saltpetre—when nothing could enter by land through the armies of four hundred thousand men hurled against France by the allied Kings, and nothing by sea, through the blockade maintained by English ships—under these circumstances the *sans-culottes* were striving to save the Revolution which was on the point of collapsing.

At the same time, all who held by the old state of things, all who had formerly occupied privileged positions and all who hoped either to regain those positions, or else create new ones for themselves as soon as the monarchic *régime* was re-established—the clergy, the nobility, the middle classes enriched by the Revolution—all conspired against it. Those who remained faithful to it had to struggle between the circle of foreign cannon and bayonets that was closing round them, and the conspirators in their midst who were trying to stab them in the back.

Seeing this, the *sans-culottes* made haste to act so that when the reaction gained the upper hand, it should find a new and regenerate France: the peasants in possession of the land, the town-worker familiarised with equality and democracy, the aristocracy and the clergy despoiled of their riches which had been their true strength, and these riches already passed into

ARBITRARY TAXATION

thousands of other hands, divided into shares, changed entirely in appearance, unrecognisable—impossible to reconstruct.

The true history of those thirteen months—June 1793 to July 1794—has not yet been written. The documents which one day will be used for writing it exist in the provincial archives, in the reports and letters of the Convention's commissioners, in the minutes of the municipalities and of the popular societies. But they have not yet been collected with the care that has been bestowed upon the documents concerning the legislation of the Revolution, and they ought to be sought for soon as they are rapidly disappearing. This would, no doubt, be the work of a life-time: but without this work the history of the Revolution will remain incomplete.*

What the historians have chiefly studied of this period is the War—and the Terror. And yet these are not the essentials. The essential factor was the immense work of distributing the landed property, the work of democratising and dechristianising France, which was accomplished during these thirteen months. To relate this immense work with all the struggles to which it gave birth in the different places, in each town and hamlet of France, will be the work of some future historian. All that we can do to-day is to recall some of the chief features of it.

The first really revolutionary measure taken after May 31 was the *forced loan from the rich* to subvent the expenses of the war. The condition of the Treasury was, as we have seen, deplorable. The war was devouring huge sums of money. The paper-money, issued in too great quantities, had already depreciated. New taxes on the poor could not produce anything. What else was left to do, if not to tax the rich ? And the idea of a forced loan, of a milliard levied on the rich—an idea which had already been mooted under the Ministry of Necker at the outset of the Revolution—germinated in the nation.

When we read to-day what contemporaries, both reactionaries

* Papers of the highest value have been destroyed recently at Clairvaux. We have found the traces of them and we have recovered some fragments of the library of " Pélarin," which had been sold to a grocer and a tobacconist in the village.

and revolutionists, said of the condition of France, it is impossible not to think that every republican, whatever his ideas might be concerning property, must have sided with the idea of a forced loan. There was no other possible way out of the difficulty. When this question was brought forward, on May 20, the tax was proposed by Cambon, a moderate; but the Girondins fell upon the proposers of the loan with unexpected violence, stirring up a shameful scene in the Convention.

This is why all that could be done on May 20 was to accept the idea of a forced loan *in principle*. As to the manner of carrying it into effect that was to be discussed later on—or perhaps never, if the Girondins succeeded in sending the "Montagnards" to the "Tarpeian Rock."

On the very night following the expulsion of the principal Girondins, the Commune of Paris resolved that the decree fixing the maximum for the price of commodities should be carried into effect without further delay, that the arming of the citizens should be proceeded with at once; that the forced loan should be levied; and that the revolutionary army should be organised and should comprise all good citizens, but exclude the *ci-devants*, that is, the ex-nobles, the "aristocrats."

The Convention lost no time in taking similar action, and on June 22, 1793, it discussed the report of Réal, who proposed the following principles for the forced loan. The *necessary* income, three thousand livres for a father of a family and fifteen hundred livres for a bachelor, was to be free from taxation. The *excessive* incomes were to contribute by progression, up to the incomes of ten thousand livres for bachelors, and twenty thousand for fathers of families. If the income were above this figure, it was to be considered as *superfluous*, and requisitioned in its entirety for the loan. This principle was adopted; only the Convention by its decree of the same day fixed the necessary income at six thousand livres for bachelors and ten thousand for the fathers of families.*

* I here follow the work of René Stourm, *Les finances de l'ancien régime et la Révolution*, 1885, vol. ii. pp. 369 *et seq.* The discussions in the Convention were very interesting. Cambon, on introducing the question on May 20, 1793, said: "I should like the Convention to open a civic loan of a milliard livres, which should be made up by the

ARBITRARY TAXATION

They perceived, however, in August, that with these sums the loan would produce less than two hundred millions,* and on September 3, the Convention had to fall back on its decree of June 22. It fixed the *necessary* income at a thousand livres for bachelors and fifteen hundred for married men, plus a thousand livres for each member of their family. The *excessive* incomes were taxed on an ascending scale which went from ten to fifty per cent. of the income. And as to the incomes above nine thousand livres, they were taxed so as never to leave more than four thousand five hundred livres of income, plus the *necessary* which we have just mentioned, no matter what the amount of the rich man's revenue was. This, however, was applied not as a permanent tax, but as a forced loan, only made for a time and under extraordinary circumstances.

A striking fact, which proves in a remarkable way the impotence of parliaments, is that although there was certainly never any government that inspired more terror than that of the Convention in the Year II. of the Republic, yet this law concerning the forced loan was never obeyed. The rich people did not pay it. The levying of the loan entailed enormous expense; but how was it to be levied upon rich people who would not pay. By seizure, by sale? For this a complicated political mechanism was required, and there was already so very much of the national property for sale? Materially, the loan was not a success; but as the advanced Montagnards meant it to prepare men's minds for the idea of equalising all wealth, and so to make it another step forward, in this respect they attained their end.

Later on—even after the reaction of Thermidor, the Directory also had recourse to two attempts in the same direction—in 1795 and in 1799. The idea of *superfluous* and *necessary*

rich and the indifferent. You are rich, *you have an opinion, which causes us expense ;* I want to bind you to the Revolution whether you like or not ; I want you to lend your wealth to the Republic." Marat, Thuriot, and Mathieu supported this proposal ; but there was a very strong opposition. It should be noted that it was a department, that of Hérault, that had taken the initiative, and set the example of a loan of this kind. Cambon mentioned it in his speech. Jacques Roux, at the Gravilliers, had already advised it on March 9.

* Stourm, p. 372, note.

incomes was making its way—and we know that progressive taxation became part of the democratic programme during the century after the Revolution. It was even applied in several countries, but in much more moderate proportions ; so moderate, indeed, that there was nothing left but the name.

CHAPTER XLVIII

THE LEGISLATIVE ASSEMBLY AND THE COMMUNAL LANDS

History of communal lands—Rise of middle-class peasants—Opposition to poorer peasants—*Active* and *passive* citizens—Appropriation of communal land by well-to-do peasants—Inaction of Assembly—Proposal of Mailhe rejected—Decree of Assembly—Indignation produced by decree—Difficulty of carrying decree into effect—Assembly frames new law to advantage of " grabbers "

THE restoration of the communal lands to the village communes and the definite abolition of the feudal laws were, as we have seen, the questions that dominated all others in rural France; quest ons of immense importance in which two-thirds of France was intensely interested, and yet so long as the Girondins, the " defenders of property " ruled the Convention, they remained in suspense.

Since the beginning of the Revolution, or rather since 1788, when a ray of hope had penetrated into the villages, the peasants had expected to regain possession of the communal lands, and had even tried to take back what the nobility, the clergy and the upper middle classes had appropriated under the edict of 1669. Wherever they could, the peasants took back these lands in spite of the terrible repression which very often followed their attempts at expropriation.

Formerly, the whole of the land—meadows, woods, waste lands, and clearings—had belonged to the village communities. The feudal lords held the right of administering justice over the inhabitants, and most of them had also the right of levying various taxes, generally consisting of three days' work and various payments, or *gifts*, in kind, in exchange for which the lords were pledged to maintain armed bands for the defence of the territory against invasions and incursions, whether of other lords or of foreigners or of local brigands.

Gradually, however, with the help of the military power they possessed, and of the clergy, who sided with them, as well as of the lawyers versed in Roman law, whom they maintained in their courts, the lords appropriated considerable tracts of land as their private property. This appropriation was gradual; it took centuries—the whole of the Middle Ages—to accomplish it, but towards the end of the sixteenth century it was accomplished. The lords were, by that time, in possession of large tracts of arable land and pastures. But still they were not satisfied.

As the population of Western Europe increased, and the land acquired a greater value, the lords, having become the King's peers, being under the protection of both King and Church, began to covet the lands still in the possession of the village communities. To take these lands by a thousand ways and under a thousand pretexts, either by force or by legal fraud, was the customary thing in the sixteenth and seventeenth centuries. Then came the ordinance of Louis XIV., *le Roi Soleil*, in 1669, to furnish the lords with a new legal weapon for the appropriation of the communal lands.

This weapon was the *triage*, which permitted the lord to appropriate *a third* of the lands belonging to the village communities that had formerly been under his jurisdiction, and the lords eagerly took advantage of the edict to seize upon the best land, chiefly the meadows.

Under Louis XIV. and Louis XV. the nobility and the Church continued to seize the communal lands under various pretexts. A monastery would be founded in the midst of virgin forests, and the peasants of their own accord would give the monks vast tracts of the forest, and this possession soon became property. Or else the lord, for a mere nothing, would obtain the right of building a farm on land belonging to the commune in the centre of uncultivated lands, with the result that he soon claimed the right of property over all, and, if need were, did not hesitate to fabricate title-deeds. In other places they took advantage of the law of enclosures (*bornage*), and in several provinces the lord who had put a fence round part of the communal lands declared himself the owner of it and received the royal sanction or the sanction of the parliaments to his rights of property over these enclosures. As the resistance of the communes to these appropriations was treated as rebellion, while the lords had protectors at Court, the theft of the communal lands, on a large and small scale, continued throughout the whole kingdom.*

However, as soon as the peasants became conscious of the approaching Revolution, they began to insist that all the appropriations made since 1669, whether under the law of *triage* or otherwise, should be declared illegal, and that the lands, which the village communes themselves had been induced by a thousand fraudulent means to give up to individuals, should be restored. In certain places, during the risings of 1789-1792, the peasants had already taken back these lands, but reaction might set in any day, and if successful the *ci-devants*—the dispossessed nobles—would again seize upon them. It was necessary, therefore, to make the restoration of the lands general and to legalise it, a measure which was strenuously opposed, not only by the two Assemblies, the Constituent and the Legislative, but also by the Convention, so long as it was under the domination of the Girondins.

It must be noted that the idea of dividing the communal lands between the inhabitants of each commune, which was often brought forward by the village *bourgeoisie*, was not at all favoured by the great mass of the peasants, no more than it is favoured in our own day by Russians, Bulgarians, Servians, Arabs, Kabyles, Hindus, or any other peasantry among whom the village community still persists. We know, in fact, that whenever a voice is raised in a country where communal property exists, demanding the division of lands belonging to the village community, it is raised in behalf of the village middle-class people, who have grown rich by some small business, and

---

* Several provincial assemblies had, prior to 1789, tried to compel the village communes to divide their lands, either in equal parts per head, or in proportion to the personal tax (*la taille*) paid by each householder. Several *cahiers* of 1789 made a similar demand. Others, on the contrary, complained of the enclosures (*bornage*) which the King had authorised in certain provinces in 1769 and 1777.

hope to appropriate the poor man's acre, as soon as the land is divided. The bulk of the peasantry is nearly always opposed to such a division.

This was also what happened in France during the Revolution. In the midst of the great mass always sinking deeper and deeper in their hideous poverty, a peasant middle class was being evolved, which was growing rich, in one way or another, and whose demands were the more readily heard by a revolutionary administration, middle class in its origin, its tastes and its point of view. These *bourgeois*-peasants were quite in agreement with the mass of the poor peasants in demanding the *restoration of the communal lands* taken by the lords since 1669, but they were against this mass when they demanded the peremptory *division* of these lands. The opposition of the poorer peasants was the stronger, because of the distinction which had been established during the course of the centuries between two classes of inhabitants, in both rural and urban communes. There were families, more or less well-to-do, who were, or said they were, descended from the first founders of each commune. These styled themselves the *bourgeois*, in Alsace *die Bürger*, the "citizens," or even simply "the families"; but there were also those who had entered the commune later on, and who were called "the inhabitants," *les menants; die Ansässigen* in Alsace and Switzerland.

Only the former had rights over the communal arable lands, and they alone in many cases shared the right of pasturage and the right over the woods, the waste lands, the forests, &c.; while the inhabitants, the *manants*, the *Ansässigen*, were often debarred all rights, and were scarcely allowed to pasture a goat on the waste land, or to pick up the fallen wood and chestnuts.

Their situation became still worse after the National Assembly had established the fatal distinction between *active* and *passive* citizens, not only for political rights but also for the election of the communal councils, the officials, and the judges. By the municipal law of December 1789, the Constituent Assembly had indeed abolished the popular village assembly, which was composed, as in the Russian *mir*, of all the heads of families in the commune, which till then had continued to meet under an elm

THE ASSEMBLY AND COMMUNAL LANDS

or in the shadow of the belfry; and instead of the folk-mote, it had introduced an elected *municipality* which could be elected by the *active* citizens alone.

From that time the appropriation of communal lands by well-to-do peasants and all sorts of middle-class people must have proceeded rapidly. It was easy, indeed, for the " active " citizens to come to an understanding among themselves about purchases of the best pieces of ground, and thus to deprive the poor commoners of the use of the common lands which were perhaps the sole guarantee of their existence. This must have been the case in the Vendée, and undoubtedly all through Brittany also, where the peasants, as may be seen from the laws of 1793, enjoyed till then extensive rights over wide stretches of waste lands, heaths and pastures—rights which the village *bourgeoisie* began to dispute when the ancient custom of communal assembly was abolished by the law of December 1789.

Under the influence of the laws made by the Constituent Assembly, the little village *bourgeoisie* began to insist more and more that the lands appropriated under the law of *triage* should be given back to the villages, and that the division of the communal lands should be decreed at the same time. They were, no doubt, quite sure that if the division were decreed by the National Assembly, it would be accomplished to the advantage of the well-to-do peasants. The poor, the "passive" commoners, would be excluded. But neither the Constituent nor the Legislative Assembly did anything until 1792. They were both opposed to any solution of the land question that might be unfavourable to the nobility, and for that reason they took no action.*

* Robespierre had already demanded in the Constituent Assembly the abolition of the ordinance of 1669, and the restitution of the communal lands which " the towns, boroughs and villages of Artois possessed since time immemorial," and to the preservation of which had mainly been due the abundance of cattle and the prosperity of agriculture and the flax industry. These lands had been taken away by the States-General of Artois for the enrichment of the administrative officials and to place them in the hands of the nobility. He demanded, therefore, the abolition of the ordinance of 1669. (*Motion de Robespierre au nom de la province d'Artois et des provinces de Flandre, d'Hainaut*

After August 10, 1792, however, the Legislative Assembly, on the eve of dissolution, felt itself obliged to do something, and what it did was for the benefit of the village *bourgeoisie*. When Mailhe brought forward, on August 25, 1792, a well-thought-out proposal for a decree to annual the effects of the ordinance of 1669, and compel the lords to restore the communal lands which had been taken from the village communes within the last two hundred years, his decree was not accepted. Instead, eleven days previously, on August 14, the Legislative Assembly, on the motion of François (of Neufchâteau), had already decreed as follows: " First, this year, immediately after the harvest, all the communal *lands* and *usages* other than woods [which meant even the grazing lands still held by the communes, over which rights of pasturage generally belonged to all the inhabitants] shall be divided among the citizens of each commune. Secondly, these citizens shall enjoy complete ownership of their respective portions. Thirdly, the communal property known as *nobody's* and *vacant* shall be equally divided between the inhabitants. And fourthly, to fix the method of division the Committee of Agriculture shall in three days propose a plan to be decreed." By this same decree the Legislative Assembly abolished also the joint liability of the commoners for the payment of dues and taxes.

It was indeed a treacherous blow dealt to communal ownership. Hurriedly drawn up, with incredible vagueness and carelessness, this decree seemed to me so extravagant that for some time I could not believe that the text, as given by Dalloz, was anything but an imperfect summary, and I searched for the complete decree. But I found Dalloz had given the exact and full text of this amazing law, which, with the stroke of a pen, abolished communal property in France and deprived those who were called inhabitants, or *Ansässigen*, of all rights over communal lands.

We can quite understand the fury provoked by this decree throughout France among the poorer of the rural population. It was understood to be an order to divide the communal lands

et de Cambrésis pour la restitution des biens nationaux envahis par les seigneurs. Imprimerie Nationale, 1791. British Museum Pamphlets.)

THE ASSEMBLY AND COMMUNAL LANDS 419

among the *active* citizens, and those "citizens" only, to the exclusion of the "inhabitants" and the poor. It was a spoliation for the benefit of the village *bourgeoisie*,* and this decree, with its third paragraph, would in itself have sufficed to rouse the whole of the Breton peasantry against the Republic.

Already on September 8, 1793, a report was read before the Assembly to state that the carrying out of this decree was so vigorously opposed by the people that it would be impossible to apply it. However, nothing was done. The Legislative Assembly separated without having abrogated it, and it was not rescinded until October by the Convention.

Seeing the difficulty of carrying the decree into effect, the Convention decided first, by the decrees of October 11-13, 1792, that "the communal lands under cultivation shall, until the time of partition, continue to be ploughed and sown as before in accordance with local customs, and the citizens who shall have done the aforesaid ploughing and sowing shall enjoy the crops resulting from their labours." †

So long as the Girondins dominated the Convention nothing better could be done. But it is very probable that the peasants —those of them, at least, to whom the purport of these counter-decrees was explained—realised that the attempt to divide the communal lands had failed for the time being. But who shall measure the harm that this threat of expropriation, still suspended over the communes, did to the Revolution ? Who shall tell the amount of hatred stirred up by it in agricultural districts against the revolutionists of the towns ?

Nor was this all. Between August 28 and September 14, on the eve of its dissolution, the Legislative Assembly had published another decree concerning the communal lands, which, if it had been upheld, would have been turned completely to the advantage of the lords. It declared, true enough, that "the unoccupied and waste lands shall be considered as belonging to the village communes, and shall be adjudged as theirs by the tribunals " ; but if the lord had appropriated these lands or part of them earlier than within the last forty years,

---

* The decree was so interpreted indeed by the law-courts (*vide* Dalloz, x. p. 265, No. 2261, note). † *Ibid*. ix. 186.

and had held them since, they remained his property.* This law, as was shown later by Fabre (deputy for the Hérault), in a report by him to the Convention, was of a very great advantage to the lords, for " nearly all the former lords were able to prove the necessary forty years' possession," and so to nullify the clauses "of this decree which were favourable to the communes." † Fabre also pointed out in this decree the injustice of Article 3, according to which the village commune could never regain possession of its lands once the lord had sold his acquired or supposed rights over them to a third person. Dalloz has, furthermore, shown clearly how difficult it was for the village communes to produce the positive and certain proofs which were demanded of them by the law-courts for reinstating them in possession of their lands.

Such as it was, the law of August 1792 was, therefore, always turned to the advantage of the "grabbers" of communal property. It was only in the Convention, and then only after the insurrection of May 31 and June 2, which ended in the expulsion of the Girondist leaders, that the question of the communal lands could again be considered in a light favourable to the mass of the peasants.

* " These lands shall be restored to the communes unless the former lords (*ci-devant seigneurs*) can prove by title-deeds or by exclusive and undisturbed *possession for forty years* that they have proprietary rights."

† *Rapport de Fabre*, p. 36. British Museum Pamphlets on the French Revolution, R. F., vol. 247.

CHAPTER XLIX

THE LANDS RESTORED TO THE COMMUNES

Law of June 11, 1793—Lands to be restored—Difficulty of partition—Details of decree—Diverse opinions of peasants—Majority of communes quickly take possession of lands—Subsequent history of communal lands

So long as the Girondins were the masters, the question of the communal lands remained as it was. The Convention did nothing to minimise the harmful effects of the decrees of August 1792, still less did it accept Mailhe's proposal concerning the lands of which the communes had been robbed.

But immediately after June 2, the Convention took up the question again, and on June 11, 1793, it passed a law which has marked an epoch in the village life of France, and has been full of consequences—more, perhaps, than any other law in French legislation.

By this law all the lands taken from the communes within the last two centuries, by virtue of the *triage* ordinance of 1669, had to be restored, as well as all those unoccupied, and waste lands, grass, marsh, heath, &c., that had been taken from the village communes in one way or another by individuals, including also those that came under the "forty years' possession" Act, decreed by the Legislative Assembly.*

---
* "All the communal lands in general," said the law of June 10-11, 1793, "known throughout the Republic under the various names of idle and waste lands, &c. (*gastes, garrigues, landes, pacages, pâtis, ajoncs, bruyères, bois communs, hermes, vacants, palus, marais, marécage, montagne*), and under any other denomination whatsoever, are the property of, and by their nature *belong to, the generality of the inhabitants, or members of the communes, or sections of the communes*. The communes shall be authorised to demand their restitution." Clause 4 of Article 25 of the ordinance concerning the "waters and forests of 1669, as well as all the edicts, declarations, decrees of the council and

However, in passing this just and necessary measure, which was to efface the effects of the spoliations committed under the old *régime*, the Convention made a false step concerning the partition of these lands. On this point there were two conflicting currents of ideas in the Convention as in every other place in France. The well-to-do peasants, who had long coveted the communal lands, of which they in many cases held portions in pledge, wanted the partition. They knew that if the lands were divided, it would be easy for them before long to buy up from the poorer peasants the plots of land which would be allotted to them. They wanted also, as we have said, the division to be made between the " citizens " alone, to the exclusion of the " inhabitants," or even of the poorer citizens—the *passive* citizens of 1789. These *bourgeois* peasants found in the Convention energetic advocates, who always pleaded in the name of property, justice and equality when they pointed out the inequality in the properties held by the different communes—which did not prevent them from defending the inequalities within the commune. These were the men who demanded compulsory division,* there being only a few, like Julian Souhait, who demanded that communal property should be maintained.

The Girondist leaders, however, were no longer there to support the advocates of division, and the purified Convention, dominated by the Montagnards, would not agree to divide the communal lands among one part only of the inhabitants; but it believed at the same time that it was doing a good thing, and acting in the interests of agriculture, by authorising the lands to be divided among the inhabitants individually. The idea which led the Convention astray was that no one in France

letters patent, which since that time have authorised the *triage*, division, partial distribution or concession of woods and forests, manorial and seigniorial, to the prejudice of the communal rights and usages . . . and all the judgments given, and acts done as resulting therefrom, are revoked and remain in this respect as null and void." " The forty years' possession, declared by the decree of August 28, 1792, as sufficient to establish the ownership of an individual, shall not in any case be allowed to take the place of the legitimate title, and the legitimate title shall not be that which emanates from feudal authority."

* *Vide* the speech of P. Lozeau concerning the communal properties, printed by order of the Convention.

LANDS RESTORED TO THE COMMUNES

should be refused a share of the Republic's land, and under the influence of this idea the Convention favoured, rather than permitted, the division of the communal lands.

The division, says the law of June 11, 1793, shall be made between all, "so much per head of the domiciled inhabitants, regardless of age or sex, absent or present."* "Every citizen, including the labourers and the domestics on the farms, domiciled for a year in the commune, shall have an equal share in this division, and for ten years the communal portion assigned to each citizen shall not be seized for debt."†

The partition, however, had to be optional. An assembly of the inhabitants, composed of all individuals having an interest in the division, of either sex and over the age of twenty-one, was to be convened on a certain Sunday, and this assembly was to decide whether the communal property should be divided, either the whole of it, or only in part. If a third of the assembly voted for the division, the division should be decided upon and could not be revoked.‡

It is easy to conceive the immense change brought about by this decree in the economic life of the villages. All the lands taken from the communes for the past two centuries, by means of *triage*, pretended debts, and frauds, could now be taken back by the peasants. The forty years' possession was no longer a title to property, the communes could go as far back as 1669 to claim their former possessions from the powerful and the crafty. And all the communal lands, including the lands restored to the peasants by the law of June 11, now belonged to all those who had lived in the commune for a year in proportion to the number of persons in each family, including the children of both sexes and aged relatives. The distinction between citizen and inhabitant was wiped out. Every one had a right to the land. It was a complete revolution.

Concerning the other part of the law that decreed the division, and its being carried into effect by the will of one-third over two-thirds of the inhabitants, it was applied only

---
* Section ii., Article 1.
† Section iii., Article 1.
‡ *Ibid.* Article 2.

in certain parts of France, and then not generally. In the North, where there was not much pasture, the peasants willingly divided the communal lands. But in La Vendée and in Brittany they violently opposed the division being made by the will of a third of the inhabitants. They meant to hold, all of them, their right of grazing, &c., over the uncultivated lands intact. In some parts of France there were numerous divisions. Thus, in the Moselle, which is a wine-growing country, 686 communes divided the communal property, 107 of them per head and 579 per family, only 119 communes remaining undivided; but in other departments, in Central and Western France, the majority of the communes kept their lands intact.

As a rule the peasants, who knew very well that if the communal lands were divided, the poorer families would soon become proletarians and poorer than ever, were in no hurry to vote for the partition.

It need hardly be said that the Convention, whose middle-class members loved so much to talk of the inequalities that would result if the communes simply retook possession of their lands, made no attempt to equalise the benefits conferred on the communes by the law of June 11. Making speeches about the poor communes that got nothing served as an excellent pretext for doing nothing and for leaving the dishonestly appropriated lands with those who had got them, but when the opportunity came for proposing something to prevent this "injustice," nothing was proposed.*

* An exception should be made in favour of Pierre Bridet (*Observation sur le décret du 28 août 1792*. Paris, 1793). He proposed something like what is to-day described as "land nationalisation." "The communal lands," said Bridet, "are national property, and consequently it is unfair to allow certain communes to possess a great deal of land while others have only a little." He proposed therefore that the State should take possession of all the communal lands, and lease them in small lots, if leaseholders were to be found; if not—in large lots, *thrown open to the enterprise of inhabitants from other districts in the neighbourhood.* All this was to be done by the Directories of the departments, which were, as we know, highly reactionary bodies representing the interests of the rich. Of course this scheme was not adopted. Since the lands belonging to each commune would have been leased (as they already were) in the first instance, to the local peasants, rich and poor, by the communes themselves, and would only in exceptional

LANDS RESTORED TO THE COMMUNES 425

What the communes, up till then, had been doing themselves was going to be handed over now to paid officials, who, most probably, would have favoured the better-off men in the province, by enabling them to enrich themselves at the expense of the village communes.

The communes that made no delay in retaking possession of their ancient lands secured them then and there, so that when reaction triumphed and the lords came back into power, they could do nothing to regain what the law had taken away from them and the peasants were holding in actual possession. But the communes that hesitated got nothing at all. For, as soon as reaction got the better of the revolutionists, as soon as the insurrection of the last of the Montagnards had been crushed on the 1st Prairial, Year III. (May 20, 1795), the first care of the reactionary Convention was to annul the revolutionary decrees of the Montagnard Convention. On the 21st Prairial, Year IV. (June 19, 1796), a decree was issued prohibiting the restitution of the communal lands to the communes.*

A year later, on May 21, 1797, a new law forbade the village communes to transfer or exchange their property by virtue of the laws of June 11 and August 24, 1793. Henceforth special legislation was required for each particular act of transference. This law was clearly meant to check the too

cases be rented by inhabitants from neighbouring districts, the scheme practically amounted to this: In order to permit a few *exceptional* middle-class men to lease lands situated in other districts and communes than their own, the State was going to step in and take the place of the communes in the administration of their lands. This is what the scheme meant. Of course, its preamble contained lofty language about justice which might appeal to socialistically inclined town-people, ignorant of the land question, and unable to examine that language more closely. But in reality the scheme tended only to create many new injustices, even worse than the old ones, and to establish numerous sinecures—all in the name of State regulation.

* " Inasmuch as the effect of the law of June 10, 1793, has given rise to numberless actions for claims . . ." since the examination of these matters under dispute would take a long time, " and since it is, moreover, urgent that the unfortunate results of the too literal interpretation of the law of June 10, 1793, should be checked, serious inconveniences from them having already been felt . . . all actions and proceedings resulting from this law are, for the time being, to be suspended, and all the present holders of the said lands are, for the time being, to be maintained in their possession " (Dalloz, ix. 195).

scandalous plundering of the communal property which went on after the Revolution.

Later still, under the Empire, there were several attempts made to abolish the legislation of the Convention. But, as M. Sagnac remarks, "the successive attempts against the laws of the Convention failed miserably." There were too many interests established on the part of the peasants for these attacks to have any effect.

On the whole, it may be said that the majority of the communes that had retaken possession of the lands filched from them since 1669 retained possession of them, while those that failed to do so before June 1796 got nothing. In revolution it is only the accomplished facts which count.

CHAPTER L

FINAL ABOLITION OF THE FEUDAL RIGHTS

Girondins oppose abolition of feudal rights—Decree of July 17
—Feudal laws abolished *en masse*—Reaction unable to prevent effect of decree—Triumph of Revolution

As soon as royalty was abolished, the Convention had to discuss in its first sittings the question of the feudal rights. However, as the Girondins were opposed to the abolition of these rights without indemnity, and yet proposed no scheme of redemption which would be binding on the lords, the whole matter remained in suspense. But this was the main, the all-absorbing question for much more than one-half of the population of France, who asked themselves with anxiety: " Is it possible that the peasant shall have to set his neck again under the feudal yoke, and again endure the horrors of famine—as soon as the revolutionary period is over ? "

We have just seen that immediately after the Girondist leaders had been expelled from the Convention, the decree which restored the communal lands to the communes was passed; but the Convention still hesitated to legislate about the feudal rights. It was only on July 17, 1793, that at last it decided to strike the great blow which was to set a seal upon the Revolution by legalising the attainment of one of its two chief objectives—the complete abolition of the feudal rights.

Royalty ceased to exist on January 24, 1793, and now, on July 17, 1793, the law of France ceased to recognise the rights of the feudal lords—the servitude of one man to another.

The decree of July 17 was quite explicit. The distinctions established by the two preceding Assemblies between the different feudal rights, in the hope of maintaining part of them, were annulled. Every right based upon the feudal law simply ceased to exist.

"All dues formerly seigniorial, feudal rights, both fixed and casual, even those reserved by the decree of August 25 last, are suppressed without indemnity," so ran the decree.* There was no exception; there remained only those rents and labour dues that were paid purely for the land, and were not of feudal origin.†

Thus the assimilation of *feudal* rents to *ground* rents, which had been established in 1789 and 1790, was completely blotted out. If any rent or obligation had a feudal origin, it was abolished irrevocably and without indemnity. The law of 1790 had declared that if any one leased a piece of land, he could purchase it by paying a sum equivalent to twenty or twenty-five times the annual rent; and this condition was accepted by the peasants. But, added the law, if besides the ground rent the owner had imposed any due of a feudal character— a fine, for instance, on all sales and inheritances, any kind of pledge or tax which represented a personal obligation on the farmer to the landlord, such as the obligation to use the mill or wine-press belonging to the lord, or a limitation on the right of sale of produce, or a tribute out of the crops, or even a payment to be made at the time of breaking the lease, or when the land changed owners—all dues, such as these, had to be redeemed at the same time as the ground rent.

But this time the Convention struck a really revolutionary blow. It would have none of these subtleties. Does your farmer hold his land under an obligation of a feudal character? If so, whatever you call this obligation, it is suppressed without indemnity. Or it may be the farmer pays a ground rent which has nothing feudal about it, but beside this rent you have imposed on him a pledge or a tax or some kind of feudal due. In that case, *he becomes the owner of the land without owing you anything whatsoever.*

But the owner might reply, the obligation was merely nominal. So much the worse. You intended to make a vassal of your farmer; he is therefore free and in full possession of the land

* Article 1 of the decree of July 17, 1793. † Article 2.

to which the feudal obligation was attached, without owing you anything. Ordinary individuals, M. Sagnac says, " either through vanity or by force of custom employed this proscribed form, and in the leases they granted stipulated for some trifling fine or small tax on sales and purchases "*—they wanted merely to play the lord.

So much the worse for them. The Convention did not inquire whether they wanted to play the lord or to become one. It knew that all the feudal dues had been trifling and customary at first, only to grow very oppressive in the course of time. Such a contract was as much tinged with feudalism as those that had served in centuries past to enslave the peasants; the Convention saw in it the mark of feudalism, and therefore it gave the land to the peasant who rented it, without asking any indemnity for it.

More than this: it ordered that " all the title-deeds which acknowledged the now abolished dues should be destroyed."† Lords, notaries, land-commissioners, had all, within three months, to bring those title-deeds and charters which gave one class power over another to the record office of their municipality, there to be thrown in a heap and burned. What the peasants had done during their revolt in 1789, at the risk of being hanged, was now to be done by law. " Five years in irons for every depository convicted of having concealed, subtracted or kept back the originals or copies of such deeds." Many deeds of that sort proved the right of feudal State-ownership over certain lands, for the State, too, had formerly its serfs, and later its vassals. But that did not matter. The feudal rights must and shall disappear. What the Constituent Assembly had done with the feudal titles—prince, count, marquis—the Convention was now doing with the *pecuniary rights* of feudalism.

Six months later, on the 8th Pluviose, Year II. (January 27, 1794), in response to numerous protests, chiefly on the part of the notaries who had recorded in the same books, and often on the same page, the dues attaching merely to the land and the feudal dues, the Convention consented to suspend

* Ph. Sagnac, *loc. cit.* p. 147.   † Article 4.

the working of Article 6, and the municipalities were permitted to keep the mixed title-deeds in their archives. But the law of July 17 remained intact, and once more, on the 29th Floreal, Year II. (May 18, 1794), the Convention confirmed the decree that all rents "tinged with the slightest trace of feudalism" were to be suppressed without indemnity.

It is most remarkable that the reaction which took the upper hand since 1794 was quite unable to abolish the effect of this revolutionary measure. It is a long way, as we have already said, from the written law to its carrying into actual effect. Consequently, wherever the peasants had not risen against their lords, wherever they had turned against the *sans-culottes*, as in La Vendée, under the leadership of the lords and the priests, wherever their village municipalities remained in the hands of the priests and the rich—there the decrees of June 11 and July 17 were not applied. In these regions the peasants did *not* regain possession of their communal lands. They did not become the owners of the lands they held on feudal lease from their ex-feudal lords. They did not burn the feudal title-deeds; and they did not even buy the nationalised lands for fear of the Church's curse.

But in many places—in a good half of the departments—the peasants did buy the national lands; here and there they even compelled the administration to sell them in small lots. They took possession of the lands they leased from their former lords, and, after planting a May-tree, they danced round it and burned all the feudal documents. They retook, in fact, their communal lands from the monks, the local *bourgeoisie* and the lords—and where this was done, the returning tide of reaction had no power over the economic revolution that was accomplished in deeds.

Reaction set in on the 9th Thermidor, and with it began the "blue" terror of the enriched middle classes. Later on came the Directory, the Consulat, the Empire, the Restoration, which swept away the greater part of the democratic institutions of the Revolution. But this part of the work accomplished by the Revolution remained: it resisted all attacks. The reaction was able to destroy, up to a certain point, the political work of the Revolution; but its economic work survived. And the new, transfigured nation, which had been formed during the revolutionary turmoil, also remained and set itself hard to work.

Another thing. When we study the economic results of the Great Revolution, as it was accomplished in France, we comprehend the vast difference there is between the abolition of feudalism accomplished bureaucratically by the feudal State itself, as was done in Prussia in 1848, or in Russia in 1861, and the abolition accomplished by a popular revolution. In Prussia and Russia the peasants were freed from feudal dues and compulsory labour only by losing a considerable part of the lands they possessed and by consenting to pay a heavy indemnity which ruined them. To become free property-owners, they impoverished themselves; while the lords, who at first resisted the reform, drew from it, at least in the fertile regions, unhoped-for advantages. Nearly everywhere in Europe the reform that abolished the feudal servitude increased the power of the lords.

In France alone, where the abolition of the feudal system was carried out by a revolution, the change has acted against the lords, as an economic and political caste, to the advantage of the great mass of the peasants.

CHAPTER LI

THE NATIONAL ESTATES

National estates—Previously benefited only middle classes—Discontent among peasants—Convention orders land to be subdivided—Decree concerning heirs—Effect of redistribution of land—Changed aspect of France

THE movement of May 31 had the same salutary effect upon the sale of the national estates. Until then these sales had been profitable mainly to the middle classes. Now the Montagnards took measures for rendering the purchase of national estates accessible to the poor who wished to cultivate the land themselves.

When the estates of the clergy, and later on those of the *émigrés*, had been confiscated by the Revolution and put up for sale, a certain part of these estates was divided at the outset into small lots, and the buyers were allowed twelve years to pay the purchase-money by instalments. But in proportion as reaction grew stronger and stronger in 1790 and 1791, and the middle classes consolidated their power, less and less facilities were offered to the poorer classes for buying the confiscated lands. Moreover, the State, being short of funds, was in need of ready money. Consequently, it was found preferable not to break up the large estates and farms, but to sell them as they were to those who bought them for speculation. True, in certain regions the peasants combined into syndicates for buying the larger estates, but the legislators did not favour such combinations, and an immense quantity of land went into the hands of speculators. The small farmers, the farm labourers, the artisans who lived in the villages, and the poor in general complained, of course, but the Legislative Assembly paid no attention to their complaints.*

Already, in 1789, the wish was expressed in several *cahiers* that the Crown lands and the mortmain estates should be divided into small farms of from four to five acres each. The people of Artois would even have no farms larger than "three hundred measures of land."† But, as Avenel had already pointed out, "neither in the speeches pronounced on this subject, nor in the decrees that were passed, do we find one single word in favour of those poorer peasants who owned no land. . . . Nobody advocated in the Assembly the organisation of popular credit for enabling these famishing peasants to buy on easy terms small lots of land. . . . Nor was any attention paid to the desire expressed by certain papers, such as the *Moniteur*, which asked that one-half of the lands offered for sale should be divided into lots, worth about 5000 francs each, so as to create a number of small peasant proprietors."‡

The result was that the lands that were put up for sale by the nation were chiefly bought by such peasants who had already some property, or else by middle-class town-people—the last circumstance producing a great deal of discontent in the villages of Brittany and La Vendée.

Thereupon came August 10. Under the menaces of the revolted poor, the Legislative Assembly tried to appease discontent by ordering that the lands confiscated from the *émigrés* should be sold in small lots of from two to four acres, to be paid for by a perpetual rent in money. However, those buyers who could pay ready money had still the preference.

On June 3, 1793, immediately after the expulsion of the Girondist leaders from the Convention, the promise was made by the National Representation, now under Montagnard influence, to give one acre of freehold land to each proletarian family in the villages; and some commissioners of the Convention actually did that, distributing small allotments to the poorest peasants. But it was only on the 2nd Frimaire,

* Ph. Sagnac, *La législation civile de la Révolution francaise*, p. 177.
† *Ibid.* p. 80.
‡ G. Avenel, *Lundis révolutionnaires*, pp. 30-40; Prof. Karéiev, p. 519.

Year II. (November 22, 1793), that the Convention issued orders to subdivide as much as possible the national estates that were put up for sale. Besides, especially favourable conditions of payment were introduced for the buyers of the estates of the *émigrés*, and these conditions were maintained until 1796, when the reactionaries, returning to power, abolished them.

It must, however, be remembered that the finances of the Republic remained all the time in a deplorable state. The taxes were coming in very irregularly, and the war absorbed thousands and thousands of million francs. The paper currency lost in value, and in such conditions the essential thing was to get ready money as quickly as possible, through the sale of the national estates, so as to be able to destroy a corresponding amount of paper-money from the previous issues. This is why the Montagnards as well as the Girondins cared less for the small agriculturist than for the means of realising as rapidly as possible the largest amounts of ready money. Whoever paid in cash continued to have preference.

And yet, notwithstanding all that, and notwithstanding all prevarications and speculations, considerable quantities of land were sold in small lots. While there were many middle-class people who suddenly made scandalous fortunes by the accumulation of national property, considerable quantities of land, in certain portions of France, and especially in the East (as has been shown by Professor Luchitzky of Kieff), passed in small lots into the hands of the poorer peasants. In this region, a real revolution was accomplished in the distribution of landed property.

At the same time, the idea of the Revolution was to strike a blow at the whole class of great landed proprietors, and completely to break up all large fortunes. For this purpose the right of primogeniture in inheritance was abolished by the revolutionary legislature. Already, on March 15, 1790, the Legislative Assembly had abolished the feudal form of inheritance, according to which the landlord transmitted his estates to one single heir—generally his eldest son. Next year (law of April 8 to 15, 1791) all legal inequalities among the different heirs were done away with. "All the inheritants of equal degree shall inherit, in equal parts, the properties which are assigned to them by law," said this decree. Next, the number of heirs was increased—collateral heirs and illegitimate children being put on the same footing as the direct heirs ; and finally, on March 7, 1793, the Convention abolished all rights " of disposing of one's property, whether in case of death, or whilst still alive, by means of agreed donation in a direct line." " All descendants will have an equal part of the properties of their deceased relatives (*ascendants*)."

The parcelling out of the estates was thus rendered obligatory in all inheritances.

What was the effect of these three great measures—the abolition of the feudal rights without compensation, the return of the communal lands to the communes, and the sale of the estates sequestrated from the clergy and the *émigrés ?* How did they affect the distribution of landed property ? This question continues to be discussed till now, and the opinions still remain contradictory. It may even be said that they vary according to the portions of France which have been the main object of study by this or that investigator.*

With all that, one fact dominates the others. Landed property *was* subdivided. In all those parts of France where the peasants joined the Revolution, considerable amounts of land passed into the hands of the peasants. And everywhere black misery—the gloomy misery of the old *régime*—began to disappear. Chronic famine which formerly used to brood over nearly one-third of France every year, was known no more in the nineteenth century.

Previous to the Revolution some parts of France suffered every year from famine. The agricultural conditions were

* In the Côte-d'Or, the estates of the clergy were bought more by the middle classes than by the peasants. But it was the reverse with the estates of the *émigrés*, which were bought in the same region mainly by the peasants. In the Laonnais, the peasants have bought more estates of the clergy than the middle classes did, while the estates of the emigrants were equally distributed between these two classes. In the North, considerable areas of land were bought by small associations of peasants (Sagnac, *loc. cit.* p. 188).

exactly what they are now in Russia. The peasant might work himself to death, but he could never have enough even of bread from one crop to the next. His ploughing was bad, his seeds were bad, and his meagre cattle could not give him the necessary manure. From one year to another the crops grew worse and worse. "Just as it is now in Russia!" one is bound to exclaim continually, while studying the documents and the works that deal with the conditions of the French peasants under the old *régime*.

But then comes the Revolution. The storm is terrible. The sufferings inflicted by the Revolution and especially by the war are unparalleled; they are truly tragical. At certain moments one sees the abyss opening that will swallow France. After that comes the Directory, followed by the wars of the Napoleonic Empire. And finally comes the reaction of the Bourbons, who are replaced upon the throne of France in 1814, by the coalition of Kings and Emperors; and with them comes the White Terror, even more terrible than the Red Terror of the Revolution. Whereupon superficial people triumphantly say: "You see, revolutions are of no use!"

There are, however, two legacies of the Great Revolution which no reaction could wipe out. France was democratised by the Revolution to such an extent that those who know France cannot stay for a while in any other country of Europe without saying to themselves: "One sees here at every step that the Great Revolution has not passed over this country. The peasant, in France, has become a man. He is no longer "the wild animal" of whom La Bruyère spoke in his *Caractères*. He is a thinking being. And the very aspect of France has been changed by the Revolution. France has become a country of relatively wealthy peasants. Even the White Terror itself was not capable of thrusting back the French peasant under the old yoke of misery. Of course there still remains too much poverty in the villages, in France as elsewhere. But this poverty is wealth in comparison with what France was a hundred and fifty years ago, and with what we still see wherever the Revolution has not yet carried its torch.

CHAPTER LII

THE STRUGGLE AGAINST FAMINE—THE MAXIMUM—PAPER-MONEY

Difficulty of feeding large towns—Activity of speculators—Situation at Lyons—Demand for maximum—Convention fixes price of wheat and food-stuffs—Danger of fixing retail prices—Maximum abolished by reactionaries—Fall in value of paper currency—Bankruptcy threatens State—Necker tries to raise money—Manufacture of false *assignats*

ONE of the great difficulties in every Revolution is the feeding of the large towns. The large towns of modern times are centres of various industries that are developed chiefly for the sake of the rich or for export trade; these two branches fail whenever any crisis occurs, and the question then arises of how these great urban agglomerations are to be fed.

France had entered upon this phase. Emigration and war, especially the war with England which prevented exportation and all the foreign trade by which such towns as Marseilles, Lyons, Nantes and Bordeaux lived, and the tendency felt by rich people to avoid making any display of their wealth in time of revolution, combined to put a stop to the manufacture of luxuries and to commerce on a large scale.

The peasants, especially those who had obtained possession of their lands, worked hard. Never was labour so energetic as in that autumn of 1791, Michelet tells us; and the harvests of 1791, 1792, and 1793 had been abundant, so that there should have been no lack of bread. But since 1788, all Europe, and France in particular, had been passing through a series of bad years—very cold winters and sunless summers. In reality there had been only one good harvest, that of 1793, and then only in half the departments. In those there had been even a surplus of wheat; but when this surplus, as well as the means of transport, had been requisitioned for the war, there was a dearth in more than half France. A sack of wheat which before that had been valued at only 50 livres in Paris, went up to 60 livres in February 1793 and to 100 and 150 livres in the month of May.

Bread, which formerly cost three sous a pound, now rose to six sous, and even to eight sous in the small towns round Paris. In the south it was famine price—ten and twelve sous a pound. At Clermont in the Puy-de-Dôme in June 1793, a pound of bread cost sixteen to eighteen sous. "Our mountain districts are in the utmost misery. The government is distributing the eighth of a *setier* per individual, and every one is obliged to wait two days for his turn," we read in the *Moniteur* of June 15, 1793.

As the Convention did nothing there were disorderly gatherings and riots in eight of the departments, and the Commissioners of the Convention were forced to fix the price of breadstuffs as the people wished. The trade of *bladier* (speculation in wheat) became at this time one of the most dangerous.

In Paris the question of feeding 600,000 persons had come to be one of life or death; for if the price of bread remained at six sous a pound, as it then was, an insurrection was inevitable and in that case grape-shot alone could prevent the pillaging of the rich men's houses. The Commune, therefore, plunged deeper into debt to the State, and expended from 12,000 to 75,000 livres a day to furnish the bakers with flour, and to keep the price of bread at twelve sous for the four-pound loaf. The Government, for its part, fixed the quantity of grain that each department and each canton should send to Paris. But the roads were in bad repair and all the beasts of burden had been requisitioned for the war. The prices of everything had gone up in proportion. A pound of meat which had formerly cost five or six sous now sold at twenty sous; sugar was ninety sous a pound, and a candle cost seven sous.

Speculators had been treated with much severity; but that did not help matters. After the expulsion of the Girondins, the Commune had succeeded in getting the Convention to close the Stock Exchange in Paris on June 27, 1793, but speculation still went on, and speculators were seen assembling at the Palais Royal wearing a special badge and marching in processions with girls to mock the misery of the people.

On September 8, 1793, the Paris Commune in desperation set seals on the houses of the bankers and "money-merchants." Saint-Just and Lebas, sent by the Convention on commission to the Lower Rhine, made an order in the Criminal Court for the house of any one convicted of jobbery to be razed to the ground. But speculation was only driven into other channels.

In Lyons the situation was worse than in Paris, for the municipality being partly Girondist, took no measures to relieve the wants of the people. "The population of Lyons at present is 130,000 souls at least ; *there are not provisions enough for three days*," wrote Collot d'Herbois to the Convention on November 7, 1793. "Our situation as regards food is desperate. We are on the brink of famine. . . ." And it was the same in all the large towns.

During this period of scarcity there were touching instances of devotion. We read, for instance, how that the sections of Montmartre and L'Homme Armé decreed a civic fast of six weeks ;* and Meillé has found in the Bibliothèque Nationale the decree of the Observatoire section dated February 1, 1792, by which all well-to-do citizens in this section were pledged not to use sugar and coffee until their more moderate price would allow the enjoyment of them to their less fortunate brethren.† Later on in the Year II. (February and March 1794), when bread went up to a very high price, all the patriots of Paris decided not to eat any more of it.

But such things could only have a moral effect in the midst of dearth. A general measure became necessary. On April 16, 1793, the administration of the Paris department had addressed a petition to the Convention demanding that the maximum price at which corn could be sold should be fixed ; and after a serious discussion, in spite of strong opposition, the Convention on May 3, 1793, decided to fix a maximum price for all grains.

* Buchez and Roux, xxxvii. 12.   † Meillé, p. 302, note.

The general intention of this decree was to place, as far as possible, the consumer in direct touch with the farmer in the markets, so that they could dispense with the middle-men. For this purpose every merchant or owner of corn and flour was bound to send from his place of residence to the municipality a declaration as to the quantity and nature of the grain in his possession. Corn and flour were no longer to be sold except in public markets established for the purpose, but the consumer might lay in provisions by the month directly from the merchants or landowners of his canton if furnished with a certificate from the municipality. The lowest prices at which the different kinds of grain had stood between January 1 and May 1, 1793, became the maximum price, above which the grain could not be sold. These prices were to be slightly decreased by degrees until September 1. Those who sold or bought at prices above the maximum were to be fined. Those who were convicted of maliciously or designedly spoiling or concealing the grain or flour, which was done even during the scarcity, were to be put to death.

Four months later it was found advisable to equalise the price of wheat all over France, and on September 4, 1793, the Convention fixed for the month of September the price of the best quality wheat at 14 livres the quintal (50 kilos. in weight, 100 by measure). This was the maximum so much cried down,* a necessity of the moment of which the royalists and Girondins made a crime to lay upon the Montagnards. The crime was all the more unpardonable because those who sympathised with the people demanded that not only should the price of wheat be fixed, but also that of the baked bread, as well as various objects of prime and secondary necessity. If society had undertaken to protect the life of the citizen, should it not also, they said with justice, protect it against those who made attempts on that life by forming coalitions to deprive it of what was absolutely necessary.

---

* It is often thought that it would be easy for a revolution to economise in the administration by reducing the number of officials. This was certainly not the case during the Revolution of 1789–1793, which with each year extended the functions of the State, over instruction, judges paid by the State, the administration paid out of the taxes, an immense army, and so forth.

The contest over this subject was, however, very keen—many of the Montagnards as well as the Girondins being absolutely opposed to the idea of fixing the price of food-stuffs, which they said was "impolitic, unpractical and dangerous." *
But public opinion prevailed, and on September 29, 1793, the Convention decided to fix a maximum price for things of first and second necessity—meat, cattle for the market, lard, butter, sweet oil, fish, vinegar, brandy, and beer.

This solution was so natural that the question of forbidding the exportation of grain, and of building granaries with this view and of fixing a maximum price for cereals and meat had already been discussed by both politicians and revolutionists since 1789. Certain towns, such as Grenoble, had decided since September 1789, to purchase grain for itself and to deal severely with monopolists. Many pamphlets to this effect were published.† When the Convention assembled, the demands for the fixing of a maximum price became pressing, and the council of the department of Paris met the magistrates of the department to discuss this question. The result was a petition which, in the name of all the people in the department of Paris, demanded that the Convention should fix a maximum price for grain. The prices of articles of secondary necessity were fixed for a year. Combustibles, candles, lamp oil, salt, soap, sugar, honey, white paper, metals, hemp, flax, woollen and cotton stuffs, sabots, shoes, tobacco, and the raw materials used in factories were comprised in this category. The maximum price at which it was permitted to sell these wares was the price each had fetched in 1790, which had been fixed by the Assemblies plus one-third, deduction being made of the fiscal and other duties to which they were then subject. This was the decree of September 29, 1793.

But at the same time the Convention legislated against the salaried classes and the poor in general. It decreed that "the

---

* *Vide* the collection in the British Museum, *Bibliothèque historique de la Révolution*, which contains the pamphlets on the Food Question, vols. 473, 474, 475.

† Momoro has published a very interesting pamphlet on this subject, in which he explains the communist principles (*Opinion de Momoro . . . sur la fixation de maximum du prix des grains dans l'universalité de la République française*).

maximum or highest figure respectively of salaries, wages, piece work or by the day, shall be fixed up to the September following, by the General Councils of the commune at the same rate as in 1790, with half that sum in addition. . . ."

It is clear that this system could not be limited. Once France had shown that she did not wish to remain under a system of freedom in commerce—and consequently in stock-jobbing and speculation which naturally followed—she could not stop at these timid experiments. She had to go further along the road to the communalism of commerce, despite the resistance which such ideas must necessarily encounter. The result of this was that, on the 11th Brumaire (November 1, 1593), the Convention discovered through the report of Barère that to fix the price at which goods should be sold by retailers was " to injure the small trades to the profit of the greater ones, and the factory-hand to the profit of the factory-owner." Then the idea was conceived that to establish the price of merchandise included in the preceding decree, it was necessary to know " the value of each on production." Adding to this five per cent. profit for the wholesale merchant, and five per cent. for the retailer, so much more for expenses of transport, the fair price was fixed at which each kind of goods should be sold.

A gigantic inquiry was begun, therefore, to establish one of the factors of value, the cost of production. Unfortunately, it was never completed, owing to the triumph of reaction, on the 9th Thermidor, when everything of that kind was abandoned. On the 3rd Nivose, Year III. (December 23, 1794), after a stormy discussion, opened by the Thermidorians, on the 18th Brumaire (November 8), the decrees concerning the maximum were repealed. This resulted in an alarming fall in the value of the paper currency : only nineteen francs were given in exchange for a hundred francs in paper, six months later the exchange was two francs for a hundred, and in November 1725 the value had sunk to fifteen sous. Meanwhile a pair of shoes cost a hundred livres and a drive in a carriage six thousand livres.*

* *Vide* Avenel, *Lundis révolutionnaires*, ch. iii., concerning the true causes of this unavoidable dearness.

PAPER-MONEY

It has been already mentioned how Necker, to procure the means of existence for the State, had had recourse at first to two loans, one for thirty, the other for eighty millions. These loans, however, not being successful, he had obtained from the Constituent Assembly an extraordinary grant of a quarter of every person's income payable once. Bankruptcy was threatening the State, and the Assembly, led by Mirabeau, voted the grant demanded by Necker. But this also produced very little.* Then, as we have seen, the idea was evolved of putting up the Church lands for sale and issuing *assignats* (paper-money), which were to be cancelled according as the sales brought in the money, thus forming a source of national revenue. The quantity of paper-money issued was to be limited to the value of the lands each time put up for sale. These *assignats* bore interest and had an inflated value.

Jobbery and money-lending no doubt tended continually to depreciate the value of the *assignats :* it could, however, be maintained more or less, so long as the maximum prices of the principal commodities and objects of prime necessity were fixed by the municipalities. But as soon as the maximum was abolished by the Thermidorian reaction the depreciation of the *assignats* was rapid. The misery caused by this among those who lived from hand to mouth can be imagined.

Reactionary historians are always ready to involve this subject, like so many others, in vagueness and confusion. But the truth is that the great depreciation of the *assignats* was only felt after the decree of the 3rd Nivose, Year III., which abolished the maximum.

At the same time, the Convention under the Thermidorians began to issue vast quantities of *assignats*, so that from six thousand four hundred and twenty millions, which were in circulation on the 3rd Brumaire, Year III. (November 3, 1794), the sum had mounted nine months later, that is, by the 25th Messidor, Year III. (July 13, 1795), to *twelve milliards*.

* As a rule, during the whole Revolution no taxes were paid in. In February 1793, the Treasury had not received anything from the tax on landed and personal property levied in 1792, and of that levied in 1791 only half had been received—about 150 millions. The remainder was still to come.

Furthermore, the princes, and above all, the Count d'Artois, had set up in England, by an ordinance of September 20, 1794, countersigned by Count Joseph de Puisaye and the Chevalier de Tinténiac, " a manufactory of *assignats*, resembling in all respects thos which had been issued, or were to be issued, by the so-called National Convention." There were soon seventy workmen employed in this manufacture, and the Count de Puisaye wrote to the committee of the Breton insurrection : " Before long you will have a million a day, and afterwards two, and more later."

Finally, on March 21, 1794, there was a discussion in the English House of Commons, in which the famous Sheridan denounced the manufacture of the false *assignats*, which Pitt had allowed to be established in England, and Taylor declared that he had seen with his own eyes the false paper-money being made. Considerable quantities of these *assignats* were offered in all the large towns of Europe in payment of bills of exchange.*

If only reaction had confined itself to these infamous secret doings, but it was even still more active in the systematic monopolisation of food-stuffs by means of purchasing the crops in advance, and in speculating in *assignats*.†

In addition, the abolition of the maximum was the signal for an increase in the price of everything, and this in the midst of terrible scarcity. One can but ask how France managed to pass through such a frightful crisis without completely going under. Even the most revolutionary authors ask themselves this.

* *Vide* Louis Blanc, Book XIII., ch. iv., which gives an excellent *Histoire du maximum ;* also Avenel, *Lundis révolutionnaires*.

† Some letters from England, addressed by royalists to their agents in France, reveal the methods by which the stock-jobbers worked. Thus we read in one of these letters : " Run up the exchange to 200 livres for one pound sterling. We must discredit the *assignats* as much as possible, and refuse all those without the royal effigy. *Run up the prices of all kinds of commodities. Give orders to your merchants to buy in all objects of prime necessity.* If you can, persuade Cott . . . ti to buy up the tallow and candles at any price, make the public pay as much as five francs a pound. My lord is well satisfied with the way in which B.t.z. (Batz) has acted. We hope that the *assassinats* (sic) will be pushed carefully. Disguised priests and women are the best for this work." (S. Thiers, *Histoire de la Révolution française*, vol. iii. pp. 144–145, 1834.)

CHAPTER LIII

COUNTER-REVOLUTION IN BRITTANY—
ASSASSINATION OF MARAT

Girondins stir up civil war—Royalist plot discovered—English prepare insurrection in Normandy and Brittany—Insurrection falls through—Weakness of republican forces—Commissioners of Convention succeed in rousing towns—Charlotte Corday—Implication of Girondins in plot—Assassination of Marat—Execution of Chalier—Character and work of Marat

ASSAILED from all sides by the coalition of European monarchies, in the midst of the tremendous work of reconstruction which she had undertaken, France found herself in the throes of a terrible crisis. And it is in studying this crisis in its details, in realising the sufferings which the people had to endure from day to day, that we realise the enormity of the crime committed by the leisured classes, when, in order to retain their privileges, they did not hesitate to plunge France into the horrors of a civil war and a foreign invasion.

Nevertheless, the Girondist leaders did not shrink after their exclusion from the Convention on June 2, 1793, from going to the provinces, to fan there, with the support of royalists and even of foreigners, the flame of civil war.

It may be remembered that after excluding thirty-one Girondist members from its midst, the Convention placed them under home-arrest, leaving them the right of going about in Paris, under the condition of being accompanied by a gendarme. Vergniaud, Gensonné, Fonfrède, remained in Paris, and from time to time Vergniaud addressed letters, full of venom, to the Convention. As to the others, they escaped and went to rouse the provinces. The royalists could not desire anything better.

Anti-revolutionary risings broke out in sixty departments—the most extreme Girondins and the royalists working hand in hand.

Since 1791 a royalist plot was already hatching in Brittany—its aim being to re-establish the old States-General of this province, and the old administration by the three orders. Tufin, Marquis de la Rouèrie-Rezière, had been placed by the emigrant princes at the head of this conspiracy. The plot, however, was denounced to Danton, who had it watched by one of his secret agents. The Marquis de la Rouèrie-Rezière was forced to go into hiding, and in January 1793, he died in La Guyaumarais, the châteaux of one of his friends, where he was buried secretly. The insurrection broke out, however, with the support of the English.

With the aid of smugglers and the *émigrés* who lived in Jersey and in London, the English Government prepared a tremendous insurrection which was to place in its hands the fortified towns of Saint-Malo, Brest, Cherbourg, and perhaps also Nantes and Bordeaux. After the Convention had decreed the arrest of the most important Girondist members, Pétion, Gaudet, Brissot, Barbaroux, Louvet, Buzot, and Lanjuinais went to Normandy and Brittany, to take the leadership of the insurrection there. On reaching Caen, they at once organised a League of the United Counties, with the intention of marching against Paris. They had the delegates of the Convention arrested, and they excited popular feeling against the Montagnards. General Wimpffen, who was in command of the Republican troops in Normandy, and who took up the cause of the insurgents, did not hide from them his royalist opinions and his intention to seek support in England; but, notwithstanding this, the Girondist leaders did not break with him.

Happily the people in Normandy and Brittany did not follow the lead of the royalists and the clergy. The towns ranged themselves on the side of the Revolution, and the insurrection, having been crushed at Vernon, fell through.*

The march of the Girondist leaders through Brittany, along the dark, walled country lanes, not daring to show themselves

* "The civic hymn of the Bretons marching against Anarchy,"

COUNTER-REVOLUTION IN BRITTANY 447

even in the smallest towns, where the republicans would have arrested them, shows how little sympathy they found, even in this Breton country, where the Convention had not won the favour of the peasants, and where the levying of recruits for the war on the Rhine was, of course, fiercely resented. When Wimpffen intended to march against Paris, Caen only furnished him with a few dozen volunteers.* In the whole of Normandy and Brittany only five to six hundred men were enlisted, and they did not even fight when they found themselves face to face with a small army arrived from Paris.

In some towns, however, especially in the seaports of Saint-Malo and Brest, the royalists found staunch supporters amongst the merchant class, and a tremendous effort was necessary for the republicans to prevent Saint-Malo from giving itself up, as Toulon had done, to the English.

One must, indeed, read the letters of the young Jullien, commissioner of the Committee of Public Welfare, and of Jeanbon Saint-André, commissioner of the National Convention, to understand how weak were the material forces of the Republic, and how willing the well-to-do classes were to uphold the foreign invaders.

Everything had been prepared to give up the fortress of Saint-Malo to the English fleet, armed as it was with 123 cannon, 25 mortars, and well stocked with cannon-ball, bombs and powder.

such was the title of the song of the Girondins, which Gaudet gives in the *Mémoires of Buzot*, pp. 68–69. Here is one of the stanzas:

> From a throne propped by his crimes,
> Robespierre, all drunk with blood,
> Points out his victims with his finger
> To the roaring Anarchist.

This Marseillaise of the Girondins demanded the death of Danton, of Pache, and of Marat. Its refrain was:

> War and death to the tyrants,
> Death to the apostles of carnage !

Of course, at the same time they themselves were demanding and preparing the slaughter of the revolutionists.

* The review of which Charlotte Corday spoke before her judges and which was to have gathered thousands of men, was a fiction, with which she expected no doubt to frighten the *sans-culottes* of Paris.

It was only the arrival of the commissioners of the Convention which rekindled the zeal of the republicans and prevented this treachery.

These commissioners did not rely upon the local administrative bodies; they knew them to be worm-eaten with royalism and "commercialism." They went straight to the Popular Society of each town, whether small or large. They proposed to this society to "purify" itself. Each member had to state openly before the whole society what he had been before 1789; what he had done since then; whether he had signed the royalist petitions of the 8000 or 20,000; what had been his fortune before 1789, and what it was at the present moment. Those who could not give satisfactory answers to these questions were excluded from the Republican Society.

After this the society became the recognised organ of the Convention. With its aid the commissioner proceeded to a similar purification in the municipality and had the royalist members and profit-mongers (*profiteurs*) excluded. Then, supported by the society, they roused the enthusiasm of the population, especially of the *sans-culottes*. They directed the enlisting of volunteers and induced the patriots to make efforts, often heroic, for the defence of the coasts. They organised republican *fêtes* and introduced the republican calendar. And when they left, to accomplish the same work elsewhere, they handed over to the new municipality the work of taking all necessary measures for the transport of ammunition, provisions, troops, when asked to do so by the commissioners of the Convention—always under the supervision of the local Popular Society with which they maintained a regular correspondence.

Very often the war demanded extraordinary sacrifices. But in each town, in Quimper, in Saint-Malo itself, the commissioners of the Convention found men devoted to the Revolution; with their aid they organised the defence. The *émigrés* and the British ships did not even dare to approach Saint-Malo or Brest.

Thus the royalist insurrection failed both in Normandy and in

Brittany. Yet it was from Caen that Charlotte Corday came to assassinate Marat. Influenced, no doubt, by all that she heard said against the Republic of the *sans-culotte* Montagnards, dazzled perhaps by the refined republican airs which the Girondins who had come to Caen gave themselves, and where she met Barbaroux, Charlotte Corday arrived on July 11 in Paris, determined to murder some one of the eminent revolutionists.

The Girondist chroniclers, who all hated Marat, the chief organiser of May 31, have made out that Charlotte Corday was a republican. This is absolutely untrue. Mademoiselle Marie Charlotte Corday d'Armont belonged to an arch-royalist family, and her two brothers had emigrated. She herself, brought up in the convent of l'Abbaye-aux-Dames at Caen, now lived with a relation, Madame de Breteville, who was only prevented by fear from openly calling herself a royalist. All the so-called "republicanism" of Mademoiselle Corday d'Armont lay in the fact that she refused once to drink the king's health, and explained her refusal by saying that she would be a republican "if the French were worthy of a Republic." That is to say, she was a constitutionalist, probably a "Feuillante." General Wimpffen even described her simply as a royalist.

Everything leads us to believe that Charlotte Corday d'Armont did not stand alone. Caen, as we have just seen, was the centre of the Federation of the United Departments, organised against the Montagnard Convention, and it is very probable that a plot had been prepared for July 14 or 15, to kill on that day "Danton, Robespierre, Marat and Company," and that Charlotte Corday knew of this. Her visit to the Girondin Duperret, to whom she handed over some leaflets and a letter from Barbaroux—then at Caen—and whom she advised to retire to Caen without delay, tend rather to represent Charlotte Corday as the tool of a plot hatched at Caen by the Girondins and the royalists.*

The original plan of Charlotte Corday had been, she said,

* That a plot existed, and that the Girondins were cognisant of it, seems clear enough. Thus, on July 10, a letter was read at the General Council of the Commune of Paris, received at Strasbourg, and forwarded to Paris by the mayor of that city, in which were the following lines:

to kill Marat on the Champ-de-Mars, on July 14, during the anniversary *fête* of the Revolution, or should he not be there, at the sitting of the Convention. But the *fête* had been put off, and Marat, who was ill, did not attend the Convention.

Then she wrote to him, begging to be received, and on obtaining no answer, she wrote again, playing this time jesuitically on his kindness, of which she knew, or of which her friends had spoken to her. In this letter she said she was unhappy, persecuted, knowing for certain that with such a recommendation she would be received.

With this note, and a dagger hidden in her scarf, she went, on July 13, at seven o'clock in the evening, to Marat. His wife, Catherine Evrard, after hesitating a little, finally allowed the young lady to enter the modest room of the people's friend.

Marat, wasted by fever for the past two or three months, after the life of a tracked wild beast which he had led since 1789, was seated in a closed bath, correcting the proofs of his paper on a board placed across the bath. It was here that Charlotte Corday d'Armont struck the Friend of the People in the breast. His death was instantaneous.

Three days later, on the 16th, another friend of the people, Chalier, was executed by the Girondins at Lyons.

In Marat, the people lost their most devoted friend. The partisans of the Girondins have represented him as a bloodthirsty madman, who did not even know what he wanted. But we know to-day how such reputations are made. The fact is, that in the dark years of 1790 and 1791, when he saw that all the heroism of the people had not been able to break the royal power, Marat began to despair, and he wrote that a few thousand aristocratic heads ought to be sacrificed to make the Revolution succeed. However, in the depth of his heart, he was not at all bloodthirsty. He only loved the people, both

" The 'Mountain,' the Commune, the Jacobin Club and the whole rascally crew are a hair's-breadth from the grave. . . . Between now and July 15 we will dance ! I hope that no other blood than that of Danton, Robespierre, Marat and Company will be shed " (I quote from Louis Blanc). On July 11 and 12, in the Girondist paper, the *Chronique de Paris*, there were already allusions to the death of Marat.

he and his heroic mate, Catherine Evrard,* with a love far deeper than that of any other prominent revolutionist, and to this love he remained true.

From the day the Revolution began, Marat took to bread and water, not figuratively speaking, but in reality. And when he was murdered, the entire fortune of the Friend of the People was a note for 25 livres (francs).

With this love of the people to guide him, Marat, who also was older than most of his revolutionist comrades, and had more experience, understood the various phases of the Revolution, and foresaw what was to come, far better than did any of his contemporaries. He was the only one, we may say, of the revolutionary leaders who had a real understanding of events and power of grasping them as a whole, in their intricate bearings on one another.†

That he had a certain amount of vanity is to be explained to some extent by the fact that he was always pursued, always tracked, even in the greatest days of the Revolution, while each new phase of the Revolution only confirmed the accuracy of his predictions. But these are mere details. The distinctive feature of his mind was that at each given moment he understood what had to be done for the triumph of the people's cause—the triumph of the people's revolution, not of an abstract theoretical revolution.

However, it must be owned that when the Revolution, after the abolition of feudal rights, had to make one more step to solidify its work—when it had to take such measures as would benefit the lowest classes by giving to every one the certainty of work and life—Marat did not fully grasp the truth in the ideas held by Jacques Roux, Varlet, Chalier, L'Ange, and many others. Having been himself unable to formulate the leading ideas of the deep communist change, of which these precursors sought the practical forms, and fearing, on the other hand, that

* "A divine woman, who, touched by his position when he fled from cellar to cellar, took in and hid the Friend of the People. To him she devoted her fortune and sacrificed her peace." Thus Michelet quotes the words of Albertine, Marat's sister, about Catherine Evrard.

† It is a pleasure to note that a study of Marat's work, neglected till this day, led Jaurès to speak with respect of this quality of the popular tribune.

France might lose the liberties she had already won, he did not give these communists the necessary support of his energy and his immense influence. He did not make himself the mouthpiece of the new movement.

"Had my brother lived," said the sister of Marat, "neither Danton, nor Camille Desmoulins "—nor the Hébertists either, we may add—" would have been guillotined."

On the whole, although Marat understood the sudden accesses of fury in the people, and even considered them necessary, at times, yet he certainly was not an upholder of terrorism as it was practised after September 1793.

CHAPTER LIV

THE VENDEE—LYONS—THE RISINGS IN SOUTHERN FRANCE

Royalist conspiracies in South—Risings against Convention—Toulon surrenders to English and Spanish fleet—Causes of rising in La Vendée—Disaffection of peasants—Ill-feeling of villages against towns—Girondins help insurrection—Plan of Vendeans—They take Saumur and Angers, but are forced to retire at Nantes—Vendeans exterminated—Risings in Provence and at Lyons—Chalier—Marseilles and other southern towns join movement—Royalists defeated—Siege and capture of Lyons—Action of republicans in Lyons—Bordeaux surrenders to Convention

IF the royalist rising failed in Normandy and Brittany, the reactionaries met with more success in the province of Poitou, in the departments of Deux-Sèvres, Vienne, and Vendée, at Bordeaux, Limoges, and partly in Eastern France, where risings against the Convention began at Besançon, Dijon and Mâcon. In these parts of France the middle classes, as we have seen, had acted with ferocity against the revolted peasants in 1789.

In the South, where royalist conspiracies had been going on for a long time, revolts broke out in several places. Marseilles fell into the hands of the counter-revolutionists—Girondins and royalists—who elected a provisory government, and intended to march against Paris. Toulouse, Nîmes and Grenoble rose also against the Convention.

Toulon surrendered to an English and Spanish fleet, which took possession of this fortress in the name of Louis XVII. Bordeaux, a trading town of great importance, seemed also to be ready to rise at the call of the Girondins; and Lyons, where the industrial and merchant *bourgeoisie* was supreme since May 29, revolted openly against the Convention, and withstood a long siege; whilst the Piedmontese, profiting by the disorder in the army, which had Lyons as its base of operations, crossed the frontier of France.

Up to the present day, the true causes of the rising in La Vendée have not been made quite clear. Of course the devotion of the peasants to their clergy, cleverly made use of by Rome, did much to foster their hatred against the Revolution. Certainly there was also in the villages of La Vendée a vague attachment to the King, and it was easy for the royalists to rouse the pity of the peasants for "the poor King who had desired only the good of the people, and had been executed by the people of Paris"; many tears also were then shed by the women over the fate of the poor child, the Dauphin, shut up in a prison. The emissaries who came from Rome, Coblentz and England, bringing with them papal bulls, royal decrees and gold, had a clear field under such conditions, above all when they were protected by the middle classes, the ex-slave-traders of Nantes, and the merchants on whom England showered promises of aid against the *sansculottes*.

And finally, there was this reason, in itself sufficient to bring whole provinces to arms—the levy of three hundred thousand men ordered by the Convention. This levy was regarded in La Vendée as a violation of the most sacred right of every human being—that of remaining in his native land.

It is nevertheless permissible to believe that there were yet other causes to rouse the peasants of La Vendée against the Revolution. Continually, whilst studying various documents of the period, one comes across such causes as must certainly have produced a feeling of resentment among the peasants against the Constituent and the Legislative Assemblies. The fact alone that the former had abolished with a stroke of the pen the folk-motes of the villages, which had existed for centuries until December 1789, as also the fact that the peasants were divided into two classes—active and passive—and that the administration of communal affairs was given to those elected by the rich only—these facts alone were sufficient to awake discontent in the villages against the Revolution, and against the towns in general and their middle classes.

It is true that on August 4 the Revolution had proclaimed in principle the abolition of feudal rights and mortmain, but the latter, it appears, no longer existed in the West, and feudal rights were only abolished on paper; and as the risings of the villages were not widespread in the western provinces, the peasants of these provinces saw that they would have to continue paying feudal dues as before.

On the other hand—and this was of great importance to the villages—the sale of the State lands, of which the greater part, all the Church lands, should have reverted to the poor, were now being bought by wealthy people in the towns, and this tended to strengthen the general ill-feeling of the villages against the towns. To this must also be added the pilfering of the communal lands for the benefit of the middle class, which was increased by the decrees of the Legislative Assembly.*

It thus happened that the Revolution, while imposing new burdens on the peasants—fresh taxes, recruiting, and requisitions—had given nothing to the villages up to August 1793, except when the peasants themselves had taken the lands of the nobles or the estates of the clergy. In consequence, a deeply seated hatred was growing in the villages against the towns, and we see indeed that the rising in La Vendée was a war declared by the villages against the towns, especially against the middle classes of the towns.†

With the help of Rome, the insurrection broke out, wild and bloody, under the guidance of the clergy. And the Convention could only send out against it some insignificant troops, commanded by generals either incapable or else interested in making the war drag on; while the Girondist deputies did their best to help the insurrection by the letters they addressed

---

* *See* ch. xxvi.

† Certain indications of a social character in the Vendean rising are to be found, says Avenel, in the work of Antonin Proust (*La Justice révolutionnaire à Niort*). It was a war of the peasants against the *bourgeois*—the peasants sending their delegates to the *bourgeois* creditors " to get the title-deeds and burn them " (*Lundis révolutionnaires*, p. 284).

to Nantes and the other towns. All these forces, acting in the same direction, made it possible for the rising to spread and finally to become so menacing that the "Mountain," in order to crush it, had recourse to the most abominable measures.

The plan of the Vendeans was to take all the towns, to exterminate the republican "patriots," to carry the insurrection into the neighbouring provinces, and then to march against Paris.

At the beginning of June 1793, the Vendean leaders, Cathelineau, Lescure, Stoflet, and La Roche-Jacquelein, at the head of 40,000 men, took the town of Saumur, which gave them command over the Loire. Then, crossing the Loire, they took Angers (June 17), and dexterously disguising their movements, they immediately marched on Nantes, the seaport of the Loire, the possession of which would have put them into direct communication with the English fleet. On June 29 and 30, their armies, rapidly massed, attacked Nantes. But in this enterprise they were routed by the republicans. They lost Cathelineau, the real and democratic leader of the rising, and they were forced to abandon Saumur and retire to the left bank of the Loire.

A supreme effort was made now by the Republic to attack the Vendeans in their own country. The war became a war of extermination, and finally twenty to thirty thousand Vendeans, followed by their families, decided to emigrate to England after crossing Brittany. They consequently crossed the Loire from south to north, and went northwards. But England had no desire to receive such immigrants, and the Bretons, for their part, received them coldly, the more so as the Breton patriots were gaining the upper hand in the towns and villages; therefore all these starving and ragged people, with their women and children, were driven back towards the Loire.

We have mentioned already the savage ardour with which the Vendeans, encouraged by their clergy, were animated at the outset of their revolt. Now, the war was becoming one of mutual extermination. In October 1793—it is Madame de la Roche-Jacquelein who writes thus—their watchword was "No quarter." On September 20, 1793, the Vendeans filled the wells at Montaigne with the bodies of republican soldiers, many of them still alive and only stunned or disabled by blows. Charette, on taking Noirmoutiers, on October 15, had all those who surrendered shot. Living men were buried up to the neck, and their captors amused themselves by inflicting all kinds of tortures on the unburied heads.*

On the other hand, when all this mass of men, women and children, driven back to the Loire, poured into Nantes, the prisons of this town began to be dangerously overcrowded. In these dens, swarming with human beings, typhoid fever and various other infectious diseases raged, and soon spread into the town which was already exhausted by the siege. Besides, just as in Paris, after August 10, the imprisoned royalists threatened to set fire to the city and to murder all the Jacobins, so the Vendeans imprisoned at Nantes likewise threatened to exterminate all the republicans as soon as the "Royal Army" of Vendeans should approach Nantes. It must be noted that the patriots numbered but a few hundreds in this town, which had gained its wealth in the slave trade and slave labour in Saint Domingo, and was losing it now that slavery had been abolished. Consequently, the patriots had to display an extraordinary vigilance and energy to prevent Nantes from being taken by a sudden attack of the " Royal Army," and the republicans from being massacred. Their efforts had been so great that the men of the republican patrols were quite worn out.

Then the cry of " Drown them all," which had already been heard in 1792, became more and more menacing. A panic,

* *See* Michelet, who studied the Vendean war from local documents on the spot. "The sad question," he says, " has often been discussed as to who had taken the initiative in these barbarous acts, and which of the two sides went furthest in such crimes. The wholesale drowning of the Vendeans in the Loire by Carrier is spoken of endlessly, but why should the massacres of Charette be passed over in silence ? Old Vendean veterans have told their doctor, who retold it to me, that never had they taken a soldier (especially one of the army that came from Mayence) without killing him under torture, provided they had time for that ; and when the men from Nantes arrived, in April 1793, at Challans, they saw nailed to a door something which resembled a great bat ; this was a republican soldier who for several hours had been nailed there, suffering terrible agonies and unable to die " (Michelet's *History of the Revolution*, Book XI. ch. v.).

which Michelet compares to the panic which takes hold of men in a plague-stricken town, seized on the poorest among the population of Nantes, and the commissioner of the Convention, Carrier, whose temperament made him only too susceptible to such a panic, let them have their own way.

The people began by drowning the arrested priests, and ended by exterminating over 2000 men, women and children, incarcerated in the prisons of Nantes.

As to La Vendée, the Committee of Public Welfare (*Comité de Salut public*), without going deeper into the scrutiny of the causes which might have brought a whole province to revolt, and contenting themselves wth a hackneyed explanation of the " fanaticism of these peasant brutes," without endeavouring to understand the peasants or to rouse their interest in the Republic, conceived the abominable idea of exterminating the Vendeans and depopulating the department.

Sixteen entrenched camps were made, and twelve " infernal columns " were sent into the country to ravage it, to burn the peasants' huts, and to exterminate the inhabitants. It is easy to conceive what a harvest such a system gave! La Vendée became a bleeding wound of the Republic, and one which bled for two years. An immense region was lost entirely to the Republic, and La Vendée was the cause of the most painful divisions between the Montagnards themselves.

The risings in Provence and at Lyons had an equally fatal influence on the progress of the Revolution. Lyons was at that time a city of industries for the wealthy. Great numbers of artist-workmen worked in their homes at weaving fine silks and also at making gold and silver embroideries.

Now, the whole of this industry came to a standstill during the Revolution, and the population of Lyons became divided into two hostile camps. The master-workers, the small employers, and the leisured classes, higher and middle, were against the Revolution; whereas the ordinary workmen, those who worked for the small employers, or who found work in the industries connected with weaving, were wholeheartedly for the Revolution, and were already kindling the

THE RISINGS IN SOUTHERN FRANCE 459

beacons of socialism, which were to flare up during the nineteenth century. They willingly followed Chalier, a mystical communist and a friend of Marat, a man of much influence in the municipal council, the democratic aspirations of which resembled those of the Paris Commune. An active communist propaganda was also being carried on by L'Ange—a precursor of Fourier and his friends.

The middle classes, for their part, listened willingly to the nobles, and above all to the priests. The local clergy had always had a strong influence at Lyons, and they were reinforced now by a number of priests who had returned from their emigration to Savoy.

Taking advantage of all this, the middle-class Girondins behind whom were the royalists, had invaded the greater, part of the sections of Lyons, and were preparing a rising against the Jacobins.

The conflict broke out on May 29, 1793. There was fighting in the streets, and the middle classes got the upper hand. Chalier was arrested, and after being tamely defended at Paris by Robespierre and Marat, he was executed on July 16, after which the repression on the part of the middle classes and the royalists became terrible. The wealthy people of Lyons who had been Girondins up till then, encouraged by the revolts in the West, now openly made common cause with the royalist *émigrés*. They armed 20,000 men and fortified the town against the Convention.

At Marseilles the Girondins had intended to support Lyons. Here they had risen after May 31. Inspired by the Girondin Rebecqui, who had come here from Paris, the sections of Marseilles, the greater part of which were also in the hands of the Girondins, had raised an army of 10,000 men, which was going to march towards Lyons, and thence to Paris, to combat the Montagnards there. Other southern towns, Toulon, Nîmes, Montauban, joined the movement, which soon acquired, as might have been expected, an openly royalist character. However, the Marseilles army was soon routed by the troops of the Republic, commanded by Carteaux, who entered Marseilles on August 25.

Rebecqui drowned himself; but a party of the defeated royalists took refuge at Toulon, and this big military port was given up to the English. The English admiral took possession of the town, proclaimed Louis XVII. King of France, and had an army of 8000 Spaniards brought over by sea, to hold Toulon and its forts.

Meanwhile an army of 20,000 Piedmontese had entered France to rescue the royalists at Lyons, and they were now coming down towards Lyons, by way of the valleys of the Sallenche, the Tarentaise, and the Maurienne.

The attempts of Dubois-Crancé, a member of the Convention, to treat with Lyons, failed, because the movement had fallen by now into the hands of the royalists, and they would not listen to any offers. The commandant Précy, who had fought among the Swiss on August 10, was one of the faithful adherents of Louis XVI. Many of the *émigrés* had also come to Lyons to fight against the Republic, and the leaders of the royalist party were contriving with an agent of the royal house, Imbert-Colomiès, as to the means of connecting the Lyons insurrection with the operations of the Piedmontese army. Finally, the Council of Public Welfare for Lyons had for secretary General Reubiès, one of the "Pères de l'Oratoire," while the commandant Précy was in touch with the agents of the royal house, and was asking them for reinforcements of Piedmontese and Austrian soldiers.

In these circumstances nothing remained to do but to besiege Lyons in due form; and the siege was begun on August 8 by seasoned troops, detached for this purpose from the army of the Alps, and with cannon brought from Besancon and Grenoble. The workmen of Lyons had no desire for this counter-revolutionary war, but they did not feel themselves strong enough to revolt. They escaped from the besieged town, and came to join the army of the *sans-culottes*, who, although they lacked bread themselves, still shared it with 20,000 of these fugitives.

In the meantime, Kellerman had succeeded, in September, in driving back the Piedmontese, and Couthon and Maignet, two commissioners of the Convention, who had raised an army of peasants in the Auvergne, armed with scythes, pickaxes and pitchforks, arrived on October 2 to reinforce Kellerman. Seven days later the armies of the Convention at last took possession of Lyons.

It is sad to record that the repression by the Republicans was terrible. Couthon apparently favoured a policy of pacification, but the terrorists got the upper hand in the Convention. It was proposed to apply to Lyons the method which the Girondin Isnard had proposed to apply to Paris—that is to say, to destroy Lyons, so that nothing but ruins should remain, which would bear the following inscription: "*Lyons made war against liberty—Lyons exists no more.*" But this absurd plan was not accepted, and the Convention decided that the houses of the wealthy were to be destroyed, and that those of the poor should be left intact. The execution of this plan was placed in the hands of Collot d'Herbois, and if he did not carry it out, this was because its realisation was practically impossible; a city is not so easily destroyed as that. But by the tremendous number of executions and the prisoners being shot "in a heap," Collot managed to surpass even the Marseilles counter-revolutionists, and did, of course, immense harm to the Revolution.

The Girondins had counted greatly on the rising in Bordeaux, and this merchant town rose indeed, but the insurrection did not last. The people were not to be carried away; they did not believe in the accusations of "royalism and Orléanism" hurled against the "Mountain," and when the Girondist members who had escaped from Paris arrived at Bordeaux, they were forced to go into hiding in this city, which in their dreams was to have been the centre of their rising. Bordeaux soon gave itself up to the commissioners of the Convention.

As to Toulon, which had been long since worked upon by English agents, and where the naval officers were all royalists, it surrendered completely to an English squadron. The few republicans of this city were imprisoned, and as the English, without losing time, had armed the forts and built new ones, a regular siege was necessary to retake the town. This was only done in the December following.

CHAPTER LV

THE WAR—THE INVASION BEATEN BACK

Reorganisation of republican army—Horrors of war—Girondist generals replaced—The war—Difficulties of republicans—Condition of France—Hopes of allies—Their successes and delays—Republicans gain courage—Victory over Austrians—Surrender of Lyons—Toulon recaptured—Vengeance of republicans

AFTER the betrayal of Dumouriez and the arrest of the Girondist leaders, the Republic had to accomplish anew the entire work of reorganising its army on a democratic basis, and it was necessary to re-elect all the superior officers, in order to replace the Girondist and royalist generals by Jacobin republicans.

The conditions under which this great change was accomplished, were so hard that only the grim energy of a nation in revolution was capable of bringing it to the desired end in face of the invasion, the internal disorders, and the underground work of conspiracies which was being carried on all over France by the rich, for the purpose of starving the *sans-culotte* armies, and handing them over to the enemy. For nearly everywhere the administration of the departments and the districts had remained in the hands of the Feuillants and the Girondins, and they did their best to prevent ammunition and provisions from reaching the armies.

It needed all the genius of the Revolution and all the youthful audacity of a people awakened from its long sleep, all the faith of the revolutionists in a future of equality, to persist in the Titanic struggle which the *sans-culottes* had to carry on against the invaders and the traitors. But how many times the exhausted nation was on the point of giving in!

If to-day war can ruin and devastate whole provinces, we

THE WAR—THE INVASION BEATEN BACK

can guess what were the ravages of war a hundred and twenty years ago, amongst a population much poorer then. In the departments adjoining the seat of the war, the harvests were cut, mostly unripe, as forage. Most of the horses and other beasts of burden were pressed into service, either on the spot or for one of the fourteen armies of the Republic. The soldiers, in common with the peasants and the poor of the towns, lacked bread. But they lacked everything else as well. In Brittany and in Alsace, the commissioners of the Convention were driven to ask the citizens of certain towns, such as Brest or Strasbourg, to take off their boots and shoes and to send them to the soldiers. All the leather that could be obtained was requisitioned, as also were all the cobblers, to make footwear, but this was still insufficient, and wooden shoes had to be distributed to the soldiers. Worse than this, it became imperative to form committees to requisition from private houses "kitchen utensils, cauldrons, frying-pans, saucepans, buckets, and other articles of brass and pewter, and also any pieces of broken brass or lead." This was done in the districts of Strasbourg.

At Strasbourg, the commissioners of the Convention and the municipal council were obliged to ask the inhabitants for clothes, stockings, boots, shirts, bed-clothes, and old linen, with which to clothe the ragged volunteers. They had also to beg for beds in private houses, where the wounded might be nursed.

But all this was insufficient, and from time to time the commissioners of the Convention found it necessary to raise heavy revolutionary impositions, which they levied chiefly from the rich. This was especially the case in Alsace, where the great landowners would not give up their feudal rights, in defence of which Austria had taken up arms. In the South, at Narbonne, one of the members of the Convention was driven to demand the services of all the men and women of the town to unload the barges and load the carts which were to transport provisions for the army.*

* It is important to note that in spite of all that reactionary historians may say about the Terror, we see by the archives in this case

Little by little, however, the army was reorganised. The Girondist generals were eliminated; younger men replaced them. Everywhere appeared new men, for whom war had never been a trade, and who came into the army with all the ardour of the citizens of a nation deeply stirred by revolution. They soon created, too, new tactics, which were later attributed to Napoleon Bonaparte, the tactics of rapid marches, and of great masses crushing the enemy in its separate armies, before they had time to effect a junction.

Miserably clothed, often in rags and barefoot, very often hungry, but inspired with the holy flame of the Revolution of Equality, the volunteers of 1793 were victorious where defeat had seemed certain.

At the same time the commissioners of the Convention displayed fierce energy in finding the means to feed, clothe and move the armies. For the greater part, equality was their principle. No doubt there were amongst these commissioners some black sheep, like Cambacerès, a future dignitary under Napoleon. There were a few fools who surrounded themselves with display, such as became later the undoing of Bonaparte, and there were also a few not above bribes. But all these were very rare exceptions. Nearly all the two hundred commissioners honestly shared the hardships and the dangers with the soldiers.

These efforts brought success, and after a very dark period of reverses in August and September, the republican armies gained the upper hand. The tide of the invasion was stemmed in the beginning of the autumn.

In June, after the treachery of Dumouriez, the army of the North was completely disorganised—its generals being ready to fight each other—and it had against it four armies representing a total of 118,000 men, English, Austrians, Hanoverians and Dutch. Forced also to abandon its entrenched camp, and to take refuge behind the Sarpe, leaving the fortresses of

that the *sans-culottes* and a few young citizens were the only ones who answered this call on their patriotism, and that " not one silk-stocking, whether man or woman," turned up on the quay of the canal. After which the commissioner limited himself to imposing on the rich " a patriotic gift " for the benefit of the poor.

THE WAR—THE INVASION BEATEN BACK 465

Valenciennes and Condé in the hands of the enemy, this army had left open the road to Paris.

The two armies which defended the Moselle and the Rhine barely numbered 60,000 fighting men, and they had against them 83,000 Prussians and Austrians, together with a cavalry corps of about 6000 *émigrés*. Custine, whose devotion to the Republic was very doubtful, abandoned the positions taken in 1792, and allowed the Germans to occupy the fortress of Mayence, on the Rhine.

In Savoy and near Nice, where 40,000 Piedmontese, supported by 8000 Austrians, had to be headed off, there was only the Alpine Army and the Army of the Maritime Alps, both completely deprived of all means of transport, in consequence of the royalist risings in the Forèz, at Lyons, and in Provence.

In the Pyrenees, 23,000 Spaniards entered France, and were opposed by only 10,000 men, who had no cannon and no provisions. With the help of the *émigrés*, this Spanish army took several forts, and threatened the whole of the Roussillon region.

As to England, she inaugurated in 1793 the policy which was followed later on during the Napoleonic wars. Without coming forward too much herself, she preferred to subsidise the allied Powers and to profit by the weakness of France in taking her colonies and ruining her maritime commerce. In June 1793, the English Government declared the blockade of all the French ports, and English vessels, contrary to the custom of international law of those days, began to seize all neutral vessels bringing provisions to France. At the same time England helped the *émigrés*, smuggled in arms and bundles of proclamations to stir up Brittany and La Vendée, and prepared to seize the ports of Saint-Malo, Brest, Nantes, Bordeaux and Toulon.

The interior affairs of France were no better. Brittany was in a ferment through the intrigues of the *émigrés* and the agents of England. In La Vendée, a hundred thousand peasants, influenced to fanaticism, were in open revolt. In the great commercial cities, such as Nantes, Bordeaux and Marseilles, the middle classes were infuriated because their business affairs had been brought to a standstill. Lyons and Provence were in the full swing of an insurrection. In the Forèz the clergy and the *émigrés* were busy sowing discord; and in Paris itself all who had grown rich since 1789, impatient to see the end of the Revolution, were preparing a fierce attack upon it.

Under these conditions, the allies felt so certain of being able soon to re-establish royalty, and of placing Louis XVII. on the throne, that they considered it a question of but a few weeks. Fersen, the confidant of Marie-Antoinette, was already discussing with his friends of whom should the Council of Regency be composed, whilst the scheme for placing the Count d'Artois at the head of the malcontents in Brittany was agreed upon between England, Spain and Russia.*

If the allies had only marched straight against Paris, they would certainly have reduced the Revolution to serious straits. But either from the fear of a new September 2, or because they preferred the possession of the fortresses won from France to a siege of Paris, they chose to stop in their advance to take Valenciennes and Mayence.

However, Mayence fought, and surrendered only on July 22. The fortress of Condé had surrendered a few days earlier, after holding out for four months; and on July 26 Valenciennes, after an assault of the allies, capitulated in its turn amidst the applause of the *bourgeoisie* who, during the siege, had been in close communication with the Duke of York. Austria took possession of these two fortified towns.

In the North, the road to Paris was open since August 10, 1793, and the allies had more than 300,000 men in all between Ostend and Bâle. What was it then that once again held back the allies and prevented them from marching against Paris, to deliver Marie-Antoinette and the Dauphin? Was it really the desire only to take first those fortresses which would remain theirs, whatever might happen in France? Was it the fear of the fierce resistance which Republican France might offer? Or was it—and this seems to us the most

* Letter to Baron de Stedinck, written on April 26, from St. Petersburg.

THE WAR—THE INVASION BEATEN BACK

probable—considerations of a diplomatic nature ? As the documents which might throw light on the French diplomacy of this period are not yet published, we are reduced to conjectures. We know, however, that during the summer and autumn of 1793, the Committee for Public Welfare was treating with Austria about the liberation of Marie-Antoinette, the Dauphin and his sister, and their aunt, Madame Elisabeth. And we know also that Danton carried on secret negotiations with the English Whigs till 1794, to stop the war with England. From day to day people were expecting in England to see Fox, the leader of the Whigs, overthrow Pitt, the Tory leader, and step into power; and twice—at the end of January 1794, during the discussion of the answer to the speech from the throne, and on March 16, 1794—it was hoped that the English Parliament would declare itself against a war with France.*

At any rate, the fact remains, that after their first successes, the allies did not march against Paris, but began to besiege the fortresses. The Duke of York began the siege of Dunkirk and the Duke of Coburg besieged Le Quesnoy.

This gave a moment of respite to the Republic, and allowed Bouchotte, the Minister of War who had succeeded Pache, time to reorganise the army which had been reinforced by a levy of 600,000 men, and to find republican officers for it. Carnot, at the same time, in the Committee of Public Welfare, tried to make the generals act together with more accord, while the commissioners of the Convention carried the flame of the Revolution to the armies.

Thus passed the month of August, during which the reverses on the frontier and in La Vendée revived the hopes of the royalists and filled with despair a good many of the republicans. However, from the first days of September 1793, the armies of the Republic, spurred by public opinion, took the offensive in the North, on the Rhine, and in the Pyrenees. This new move was crowned with success in the North, where the Duke of York, furiously attacked by the French at Hondschoote,

* G. Avenel, *Lundis révolutionnaires*, p. 245. Avenel even attributes the fall of Danton to the failure of this diplomacy, which had always been opposed by Robespierre and Barère.

was forced to abandon the siege of Dunkirk; but elsewhere the results were for the time indecisive.

The Committee of Public Welfare at once took advantage of the first military successes to demand and obtain from the Convention almost dictatorial powers—to be retained "as long as peace is not concluded." But what helped most in arresting the advance of the invasion was that, seeing everywhere new leaders, openly republican, rise from the ranks and reach the highest positions in a few days, and seeing also the commissioners of the Convention marching themselves sword in hand at the heads of attacking columns, the soldiers were inspired with fresh courage and achieved wonders of valour.

On October 15 and 16, in spite of very heavy losses, they gained at Wattignies the first great victory over the Austrians. This victory was won, we may say literally, by the bayonet, for the village of Wattignies changed hands as often as eight times during the battle. As a result of this defeat, the Austrians raised the siege of Maubeuge, and the victory won at Wattignies had the same influence on the course of events as the victory of Valmy had had in 1792.

Lyons, as we saw, was forced to surrender in October, and in December Toulon was retaken from the English, after an assault which was begun on the 8th Frimaire of the Year II. (November 28, 1793), and lasted till the 26th Frimaire (December 16), when the "English redoubt" and the forts of Eguillette and of Balagnier were taken by assault. The English squadron set fire to the French vessels harboured in the port, as well as to the arsenals, the docks and the powder magazines and, leaving the roadstead, abandoned the royalists, who had delivered Toulon to them, to the vengeance of the republicans.

Unhappily this vengeance was terrible, and left deep traces of hatred in many hearts. One hundred and fifty persons, mostly naval officers, were shot in batches, after which came the detailed vengeance of the revolutionary courts.

In Alsace and on the Rhine, where the armies of the Republic had to fight the Prussians and the Austrians, they were forced

THE WAR—THE INVASION BEATEN BACK

from the beginning of the year's campaign to abandon their line of defence round Wissemburg. This opened the road to Strasbourg, where the *bourgeoisie* was calling on the Austrians and pressing them to come and take possession of the town in the name of Louis XVII. But the Austrians had no desire to strengthen royalty in France, and this gave time to Hoche and Pichegrue, aided by Saint-Just and Le Bas, who represented the Convention, to reorganise the army and take the offensive themselves.

However, winter was already approaching, and the campaign of 1793 ended, without there being any new successes to record on either side. The Austrian, Prussian, Hessian, Dutch, Piedmontese and Spanish armies remained on the French frontiers, but the energy of the allies was spent. Prussia even wished to retire from the alliance; and England had to bind herself at The Hague (April 28, 1794) to pay the Prussian King a sum of 7,500,000 francs, and to send in a yearly contribution of 1,250,000 francs, before Prussia would agree to maintain an army of 62,400 men to fight France.

The following spring, therefore, the war was to recommence; but the Republic could now struggle under far more favourable conditions than in 1792 and 1793. Thanks to the enthusiasm with which it had inspired the poorest classes, the Revolution was freeing itself little by little from those external enemies who had sought to crush it. But at what a price when we consider the sacrifices this entailed—the internal convulsions, the alienation of liberty, which in the end killed this very same Revolution and delivered France up to the despotism of a military "saviour."

CHAPTER LVI

THE CONSTITUTION—THE REVOLUTIONARY MOVEMENT

Committee formed to frame new Constitution—Plans of Girondins—Struggle between Girondins and Montagnards—Girondins try to strengthen power of *Directoires*—Girondist scheme rejected—Constitution of Montagnards—It is accepted by Convention—Dictatorship of Committees of Public Welfare and Public Safety

It has been necessary to narrate at some length the counter-revolutionary risings in France and the varied events of the frontier wars before returning to the legislative activity of the Convention and the events which subsequently unfolded themselves in Paris. Without some knowledge of the former, the latter would be incomprehensible. The truth is, the war dominated everything; it was absorbing the best forces of the nation, and was paralysing every effort to render the Revolution more advantageous to the masses of the people.

The chief aim with which the Convention had been convoked was the elaboration of a new republican Constitution. The monarchist Constitution of 1791, that had divided the country into two classes, one of which was deprived of all political rights, could not be maintained any longer: in fact, it had ceased to exist. Consequently, as soon as the Convention assembled (September 21, 1792), it set to work on a new Constitution, and on October 11 a special committee was elected for this purpose. It was composed, as might have been expected, chiefly of Girondins (Sieyès, the Englishman, Thomas Paine, Brissot, Pétion, Vergniaud, Gensonné, Condorcet, Barère, and Danton). The Girondin Condorect, a celebrated mathematician and philosopher, who as far back as 1774 had

THE CONSTITUTION

been working with Turgot at political and social reforms, and who was one of the first, after the flight of Varennes, to declare himself a republican, was the chief author of the constitutional scheme placed by the committee before the Convention, and of a Declaration of the Rights of Man and Citizen which accompanied this scheme.

It is obvious that in a legislative body of deputies, the first question to arise, as soon as there was any mention of a new Constitution, was the question as to which of the two parties struggling for power would profit by this new law. The Girondins wished to turn it into a tool which would enable them to put a brake on the Revolution, so that it should not go further than it went on August 10; to shatter the power of the revolutionary Commune of Paris, and of the revolutionary communes in the country, and to crush the Montagnards. And the Montagnards, who did not consider the work of the Revolution accomplished, naturally had to prevent the Girondins from turning the Constitution into an instrument for opposing the further development of the Revolution.

Even before the condemnation of Louis XVI. the Girondins had pressed the Convention to accept their Constitution, in the hope of saving the King. And later on, in March and in April 1793, when they saw communistic efforts budding amongst the people and directed against the rich, they pressed the Convention all the more to accept Condorcet's scheme; whilst the Montagnards did all they could to postpone the final discussion, until they had succeeded in paralysing the Girondins and the royalists. It must also be said that the Constitution, which had roused so much enthusiasm in 1789, had already lost much of its interest for the revolutionists, especially since the decrees of August 10 and 11 had abolished the distinction between passive and active citizens. If the Girondins did attach any importance to it, it was " to restore order," to diminish the influence that the revolutionists exercised in the provinces through the medium of the municipal councils, and, in Paris, through the Commune.

The municipal law of December 1789 had given the municipalities considerable power—the greater because the provincial representatives of the central power had been abolished. And we have seen how the sections of Paris, which acted as independent municipalities, succeeded in conquering extensive administrative rights, when it became necessary to repel invasion, to enlist volunteers, to provision the armies, and to keep a watch on the royalist plots.

In the municipalities and the sections, the Revolution of 1793 had found its best support, and it is easy to understand that the Montagnards did their utmost to retain this powerful instrument of their influence.*

But this is also why the Girondins, in their scheme for a Constitution, which the rising of May 31 alone prevented them from imposing on France, had taken care to destroy the communes, to abolish their independence, and to strengthen the power of the *Directoires* of the departments and the districts, which were the organs of the landlord and the middle classes. To achieve this, the Girondins demanded the abolition of the large communes and the communal municipalities, and the creation of a third and new series of bureaucratic bodies—the *directoires du canton*, which they described as "cantonal municipalities."

If this scheme had been adopted, the communes, which represented not mere wheels of the administration, but bodies possessing lands, buildings, schools, &c., in common, would have disappeared. Their place would have been taken by purely administrative bodies. As the village municipalities very often took the side of the peasants, and the municipalities of the large towns, as also their sections, often stood for the interests of the poor citizen, the Girondins intended to hand over the local government to the middle classes, and they hoped to achieve their end by creating the cantonal municipalities, which would depend much more upon the eminently bureaucratic and

* When, on March 7, 1793, the Defence Committee, alarmed at the desperate situation of France in face of the invasion, called the ministers and the Commune of Paris to consult together, Marat, in summing up what was already being done, told them " that in such a crisis, the *sovereignty of the people was not indivisible*: that each commune was sovereign in its own territory, and that the people had the right to take such steps as were necessary for their welfare " (*Mémoires de Thibaudeau;* Michelet, Book X. ch. i.).

reactionary Directories of the departments than upon the poorer classes of the people.

On this extremely important point the Girondist and the Montagnard schemes of Constitution were thus entirely opposed to each other.

Another alteration, and a very important one, which the Girondins endeavoured to introduce and the Constitutional Committee rejected, was the introduction of two houses of parliament, or, in default of this, the division of the legislative body into two sections, as was done later in the Constitution of the Year III. (1795), after the reaction of Thermidor had set in and the Girondins had returned to power.

It is true that the Girondist scheme for a Constitution seemed in some ways very democratic, in the sense that it left to the primary assemblies of electors, not only the choice of their representatives, but also the choice of functionaries of the Treasury, of the Courts of Justice, including the High Court, and also the ministers,* and that it introduced the *referendum*, or direct legislation. But the nomination of ministers by the electoral bodies (admitting that it would be possible in practice) would only have succeeded in creating two rival authorities, the Chamber and the Ministry, both nominees of the universal suffrage, whilst the *referendum* was hemmed in by most complicated rules that made it illusory.†

And finally this scheme of a constitution, and the Declaration of Rights which had to precede it, established, in a more concrete way than the Constitution of 1791, the rights of the citizens—*i.e.*, his liberty of religious belief and worship, freedom of the

* Each Primary Assembly had to nominate seven ministers, and the administration of the department would form with these names a list of thirteen candidates for each Ministry. Then, the Primary Assemblies, convoked for a second time, would elect the ministers from these lists.

† An excellent summary of the two Constitutions, the Girondin and the Montagnard, and of all concerning them, will be found in Aulard's *Histoire Politique*, 2nd part, ch. iv. I follow this summary for the facts, but the responsibility for the appreciation is mine. Thus I disagree, as may be seen, with M. Aulard in his appreciation of the Girondin project regarding the " cantonal municipalities." Far from tending to " seriously organise the commune," this project tended, in my opinion, to destroy it, so as to replace it by a body bureaucratic rather than popular.

press, and all other ways of spreading his thoughts. As to the communist tendencies which were coming to the front among the masses, the Declaration of Rights limited itself to acknowledging that " aid to the poor is a sacred debt owed to them by society, and that society owes education to all its members equally."

One can well understand the apprehension that this project raised when it was laid before the Convention on February 15, 1793. The Convention, influenced by the Montagnards, sought to withhold its decision as long as possible, and asked that other projects should be sent in. It also nominated a new commission—the Commission of the Six—to analyse the various projects which might be submitted, and on April 17, the report having been made by the new commission, the discussion began in the Convention. Robespierre pronounced a long discourse which was, as has been remarked by M. Aulard,[*] certainly slightly tinged with what we call " socialism." " We should," said Robespierre, " declare that the right of property is limited, as all others, by the obligation of respecting the rights of the others ; that the right of property must not be injurious either to the security or to the liberty, or to the existence, or to the property of other men ; and that every trade which violates this principle is essentially illicit and immoral." He demanded also that the right to work be proclaimed, though in a very modest form. " Society," he said, "is bound to provide for the subsistence of all its members, either in procuring work for them, or in guaranteeing the means of existence to those who are unable to work."

But where the ideas of the Montagnards differed entirely from those of the Girondins was when it came to discussing, on May 22, the abolition of communal municipalities, and the creation of cantonal councils of administration. The Montagnards were decidedly against this abolition, the more so as the Girondins wished to destroy also the unity of Paris and of its Commune, and demanded that each town of more than 50,000 inhabitants should be divided into several municipalities. On this point the Convention took up the opinions of the Monta-

[*] *Histoire Politique,* p. 291.

gnards and rejected the Girondist project of cantonal municipalities.

The Constitution of the Montagnards—and herein lies its distinctive feature—maintained the municipalities intact. "Could we," said Hérault de Séchelles, "give up the municipalities, however great their number? To abolish them would have been an ingratitude towards the Revolution and a crime against liberty. Nay, it would be to *annihilate completely popular government.*" "No," he added, after having uttered some sentimental phrases, "no, the idea of suppressing municipalities can only have been born in the heads of the aristocrats, whence it transferred itself into those of the Moderates." *

For the nomination of representatives the Montagnard Constitution introduced direct manhood suffrage by ballot in each district (50,000 inhabitants). For the nomination of the administrators of the departments and those of the districts, the suffrage was to be in two degrees, and in three degrees for the nomination of the twenty-four members of the Executive Council (the Ministry) which was to be renewed each year. The Legislative Assembly was to be elected for one year only, and its acts were to be divided into two categories: the decrees, to be carried into effect at once; and the laws, for which the people could demand the *referendum*.

However, in the Montagnard Constitution, as well as in the Girondin scheme, the right of *referendum* was illusory. To begin with, nearly everything could be done by decrees, and this excluded the *referendum*. Then, to obtain the *referendum* it was necessary that "in half of the departments, plus one-tenth of the Primary Assemblies of each department, regularly constituted," an objection should be formulated against a new law, during the forty days after the promulgation of the proposed law.

Finally, the Constitution guaranteed to all Frenchmen "equality, liberty, safety, inviolability of property, the security

* It is interesting to notice that in Russia also, the enemies of the commune are at the present day partisans of the canton (*Vsessoslovnaya volost*), and that they oppose it to the village communes, whose lands they covet.

of the national debt, free worship, common education, public relief, unrestricted liberty of the press, the right of petitioning, the right of forming popular societies, and enjoyment of all the rights of man."

As to the social laws which the people awaited from the Constitution, Hérault de Séchelles promised these later. Order first: they would see later on what they could do for the people; upon this the majority of the Girondins and Montagnards were in perfect agreement.

On June 24, 1793, this Constitution was accepted by the Convention, and was immediately submitted to the Primary Assemblies, which pronounced themselves with great unanimity and even enthusiasm in favour of it. The Republic was then composed of 4944 cantons, and when the votes of 4420 cantons were known, it appeared that the Constitution had been accepted by 1,801,918 voices against 11,610.

On August 10, the Constitution was proclaimed in Paris with much pomp, and in the departments it became an effective means of paralysing Girondist risings. These no longer had a pretext, since the calumnies which the Girondins spread everywhere about the Montagnards wishing to re-establish royalty, with a Duke of Orléans on the throne, had fallen through. On the other hand, the Constitution of June 24, 1793, was so well received by the majority of the democrats that it subsequently became the creed of democracy for nearly a century.

The Convention which had been convoked for the special purpose of giving a republican Constitution to France had now only to lay down its powers. But it was obvious that under the circumstances, invaders holding part of the country, and the war having to be carried on with an energy far surpassing the means at the disposal of the Republic, and in the face of risings in La Vendée, at Lyons, in Provence, and elsewhere, the Constitution could not be applied. It was impossible for the Convention to disperse, and to leave the Republic to run the risks of new elections.

Robespierre developed this idea before the Jacobin Club on the very morrow of the promulgation of the Constitution, and the numerous delegates who had come to Paris to assist at this

THE REVOLUTIONARY MOVEMENT 477

promulgation held the same opinion. On August 28, the Committee of Public Welfare expressed the same opinion before the Convention, which, after hesitating for six weeks, finally decreed, when the Republican Government had obtained its first successes at Lyons—that is to say, on October 10, 1793—that *the government of France should remain " revolutionary " till the conclusion of peace.*

This meant to maintain, in fact, if not by right, the dictatorship of the Committees of Public Welfare and General Safety, which had just been strengthened in September by the law of suspects and the law dealing with revolutionary committees.

CHAPTER LVII

THE EXHAUSTION OF THE REVOLUTIONARY SPIRIT

Revolutionary leaders afraid to move—Commune of Paris—Montagnards—Inactivity of Convention—Commissioners of Convention work only to strengthen Montagnard *régime*

THE movement of May 31, 1793, had made it possible for the Revolution to complete the work which proved to be its principal achievement: the final abolition, without redemption, of feudal rights, and the abolition of royal despotism. But, this done, the Revolution was coming to a standstill. The mass of the people were willing to go further; but those whom the tide of Revolution had carried to the head of the movement dared not advance. They did not wish the Revolution to lay hands on the wealth of the middle classes, as it had on that of the nobility and clergy, and they strained all their power to moderate, to arrest, and eventually to crush the movement that was beginning in this direction. Even the more advanced and the more sincere among them, as they gradually neared power, developed the greatest consideration for the middle classes, although they hated them. They stifled their own aspirations towards equality, they even considered what the English middle classes might say of them. In their turn they became "statesmen," and laboured to build up a strong centralised government, whose component parts should obey them blindly. They succeeded in erecting this power over the corpses of those whom they had found too advanced, but they realised, when they themselves mounted the scaffold, that in destroying the advanced party, they had killed the Revolution.

After having sanctioned by law what the peasants had demanded during the last four years, and had already achieved here and there, the Convention was incapable of undertaking anything more of importance. Except in matters of national defence and education, its work henceforth was sterile. The legislators sanctioned, it is true, the formation of revolutionary committees and decided to pay those of the poor *sans-culottes* who gave their time to serve on the sections and the committees; but these measures, apparently so democratic, were not measures of revolutionary demolition or creation. They were but means for organising the power of the State.

It was outside the Convention and the Jacobin Club—in the Commune of Paris, in certain sections of the capital and of the provinces, and in the Cordeliers' Club, that a few men were to be found who understood that to secure the victories already gained, it was necessary to march further still, and they endeavoured therefore to formulate the aspirations of a social character which were beginning to appear among the masses.

They made a bold attempt at organising France as an aggregate of forty thousand communes, regularly corresponding amongst themselves, and representing so many centres of extreme democracy,* which should work to establish the real equality—*l'égalité de fait*, as used then to be said, the " equalisation of incomes." They sought to develop the germs of municipal communism which the law of maximum had recognised; they advocated the nationalisation of the trade in prime commodities as the best means for combating the monopolists and the speculators. And they attempted, finally, to prevent the formation of large fortunes, and to distribute those already amassed. But, once they had reached power, the revolutionists from the middle classes took advantage of the force that had

* The municipal function was " the last term of the Revolution," as Mignet has so well said (*Histoire de la Révolution française*, 19th edition, vol. ii. p. 31). " Opposed in its aims to the Committee of Public Welfare, it desired, *in lieu of the ordinary dictatorship, the most extreme local democracy,* and in the place of creeds the consecration of the grossest disbelief. Anarchy in politics and atheism in religious affairs, such were the distinctive features of this party and the means by which they counted on establishing its power." It must, however, be remarked that only a part of the " anarchists " followed Hébert in his anti-religious campaign, while many left him on realising the force of religious spirit in the villages.

been constituted in the hands of the two Committees of Public Welfare and General Safety, whose authority grew with the dangers of the war, and they crushed those whom they named the *Enragés*—only to succumb in their turn, in the month of Thermidor, to the attacks of the counter-revolutionary middle classes.

So long as the Montagnards had to struggle against the Girondins, they sought the support of the popular revolutionists. In March and in April 1793, they appeared ready to go far in company with the proletarians. But having entered into power, most of them thought only of establishing a "midway" party, taking a stand between the *Enragés* and the counter-revolutionists, and they treated as enemies those who stood for the aspirations of the people towards equality. They crushed them by frustrating all their attempts at organising themselves in the sections and the communes.

The fact is that the Montagnards, with one or two exceptions, had not even the comprehension of popular needs indispensable in constituting a party of democratic revolution. They did not understand the proletarian, with his troubles, his often starving family, and his still vague and formulated aspirations after equality. It was rather the individual in the abstract, the unity of a democratic society that interested them.

With the exception of a few advanced Montagnards, when a commissioner of the Convention arrived in a provincial town, the questions of employment and prosperity within the Republic and the equal enjoyment of available commodities by all interested him but little. Having been sent to organise resistance to the invasion and to rouse the patriotic feeling, he acted as a democratic official for whom the people were but the tools which were to help him to carry out the plans of the Government.

If he presented himself at the local Popular Society, it was because, the municipality being "worm-eaten with aristocracy," the Popular Society would help him to "purify the municipality," with a view to organising the national defence and arresting the traitors

If he imposed taxes on the rich, often very heavy ones, it was because the rich, "worm-eaten with commercialism," were in sympathy with the Feuillants or the Federalists and were helping the enemy. It was also because by taxing them, means were provided to feed and clothe the armies.

If he proclaimed equality in some town, if he forbade the baking of white bread and recommended the inhabitants to use black or bean-bread only, he did so in order that the soldiers might be fed. And when some agent of the Committee of Public Welfare organised a popular *fête*, and wrote afterwards to Robespierre that he had united a certain number of young women and young patriots in wedlock, it was yet another stroke of military patriotism. It is remarkable, therefore, when we now read the letters of the deputy commissioners of the Convention, addressed to the Convention or the Committee of Public Welfare, that we find nothing in them about the great questions which were then so interesting to the peasants and the working men.* That military matters and those of provisioning the armies should predominate in this correspondence is quite natural. But the time was one of revolution, and the commissioners must have continually come across subjects of vital importance to the Revolution—the more so as they spoke in their letters of public feeling, of the reception given to the Montagnard Convention and its Constitution, of the difficulties of finding provisions for the armies, and of the scarcity of available means of subsistence. And yet the great economic questions, which were of such immense importance for the poor, seem to have interested only three or four of the commissioners.

The Convention had at last abolished the feudal rights, and had ordered the burning of the title-deeds—an operation which was carried out with much ill-will; and it had authorised the village communities to recover possession of those lands which had been taken from them, under various pretexts, during the past two hundred years. It is evident that to carry out these measures, and to carry them out at once, would have been the

* These letters may be found in the *Recueil des Actes du Comité de Salut Public*, published by T. Aulard. Paris, 1889 and following years; also in Legros, *La Révolution telle qu'elle est : Correspondance du Comité de Salut Public avec ses généraux*, 2 vols., Paris, 1837.

way to rouse the enthusiasm of the masses for the Revolution. But in the letters of the commissioners scarcely anything can be found on this subject.* The younger Jullien, in his most interesting letters, addressed to the Committee of Public Welfare and to his friend and patron, Robespierre, only once mentions that he has had the feudal title-deeds burnt.† In the same way only a passing mention of this subject is made once by Collot d'Herbois.‡

Even when the commissioners speak of the supplies of food —and they have often to do so—they do not go to the root of the question. There is but one letter of Jeanbon Saint-André, dated March 26, 1793, which is an exception; but even that letter is anterior to the movement of May 31 : later on, he too turned against the advanced revolutionists.§

Writing from the Lot-et-Garonne, one of the departments most in sympathy with the Revolution, Jeanbon begged his colleagues in the committee not to blind themselves to the dangers of the situation : "It is such," said he, "that if our courage does not bring forth one of those extraordinary events which rouse public opinion in France and give it new strength, there is no more hope. The disturbances in La Vendée and in the neighbouring departments are no doubt such as to cause anxiety, but they are really dangerous only because the sacred enthusiasm for liberty is being stifled in every heart. Everywhere men are weary of the Revolution. The rich hate it, the poor lack bread . . ." and "all those who were until now termed 'moderates,' who made some sort of common cause

---

* The letters published in the collection of Aulard, or in that of Legros, are palpitating with interest in every way ; but I have sought in vain for traces of activity of the commissioners in this direction. Only Jeanbon Saint-André, Collot d'Herbois, Fouché, and Dubois Crancé sometimes touch on the great questions which so interested the peasants and the proletarians in the towns. It may be that there are other letters of commissioners which I do not know ; but what seems to me certain is that the greater part of the Commissioners took but little interest in these matters.

† *Une Mission en Vendée.*

‡ Aulard, *Recueil des Actes du Comité de Salut Public,* vol. v. p. 505.

§ This letter is signed by the two commissioners, Jeanbon and Lacoste, who had been sent to this department ; but it is in the writing of the former.

with the republicans, and who at least desired some kind of revolution, no longer wish for it now. . . . Let us say it openly, they desire a counter-revolution. Should a new Convention be summoned, the French people would either refuse to elect it, or they would elect one entirely opposed to the principles of liberty. Even the municipal councils are weak or corrupted." Such, at least, they were found to be in all the districts that these two representatives had visited.

Jeanbon thus demanded broad and rigorous measures. And at the end of his letter he again referred to this subject in a postscript. " The poor man," said he, " has no bread. Although grain is not lacking, it has been hoarded. It is imperative to help the poor to live, if you want them to help you to uphold the Revolution. . . . We think that a decree ordering *a general levy of all kinds of grain* would be very good, especially if a clause be added establishing public granaries, formed with the superfluous stock of private persons." Jeanbon Saint-André implored Barère to take the lead in these matters.*
But how was it possible to arouse interest in the Convention for such things ?

The strengthening of the Montagnard *régime* was what most of all interested the commissioners. However, like all statesmen who preceded, like all who will succeed them, it was not in the general well-being and happiness for the great mass of the people that they sought a foundation. It was in the weakening and, at need, in the extermination of the enemies of this *régime*. They soon welcomed the Terror, as a means of crushing the enemies of the democratic Republic ; but never do we see them welcoming broad measures of great economic change, not even those for which they had themselves voted under the pressure of circumstances.

* *Actes du Comité de Salut Public*, published by Aulard, vol. iii. pp. 533-534.

CHAPTER LVIII

THE COMMUNIST MOVEMENT

Egalité de fait—Socialistic problems—Proposition of Billaud-Varenne—Communalist movement—*Means of subsistence* and *land question*—Leading apostles of communism—Jacques Roux—Leclerc—Varlet—Boissel—Babeuf

In the *cahiers* of 1789, ideas were already to be found which, as Chassin has pointed out, would to-day be classed as socialistic. Rousseau, Helvetius, Mably, Diderot and others had already dealt with the inequalities of fortunes and the accumulation of superfluous wealth in the hands of the few, as the great obstacle to the establishment of democratic liberty. These ideas came once more to the front during the first hours of the Revolution.

Turgot, Sieyès and Condorcet asserted that the equality of political rights meant nothing *without real equality in fact* (*égalité de fait*)! This, said Condorcet, was the "final aim of social art, since inequality in riches, inequality of state, and inequality of education are the main cause of all evils."* And the same ideas found an echo in several *cahiers* of the electors in 1789, who demanded the right of all to the possession of the land, or "the equalisation of wealth."

It may even be said that the Parisian proletariat had already formed a conception of its class interests and had found men to express them well. The idea of separate classes, having opposing interests, is clearly stated in the *cahiers des pauvres* of the district of Saint-Etienne-du-Mont, by a certain Lambert,

---

* Already Cabet, in his Appendix to *Voyage en Icarie*, edition of 1842, had pointed out, with quotations in support, this characteristic of the eighteenth-century thinkers; of recent works see André Lichtenberger, *Le Socialisme et la Révolution française*, Paris, 1899.

"a friend of those who have nothing." Productive work, adequate salaries (the *living wage* of the modern English Socialists), the struggle against the *laisser faire* of the middle-class economists, and a plain distinction traced between the social question and the political one—all these are to be found in this *cahier des pauvres*.*

But it was chiefly after the taking of the Tuileries, and still more after the execution of the King—in February and in March 1793—that these ideas began to be openly propagated. It would even seem—so at least it is said by Baudot—that if the Girondins appeared as such passionate defenders of property, it was because they feared the influence which the propaganda of equality and communism was acquiring in Paris.†

A few Girondins, especially Rabaut de Saint-Etienne and Condorcet, fell under the influence of this movement. Condorcet, on his death-bed, was working out the scheme of a "mutuality" (*mutualité*), *i.e.*, of a mutual insurance league amongst all citizens, against eventualities which might throw the relatively well-off worker into conditions under which he would be forced to sell his work at no matter what price. As to Rabaut, he demanded that the great fortunes be taken from the rich, either by means of a progressive tax or by a law which would cause the natural flow of the rich man's superfluous wealth "into establishments of public utility."

* "There has never been and there will never be any but two really distinct classes of citizens, the property-owners and those who have no property—of whom the former have everything and the latter nothing," so it was said in the *cahier des pauvres*. "Of what use will a wise constitution be to a nation reduced by hunger to the state of skeletons?" queried the author of the *Quatre cris d'un patriote*. (Chassin, *Le Génie de la Révolution*, Paris, 1863, vol. i. pp. 287, 289.)

† We find in the *Notes historiques sur la Convention nationale, le Directoire, l'Empire et l'exil des votants*, by M. A. Baudot, edited by Mme. Edgar Quinet (Paris, 1893), a very interesting note where it is said that Ingrand's opinion about the system "of common property" (communism), developed by Buonarroti, "was brought forward some time before the events of June 20 ; and that these events owed their origin to this spirit of association" (pp. 10–11). Pétion is said to have warned a great number of deputies about it. "It seems," continues Baudot, "that the Girondins put so much acrimony and bitterness into their policy from fear of seeing the doctrine of the communists predominate." Later on certain members of the Convention took up these ideas, as is known, and joined the conspiracy of Babeuf.

"Great riches are a drawback to liberty," he wrote, repeating a saying very much in vogue at that time. Even Brissot at one time tried to come to some sort of agreement with this popular theory—which soon after he attacked with ferocity.*

A few Montagnards went further. Thus Billaud-Varenne, in a tract published in 1793, spoke openly against great wealth. He protested against Voltaire's idea that the worker should be spurred to work by hunger, and he demanded that it be declared that no citizen should henceforth be permitted to possess more than a fixed amount of land, and that no one be allowed to inherit more than from 20,000 to 25,000 livres.† He understood that the primal cause of social ills lay in the fact that there were men who existed "in a direct but not mutual dependency upon some other human being. For this is the first link in the chain of slavery." He derided small peasant proprietorship which some wished to introduce for the poor, "whose existence in such conditions would never be anything but precarious and miserable." A cry was making itself heard, he said later on (p. 129) : "*War to the châteaux, peace to the huts!* Let us add to this the consecration of this fundamental rule : Let there be no citizen who can dispense with employment, and let there be no citizen unable to learn a trade and practise it."

Billaud-Varenne's proposition concerning inheritances was taken up, as is known, by the International Working Men's

* The better to fight "the division of lands proposed by anarchists or the *Coblentzians*" (Robespierre afterwards took up this insinuation of Brissot's against the communists and made it his own), Brissot declared, in December 1792, that *the equality of the rights* of citizens would be a fiction if the laws did not abolish and prevent the too great real inequalities among the citizens. But such institutions, favourable to "equality," added Brissot, "must be introduced without commotion, without violence, without showing disrespect to the first of all social rights, the right of property."

† Speaking of property, he represented it in this interesting guise. "Property," said he, "is the pivot of civil associations. It is well known that, especially in a great empire, the balance of fortunes cannot be quite exact and immovable, and that the impulse of an immense commerce, aided by a vast industry and by riches produced by agriculture necessarily keep it continually oscillating ; but the balance should never fall on either side too decidedly." (*Les éléments de républicanisme*, Paris, 1793, p. 57. Pamphlets of the British Museum, vol. F. 1097.)

Association at its Congress at Bâle in 1869. But it must be said that Billaud-Varenne was one of the most advanced among the Montagnards. Some, as for instance, Lepelletier, limited themselves to asking what the International asked under the name of "integral education"—that is to say, the teaching of a handicraft to each young man; whilst others limited themselves to asking for "the revolutionary restitution of properties," or the limitation of the right of property.

It is, however, chiefly outside the Convention—amongst the people, in some sections, such as that of Gravilliers, and in the Cordeliers' Club—certainly not among the Jacobins—that one must look for the champions of the communalist and communist movements of 1793 and 1794. There was even an attempt at free organisation among those who were known at that time as the *Enragés*—that is to say, the extremists—those who aimed at a revolution that would tend towards equality. After August 10, 1792, there was founded—apparently at the suggestion of the federates who had come to Paris—a sort of league between the delegates of the forty-eight sections of Paris, the General Council of the Commune and the "United Defenders of the eighty-four departments." And when in February 1793 the movements against stock-jobbers began, of which we have already spoken,* the delegates of this league demanded from the Convention, on February 3, energetic measures against stock-jobbing. In their address can already be seen a germ of the idea which later on was the base of Proudhon's Mutualism and his Bank of the People: the idea that all profit resulting from exchange in the banks, if there be any profit, should return to the whole nation—not to separate individuals—since they are produced by *public confidence of all in all.*

Our knowledge about the different movements which were going on among the people of Paris and of the large towns in 1793 and 1794 still remains imperfect. It is only now that they are being studied. But what is indisputable is, that the communist movement represented in Jacques Roux, Varlet, Dolivier, Chalier, Leclerc, L'Ange (or Lange), Rose Lacombe,

* Chap. xliii.

Boissel, and some others, was of a depth which passed unperceived at first, but which Michelet had already surmised.*

It is obvious that communism in 1793 did not appear with that completeness of doctrine which is found with the French followers of Fourier and Saint-Simon, and especially with Considérant, or even Vidal. In 1793, communist ideas were not worked out in the quiet of a private study; they were born from the needs of the moment. This is why the social problem showed itself during the Great Revolution especially in the form of a question about the *means of subsistence*, and of a *land question*. But in this also lies what makes the *communism* of the Great Revolution superior to the *socialism* of 1848 and of its later forms. It went straight to the root in attacking the *distribution of produce*.

This communism certainly appears fragmentary to us, especially as stress was laid by its exponents upon its different separate aspects; and there always remained in it what we might call *partial* communism. It admitted *individual possession* side by side with *common property*, and while proclaiming the right of all to the entire sum of the fruits of production, it yet recognised an individual right to the " superfluous," by the side of the right of all to the products of " first and second necessity." Nevertheless the *three principal aspects* of communism are already to be found in the teachings of 1793: *Land* communism, *industrial* communism, and communism in *commerce* and in *credit*. And in this, the conception of 1793 was broader than the one of 1848. For, if each one of the agitators of 1793 usually laid more stress on one of these aspects than on the others, these three aspects do not exclude one another. On the contrary, being born from the same conception of equality, they complete each other. At the same time the agitators of the Great Revolution endeavoured to attain the practical carrying out of their idea by the action

---

* It is probable that besides the advocating of communism in the sections and Popular Societies, there were also, from August 10, 1792, attempts to constitute secret communist societies, which were extended afterwards, in 1795, by Buonarroti and Babeuf, and which, after the revolution of July 1830, gave birth to the secret societies of the Blanquists.

of local forces, by immediate practical realisation, while at the same time they tried to start some sort of a direct union of the 40,000 communes. In Sylvain Maréchal one finds even a vague aspiration towards what we describe now as anarchist communism—expressed, of course, with much caution, for one risked paying with one's head for the use of too frank language.

The idea of reaching communism by means of a conspiracy through a secret society which should grasp the reins of government—the idea of which Babeuf became the apostle—was formulated later on, in 1794 and 1795, when the Thermidor reaction had crushed the ascending movement of the Great Revolution. This was the result of a loss of force—not an effect of the growing power of the years from 1789 to 1793.

Of course there was plenty of declamatory effect in the preachings of the popular communists. It was a fashion of the times—one to which our modern orators also pay a tribute. But everything that is known about the communists of the Great Revolution tends to show them as men profoundly devoted to their ideas.

Jacques Roux had been a priest. He was extremely poor and lived with his sole companion, a dog, almost entirely on his income of two hundred livres (francs) in a gloomy house in the centre of Paris,* and preached communism in the workingmen's quarters. He was very popular in the Gravilliers section to which he belonged, and had great influence on the Cordeliers' Club—until the end of June 1793, when his influence was destroyed by the intervention of Robespierre. As to Chalier, we have already seen the power which he had in Lyons, and we know through Michelet that this mystic-communist was a remarkable man—even more a "friend of the people" than Marat. He was simply adored by his pupils. After his death, his friend Leclerc came to Paris and continued the propaganda of communism with Roux, Varlet, a young Parisian working man, and Rose Lacombe, a leader of the women revolutionists. About Varlet practically nothing is known, except that he was popular among the poor of Paris.

* Jaurès, *La Convention*, p. 1069 (notes of Bernard Lazare).

His pamphlet, *Déclaration solennelle des droits de l'homme dans l'état social*, published in 1793, was very moderate in tone.* But it must be remembered that with the decree of March 10, 1793, hanging over their heads, the revolutionists did not dare to say in print everything they thought.

The communists also had their theorists, such as Boissel, who published his *Catéchisme du genre humain* in the early days of the Revolution, and a second edition of the same work in 1791; the anonymous author of a work published also in 1791 and entitled *De la propriété, ou la cause du pauvre plaidée au tribunal de la Raison, de la Justice et de la Vérité;* and Pierre Dolivier, curé of Mauchamp, whose remarkable work, *Essai sur la justice primitive pour servir de principe générateur au seul ordre social qui peut assurer à l'homme tous ses droits et tous ses moyens de bonheur*, was published at the end of July 1793 by the citizens of the Commune of Anvers, a district of Etampes.†

There was also L'Ange (or Lange), who was, as Michelet had already pointed out, a real precursor of Fourier. Babeuf was also in Paris in 1793. He was employed under the protection of Sylvain Maréchal in the administration of the means of subsistence, and made a secret communist propaganda. Forced to stay in hiding, since he had been prosecuted for a supposed

---

* He limited himself to asking in this declaration that the right of possession of land be limited ; that the enormous inequality of fortunes be abolished " by fair means," so that the poor could protect themselves from oppression by the rich, and that " the possessions amassed at the cost of the public, by theft, stock-jobbing, monopoly, &c., should become national property, the instant society obtained conclusive and reliable proofs of peculation." (Pamphlets in the British Museum, F. 499.) In another pamphlet, *Vœux formés par des français libres*, &c., he also asked for severe laws against monopolists (same collection, F. 65.)

† In his *Discours sur les moyens de sauver la France et la liberté*, delivered at the time of the elections for the Convention (this pamphlet may be found at the Bibliothèque Nationale), Jacques Roux maintained that a prolonged dictatorship means the death of liberty, and he wished (pp. 42 and 43) that it should be made obligatory for the great landowners to be allowed to sell their harvest only in those markets indicated to them in their respective districts ; " establish," he said, " in all the cities and large market towns public stores where the price of goods will be established by public auction (*au concours*)." Michelet, who had already mentioned this *Discours* (Book XV. ch. vi.), added that this doctrine of Roux was very popular in the Gravilliers, Arcis, and other sections of the Centre de Paris.

forgery—wrongly prosecuted by the middle classes, as has been proved by Deville, who has found the original minutes of the trial*—he was compelled to be very discreet.†

Later on communism was connected with Babeuf's conspiracy. But Babeuf, so far as one may judge from his writings and letters, was only an opportunist of the communism of 1793. His conceptions, as well as the means of action which he advocated, belittled the idea. While it was well understood by many that a movement having a communist tendency would be the only means to assure the victories of the democracy, Babeuf, as one of his recent apologists—quite correctly—put it, sought to shuffle communism into democracy (*glisser le communisme dans le démocratie*). While it had become evident that democracy would lose its victories if the people did not enter the arena with its demands and ideals, Babeuf wanted *democracy first*, and then to introduce communism into it, little by little.‡

Altogether Babeuf's conception of communism was so narrow, so unreal, that he thought it possible to reach communism by the action of a few individuals who were to get the Govern-

* *Thermidor et Directoire*, 1794-1799 (*Histoire socialiste*, vol. v. pp. 14 and following).

† In his *Catéchisme*, Boissel already expounded the ideas which became current among socialists towards 1848. Thus, to the question " Which are the principal institutions of this mercenary, homicidal, anti-social State ? " he answers, " Property, marriage, and religions are what men have invented, established, and consecrated to legitimate their impostures." In specifying the things over which men have extended their property rights, he said : " It is those things of which they have thought it necessary to become possessed, or to make others believe that they were possessed, such as lands, women, even men, the sea, the rivers, and mountains, the sky, the nether regions, the gods themselves, out of whom they have always made and still make capital." He was not tender either to the laws, of which he said : " They are the obligations which the strong, the more shrewd, the more cunning have imposed on the weaker, in order to maintain their disastrous institutions, or even to prevent the bad effects of these institutions, so far as it was possible." His definitions of authority and justice might be accepted by modern anarchists. See *Le Catéchisme du genre humain pour l'établissement essentiel et indispensable du véritable ordre moral et de l'éducation sociale des hommes*. (Paris 1789). p. 132. Pamphlets of the British Museum, F. 513 (3).)

‡ Thus, for instance, the people, armed with a democratic Constitution, would veto all the laws, until the maintenance of all citizens should be assured by law !

ment into their hands by means of the conspiracy of a secret society. He went so far as to be ready to put his faith in one single person, provided this person had a will strong enough *to introduce communism, and thus save the world!* A sad illusion, which paved the way for Bonaparte and, continuing to be cherished by a great number of socialists during the whole of the nineteenth century, gave us Cæsarism—the faith in a Napoleon or a Disraeli—the faith in a saviour which still persists even to this day.

CHAPTER LIX

SCHEMES FOR THE SOCIALISATION OF LAND, INDUSTRIES, MEANS OF SUBSISTENCE AND EXCHANGE

Communist movement and land—Economic importance of land—Agrarian proposals—View of Dolivier—Industrial demands—Proposals of L'Ange—Problem of means of subsistence—Question of exchange of produce—Summary of situation—Evils of repression

THE dominating idea of the communist movement of 1793 was, that the land should be considered as the common inheritance of the whole nation, that every citizen should have a right to the land, and that the means of existence should be guaranteed to each, so that no one could be forced to sell his or her work under the threat of starvation. "Actual equality" (*l'égalité de fait*), which had been much spoken of during the eighteenth century, was now interpreted as the affirmation of an equal right of all to the land; and the great transfer of lands which was going on through the sale of the national estates awakened a hope of a practical realisation of this idea.

It must be borne in mind that at this time, when the great industries were only just beginning to grow, the land was the chief instrument of exploitation. By the land the landowner held the peasants in his hands, and the impossibility of owning a scrap of land compelled the peasants to emigrate to the towns, where they became the defenceless prey of the factory-owners and the stock-jobbers.

Under such circumstances the minds of the communists necessarily turned to what was described then as the "agrarian law"—that is to say, to the limitation of property in land to a certain maximum of area, and towards the recognition of the right of every inhabitant to the land. The land-grabbing that was then practised by speculators during the sales of the national estates could but strengthen this idea; and while some demanded that each citizen desiring to cultivate land should have the right to receive his share of the national property, or at least to buy a part of it under easy conditions of payment—others, who saw further ahead, demanded that all the land should again be made communal property and that every holder of land should get only the right of temporary possession of that land which he himself cultivated, and only for so long as he cultivated it.

Thus Babeuf, fearing perhaps to compromise himself too much, demanded the equal division of communal lands. But he also wanted the "inalienability" of the land, which meant the retention of the rights of the commune, or of the nation, over the land, *i.e.*, *possession* by the individuals, not *ownership*.

On the other hand, at the Convention, during the debate on the law on the partition of communal lands, Julien Souhait opposed the final partition proposed by the Agricultural Committee, and he certainly had on his side the millions of poor peasants. He demanded that the division of communal lands, in equal portions, among all, should be only temporary, and that they might be *redivided after certain periods of time.* The *use* only would be conceded in this case to separate individuals, as it is in the Russian *Mir*.

Dolivier, a curé of Mauchamp, following a similar line of thought, expressed, in his *Essai sur la justice primitive*, "two immutable principles: the first, that the land belongs to all in general and to no one in particular; and the second, that each has the exclusive right to the produce of his labour." But as the land question dominated all others at this time, he preferred to dwell especially on the first of these two propositions.

"The land," he said, "taken as a whole, must be considered as the great common-land of nature "—the common property of all; "each individual must have the right of sharing in the great *common-land (au grand communal)*. One generation has no right to make laws for the next, or to dispose of its sovereign rights; how much stronger, then, the reason for not disposing of its patrimony!" And further: "Nations alone, and by sub-division the communes, are the real owners of their land."*

In fact, Dolivier recognised a right of property, transmissible by inheritance, in the case of movable property only. As to the land, no one should be allowed to possess any part of the common property, except what he with his family could cultivate—and then only as a temporary possession. This, of course, would not prevent common cultivation being done by the commune, side by side with farms cultivated individually. But Dolivier, who knew village life well, disliked the farmers as much as the big landowners. He demanded "the complete subdivision of the big farms"; "the utmost division of land among all those citizens who have none, or who have not enough of it. This is the only adequate measure which can put life into our villages, and bring comfort to all the families now groaning in misery, through a lack of means for rendering their work remunerative.... The land," he added, "will be better cultivated, domestic resources will be more numerous, and the markets consequently more abundantly supplied; we shall get rid of the most abominable aristocracy, that of the farmers." He foresaw that greater agricultural well-being would be attained in this way, and that there would never again be any need of regulating the prices of the means of subsistence by laws, which "is necessary under the present circumstances, but nevertheless is always inconvenient."

The socialisation of industries also found champions, especially in the Lyons region. The Lyons workers demanded that wages should be regulated by the commune, and that the wages should be such as to guarantee subsistence. It was the "living wage" of modern English socialists. Besides, they demanded the nationalisation of certain industries, such as mining. The

* As this work of Dolivier is not in the British Museum I quote from Jaurès. His other work, *Le vœu national, ou système politique propre à organiser la nation dans toutes ses parties* (Paris, 1790), is only interesting because of the idea of organising the nation from the bottom upwards.—Pamphlets of the British Museum, F. 514 (4).

proposition was also put forward that the communes should seize upon the industrial enterprises abandoned by the counter-revolutionists, and work them on their own account. On the whole the idea of the commune becoming a producer of all sorts of commodities was very popular in 1793. The utilisation of the large tracts of uncultivated land in the parks of the rich, for communal market gardening, was a widespread idea in Paris, and Chaumette advocated it.

It is evident that much less interest was taken then in industry than in agriculture. Nevertheless, Cusset, a merchant whom Lyons had elected member of the Convention, already spoke of the nationalisation of industries, and L'Ange elaborated a project of a sort of " phalanstery," where industry would be combined with agriculture. Since 1790 L'Ange had carried on an earnest communist propaganda at Lyons. Thus, in a pamphlet, dated 1790, he put forward the following ideas: " The Revolution," he wrote, " was going to be a salutary change; but then it was spoiled by a change of ideas, by means of the most abominable abuse of riches. The sovereign (that is, the people) has been transformed." " Gold," he wrote further, " is useful and beneficial in laborious hands, but it becomes dangerous when it accumulates in the coffers of capitalists. ·Everywhere, sire, wherever your Majesty may look, you will see the land cultivated, but by us; it is we who till it, we who have been the first owners of the land, the first and the last effective possessors of it. The idle who call themselves landowners can but collect the *surplus of our subsistence*. This proves, at least, our rights to co-proprietorship. But if, then, we are co-proprietors, and *the sole cause of any income, the right of limiting our consumption, and of depriving us of the surplus, is the right of a plunderer*," which is, to my mind, a very concrete conception of the " surplus value."*

* *Plaintes et représentations d'un citoyen décrété passif, aux citoyens décrétés actifs*, by M. L'Ange (Lyons), 1790, p. 15 (Bibliothèque Nationale of Paris). For the more or less socialistic ideas of the *Cercle Social* founded by the Abbé Fauchet, and whose organ was *La Bouche de fer* see, vide A. Lichtenberger, *Le Socialisme et la Révolution française*, ch. iii. p. 69.

SCHEMES FOR SOCIALISATION

Reasoning always from facts—*i.e.*, from the crisis in the means of livelihood through which France was passing—he proposed a system of subscription of all the would-be consumers, entitling them to buy at fixed prices the whole of the crop—all this to be reached by means of free association, gradually becoming universal. He also wanted to see common stores, whereto all the cultivators could carry their produce for sale. This was, as we see, a system which avoided in the commerce of commodities both the individualist monopoly and the obligatory State system of the Revolution. It was the precursor of the present system of co-operative creameries united to sell the produce of a whole province, as may be seen in Canada, or of a whole nation, as is the case in Denmark.

On the whole, it was the problem of the means of subsistence that was the preoccupation of the communists of 1793, and led them to compel the Convention to pass the law of *maximum*, and also to formulate the great principle of the *socialisation of the exchange of produce—the municipalisation of trade*.

In fact, the question of the trade in cereals was foremost all over France. "Full freedom in the grain trade is incompatible with the existence of our Republic," said the electors of Seine-et-Oise before the Convention in November 1792. "This trade is carried on by a minority with a view to its own enrichment, and this minority is always interested in bringing about artificial rises in price, which invariably make the consumer suffer. All partial measures against this speculation are dangerous and impotent," these electors said; "it is half-way measures that will ruin us." All the trade in grain, *the entire provisioning must be carried on by the Republic*, which will establish "a fair proportion between the price of bread and the price of a day's labour." The sale of the national estates having given rise to abominable speculations on the part of those who bought these lands, the electors of Seine-et-Oise demanded the limitation of the size of the farms and the nationalisation of trade.

"Ordain," they said, "that no one shall be allowed to undertake to farm more than 120 arpents of 22 feet to the perch;*

---
* About 120 acres.

that no landowner be allowed to cultivate more than one such farm, and that he will be obliged to lease out any others he may possess." And they added: " Place, moreover, the duty of providing the necessary food-stuffs for each part of the Republic in the hands of a central administration chosen by the people, and you will see that the abundance of grain and the fair proportion between its price and the day's wage will restore peace, happiness and life to all citizens."

It is evident that these were not ideas from the brain of a Turgot or a Necker; they were born of life itself.

It is interesting to note that these ideas were accepted both by the Committee of Agriculture and that of Commerce, and were developed in their report on the means of subsistence laid before the Convention.* In fact, they were applied, at the instance of the people, in several departments of the Berry and the Orléanais. In the department of Eure-et-Loir, on December 3, 1792, the commissioners of the Convention were nearly killed by the people, who said : " The middle classes have had enough, it is now the turn of the poor workers."

Later on, similar laws were violently advocated by Beffroy (Aisne), and the Convention, as we saw already when referring to the law of " maximum,"† attempted to socialise on an immense scale all trade in objects of prime and secondary necessity, for the whole of France, by means of national stores, and by establishing in every department what would be found to be " fair " prices for all commodities.

We thus see, budding during the Revolution, the idea that *commerce is a social function;* that it must be socialised, as well as the land and the industries—an idea which was to be elaborated later on by Fourier, Robert Owen, Proudhon, and the communists of the 'forties.

We perceive even more. It is clear to us that Jacques Roux, Varlet, Dolivier, L'Ange, and thousands of town and country folk, agriculturists and artisans, understood, from a practical

---

* " Report and project of a decree on subsistences," presented by M. Fabre, deputy of the department of the Hérault.
† Chap. lii.

SCHEMES FOR SOCIALISATION

point of view, the problem of the means of subsistence infinitely better than the Convention. They understood that taxation alone, without the socialisation of the land, the industries and the commerce of the nation would remain a dead letter, even if it were backed up by a legion of repressive laws and by the revolutionary tribunal.

It was the system of selling the national estates adopted by the Constituent Assembly, the Legislative Assembly and the Convention, that had created those rich farmers whom Dolivier considered, and quite rightly, as the worst form of aristocracy. The Convention did not begin to notice this until 1794. But then, the only thing they were able to do was to arrest the farmers in hundreds and to send them to the guillotine as monopolists (*accapareurs*). However, all these Draconian laws against monopoly (such as the law of July 26, 1793, which prescribed the searching of all lofts, cellars, and barns belonging to farmers) resulted only in spreading in the villages hatred against the towns, and against Paris in particular.

The revolutionary tribunal and the guillotine could not make up for the lack of a constructive communist theory.

CHAPTER LX

THE END OF THE COMMUNIST MOVEMENT

Montagnards and communists—Attitude of Hébert—Of Billaud-Varenne—Obstacles to communism—Assemblies and land—Communal land given to well-to-do peasants—Jacques Roux and Robespierre—Roux prosecuted—Reply to communism of Committee of Public Welfare—Resolutions passed by communists—Convention defends middle class and suppresses communism

PREVIOUS to May 31, when the Montagnards saw the Revolution brought to a standstill by the opposition of the Girondins, they sought the support of the communists, and of the *Enragés* in general. In those days, Robespierre, in the proposed Declaration of Rights which he read before the Convention on April 21, 1793, expressed himself in favour of a limitation of the rights of property, and Jeanbon Saint-André, Collot d'Herbois, Billaud-Varenne, and several others tried to make terms with the communists. If Brissot, in his savage attacks on the Montagnards, described all of them as "anarchists" and "destroyers of property," it was only because at that time the Montagnards had not yet tried to separate themselves definitely from the *Enragés* and the communists.

However, immediately after the disturbances in February 1793, the Convention assumed a threatening attitude towards the communists. Acting on a report by Barère, in which he already represented the communist agitation as the work of the clergy and the *émigrés*, the Convention, notwithstanding the opposition of Marat, enthusiastically voted, on March 18, 1793, " the penalty of death for whomsoever should propose *an agrarian law*, or any subversion whatsoever of landed property, whether communal or individual."

Still, they were forced to conciliate the *Enragés*, since they needed the support of the people of Paris against the Girondins, and in the most active sections of Paris the *Enragés* were very popular. But once the Girondins had been overthrown, the Montagnards turned against those who wished for "the Revolution in deeds, after it had been accomplished in thought," and crushed them in their turn.

It is much to be regretted that there was no one among the educated men of the time who could formulate the communist ideas in a complete and comprehensive form, and make himself heard. Marat might have done so, had he been allowed to live; but he had been assassinated on July 13. As to Hébert, he was too easy-going a man to take upon himself a task of this nature: he belonged too much to the society of the gay middle classes of Holbach's school ever to become a champion of the anarchist communism which was springing up among the masses. He could adopt the language of the *sans-culottes*, as the Girondins had adopted the red woollen cap of the poor, and their familiar "thee" and "thou" in speech, but, like them, Hébert was too little in sympathy with the people to understand and to express the popular aspirations. In fact, he allied himself with the "Mountain" to crush Jacques Roux and the *Enragés* together.

Billaud-Varenne seemed to understand, better than the other Montagnards, the need of profound changes in a communistic direction. He understood at one time that a social revolution ought to have been going abreast with the political revolution. But he, too, had not the courage to enter the ranks for this cause. He took a place in the Government and ended by doing as all the other Montagnards did, when they said: "*The Republic first, social measures will come later.*" But there they got stranded, and there the Republic was stranded as well.

The fact is, that the Revolution, by its first measures, had roused too many interests and too much cupidity to make it possible for communism to develop. The communist ideas about landed property were running counter to all the widespread interests of the middle classes, who had bought national estates, or were wildly speculating in them.

The legislators of the Constituent and the Legislative Assemblies, as we have already mentioned, had seen in these sales a means of enriching the middle classes at the cost of the clergy and the nobility. As to the masses of the people, they did not think much about them. Ready money being badly needed in the Exchequer, the national estates were sold recklessly, *avec fureur*, as Avenel says, in 1790 and 1791, to the middle class, or to the rich peasants—even to English and Dutch companies, which bought with an eye to speculation. And when the purchasers, who paid only 20 or even only 12 per cent. of the whole price at the moment of the purchase, had to pay the next instalment, they did all they could to avoid paying anything more, and very often they succeeded.

However, as the peasants who had been unable to obtain any of these lands were complaining bitterly, the Legislative Assembly, in August 1790, and later on, by the decree of June 11, 1793,* the communal lands—the only hope for the poorer peasant —were flung by the Convention to the better-off peasants as their prey.† The Convention promised also that the confiscated land of the *émigrés* should be divided into lots of one to four acres, to be sold to the poor for a perpetual rent which was to be paid in money, and could be redeemed at any time. It was even decreed, towards the end of 1792, that national lands to the amount of a thousand million livres worth, should be reserved for the *sans-culotte* volunteers who had enlisted in the armies, and be sold to them under favourable conditions. But nothing of the kind was done. This decree remained a dead letter, just as hundreds of other decrees of those times.

And when Jacques Roux spoke before the Convention, on June 25, 1793—less than four weeks after the rising of May 31 —denouncing stock-jobbing and demanding laws against the speculators, his speech was received with angry howls, and

* *See* chap. xlviii.
† Most historians have described this measure as a favourable one to the peasants. In reality, it meant depriving the poorest of the sole inheritance which was left them. This is why the measure met with so much opposition when it came to its application.

Roux himself was hooted out of the Convention.* Besides, as he attacked the "Mountain" in his speeches, and enjoyed a great influence in his own section, Les Gravilliers, as well as in the Cordeliers' Club, Robespierre, who never went near this Club, visited it on the night of June 30, after the riots of the 25th and 27th directed against the soap merchants, in company with Hébert, Collot d'Herbois, and several others, as a delegation from the Jacobin Club, and they got Roux and his friend Varlet struck off the list of the Cordeliers.

From that day Robespierre never ceased slandering Jacques Roux. As this Cordelier-communist severely criticised the Revolution for having done nothing so far for the people, and would say occasionally in his criticisms—just as the socialists of our own day often do—that the people suffered more under the Republic than under monarchy, Robespierre, whenever he spoke of Roux, never failed to describe him as a "base priest" who had sold himself to the foreigners, a "scoundrel" who "endeavoured to excite baneful disturbances to injure the Republic."

From June 1793, Jacques Roux might have considered himself doomed. He was first accused of being the instigator of

---

* "It is the rich," said Jacques Roux, "who have reaped for the last four years the advantages of the Revolutions; it is the merchant aristocracy, more terrible than the noble aristocracy, which oppresses us, and we do not see any limit to their extortions, for the price of goods is growing to an alarming extent. It is time that the death-struggle between the selfish and the hard-working classes should come to an end. . . . Are the possessions of knaves to be held more sacred than human life? *The necessities of life must be at the disposition of administrative bodies, just as the armed forces are at their disposition.*" Roux reproached the Convention with not having confiscated the fortunes acquired since the Revolution by the bankers and monopolists, and he said that the Convention having decreed "a forced loan of a thousand million livres to be levied upon the rich, *the capitalist and the merchant will the next day raise this sum from the* sans-culottes, *thanks to the monopolies and the powers of extortion they will retain if the monopolies of commerce and forestalling are not destroyed.*" He very clearly saw the danger of such conditions for the Revolution, when he said: "The stock-jobbers get possession of the factories, of the seaports, of every branch of commerce, of all produce of the land, and they cause the friends of justice to die of hunger, thirst and exposure, or else force them into the arms of despotism." (I quote from the text of Roux' speech, found by Bernard Lazare, and communicated to Jaurès.)

the riots against the soap merchants. Later on, in August, when he was publishing with Leclerc a paper, *L'Ombre de Marat*, Marat's widow was persuaded to prosecute him for using this title; and finally he was accused of having embezzled a small cheque which he had received for the Cordeliers' Club, while it is quite certain, as Michelet has said, that "disinterestedness was the special characteristic of these fanatics," and that among all the well-known revolutionists, "Roux, Varlet, and Leclerc were distinguished as models of probity." Roux' section of the Gravilliers vainly demanded from the Commune the abandonment of these prosecutions, offering that its members should give securities for him. The women revolutionists did likewise—and their club was suppressed by the Commune. Finally, he was released, but the prosecution was not stopped.

Full of indignation at the persistent persecutions, Roux and his friends went on the evening of August 19 to the Gravilliers section to which they belonged, and deprived the president and the secretaries of their offices. Roux was nominated president. Upon this, Hébert denounced Roux before the Jacobin Club, on the 21st, and when the matter was brought before the Council of the Commune, Chaumette accused him of "an attempt against the sovereignty of the people," and spoke of capital punishment. Roux was prosecuted, but his section obtained from the Commune his release on August 25. The inquiry, however, was continued, and the charge of theft was brought forward; so that on January 14, 1794 (23rd Nivôse), Roux was sent before a common police court.

This court declared itself incompetent to pronounce upon such serious indictments as those brought against Roux—meaning the affair of the Gravilliers section—and ordered him to be sent before the revolutionary tribunal. Knowing what that meant, Roux stabbed himself in court thrice with a knife. The president of the court hastened to his assistance and displayed much friendliness towards him, even giving him the kiss of civic brotherhood, before he was removed to the Bicêtre prison. In the prison infirmary Roux "tried to exhaust his strength," as it was reported to the procurator of the Revolutionary Tribunal, Fouquier-Tinville, by opening his wounds; and finally he succeeded in stabbing himself once more, this time mortally, through the lung. The record of the post-mortem is dated "1st Ventôse," *i.e.*, February 19, 1794.*

The people of Paris, especially in the sections of the centre of the city, understood now that their hopes of "practical equality" were over. Gaillard, a friend of Chalier, who had been kept by the Girondins in prison, at Lyons, during the siege, and who had come to Paris after Lyons had been taken by the Montagnards, also killed himself three weeks later, when he learned that Leclerc had been arrested together with Chaumette and the Hébertists.

In reply to all these demands of communism, and seeing that the masses were abandoning the Revolution, as they found that little attention was paid to their demands, the Committee of Public Welfare issued on the 21st Ventôse (March 11, 1794), a circular, written in a pompous style and addressed to the commissioners of the Convention in the provinces. But the conclusions of both this high-flown circular and the famous speech pronounced two days later (23rd Ventôse) by Saint-Just, were very poor. The Convention offered nothing but charity—scanty charity—to be provided for the destitute by the State.

"A great blow was necessary to overthrow the aristocracy," so the circular ran. "The Convention has struck it. Virtuous poverty must recover the property which criminals had taken away from it. . . . It is necessary that terror and justice should strike in all directions at the same time. The Revolution is the work of the people. It is time the people should enjoy its fruits" . . . and so on. But in reality the Convention did nothing in this direction. The decree of the 13th Ventôse Year II. (February 3, 1794), of which Saint-Just spoke in high-flown terms, amounted to this: Each commune was to make a list of its destitute "patriots"—and later on the Committee of Public Welfare would make a report to the Convention about the means of giving them certain compensation out of the estates of the enemies of the Revolution. They would be given

* Jaurès, *Histoire socialiste, La Convention*, pp. 1698 and 1699.

full ownership of about one acre each.* As to the old people and the infirm, the Convention decided on the 22nd Floréal (May 11), to open for them a Book of National Charity, in which both the old and the infirm peasants were to be registered for a yearly allowance of 160 livres (francs), the old or infirm artisans for 120 livres, and the old mothers and widows for 80 and 60 livres respectively.

It is hardly needful to say that this promised acre of land looked like mockery to the peasants. Moreover, apart from a few localities, the decree was never applied. Those who had seized nothing for themselves got nothing.

It must be added, however, that some of the Commissioners of the Convention, namely, Albitte, Collot d'Herbois, and Fouché at Lyons, Jeanbon Saint-André at Brest and Toulon, Romme in the Charente, had shown in 1793 a certain tendency towards socialising various commodities. And when the Convention decreed, on the 16th Nivôse, Year II. (January 5, 1794), that in towns besieged, blockaded or surrounded by the enemy, all materials, goods, and means of subsistence of all sorts, must be shared in common"—" there was a tendency," as M. Aulard says, " to apply this law to towns which were neither besieged nor blockaded, nor surrounded." †

The Convention, or, to be more correct, its Committees of Public Welfare and Public Safety, certainly succeeded in suppressing in 1794 the communist manifestations. But the spirit of the revolution impelled the French nation towards such measures, and under the pressure of events a great work of levelling and an unmistakable display of the communist spirit took place, more or less, all over France, during the Year II. of the Republic.‡

Thus, on the 24th Brumaire, Year II. (November 14, 1793),

* One *arpent*—a measure the size of which varied in different parts of France from one acre to one acre and a quarter.
† *Histoire politique*, chap. viii. ii.
‡ " This is why," Aulard wrote, " one looks vainly for the appearance of socialist theories at this moment of severe repression. But the sum total of partial and empiric measures which are taken, of laws which are passed under the pressure of the moment, and of provisory institutions introduced by the revolutionary government, is bringing about a state of things which prepares men's minds, even though the voice

the representatives of the Convention at Lyons, Albitte, Collot d'Herbois and Fouché, passed a resolution, which even began to take effect, whereby all the infirm, the old, the orphans, and the destitute citizens had to be "lodged, clothed, and fed at the cost of the rich in their respective cantons." Moreover, "labour, as well as the implements needful in their trades, had to be provided for the citizens capable of work." The commodities placed at the disposal of the various citizens—wrote these commissioners in their circulars—must be in proportion to their labour, their diligence and the ardour they display in the service of the mother country. Many commissioners of the Convention passed similar resolutions. Thus Fouché levied heavy taxes on the rich to feed the poor. It is also certain—as M. Aulard says—that many commissioners had begun to practise collectivism, or, we should say, municipal communism.*

The idea that the State ought to take over the factories abandoned by their owners, and work them, was expressed more than once. Chaumette developed it in October 1793, when he demonstrated the bad effects of the law of the "maximum" upon certain industries; and Jeanbon Saint-André had taken into the hands of the Government a certain mine of Carhaix, in Brittany, in order to secure a living for the workers.

However, if certain of the representatives of the Convention in the provinces really took, in 1793 and 1794, equalitarian measures, and were inspired with the idea of "limitation of incomes," the Convention itself remained a defender of the interests of the middle classes, and there must be some truth in the remark of Buonarotti, who wrote in 1842, that the fear of the Convention, lest Robespierre and his group should begin taking measures that would favour the equalitarian instincts of the people, contributed to the downfall of this group on the 9th Thermidor.*

of the socialists is not heard, for a social revolution, and begins a partial accomplishment of it."

* *Observations sur Maximilien Robespierre*, in *La Fraternité, journal mensuel exposant la doctrine de la communauté*, No. 17, September 1842.

CHAPTER LXI

THE CONSTITUTION OF THE CENTRAL GOVERNMENT—REPRISALS

Committees of Public Welfare and Public Safety—Condition of Paris—Power of old *régime*—Middle classes in opposition to Revolution—Paper-money forbidden by Convention—Weakening of Commune—Convention and sections—" Law of suspects "—Jacobins obtain power—Robespierre and expelled Girondins—Report of Saint-Just—Central Government established—Military situation—Republican reverses—Massacres of Republicans—Attempts to rescue Marie-Antoinette—Her trial ordered, but postponed—Her execution—Condemnation of arrested Girondins—Others follow—Beginning of Terror

SINCE May 31 and the arrest of the principal Girondin members, the "Mountain" had patiently worked during the summer of 1793 at the constitution of a strong Government, concentrated in Paris and capable of grappling with the foreign invasion, the revolts in the provinces, and any popular risings that might occur in Paris itself under the guidance of the *Enragés* and the communists.

We have seen that in April the Convention had entrusted the central power to a Committee of Public Welfare, and after May 31 it continued to strengthen this committee with new Montagnard elements.* And when the application of the

* The Committee of Public Welfare which at first had been Dantonist, became after May 31 more and more Robespierrist. Saint-Just and Couthon had already become members on May 30; and Jeanbon Saint-André joined on June 12; Robespierre entered it on July 27. Carnot and Prieur (of the Côte-d'Or) were admitted on August 14, and Collot d'Herbois and Billaud-Varenne on September 6, after the rising of the 4th and 5th of that month. Three parties could be distinguished in this committee: the *terrorists*, Collot d'Herbois and Billaud-Varenne; the workers, Carnot for the war, Prieur for military engineering and armament, and Lindet for the provisioning of the army; and "the

CONSTITUTION OF THE GOVERNMENT

new Constitution was put off till the termination of the war, the two committees—of Public Welfare and of General Safety—continued to concentrate power in their hands, while pursuing a moderate policy—that of standing midway between the advanced parties, represented by the *Enragés* and the Commune of Paris, and the followers of Danton, behind whom stood the Girondins.

In this work of concentration of power the two committees were strongly seconded by the Jacobins, who were extending their sphere of action into the provinces and were closing up their ranks. From eight hundred in 1791, the number of societies affiliated to the Jacobin Club of Paris rose to eight thousand in 1793, and each one of these societies became a support of the republican middle classes; they were also nurseries whence the numerous officials of the new bureaucracy were drawn, and police centres which the Government used for discovering its enemies and for getting rid of them.

Besides, forty thousand revolutionary committees were formed in the towns and the village communes, as well as in the sections, and all these communities, which mostly stood, as Michelet had already noticed, under the leadership of educated middle-class men—very often officials of the old *régime*—were soon subordinated by the Convention to the Committee of General Safety, while the sections themselves, as also the Popular Societies, were as rapidly transformed into organs of the central government, so as to become mere branches of the republican hierarchy.

Meanwhile the state of Paris was far from reassuring. The energetic men, the best revolutionists, had enlisted in 1792 and 1793 in the army, and had gone to the frontiers or to La Vendée, while the royalists were beginning to lift their heads. Taking advantage of the slackened supervision of the sections, they returned in great numbers to Paris. In August, the

men of action," Robespierre, Saint-Just and Couthon. The Committee of Public Safety, which represented the State police, consisted chiefly of functionaries of the old *régime*. One is even tempted to ask oneself whether many of these men had not retained their former sympathies. The Public Prosecutor of the revolutionary tribunal, Fouquier-Tinville, was entirely subservient to the Committee of Public Safety, whose orders he came to receive every evening.

extravagant luxury of the old *régime* suddenly made its reappearance. The public gardens and the theatres were crowded with "muscadins".* In the theatres royalist plays were cheered vociferously, while republican plays were hissed. In one of the former, the Temple prison and the rescue of the Queen were represented, and it needed but little for the escape of Marie-Antoinette to become an accomplished fact.

The sections were overrun by Girondist and royalist counter-revolutionists. And when the young workmen and artisans, weary after their long day's work, assembled in the general meetings of the sections, the young men of the middle classes, armed with cudgels, came to these meetings, and carried the voting at their will.

Of course the sections would have withstood these incursions, as they had already done once before, by each helping the neighbouring sections, but the Jacobins regarded the power of the sections with jealousy, and made use of the first opportunity to paralyse them. That opportunity was not long in coming.

Bread still continued scarce and dear in Paris, and on September 4 crowds began to assemble round the Hôtel de Ville, with cries of "We want bread!"† These cries were becoming threatening, and it needed all the popularity and good-humour of Chaumette, the orator most loved by the poor of Paris, to soothe the crowd. Chaumette promised to provide bread, and to have the administrators charged with provisioning Paris arrested. By these promises he staved off a rising, and the next day the people only sent deputations to the Convention.

The Convention, however, neither knew nor wished to deal with the true causes of this movement. All it did was to threaten the counter-revolutionists with drastic measures, and to strengthen the central government. In fact, neither the Convention, nor the Committee of Public Welfare, nor

---

* A nickname given to extravagantly dressed dandies of the wealthier classes.

† It is possible, even probable, that royalists, too (like Lepître), worked in the sections to foment this movement. It was an old ruse of the reactionists. But to say that this movement was the work of reactionaries was as absurd and as jesuitical as to say, for instance, that the movements of 1789 were the work of the Duke of Orléans.

CONSTITUTION OF THE GOVERNMENT 511

even the Commnne—the existence of which, it must be said, was already threatened by the committee—showed any capacity for facing the situation. There was no one to express the communist ideas which were growing among the people, with the same vigour, the same daring and precision that Danton, Robespierre, Barère, and so many others had used in expressing the aspirations of the early days of the Revolution. The advocates of " strong government "—middle-class mediocrities, more or less democratic in their views—were steadily gaining the upper hand.

The truth is, that the old *régime* st ll retained an immense power, and this power had been augmented lately by the support it had found among precisely those on whom the Revolution had poured its gifts. To shatter this power, a new, popular and equalitarian revolution was necessary; but the greater number of the revolutionists of 1789-1792 wanted no such thing. The majority of the middle classes, who had held revolutionary views in 1789-1792, now considered that the Revolution was going too far. Would this Revolution be able to prevent the "anarchists" from "levelling wealth"? Would it not make the peasants too comfortable? so comfortable that they would refuse to work for the purchasers of the national lands? Where, then, should they find the labourers to get profits from their estates? For if the buyers had put millions into the Treasury to buy national lands, it was certainly with the intent of getting profits out of them, and what was to be done if there were no more unemployed proletarians in the villages?

The Court party and the aristocracy, threfore, had now as allies a whole class of men who had bought national lands, troops of the so-called "black gangs" (*les bandes noires*) who were speculating in the purchase and sale of the national estates, crowds of contractors speculating in the supplies for the army, and multitudes of stock-jobbers speculating in the paper-currency and in all the necessaries of life. All of them had made their fortunes, and they were in a hurry now to enjoy them unhindered—to put an end to the Revolution, on one condition only, that the properties they had bought and the fortunes they had amassed should not be taken from them. A newly created crowd of lower middle-class people backed them up in the villages. And all of them cared but little as to the kind of Government they were to have, *provided it was strong*, provided it could keep the *sans-culottes* in order and withstand England, Austria and Prussia, which otherwise, if victorious, might try to restore to their previous owners the properties taken by the Revolution from the clergy and the emigrant royalists.

Consequently, the Convention and the Committee of Public Welfare, seeing that their authority was endangered by the Commune and the sections, had every facility for taking advantage of the lack of cohesion in the movement of the first days of September, and for giving new powers to the central government.

The Convention decided, it is true, to stop the trade in paper-money, by forbidding it on pain of death, and a " revolutionary army " of 6000 men was organised, under the command of the Hébertist Ronsin, for the purpose of checking the counter-revolutionists and requisitioning in the villages victuals wherewith to feed Paris. But as this measure was not followed by any vital act which would have given the land to those who wished to cultivate it themselves, or would have helped them to cultivate it, the requisitions of the revolutionary army became another cause of hatred in the villages against Paris, and resulted only in increasing the difficulties of providing food-stuffs for the capital.

For the rest, the Convention did not go beyond uttering threats of a " Terror," and endowing the Government with fresh powers. Danton spoke of an " armed nation " and menaced the royalists. " Every day," he said, " some aristocrat, some scoundrel ought to pay with his head for his crimes." The Jacobin Club demanded the arraignment of the arrested Girondins. Hébert spoke of an " itinerant guillotine." The revolutionary tribunal was going to be rendered more efficacious, and searches in private houses were allowed to be made, even at night.

At the same time, while threatening the nation with a reign

of terror, measures were taken to weaken the Commune. As the revolutionary committees of the sections, which held powers of judicial police, including that of arrest, had been accused of various abuses of these powers, Chaumette succeeded in placing them under the surveillance of the Commune and in making them eliminate their less reliable members; but twelve days later, on September 17, 1793, the Convention, becoming jealous of the thus increased power of the Commune, took away this right from its rival, and the revolutionary committees were now placed under the direct supervision of the Committee of Public Safety—that sinister force of secret police which grew by the side of the Committee of Public Welfare, threatening soon to absorb it.

As to the sections, under the pretext that they were being invaded by counter-revolutionists, the Convention decided, on September 9, that the number of their general meetings should be reduced to two a week; and to gild the pill, two francs a meeting were allotted to those of the *sans-culottes* who attended these assemblies, and who lived only by the work of their hands—a measure which has often been put forward as very revolutionary, but which the sections seem to have judged differently. A few of these (the Contract social, the Halle-aux-blés, the Droits de l'homme, under the influence of Varlet) refused the indemnity and condemned the principle; whilst others, as Ernest Mellié has shown, only made very moderate use of this allowance.

On September 19, the Convention increased the arsenal of repressive laws by the terrible "law of suspects." This law made possible the arrest as suspects of all *ci-devants*—dispossessed nobles—of all those who might show themselves "partisans of tyranny or federalism," of all who "do not fulfil their civil duties"—whosoever, in fact, had not continually shown devotion to the Revolution. Louis Blanc and all the admirers of the State describe this law as a measure of "tremendous policy" (*formidable politique*), whereas in reality it simply revealed the incapacity of the Convention to continue in the direction that has been opened and traced by the Revolution. It also prepared the way for the terrible overcrowding of the prisons, which led later on to the drowning (*noyades*) of prisoners by Carrier in Nantes, to the wholesale shooting by Collot in Lyons, to the *fournées* (batches) of June and July 1794 in Paris, and more than anything else prepared the downfall of the Montagnard *régime*.

As a formidable government thus grew up in Paris, terrible struggles inevitably arose between the various political factions, to decide in whose hands this powerful weapon should be. On September 25, a free fight took place at the Convention between all the parties, the victory remaining with those who represented the party of the golden mean among the revolutionists —with the Jacobins and Robespierre their faithful representative. Under their influence, the revolutionary tribunal was constituted from their nominees.

Eight days later, on October 3, the new power asserted itself. On that day, Amar, member of the Committee of Public Safety, was forced to make, after much hesitation, his report about the Girondins who had been expelled on June 2 from the Convention, in which he demanded that they should be sent before the revolutionary tribunal ; and either from fear or from some other consideration, he now went a good deal further the other way, and demanded, besides the thirty-one men whom he accused, the prosecution also of seventy-three Girondist deputies who had protested in June against the violation of the national representation in the Convention, but had continued to sit. To every one's great astonishment Robespierre violently opposed this proposition. It was not the rank and file, said he, who should be punished ; it sufficed to punish their leaders. Supported as he was by both the Right and by the Jacobins, he carried his point with the Convention, and thus gained the aureole of a conciliator, capable of dominating both the Convention and the two committees.

A few days more and his friend Saint-Just read before the Convention a report, in which, after complaining of corruption, and of the tyranny of the new bureaucracy, he made allusions to the Commune of Paris—Chaumette and his party—and concluded with a demand that "the revolutionary government be maintained till peace be concluded."

CONSTITUTION OF THE GOVERNMENT

The Convention accepted his conclusions. The central government was thus definitively constituted.

Whilst these struggles were taking place in Paris, the military situation offered a most gloomy prospect. In August, an order for a levy had been issued, and Danton having again recovered his energy and his penetration of the people's mind, had the splendid inspiration of putting the entire work of enlistment into the hands, not of the revolutionary bureaucracy, but of the eight hundred confederates who had been sent to Paris by the primary electoral assemblies to signify their acceptance of the Constitution. This plan was adopted on August 25.

However, as one-half of France had no desire for war, the levy progressed but slowly; both arms and ammunition were lacking.

There was a series of reverses at first, in August and September. Toulon was in the hands of the English, Marseilles and Provence were in revolt against the Convention; the siege of Lyons was still going on—it continued till October 8—and in La Vendée the situation was not improving. It was only on October 16 that the armies of the Republic gained their first victory, at Wattignies, and on the 18th that the Vendeans, beaten at Chollet, crossed the Loire to march northwards. But still the massacres of the republicans did not cease, and at Noirmoutiers, Charette shot all who surrendered to him.

It is easy to understand that at the sight of all this bloodshed, of the superhuman efforts made by France to liberate its territory from the invaders, and the incredible sufferings of the great mass of the French people, the cry of " Strike the enemies of the Revolution, high or low!" came from the hearts of the revolutionists. A nation cannot be oppressed beyond endurance without awakening revolt.

On October 3 the order was given to the revolutionary tribunal for the trial of Marie-Antoinette. Since February there had been continual talk of attempted rescues of the Queen. Several of these, as we know to-day, very nearly succeeded. The municipal officers whom the Commune put in charge of the Temple were continually being won over by partisans of the royal family. Foulon, Brunot, Moelle, Vincent, and Michonis were amongst them. Lepître, an ardent royalist, was in the service of the Commune and attracted attention in the sections by his advanced opinions. Another royalist, Bault, had obtained the post of warder in the Conciergerie prison, where the Queen was now kept. An attempted escape had fallen through in February; but another attempt, organised by Michonis and the Baron de Batz, came very near succeeding. After the discovery of this attempt (July 11) Marie-Antoinette was first separated from her son, who was placed in the keeping of the cobbler Simon. The Queen was then transferred (August 8) to the Conciergerie. But the attempts to rescue her continued, and a Knight of Saint-Louis, Rougeville, even succeeded in penetrating to her, whilst Bault, as warder, kept up relations with the outer world. Every plan for her liberation produced great excitement among the royalists, who threatened a *coup d'état* and the immediate massacre of the conventionals and all patriots in general.

It is very likely that the Convention would not have postponed the trial of Marie-Antoinette till October had it not hoped to stop the invasion of the allied monarchs as a condition of the Queen's liberation. It is known, indeed, that the Committee of Public Welfare had given (in July) instructions in this sense to its commissioners, Semonville and Maret, who were arrested in Italy by the governor of Milan; and it is also known that the negotiations for the liberation of the Crown Princess were carried on still later.

The efforts of Marie-Antoinette to call into France a German invasion, and her betrayals to facilitate the victory of the enemy, are too well known—now that her correspondence with Fersen has been published—for it to be worth while to refute the fables of her modern defenders who wish to prove that she was almost a saint. Public opinion was not mistaken in 1793, when it accused the daughter of Marie-Thérèse of being even more guilty than Louis XVI. She died on the scaffold on October 16.

The Girondins soon followed her. It will be remembered that when thirty-one of them were arrested on June 2, they had been allowed the liberty of moving about in Paris, under the

CONSTITUTION OF THE GOVERNMENT

condition of being escorted by a gendarme. There was so little idea of taking their lives that several well-known Montagnards had offered to go to the departments of the arrested Girondins, to be kept there as hostages. But most of the arrested Girondins had escaped from Paris and had gone to preach civil war in the provinces. Some roused Normandy and Brittany, others urged Bordeaux, Marseilles, and Provence to revolt, and everywhere they became the allies of royalists.

At this time, of the thirty-one arrested on June 2, only twelve remained in Paris. Ten more Girondins were added to these, and the case was brought into Court on the 3rd Brumaire (October 22). The Girondins defended themselves with courage, and as their speeches seemed likely to influence even the picked jury of the revolutionary tribunal, the Committee of Public Welfare hurriedly obtained from the Convention a law on the "acceleration of the pleadings" in Court. On the 9th Brumaire (October 29), Fouquier-Tinville had this new law read before the Court, the case was closed, and the twenty-two Girondins were condemned. Valazé stabbed himself, the others were executed on the morrow.

Madame Roland, the real inspirer of the Girondist party, was executed on the 18th Brumaire (November 8); the ex-mayor of Paris, Bailly, of whose connivance with Lafayette in the massacre of July 17, 1791, there was no doubt, Girey-Dupré from Lyons, the Feuillant Barnave, won over by the Queen while he accompanied her from Varennes to Paris, soon followed them, and in December the Girondin Kersaint and Rabaut Saint-Etienne mounted the scaffold, as also did Madame Dubarry of royal fame. Roland and Condorcet committed suicide.

Thus began the Terror, and once begun, it had to follow its inevitable course of development.

CHAPTER LXII

EDUCATION—THE METRIC SYSTEM—THE NEW CALENDAR—ANTI-RELIGIOUS MOVEMENT

Education—Three-grade system—Metric system—Its importance—The Republican calendar—Its connection with Church—Severe laws against priests—First attempts at "dechristianisation"—Encouraged by Convention—Bishop Gobel's renunciation—Enthusiasm of Assembly—Movement spreads—*Fête* of Liberty and Reason—Opposition of Robespierre—Conduct of Danton—Robespierre and Danton—Triumph of Catholicism—*Fête* of the Supreme Being—Prelude to 9th Thermidor

AMIDST all these struggles, the revolutionists did not lose sight of the great question of national education. They tried to lay its foundations on principles of equality. An enormous amount of work was actually done in this direction, as may be seen by the documents of the Committee of Public Instruction, recently published.* The admirable report of Michel Lepelletier on education, found after his death, was read before the Convention, and a series of measures for a three-grade system of education—primary schools, central schools and special schools—was adopted.

But the greatest intellectual monument of this period of the Revolution was the metric system. This system did much more than simply introduce into the subdivisions of linear, surface, volume, and weight measures, the decimal system which is the basis of our numeration—which of itself would have gone a good way towards the simplification of mathe-

---

* *Procès-verbaux du Comité d'instruction publique de l'Assemblée législative* and *Procès-verbaux du Comité d'instruction publique de la Convention nationale*, published, with notes and prefaces, by James Guillaume (Paris, 1889–1907), 7 vols.

THE NEW CALENDAR

matical instruction, and helped to develop the mathematical turn of mind. It also gave to the fundamental measure, the *mètre*, a length (one forty-millionth part of the earth's meridian) which could always be re-established with a very fair degree of accuracy, in case our measures should be lost in future ages, as those of the old civilisations have been lost—and this very fact opened up new vistas for thought. Besides, by establishing a simple ratio between the units of length, surface, volume and weight, the metric system prepared the mind of the next generation for the great victory of science in the nineteenth century—its certainty as to the unity of physical forces and the unity of Nature.

The new Republican calendar was a logical outcome of the metric system. It was adopted by the Convention, after two reports by Romme, read on September 20 and October 5, and another report of Fabre d'Eglantine, read on November 24, 1793.* The new calendar inaugurated also a new era in the reckoning of years, which was to begin with the proclamation of the Republic in France, on September 22, 1792, which was also the autumn equinox. The Christian week was abandoned. Sunday disappeared—the day of rest being each tenth day, the *decadi*.†

This decision of the Convention, which struck out the

---

* The Republican year was divided into twelve months, each of thirty days, the names for which were found by Fabre d'Eglantine: *Vendémiaire*, *Brumaire* and *Frimaire* for the autumn, from September 22 till December 20; *Nivôse*, *Pluviôse* and *Ventôse* for the winter, from December 21 till March 20; *Germinal*, *Floréal* and *Prairial* for the spring, from March 21 till June 18; and *Messidor*, *Thermidor* and *Fructidor* for the summer, from June 19 till September 16. Five extra days, called the *sans-culottides*, September 17, 18, 19, 20 and 21, completed the year. Each month was divided into three decades, and the days were called *primidi*, *duodi*, *tridi*, &c., the day of rest being the tenth day, the *decadi*.

† The idea of establishing the new calendar on an astronomical conception was certainly excellent (the idea of placing the five surplus days all at the end of the year was not so good) and the names of the months were very well chosen; but besides all the objections which were bound to be made against this calendar, because it glorified the Revolution, it is very probable also that the idea of replacing the week of *seven* days (the quarter of a lunar month) by one of *ten* days, too long for our customs, was and will be an obstacle to its general acceptance.

Christian calendar from our daily life, necessarily emboldened those who saw in the Christian Church and its servants the chief support of servitude. The experience they had had with the clergy who had taken the Oath to the Constitution had proved the impossibility of winning over the Church to the cause of progress. Consequently the question of abolishing the payment of the clergy by the State, and of leaving the expense of supporting the ministers of their various cults to the members of these cults themselves, necessarily arose. Cambon had already brought it before the Convention in November 1792. But on three different occasions the Convention decided to retain a National Church, subject to the State and paid by it—while it treated the refractory priests (who had not taken the oath) with great severity.

Against these priests very severe laws were passed: deportation for those unsworn, and, from March 18, 1793, death for those who should take part in disturbances in connection with the recruiting, and those who should be found on the Republic's territory after having been condemned to deportation. On October 21, 1793, even more expeditious laws were decreed, and deportation became applicable also to the constitutional, sworn priests, if they were accused of "incivism" by six citizens of their canton. This proved the growth of a conviction in France that the *jureurs* (the priests who had taken the oath) were often quite as dangerous as the *non-jureurs* or *papistes*.

The first attempts of "dechristianisation" were made at Abbeville and at Nevers.* The commissioner of the Convention, Fouché, who was at Nevers and who acted no doubt in agreement and perhaps under the influence of Chaumette, whom he met in this town, declared, on September, 26, 1793, war "against all superstitious and hypocritical worship," as also the desire to substitute for them "a worship of the Republic and of natural morality."† A few days after the introduction

---

* In this account I follow closely the excellent monograph of Professor Aulard, *Le Culte de la Raison et le Culte de l'Etre suprême*, 2nd edition (Paris, 1904). An abridgment of this work is to be found also in his *Histoire politique*, 2nd edition, p. 469 and following.

† He also issued an order by the force of which " any minister of any cult, or priest pensioned by the nation, is bound to marry, or to

of the new calendar he issued, on October 10, a new order, according to which the ceremonies of various cults might only be practised inside their respective temples. All "religious emblems on the high roads," &c., were to be destroyed, the priests were no longer to appear in their vestments anywhere except in their churches, and, finally, burials were to be conducted without any religious ceremony, in fields planted with trees, " beneath the shadow of which shall be erected a statue representing Sleep. All other emblems shall be destroyed," and " the gates to this field, consecrated with religious respect to the shades of the dead, shall bear this inscription : ' Death is eternal sleep '." He also explained the meaning of these decrees to the people, by means of materialist lectures.

At the same time, Laignelot, another commissioner of the Convention, transformed the parish church in Rochefort into a Temple of Truth, where eight Catholic priests and one Protestant minister came to " renounce " their orders on October 31, 1793. At Paris, on October 14, at the instigation of Chaumette, external religious practices were forbidden, and on the 16th the order issued by Fouché on burials was adopted in principle by the Commune.

That this movement was in no way a surprise, and that men's minds had been prepared for it by the Revolution itself and its forerunners, is self-evident. Encouraged now by the acts of the Convention, the provinces threw themselves enthusiastically into the movement of dechristianisation. Following the lead of the borough of Ris-Orangis, the whole district of Corbeil renounced Christianity, and this step received the approbation of the Convention, when deputies from Corbeil arrived on October 30 to report what had been done.

Six days later, deputies from the commune of Mennecy presented themselves at the Convention, attired in copes. They, too, were well received, and the Convention recognised the " right that all citizens have to adopt whatsoever worship suits them best, and to suppress those ceremonies which displease them." A deputation from Seine-et-Oise asking

adopt a child, or to keep an incapable old person, on pain of being divested of his offices and pensions " (Aulard, *Culte de la Raison*, p. 27).

that the Bishop of Versailles, who had recently died, should not be replaced, was also received with due honours.

The Convention encouraged the movement against Christianity not only by its attitude towards dechristianisation, but also by the use to which it put the Church treasures, brought to it by the inhabitants—including the shrine of the Church of Sainte-Geneviève, which was transferred, by order, to the Mint.*

Encouraged undoubtedly by this attitude of the government, Anacharsis Cloots and Chaumette then took another step forward. Cloots, a Prussian baron, who had wholeheartedly espoused the cause of the Revolution, and who advocated with courage and sincerity an International Federation of all peoples, and the *procureur* of the Commune, Chaumette, who was a true representative of the Paris working man, persuaded Gobel, the Bishop of Paris, to lay down his ecclesiastical duties. Having received the consent of the Episcopal Council, and having announced his decision to the department and to the Commune, Gobel came in state on the 17th Brumaire (November 7, 1793), accompanied by eleven of his vicars, and followed by the mayor Pache, the *procureur* Chaumette, and by two members of the department, Momoro and Lullier, to the Convention, to divest himself openly of his prerogatives and titles.

His speech on this occasion was full of dignity. Revering as he did "the eternal principles of equality and morality, the necessary foundations of every truly republican government," he now obeyed the voice of the people and renounced the practice of "the functions of a minister of the Catholic faith." Depositing his cross and his ring, he accepted and put on the red cap which one of the members handed him.

The Assembly was seized thereupon with an enthusiasm which could only be compared to that of the night of August 4. Two other bishops, Thomas Lindet and Gay-Vernon, and some other ecclesiastical members of the Convention, rushed to the tribune to follow the example of Bishop Gobel.

* It will be remembered that the Constituent Assembly had already made similar decisions.

Abbé Gregoire, however, refused to join them. As to Sieyès, he declared that for many years already he had abandoned all ecclesiastical forms, that he had no other faith than that of liberty and equality, and that his prayers had long since called for the triumph of reason over superstition and fanaticism.

The result of this scene in the Convention was tremendous. The whole of France and all the neighbouring nations heard of it. And everywhere, among the governing classes, there rose a flood of hatred against the Republic.

In France, the movement spread rapidly to the provinces. Within a few days several bishops and a great number of clergy had divested themselves of their titles, and their abdications were at times the occasion of striking scenes. It is touching, indeed, to read, for instance, the following description of the abdication of the clergy at Bourges, which I found in a local pamphlet of the period.*

Having mentioned a priest, J. Baptiste Patin, and Julien-de-Dieu, a member of the Benedictine Order, who came to lay down their ecclesiastical prerogatives, the author of the pamphlet continues: " Privat, Brisson, Patrou, Rouen and Champion, all metropolitan *ex-curés*, were not the last to step into the arena; Epsic and Calende, Dumantier, Veyreton, ex-Benedictines, Rauchon and Collardot came after them; the ex-canon Desormaux, and Dubois, his companion, bent beneath the burden of years, followed them with slow steps, when Lefranc exclaimed: ' Burn, burn the credentials of our priesthood, and may the very memory of our past state disappear in the flames which consume them. I lay upon the altar of our fatherland this silver medal; it bears the image of the last of those tyrants who, by reason of the scheming ambition of the clergy, was called " most Christian ".' All the documents of priesthood were then burnt in a pile; and a thousand cries arose: ' Perish for ever the memory of the priests! Perish for ever Christian superstition! Long live the sublime religion of Nature!' " After which the pamphlet

* *Extraits du registre de la Société populaire de Bourges. Séance du quintidi 25 brumaire de l'an deuxième de la République française, une et indivisible* (November 15, 1793). Pamphlets of the British Museum, F. 16 (7).

enumerates the patriotic gifts. This list is really touching. Presents in linen and silver shoe-buckles are very numerous. The patriots and the "brothers" were poor. They gave what they could.

On the whole the anti-Catholic feeling, in which a "religion of Nature" was blended with patriotic sentiments, seems to have been far deeper than one was led to think before consulting the documents of the period. The Revolution made men think, and gave courage to their thoughts.

In the meantime, the Department and the Commune of Paris decided to celebrate the following *decadi*, the 20th Brumaire (November 10), in Notre Dame itself, and to organise a *Fête of Liberty and Reason*, during which patriotic hymns were to be sung before the statue of Liberty. Cloots, Momoro, Hébert and Chaumette carried on an active propaganda among the popular societies, and the *fête* was entirely successful. This *fête* has been so often described that we need not dwell on the details. It must be mentioned, however, that in representing "Liberty" a living creature was preferred to a statue, because, said Chaumette, "A statue would also have been a step towards idolatry." As Michelet had already remarked, the founders of the new faith recommended "the choice, for the fulfilment of so august a part, of persons whose character makes them chastely beautiful, and whose strictness of habits and views repudiates any base idea." Far from being a gay mockery, the *fête* was rather a "chaste ceremony, cheerless, dull and tedious," says Michelet,* who was, it is known, very favourably inclined towards the dechristianisation movement of 1793. But the Revolution, he said, was already "old and weary, too old to engender anything new." The attempt of 1793 was not born of the fiery enthusiasm of Revolution, "but of the dialectical schools of the Encyclopedic times." Indeed, it closely resembled the modern Ethical Societies' movement, which also remains out of touch with the masses.

What chiefly strikes us to-day is that the Convention, notwithstanding the requests which came from all quarters, refused to broach the great question, the abolition of salaries

---

* Book XIV., chap. iii.

ANTI-RELIGIOUS MOVEMENT

for priests paid by the State. On the contrary, the Commune of Paris and its sections openly put into practice dechristianisation. In every section one church was dedicated to the cult of Reason. The General Council of the Commune even risked hastening events. In reply to a religious speech by Robespierre, delivered on the 1st Frimaire,* the Council issued on the 3rd Frimaire (November 23), under the influence of Chaumette, an order by which all churches or temples of all religions in Paris were to be immediately closed; the clergy were made individually responsible for religious disturbances; the Revolutionary Committees were invited to keep a watch on the clergy; and a resolution was made to demand that the Convention exclude the clergy from any form of public service. At the same time a course of "morality" lectures was established, to prepare the preachers of the new cult. It was also decided to destroy the bell towers, while in various sections *fêtes* of Reason were organised, during which the Catholic faith was ridiculed. One section burnt some missals, and Hébert burnt some relics at the Commune.

In the provinces, says Aulard, nearly all the towns, especially in the south-west, seemed to rally round the new rationalist faith.

Yet the government, that is to say, the Committee of Public Welfare, from the very beginning showed a decided opposition to this movement. Robespierre combated it openly, and when Cloots came to tell him with enthusiasm of the abdication of Gobel, he showed his displeasure roughly, asking what the Belgians, whose union with France was desired by Cloots, would say to it.

For a few days, however, he kept quiet. But on November 20 Danton returned to Paris, after a prolonged stay at Arcis-sur-Aube, where he had retired with his young wife, whom he had married in church immediately after the death of his first wife. The next day, the 1st Frimaire (November 21), Robespierre pronounced at the Jacobin Club his first speech, and a very violent one, against the worship of Reason. The Convention, he said, would never take the rash step of forbidding

* See further.

the practice of the Catholic faith. The liberty of religion would be maintained, and the persecution of the peaceful priests would not be permitted. He then pointed out that the belief in a " great Being watching over oppressed innocence and punishing crime " was entirely popular, and he treated the dechristianisers as traitors, as agents of the enemies of France, who wished to repel those foreigners whom the cause of humanity and common interests attracted towards the Republic.

Five days later Danton spoke almost to the same effect in the Convention, and attacked the anti-religious processions. He demanded that a limit be fixed to such manifestations.

What had occurred during these few days to draw Robespierre and Danton together ? What new combinations, diplomatic or otherwise, presented themselves at this moment, to call Danton to Paris and to induce him to oppose himself to the dechristianising movement, while he was a true disciple of Diderot, and did not cease to affirm his materialistic atheism even on the scaffold ? This move of Danton's is the more striking because during the first half of the month of Frimaire the Convention continued to view the dechristianisers favourably.* On the 14th Frimaire (December 4) the " Robespierrist " Couthon had displayed some more relics from the tribune of the Convention and mocked at them.

The question therefore arises, Was not Robespierre making use of some new turn in the negotiations with England to influence Danton and to freely express his views on religion which had always remained dear to this deistic disciple of Rousseau ?

Towards the middle of the month, Robespierre, reinforced by the support of Danton, decided to act, and on the 16th Frimaire (December 6) the Committee of Public Welfare came before the Convention to demand a decree concerning religious liberty, the first article of which forbade " all violence and measures against the liberty of religions." Was this measure dictated by the fear of revolt in the villages, where the closing

* Aulard, *Histoire politique*, p. 475.

ANTI-RELIGIOUS MOVEMENT 527

of the churches was usually very badly received,* or were there other reasons, unknown to us—the fact remains, at any rate, that from that day Catholicism triumphed. The Robespierrist Government took it under its protection, and once again Catholicism became the State religion.†

Later in the spring, Robespierre and his followers went still further: they made an attempt to oppose to the worship of Reason a new worship, that of the Supreme Being, conceived after the fashion of the *Vicaire savoyard* of Rousseau. This worship, however, in spite of governmental support and the prospect of the guillotine for its adversaries, became confused with the cult of Reason, even though it was called the cult of the Supreme Being, and under this name—Aulard says—a half-deistic and half-rationalistic cult continued to spread up to the time when the reaction of Thermidor got the upper hand.

As to the *fête* of the Supreme Being which was celebrated with great pomp in Paris on the 20th Prairial (June 8, 1794), and to which Robespierre, posing as the founder of a new State religion, which was to combat atheism, attached much importance—this *fête* was as beautiful, it appears, as a popular theatrical performance can be, but it called forth no echo in the feelings of the people. Celebrated as it was by the wish of the Committee of Public Welfare—soon after Chaumette and Gobel, who had all the sympathies of the masses with them, had been executed for their irreligious opinions by this committee—the *fête* wore too much the character of a bloody triumph of the Jacobin government over the advanced spirits among the people and the Commune, to be agreeable to the people. And by the openly hostile attitude of several members of the Convention towards Robespierre, during the *fête* itself, it became the prelude of the 9th Thermidor—the prelude of the grand finale.

* Several letters of commissioners mention this. Most of them, as those of Dartygoëyte, Lefiot, Pflieger and Garnier, are, however, posterior to the decree. (*Actes du Comité de Salut Public*, published by Aulard, vol. ix., pp. 385, 759, 780.)

† As several commissioners of the Convention had taken very stringent measures against the Catholic religion, the Convention added, however, a paragraph to this decree to say that it did not intend to censure *what had been done up to that day* by its representatives.

CHAPTER LXIII

THE SUPPRESSION OF THE SECTIONS

Position of sections—" Popular societies "—Opposition of Jacobins—Attitude of Robespierre—Sections gradually deprived of their powers—Control of police—Revolutionary committees subordinated to Committee of Public Safety—State absorbs sections—Revolution doomed

TOWARDS the end of 1793, two rival powers stood facing one another: the two committees—of Public Welfare and of Public Safety—which governed the Convention, and the Commune of Paris. Yet the real strength of the Commune lay neither in its extremely popular mayor Pache, nor in its equally popular *procureur* Chaumette, nor yet in his deputy Hébert, nor in its General Council. It was to be found in the sections. And therefore the central government was steadily endeavouring to subject the sections to its authority.

After the Convention had withdrawn the "permanence" of the sections of Paris; that is to say, their right of calling their general meetings as frequently as they chose, the sections began to found "popular societies" or "sectional societies." But these societies were viewed very unfavourably by the Jacobins, who in their turn were becoming "government men." Therefore, at the end of 1793, and in January 1794, there was much talk in the Jacobin Club against these societies —the more so as the royalists were making a united effort to invade and to capture them. "Out of the corpse of monarchy," said Simond, one of the Jacobins, "came an infinite number of poisonous insects, who are not sufficiently stupid to attempt its resurrection, but who try nevertheless

THE SUPPRESSION OF THE SECTIONS

to prolong the convulsions of the political body."* In the provinces especially, these "insects" were successful. An enormous number of *émigrés*, continued Simond, "lawyers, financiers, agents of the *ancien régime*," overran the country, invaded the popular societies and became their presidents and secretaries.

It is evident that the popular societies, which in Paris were merely the same sections under another name,† would have easily "purified" themselves by excluding from their midst the disguised royalists, and then have continued the work of the sections. But their entire activity displeased the Jacobins, who viewed with jealousy the influence of these "new-comers" who "vied with them in patriotism." "If one believed them," said the same Simond, "the patriots of 1789 . . . are nothing but overtaxed or worn-out beasts of burden who ought to be slaughtered because they can no longer keep pace with the novelties in the political life of the Revolution." And he betrayed the fears of the middle-class Jacobins when he spoke of the "fourth legislative body" which these new-comers would have liked to convoke, in order to go further than the Convention. "Our greatest enemies," added Jeanbon Saint-André, "are not without; we see them: they are amongst us; *they wish to carry revolutionary measures further than we do*."‡ Thereupon Dufourney spoke against all the sectional societies, and Deschamps called them the *petites Vendées*.

As to Robespierre, he hastened to bring forward his favourite argument—foreign intrigues. "My suspicions," said he, "were only too true. You see that the hypocritical counter-revolutionists are dominant in them. Prussian, English and Austrian agents want, by these means, to annihilate *the authority of the Convention and the patriotic ascendency of the Jacobin Society*."§

---

* *Jacobins*, vol. v., p. 623.
† See, for instance, in Ernest Mellié's work, the statutes of the popular society organised by the Poissonnière section.
‡ *Jacobins*, vol. v., pp. 624, 625.
§ *Jacobins*, sitting of December 26, 1793, vol. v., p. 578. Momoro, a member of the Cordeliers' Club, having hazarded the remark that the

The hostility of the Jacobins against the popular societies was evidently nothing but hostility against the sections in Paris and against all similar organisations in the provinces, and this hostility was but an expression of similar feeling in the Central Government. Consequently, as soon as the Revolutionary Government was established by the decree of the 14th Frimaire (December 4, 1793), the right to elect justices of the peace and their secretaries—a privilege which the sections had enjoyed since 1789—was taken from them. The magistrates and their secretaries were henceforth to be nominated by the General Council of the department.* Even the right of the sections to nominate their relief committees, and of themselves to organise relief work, which they had turned, as we saw, to such good account, was taken from them in December 1793, and given to the Committees of Public Welfare and Public Safety. The popular organisation of the Revolution was thus struck at its very root.

But it is especially in the concentration of police functions that the leading idea of the Jacobin government appears in full. We have seen the importance of the sections as parts of the life of Paris, both municipal and revolutionary;† we know what they were doing for the provisioning of the capital, the enlisting of volunteers, the raising, arming and despatching of volunteer regiments, the manufacture of saltpetre, the organisation of labour, the care of the poor, &c. But besides these functions the sections of Paris and the provincial popular societies also performed police duties. This had dated, in Paris, from July 14, 1879, when the citizens had themselves formed their district committees, in order to take charge of the duties of the police. Later on, the law of September 6, 1789, confirmed them in the discharge of these duties, and in the following October the municipality of Paris, still a provisional body at this period, founded its secret police under

members of the Cordeliers' Club had often questioned their right to prevent the formation of popular societies, since "the right to assemble in popular societies is sacred," Robespierre answered curtly: "Everything demanded by the public welfare is certainly right."

* Decrees of the 8th Nivôse (December 28, 1793), and of the 23rd Floréal (May 12, 1794). † Chap. xxiv.

THE SUPPRESSION OF THE SECTIONS

the name of "The Search Committee." The municipal government, sprung from the Revolution, thus revived one of the worst traditions of the *ancien régime*.

After August 10 the Legislative Assembly decreed that all the police duties of " public safety " should pass to the councils of the departments, the districts and the municipalities, and a Committee of Supervision was established, with its subordinate committees in every section ; but as, by degrees, the struggle between the revolutionists and their enemies became keener, these committees were overwhelmed with work, and on March 21, 1793, new revolutionary committees, each made up of twelve members, were established in every commune and in every section of the communes of the large towns, which, like Paris, were divided into sections.*

In this way, the sections, through the medium of their revolutionary committees, became police bureaux. The duties of these revolutionary committees were limited, it is true, to the supervision of strangers ; but they soon acquired rights as extensive as those of the secret police in monarchical States. At the same time one can see how the sections, which, to begin with, had been organs of the democratic revolution, became gradually absorbed by the police functions of their committees, and how these latter, becoming less and less municipal bodies, changed into mere police officials, subordinate to the central police, which was in its turn subject to the Committee of Public Safety.†

The two committees—of Public Welfare and of Public Safety—separated the revolutionary committees more and more from their rival, the Commune, which in this way they weakened, and by disciplining them to obedience they transformed them into machinery of the State. Finally, under the pretext of suppressing abuses, the Convention transformed them into salaried officials ; and at the same time it subordinated the 40,000 revolutionary committees to the

---

* See the rights given by the section of the Panthéon to its committee, quoted by Ernest Melliè, *loc. cit.*, p. 185.

† See the work of Ernest Melliè, p. 189 *et seq.* for very interesting details on the "Committee of Public Welfare of the Department of Paris"—an organ of the secret police—and other similar information.

Committee of Public Safety, to which it gave also the right of "purifying them," and even of nominating their members.

The State's seeking to centralise everything in its own hands, as the monarchy had done in the seventeenth century, and its depriving the popular organisations of such rights as the nomination of the judges and the administration of relief work, as well as of all other administrative functions, and its subjecting them to its bureaucracy in police matters, meant the death of the sections and of the revolutionary councils.

After these changes had been made, the sections of Paris and the popular societies in the provinces were really dead. The State had swallowed them. *And their death was the death of the Revolution.* Since January 1794, public life in Paris had been destroyed, says Michelet. "The general assemblies of the sections were dead, and all their power had passed to their revolutionary committees, which, themselves being no longer elected bodies, but simply groups of officials nominated by the authorities, had not much life in them either."

Now, whenever it might please the Government to crush the Commune of Paris, it could do so without fear of being itself overthrown. And this it really did in March 1794 (Ventôse of the Year II.).

CHAPTER LXIV

STRUGGLE AGAINST THE HEBERTISTS

Robespierre foretells end of Revolution—Causes of its termination — Hébert — Chaumette and Hébertists — Increased power of Committees of Public Welfare and Public Safety—The struggle for power—Robespierre and Danton—Camille Desmoulins—Robespierre attacks Cloots—State of insurrection in Southern France—Fabre d'Eglantine and Bourdon—Attempt to rouse Convention against Committee of Public Welfare—Fabre d'Eglantine demands arrest of three Hébertists—Cordeliers side with Hébertists—Toulon recaptured—Series of republican successes—Authority of Committee of Public Welfare restored—Arrest of Fabre d'Eglantine—False accusations against him—He is executed—Struggle between revolutionary factions continues—Influence of masonic lodges on Revolution,

As early as December 1793, Robespierre spoke of the coming end of the revolutionary Republic—" Let us be careful," he said, " for the death of the fatherland is not far off." * Nor was he alone in foreseeing it ; the same idea recurred frequently in the speeches and letters of the revolutionists.

The fact is, that a revolution that stops half-way is sure to be soon defeated, and at the end of 1793 the situation in France was, that the Revolution, having been arrested in its development, was now wearing itself out in internal struggles and in an effort, as fruitless as it was impolitic, to exterminate its enemies while it was mounting guard over their property.†

* *Séances du club des Jacobins*, edited by Professor Aulard ; sitting of December 12, 1793, vol. v., p. 557.

† Michelet understood this very well, when he wrote a few lines, full of sadness (Book XIV., chap. i.), in which he recalled the words of Duport, "Plough deeply," and said that the Revolution was bound to fail because both the Girondins and the Jacobins were political revolutionists who marked only "two different degrees on the same line." The most advanced of them, Saint-Just, he added, never ventured to

By the very force of events, France was drifting towards a new movement imbued with a communist spirit. But the Revolution had allowed a "strong government" to be constituted, and this government had crushed the *Enragés* and gagged those who dared to hold similar opinions.

As to the Hebertists who predominated in the Cordeliers' Club and in the Commune, and had succeeded in invading, through Bouchotte, the Minister of War, the offices of his department, their ideas on government led them in paths remote from an economic revolution. It is true that Hébert had at times expressed communist sentiments in his paper,* but to terrorise the enemies of the Revolution and to have the government seized by his party seemed to him far more important than to solve the questions of food, the land and organised labour. The Commune of 1871 also produced this type of revolutionist.

So far as Chaumette was concerned, by his popular sympathies and his manner of life he might almost have been ranked with the Communists. At one time he was indeed under their influence. But he was closely connected with the party of Hébertists, and this party was not in the least enthusiastic about Communism. They never tried to arouse a powerful manifestation of the people's *social will*. Their idea was to attain power by means of a new "weeding out" of the Convention: to get rid of the "worn out, the broken limbs of the Revolution," as Momoro used to say, and to compel the Convention to submit to the Commune of Paris, by means of a new May 31, supported this time by the military force of the "revolutionary army." *Later on they would see what was to be done.*

In this, however, the Hébertists had miscalculated. They did not realise that they had to deal now with two serious powers: a Committee of Public Welfare which during the attack religion or education or to go to the root of social questions; one can hardly make out what were his views on property. "The Revolution," said Michelet, "thus failed to take the character of a religious or a social revolution, which would have consolidated it by giving it support, vigour and depth."

* Tridon has given some such extracts in his sketch *Les Hébertistes* (Œuvres diverses de G. Tridon, Paris, 1891, pp. 86–90).

STRUGGLE AGAINST THE HEBERTISTS

past six months had become a force in the Government and had won general approval for the intelligent way in which it had directed the war; and a Committee of Public Safety, which had grown very powerful, since it had concentrated in its hands a wide system of police, and thus had the power to send whomsoever it wished to the guillotine. Besides, the Hébertists began to fight on ground where they were bound to be defeated —the ground of Terrorism. Here they had to meet the rivalry of a whole world of Government officials, even those who, like Cambon, considered Terrorism necessary for conducting the war. Terrorism is always a weapon of government and the government of the day turned it against them.

It would be tiresome to recount here all the intrigues of the different parties that struggled for power during the month of December 1793, and the first months of 1794. Suffice it to say that four groups or parties were then in the field: the Robespierrist group, consisting of Robespierre, Saint-Just, Couthon, and their friends, the party of the "worn out"; politicians who grouped themselves round Danton (Fabre d'Eglantine, Phélippeaux, Bourdon, Camille Desmoulins, and others); the Commune, which was in agreement with the Hébertists; and finally, those members of the Committee of Public Welfare (Billaud-Varenne and Collot d'Herbois) who were known as *terrorists*, around whom were grouped men who did not wish to see the Revolution lay down its arms, but did not want either that Robespierre, whom they secretly opposed, or the Commune and the Hébertists should gain the upper hand.

Danton was, in the eyes of the revolutionists, a man completely used up, but they saw in him a real danger, since the Girondins stood behind him, pushing themselves forward under cover of his great popularity. At the end of November, however, we saw Robespierre and Danton marching hand in hand against the anti-religious movement; and when it was Danton's turn to submit to a public examination of his life before the Jacobin Club, which was then "weeding itself out," Robespierre again held out his hand to him. He did even more: he identified himself with Danton.

On the other hand, when Camille Desmoulins, who as a

journalist excelled in calumny, issued, on the 15th and 20th of Frimaire (December 5 and 10), the two first numbers of his *Vieux Cordelier*, in which he attacked Hébert and Chaumette in the vilest manner, and started a campaign in favour of an abatement in the prosecution of the enemies of the Revolution, Robespierre read both these numbers before publication and approved them. During the examination of Desmoulins' life at the Jacobin Club, he also defended him. This meant that for the moment he was ready to make certain concessions to the Dantonists, provided they helped him to attack the party of the Left—the Hébertists.

This they did quite willingly and with much violence, by the pen of Desmoulins in his *Vieux Cordelier*, and through the organ of Phélippeaux and at the Jacobin Club, where the latter bitterly attacked the conduct of the Hébertist generals in the Vendée. Robespierre worked in the same direction against Anacharsis Cloots, an influential Hébertist, whom the Jacobins had even elected president at that moment, attacking him with quite religious fanaticism. When it was Cloots' turn to undergo the civic examination of his life, Robespierre pronounced a speech against him, full of venom, in which he represented this pure idealist and worshipper of the Revolution, this inspired propagandist of the International union of all the *sans-culottes*, as a traitor, and that because he had had business relations with the bankers Vandenyver, and had taken some interest in them when they were arrested as suspects. Cloots was expelled from the Jacobin Club on the 22nd of Frimaire (December 12) and so became a victim marked for the scaffold. He was, in fact, arrested a fortnight later.

The insurrection in Southern France dragged on in the meantime, and Toulon remained in the hands of the English; so that the Committee of Public Welfare was accused of incapacity and it was even rumoured that it intended to give up Southern France to the counter-revolution. There were days when the Committee was but a hair's-breadth from being overthrown, "sent to the Tarpeian Rock"—which would have been a victory for both the Girondins and the "moderates," that is to say, for the counter-revolutionists.

STRUGGLE AGAINST THE HEBERTISTS

The soul of the campaign carried on in political circles against the Committee of Public Welfare was Fabre d'Eglantine, one of the "moderates," seconded by Bourdon (of the Oise) a Dantonist, and between the 22nd and the 27th Frimaire (December 12-17) a serious attempt was made to rouse the Convention against its Committee of Public Welfare, and to impeach it.

However, though the Dantonists plotted against the Robespierrists, both parties joined hands to attack the Hébertists. On the 27th Frimaire (December 17) Fabre d'Eglantine made a report at the Convention demanding the arrest of three Hébertists: Ronsin, the general of the "revolutionary army" in Paris; Vincent, secretary general of the War Office, and Maillard, who had led the women to Versailles on October 5, 1789. This was the first attempt of the "party of clemency" to make a *coup d'état* in favour of the Girondins and a more moderate government. All those who had made fortunes by the Revolution were now in a hurry, as we have already said, to return to a state of "order," and to reach this goal they were prepared to sacrifice the Republic, if need be, and to establish a constitutional monarchy. Many, like Danton, were weary of mankind, and said to themselves: "It is time to put an end to all this," while others—and these are the most dangerous to all revolutions—losing faith in the Revolution, prepared to meet half-way the reaction which they already saw coming.

The arrest of the three Hébertists would have been granted without difficulty by the Convention, but for the fear of recalling the arrest of Hébert in 1793.* It would have become obvious that a *coup d'état* was preparing in favour of the Girondins who would serve in their turn as a stepping-stone to reaction. The publication of the third number of the *Vieux Cordelier*, in which Desmoulins, under names borrowed from Roman history, denounced the whole revolutionary government, helped to unmask the intrigue, for all the counter-revolutionists in Paris suddenly lifted their heads after reading this number, and openly predicted the speedy end of the Revolution.

* *Vide* chap. xxxix.

The Cordeliers immediately took up the cause of the Hébertists, but found no other basis for their appeal to the people than the necessity for acting more severely against the enemies of the Revolution. They too identified the Revolution with *Terrorism*. They carried the head of Chalier about Paris and began to prepare the people for a fresh May 31 rising, with the intention of bringing about a new "purification" of the Convention, and the removal of its "worn-out and its broken limbs." But as to what they intended to do on attaining power—what direction they would try to give to the Revolution—nothing was said about that.

Once the fight was begun in such conditions, it was easy for the Committee of Public Welfare to parry the blow. They by no means rejected Terror as an arm of Government. In fact, on the 5th Nivôse (December 25), Robespierre had made his report on the revolutionary government, and if the substance of this report was the necessity of maintaining the balance between the too advanced parties and the too moderate ones, its conclusion was *death to the enemies of the people!* Next day he demanded, moreover, a greater rapidity in the pronouncement of sentences by the revolutionary tribunal.

About the same time it became known in Paris (on the 4th Nivôse—December 24) that Toulon had been retaken from the English; on the 5th and 6th of the same month (December 25 and 26) that La Vendée was crushed at Savenay; on the 10th that the army of the Rhine, having taken the offensive, had retaken the lines of Wissembourg from the enemy; and on the 12th Nivôse (January 1, 1794) that the blockade of Landau was raised and that the German army had recrossed the Rhine.

A whole series of decisive victories had thus been won, and they strengthened the Republic. They also restored the authority of the Committee of Public Welfare. Camille Desmoulins in his fifth number hastened to make amends for his recent articles, but still continued to attack Hébert violently, a proceeding which turned the meetings of the Jacobin Club in the second decade of Nivôse (from December 31 to January 10, 1794) into personal attacks ending in free fights. On January 10, the Jacobins passed a resolution excluding Desmoulins from

STRUGGLE AGAINST THE HEBERTISTS 539

their club, and only Robespierre's great popularity enabled him to induce the society not to carry it into effect.

On the 24th Nivôse (January 13) the committees decided to strike a blow and to terrify the camp of their detractors by ordering Fabre d'Eglantine to be arrested. The pretext was an accusation of forgery, and it was announced loudly that the committees had succeeded in discovering a great plot, the aim of which was to discredit the nation's representatives.

It is now known that the accusation which served as a pretext for the arrest of Fabre—that of having falsified a decree of the Convention to the advantage of the powerful Indian Company—was false. The decree dealing with the Indian Company had indeed been falsified, but by Delaunay, another member of the Convention. The document still exists in the archives, and since its discovery by Michelet, it has been proved that the falsification was in Delaunay's handwriting. But at the time of Fabre's arrest, Fouquier-Tinville, the public prosecutor of the revolutionary tribunal, and of the Committee of Public Safety, did not allow the document to be produced either before or during the trial in court, and Fabre perished as a forger, because the Government simply wanted to get rid of a dangerous foe. Robespierre took good care not to interfere.*

* The affair was a complicated one. The royalists had in their service a very clever man, the Baron de Batz, who by his courage and skill in escaping from pursuit had acquired an almost legendary reputation. This Baron de Batz, after having worked a long time for the escape of Marie-Antoinette, undertook to incite certain members of the Convention to make large fortunes by going into stock-jobbing—money having to be provided for these operations by the Abbé Espagnac. For this purpose Baron de Batz assembled in his house on a certain day Julien (of Toulouse), Delaunay and Bazire (a Dantonist). The banker Benoît, the poet Laharpe, the Comtesse de Beaufort (Julien's mistress), and Chabot (the unfrocked priest who at one time had been a favourite of the people, but who had since married an Austrian lady, a sister of the banker Frey) were also of the party. Besides, an attempt was made by the same man to win over Fabre, and Delaunay was actually won over in favour of the Indian Company. This company was attacked in the Convention, which ordered the liquidation of the company to be proceeded with at once by special commissioners. The wording of this decree had to be written by Delaunay, who wrote indeed a draft of the decree, and this draft was signed by Fabre, who made a few alterations in it in pencil. But other alterations *to the advantage of the company* were subsequently made, in ink, by Delaunay, on the same draft, and this draft, which was

Three months later, Fabre d'Eglantine was executed, as were also Chabot, Delaunay, the Abbé d'Espagnac, and the two brothers Frey, the Austrian bankers.

Thus the mortal struggle between the different factions of the revolutionary party went on, and one easily understands how the foreign invasion and all the horrors of civil war in the provinces were bound to render this struggle more and more violent and sanguinary. A question, however, necessarily arises: What prevented the struggle between the parties from taking the same sanguinary character at the very beginning of the Revolution? How was it that men, whose political views were so widely different as those of the Girondins, of Danton, Robespierre and Marat, had been able to act in concert against royal despotism?

It appears very probable that the intimate and fraternal relations which had been established at the approach of the Revolution in the masonic lodges of Paris and the provinces, between the leading men of the time, must have contributed to bring about such an understanding. It is known, indeed, from Louis Blanc, Henri Martin, and the excellent monograph of Professor Ernest Nys,* that nearly all revolutionists of renown were freemasons—Mirabeau, Bailly, Danton, Robespierre, Marat, Condorcet, Brissot, Lalande, and many others were masonic brothers, and the Duke of Orléans (Philippe-Egalité) remained its national Grand Master down to May 13, 1793. On the other side, it is also known that Robespierre, Mirabeau, Lavoisier, and probably many more belonged to the lodges of the Illuminates, founded by Weishaupt, whose aim was " to free the nations from the tyranny of princes and priests, and as a first step, to free the peasants and the working men from serfdom, forced labour and guilds."

It is quite certain, to quote M. Nys, that " by its humanitarian tendencies, its firm belief in the dignity of man, and by its principles of liberty, equality and fraternity," freemasonry never submitted to the Convention, was made to pass for the decree itself.

* Ernest Nys, *Idées modernes : Droit International et Franc-maçonnerie.* Bruxelles, 1908.

STRUGGLE AGAINST THE HEBERTISTS

had helped immensely to educate public opinion in the new ideas—the more so that, thanks to it, in every part of France meetings were held, at which progressive ideas were expounded and applauded, and, what was much more important than is usually thought, men learned to discuss and to vote. "The union of the Three Estates in June 1789, and the movement on the night of August 4, were most probably prepared within the masonic lodges." *

This preliminary work must also have established personal relations and habits of mutual respect between the men of action, apart from the always too narrow party interests, and thus enabled the revolutionaries of different opinions to act with a certain unity, for four years, in the abolition of royal despotism. It was only later, towards the end of the Revolution, when their personal relations were subjected to the severest trials—especially after the freemasons themselves were divided upon the question of royalty—that these links were broken. And then the struggles began to be of the ferocious character they assumed before the fall of the Montagnards.

* E. Nys, *loc cit.* pp. 82, 83.

CHAPTER LXV

FALL OF THE HEBERTISTS—DANTON EXECUTED

Struggle between revolutionists and counter-revolutionists continues—Robespierre and commissioners of Convention—Triumph of Hébertists—Great speech of Saint-Just—He advocates Terrorism—His attack on Dantonists—Action of Cordeliers—Arrest of Hébertist leaders—Further arrests of Chaumette, Pache, Clootz and Leclerc—Success of the Government—Execution of Hébertists and others—Royalist rejoicing—End of struggle between committees and Commune—Committees arrest Danton, Desmoulins, Phélippeaux and Lacroix —They are executed—Effect of executions on Paris—End of Revolution in sight

THE winter thus passed in veiled struggles between the revolutionists and the counter-revolutionists, who every day lifted their heads higher and more boldly.

In the beginning of February, Robespierre made himself the mouthpiece of a movement against certain commissioners of the Convention who had acted, as Carrier did at Nantes and Fouché at Lyons, with appalling fury against the revolted towns, and who had not discriminated between the instigators of the revolts and the men of the people who had been dragged into them.* He demanded that these commissioners should be recalled, and he threatened them with prosecution, but this movement came to nothing. On the 5th Ventôse (February 23) Carrier was amnestied by the Convention—and Carrier being the greatest sinner, this meant, of course, that the faults of all the other commissioners, whatever they might have been, were pardoned. The Hébertists triumphed. Robespierre and Couthon were both ill, and did not appear for a few weeks.

* It is known that the young Julien had written to him quite frankly about the excesses of certain commissioners, and especially of those of Carrier (vide *Une mission en Vendée*).

In the meantime Saint-Just, returned from visiting the armies, delivered before the Convention, on the 8th Ventôse (February 26), a great speech which produced a strong impression and still more embroiled matters. Far from advocating clemency, Saint-Just adopted the Terrorist programme of the Hébertists. He, too, menaced the foes of the Republic—even more vigorously than the Hébertists had ever done. He promised to direct the attack on the "worn-out party," and singled out, as the next victims of the guillotine, the Dantonists—" the political party which always speaks of moving with slow steps, deceives all parties, and prepares the return of reaction; the party which speaks of clemency because its members know that they are not virtuous enough to be terrible." Once he stood on this ground of republican probity Saint-Just could speak of course with authority, while the Hébertists who—in their words at least—scoffed at probity, gave their enemies the possibility of confounding them with the crowd of "profitmongers" (*profiteurs*) who only saw in the Revolution their personal enrichment. As to the economic questions, the tactics adopted by Saint-Just in his report of the 8th Ventôse was to accept, though very vaguely, some of the ideas of the *Enragés*. He confessed that until then he had not thought of these questions. "The force of circumstances," he said, "leads us perhaps to conclusions of which we had not thought." But now that he thinks of them, he still does not wish to injure great fortunes: he objects to them only because they are in the hands of the enemies of the Revolution. "*The estates of the patriots are sacred*," he says, "but the lands of the conspirators are there for the poor." Still he expresses some ideas upon landed property. His intention is that the land should belong to those who cultivate it: let the land be taken away from those who for twenty or fifty years have not cultivated it. He would like to see a democracy of virtuous small landowners living in modest ease; and he asks that the landed estates of the conspirators be seized and given to the poor. There can be no liberty so long as there are beggars and paupers, and so long as the civil (he means the economic) relations in society produce desires that are contrary to the established form of government, "*I defy you*," he says, "*to establish liberty, so long as the poor can be roused against the new order of things*, and I defy you to do away with poverty, so long as we have not made it possible for every one to be able to own land. . . . Mendicity must be abolished by distributing the national estates to the poor." He spoke also of a sort of national insurance : of a "national public domain established for repairing the misfortunes that may happen to the social body." This domain would be used to reward virtue, to repair individual misfortunes, and for education.

And with all this was mingled a great deal of Terrorism. It was Hébertist Terrorism, slightly tinged with socialism. But his socialism had no backbone in it. It consisted rather of maxims than of legislative schemes. It is obvious, moreover, that Saint-Just's aim was chiefly to prove, as he himself said, "that the 'Mountain' still remains the summit of the Revolution." It will not allow others to surpass it. It will execute the *Enragés* and the Hébertists, but it may borrow something from them.

Through this report, Saint-Just obtained two decrees from the Convention. One was in reply to those who called for clemency: the Committee of Public Safety was invested with the power of liberating "the detained patriots." The other decree was meant apparently to go even further than the Hébertists ever intended to go, and at the same time to tranquillise the purchasers of national estates. The estates of the patriots were to be sacred; but those of the enemies of the Revolution were to be confiscated for the benefit of the Republic. As to the enemies themselves, they were to be detained until peace was concluded, and then they would be banished. Those who wished the Revolution to advance further in a social direction were thus befooled. Nothing came of this discourse but the words.

Thereupon the Cordeliers decided to act. On the 14th Ventôse (March 4) they covered with a black veil the board inscribed with the Rights of Man which was hung up in their club. Vincent spoke of the guillotine, and Hébert spoke against Amar, one of the Committee of Public Safety, who was hesitating to send sixty-one Girondins before the revolutionary tribunal. In ambiguous phrases he even alluded to Robespierre —not as an obstacle to serious change, but as a defender of Desmoulins. It thus meant applying to all evils no remedy but Terrorism. Carrier let slip the word "insurrection."

But the people of Paris did not move and the Commune refused to listen to the appeal of the Hébertist Cordeliers. Then during the night of the 23rd Ventôse (March 13) the Hébertist leaders—Hebert, Momoro, Vincent, Ronsin, Ducroquet and Laumur—were arrested, and the Committee of Public Welfare spread by the agency of Billaud-Varenne all kinds of fables and calumnies about them. They had meant, said Billaud, to massacre all the royalists in the prisons; they were going to plunder the Mint; they had buried food-supplies in the ground in order to starve Paris!

On the 28th Ventôse (March 18) Chaumette, the procurator of the Commune, whom the Committee of Public Welfare had dismissed on the previous day and replaced by Cellier, was also arrested. The mayor Pache was deprived of office by the same committee. Anacharsis Cloots had already been arrested on the 8th Nivôse (December 28)—the accusation being that he had sought information as to whether a certain lady was on the list of suspects. Leclerc, a friend of Chalier, who had come from Lyons and had worked with Jacques Roux, was implicated in the same charge.

The Government triumphed.

The true reasons of these arrests among the advanced party we do not yet know. Had they made a plot with the intention of seizing the power by the help of the "revolutionary army" of Ronsin? It was possible, but up to now we know nothing definite of this affair.

The Hébertists were sent before the revolutionary tribunal, and the committees had the baseness to make up what was known then as an "amalgam." In the same batch were included bankers and German agents, together with Momoro, who since 1790 had become known for his Communist ideas, and who had given absolutely everything he possessed to the Revolution; with Leclerc, the friend of Chalier, and Anacharsis Cloots, "the orator of mankind" (*orateur du genre humain*), who in 1793 had already foreseen the Republic of Mankind and had dared to speak of it.

On the 4th Germinal (March 24) after a purely formal trial which lasted three days, they were all executed.

It is easy to imagine what rejoicings took place on that day among the royalists, with whom Paris was crowded. The streets were overflowing with " muscadins " attired in the most *impayable* fashion; who insulted the condemned victims while they were being dragged in dust-carts to the Place de la Révolution. The rich paid absurd prices to have seats close to the guillotine, so that they might enjoy fully the death of the editor of the *Père Duchesne*. "The square was turned into a theatre," says Michelet, "and round about there was a kind of fair, in the Champs-Elysées, where gaily dressed crowds circulated among the improvised shops and tents." The people did not appear on that day; gloomy and heavy-hearted, the poor remained in their slums. They knew that it was their friends who were being murdered.

Chaumette was guillotined a few days later, on the 24th Germinal (April 13) with Gobel, the bishop of Paris, who had resigned his bishopric. They had both been accused of impiety. The widow of Desmoulins and the widow of Hébert were included in the same batch. Pache was spared, but he was replaced as mayor by Fleuriot-Lescaut, an insignificant man, and the procureur Chaumette, first by Cellier, and then by Claude Payan, a man devoted to Robespierre and more interested in the Supreme Being than in the people of Paris.*

The two committees—of Public Safety and of Public Welfare—had thus got the better of their rival, the Commune of Paris. The long struggle which this centre of revolutionary

* The law of the 14th Frimaire (December 4), which had established the " Revolutionary Government " had replaced the elected *procureurs* of the communes by *agents nationaux*, nominated by the Committee of Public Welfare. Chaumette, having been confirmed in his functions by the committee, became thus a " national agent." Then, on the day when the Hébertists were arrested, *i.e.*, on the 23rd Ventôse (March 13), the Committee of Public Welfare obtained from the Convention a new law which allowed them to replace provisionally those functionaries, elected by the Communes, of whom they wanted to get rid. In virtue of this law the committee, having removed Pache, the mayor of Paris, nominated Fleuriot-Lescaut in his place.

FALL OF THE HEBERTISTS

initiative had sustained since August 9, 1792, against the official representatives of the Revolution, had come to an end. The Commune, which for nineteen months had been as a beacon to revolutionary France, was about to become a mere particle of the State machinery. After this, the end was already in sight.*

However, the royalists were so triumphant after these executions that the committee felt themselves outdone by the counter-revolutionists. Now, it was they who were asked to ascend the " Tarpeian Rock "—so dear to Brissot. Desmoulins, whose behaviour on the day of Hébert's execution was abominable (he himself has told all about it), issued a seventh number of his *Vieux Cordelier*, directed entirely against the revolutionary *régime*. The royalists indulged in foolish manifestations of joy, and urged Danton to attack the committees. The crowd of Girondins who had covered themselves with the mantle of Danton were going to take advantage of the absence of the Hébertists to make a *coup d'état*—and this would have meant the guillotine for Robespierre, Couthon, Saint-Just, Billaud-Varenne, Collot d'Herbois and all the leading Montagnards. The counter-revolution might have been already victorious by the spring of 1794, but the committees decided to deal a blow to the Right, and to sacrifice Danton.

During the night of March 30 (the 9th Germinal) Paris was stupefied to learn that Danton, Desmoulins, Phélippeaux and Lacroix were arrested. Acting on a report laid before the Convention by Saint-Just (drawn up after a rough draft given him by Robespierre which has been preserved till now), the Assembly immediately gave the order for the prosecution of

---

* With Pache and Chaumette disappeared the two men who in the minds of the people best symbolised the *popular revolution*. When the delegates who had been sent from the departments came to Paris to signify the acceptance of the Constitution, they were surprised to find Paris quite democratic, says Avenel (*Anacharsis Cloots*, vol. ii. pp. 168-169). The mayor, " Papa Pache," came from the country with a loaf of bread in his pocket ; Chaumette, the *procureur* of the Commune, " lives in one room with his wife, who mends old clothes. ' Come in,' they reply to whoever knocks at their door—just as it was at Marat's." The " Père Duchesne," the " orator of mankind "—all these men were equally accessible. These were the men who were now taken from the people. . . .

Danton and his arrest. The "Marsh" obediently voted as it was told to vote.

The Committees again made an "amalgam"—or "batch"—in order to bewilder public opinion, and sent before the revolutionary tribunal, Danton, together with Desmoulins, Bazire (whose name we saw as a visitor of the Baron de Batz), Fabre, accused of forgery, Lacroix, accused of robbery, Chabot, who acknowledged that he had received (without having spent them) a hundred thousand francs from the royalists for some unknown affair, the forger Delaunay, and the go-between of de Batz's conspiracy, Julien (of Toulouse).

The pleadings before the tribunal were suppressed. When the vigorous defence of Danton threatened to provoke a popular rising, the judges would not permit him or the others to speak, and pronounced the death sentences.

On the 16th Germinal (April 5) they were all executed.

One can well understand the effect produced on the population of Paris and the revolutionists in general by the fall of the revolutionary Commune of Paris, and the execution of men such as Leclerc, Momoro, Hébert, and Cloots, followed by that of Danton and Camille Desmoulins, and finally that of Chaumette. These executions were considered in Paris and in the provinces as the end of the Revolution. In political circles it was known that Danton was the rallying-point of the counter-revolutionists. But for France in general he remained the revolutionist who had always been in the vanguard of all popular movements. "If these men are traitors, whom then shall we trust?" the people asked themselves. "But are they traitors?" others questioned. "Is this not a sure sign that the Revolution is nearing its end?"

Certainly it was such a sign. Once the upward movement of the Revolution was arrested; once a force could be found that was able to say: "Further thou shalt not go," and that at a moment when the most essential demands of the people were seeking expression—once this force had succeeded in crushing those who tried to formulate the claims of the masses, the true revolutionists knew well that this was indeed the death-agony of the Revolution. They were not deceived by Saint-Just, who told them that he, too, was coming to think like those whom he sent to the scaffold. They understood that it was the beginning of the end.

In fact, the triumph of the committees over the Commune of Paris was the triumph of *order*, and during a revolution the triumph of order is the termination of the *revolutionary* period. There might still be a few more convulsions, but the Revolution was at an end.

And the people who had made the Revolution finally lost all interest in it. They stood aside to make way for the "muscadins."

CHAPTER LXVI

ROBESPIERRE AND HIS GROUP

Position and influence of Robespierre—Causes of his power—
His incorruptibility—His fanaticism—His accusation against
Fabre—His character and policy

ROBESPIERRE has been often mentioned as a dictator; his enemies in the Convention called him "the tyrant," and it is true that as the Revolution drew to a close Robespierre acquired so much influence that he came to be regarded both in France and abroad as the most important person in the Republic.

It would, however, be incorrect to represent Robespierre as a *dictator*, though certainly many of his admirers desired a dictatorship for him.* We know, indeed, that Cambon exercised considerable authority within his special domain, the Committee of Finance, and that Carnot wielded extensive powers in matters concerning the war, despite the ill-will borne him by Robespierre and Saint-Just. But the Committee of Public Safety was too jealous of its controlling power not to have opposed a dictatorship, and, besides, some of its members detested Robespierre. Moreover, even if there were in the Convention a certain number who were not actually averse to Robespierre's preponderating influence, these would have been none the less unwilling to submit to the dictatorship of a Montagnard so rigorous as he in his principles. Nevertheless, Robespierre's power was really immense. Nearly every one of his enemies as well as his admirers felt that the disappearance of his party from

---

* The *Notes historiques sur la Convention nationale*, by Marc Antoine Baudot (Paris, 1893), may be of little value, but Saint-Just's proposal to appoint Robespierre dictator to save the Republic, which Baudot mentions (p. 13), is by no means improbable. Buonarotti speaks of it as of a well-known fact.

the political arena would mean, as indeed it proved, the triumph of reaction.

How then is the power of Robespierre and his group to be explained ? First of all, Robespierre had been incorruptible in the midst of a host of men who readily yielded to the seductions of riches and power, and this is a very important trait in time of revolution. While the majority of the middle-class men about him shared in the spoils of the national estates when they were put up for sale by the Revolution, and took part in the stock-jobbery; while thousands of Jacobins secured posts under Government for themselves, Robespierre remained an upright judge, steadfastly reminding them of the higher principles of republicanism and threatening those keenest after spoil with the guillotine.

In all he said and did during those five troubled years of revolution, we feel even now, and his contemporaries must have felt it still more, that he was one of the very few politicians of that time who never wavered in their revolutionary faith, nor in their love for the democratic republic. In this respect Robespierre was a real force, and if the communists had been able to oppose him with another force equal to his own in strength of will and intelligence, they would undoubtedly have succeeded in leaving a far deeper impress of their ideas on the Great Revolution.

These qualities, however, which even his enemies acknowledge in Robespierre, would not suffice alone to explain the immense power he possessed towards the end of the Revolution. The fact is, his fanaticism, which sprang from the purity of his intentions, kept him incorruptible in the midst of a widespread corruption. At the same time, he was striving to establish his authority over men's minds, and to accomplish this he was ready, if necessary, to pass over the dead bodies of his opponents. In the work of establishing his authority he was powerfully seconded by the growing middle classes as soon as they recognised in him the " happy mean "—equally removed from the extremists and the moderates—the man who offered them the best guarantee against the " excesses " of the people.

The *bourgeoisie* felt that here was a man who by the respect he inspired in the people, the moderate scope of his aims and his itch for power, was just the right man to establish a strong government, and thus put an end to the revolutionary period. So long, therefore, as the middle classes had anything to fear from the advanced parties, so long did they refrain from interfering with Robespierre's work of establishing the authority of the Committee of Public Welfare and of his group in the Convention. But when Robespierre had helped them to crush those parties, they crushed him in his turn, in order that middle-class Girondins should be restored to power in the Convention, after which the Thermidorean reaction was developed to its fullest extent.

Robespierre's mind was admirably suited for the *rôle* he was required to play. To be convinced of this, one has only to read the rough draft of the deed of accusation against the Fabre d'Eglantine and Chabot group, which is written in Robespierre's own hand, and was found among his papers after the 9th Thermidor. This document characterises the man better than any amount of arguments.[*]

"Two rival coalitions have been quarrelling, to the public scandal, for some time past," it begins. "One of them is inclined to moderation and the other to excesses which are practically working against the Revolution. One declares war against all energetic patriots and preaches indulgence for conspirators, the other artfully slanders the defenders of liberty, and would crush, one by one, every patriot who has ever erred, while remaining at the same time wilfully blind to the criminal plottings of our most dangerous enemies. . . . One tries to abuse its credit with or its presence in the National Convention [Danton's party], the other misuses its influence with the popular societies [the Commune and the *Enragés*]. One wants to obtain from the Convention dangerous decrees and measures of oppression against its adversaries; the other makes use of dangerous language in public assemblies. . . . The triumph

---

[*] It was Robespierre who prepared the rough draft of the accusation against this group, but he made Saint-Just his mouthpiece. Vide *Papiers inédits trouvés chez Robespierre, Saint-Just, Payan, &c., supprimés ou omis par Courtois, précédé du rapport de ce dernier à la Convention nationale*, vol. i., p. 21 *et seq.* Paris, 1828.

of either party would be equally fatal to liberty and national authority. . . ." And Robespierre goes on to say how the two parties had attacked the Committee of Public Welfare ever since its formation.

After charging Fabre with preaching clemency, in order to conceal his own crimes, he adds : " The moment no doubt was favourable for preaching a base and cowardly doctrine, even to well-disposed men, when all the enemies of liberty were doing their utmost on the other side; when a venal philosophy, prostituted to tyranny, neglected thrones for altars, opposed religion to patriotism,* made morality contradict itself, confounded the cause of religion with that of despotism, the Catholics with the conspirators, and tried to force the people to see in the revolution not the triumph of virtue but the triumph of atheism—not the source of happiness, but the destruction of moral and religious ideas."

We can see plainly from these extracts that if Robespierre had not the breadth of view and boldness of thought necessary for the leader of a party during a revolution, he possessed in perfection the art of inciting an assembly against this or that person. Every phrase in his deed of accusation is a poisoned arrow that hits the mark.

The most striking point in all this is the fact that Robespierre and his friends did not realise the part the " Moderates " were making them play until the time had come for their own overthrow. "There is a scheme to incite the people to level everything," his brother writes to him from Lyons. " If care is not taken, everything will be disorganised." And Maximilien Robespierre could see no further than his brother. In the efforts of the advanced party he saw only attacks on the Government of which he was a member. Like Brissot, he accused them of being the tools of the London and Viennese Cabinets. The attempts of the Communists were for him only " disorganisation." It was necessary to " take care " of them—to crush them by the Terror.

* We see in Aulard's *Le Culte de la Raison et le Culte de l'Etre suprême* how, on the contrary, the movement against Christianity was linked with patriotism.

"What are the means of ending the civil war ?" he asks in a note. And he replies :

"To punish the traitors and conspirators, especially the guilty deputies and administrators.

"To send patriotic troops under patriot leaders to subdue the aristocrats of Lyons, Marseilles, Toulon, the Vendée, the Jura, and every other region where the standard of revolt and royalism has been set up.

"And to make terrible examples of all the scoundrels who have outraged liberty and shed the blood of patriots." *

It is not a revolutionist who speaks but a member of a Government using the language of all Governments. This is why Robespierre's whole policy, after the fall of the Commune until the 9th Thermidor, remained absolutely sterile. It did nothing to prevent the impending catastrophe, it did much to accelerate it. It did nothing to turn aside the daggers which were being secretly whetted to strike the Revolution ; it did everything to make their blows mortal.

* *Papiers inédits*, vol. ii., p. 14.

CHAPTER LXVII

THE TERROR

Steps taken by committees to increase their power—War with England—Condition of provinces—Burning of Bedouin—Special commission formed to deal with arrested citizens—Robespierre's law of 22nd Prairial—Effect of law—Aim of Robespierre—Attempts on his life—Arrests and executions—Terror—Hatred of Jacobin government

AFTER the downfall of their enemies of the Left and of the Right, the committees continued to concentrate more and more power in their own hands. Up to that time there had been six Government departments, which were indirectly subordinate to the Committee of Public Welfare through the intermediary of the Executive Committee composed of six ministers. On the 12th Germinal (April 1) the State departments were suppressed and their place taken by twelve Executive Commissions, each of them under the supervision of a section of the committee.* Furthermore, the Committee of Public Welfare obtained the right of recalling by its own authority the commissioners of the Convention. And finally, it was decided that the supreme revolutionary tribunal should sit in Paris under the eye of the committees. Those who were accused of conspiracy, in any part of France, were to be brought to Paris for trial. At the same time measures were taken for purging Paris of all dangerous elements. All *ci-devants* (dispossessed nobles) and all the foreigners belonging to the nations at war with France, with a few indispensable exceptions, were to be expelled from Paris.†

---

* As James Guillaume has shown, the majority of these Commissions had already been formed successively since October 1793. *Procès-verbaux du comité d'instruction publique de la Convention*, vol. iv., Introduction, pp. 11, 12.

† Decrees of the 26th and 27th Germinal.

The other great pre-occupation of the Government was the war. In January 1794, there had still been hope that the opposition party in the English parliament supported by a considerable number of people in London and several influential members of the House of Lords, would prevent the Prime Minister, Pitt, from continuing the war. Danton must have shared this illusion—which was one of the crimes imputed to him. But Pitt carried the parliamentary majority with him against " the impious nation," and since the beginning of spring England, and Prussia whom she subsidised, pushed on the war vigorously. There were soon four armies, 315,000 strong, massed on the frontiers of France, confronting the four armies of the Republic, which numbered only 294,000. But by this time the armies of France were Republican armies, democratised, with tactics of their own elaborated, and they were not long in gaining the upper hand over the allied Powers.

The darkest spot, however, was in the condition of things in the provinces, especially in the South. The indiscriminate extermination of all the counter-revolutionists—both the leaders and their irresponsible followers—to which the local Jacobins and the commissioners of the Convention had resorted when their party triumphed, aroused such bitter hatred that it was war to the knife everywhere. To make matters still more difficult, there was no one either on the spot or in Paris who could have suggested any remedy but extreme measures of repression. Here is an instance in point.

The department of the Vaucluse had always been full of royalists and priests; and it happened that in Bedouin, one of these remote villages at the foot of Mont Ventoux which had never forsaken the old *régime* nor concealed the fact, " the law had been scandalously outraged." On May 1, the " Tree of Liberty " had been cut down and " the decrees of the Convention dragged through the mud." Suchet, the local military chief, who was presently to become an imperialist, wished to make a terrible example of the village and demanded its destruction. Maignet, the commissioner of the Convention, hesitated and applied for instructions to Paris, whence came the order " Punish severely," whereupon Suchet set fire to the

THE TERROR

village and 433 houses were rendered uninhabitable. With such a system one can easily imagine that there would be no choice but to "punish severely."

So it was in reality. A few days later, it being found impossible to transfer to Paris all the arrested citizens, for, as Maignet said, it would have required an army and a commissariat to do it, Couthon proposed a special commission to deal with them. This commission was to be formed of five members to sit at Orange and try the enemies of the Revolution in the departments of the Vaucluse and the Bouches-du-Rhône. The two committees agreed to the proposal.* Robespierre with his own hand drew up the instructions for this commission, and these instructions presently served as a model for his law of Terror issued on the 22nd Prairial.†

A few days later, Robespierre enlarged upon these principles before the Convention, saying that hitherto they had shown too much consideration for the enemies of liberty and that they must now go beyond the judicial forms and simplify them.‡ And two days after the *Fête* of the Supreme Being he proposed, with the consent of his colleagues on the Committee of Public Welfare, the famous law of the 22nd Prairial (June 10)—concerning the reorganisation of the revolutionary tribunal. By virtue of this law, the tribunal was to be divided into

---

* I here follow the account given by Louis Blanc (Book XII., chap. xiii.), whom no one can accuse of being hostile to the Robespierre group.

† "The enemies of the Revolution," said this instruction, "are those who by any means whatever and under no matter what pretext have tried to hamper the progress of the Revolution and prevent the establishment of the Republic. The due penalty for this crime is death ; the proofs requisite for condemnation are *all information, of no matter what kind*, which may convince a reasonable man and a friend of liberty. The guide for passing sentences lies in the conscience of the judge, enlightened by love of justice and of his country, their aim being the public welfare and the destruction of these enemies of the fatherland."

‡ "They wish to govern revolutions by lawyers' subtleties ; conspiracies against the Republic were being treated as if they were actions between private individuals. Tyranny slays and liberty pleads ! And the Code made by the conspirators is the law by which they are judged ! . . ." "The only delay in punishing the enemies of the fatherland should be until such time as they are found out : it is not so much a question of punishing as of destroying them."

sections, each composed of three judges and nine jurors. Seven of their combined number were to be sufficient for making decisions. The rules for passing sentence were to be those which have just been described as contained in the instructions to the commission at Orange, except that among the crimes deserving of death they included also the spreading of false news to divide or stir up the people, the undermining of morality and the corrupting of the public conscience.

It is evident that to decree such a law was to sign the bankruptcy of the revolutionary Government. It meant doing under a pretext of legality what the people of Paris had done in an insurrection and in a moment of panic and desperation during the September days. And the effect of the law of the 22nd Prairial was to bring the counter-revolution to a head in six weeks.

Was Robespierre's purpose in drawing up this law only to strike at those members of the Convention whom he believed to be most harmful to the Revolution, as some historians have tried to prove? His withdrawal from the business of government after the discussions in the Convention had proved that the Assembly would not allow itself to be bled by the committee without defending its members, gives an air of probability to this supposition. But the well-established fact that the instructions to the commission at Orange had also emanated from Robespierre upsets this theory. It is more probable that Robespierre simply followed the current of the moment, and that he, Couthon and Saint-Just, in agreement with many others, including Cambon, wanted to use the Terror as a general weapon of warfare as well as a menace to some members of the Convention. In reality, without mentioning Hébert, they had been steadily approaching this law since the decrees of the 19th Floréal (May 8) and 9th Prairial (May 28) which dealt with the concentration of authority. It is also very probable that the attempt of Ladmiral to kill Collot d'Herbois and the strange affair of Cécile Renault helped to secure the acceptation of the law of the 22nd Prairial.

Towards the end of April there had been a series of executions in Paris which must have stimulated to a high degree the hatred on the royalists' side. After the "batch" guillotined on the 24th Germinal (April 13), which included Chaumette, Gobel, Lucile Desmoulins, the widow of Hébert, and fifteen others, they had executed d'Eprémesnil, le Chapelier, Thouret, old Malesherbes, the defender of Louis XVI. at his trial, Lavoisier, the great chemist and good republican, and the sister of Louis XVI., Madame Elisabeth, whom they might have set at liberty at the same time as her niece, without in the least endangering the Republic.

The royalists were much infuriated by this, and on the 7th Prairial (May 25) a certain Ladmiral—an office-keeper aged fifty —went to the Convention intending to kill Robespierre. Ladmiral, however, fell asleep during a speech by Barère and missed the "tyrant." He therefore fired instead at Collot d'Herbois as he was mounting the stairs to his lodging. A struggle ensued between the two men in which Collot disarmed Ladmiral.

The same day, Cécile Renault, a girl of twenty, the daughter of a royalist stationer, entered the courtyard of the house where Robespierre lodged with the Duplays, and insisted on seeing him. Her intentions were suspected and she was arrested. Two small knives were found in her pocket and her incoherent answers were interpreted as meaning that she had intended to make an attempt on Robespierre's life. If it was so, the whole affair was very childish; but these two attempts probably served as an argument in favour of the Terrorist Law.

At any rate the committees took advantage of both incidents to make a huge "amalgam." They had the father and brother of the young girl arrested, and several persons whose sole crime was that they had known Ladmiral more or less intimately. In the same "batch" they included Madame Saint-Amaranthe, who kept a gambling-house to which many people were attracted by the beauty of her daughter, Madame de Sartine. As the establishment had been frequented by all sorts of people, among others by Chabot, Desfieux, Hérault de Séchelles, and visited, it seems, by Danton and apparently by a younger brother of Robespierre, the affair was made out to be a royalist conspiracy, in which it was attempted to implicate Robespierre himself. They also dragged in old Sombreuil, whom Maillard had saved during the September massacres, the actress Grand'-Maison, a mistress of Baron de Batz, Sartino, "a knight of the dagger," and along with these notables a poor innocent little dressmaker, seventeen years old, named Nicolle.

Under the new law of the 22nd Prairial, the trial was soon over. This time the "batch" numbered fifty-four persons, who all went to the scaffold in red smocks of parricides, their execution lasting two hours. This was the first outcome of the new law, which every one called Robespierre's law, and at one stroke it made the rule of the Terrorists detested by all Paris.

One can imagine the state of mind of those who had been arrested as "suspects" and flung into prisons in the capital, when they heard the terms of the new law and its application in the case of the fifty-four red-smocks (*les chemises rouges*). A general massacre to clear out the prisons was expected, as at Nantes and Lyons, and preparations were being made by the prisoners to resist. It is even probable that a rising was planned.* The number of accused persons tried at one time rose to one hundred and fifty, who were executed in three "batches"—convicts and royalists going to the scaffold together.

It is useless to dwell upon these executions. Suffice it to say that from April 17, 1793, the day when the Revolutionary Tribunal was established, until the 22nd Prairial in the Year II. (June 10, 1794), that is, within fourteen months, the tribunal had sent 2607 persons to the guillotine in Paris; but after the passing of the new law, within forty-six days from the 22nd Prairial to the 9th Thermidor (July 27, 1794) the same tribunal caused 1351 to perish.

The people of Paris soon sickened with the horror of seeing the procession of tumbrils carrying the condemned to the foot of the guillotine, where it was as much as five executioners could do to empty them every day. There was no longer room in the cemeteries to bury the victims, and vigorous protests were raised

* A search made in the prisons led to the seizure of sums of money amounting to 864,000 livres, exclusive of jewels, which brought the total value up to something like 1,200,000 livres possessed by the suspects in prison.

each time a new cemetery was opened in any of the faubourgs. The sympathies of the working people were now turned to the victims of the guillotine all the more because those struck down belonged chiefly to the poorer classes—the rich having emigrated or concealed themselves. As a fact, among the 2750 guillotined persons of whose social status Louis Blanc found record only 650 belonged to the well-to-do classes. It was even whispered that on the Committee of Public Safety there was a royalist, an agent of Baron de Batz, who urged on the executions so as to render the Republic detested.

One thing is certain; each new " batch " of this kind hastened the fall of the Jacobin Government. The Terror had ceased to terrorise, a thing which statesmen cannot understand.

CHAPTER LXVIII

THE 9TH THERMIDOR—TRIUMPH OF REACTION

Causes of overthrow of Robespierre—Evils of transfer of land—Republican successes abroad—Terror continues—Dantonists, Girondins and " Marsh " unite to overthrow Robespierre—Unpopularity of Committee of Public Welfare—Robespierre attacks Barère and Fouché—His speech in Convention—Effect of speech—9th Thermidor—Arrest of Robespierre and his associates—Efforts of Commune—Capture of Hôtel de Ville—Execution of Robespierre and Terrorists—End of Revolution—Reactionaries continue executions—Attempted rising of workers—Execution of last of Montagnards—Triumph of middle classes—Royalist manifestations—Massacres of revolutionists—Reaction succeeded by Directory—Final effort of revolutionists—Napoleon proclaims himself Emperor

IF Robespierre had many admirers, who adored him, he had also quite as many enemies, who utterly detested him and lost no opportunity of making him odious by attributing to him all the horrors of the Terror. Nor did they neglect to render him ridiculous by connecting him with the doings of an old mad mystic, Catherine Théot, who called herself " the Mother of God."

But still it is evident that it was not personal enmities which overthrew Robespierre. His fall was inevitable, because he represented a *régime* that was on the point of foundering. After the Revolution had passed through its ascendant phase, which lasted until August or September 1793, it entered upon its descendant phase. It was now passing through the Jacobin *régime* of which Robespierre was the supreme expression, and in its turn this *régime* had to give place to the men of " law and order," who were longing to put an end to the unrest of revolution, and were only waiting for the moment when they could overthrow the Terrorists of the "Mountain" without provoking an insurrection in Paris.

We cannot overestimate all the evil resulting from the fact that in economic matters the Revolution was based on personal gain. A revolution should include *the welfare of all*, otherwise it is certain to be crushed by those very persons whom it has enriched at the expense of the nation. Whenever a shifting of wealth is caused by a revolution, it ought never to be for the benefit of *individuals*, but always for the benefit of *communities*. Yet it was on this point precisely that the Great Revolution fatally erred.

The estates, which were confiscated from the church and the nobility, were given to private persons, whereas they should have been restored to the villages and the towns, because they had formerly belonged to the people—being, as they were, the lands which individuals had fastened upon under the protection of the feudal system. There have never been any cultivated lands of seigniorial or ecclesiastic origin. Apart from a few monastic communities, neither lords nor priests had ever with their own hands cleared a single acre. The people, those called *vilains* or *manants*, had cleared every square yard of cultivated soil. It was they who had made it accessible, habitable, and given value to it, and it was to them it should have been restored.

But, acting in the interests of a middle-class State, the Constituent and Legislative Assemblies, and even the Convention too, acknowledged the legal claims of lord, convent, cathedral, and church to lands which in former times had been appropriated by those props of the then growing State, and they took possession of these lands and sold them chiefly to the middle classes.

It can be imagined what a scramble for a share in this booty took place when estates, of which the total value amounted to from ten to fifteen thousand millions of francs, were on sale for several years under conditions extremely favourable to the purchasers—conditions which could be rendered still more advantageous by currying favour with the new local authorities. In this way the famous "black bands" were formed in the provinces, against which all the efforts of the Convention's commissioners were powerless.

The pernicious influence of these pilferers, reinforced by the Paris stock-jobbers and the army contractors, spread by degrees to the Convention itself, where the honest men among the Montagnards found themselves confronted by "profitmongers" and helpless against them. What was there to oppose to them ? Once the *Enragés* were crushed and the sections of Paris paralysed—what remained in the Convention beside the "Marsh"?

The victory of Fleurus, won on June 26 (8th Messidor) over the combined forces of Austria and England—a victory which ended the campaign in the North for that year—and the successes gained by the Republic's armies in the Pyrenees, the Alps, and on the Rhine, as well as the arrival of a transport laden with wheat from America—at the cost, be it said, of several battleships—these successes served in themselves as powerful arguments with the "moderates," who were anxious to restore order. "What," said they, "is the good of a revolutionary government, now that the war is almost over ? It is time to go back to legal conditions, and to put an end to government by revolutionary committees and patriotic societies in the provinces. It is time to restore order and to close the period of revolution!"

But the Terror, so generally attributed to Robespierre, far from relaxing, was still fully maintained. On the 3rd Messidor (June 21), Herman, a government official, "*commissaire des administrations civiles, police et tribunaux,*" a man much attached to Robespierre, sent in a statement to the Committee of Public Welfare, asking permission to inquire into the plottings among the prisoners and hinting that "it might be necessary presently to purge the prisons." He was authorised by the committee to hold the inquiry, and forthwith began the sending of those horrible "batches," those cartloads of men and women to the guillotine, a sight more abominable to the Parisians than the September massacres. These executions were all the more odious because no one knew where they would end, and because they went on in the midst of balls, concerts, and other festivities given by the class that had so recently grown rich, and amid the derision of the royalist *jeunesse dorée*, who grew daily more aggressive.

Every one must have felt that this state of things could not last, and the Moderates in the Convention took advantage of it. Dantonists, Girondins, and the members of the "Marsh," joined ranks, and concentrated their forces on Robespierre's overthrow, as the first point to be gained. The condition of Paris favoured their designs, as the Committee of Public Welfare had succeeded in crippling the sections—the true centres of the popular movements.

On the 5th Thermidor (July 23) the general council of the Commune, in which Payan, an intimate friend of Robespierre, was now all powerful, did much to injure its popularity by issuing a decree that was absolutely unjust to the workers. The council ordered in all the forty-eight sections the proclamation of the maximum, which was to fix the limit of the workers' wages. As we have seen, the Committee of Public Welfare had already made itself unpopular with the sections by destroying their autonomy, and appointing the members of several of their committee.

The moment, therefore, was ripe for attempting a *coup d'état*.

On the 21st Messidor (July 9) Robespierre had at length decided to begin the attack upon his enemies. Eight days previously he had been complaining at the Jacobin Club of the war that was being waged against him personally. He now went into particulars, and made some allusions to Barère—that very Barère who until then had been the pliant instrument of his faction, whenever a bold stroke had been needed in the Convention. Two days later, again at the Jacobin Club, he made a direct attack on Fouché for his terrible doings in Lyons, and succeeded in having him summoned to answer for them before the club.

By the 26th Messidor (July 14) war was declared, as Fouché had refused to appear before the Jacobins. As to the attack on Barère, it meant also an attack on Collot d'Herbois and Billaud-Varenne, as well as on two powerful members of the Committee of Public Safety, Vadier and Voulland, who often conferred with Barère and had collaborated with him in the business of the prison plots.

All those of the Left, therefore, who felt themselves threatened —Tallien, Barère, Vadier, Voulland, Billaud-Varenne, Collot d'Herbois, Fouché—banded themselves together against the "triumvirs"—Robespierre, Saint-Just and Couthon. Moderates, such as Barras, Rovère, Thirion, Courtois, Bourdon, and the rest, who, for their part, would have liked to see the downfall of the whole "Mountain," including Collot d'Herbois, Billaud-Varenne, Barère, Vadier and the others, no doubt said to themselves that it was best to begin by attacking the Robespierre group, as, once that was overthrown, the rest could be easily managed.

The storm burst in the Convention on the 8th Thermidor (July 26, 1794). It must have been expected, for the hall was thronged. Robespierre attacked the Committee of General Safety in a carefully prepared speech and charged it with conspiring against the Convention. He was there, he said, to defend the Convention and himself against slanders. He also defended himself against the charge of dictatorial tendencies, and he did not try to be conciliatory towards his adversaries— even towards Cambon, of whom he spoke, as well as of Mallarmé and Ramel, in terms borrowed from the *Enragés*, calling them "*Feuillants*, aristocrats, rascals."

He was permitted to finish, because people were anxious to know his conclusions, and when he had expressed them it was perceived that in reality he was asking for an increase in his own authority and that of his group. There was no new outlook, no new programme in his speech. It was only the demand of a Government member for more power—still more power, to be used for purposes of repression.

"What is the remedy for the evil?" he said in conclusion. "The punishment of the traitors, a complete reconstruction of the Committee of General Safety, the purification of that committee and its subordination to the Committee of Public Welfare; the purification of the Committee of Public Welfare itself; and unity of Government under the authority of the National Convention which was the centre and the judge."

THE 9TH THERMIDOR

It was understood then that he confined himself to asking for more authority to be vested in his triumvirate, to be used against Collot and Billot, Tallien and Barère, Cambon and Carnot, Vadier and Voulland. The conspirators of the Right must have rubbed their hands. They had only to let Tallien, Billot-Varenne and the other Montagnards act.

The evening of the same day the Jacobin Club rapturously applauded Robespierre's speech and made a furious demonstration against Collot d'Herbois and Billaud-Varenne. It was even proposed to march against the two committees. But nothing went beyond mere talk. The Jacobin Club had never been a centre of action.

During the night Bourdon and Tallien secured the support of the Conventionals of the Right, and apparently the plan agreed upon was to prevent Robespierre and Saint-Just from speaking.

The next day, the 9th Thermidor, as soon as Saint-Just rose to read his statement—which, by the way, was very moderate, for it only asked for a revision of Government procedure—Billaud-Varenne and Tallien would not allow him to read it. They demanded the arrest of the "tyrant," meaning Robespierre, and shouts of "Down with the tyrant!" were re-echoed by the whole of the "Marsh." Robespierre attempted to speak, but he, too, was prevented. An order was given for his prosecution, including his brother, Saint-Just, Couthon and Lebas, and they were immediately arrested and taken off to different prisons.

Meanwhile Hanriot, the chief of the National Guard, followed by two aides-de-camp and some gendarmes, was galloping through the streets in the direction of the Convention, when two of the members of the Convention, seeing him pass in the Rue Saint-Honore, had him arrested by six of the very gendarmes under his command.

The General Council of the Commune did not meet until six o'clock in the evening. It then issued an appeal to the people, calling on them to rise against Barère, Collot, Bourdon and Amar, and Coffinhal was despatched to deliver Robespierre and his friends who, it was thought, were kept under arrest in the building occupied by the Committee of General Safety, but Coffinhal found there only Hanriot, whom he released. As to Robespierre, he had been taken first to the Luxembourg, but the officials there refused to receive him; and, instead of going straight to the Commune, and casting in his lot with the party of insurrection, he went to the Police Office on the Quai des Orfèvres, and remained doing nothing. Saint-Just and Lebas went as soon as they were free to the Commune, and Coffinhal, again sent by the Council to seek Robespierre, had to force his hand to compel him to go to the Hôtel de Ville, which he reached about eight o'clock.

The Council of the Commune began to arrange for a rising, but it became clear that the sections had no mind to rise against the Convention in favour of those whom they charged with having guillotined Chaumette and Hébert, killed Jacques Roux, ejected Pache from office, and destroyed the autonomy of the sections. Paris, moreover, must have felt that the Revolution was dying out, and that the men for whom the Council of the Commune appealed to the people to rise were in no way representative of the popular cause.

By midnight the sections had made no sign of stirring. Louis Blanc says that they were in a state of division, their civil committees being unable to come to agreement with the revolutionary committees and the General Assemblies. The fourteen sections that obeyed the Commune in the first instance did nothing, while eighteen were hostile, and of these, six were in the immediate neighbourhood of the Hôtel de Ville. The men of Jacques Roux' section, the Gravilliers, even formed the first nucleus of one of the two columns that marched upon the Hôtel de Ville at the order of the Convention.*

* The sections, M. Ernest Mellié says, took no initiative, but tamely followed their committees, the members of which were dependent on the Committees of Public Welfare and General Safety. They were left no part in politics. . . . They had even been forbidden to call themselves primary assemblies; on the 20th Floréal, Year II. (May 9, 1794), Payan, the national agent of the Commune, who had taken the place of Chaumette, warned them by letter that, under a revolutionary government, there were no primary assemblies. . . . This was to remind them that their abdication was complete (pp. 151, 152). After recounting the successive purifications to which the sections had submitted to make themselves acceptable to the Jacobins (p. 153), M.

In the meantime, the Convention was declaring the insurgents and the Commune outlaws, and when this declaration was read in the Place de la Grève, Hanriot's artillerymen, who had been posted there with nothing to do, slipped away one by one. The Place was quite deserted when shortly afterwards the Hôtel de Ville was invaded by the columns from the Gravilliers and the Arcis. A young gendarme, who was the first to enter the room in which were Robespierre and his friends, fired a pistol-shot which broke Robespierre's jaw. The Hôtel de Ville, the very centre of the resistance, was thus taken without a blow being struck in its defence. Thereupon Lebas killed himself, the younger Robespierre tried to kill himself by leaping through a window from the third story; Coffinhal caught hold of Hanriot, whom he accused of having lost their cause, and hurled him out of window; Saint-Just and Couthon allowed themselves to be arrested quietly.

The next morning, after a mere form of identification, they were all executed, to the number of twenty-one. They went to their death in the Place de la Révolution by a long route amid the insults of counter-revolutionary crowds. The fashionable people who hastened to enjoy the spectacle were even more festive than on the day of the execution of the Hébertists. Windows were let at fabulous prices, and the ladies who sat in them wore full dress. Reaction was triumphing. The Revolution had come to an end.

Here we, too, shall pause, without narrating the details of the orgies under the White Terror, which began after Thermidor, or the two attempts at insurrection against the new *régime :* the movement of Prairial in the Year III. and the conspiracy of Babeuf in the Year IV.

Mellié concludes with these words : " Michelet was right, therefore, in saying that by this time the assemblies of the sections were dead and that all power had passed over to the revolutionary committees, which, being themselves nominated by the Government, had no longer any vitality either " (pp. 154, 155). On the 9th Thermidor (and of this M. Mellié has found the proofs in the Archives), in nearly all the sections the revolutionary committees were assembled to await the orders of the Government (p. 169). It is not surprising, therefore, that the sections did not take action against the Thermidoreans.

The opponents of the Terror, who were always talking of clemency, wanted it only for themselves and their friends. The first thing they did when they came into power was to execute all the partisans of the Montagnards whom they had overthrown. In the three days, the 10th, 11th, and 12th Thermidor (July 28, 29, and 30) there were a hundred and three executions. Denunciations poured in from the middle classes and the guillotine was working hard—this time on the side of reaction. From the 9th Thermidor to the 1st Prairial, in less than ten months, seventy-three Montagnard representatives were condemned to death or imprisoned, while seventy-three Girondins re-entered the Convention.

It was now the turn of the real " Statesmen." The " maximum " on commodities was speedily abolished, which produced a violent crisis, during which stock-jobbing and speculation attained gigantic proportions. The middle classes held high holiday, as they did again later on after June 1848 and May 1871. The *jeunesse dorée* organised by Fréon ruled Paris, while the workers, seeing that the Revolution was vanquished, crept back to their hovels to meditate on the chances of the next upheaval.

They attempted to rise on the 12th Germinal, Year III. (April 1, 1795), and again on the 1st Prairial (May 20) demanding bread and the Constitution of 1793. On this occasion the faubourgs showed much spirit, but the middle classes had had time to organise their forces. The revolutionary tribunal had been abolished, so the last of the Montagnards—Romme, Bourbotte, Duroy, Soubrancy, Goujon and Duquesnoy—were condemned to death by a military commission and executed.

Thenceforth the middle classes remained masters of the Revolution and the descendant phase continued. The reaction soon became frankly royalist. The *troupe dorée* no longer remained concealed, but openly wore the grey coat with the green or blue colour of the *Chouans* * and ill-treated all those known as " terrorists "—that is to say, all republicans. There were persecutions both wholesale and retail. Whoever had assisted in any way in the execution of the King—or in his

* The Breton royalists.

arrest after the flight to Varennes, whoever had taken any part whatever in the assault on the Tuileries, was pointed out to the royalists and life made insupportable for him.

In the departments, especially in the South, the "Compagnies du Jésus," the "Compagnies du Soleil" and other royalist organisations practised wholesale reprisals. In the prisons at Lyons, Aix and Marseilles they killed all those who had taken part in the former government. Mignet says: "Nearly every place in the South had its second of September," and that, of course, means its royalist second of September. Besides these wholesale massacres, the members of the above-named Societies of Jesus and the Sun held individual man-hunts. In Lyons, whenever they found a revolutionist who had escaped their massacres, they killed him and threw the body into the Rhône without any pretence at a trial. Similar deeds were enacted in Tarascon.

The reaction increased until at last the Convention broke up on the 4th Brumaire, Year IV. (October 26, 1795). The Directory succeeded it and prepared the way for the Consulate first and the Empire afterwards. The Directory was a terrible orgy of the middle classes, in which the fortunes acquired during the Revolution, especially during the Thermidorean reaction, were squandered in unbridled luxury. For, if the Revolution had put in circulation eight milliards of paper-money, the Thermidorean reaction went ten times as fast in that direction, for it issued the amazing sum of thirty milliards in paper *within fifteen months*. By this we can calculate the amount of the fortunes which had been accumulated by the "profit-mongers," thanks to these tremendous issues of paper-money.

Once again, in May 1796, the revolutionary Communists under the leadership of Babeuf tried to get up an insurrection through their secret society, but they were arrested before it was ripe. An attempt to raise the camp at Grenelle on the night of the 23rd Fructidor, Year IV. (September 9, 1796), also failed. Babeuf and Darthé were condemned to death, and killed themselves with a dagger on the 7th Prairial, Year V. But the royalists had their failure too, on the 18th Fructidor, Year V. (September 4,

1797), and the Directory lasted until the 18th Brumaire, Year VIII. (November 9, 1799).

On that day Napoleon Bonaparte carried out his *coup d'état*, and national representation was completely suppressed by the *ex-sans-culotte*, who had the army on his side.

The war, which had lasted seven years, had thus come to its logical conclusion. On the 28th Floréal, Year XII. (May 18, 1804), Napoleon proclaimed himself Emperor, and then war broke out again, to last with brief intervals until 1815.

CONCLUSION

WHEN one sees that terrible and powerful Convention wrecking itself in 1794–1795, that proud and strong Republic disappearing, and France, after the demoralising *régime* of the Directory, falling under the military yoke of a Bonaparte, one is impelled to ask: " What was the good of the Revolution if the nation had to fall back again under despotism ? " In the course of the nineteenth century, this question has been constantly put, and the timid and conservative have worn it threadbare as an argument against revolutions in general.

The preceding pages supply the answer. Those who have seen in the Revolution only a change in the Government, those who are ignorant of its economic as well as its educational work, those alone could put such a question.

The France we see during the last days of the eighteenth century, at the moment of the *coup d'état* on the 18th Brumaire, is not the France that existed before 1789. Would it have been possible for the old France, wretchedly poor and with a third of her population suffering yearly from dearth, to have maintained the Napoleonic Wars, coming so soon after the terrible wars of the Republic between 1792 and 1799, when all Europe was attacking her ?

The fact is, that a new France had been constituted since 1792–1793. Scarcity still prevailed in many of the departments, and its full horrors were felt especially after the *coup d'état* of Thermidor, when the maximum price for all foodstuffs was abolished. There were still some departments which did not produce enough wheat to feed themselves, and as the war went on, and all means of transport were requisitioned for its supplies, there was scarcity in those departments. But everything tends to prove that France was even then producing much more of the necessaries of life of every kind than in 1789.

Never was there in France such energetic ploughing, Michelet tells us, as in 1792, when the peasant was ploughing the lands he had taken back from the lords, the convents, the churches, and was goading his oxen to the cry of "*Allons Prusse! Allons Autriche!*" Never had there been so much clearing of lands —even royalist writers admit this—as during those years of revolution. The first good harvest, in 1794, brought relief to two-thirds of France—at least in the villages, for all this time the towns were threatened with scarcity of food. Not that it was scarce in France as a whole, or that the *sans-culotte* municipalities neglected to take measures to feed those who could not find employment, but from the fact that all beasts of burden not actually used in tillage were requisitioned to carry food and ammunition to the fourteen armies of the Republic. In those days there were no railways, and all but the main roads were in the state they are to this day in Russia—well-nigh impassable.

A new France was born during those four years of revolution. For the first time in centuries the peasant ate his fill, straightened his back and dared to speak out. Read the detailed reports concerning the return of Louis XVI. to Paris, when he was brought back a prisoner from Varennes, in June 1791, by the peasants, and say: "Could such a thing, such an interest in the public welfare, such a devotion to it, and such an independence of judgment and action have been possible before 1789?" A new nation had been born in the meantime, just as we see to-day a new nation coming into life in Russia and in Turkey.

It was owing to this new birth that France was able to maintain her wars under the Republic and Napoleon, and to carry the principles of the Great Revolution into Switzerland, Italy, Spain, Belgium, Holland, Germany, and even to the borders of Russia. And when, after all those wars, after having mentally followed the French armies as far as Egypt and Moscow, we expect to find France in 1815 reduced to an appalling misery and her lands laid waste, we find, instead, that even in its eastern portions and in the Jura, the country is much more prosperous than it was at the time when Pétion, pointing out to Louis XVI. the luxuriant banks of the Marne, asked him if there was anywhere in the world a kingdom more beautiful than the one the King had not wished to keep.

The self-contained energy was such in villages regenerated by the Revolution, that in a few years France became a country of well-to-do peasants, and her enemies soon discovered that in spite of all the blood she had shed and the losses she had sustained, France, in respect of her *productivity*, was the richest country in Europe. Her wealth, indeed, is not drawn from the Indies or from her foreign commerce : it comes from her own soil, from her love of the soil, from her own skill and industry. She is the richest country, because of the subdivision of her wealth, and she is still richer because of the possibilities she offers for the future.

Such was the effect of the Revolution. And if the casual observer sees in Napoleonic France only a love of glory, the historian realises that even the wars France waged at that period were undertaken to secure the fruits of the Revolution—to keep the lands that had been retaken from the lords, the priests and the rich, and the liberties that had been won from despotism and the Court. If France was willing in those years to bleed herself to death, merely to prevent the Germans, the English, and the Russians from forcing a Louis XVIII. upon her, it was because she did not want the return of the emigrant nobles to mean that the *ci-devants* would take back the lands which had been watered already with the peasant's sweat, and the liberties which had been sanctified with the patriots' blood. And France fóught so well for twenty-three years, that when she was compelled at last to admit the Bourbons, it was she who imposed conditions on them. The Bourbons might reign, but the lands were to be kept by those who had taken them from the feudal lords, so that even during the White Terror of the Bourbons they dared not touch those lands. The old *régime* could not be re-established.

This is what is gained by making a Revolution.

There are other things to be pointed out. In the history of

all nations a time comes when fundamental changes are bound to take place in the whole of the national life. Royal despotism and feudalism were dying in 1789; it was impossible to keep them alive; they had to go.

But then, two ways were opened out before France: reform or revolution.

At such times there is always a moment when reform is still possible; but if advantage has not been taken of that moment, if an obstinate resistance has been opposed to the requirements of the new life, up to the point when blood has flowed in the streets, as it flowed on July 14, 1789, then there must be a Revolution. And once the Revolution has begun, it must necessarily develop to its last conclusions—that is to say, to the highest point it is capable of attaining—were it only temporarily, being given a certain condition of the public mind at this particular moment.

If we represent the slow progress of a period of evolution by a line drawn on paper, we shall see this line gradually though slowly rising. Then there comes a Revolution, and the line makes a sudden leap upwards. In England the line would be represented as rising to the Puritan Republic of Cromwell; in France it rises to the *Sans-culotte* Republic of 1793. However, at this height progress cannot be maintained; all the hostile forces league together against it, and the Republic goes down. Our line, after having reached that height, drops. Reaction follows. For the political life of France the line drops very low indeed, but by degrees it rises again, and when peace is restored in 1815 in France, and in 1688 in England—both countries are found to have attained a level much higher than they were on prior to their Revolutions.

After that, evolution is resumed: our line again begins to rise slowly: but, besides taking place on a very much higher level, the rising of the line will in nearly every case be also much more rapid than before the period of disturbance.

This is a law of human progress, and also a law of individual progress. The more recent history of France confirms this very law by showing how it was necessary to pass through the Commune to arrive at the Third Republic.

CONCLUSION

The work of the French Revolution is not confined merely to what it obtained and what was retained of it in France. It is to be found also in the principles bequeathed by it to the succeeding century—in the line of direction it marked out for the future.

A reform is always a compromise with the past, but the progress accomplished by revolution is always a promise of future progress. If the Great French Revolution was the summing up of a century's evolution, it also marked out in its turn the programme of evolution to be accomplished in the course of the nineteenth century.

It is a law in the world's history that the period of a hundred or a hundred and thirty years, more or less, which passes between two great revolutions, receives its character from the revolution in which this period began. The nations endeavour to realise in their institutions the inheritance bequeathed to them by the last revolution. All that this last could not yet put into practice, all the great thoughts which were thrown into circulation during the turmoil, and which the revolution either could not or did not know how to apply, all the attempts at sociological reconstruction, which were born during the revolution, will go to make up the substance of evolution during the epoch that follows the revolution, with the addition of those new ideas to which this evolution will give birth, when trying to put into practice the programme marked out by the last upheaval. Then, a new revolution will be brought about in some other nation, and this nation in its turn will set the problems for the following century. Such has hitherto been the trend of history.

Two great conquests, in fact, characterise the century which has passed since 1789–1793. Both owe their origin to the French Revolution, which had carried on the work of the English Revolution while enlarging and invigorating it with all the progress that had been made since the English middle classes beheaded their King and transferred his power to the Parliament. These two great triumphs are: the abolition of serfdom and the abolition of absolutism, by which personal liberties have been conferred upon the individual, undreamt of by the serf of the lord and the subject of the absolute king, while at the same time they have brought about the development of the middle classes and the capitalist *régime*.

These two achievements represent the principal work of the nineteenth century, begun in France in 1789 and slowly spread over Europe in the course of that century.

The work of enfranchisement, begun by the French peasants in 1789, was continued in Spain, Italy, Switzerland, Germany, and Austria by the armies of the *sans-culottes*. Unfortunately, this work hardly penetrated into Poland and did not reach Russia at all.

The abolition of serfdom in Europe would have been already completed in the first half of the nineteenth century if the French *bourgeoisie*, coming into power in 1794 over the dead bodies of Anarchists, Cordeliers, and Jacobins, had not checked the revolutionary impulse, restored monarchy, and handed over France to the imperial juggler, the first Napoleon. This ex-*sans-culotte*, now a general of the *sans-culottes*, speedily began to prop up aristocracy; but the impulsion had been given, the institution of serfdom had already received a mortal blow. It was abolished in Spain and Italy in spite of the temporary triumph of reaction. It was closely pressed in Germany after 1811, and disappeared in that country definitively in 1848. In 1861, Russia was compelled to emancipate her serfs, and the war of 1878 put an end to serfdom in the Balkan peninsula.

The cycle is now complete. The right of the lord over the person of the peasant no longer exists in Europe, even in those countries where the feudal dues have still to be redeemed.

This fact is not sufficiently appreciated by historians. Absorbed as they are in political questions, they do not perceive the importance of the abolition of serfdom, which is, however, the essential feature of the nineteenth century. The rivalries between nations and the wars resulting from them, the policies of the Great Powers which occupy so much of the historian's attention, have all sprung from that one great fact—the abolition of serfdom and the development of the wage-system which has taken its place.

The French peasant, in revolting a hundred and twenty years

CONCLUSION 579

ago against the lord who made him beat the ponds lest croaking frogs should disturb his master's sleep, has thus freed the peasants of all Europe. In four years, by burning the documents which registered his subjection, by setting fire to the châteaux, and by executing the owners of them who refused to recognise his rights as a human being, the French peasant so stirred up all Europe that it is to-day altogether free from the degradation of serfdom.

On the other hand, the abolition of absolute power has also taken a little over a hundred years to make the tour of Europe. Attacked in England in 1648, and vanquished in France in 1789, royal authority based on divine right is no longer exercised save in Russia, but there, too, it is at its last gasp. Even the little Balkan States and Turkey have now their representative assemblies, and Russia is entering the same cycle.

In this respect the Revolution of 1789-1793 has also accomplished its work. Equality before the law and representative government have now their place in almost all the codes of Europe. In theory, at least, the law makes no distinctions between men, and every one has the right to participate, more or less, in the government.

The absolute monarch—master of his subjects—and the lord —master of the soil and the peasants, by right of birth—have both disappeared. The middle classes now govern Europe.

But at the same time the Great Revolution has bequeathed to us some other principles of an infinitely higher import; the principles of communism. We have seen how all through the Great Revolution the communist idea kept coming to the front, and how after the fall of the Girondins numerous attempts and sometimes great attempts were made in this direction. Fourierism descends in a direct line from L'Ange on one side and from Chalier on the other. Babeuf is the direct descendant of ideas which stirred the masses to enthusiasm in 1793; he, Buonarotti, and Sylvain Maréchal have only systematised them a little or even merely put them into literary form. But the secret societies organised by Babeuf and Buonarotti were the origin of the *communistes matérialistes* secret societies through which Blanqui and Barbès conspired under the *bourgeois* monarchy of Louis-Philippe. Later on, in 1866, the International Working Men's Association appeared in the direct line of descent from these societies. As to "socialism" we know now that this term came into vogue to avoid the term "communism," which at one time was dangerous because the secret communist societies became societies for action, and were rigorously suppressed by the *bourgeoisie* then in power.

There is, therefore, a direct filiation from the *Enragés* of 1793 and the Babeuf conspiracy of 1795 to the International Working Men's Association of 1866–1878.

There is also a direct descent of ideas. Up till now, modern socialism has added absolutely nothing to the ideas which were circulating among the French people between 1789 and 1794, and which it was tried to put into practice in the Year II. of the Republic. Modern socialism has only systematised those ideas and found arguments in their favour, either by turning against the middle-class economists certain of their own definitions, or by generalising certain facts noticed in the development of industrial capitalism, in the course of the nineteenth century.

But I permit myself to maintain also that, however vague it may have been, however little support it endeavoured to draw from arguments dressed in a scientific garb, and however little use it made of the pseudo-scientific slang of the middle-class economists, the popular communism of the first two years of the Republic saw clearer, and went much deeper in its analyses, than modern socialism.

First of all, it was communism in the consumption of the necessaries of life—not in production only; it was the communalisation and the nationalisation of what economists know as consumption—to which the stern republicans of 1793 turned, above all, their attention, when they tried to establish their stores of grain and provisions in every commune, when they set on foot a gigantic inquiry to find and fix the true value of the objects of prime and secondary necessity, and when they inspired Robespierre to declare that *only the superfluity of food-*

CONCLUSION

stuffs should become articles of commerce, and that what was necessary belonged to all.

Born out of the pressing necessities of those troublous years, the communism of 1793, with its affirmation of the right of all to sustenance and to the land for its production, its denial of the right of any one to hold more land than he and his family could cultivate—that is, more than a farm of 120 acres—and its attempt to communalise all trade and industry—this communism went straighter to the heart of things than all the minimum programmes of our own time, or even all the maximum preambles of such programmes.

In any case, what we learn to-day from the study of the Great Revolution is, that it was the source and origin of all the present communist, anarchist, and socialist conceptions. We have but badly understood our common mother, but now we have found her again in the midst of the *sans-culottes*, and we see what we have to learn from her.

Humanity advances by stages and these stages have been marked for several hundred years by great revolutions. After the Netherlands came England with her revolution in 1648–1657, and then it was the turn of France. Each great revolution has in it, besides, something special and original. England and France both abolished royal absolutism. But in doing so England was chiefly interested in the personal rights of the individual, particularly in matters of religion, as well as the local rights of every parish and every community. As to France, she turned her chief attention to the land question, and in striking a mortal blow at the feudal system she struck also at the great fortunes, and sent forth into the world the idea of nationalising the soil, and of socialising commerce and the chief industries.

Which of the nations will take upon herself the terrible but glorious task of the next great revolution ? One may have thought for a time that it would be Russia. But if she should push her revolution further than the mere limitation of the imperial power ; if she touches the land question in a revolutionary spirit—how far will she go ? Will she know how to avoid the mistake made by the French Assemblies, and will she socialise the land and give it only to those who want to cultivate it with their own hands ? We know not : any answer to this question would belong to the domain of prophecy.

The one thing certain is, that whatsoever nation enters on the path of revolution in our own day, it will be heir to all our forefathers have done in France. The blood they shed was shed for humanity—the sufferings they endured were borne for the entire human race ; their struggles, the ideas they gave to the world, the shock of those ideas, are all included in the heritage of mankind. All have borne fruit and will bear more, still finer, as we advance towards those wide horizons opening out before us, where, like some great beacon to point the way, flame the words—LIBERTY, EQUALITY, FRATERNITY.

INDEX

ABBAYE (prison), soldiers released from, 69; attacked by Federals, 297; massacres at, 299
Absolutism, abolition of, 577–79
Acapts, 203
Agrarian Law, fear of, 169; progress of, 242; repudiated by "Gironde," 342; meaning of, 403–4; supporters penalised, 500
Agrier, 203
Aiguillon, Duc d', against feudalism, 121
Albitte, socialism of, 506, 507
Allier, Claude, organises conspiracy, 250, 251
Allies, mistake of, 466
"Amalgams," 545, 548, 549
Amar, reports on Girondins, 514; attacked, 544
America, North, inspires liberty, 21 *et seq.*; young Republic of, 141
"Ami du Peuple," 395
Anarchism, principles of, 184; beliefs of, 354–55; modern, 365
Anarchists, 4, 13; side with people, 346; persecution of, 347; denounced by Brissot, 350, 392; influence of, 353, 357; attacked by Girondins, 359; called Coblentzians, 486; called Levellers, 511
Anarchy defined by Brissot, 351; in politics, 479
"Ancien régime," vices of, 149
Angremont d', conspiracy of, 293
"Annales patriotiques," *quoted*, 305, 307–8
"Ansässigen," 416; deprived of rights, 418

Archbishop of Arles, tried and executed, 302
Archives, National, records of peasant risings in, 39
Archives of France, vi., provincial, importance of, 409
Argenson, d', *cited*, 12
Argonne, Forest of; Prussians halt in, 325
Aristocracy, worst form of, 499
Arles, Archbishop, accused of massacre, 302
Armies, Four, of France, 556
Arms, search for, 294
Army, French, weakness of, 284; unreliability of, 290; corruption in, 223, 329
German, enters France, on frontier, 323, 324–25; retreat of, 325; recrosses Rhine, 538
of Republic (Fr.), condition of, 462–63; disorganisation and tactics of, 464; retreat of, 465; reorganisation of, 410, 515
Artois, Count d', plans *coup d'état*, hated, 70; escape of, 91; protests against Constitution, 238; in exile, 248; manufactures *assignats*, 444; heads Breton rising, 466
land system in, 417, 433
Assemblies, electoral, in Paris, 47; of Notables, 29, 33, 109; of Representatives, 186; of Commissioners, 273; Village, 416; Communal, 417
Assembly, Constituent, character of, 172; maintains mortmain, 201; reaction in, 202; protects property, 203, 204; imposes redemption, 210;

INDEX

Assembly, Constituent—*continued*
opposes popular revolution, 214; reinstates King, 233; dissolves, 234; decrees on land, 277; recognises money as merchandise, 374; opposes land solution, 417; abolishes titles, 429; mistakes of, 499

Legislative, sells communal lands, 21; opposes people, 214, 217; formation of, 234; servility of, 237; proceeds against Count de Provence, 239; moderation of, 256; King takes refuge in, 275; threatened, 278, 307; bad policy of, 279; dissolution of, 280; declares against monarchy, 306-7; dissensions in, 315; members bought, 332; disappoints peasants about land, 417; laws of, 418-20; sells *émigrés'* lands, 435; mistake of, 499; sells communal lands, 502

National, inevitability of, 33; enthusiasm in, 118 *et seq.*; condemns riots, 120; temporises over feudal rights, 131; work of, 135, 173; resolutions of, 135; effect on peasants, 136; composition of, 148, 162; threatened, 152; fears people, 159; method of electing, 163-64; opposition to, 167; King's intentions towards, 175; concocts municipal constitution, 184-85; lessens power of Districts, 191; destroys feudalism, 198; resolutions of 200 legalises feudalism, 205; ignores King, 232; reaction in, 232-33; suppresses Lafayette's letter, 245; absolves Lafayette, 285; yields to threats, 288; libels on, 289. *Vide* National

Assignats, *vide* Paper-currency, issue of, 44, 171, 371; depreciation of, 434, 442-3; forging of, 444

Atheism, 479

Avenel, *cited*, 327; *quoted*, 433, 455, 502, 547
August 4, renunciations of, 118 *e seq.*
Aulard,'research by, v., *quoted*, 39, 101, 217, 220, 245, 298, 316, 319, 365, 366, 367, 473, 506, 507, 521, 525; *cited*, 481, 482, 483, 526, 527
Aumont, Duke d', refuses command of National Guards, 76
Austria, army, on frontier, 224; urged to invade, 239; war declared against, 240
"Austrian Committee," 283
Author, *cited*, 40
Autonomy of towns, 100

BABEAU, *quoted*, 98, 99
Babeuf, apostle of communism, 489, 490, 491, 492, 494, 579; conspiracy of, 485, 569, 571; suicide of, 571
Bachmann (Commander of Swiss), escapes punishment, 293
Bailly (Mayor of Paris), President of Assembly, 56; pins tricolour in King's hat, 91; on Municipal Council, 101; *quoted*, 152; importance of, 160; plans organisation, 183; agrees to free assembly, 184-85; demands dismissal of ministers, 192; execution of, 517; a freemason, 540
Balkan States, *cited*, 579
Banalités, 37, 129, 131, 202
Bankruptcy of State, 33, 149, 168
Banquets, October 1 and October 3, 1789, 152, 153
Barbaroux, justifies massacres, 321; favours centralisation, 367; stirs up revolt, 368, 446
Barbès, secret society of, 580
Barbot, Berthelet de (Abbé), narrative of, 302
Barentain (Keeper of Seals), addresses States General, 51-52, 54; hooted by people, 56
Barère, suggests Commission of Twelve, 397; report of, 441, 500; takes lead, 483; daring

INDEX

Barère—*continued*
of, 511; attachment to Robespierre, 565, 567
Barnave, silence of, 35; member of Breton Club, 61; in middle-class triumvirate, 162; won over by King, 332; executed, 517
Bastille, taking of (July 14, 1789), official account, 57; true version, 58; 78 *et seq.*, 87
Batz, Baron de, conspires with Count d'Artois, 444; organises Queen's escape, 516; cleverness of, 539; agent of, on Committee of Public Safety, 561
Baudot, *quoted*, 369; explains Girondins' defence of property, 485; *cited*, 550
Bault, warder of Queen, 516
Bayon, pursues King, 228
Bazire, tries to stop massacres, 299; in royalist plot, 539; tried and executed, 548
Beauvais, Bishop of, stoned, 56
Beck, Baron de, Prussian Minister, objects to clemency, 335
"Bed of Justice," 25-26
Bedoin, burning of, 556
Beffroy, communism of, 498
Beggary, increase of, 30
Benoît (banker) in Royalist plot, 539
Bernardins, the massacre of convicts at, 303
Bernier, heads Council of Insurrection, 386
Berthier, arrested, 92; trampled to death, 93; effect of death, 100; memory of, 149
Besançon, rising at, 27
Besenval, Marquis de, commands troops in Paris, 72, 78, 80
Betrayals, 282 *et seq.*
Beuvron, Duchess de, boasts of, 65
Bicêtre (prison), loathed by people, 79; massacres at, 303
Billaud-Varennes, in war-council, 305; against wealth, 486; makes terms with Communists, 500; insight of, 501; on Committee of Public Welfare, 535; slanders Hébertists, 545; attacked by Robespierre, 565-67

"Blackgangs" (*Bandes noires*), speculations of, 511
Blanc, Louis, *quoted* and *cited*, 59, 62, 134, 161, 172, 227, 299, 321, 366, 367, 444, 450, 557, 568; as authoritarian, 194; criticises Robespierre, 243-44; on leaders, 272; excellent at description, 274; criticises Brissot, 356; cites law of suspects, 513; on freemasons, 540; guillotine statistics of, 561
"Blancs," origin of, 290
Blanqui, secret society of, 580
"Blue Terror," 430
Boissel, communism of, 488; *Catéchisme* of, 490; *note*, 491
Bonaparte, Napoleon, vanity of, 464; way paved for, 492; *coup d'état* of, 572
Boncerf, *quoted*, 130-31
"Bonnet rouge" (cap of liberty), 308
Bonneville, appeals to arms, 69
Book of National Charity, 506
"Bornage," 414-15
"Bouche de fer sec," 85
Boucheron, *quoted*, 85
Bouchotte, Minister of War, 467, 534
Bouillé, Marquis de, in royalist plot, 153; commands army of east, 223; massacres at Metz, 224-25
Bourbotte, executed, 570
Bourdon (of the Oise), *quoted*, 369; as Dantonist, 535; attacks Commission of Public Welfare, 537
Bourgeoisie, prosperity of, 376; peasant, 416; power of, 578; *vide* middle classes
Bourges, priests abdicate at, 523
"Bread for all" (1793), 355
Bread, scarcity of, 235; prices of, 438 *et seq.*
Breda, taken by Dumouriez, 383
Brest, federals from, 272
Breteuil, Baron de, effigy of, burned 29; plots with Court, 65, 153; changes prison into granary, 79; corresponds with Fersen, 335

Bretons, civic hymn of, 446
Bridet, Pierre, proposes land nationalisation, 424
Brienne, Loménie de (Archbishop of Sens), Minister, 28, 33
" Brigands," legend of the, 114, 116, 207
Brisson, ex-*curé*, resigns, 523
Brissot, municipal constitution of, 184; politics of, 197; against people, 241; against Republic, 284; *quoted*, 293; house of, searched, 295, 307; *cited*, 305; negotiates with England, 327; accused by Billaud-Varenne, 338; leads " Gironde," 341; defends property, 341; rival of Robespierre, 344, 367; pamphlets of, 346, 349 *et seq.*; attacks Revolutionists, 347; on crimes of Anarchists, 354 *et seq.*; knows England, 382; " To his Constituents," 392; stirs up revolt, 446; on Commission of Constitution, 470; attacks communism, 486; attacks Montagnards, 500; a freemason, 540
" Brissotins," 399
British Museum, Pamphlets in, vi., 224, 338, 420, 441, 490, 491, 523
Brittany, risings in, 26 *et seq.*; disturbances in, 39; counter-revolution in, 383, 445; discontent in, 433
Broglie, Marshal de, plots with Court, 65; defied by people, 70; threatens Paris, 71, 80; fails King,' 91; plans *coup d'état*, 92
Brunot, won over by Royalists, 516
Brunswick, D. of, intrigues of, 290; fear of, 292; aspires to throne 307-8; marches on Coblentz, 324; defeat of, 325; negotiations with, 331; mildness of, 335
Brussels, *émigrés* at, 17
Bruyère, La, *quoted*, 436
Buchez and Roux, *quoted* and *cited*, 127, 128, 135, 152, 187, 299, 300, 304-5, 314, 439

Buonarotti, explains 9th Thermidor, 507; *cited*, 550; commission of, 579
" Bureau de Ville," 186
Buzot, protests against martial law, 161; *cited*, 344; stirs up revolt, 446; *Mémoires* of, *quoted*, 447

CAFÉ du Caveau, patriots enrol at, 70
Cahier Général, 36; d'Aval, Song in, 113
Cahiers de doléances, 35; moderation of, 36; pamphlet on, 37; demand destruction of Bastille 79; delayed, 103; on elections, 112; socialism in, 484-85
" Ça ira " sung by volunteers, 323, 324
Calendar, Republican, 519
Calende, ex-*curé*, resigns, 523
Calonne, effigy burned, 26, 29; convokes Assembly of Notables (1787), 33; dismissed, 33
Cambacerès, advises Convention, 385; disloyalty of, 464
Cambon, ideas on landed property, 327; issues new paper-currency, 380; proposes forced loan, 396, 410, and disestablishment of church, 520; as Terrorist, 535; authority in finance, 550; abused by Robespierre, 566-67
Campan, Mme., disclosures of, 155
Canton (system), partisans of, enemies of Commune, 475
Carmelite Convent, massacre at, 302
Carnot, authority in war, 550; attacked by Robespierre, 550
Carra, *quoted*, 307; denounced by Robespierre, 307-8
Carrier, drowns prisoners at Nantes, 457; amnestied, 542; advocates insurrection, 545
Carteaux commands Rep. troops, 459
Cathelineau, Vendean leader, 386, 456
Catherine II. (Russia) helps counter-revolution, 253

Catholicism, triumph of, 527
Cassagnac, Granier de, *cited*, 296, 302
Casuels, 203
Cazotte, saved by Maillard, 301; daughter of, 302
Cellier arrested, 545; succeeds Chaumette, 546
Centralisation, evils of, 149
Chabot, silenced, 285; tries to stop massacres, 299; motion of, 306; tried and executed, 540, 548
Chalier, represents people at Lyons, 377; leads workers and arrested, 459; head carried through streets, 538; forefather of Fourierism, 579
Chambery, taken, 326
Chambon succeeds Pétion, 322
Champerty (*champart*), 203, 209
Champion (ex-*curé*), resignation of, 523
Champs-de-Mars, *Fête* in, 178; massacre in, 179, 233, 257
Chapelier, Le, guillotined, 559
Charette, urges peasants to kill Republicans, 387; brutality of, 457; massacres prisoners, 515
Charles I. (England), influence of history on Louis XVI., 91, 151
Charrier, chief of counter-revolution, 250
Chartres, Duke de, candidate for throne, 308, 326, 331; intrigues with Dumouriez, 326, 387; fails with soldiers, 388
Chassin, *quoted* and *cited*, 36, 42, 43, 44, 69, 73, 79, 386, 484, 485
Châteaux burned, 42, 95, 113, 115, 135, 207, 252
Châtelet (prison), revolt in, 73
Châtellier, du, *cited*, 40; *quoted*, 126
Chaumette, *quoted*, 245, 246, 273, 396; Procurator of Commune, 322, 364; law of maximum of, 375; demands revolutionary tribunal, 385; promotes income tax, 396; advocates market-gardening, 496; accuses Roux, 504; arrested,

Chaumette—*continued*
505; promises bread, 510; purifies revolutionary committees, 513; new cult preached, 520, 522; organises *fête*, 524; guillotined, 527, 546; communism of, 534; attacked by Desmoulins, 536; arrested, 545; character, 547
"Chemises Rouges," 560
Chevalier, François, describes massacre in Vendée, 386
Chèvremont, *cited*, 395
Chiennage, 202
Chiffonistes, 251
Chollet, Vendeans defeated at 515
Chouans, costume of, 570
"Chronique de Paris," *cited*, 305, 307; foretells Marat's death, 450
Church, tithes relinquished, 132; property, value of, 169; expropriation of—lands voted, 170, and speculation in, 171; liquidation of property, 185; treasures sent to Mint, 522
Ci-devants, expelled from Paris, 555
"Citizen Kings," 157
Citizens, "active and passive," 163 *et seq.*, 191, 212; respon- of, 209
Civic Fasts, 439
Civil War, avoided, 306; fear of, 384
Clairvaux, papers found at, 409
Claude Payan, Mayor of Paris, 546
Clavière (Girondist Minister of Finance), 240, 318; dismissed, 244
Clermont-Tonnerre dissolves Grenoble *parlement*, 27
Clive, Ed. Le, *cited*, 40; *quoted*, 114
Cloots, Anacharsis, advocates internationalism, 522; organises *Fête* of Liberty, 524; enthusiasm of, 525; attacked by Robespierre, 536; charge against, 545, guillotined, 546
Club, Breton, revolutionary centre, 60, 61, 64 (*vide* Jacobins)
Constitutional, formed, 43
Cordeliers' (*vide* Cordeliers)

INDEX

"Coalition of Kings," 336
Coblentz, *émigrés* at, 17, 248, 249, 332
Coburg, Duke of, proclamation, 388; besieges Le Quesnoy, 467
Coffinhal, tries to save Robespierre, 567
Collardot resigns, 253
"Collectivism," founders of, 11, 253
Colonies, English, revolt of, 22
Combes, Anacharsis, *cited*, 40; *quoted*, 114
"Commerçantistes," 253
Commerce, a social function, 498
Commission of Twelve, 347; consternation of, 292; prosecution of sections, 397; suppressed, 400, 403
of Six, 399, 474
Commissioners of Convention, supervise war, 389; levy toll from rich, 463; march sword in hand, 468; functions of, 480–81; defects of, 482; attacked by people, 498; treat with foreign Courts, 516; stringent measures of, 527
of Departments, 366
of Sections, 314
Committee, Agricultural, 494, 498;
Civil (of Districts), 182
of Commerce, 498
of Defence, 472
District assumes police duties, 530
Feudal, report of, 200
to frame Constitution, 470
of General Safety, *vide* Public Safety
Insurrectionary, good sense of, 274; wins Commune, 388
of Militia, 82
Permanent, 69; illegality of, 128
of Public Instruction, 518
of Public Safety (April 1793), 319; deterioration of, 365; ferocity of, 394–95, 458; dictatorship of, 471; authority of, 480; suppresses Communism, 506;

Committee of Public Safety—*continued*
power of, 508; policy of, 509; constitution of, 509; incapacity of, 511; jealous of Commune, 512, 550; sinister force of, 513; organises relief works, 530; controls police, 531; new power given to, 544; triumph of, 546; used by Robespierre, 550; unpopularity of, 565
of Public Welfare, deteriorates, 365; formed, 388–89; treats with Austria, 467; dictatorship of, 468, 477, 480; pompous circular of, 505; suppresses communism, 506; constitution of, 508–9; power of, 508, 534–35; policy of, 509; opposes cult of Reason, 525; demands decree on religious liberty, 526; accused of incapacity and treachery, 536–37; authority restored, 538; parries attack, 538; slanders Hébertists, 545; attacked by Robespierre, 566
Revolutionary, orders arrest of Girondins, 403
Search, 531
of "Subsistence," 53; report of, 63
Watch, of Commune, 301
Committees, Civic, functions of, 193–94
Revolutionary, 477
Commune, definition of, 189–90; *Actes de la*, 186
of Paris, 77, 183; popular work of, 180 *et seq.*; divisions of, 182; coerces National Assembly, 187; functions of, 219; attacks property, 245; Revolutionary, 273; Insurrectionary, 275; power of, 281, 357; holds King prisoner, 283; threatens massacre, 288; foresight of, 292; opposes Directory, 292; releases prisoners, 294; attacked by Assembly, 295; **rings**

Commune of Paris—*continued*
tocsin, 296; protects prisoners, 298 *et seq.*; stops massacres, 303; how constituted, 312; at Hôtel de Ville, 315; authority of, 319; attacked by Gironde, 317; honesty questioned, 320; success of attack on, 322; constitution of (1793), 322; demands trial of King, 332; differs from Convention, 340; dissolution demanded, 347; anarchists rally round, 353; dissolution of, 364; hoists black flag, 383; backs Jacobin Triumvirate, 384; collaborates with "Mountain," 388; decrees progressive income tax, 396; opposes Terror, 400; levies tax on rich, 403; fixes maximum and reorganises army, 410; power of, destroyed, 472, 532; real strength of, 528; separated from Sections, 531; agrees with Hébertists and downfall of, 547
of France, 176
of Strasbourg, 105
Communes, administration and creation of, 165; federation of, 315
Peasant, joint responsibility of, 210, 279
Village, composition of (1789), 211
Communism, signs of, 41; importance of, 101; Godwin's, 327; supporters of, 451; of Republic, 362–63, 580; efforts towards, 369; tendencies towards, 474; warnings against, 485; in Revolution, 488–89, 579; at Lyons, 496
Constructive, need of, 499
Communist Movement (1891), 363; 484 *et seq.*, 500 *et seq.*; representatives of, 487
Communists, threatened by Convention, 500; of the "Forties," 498

"Compagnies de Jesus," massacres by, 571
du Soleil," massacres by, 571
"Compromising auxiliaries," 74–75
Conches, J. Feuillet de, *quoted*, 28, 135
Conciergerie (prison), attacked, 298
Queen in, 516
Condé, Prince de, plans *coup d'état* 54, 65
occupied by Austrians, 387
Condorcet, municipal scheme of, 192; sincerity of, 243; supports Republic, 307; defends free trade, 373; and equality, 484; author of Constitution, 470; communism of, 485; suicide of, 517; a freemason, 540
"Confederation of Clubs," 151
Confederation, National, 188
"Conquest of Power," 196–97
Considérant, communism of, 488
Conspiracies, at Grenoble; 248; in South, 248
"Conspiracy of the Right," 567
Constitution, discussed, 20, 68; of 1791, 102, 343; oath to, 178; *quoted*, 192; function of, 256; framing of, 470 *et seq.*; democratic character of and summary of, 473; Montagnards', 475; proclaimed, 476
Constitutional Government, first conditions of, 160; guarantees of, 475
Constitutionalists, royalist, limitations of, 36
Conti, Prince de, plans *coup d'état*, 54
Convention, National, contests in, 14; abolishes feudal system 210; convoked, 280; how elected, 309; three parties in; abolishes royalty, 310; Conservatives in, 311; cowardice of, 316; conflicts with, 318 *et seq.*; orders prosecution for massacres, 321; defies monarchies, 327; sovereign rights of, 333; decrees King's trial, 337; publishes pamphlets, 338; votes on King's sentence, 339; differs from Commune, 340;

590 INDEX

Convention, National—*continued*
inactivity of, 362, 424; purification of, 364, 385; struggle in, 369; raises bread fund, 375; middle-class power in, 376; levies men, 380; tries to grasp judicial power, 385; helplessness of, 386; grasps executive power, 388; treachery in, 390; child of Revolution, 391; battles in, 395–97; besieged by people, 400, 402; galleries opened to public, 403; tries to overawe people, 404; legislative work of, 407; false step of, 422; legislative stability of, 426; abolishes pecuniary rights, 429; breaks up large estates, 434; fixes maximum, 439–441; Commissioners, zeal of, 448; work finished, 476–79, 481; attempts socialisation, 498; mistakes of, 499; threatens Communists, 500; defends middle classes, 507; checks speculation, 512; jealous of Commune, 513; free fight in, 514; accepts Revolutionary Government, 515; receives resignation of bishops, 522–23; refuses to broach question of priests' pay 524–25; storm in, 566; dissolves, 571; wrecking of, 573

Co-proprietorship, 496

Corday, Charlotte d'Armont, 447, 449–50

Cordeliers, demand Republic, 232; reaction among, 238; attack property, 245; aid Fraternal Societies, 257; favour Republic, 284; support rising, 291; reinforce Jacobin Club, 317; champion communism, 487; action of, 538, 544
Club of, 197; anarchists in, 353; Robespierre visits, 503; Hébertists in, 534

Corney, Ethis de, parleys with de Launey, 83, 84, 85

Corporations of Guilds, abolished, 19

Correspondence bureaux, 182

Cost of production, inquiry into 442

Council, General, of Paris Commune, suppressed, 190; elected by people, 287; attacked, 295; change in, 364; hastens events, 525; appeals to people, 567
General of Departments, constitution of, 166; functions of, 530–31
General Revolutionary, 402
Ministerial, 318–19
Municipal, pays members, 371
Provisory Executive, 389
of the Three Hundred, 160

Councils, of Departments, 166; functions of, 530; take police duties, 531
local, election of, 164
take pledge against violence, 401

Counter-revolution, 176, 220, 221, 223, 245, 247, 251, 363–64, 404, 445 537, 556

Coup d'état, of August 10, 275
of Counter-revolution, 256
of Court, 54, 56, 57 *et seq.*, 68, 71; fails, 87; doubted, 91, 154; supported by foreign Courts, 244
of Girondins, 359, 537
of Napoleon III., 336
of Thermidor 311, 317, 341

Coupe, abolished, 114

"Courrier Français," *quoted*, 113
Parisien," *quoted*, 128
de Versailles et de Paris," *quoted*, 63

Court, rejects overtures, 48; middle class supports, 76–77; stupidity of, 89; intrigues with foreigners, 162
Party, 58
Plots, 64, 65 *et seq.*, 150, 274; evidence of, 283

Courtois, *cited*, 552

Couthon, report on land laws, 277; criticises "Gironde," 344; raises army of peasants, 460–61; favours pacification, 461; mocks relics, 526; Robespierrist, 535; arrested, 567

Crown Lands, division of, 433

INDEX

"Culottes dorées" invade Sections, 371
"Cult of Supreme Being," 527
Currents, Two, of Revolution, 1 *et seq.*
  popular, 195
Cusset, advocates nationalisation of industries, 496
Custine, commands Republican army, 326; retreats, 387, 465

DALLOZ, *cited*, 199, 205; *quoted*, 198, 418-19
Danton, silence of, 35; rouses people, 154; inspires masses, 183; policy of, 192; demands dismissal of ministers, 192; persecution of, 234; in London, 235; inactivity of, 273; supports Sections, 291; courage of, 292; orders search for arms, 294; saves prisoners, 298 *et seq.*; Minister of Justice, 318; forced to resign, made Minister of Foreign Affairs, 319; libelled, negotiates with D. of Brunswick, 325; frustrates plots in Brittany, 326; treats with England, 327; parleys with Prussians, 331; demands King's condemnation, 338; stays with army, 338; respects property, 343; believes in English Whigs, 382; appeals for unity and patriotism, 383; incites rising, 384; insists on action, 385; tries to win back Dumouriez, 387; activity of, 389; tries compromise, 392; opposes Terror, 400; secret negotiations of, 467; daring of, 511; speaks of "armed nation," 512; renews energy, 515; returns to Paris, 525; attacks atheism, 526; group of, 535; weary of mankind, 537; a freemason, 540; arrested, tried and executed, 548; illusion of, 556
Dauch, Martin, refuses oath in Tennis Court, 56
Daudet, Ernest, *quoted*, 248, 251

Daunon, speaks in favour of King, 338
Dauphiné, insurrections in, 27; executions in, 128, 166
Debt, National, 171
Declaration of Rights, 22, 163, 473, 500
Decrees (1790), re-establish feudalism, 201; spurious, 207
"Defenders of property," 197
Delaunay, forgery of, 539; trial of, 548
Demeunier proposes joint redemption, 134
Democracy, influence of, 147
Departments, Government, 160
Deputies, flight of, 292
Deschamps against Sections, 529
Desèze defends King, 338
Desmoulins, Camille, speech of, 57 appeals to arms, 72; exults, 159; despairs, 235; a Dantonist, 535; calumnies of, 536-37, 538, excluded from Jacobin Club, 539; rejoices at Hébertists fall, 547; arrested, tried, executed, 548 Lucile, journal, *cited*, 273; guillotined, 548
Desormaux, ex-canon, resigns, 523
Dessonville conspires, 293
"Deux Amis de la Liberté," *quoted*, 79, 94, 127; *cited*, 227
Deville, proves injustice to Babeuf, 491
Dictatorship, military, forced on France, 328
Diderot, socialistic ideas of, 484
Dietrich congratulates new *régime* at Strasbourg, 105
Dijon, riots at, 23
"Direct action," 190
"Direct Self-Government," 183
Directories, revolutionary, 216; favours counter-revolution,364; strengthened, 472
Directory, attempts progressive taxation, 411; succeeds Convention, 571
Disorder, the use of, 345
"Distribution of Produce," 488
Districts of Paris organise resistance, 69, 180 *et seq.*; autonomy of, 182

Dolivier, Pierre, sympathises with people, 242; favours agrarian law, 243; on land question, 494-95; insight of, 498-99
" Don gratuit," 39
Doniol, *quoted*, 111
Dragoons fraternise with people, 70
Drouet pursues and captures King, 227 *et seq.*
Droz, *quoted*, 48, 79
Dubarry, Madame, guillotined, 517
Dubois (Minister), house of, burned, 28
Dubois (*curé*), resigns, 523
Dubois-Crancé treats with Lyons, 460
Ducos accuses " Mountain," 337
Ducroquet arrested, 545
Dufourney against sectional societies, 529
Dulaure, *cited*, 40
Dumantier resigns, 253
Dumas, letter of, 80
Dumouriez at Caen, 65; treachery of, 236, 380, 381, 383, 387, 388; Minister of Foreign Affairs, 240; supports Duke de Chartres, 308, 326, 387; plans invasion of Belgium, 324; victory of, at Valmy, 325; intrigues with Jacobins, 326; enters Belgium, 326; hastens to Paris, 338; defeat of, at Neerwinden, 346; beguiled by Pitt, 382; suspected, 383; makes pact with Austrians, 383; retreats, 387; treachery of, confirmed, 388; frustrated,, 390
Duperret receives Ch. Corday, 449
Duport, Adrien, arms middle classes, 117; forms "Confederation of Clubs," 151; in Moderate Triumvirate, 162; *quoted* by Michelet, 533
Duquesnoy executed, 570
Duranthon, Minister for Justice, 240
Duroy executed, 570
Dusaulx, *quoted*, 73; tries to stop September massacres, 299

EDICTS forged, 23
Education, scheme of, 517
Egalité de fait, 403, 479, 493

Eglantine, Fabre d', points out injustice of land laws, 420; names months for Republican Calendar, 519; a Dantonist, 535; attacks Committee of Public Welfare, 537; arrested, 539; guillotined, 540
Elections, qualifications for, 164; new law for, 277
Elisabeth, Mme., letter on feudal rights, 135; negotiations concerning, 331; guillotined, 559
Emigration of nobility, 238-39
Emigrés (emigrant nobles) abandon King, 17; arrest of, 92; speculate, 219; decrees against 235; intrigues of, 238; ordered to return, 239; activity of, 245; obstinacy of, 249; at Chambéry, 250; return to Paris, 290; falsehoods of, 324; flock to Turin, 383; in Jersey, 384; fight at Lyons, 460
Enclosure Acts, effect of, 97
Encyclopedists, influence of, 170
England, example of, 8; war with, 22, 381; helps counter-revolution, 251-52; attacks west of France, 253; *rôle* of, 327; policy of, 328, 465; as model for Girondins, 343; aims at French sea-power, 381 *et seq.*; effect of war with, 437; false *assignats* made in, 444; subsidises Prussia, 469
English Ambassador, testimony of, 75
Government helps Royalists, 446
Revolution taken as model, 196
Enragés (Extremists), character of, 362; support Varlet and Roux, 372; insight of, 373; used against " Gironde," 376; inspire people, 385; lead in Paris, 388; demand " Terror," 400; defend property, 401; desire equality, 487; conciliated, 500; suppressed, 345, 534
Entraigues, d', *Les Droits des Etats-Généraux*, by, 46
Epsic (Benedictine) resigns, 523

INDEX

"Equalisation of Wealth," 241, 243, 484
Equality, doctrine of, 143; opposed, 147; aim of poor, 277; era of, 315; danger to property of, 349; effort towards, 369
Erckmann and Chatrian, *cited*, 38
Espagnac, Abbé d', executed, 540
Espréminil, d', opposes old *régime*, 35; injured by crowd, 55; guillotined, 559
Estaing, Count d', letter of, to Queen, 227
Eudistes refuse oath to Constitution, 294
Europe indebted to French peasants, 578-79
Everard, Catherine, eulogy of, 450
Evolution, 102, 576
Exchequer Court, protest by, 26
Existence, sacredness of, 405
"Expropriation," fear of, 170
Extremists, *vide Enragés*

"Families," the, 416
Famine extent of, 46 *et seq.*; "Compact," 149; in 1792, 328; all over France, 362; increase of, 395; disappearance of, 435-36; struggle against, 437 *et seq.*
Farms, limitation of, 497-98
Faubourgs, St. Antoine and St. Marceau, attack Tuileries, 276
Fauchet, Abbé, founds "Cercle Social," 496
Federalism of Girondins, 365, 366
Federals from Brest and Marseilles, 272, 275
Federation of counter-revolution, 250; of districts, 183-84, 187
Fersen, Count, correspondence of, 155, 335, 516; discusses Council of Regency, 466
Festivals, popular, 177
Fête of Federation, 174 *et seq.*, 187, 223; gives firm basis to Revolution, 250
 of Liberty and Reason, 524
 of Supreme Being, 527
Feudal Law, Sagnac *quoted* on, 205-6; renewed, 202 *et seq.*
 Dues, 37 *et seq.*, 99 *et seq.*;

Feudal Dues—*continued*
 redemption of, 201; exacted 207; enumerated, 202 *et seq.*; sacredness of, 210; abolished, 278; question of, 361
 Legislation (1790), 205 *et seq.*; 209 *et seq.*
 Rights, linked with royalty, 60; in towns, 99; effect of, 111; upheld, 129 *et seq.*; abolition pronounced, 134; but delayed, 195 *et seq.*; retention of, 278; final abolition of, 427 *et seq.*
"Feudal Seizure" abolished, 210
Feudal System, hatred of, 14, 414; broken at Strasbourg, 105; decrees against, 210; land under, 413 *et seq.*
 Taxes refused, 44
Feudalism, survivals of, 36, 255; re-established, 201
Feuillants, Club of, 221; position of, 238; fight patriots, 252; oppose Republic, 308; treachery of, 462
Fils de famille, battalions of, 383
Finances, condition of, 32; difficulties of, 168 *et seq.*
Flammermont, *quoted*, 71, 74, 80, 84, 85
Flanders, regiment of, 153
Flesselles (Provost of Merchants] corresponds with Court, 65; disarms people, 76-77; shot, 86-87
Fleuriot-Lescaut succeeds Pache, 546
Fleurus, victory of, 564
Fonfrède arrested, 445
Force, La (prison), attacked, 73, 298
"Forced loans," 242, 409-10; in Hérault, 411
"Forty Years' Possession Act," 421, 423
Foubert, M. L., *quoted*, 189, *cited*, 191
Fouché, socialism of, 506-7; on burial, 521; attacked by Robespierre, 565
Foulon, arrested, 92; hanged, 93; effect of death of, 100, 149

Fouquier-Tinville, Public Prosecutor, 509 ; "accelerates pleadings," 517
Fourier, ideas of, 373 ; followers of, 488 ; teaching of, 498
Fourierism, descent of, 579
Fournées (" batches "), 514 ; horror of, 561, 564
Fournier inspires people, 385
" Fourth Legislative Body," 529
Fox, Charles James, hopes in, 467
France, financial ruin of, 22 ; unification of, 177-78 ; transformation of, 346 ; divided into hostile camps, 361-62 ; regenerated, 408-9, 574 ; democratised, 436 ; interior condition of, 465-66 ; organised in communes, 476 ; communist spirit in, 506 ; dechristianising of, 519-21 ; productivity of, 575
Franc-fief, 59
François (of Neufchâteau), motion of, 279 ; tries to stop massacres 299 ; proposes division of communal lands, 418
Frankfort-on-the-Maine, occupied by *sans-culottes*, 326
Fraternal societies, task of, 257
" Fraternité, La," *quoted*, 509
Freedom of opinion, 143
Freemasons, Brotherhood of, revolutionaries in, 331
Free trade, in grain, 19 ; opposed, 497
Fréon organises *jeunesse dorée*, 570
Fréron persecuted, 234
Freys (Austrian Bankers), in plot, 539 ; executed, 540
" Fury of purification," 303

GABELLE (salt tax) abolished, 169
Gaillard, suicide of, 505
Gamain reveals secret safe, 293, 332
Game laws, 59 ; abolished, 121, 126, 133
Garat succeeds Danton, 319
Gardes françaises, *vide* Guards
Garnier, letters of, 527
Gay-Vernon, Bishop, resigns, 522
Gazette de Paris, editor of, recruits Royalists, 248

Geneva, emancipation of, 44
Gensonné accused, 338 ; fails Danton, 387 ; under home-arrest, 445 ; on Constitution Committee, 470
German armies, expected in Paris, 256 ; influence of, 257
Germany, comparison with, 214 ; attacks Alsace and Lorraine, 253
Gertruydenberge taken, 383
Girant, evidence of, 321
Girey-Dupré executed, 517
" Gironde," the, programme of, 62 ; defends property, 106, 358 ; composition of, 310, 311 ; protects King, 312 ; impotence of, 319 ; opposes King's trial, 333 ; *versus* " Mountain," 340 *et seq.* ; tries to end Revolution, 359 ; rallies reaction, 363 ; necessary to crush, 378 ; sends volunteers, 379 ; hostility to, 402
Girondins, party of, 197, 310 ; position of, 238 ; agree with Court, 241 ; ministry of, 240, 244, 292, 318 ; fight Anarchists, 252, 384 ; indecision of, 276 ; attitude towards massacres, 304-5 ; ready to admit foreign troops, 307 ; power of, 311 ; work against Revolution, 319 *et seq.*, 348 *et seq.* ; try to form reactionary guard, 321 ; expelled, 322, 398, 404 ; favour war, 323 ; attack Convention, 327 ; accuse " Mountain," 333 ; try to save King, 336-37 ; policy and aims of, 341-42, 389 ; characteristics of, and hatred for people, 344, 348 ; methods of, 346 ; intrigues of, 347 ; dreams of, 348 ; object to equality, 352 ; programme of, 359 ; Robespierre's opinion of, 360 ; ambition of, 369 ; attack sections, 371 ; accuse " Mountain," 375; printing-presses of, smashed, 385 ; fall inevitable, 390 ; persecute Marat, 393 ; failure of, 395 ; incite departments against Paris, 397, 406 ; out-

INDEX

Girondins—*continued*
lawed, 406; result of expulsion, 407; opposed to "maximum," 441; stir up revolt, 445, 455-56; work with Royalists, 446; discouraged by Bretons, 447; *Marseillaise* of, 447; defeat of, 459; in hiding, 461; treachery of, 462; in framing Constitution, 470 *et seq.*; use Constitution, 471; divide legislative body, 473; ideas of, 474; spread calumnies, 476; prosecution of, demanded, 514; execution of, 22, 517; similarity with Jacobins, 533
Glezen, 60
Gobel (Bishop of Paris) resigns, 522; guillotined, 527, 546
Godwin, W., *cited*, 184, 327, 373
Goethe at Battle of Valmy, 325
Gorsas, *quoted*, 63
Goujon executed, 570
Government centralised, 318; federative, 367
Revolutionary, 384, 508 *et seq.*, 545, 555
Grand Châtelet (prison), thieves massacred at, 303
Grand'-Maison (actress) guillotined, 560
Grave, War Minister, 24
"Great Unknown," 272-73
Grégoire, Abbé, 61; report of, 200; refuses to resign, 523
Grenelle, attempt to raise camp at, 571
Grenoble insurrection, 27
Guadet, silence of, 35; stratagem of, 245; report of, 295; speech of, 296; motions of, 307; accused, 338; fails Danton, 387; stirs up revolt 446
Guards, French, refuse to fire, 64; distribute bread, 71; fire on German regiment, 72
Municipal, "restore order," 108
National (faithful to King), formation of, 160; *passive* citizens excluded from, 160; disperse, 274-75; supports

Guards, National—*continued*
people, 275; refuse to stop massacres, 300; officers of, dismissed, 314; controlled by middle classes, 401
Guillaume, helps capture King, 227
James, thanks to, vii; on Resolutions of National Assembly, 137 *et seq.*; on democratic beliefs, 142; *quoted*, 143; *cited*, 199, 518, 555

HANRIOT, General of National Guard, 402; terrorises Convention, 404; arrested, 567; released, 568
Hardy (English bookseller), *quoted*, 68, 70
Harvests, effect of, 110, 328
Hassenfratz excuses pillage, 401
"Haves and Have-Nots," 354
Hébert, 305; commissioner of Convention, 273; Procurator of Paris Committee, 364; arrested, 397; anti-religious campaign of, 479; character of, 501; denounces Roux, 504; recommends itinerant guillotine, 512; organises *fête*, 524; burns relics, 525; communism of, 534; attacked by Desmoulins, 536; attacks Amar, 544; arrested, 347, 544; guillotined, 545
Hébertists, struggle against, 533 *et seq.*; miscalculation of, 534; arrest of, 537; fall of, 542 *et seq.*
Helvetius, socialism of, 484
Henri Quatre, statue saluted, 29
Herbois, Collot d', President of National Convention, 309; *quoted*, 439; ordered to destroy Lyons, 479; alludes to title-deeds, 482; makes terms with communists, 500; socialism of, 506-7; on Committee of Public Welfare, 535; attempt to kill, 558-59; attacked by Robespierre, 565-67
Herman proposes to purge prisons, 564

INDEX

High Court (Orleans), safeguards conspirators, 293
Historians, omissions, 24, 134; shortcoming of, 94-95; ignore counter-revolution, 249; embroideries of, 304; limitations of, 306, 409
Hobbes, *cited*, 6
Hoche takes the offensive, 469
Holbach, school of, 501
Holland threatened, 328, 382
Hondschoote, Duke of York attacked at, 467
Hôtel des Invalides, attack on, proposed, 70; arms seized at, 77; attacked, 80
de Ville, congratulates Assembly, 61; becomes centre of Revolution, 69-74
Hue, de, Commander of Swiss Guards, letter of, 82; saved, 86
Huez, de (Mayor of Troyes), killed by peasants, 107
Hulin attacks Bastille, 85, 86
Hume, *cited*, 6

ILLUMINATES," vow of, 540
Imbert-Colomiés, royalist agent, 460
Imperative Mandate,".185
Income tax, details of, 410-11
Indian Company, power of, 539
Industries, socialisation of, 493 *et seq.*; nationalisation of, 495-96
Insurrection, *vide* Risings; cause of, 41; uncertainty of, 401
Intellectuals," retrogression of, 243; disbelieve in Revolution, 256; compared with Radicals, 256; inclined to monarchy, 331
International Working Men's Association, 580; Congress (Bâle, 1869), 487
Interregnum, 282 *et seq.*
Invasion, foreign, 181, 238; supported by foreign Courts, 324
Isnard, President of Convention, 397; threatens to obliterate Paris, 398, 461

JACOBINS, reaction of, 221, 238; repudiate Republic, 232; support war, 240; attacked by Lafayette, 244; poverty of, 252; mistaken idea about, 257; advanced party of, 272; threatened, 275, 283; punishment of, planned, 289; support advanced revolutionists, 317; intrigue with Dumouriez, 326; extermination planned by Fersen, 335; "do not understand poor,"374; pledged to defend property, 401; support Committees of Public Welfare and General Safety, 508; jealous of sections, 510
Club (Paris), silence of, 284; electors meet at, 309; declares. itself Republican, 310; weapon of "Mountain," 316-17; reinforced by Cordeliers, 317; revokes decrees against Duke of Orléans, 337; influence of, 400; affiliation with, 508; demands trial of Girondins, 512; against Popular Societies, 528; "purification" of, 535; Robespierre complains to, 565
Government concentrate police functions, 530
Republicans, officer army, 462
Jacqueries, 15; necessity of, 52; character of, 115
"Jacques Bonhomme," 110
Jalès, confederation of, corresponds with King and *emigrés*, 250
Jaurès, *cited*, 24, 365, 374, 505; shows error of Michelet, 338; quoted on communist movement, 373; on Marat, 395
Jeanbon, *vide* Saint-André
Jemmapes, victory at, 326
Jewish question, 185
Julien-de-Dieu (Benedictine) resigns, 523
Jullien (Commissioner), letter of, 447; burns title-deed, 482; in Royalist company, 539; trial of, 548; describes *noyades* at Nantes, 542

INDEX

Jullien—*continued*
  Madame, letters *quoted*, 221, 274, 286–87; *cited*, 344
July 14 (1790), consequences of, 88 *et seq.*; importance of, 177
June 2 (1793), rising of, 403
Jura, wheat convoys plundered in, 42
Jureurs and *non-jureurs,vide* Priests, 520
" Justices of Peace," 102

KARÉEFF, Professor, *quoted*, 39
Kellerman repulses Piedmontese, 460; reinforced by Commissioners, 461
Kérengall, Le Guen de, denounces feudalism, 123
Kersaint, report of, 290; embraces Danton, 343; executed, 517
King, power of, limited, 335
Kings, right divine of, destroyed, 336
King's Council, decree of (April 3, 1789), 63
Klinckovström, Baron R. M. de, *cited*, 335
Knights of Malta, help counter-revolution, 253
  of the Poignard, 246

LACOMBE, Rose, communist, 487; leader of revolutionary women, 489
Lacoste, Minister for Marine, 240; letter of, 482
Lacroix, Sigismund, *quoted*, 182, 183, 184, 186, 187, 188, 192; arrested, 547; tried, 548
Ladmiral tries to kill d'Herbois, 558–59; guillotined, 559
Lafayette (Commander of National Guard), plots with Court, 65; on Municipal Council, 101; at Versailles, 156; importance of, 160; intrigues, 227; chief of Feuillants, 244; supports royalty in letter, 245; absolved, 274; suspected, 285–86; denounces Jacobins, 286; sides with Royalty, 286; treachery discovered, 289; fate of, 289; plans invasion of Belgium, 324; treachery of, 380–81
Lagny, J. de, helps capture King, 228

Laignelot turns church into Temple of Truth, 521
Lalande, a freemason, 540
Lally-Tollendal, letter to King of Prussia, 286
Lamballe, Princess de, killed, 299; only woman massacred, 302
Lambesc, Prince de, carriage burned, 75
Lambert, " friend of those who have nothing," 484–85
Lameth, in Triumvirate of Moderates, 162; won over by King, 332
Lamoignon (Minister), house burned, 28
Land, registers, destruction of, 40, 429; question, 52, 488; in America, 143; confiscation of, 196; importance of, 493; socialisation of, 493 *et seq.*; speculation in, 493; inalienability of, 494; theories on, 495, 543; sales of, bad results, 502; mistakes in, 563 *et seq.*
  Communal, robbery of, 195; question of, 211, 212, 361; seizure of, 414 *et seq.*; restoration of, opposed, 415; division of, 418; division of, rescinded, 419; " grabbed," 420; restoration of, 421; partition of, 422–23 *et seq.*; transferred, 425
  of *émigrés*, sale of, 277, 279, 280, 396
  " Hunger," 14
  Laws, 199, 277–78
  Ownership, 345, 346
  Pensioners', not reserved, 380
  System (in Artois), 417
  Taxes, 199
Landau, blockade raised, 538
Landed property, subdivision of, 435
Lange, precursor of Fourierism, 373, 459, 490, 496, 497, 498, 579
Lanjuinais, founds Breton Club, 60; stirs up revolt, 446
Laumur arrested, 545
Launey, Marquis de (Governor of Bastille), 79; defends Bastille, 81 *et seq.*; capitulates, 85; killed, 86; memory of, 149

Laussel, leads people at Lyons, 377
Lauzun, commands Republican army, 326
Lavergne, Commandant, letter to, 290
Lavoisier guillotined, 559
"Law of Suspects," 477, 513
Law, municipal and administrative, 165; ignored, 193
Laws, social, 476
"Leaders of Thought," cowardice of, 285
"League of United Counties," 446
Le Bas (Commissioner), sent to Lower Rhine, 439; in fighting line, 469
Lebrun, in Girondist Ministry, 318
Lechapelier, founds Breton Club, 60
Leclerc, disciple of J. Roux, 489; arrested, 505, 545
Leflot, letters of, 527
Lefranc, priest, resigns, 523
Legacy duties, 242
Legends, use of, 103; historic, 118–19; revolutionary, 302
Legislation, difficulties of, 215, 216
Legros, *cited*, 481
Lemp, Mayor of Strasbourg, house burned, 103
Lenfant, Abbé, saved, 301
Lenôtre, M. G., *cited*, 228
Lepelletier demands "integral education," 487; report of, on education, 518
Lescure, Vendean leader, 456
Lescuyer, murder of, 321
Levellers, *vide* Anarchists
Leymarie, *cited*, 40
Liberty, drawback to, 486; religious 526
Lichtenberger, A., *cited*, 496
Liége, military depôt, 382; taken by Austrians, 383
Lille, military riots at, 223
Lindet, Robert, 385
Thomas, 522
"Living Wage," 495
Lods et ventes, 203
Longwy invested, 290; surrender of, 292, 296, 298, 324
Louis XIV. ordinance of, 414
Louis XV., misery under, 22

Louis XVI., accession of, 2; reforms under, 19–20; opposes representative Government and dismisses Turgot, 20, 21; real character of, 21; good intention of, 23; yields, 31; convokes States - General, 33; opposes reform, 50 *et seq.*; policy of, 59; served by Commons, 62; intentions towards, 65; duplicity of, 71; visits Paris, 90; plots escape, 91; "best of Kings," 106; heads counter-revolution, 137; refuses sanction to Declaration of Rights of Man, 146; flight of, planned, 150 *et seq.*; feeling towards, 155; made prisoner, sanctions Declaration of Rights of Man, 157; in Paris, 173; takes oath, 178; explains property, 198; remonstrates with National Assembly, 200; thanks Bouillé for massacre, 225; flees to Varrenne, 226 *et seq.*; brought back, 229 *et seq.*; intentions of, 230–31; treachery of, 234, 239; refuses to sanction decrees, 235; secret safe of, 236, 293; tries to reestablish Three Orders, 237; calls Girondist Ministry, 240; foreign correspondence of, 245; plots of, 248-49; authority limited of, 256; takes refuge in Assembly, 275; imprisoned with family in Temple, 276, 280, 283, 284; position of, 280; intrigues of, 290; protected by Girondins, 312; suspended, 318; negotiations in favour of, 325; fate of, 328–30 *et seq.*; speculations of, 328; trial of, 330 *et seq.*; pitied by people, 330; indifference to, of foreign Courts, 331; disbanded guards in pay of, 332; treason of, 333; letter to Emperor of Austria, 334; death of, a necessity, 335; crime of, 336; interrogation of, 337; defence of, 338; found guilty and executed, 339;

INDEX

Louis XVI.—*continued*
Girondist plot in favour of, 349; effect of execution, 370; in England, 381, 382; beloved in La Vendée, 454

Loustalot, harangues crowd, 69, 71; heads deputation, 152; rouses people, 154; *quoted*, 220

Louvet, "Robespierride" of, 346; in Brittany, 368; stirs up revolt, 446

Lozeau, P., speech of, 422

Luckner, joins Lafayette, 286

Lyons, revolt at, 25; massacre at, 321, 404; a Royalist centre, 377; struggle at, 378; counter-revolution in, 383; reaction in, 458-59; siege of, 460; taken by Republicans, 461, 468; champions socialistic industry, 495; communism at, 496

MABLY, *cited*, 6, 12; socialism of, 484

Mack (Colonel in Austrian Army), promise of Dumouriez to, 388

Maignet, raises army of peasants, 460-61; "punishes severely," 556-57

Mailhe, revolutionary measure of, 280; demands reprieve of King, 339; proposes restoration of communal lands, 418, 421

Maillard, leads women to Versailles, 154; saves Cazotte, 301; and forty-three others, 302; tribunal of, 372

Mainmortes, 129 *et seq*.

Malesherbes, defends King, 337; guillotined, 559

Mallarmé abused by Robespierre, 566

Malouet, leads reaction, 56; plots against people, 154

Manants, 416

Manifesto of Leagued Kings, 295

Manorial Justice, 37
Courts, abolition of, 121

Manuel, report of, 299; tries to stop massacres, 300

Marat, rouses people, 154; protests against martial law, 161; queries people's joy, 178; inspires revolt, 183; order to arrest, 222; persecuted, 234; despair of, 234-35; insight of, 256, 293; denounces traitors, 295; circular by, 303; advises people, 307; list of, 309; despairs of France's salvation, 310; loved by people, 320; against war, 323; protests against Republic's right to kill King, 334; accused, 347; *quoted*, 367; takes up cause of poor, 374-75; policy of, 392 *et seq.*; Girondins order arrest of, 393; people's defence of, 394; character of, 394; acquittal of, 395; writing, *quoted*, 395; opposes Terror, 400; rings tocsin, 401-2; addresses Jacobins, 404; supports forced loan, 411; murder of, 450; disinterestedness and nobility of, 450-51; no terrorist, 452; on sovereignty of people, 472; opposes death penalty for communists, 500; loss to Revolution, 501; arrested in Italy, 516; a freemason, 540

"Marc of Silver," 164, 185

Maréchal Sylvain, communism of, 489, 579; employs Babeuf, 490

Marie-Antoinette (Queen), letter to Count de Mercy, 28; leads Court, 58; understood by people, 61; feasts foreign troops, 88; character of, 89, 335; insulted, 90; hated, 151; fêtes soldiers, 153; disdains King, 155; corresponds with Fersen, 155, 334; in personal danger, 156; takes oath, 178; letter of, 235; pitied by people, 330; negotiations about, 331; plots with Austria, 334; tried, 515; executed, 516

Marmontel, *quoted*, 75

Marseillaise hymn by Rouget de l'Isle, 324

Marseilles resists Revolution, 251; federals from, 272; votes for dethronement, 274; demands Republic, 310
"Marsh" or "Plain," 310; composition of, 311; obeys Robespierrists, 547
Martial Law, 160, 209, 221, 257
Martin, Henri, on freemasons, 540
Mascarats, revolt of, 24
Masonic lodges, 540
Massacres, at Lyons, 321, 404, 514; in Champ-de-Mars (July 17, 1791), 179, 257; September, 297 *et seq.*; numbers slain in, 303; of 1848 and 1871, 368; at Machecoul, 387
Mathieu, supports forced loan, 411
Maubeuge, Austrians raise siege of, 468
Maury, Abbé, almost slain, 55
"Maximum," 36, 207, 208, 241, 361, 372; Chaumette's law of, 375-76; fixed by Convention, 439; law of, 497-98; abolished, 570
Mayence occupied by *sans-culottes*, 326
"Means of Subsistence," 493 *et seq.*; problem of, 497
Exchange, 493 *et seq.*
Méhée fils (Fehlemési), *quoted*, 297, 300
Mellié, Ernest, *quoted* and *cited*, 183, 314, 315, 439, 513, 529, 568
Mercure de France, *quoted*, 70, 152, 242
Mercy, Count de, plots, 153; reveals English policy, 381; severity of, 335
Metric system, importance of, 518-19
Michelet, v.; excellent description by, 274; *quoted*, 282, 303, 306; criticises Jacobins, 316-17; criticises Gironde, 319; errors of, 338; on King's mendacity, 337; on communist movement, 373; on Dumouriez, 381-82; on hunting Republicans, 386; *quoted*, 437, 451, 452; on Vendean War, 457-58; *cited*, 488; defends Cordeliers, 504;

Michelet—*continued*
on middle-class leadership, 508; on *Fête* of Liberty and Reason, 524; on death of Revolution, 532; on Jacobins and Girondins, 533; on executions, 546; on Sections, 569; on peasants during Revolution, 574
Michonis, plans Queen's escape, 516
Middle classes, Third Estate or *bourgeoisie*, idea of, 5 *et seq.*; practical programme of, 10; schemes of, 30 *et seq.*; moderation of, 44; in revolution, 47; fear of masses, 58, 75, 81, 106, 158; form militia, 76; betray people, 77; work of, 96; arming of, 128; brutality of, 128; Liberalism of, 144; disband people, 158 *et seq.*; organise government, 162, 163; great fortunes of, 169; speculations of, 171; current of, 195; position of, 196; take arms, 208; legislation of, 214, 215, 218; reaction of, 222; intrigues of, 227; against Republic, 243; joy of, 287; work with counter-revolution, 291; intention of, 356; terror of, 370; hatred of people, 397; power of, 401; plots of, 488
Mignet, *quoted*, 91-92, 479, 571
Militia, armed (1789), 27, 40, 76
Mi-lods, 203
"Ministère sans-culotte," 240
"Ministers for Paris," 76
Mir, Russian, comparison with, 416; land under, 494
Mirabeau, speech of, 55, 88; member of Breton Club, 60; deserts people, 62; petitions King, 66; as Constitutionalist, 151; bought, 161, 162, 175; treachery of, 332; a freemason, 540
Moderates wish municipalities suppressed, 475
"Moderation," 310
Moelle, won over by Royalists, 516
Moleville, Bertrand de, 26, 28; opposes constitution, 240; tried and acquitted, 302
Mombelles, Mme., letter to, 135

INDEX

Momoro, pamphlet on "maximum," 44; organises *fête*, 524; speaks for sections, 529; crime of, 545; arrested, 545
Monarchy, revival of, 222
Monastic Orders suppressed, 170
Monéage, 202
Monge, Gironde minister, 318
Moniteur, Royalist plans in, 295; approved September massacres, 305; advocates peasant proprietorship, 433
Monopolists, rise of, 30; buy up wheat, 63; killed, 208
Monopoly, laws against, 499
Mons, defeat at, 298
"Montagnards," division of, 362; prepare to equalise wealth, 411; break up large estates, 432; give acre to proletarians, 434-35; oppose "maximum," 441; carry on Revolution, 471; ideas of, 474; policy of, 480; *régime* of, 483; *volte face* of, 500; mistake of, 501
Montesquieu, cited, 6, 191
Montesquiou, commands army in south, 326
Montmorin (Keeper of Civil List), compromising papers of, 288; acquitted, 295; "blood" of, 301
"Moral Insurrection," 401
Mortimer-Ternaux, cited, 314, 365
Mortmain abolished, 20
Mounier, agent of *émigrés*, 296
"Mountain," The, influenced by Commune, 273; conspires, 293; composition of, 310-11; power of, 316; success of attack on, 322; tries to introduce land reform in Belgium, 327; resolved on King's condemnation, 336; *versus* Gironde, 340 *et seq.*; programme of, 345; attacked by Gironde, 346; reproaches Gironde, 358; allays panic, 384; collaborates with Commune, 388; appeals to people, 392; policy of, 508
Municipal function, 479
institutions, 98 *et seq.*
law of December 1789, 471
organisation, 158, 189

Municipalisation of trade, 497
Municipalities, centres of Revolution, 166; cantonal, creation of, 472-73
Municipality elected, 417
"Muscadins," 510, 546, 549
Mutual Insurance scheme, 485

NANGIS, people refuse taxes at, 70
Nantes, slave trade of, 457; Carrier's *noyades* at, 514
Napoleon I., *vide* Bonaparte
Napoleon III., *coup d'état* of, 336
Narbonne supports Constitution, 240
Nation, French, unification of (1790), 177
National Assembly, composition of, 13; tardiness of, 43; Third Estate declares itself to be, 56; congratulations and militant addresses to, 61; loyal to King, 62; true character of, 63; fears people, 63; servility of, 64, 66; inactivity of, 65; marked members of, 65; impotence of, 67 *et seq.*; alarms in, 70, 89; struggle of, 101 *et seq.*; members of, threatened, 149; suppresses soldiers' agitation, 223-25; soldiers send delegates to, 224; Chaumette's estimate of, 246
Debt, amount of, 33; consolidation of, 53
Estates, 432 *et seq.*
Guard organised, 76; *vide* Guards
Lands, speculations in, 511; *vide* Lands
Life, changes in, 576
Representation, 20; defect of, 51; sacredness of, 400
Unity, scheme of Anarchists for, 350
Necker, Minister, 20; policy of, 21; dismissed, 21; recalled, 28, 34; as financier, 31 *et seq.*; his "Compte rendu," 32; three hours' speech of, to States-General, 51 *et seq.*;

Necker—*continued*
compromise of, 54; insight of, 55; dismissed again, 57, 65; tries to avert famine, 62–63; insulted by Court, 71; bust carried in procession, 72; proposes to diminish seigniorial prerogative, 197–98; orders Marat's arrest, 222
Neerwinden, defeat at, 346, 387
Newspapers, scarcity of, 102
Nineteenth Century, cited, 40; quoted, 199
Nivière-Chol leads middle-class revolt in Lyons, 377
Noailles, Viscount de, speaks against feudalism, 119 *et seq.*
Nobility, luxury of, 17; property rights of, 122 *et seq.*
Noirmoutiers, prisoners shot at, 515
" Noirs," gathering of the, 290
Notables, Assembly of, 39; *vide* Assembly
Noyades of Nantes, 457, 458, 514
Nys, Ernest, thanks to, vii., monograph of, on freemasons, *quoted*, 540–41

OCTOBER 5 and 6 (1789), Paris Insurrection, 146 *et seq.*
Old age pensions, 506
!' Ombre de Marat, L'," 504
Orange, Commission at, 557–58
Order, triumph of, 549
Ordinance of 1670, 20
Orléans, Duke of, plot against, 64, 65; popularity of, 69; bust carried in ·procession, 72; dreams of, 150; disgrace of, 161; intrigues of, 227–28; expects crown, 231; candidate for throne, 331; Grand Master of freemasons, 540
Owen, Robert, teaching of, 498

PACHE (Mayor of Paris), succeeds Chambon, 322, 364; demands revolutionary tribunal, 385; opposed to Terror, 400; deprived of office, 545; spared, 546; character of, 547

Paine, Thomas, sincerity of, 243; on Constitution .Committee, 470
Palais Royal, revolutionary focus, 49, 61, 70, 72; deputation from, 152
Pamphlets, revolutionary, 24, 46, 53; *vide* British Museum
Pan, Mallet du, *quoted*, 223, 242
Panis, signs appeal of Commune, 301
Pannetier, leads attack on Bastille, 82, 83
Paper-currency (*vide* Assignats]: under Directory, 571
Paris, hunger riots in, 23, 28, 46 (*vide* Riots); clerks and populace of, 29; centre of Revolution, 67; thieves hanged in, 77; ammunition kept in, 77; misery in, 92; scarcity in, 149; feared, 151; insurrection breaks out in, 154; districts of, 171; reaction in, 200; sections of, 215; municipality demands Republic, 232, 310; reaction in, 233, 509; full of conspiracies, 245; rises August 9 and 10, 275; laments her dead, 282; to be burned, 290; searched for arms, 294; purified, 303; revolutionary energy of, 324; threatens Convention, 333; panic in, 383, 384; rising needed in, 383; fury of, 388, 403, 404; hated by farmers, 499; executions in, 514; inactive, 545; " purification " of, 555
Parlement of Paris banished to Troyes, 26; recalled, 29
of Rennes, 26
Parlements (Courts of Justice], closing of, 24, 25 *et seq.*; disturbances about, 39; suspension of, 163; support reaction, 166
Parliament, English, friends of French Republic in, 556
Prussian, uselessness of, 45
Passeret (King's secretary) hooted, 56
Patin, J. Baptiste, resigns, 523
!' Patriote française," *cited*, 305 347

INDEX

Patriots, beaten at Arles, 251; mutilated by Uhlans, 251; form league of defence, 252
Patrou, resigns, 523
Payan, exasperates workers, 565
Peasant Risings (*vide Jacqueries*), 2, 28, 29, 40, 44, 46, 52, 112 *et seq.*, 159, 177, 198, 207, 208
Peasants, misery of, 17; oppose export of grain, 26; not represented in Assembly, 51; slaughter of, 127; illegal executions of, 128; disappointment of, 132 *et seq.*; refuse to pay taxes, 149, 150; Draconian laws for, 199, 208, 209; hardships of, 202; difficulties of, 204; repression of, 211; courage of, 228; deprived of political rights, 234; refuse to pay feudal dues, 279; oppose foreign invasion, 324; condition of (in 1793), 393; regain communal lands, 413; oppose division of lands, 415; rights of disputed, 417; admitted, 418; anger of, 418-19; advantages gained by, 431; industry of, 437; discontented in La Vendée, 454; energy of (1792), 574
Pecqueur, collectivism of, 11-12, 363
Pélarin Library, fragment found of, 409
Peltier, lies of, 304
People, first; conflict with rich, 48; feared, 55; in revolt, 56, 61, 63-64; take arms, 68; slaughtered, 85; character of, 89; change in, 179; vigilance of, 196; needs of, 218; intelligence of, 256; despair of, 287; victory of, 287-88; belied, 293; power of, 312, 357; devotion of, 313; offer hostages to Convention, 404; sovereignty of, 472; social will of, 534
"Père Duchesne," edited by Chaumette, 322
"Pères de l'Oratoire," 460
Permanent Committee, 76, 81, 84, 182, 190-91

Personal servitude suppressed, 20
Rights over peasants, 37
Pétion (Mayor of Paris), member of Breton Club, 61; proposes loan, 63; tries to save Princess de Lamballe, 299; during September massacres, 305; imprisoned, 314; resigns, 322; accused, 338; "Letter to Parisians" by, 378; stirs up revolt, 446; on Council of Commune, 470
"Petitions of Eight Thousand and Twenty Thousand," 309
Pflieger, letters of, 527
Phélippeaux, a Dantonist, 535; attacks Hébertist generals, 536; arrested, 547
Philosophers, influence of, 1, 2
Philosophy, scientific, 9
Picard, Abbé, escape of, 297
Pichegrue, attacks invaders, 469
Piedmontese, enter France, 460
Pikemen, save prisoners, 302
Pikes, forging of, 73, 77
Pillaging, rareness of, 75
Pitt, policy of, 48; money of, 252; overthrow hoped for, 467; against "impious nation," 556
"Plain" or "Marsh," right wing of Convention, 315
"Pleas," 203
"Plenary Court," 25
Polignac, Duchess de, effigy burned, 29; people's opinion of, 61; letter of, 65; hatred for, 70; intrigues of, 86, 88; insulted, 90; exiled, 91
Politics, study of, 6
Poor, relief of, 185, 193-94; neglected by Convention, 505
Pope, aids counter-revolution, 384
Popular Societies, 252, 257, 365, 400, 448, 480
Pougatchoff, leads Russian peasants (1773), 2
Power, demoralisation of, 478
Précy, commandant at Lyons, 460
Press, attitude of, towards September massacres, 305
Priests, intrigues of, 238; decrees against, 239, 280; join counter-

Priests—*continued*
  revolution, 250; protected by "patriots," 252; massacre of, 297; incite Vendéan rising, 336; enemies of Jacobins, 405; refuse oath to Constitution, 520; lay down prerogatives, 522-23
Primogeniture, abolished, 434-35
Princes, intrigues of, 58
Prisons, conspiracies in, 56, 298; *vide* Massacres, September
Privat (*curé*) resigns, 523
Profiteurs, 543
Proletarians, part played by, 391, 484
Property, protection of, 74; sacredness of, 122 *et seq.*, 143, 198, 342, 343, 368; rights of, 136; substituted for Fraternity by Girondins, 343; movement against, 373; guaranteed, 401; superfluous, 405; defended, 500; of "patriots" respected, 544
Proudhon, *quoted*, 189; ideas of, 373; his Bank of People, 487; teaching of, 498
Proust, Antonin, explains Vendéan revolt, 455
Provence, large towns in, abolish flour tax, 41
  Count de, "Monsieur," intrigues of, 161, 162; protests against Constitution, 238; in exile, 248
Provinces, importance of, 247
Provincial histories, importance of, 40
  Assemblies, discussions in, 32
Prudhomme, plain speaking of, 235; "Révolutions de Paris," paper of, *cited*, 305
Prussia, King of, advises concessions, 249
Public force, basis of, 144
Puisage, Count J. de, countersigns false *assignats*, 444

!! QUATRE cris d'un patriote," 485
Quinet, Edgar, *quoted*, 35
Quint, 203

RAMEL, abused by Robespierre, 566
Rauchon, priest, resigns, 523
Reaction, revival of, 153; rampant, 158 *et seq.*; organised, 213; in Paris, 233, 235; progress of, 255; forces of, 408
Reason, Cult of, 521-25
Rebecqui (Girondin) stirs up Marseilles, 459; drowns himself, 460
Redemption, 39; "*rachat au denier* 30," 119, 122; difficulties of, 199; of feudal dues, 277-78
"Red Terror," 311, 436
Referendum, 473
Reforms, under Turgot, 19
Regnal, *cited*, 40
Relevoisons, 203
Reliefs, 203
Religion democratised, 7
Religious hatred, 249
Renault, Cecile, strange affair of, 558-59
Rennes, *parlement* of, 26; magistrates disqualified at, 167
Renunciation, legend of, 134 *et seq.*
Republic, enemies of, 170; people's service to, 179; France impelled towards, 310; of middle classes, 343; Breton peasants against, 419; strengthened, 538
Republican soldiers, torture of, 457
Republicans, massacre of, 386; persecution of, 571
Requint, 203
Reubiés, General, Secretary of Lyons Committee of Public Welfare, 460
Reuss, Rodolphe, *cited*, 99
"Réveillon Affair," 47 *et seq.*
"Révolte, La," *cited*, 40, 199
Revolution, definition of, 2, 3; need of enthusiasm in, 124; meaning of, 242; made by minorities, 363; alternatives offered to, 369; makes men think, 524; evils of, 563; benefits of, 573 *et seq.*
  Great French, history of, incomplete, v.; heroes of, 35 map of, 111; great dates of

INDEX

Revolution, Great French—*continued*
118, 391; good humour of, 178; true picture of, 210–11; logical sequence of, 311; aims of, 323; not supported in Belgium, 327; chief work of, 392; complete on land question, 423; economic results of, 431; legacies of, 436, 577; expenses of, 440; devotion to, 448; social problem in, 488–89; interests roused by, 501; work of people, 505; middle classes enriched by, 511, 537; source of modern social ideas, 581; various phases of, *vide* Chapter index
— American, influence of, 21
— English, contrasted, 3; 96 *et seq.*, 581; part played by people in, 4; lesson of, 6
— popular power of, 145
— Russian, 17
— in Savoy, 326
Revolutions of 1848 and 1870, 336
"Revolutions de Paris," 220, 242, 305
Revolutionists, type of (1871), 534
Rigby, Dr., letter of, 74
Right of poor, 376
— of property, limitation of, 487
"Right to Work," 194, 343
"Rights of Man," *vide* Declaration; veiled in black, 544
Riots, hunger, 19 *et seq.*; at Dijon, Auxerre, Amiens, Lille, Pontoise, Passy, St.-Germain, 23; at Poitiers, Vizille, Cevennes, Vivarais, Gévaudan, 24; at Lyons, 25; in Paris, 26, 27, 29; spread of, 41 *et seq.*; bloodless character of, 42; influence elections, 42; at Villejuif, 48
Rising, of May 31-June 2 (1793), 361 *et seq.*, 391, 399
Risings, in Besançon, Provence, Languedoc, Béarn, Flanders, Franche-Comté, Burgundy, 27 *et seq.*; in country districts, 35 *et seq.*; in Strasbourg, &c., 103 *et seq.*
— Agrarian, 97

Risings—*continued*
character of, 111 *et seq.*; spread of, 116
— Peasant, 109 *et seq.*
— popular influence of, 94–96
— of Royalists, unsuccessful, 253; in La Vendée, 384; in Provence and Lyons, effects of, 458
— Urban, 95
Robert, *quoted*, 242; persecuted, 234
Robespierre, silence of, 35; member of Breton Club, 61; protests against martial law, 161; insight of, 240, 307; opposes Agrarian law and Republic, 243; fears people, 244; inactivity of, 273; denounces Carra, 307; Vice-president of Convention, 309; supported by "Marsh" or "Plain," 311; "golden mean of the Mountain," 317; against war, 323; opinion on regicide, 334; rival of Brissot, 344; satirises Girondins, 344; moderation of, 345; speech, on April 10, 360; development of, 362; belief in "foreign money," 375; attacks "Gironde," 376; policy of, 392; declares for insurrection, 398; opposes "Terror," 400; demands suppression of "Twelve" and trial of "Twenty-Two," 403; advocates restoration of communal lands, 417; socialistic speech of, 474; reads Declaration of Rights, 500; attacks Roux and Varlet, 503; "La Fraternité's" observations on, 507; daring of, 511; opposes prosecution of obscure Girondins, 514; represents Jacobins, 514; religious speech of, 525; opposes Cult of Reason, 525–26; accuses sections of foreign intrigues, 529; on public welfare, 529; foresees end of Republic, 533; group of, 535; reports on Revolutionary Government, 538; popularity of, 539; a freemason, 540;

Robespierre—*continued*
  attacks commissioners, 542;
  position and power of, 550 *et
  seq.*; incorruptibility of, 551;
  bourgeoisie's respect for, 552;
  letter from his brother, 553;
  drafts accusation of F. d'Eglantine, 547, 552; suspicions
  of, 553; notes on "Terrorism"
  of, 554; enemies of, 562;
  cabal against, 565 *et seq.*;
  attacks "Left," 566; arrest of,
  567; stupor of, 568; identification and execution of, 569
Rochambeau, Count de, refuses
  arms to middle classes, 103
Roche-Jacquelein, La, Vendean
  leader, 456
  Mme. de, letter *quoted*, 456
Rochefoucauld, supports Court, 245
Roland, silence of, 35; politics of,
  197; Minister for Interior,
  240; dismissed, 244; house
  of, searched, 295, 307;
  address of, 296; justifies
  massacres, 304, 321; again
  Minister, 318; resigns after
  execution of King, 319;
  influence of, 319; examines
  King's secret papers, 332;
  leader of "Gironde," 341;
  absurd plan of, 349; arrest
  of, ordered, 403; suicide of,
  517
  Mme., influence of, 240; guillotined, 517
Rome helps revolt in La Vendée,
  455
Romme, execution of, 570
Ronsin, organises "revolutionary
  army," 512; arrested, 545
Rosière, Thuriot de la, District
  delegate, 82, 83, 84
Rouen, insurrection at, 24
  (priest) resigns, 523
Rouërie, Marquis de, plots in Brittany, 320, 326; heads conspiracy, 446
Rousseau, J. J., influence of, 6, 12;
  cited, 191; socialism of, 484
Roux, Jacques, ex-priest and
  popular leader, 372; inspires people, 385; advises
  forced loan, 411; communism

Roux, Jacques—*continued*
  of, 489; insight of, 498-99;
  denounces stock - jobbing,
  502-3; struck off Cordeliers'
  list, 503; false charge
  against, 504; trial and
  suicide of, 504-5
Xavier, *quoted*, 114
"Royal dictature," 209
Royal family, negotiations concerning, 331
  Session, 55, 59
Royalists, plot of, 290; letters to
  agents, 444; where successful,
  453; rejoicings of, 547; fury
  of, 559
Royalty, as shield of property, 66;
  tools of, 175; downfall of,
  229-30, 285; abolished *de
  facto*, 276
Russia, peasants in, 17, 18; comparison with, 165, 212, 213,
  214, 356, 436, 475, 574; joint
  responsibility in, 279; absolutism dying in, 579; future of,
  581

SAGESSE, Sœurs de la, Royalist
  emissaries, 336
Sagnac, M., *quoted*, 134, 199, 204,
  205, 206, 207, 426, 435
Saint-Amaranthe, guillotined, 559
Saint-André, Jeanbon, letters of,
  447; warning of, 482; demands
  bread and "Terror," 483;
  makes terms with communists,
  500; socialism of, 506-7;
  opposes sections, 529-30
"Saint Bartholomew of property,"
  119, 126, 198
Saint-Etienne, Rabaud de, 46; communism of, 485; executed,
  517
Saint-Georges, Commandant, house
  of, burned, 107
Saint-Huruge, Marquis of, proposes march on Versailles, 152
Saint-Just, theory of, about King,
  334; proves King's treachery,
  338; opposes petition against
  stock - jobbing, 374; with
  army, 439; pleads for "destitute patriots," 505; demands
  Revolutionary Government,

INDEX

Saint-Just—*continued*
514; a Robespierrist, 535; adopts Terrorism, 543-44; mouthpiece of Robespierre, 552; shouted down, 567; arrested and executed, 569
Saint-Lazare, monastery attacked, 73, 75
Saint-Malo, attempt to surrender, to English, 447
Saint-Méard, J. de, *cited*, 299; *quoted*, 303
Saint-Simon, followers of, 488
Salle, Marquis de la, commands National Guard, 76
Salmour, Count de, *quoted*, 74, 80
Salpêtrière (prison), massacre at, 303
Samichon, E., *quoted*, 20
Sans-culottes, volunteer for war, 280; outnumbered in sections, 371; "happiness and comfort" for, 405; patriotism of, 463-64; enfranchisement of Europe by, 578
Santerre, ordered to stop massacres, 300; at war, 305
Sardinia, invades France, 253, 383
Sartino (Knight of Poignard), guillotined, 560
Sauce, grocer, King in shop of, 228-29
Schwendt, supports Revolution, 105
"Scientific socialism," 363
Séchelles (of Hérault), municipal integrity of, 475-76
Second Empire, comparison with, 215
Secret police, revival of, 531
Sections (of Paris), 180 *et seq.*; creation of, 188; under new law, 189 *et seq.*; General Assembly of, position of, 190; centres of Revolution, 193; new function of, 312-13; federation of, 312; demand dethronement, 314; attacked by Gironde, 322; prepare rising, 399-400; pledged to defend property, 401; conquer rights, 472; overrun with Royalists, 510; attacked by Convention, 513; suppression of, 528 *et seq.*; perform police duties, 530; divisions among, 568

Seigniorial exactions, 18
justice in cities, 38
Seligman, E., *cited*, 20
Sens, Archbishop of Minister, 28 (*vide* Brienne)
September Days, horror of, 384 (*vide* Massacres)
Serfdom, abolished on King's estates, 36; essence of, 129 *et seq.*; general abolition of, 577-79
Sergent, signs appeal to Commune, 301
Servan, War Minister, 240, 244, 305, 318
Sheridan, R. B., denounces forging of *assignats*, 444
Sieyès, silence of, 35; famous pamphlet of (*Qu'est-ce que le tiers-état?*), 43, 46; motion of, 53; member of Breton Club, 61; proposals of, 143, 163; defends free trade, 373; on special committee, 470; defends equality, 484; adopts new cult, 523
Simmoneau (Mayor of Etampes) killed, 242
Simon (cobbler), Dauphin put in charge of, 516
Simond, *quoted*, 528, 529
"Sixteen Commissioners," 192, 193
Smith, Adam, influence of, 8
Social demands, 370 *et seq.*
distinctions, danger of, 143; abolished, 144
"Socialisation of Exchange and Produce," 497
"Socialism," origin of, 11-12, 13, 459; modern, 580
Societies, Fraternal, 222, 365
Popular, 222, 448, 528
Society of the Indigent, 252
Soëtc, 203
Soldiers, distrusted, 81; as citizens, 223; meeting of, 224; fraternise with peasants, 229
Sombreuil, commands Invalides, 80; saved, 301; legend about daughter, 302; guillotined, 559
Somnier, *cited*, 40; *quoted*, 114
Soubrancy, executed, 570

INDEX

Souhait, Julian, demands maintenance of communal property, 422; opposes portioning land, 494
Soul, Albert, *cited*, 382
Spaniards, attack South, 253; 8000 in Toulon, 460; 23,000 in France, 465
Speculations, in Church property, 255; in land, 279, 404; in wheat, 329; in necessities, 372; in *assignats*, 373
Speculators, protected, 63
Spires, taken by Republican army, 326
Stamp duty, 25
State, sphere of action of, 196
States, modern, structure of, 5 *et seq.*; centralisation of, 7
States-General, 29, 30, 33–34, 39, 43, 48; Third Estate in, 39; of Brittany, 42; rely on Paris, 49; opening of, 50 *et seq.*
"Statesmen," 311, 338, 570
Statute labour abolished, 19, 37
Stedinck, Baron de, letter to, 466
Stock Exchange closed, 438
Stock-jobbers, pernicious influence of, 584
Stock-jobbing, essence of, 372; effect of, 374; prohibited, 439, 487
Stourm, Réné, *cited*, 410–11
Strasbourg, *cahier* of, 99; rising in, 103 *et seq.*; in danger of invasion, 469
Strobel, *cited*, 40; *quoted*, 113
Students fraternise with people, 27
Suchet, severity of, 566
Suffrage restricted, 234
"Surplus value," Lange's explanation of, 496
Swiss, soldiers, refuse to fire, 27; regiment defends Bastille, 82; Guards faithful to King, 274; treachery of, to people, 276; in Paris, 290; massacre of, 298

Taille (entail), 59; (personal tax), 415
Taine, complacency of, 23; superficiality of, 39; *quoted*, 41; exaggeration of, 74; "shocked," 102; disparagement of, 177

Talleyrand (Bishop of Autun), proposition of, 169; supports Court, 245
Tallien, report to Assembly, 300; report of, 300, 302; attacked by Robespierre, 567
"Tarpeian Rock," 346, 347, 359; for Girondins, 372
Tasque, 203
Tax, on bread and meat, 36
Taxation, progressive, 396, 485
Taxes, limitation of, 37 (*note*), 53
Taxpayers, joint liability of, 20
Taylor, sees false *assignats* made, 444
Tennis Court, oath in, 54 *et seq.*
Terrage, 203
Terriers (land registers), 199
"Territorial subvention," 25
"Terror," use made of, 117; need of, 253–54; counter-revolutionary, 306; welcomed, 483; begun, 517, 555 *et seq.*; Law of (22nd Prairial) 557; maintenance of, 564
Terrorism, used politically, 535
Theatres, political plays in, 510
Théot, Catherine, mad mystic, 562
Thermidor, reaction of 9th, 430; reaction triumphs, 562
Thibaudeau, *quoted*, 367
Thiers, famine at, 40
Thiers, M., *quoted*, 444
Third Estate, opportunity of, 7–8; composition of, 34; issues *cahiers*, 35; and middle classes, 38; and poorer classes, 39; determination of, 44; position of, 52, 115; demand union, 53; Constitution, 54 *et seq.*; resistance of, 54 *et seq.*; King opposed to, 59; sagacity of, 214; reaction of, 243
Third Republic, progress to, 576
Thouret, silence of, 35; guillotined, 559
Three Estates, union of, 43, 62; separation of, 54
Thuriot, supports forced loan, 411
Tinténiac, Chevalier de, countersigns false *assignats*, 444
Tithes "solites and insolites," 37 (*note*); destruction of deeds, 114; abolition of, 119 *et seq.*; iniquity of, 132

INDEX

Tocqueville, veracity of, 18
Toll-gates, removed, 19; burned, 71
Tolls, suppressed, 203
Torture, abolished, 20
Toulon, surrendered to English, 447; surrender of, 453, 460; retaken from English, 468, 538
Tour de la Glacière, tragedy of, 321
Touzel, Mme., saved by Commune, 299; *cited*, 306
Town Council of Paris, 76
Treizains, 203
Triage, 414, 421
Tribunal, Revolutionary, 301, 372; demanded, 385; rapidity of, 538; abolished, 570
Tridon, *cited*, 534
Triumvirate, of Duport, Lameth and Barnave, 162
  of Danton, Marat, and Robespierre, 319, 321, 322; attacked by Gironde, 320; effect of attacks, 320; threatened by Girondins, 359
Tronchet, defends King, 337
Troops, refuse to fire, 56
Tuileries, invasion of, 210; taking of, 278; numbers slain in, 282
Türckheim, resigns, 106
Turgot, creator of political economy, 8; as economist, 19, 23; representative government, 20; foresight of, 21; explains riots, 25; reforms rejected, 31; reforms of, 38; as Minister, 52; on equality, 484
Turkey, representative Government in, 579

"UNITED defenders" appeal to Convention, 373
United States, recognised by France, 22

VADIER, attacked by Right, 565, 567
Valazé, suicide of, 517
Vallet, Gabrielle, recognises King, 228
Valmy, battle of, 325
Varenne, Maton de la, *cited*, 303, 306

Varennes, flight to, 226 *et seq.*; threatened, 335
Varlet, arrest of, 347; leader of people, 372; inspires people, 385; arrested, 397; communism of, 489; pamphlet of, 490; insight of, 498–99; struck off Cordeliers, 503; condemns payment of members, 513
Vaucluse, Royalist centre, 556
Vendean leaders, defeat of, 456; brutalities of, 457
Vendée, against Revolution, 176; insurrection in, 247; rising in, 328, 334, 383; massacre of Republicans in, 386; reaction in, 430; rising in, 453 *et seq.*; result of suppression in, 458; crushed at Savenay, 538
Venterolles, 203
Verdun, siege of, 296; surrender of, 324
Vergniaud, 35; demands suspension of King, 276; leader in "Gironde," 341; tries to pacify people, 402; under home-arrest, 445; on Convention Committee, 470
Vernon, insurrection crushed at, 446
Versailles, King and Ministers insulted at, 23; plots at, 43; intrigues in, 64; *fête* at, 88 *et seq.*; march on, planned, 152; march on, 154 *et seq.*
Veto, opposition to, 147 *et seq.*; suspensive, 148; royal, 188
Veyreton, resigns, 253
Vic and Vaissete, *quoted*, 28; *cited*, 40
Vidal, as authoritarian, 194; collectivism of, 363; communism of, 488
Vieux Cordelier, 536–38; exults, 547
Village Communes, suppressed, 165
Village, economic life of, 423
Vincennes, donjon transformed, 79
Vincent, won over, 516; advocates guillotine, 544; arrested, 545
Vivarais, adheres to royalty, 253
"Vive la Liberté," cry of, 41

Voltaire, 6; idea, 486
Volunteers (*sans-culottes*), 280; equipment of, 291, 320; enthusiasm of, 323; two battalions of, sacrificed, 326; for La Vendée, 364; evil treatment of, 379; civic feast for, 383; ragged but victorious, 463-64; lands not reserved for, 502
Vote, capitative, granted, 54
Voulland attacked, 565

WAR, reason for, 24; fatal to Revolution, 241; opposition to and unreadiness for, 323; terrible effects of, 328; preparations for, 379; onus of, laid on Republic, 382; requirements of, 408; difficulties of the, 462 *et seq.*; end of, 564
Watch Committee, circular of, 303; attacked by Gironde, 320; justifies expenditure, 321
Wattignies, victory of, 468; first victory of Republic, 515

Weber, the Austrian, acquitted, 302; *cited*, 306
Weishaupt, founder of Illuminates, 540
Westermahn, escorts Prussians on retreat, 325
Wheat, prices of, 104
"White Terror" (1794), 272, 276; under Bourbons (1814), 306; partisans of, 311, 336, 436, 569
Wimpffen, General, Commander in Normandy, 446-47
Wissemburg, abandoned, 469; retaken, 538
Women, in revolution, 27; club of, suppressed, 504
Workers, under arms, payment of, 403

YORK, Duke of, candidate for throne, 308; besieges Dunkirk, 467; abandons siege, 468
Young, Arthur, "Travels in France," *quoted*, 11, 43, 53, 56, 68, 70, 116; *cited*, 102

THE COMING OF WORLD WAR THREE
VOL. 1
From Protest to Resistance/The International War System
by Dimitrios I. Roussopoulos

This profound and timely work analyses the various forces which bring us ever closer to nuclear annihilation. It also takes the reader on a tour of the numerous anti-nuclear and disarmament organisations worldwide and identifies the myriad political issues contributing to international tension.

Since the works of British historian E.P. Thompson are not widely read in North America, Roussopoulos serves some purpose in presenting similar views.
Choice

The author's discussion of the causes and possible prevention of World War Three are penetrating and provocative.
Vancouver Sun

An extremely important book.
Ottawa Citizen

Offers a detailed description of the activities of the anti-nuclear campaign of the 1980's...provides an information resource not readily available elsewhere.
Canadian Book Review Annual

...a penetrating study of the factors leading to a very probable disaster...goes well beyond analysis and warning, to an inquiry into what is being done and what should be done to compel a reversal of course.
Noam Chomsky

299 pages
Paperback ISBN: 0-920057-02-0 $14.95
Hardcover ISBN: 0-920057-03-9 $29.95
International Politics/Sociology

BLACK ROSE BOOKS
has published the following books of related interests

Peter Kropotkin, Memoirs of a Revolutionist, introduction by George Woodcock
Peter Kropotkin, Mutual Aid, introduction by George Woodcock
Peter Kropotkin, The Great French Revolution, introduction by George Woodcock
Peter Kropotkin, The Conquest of Bread, introduction by George Woodcock
  other books by Peter Kropotkin are forthcoming in this series
Marie Fleming, The Geography of Freedom: The Odyssey of Elisée Reclus, introduction by George Woodcock
William R. McKercher, Freedom and Authority
Noam Chomsky, Language and Politics, edited by C.P. Otero
Noam Chomsky, Radical Priorities, edited by C.P. Otero
George Woodcock, Pierre-Joseph Proudhon, a biography
Murray Bookchin, Remaking Society
Murray Bookchin, Toward an Ecological Society
Murray Bookchin, Post-Scarcity Anarchism
Murray Bookchin, The Limits of the City
Murray Bookchin, The Modern Crisis
Edith Thomas, Louise Michel, a biography
Walter Johnson, Trade Unions and the State
John Clark, The Anarchist Moment: Reflections on Culture, Nature and Power
Sam Dolgoff, Bakunin on Anarchism
Sam Dolgoff, The Anarchist Collectives in Spain, 1936-39
Sam Dolgoff, The Cuban Revolution: A critical perspective
Thom Holterman, Law and Anarchism
Etienne de la Boétie, The Politics of Obedience
Stephen Schecter, The Politics of Urban Liberation
Abel Paz, Durruti, the people armed
Juan Gomez Casas, Anarchist Organisation, the history of the F.A.I.
Voline, The Unknown Revolution
Dimitrios Roussopoulos, The Anarchist Papers
Dimitrios Roussopoulos, The Anarchist Papers 2

send for a complete catalogue of books
mailed out free
BLACK ROSE BOOKS
3981 boul. St-Laurent, #444
Montréal H2W 1Y5, Québec, Canada

Printed by
the workers of
Editions Marquis, Montmagny, Québec
for
Black Rose Books Ltd.

www.ingramcontent.com/pod-product-compliance
Lightning Source LLC
Chambersburg PA
CBHW021845300426
44115CB00005B/17